Herbert Feigl

MIND, MATTER, AND METHOD

Essays in Philosophy and Science in Honor of
HERBERT FEIGL

\(\(\)\)\)

EDITED BY PAUL K. FEYERABEND AND GROVER MAXWELL

UNIVERSITY OF MINNESOTA PRESS · MINNEAPOLIS

Library of Congress Catalog Card Number: 66-13467

PUBLISHED IN GREAT BRITAIN, INDIA, AND PAKISTAN BY THE OXFORD
UNIVERSITY PRESS, LONDON, BOMBAY, AND KARACHI, AND IN CANADA
BY THE COPP CLARK PUBLISHING CO. LIMITED, TORONTO

Table of Contents

Part II. Induction, Confirmation, and Philosophical Method

Part III. Philosophy of the Physical Sciences

MIND, MATTER, AND METHOD

PAUL K. FEYERABEND

⎩⎩⎭⎭

Herbert Feigl: A Biographical Sketch

I first met Herbert Feigl in 1954, in the pleasant and stimulating atmosphere of a Vienna coffeehouse. I was then an assistant to Arthur Pap, who had come to Vienna to lecture on analytic philosophy and who hoped, perhaps somewhat unrealistically, that he would be able to revive what was left from the great years of the Vienna Circle and the analytic tradition there. His need for an assistant most happily coincided with my own need for a job. This was not an ordinary job, however. After a lecture, which frequently turned into a heated debate with the attending metaphysicians, we would both retire to the *Professorenzimmer* of the department of philosophy and discuss what had just happened. Pap was alternately depressed and incensed at what he thought was the impertinence of those who approached philosophical problems without any knowledge of logic and of analytical techniques, and he contrasted their easily produced *Sprachträumereien*[1] with the much more modest results which analytic philosophers had achieved by hard work. Soon we would be in the middle of some analysis ourselves, continue the discussion on our way to Pap's home, and on through dinner, and it was sometimes after midnight when we reluctantly called it a day.

Feigl's papers, especially his "Existential Hypotheses" [2], were a frequent source of material in these discussions, as they had been for years in a small group that had assembled around Victor Kraft, the only remaining member of the Vienna Circle. This group, for whose organization I had been responsible, set itself the task of considering philosophi-

[1] This is Pap's own expression. Cf. the introduction of [6].

[3]

cal problems in a nonmetaphysical manner and with special reference to the findings of the sciences. We had started with the theory of relativity and had investigated in great detail the merits of the original point of view of Lorentz. Yet the problem of the existence of theoretical entities soon became *the* problem. Kraft himself took the position (which he has since explained in detail in his superb *Erkenntnislehre* [5]) that solipsism was a possible point of view and that realism could not be *proved* by philosophical reasoning. Hollitscher, who occasionally visited the circle, tried to show that science and common sense both needed and *actually used* the assumption of a real external world. We were not satisfied by his arguments, for we thought, in accordance with Kraft's ideas, that it was *possible* to interpret science in a positivistic manner and that such an interpretation did not require an external world. Elizabeth Anscombe for some time tried to convince us that analyzing the way in which children learn object-words could point the way to a solution, but we neither understood the solution nor thought this kind of nonempirical child psychology to be relevant to our problem.

Not even a brief and quite interesting visit by Wittgenstein himself (in 1952) could advance our discussion. Wittgenstein was very impressive in his way of presenting concrete cases, such as amoebas under a microscope (I cannot now recall the reason why this example was used), but when he left we still did not know whether or not there was an external world, or, if there was one, what the arguments were in favor of it. "You philosophers," said one of the participating engineers in despair, "are all alike. There you tell us that Wittgenstein has turned philosophy upside down. But what does he do? He talks just as much as everyone else in this profession and can't give a straightforward answer to a straightforward question." It was at this stage of confusion and uncertainty that our attention was directed toward Feigl's "Existential Hypotheses." Our debates now took a completely new turn. This paper, taken together with Kraft's own contributions and with the ideas which Popper had explained to us on the occasion of his visits to the Alpbach Summer University in the summers of 1948 and 1949, greatly diminished our doubts about realism. There were still some points which were not entirely clear, and I wished for an opportunity to discuss the matter with Feigl in person. Another problem that had come up both in Pap's classes and in Kraft's circle and that seemed to be connected with the realism-positivism issue concerned the application of the calculus of probabilities.

[4]

My desire to put my questions to Feigl himself was to be satisfied sooner than I thought. In 1954 he happened to be in Vienna, and Pap arranged for us to meet in the charming garden of a coffeehouse near the university. As I said above, probability had been a favorite topic both in Pap's seminar and in his lectures. His presentation made it appear that the difficulties of the earlier views had been finally overcome and that here, as in other fields, more precise definition and axiomatization had led to the solution or else to the elimination of problems which had seemed to be due solely to the vagueness of the earlier and more "philosophical" ideas. It seemed that here, as in other fields, the strife caused by ignorance had been replaced by the calm of genuine knowledge. This was the attitude which I had adopted myself, and I thought that all I needed was enlightenment on some recondite details which I still did not understand.

It was, therefore, quite a shock to hear Feigl expound fundamental difficulties and to hear him explain in perfectly simple language without any recourse to formalism why the problem of application was still without a solution. Formalization, then, was not the last word in philosophical matters. There was still a task for philosophy in the traditional sense! There was still room for fundamental discussion—for speculation (dreaded word!); there was still a possibility of overthrowing highly formalized systems with the help of a little common sense! These ideas whirled through my head as the discussion proceeded.

Of course, Feigl's objections were not unknown to the philosophical community. It was well known that he had not agreed with the more radical theses of the Vienna Circle and that he had never given up the position of philosophical realism, not even at the time when it was most unfashionable to be a realist. It was well known that he was a philosopher not easily impressed by fashions, by philosophical "revolutions," and that he would keep his head even when everyone else was proclaiming the "end" of some position or other. Much later I came to profit from the objections which he untiringly raised against my own somewhat rash proclamations of philosophical faith and which forced me to turn these proclamations first into sketches for possible arguments, then into bad arguments, then into better arguments, never allowing me to be satisfied or to regard the matter as closed. And I was also to realize that the achievements of that unique institution, the Minnesota Center for the Philosophy of Science, the interesting discussions which took place here among philosophers of creeds so widely different would have been quite impossible without Feigl's example, which forced us to argue when we might have been inclined to produce philosophical perorations.

Herbert Feigl was born in Reichenberg (then in Austria-Hungary) in the area of the Sudetenland, which today is part of Czechoslovakia, on December 14, 1902. Originally oriented to become a technological chemist, he was increasingly attracted by purely theoretical subjects. At the age of sixteen he happened upon an article on the special theory of relativity which fascinated him but did not inhibit his critical sense: he set out to refute the theory. In the course of these attempts he learned a good deal of mathematics and physics, and he also realized that the theory was logically flawless and empirically highly plausible. His interests in theoretical physics and philosophy aroused (a distant relative, Dr. Egmont Münzer, a personal friend of Einstein's, had referred him to Moritz Schlick's *Space and Time in Contemporary Physics*), he went to the University of Munich in 1921, where he took courses in physics from Willy Wien, Leo Graetz, and Arnold Sommerfeld and in physical chemistry from Kurt Fajans, and listened to some philosophers, Erich Becher and Ludwig Pfänder, whose phenomenological approach he found "completely sterile." Reading Edgar Zilsel's *Das Anwendungsproblem* made him realize that he wanted to embark on a career in philosophy. As soon as he learned that Schlick was to accept a major chair in philosophy at the University of Vienna in 1922 he became a student there—half a year before Schlick arrived. He continued his studies in mathematics (with Hans Hahn), theoretical physics (with Hans Thirring), and psychology (with Karl Bühler). In Schlick he found not only a great teacher but soon enough a warm, fatherly friend. During the autumn of 1922 Feigl wrote a long essay on "The Philosophical Significance of Einstein's Theory of Relativity" for which he obtained a prize in a then current competition (with Max von Laue, Schlick, and Ernst von Aster as judges).

In many respects, 1924 was to be a decisive year. It was then that, owing mainly to the initiative of Waismann and Feigl, Schlick assembled a Thursday evening discussion group which soon after developed into the famous (and sometimes notorious) Vienna Circle. From then on Feigl's biography and the history of modern philosophy intersect at many points.

Feigl participated in the Vienna Circle until his emigration in 1930. He formed a close friendship with Rudolf Carnap, but by no means did he accept all of Carnap's ideas. Against the phenomenalism of *Der Logische Aufbau der Welt* he maintained a critical realism similar to the realism of Aloys Riehl, Oswald Külpe, and, above all, the Schlick of the *Allgemeine Erkenntnislehre*. Later on he was also to criticize Carnap's inductive logic and to suggest a solution of his own for the problem of induction. On both of these topics his point of view was closer to that of Karl R. Popper, whom he met for the first time in 1930. Popper's *Logik der Forschung* contained an incisive criticism of the idea of a meaning criterion and the notion of a positivistic basis of knowledge, as well as of the then current views on probability. This book was a thoroughly abridged version of an earlier manuscript, "Die Beiden Grundprobleme der Erkenntnistheorie," which was never published but which was discussed with Feigl and Carnap and which influenced both. (Compare for example [1].) Unfortunately the Vienna Circle had already found its bible, Wittgenstein's *Tractatus Logico-Philosophicus*, and its philosophy had been defined thereby. Arguments like those of Feigl and Popper therefore could perhaps cause some minor modifications,[2] but they could not bring about a major revision. Popper's book had appeared too late.[3]

Wittgenstein himself, who exerted such a decisive influence upon the Circle, did not participate in its discussions. Quite generally he was reluctant to converse about philosophical topics. But he would occasionally spend an evening in Schlick's house, together with Feigl and with Waismann (whom he later accused of plagiarism), where he might even take up and discuss a philosophical point. In conversations with Feigl, Wittgenstein would often start with a long outburst of criticism against Carnap; having thus unburdened himself, he would then contribute a great deal to illuminating and constructive argument. One evening in 1929, Feigl told me, he, Waismann, and Wittgenstein attended a lecture by the mathematician Jan Brouwer. Wittgenstein, at that time preoccupied with architecture, was scarcely interested in philosophy—Waismann and Feigl had to use strong persuasion in order to get him to Brouwer's lecture. The lecture, which was afterwards discussed in a Vienna café,

[2] Many of these modifications were silently dropped later on. Contemporary empiricism is therefore much less radical than was the empiricism of the thirties, and much less coherent. For this point cf. my [4], pp. 34ff.

[3] It was Feigl's belief that an earlier publication of the *Logik der Forschung* or of some other abridged version of the "Grundprobleme" would have decisively changed the history of the Vienna Circle. "We made a mistake," said he, "to choose Wittgenstein as our bible." (Private communication to Karl R. Popper.)

seemed to have made a great impression upon Wittgenstein and he returned to its discussion again and again. This may have been a decisive moment, or perhaps *the* decisive moment, in Wittgenstein's further development, and especially in the transition to his later philosophy. Although he always resented being reminded of, or compared to, Brouwer, the interpretation of his "new" philosophy as a constructivism that has been extended to the *whole* of language (rather than applied to part of it, viz., mathematics) is highly plausible, especially when one considers the examples used by him (e.g., the development of π) which can also be found in Brouwer.

From 1925 to 1927 Feigl worked on his doctoral dissertation, "Chance and Law: An Epistemological Investigation of Induction and Probability in the Natural Sciences." This thesis, which is available in a German manuscript only, pinpoints difficulties of the *Anwendungsproblem* which are as topical today as they were forty years ago. Having received his degree (*summa cum laude*), he was appointed lecturer at the *Volkshochschule Wien*, where he started with five students in a course in astronomy and ended up in 1930 with 250 students in the philosophy of science.

The following years, up to the founding of the Minnesota Center for the Philosophy of Science, are so full of events that only some of them can be related in telegram style.

1929: publication of *Theorie und Erfahrung in der Physik*, a book that was praised by many scholars, including Einstein and Pauli; visit to the Dessau Bauhaus and discussions with Klee and Kandinsky. This visit had been arranged by the energetic Neurath, who thought that the new philosophy of the Vienna Circle and the radicalism of the Bauhaus had much to offer to each other. Feigl thus became the first "missionary" of logical positivism.

1930: immigration to America and a Rockefeller Fellowship. Work with Bridgman on the foundations of physics.

1931–1932: lecturer at the State University of Iowa. 1933: assistant professor. 1938: associate professor.

1940: second Rockefeller Fellowship; work at Columbia and Harvard universities on the methodology of scientific explanation. This included discussions with Bertrand Russell, Rudolf Carnap, Alfred Tarski, Richard von Mises, W. V. Quine, I. A. Richards, E. G. Boring, Philipp Frank, and S. S. Stevens, all of whom were at Harvard at that time. During the same year, Feigl accepted the offer of a position as professor of philosophy at the University of Minnesota. He was also visiting professor at the University of California in Berkeley in 1946 and 1953, at Columbia University in 1950, and at the University of Hawaii in 1958.

It was at Minnesota that he finally realized his ambition to establish a center for advanced studies in the philosophy of science. The generous support of the Louis W. and Maud Hill Family Foundation made it possible to bring scholars from all over the world to this research institute at the University of Minnesota. One often wonders which has contributed more to the success of this unique institution—the philosophical excellence of the many visitors, or the genial atmosphere of the Center. It is not always possible to prevent philosophical discussions from turning into disappointing and nerve-racking quarrels. Even positivists have their "existential commitments," and it is not easy to remain calm when such commitments run into the danger of being exposed as ill-founded prejudices. Nor is it easy, in such discussions, to remain close to the topic chosen and to obtain results. The atmosphere at the Center, and especially Feigl's own attitude, his humor, his eagerness to advance philosophy and to get at least a glimpse at the truth, and his quite incredible modesty, made impossible from the very beginning that subjective tension that occasionally accompanies debate and that is liable to turn individual contributions into proclamations of faith rather than into answers to the questions chosen. The critical attitude was not absent; on the contrary, one now felt free to voice basic disagreement in clear, sharp, straightforward fashion. The discussions were, and still are, in many respects similar to the earlier discussions in the Vienna Circle. The differences are that things are seen now to be much more complex than was originally thought and that there is much less confidence that a single, comprehensive empirical philosophy might one day emerge.

Many hours are devoted to the analysis of specific theories, and the attempt is made both to obtain some guidance from the sciences concerning general philosophical principles and to advance the cause of the sciences themselves. The idea which was held by some empiricists that philosophy can only clarify concepts and cannot and should not contribute toward the solution of problems of physics or psychology has never been taken very seriously at the Center, and so close is the contact with the sciences that a physicist critical of the general trend of thinking in quantum theory suggested that the Center might become an anti-Copenhagen school. This suggestion is somewhat misleading, for there is variety enough among the participants to allow also for strong support of Bohr and his followers.

Metaphysics is no longer excluded. What is sought now is a way of defining its proper place in the scientific enterprise. A new philosophy has not yet emerged, but what has emerged is an attitude calling for critical and concrete discussion, an attitude of being prepared to examine any suggestion, however "metaphysical," and in this way to test its philosophical value.

Another difference is that it is no longer possible to utilize the charm of Viennese coffeehouses for advancing the cause of empiricism. But those preferring a more informal background for debate soon chose the Tempo Bar and Restaurant as a nocturnal meeting point, and here the pleasures of good food, good drinks, attractive waitresses, only slightly diminished by the noise emanating from the Hammond organ, very often led to the quick solution of a puzzle that had been turned inside out unsuccessfully for a considerable time in more academic settings.

Many philosophers and scientists have participated in the discussions of the Center. Among them are H. Gavin Alexander (later at the University of Manchester), Bruce Aune (now at the University of Pittsburgh), Kurt Baier (now at Pittsburgh), H. G. Bohnert (University of California), C. D. Broad (Cambridge), Roger Buck (now at Indiana University), Robert Bush (Pennsylvania), Rudolf Carnap (Los Angeles), Roderick Chisholm (Brown University), Lee J. Cronbach (Illinois), Helena Eilstein (Poland), Albert Ellis, Paul K. Feyerabend (California), Antony Flew (Keele), Else Fraenkel-Brunswik, Erik Gotlind (Uppsala), Adolf Grünbaum (Pittsburgh), N. R. Hanson (now at Yale), Starke Hathaway (Minnesota), E. L. Hill (Minnesota), Carl G. Hempel (Princeton), Roman Ingarden (Poland), Abraham Kaplan (now at Michigan), Howard Kendler (New York), Sigmund Koch (Duke), Alfred Landé (Ohio State), Gardner Lindzey (now at Texas), Kenneth MacCorquodale (Minnesota), Henry Margenau (Yale), Grover Maxwell (Minnesota, staff member of the Center), Paul E. Meehl (Minnesota, staff member of the Center), Henryk Mehlberg (Chicago), Ernest Nagel (Columbia), Paul Oppenheim (Princeton), Arthur Pap (Yale), Alberto Pasquinelli (Italy), Stephen Pepper (Berkeley), Karl R. Popper (London), Hilary Putnam (now at Harvard), S. R. Reid, B. F. Ritchie (Berkeley), William Rozeboom (now at Wesleyan, Connecticut), Gilbert Ryle (Oxford), Richard Schlegel (now at Michigan State), George

Schlesinger (Canberra), Michael Scriven (Indiana, former staff member of the Center), Wilfrid Sellars (Pittsburgh, former staff member of the Center), Kenneth W. Spence (now at Texas), P. F. Strawson (Oxford), D. L. Thistlethwaite (now at Vanderbilt), L. L. Whyte (London), Donald R. Yennie (now at Cornell), Wolfgang Yourgrau (now at Denver University), and Karl Zener (Duke). The results of the discussions have been published in the volumes of the *Minnesota Studies in the Philosophy of Science*, in papers appearing separately in such publications as *Current Issues in the Philosophy of Science* (edited by Feigl and Maxwell), the *Pittsburgh Studies in the Philosophy of Science*, the *Delaware Publications in the Philosophy of Science*, and in *Philosophical Studies* (a journal that is edited by Herbert Feigl in collaboration with Wilfrid Sellars) and other philosophical and scientific journals. They provide only partial evidence of the work done by guests, by Grover Maxwell, the only current resident staff member of the Center besides Feigl, and, above all, by Feigl himself and his former Center associates Michael Scriven (until 1956) and Wilfrid Sellars (until 1958).

The work in the Center, although almost all-consuming, does not exhaust Feigl's activity. He is an extremely popular lecturer and is much in demand by professional philosophers and various scientific groups, as well as by laymen. His wit and his ability to put complex problems in simple language have convinced many doubters among scientists (who are often likely to frown upon what they think is useless mental gymnastics) and among laymen that philosophy cannot be such a monster after all, and he has also done a great deal to allay the fairly prevalent impression that an empiricist is bound to be a dry and unimaginative bore.

Among Feigl's more recent official functions let me mention these: in 1954 he was one of the main invited speakers at the International Congress for the Philosophy of Science in Zurich; in 1958 he was the guest speaker of the American Psychological Association in Washington where he was given an enthusiastic reception by an audience of more than 3500 psychologists. (For some time previous to this, Feigl's interests had been concentrated in the philosophy of psychology. In 1947 he had obtained a Guggenheim Memorial Foundation grant for study of the methodological aspects of psychology. Since then he has devoted more and more time to the study of psychology. Some of the results are contained in his monumental essay "The 'Mental' and the 'Physical' " [3].) In 1959 he was elected a vice president of the American Association for the Advancement of

Science and chairman of its section L (for history and philosophy of science). He organized the program for a four-day meeting in Chicago (December 27–30, 1959) that became a model for similar meetings to be held thereafter. A large part of the proceedings grew out of previous Center activities. They are available in print in *Current Issues in the Philosophy of Science* (New York: Holt, Rinehart, and Winston, 1961). In the autumn of 1961 Feigl participated in the International Seminars of the European Forum at Alpbach in the Tyrol. In that year he was also elected vice president of the Western Division of the American Philosophical Association; in 1962 he became its president. He is a member of the Governing Board of the Philosophy of Science Association and of the U.S. National Committee of the International Union for the Philosophy of Science. In 1963 he was elected chairman of the section for epistemology and philosophy of science at the International Congress for Philosophy in Mexico City. He returned to the University of Mexico in the spring of 1964 for a series of lectures and symposia. That summer he returned to Alpbach to direct a seminar on the more recent development of analytic philosophy (together with Paul K. Feyerabend). The same conference also saw a rather dramatic "confrontation" of dialectical materialism (represented by the well-known Marxist philosopher Ernst Bloch and by the Czech philosopher Tlusty), idealism (represented by Professor Günther Rohrmoser of Frankfurt), and logical empiricism (represented by Feigl and Rudolf Carnap). Feigl's arguments were very favorably received, both on television and off, and the printed version of the debate promises to become a bestseller on the continent. In the same summer Feigl also attended a conference on analytic statements at Salzburg. Later in the year he taught at the Vienna Institute for Advanced Studies. In January of 1965 he traveled through Italy, Greece, Turkey, Israel, India, Malaysia, and Hong Kong, conferring with philosophers of science—frequently with the one and only philosopher of science in the locality—along the way, and arriving in Australia in March. He participated in conferences and gave lectures at various universities in Australia and returned to Minnesota in July of 1965.

All these activities are carried out with a unique combination of rationality and humor; they are guided by an artist's delight in the beauty of a well-constructed argument and a philosopher's deep devotion to the search for truth. We, the editors of this volume, and all those who have been fortunate enough to learn from him, as pupils and as friends, unite in the wish that we may be allowed to profit from our contact with him for many years to come.

REFERENCES

1. Carnap, Rudolf. "Ueber Protokollsätze," *Erkenntnis*, 3:215–228 (1933).
2. Feigl, Herbert. "Existential Hypotheses: Realistic versus Phenomenalistic Interpretations," *Philosophy of Science*, 17:35–62 (January 1950).
3. Feigl, Herbert. "The 'Mental' and the 'Physical,'" in *Minnesota Studies in the Philosophy of Science*, Vol. II, Herbert Feigl, Michael Scriven, and Grover Maxwell, eds., pp. 370–497. Minneapolis: University of Minnesota Press, 1958.
4. Feyerabend, P. K. "Explanation, Reduction, and Empiricism," in *Minnesota Studies in the Philosophy of Science*, Vol. III, Herbert Feigl and Grover Maxwell, eds., pp. 28–97. Minneapolis: University of Minnesota Press, 1962.
5. Kraft, Victor. *Erkenntnislehre*. Vienna: Springer Verlag, 1960.
6. Pap, Arthur. *Analytische Erkenntnistheorie*. Vienna: Springer Verlag, 1955.

Part I

PHILOSOPHY OF MIND AND RELATED ISSUES

BRUCE AUNE

\\\()))

Feigl on the Mind-Body Problem

Feigl's "The 'Mental' and the 'Physical' " [3] is the most comprehensive treatment in recent years of the tangle of puzzles that makes up the traditional mind-body problem. Not only does it contain detailed appraisals of the merits and defects of the most important positions taken on the problem, but the critical analyses it contains reflect the work of thinkers of an exceptionally wide range of philosophical orientation. The importance of the essay is therefore considerable: it rates high even as a compendium of informed opinion on a problem that has vexed philosophers for centuries. But quite apart from this, the solution it proposes to an important strand of the problem is highly original; and though, as I shall argue, it is not wholly successful, it points the direction in which a satisfactory solution is most likely to be found. In what follows I shall examine Feigl's position on this strand of the problem, which constitutes the age-old puzzle about the relation between "raw feels"—that is, itches, pangs, feelings, sense impressions—and the cortical occurrences, or brain states, on which we have reason to think their existence depends.

I

Feigl's conception of what he calls "raw feels" is considerably complicated. He is convinced, to begin with, that his knowledge of his own feelings and sense impressions is direct and immediate, and that this knowledge can be expressed in an "absolutely private" language—a language,

NOTE: This essay was written in 1961 with the aid of a summer grant awarded by the Productive Work Committee of Oberlin College.

[17]

that is, which no one other than himself could possibly understand. His private, phenomenal language can even be extended, he thinks, so as to provide a rational reconstruction of the entire language of science. This may sound as though he is a phenomenalist of the *Aufbau* sort, but he is not. For even in his enriched private language the term "physical object" would be taken to refer, not to a set of actual and possible sense impressions, but to an independent thing, perhaps a collection of molecules, which, when in contact with his or another's body (also conceived as a theoretical entity), produces the relevant sense impressions. Feigl thinks that any good epistemological analysis of the language of science should show that all empirical concepts are ultimately based on the analyst's private data, for such data form the "deepest level of [empirical] evidence" (see [3], pages 392, 443).

While he believes that all significant knowledge claims can be reconstructed on this private, phenomenal basis, he does not actually try to do it himself; he merely indicates the way in which he thinks it *could* be done. As I have just remarked, this would in his opinion be accomplished by construing persons, physical objects, and so on as theoretical entities, or collections of such, related in various ways to one another and having effects on the analyst which turn up, phenomenally, in his private sensory field.

Now, as a realist, Feigl not only accepts the idea that there are other people standing in objective spatiotemporal relations to one another, but even agrees that they have a language, different from his private one, which he can hear and understand. This latter language is essentially intersubjective, that is, such that every statement formulated in terms of it is, in principle, capable of confirmation by more than one person. As a consequence of this, the statements it enables him to make about other people's feelings must be confirmable with respect to the behavior they can be observed to exhibit in a certain range of circumstances. For him, as for most contemporary thinkers, this means that familiar, nonprivate words like "feeling" or "sense impression" must be understood as referring to something that is intimately bound up with observable behavior. This, of course, is a thesis of philosophical behaviorism; the behaviorist simply adds, first, that private languages are impossibilities, that the only true languages are the intersubjective ones, and second, that even a person's feelings and sensations are nothing but behavior or dispositions to exhibit behavior.

Feigl rejects this reductionistic addendum, however. For him a feeling —even as describable in the intersubjective language—is a condition or occurrence, not just a pattern of behavior or a mere disposition to behave in a certain way. Since statements about such feelings must be publicly confirmable, these occurrences must be identifiable in the light of their observable effects or manifestations, but they are not therefore *reducible* to such manifestations. To assume that they are so reducible is to confuse, as Feigl says, the evidence for a statement with the statement's reference. Thus, in Feigl's view a sense impression or feeling is definable, with respect to the public language, as a state or condition of a person that results from a certain kind of stimulation and in turn disposes him to behave in a certain way. As so definable, such states or conditions are theoretical with respect to the public observation language, that is, to that part of the intersubjective language which is used to speak of things that are called "observable" in that language—things like birds, trees, or meter readings.

Using a term from molar behavior theory that is used to refer to similar nonobservable conditions, Feigl calls sensations and feelings, as they are describable in the public language, "central states." He uses this term because, as a scientific empiricist with reconstructionist leanings, he is far more interested in the language of science than in the language of everyday life; for scientific language, being technical and relatively precise, is presumably capable of exact characterization—and this, he believes, cannot be done for the constantly changing and metaphor-ridden language of the common man. Still, when he remarks that terms like "feeling" and "sense impression" refer to central states, he is expressing his conviction that, pictorial appeals and so forth aside, such terms play a role in everyday language that is analogous to the role of certain so-called theoretical terms in a scientific language of molar behavior theory. Whether this conviction is justified is a question I shall consider later on.

Since, however, Feigl thinks that feelings and sense impressions are describable in two radically different languages, namely, his private language and the language of everyday life, the strand of the mind-body problem that worries him the most thus concerns the relation between occurrences described in three logically distinct ways. These are his private phenomenal data, the sensations ascribed to him by educated common sense or the central states ascribed to him in the language of molar behavior theory, and certain occurrences in his cerebral cortex, on which

[19]

the existence of his sensations as publicly describable occurrences presumably depends.

Feigl begins the long, complicated argument leading to the resolution of his problem with a number of considerations designed to show that the "acquaintancewise possibly unknown states which the behaviorist must introduce for the sake of a theoretical explanation of overt behavior, and to which he (no longer a 'radical' behaviorist) refers as the central causes of the peripheral behavior symptoms and manifestations, may well be *identical* with the referents of the phenomenal (acquaintance) terms used by his subject in introspective descriptions of his (the subject's) direct experience" (page 436). But his reasoning at this point seems a little disjointed. For when he adds that "in ordinary communication about our respective mental states, we make this assumption of identity quite unquestioningly" (*ibid.*), he *suggests* that each person introspects in his own private language but ascribes sensations to others in the admittedly very different language of common life. Yet if the common assumption he alludes to concerns our common-sense belief that we can talk about the feelings that other people have and describe to us, then it really adds no weight to the thesis he is trying to defend. For in discussing introspective descriptions he is concerned with the reference of terms in absolutely private languages, and in describing these languages he has made it clear that private, phenomenal statements cannot be expressed overtly—since their overt expression would provide clues to their meaning (compare page 402).

Now if he is serious in his view that phenomenal statements cannot be expressed overtly and that introspection is always done in a phenomenal language, it follows at once that introspective reports cannot be expressed in audible terms. But this consequence makes his position very difficult to accept. For it seems perfectly clear that people do in fact make overt introspective reports; indeed, our chief reason for thinking that they do introspect is based on the reports, or avowals, that we hear them make. And if avowals like "I have a headache" or "The back of my hand tingles" are not to count as expressing introspective knowledge, it is by no means clear what they do express. It seems to me—in part because I do not happen to have a special phenomenal language myself—that it is much more natural, and in fact far easier, to forget about private languages and assume that one at least *can* introspect in the language one uses in speaking of the feelings of others.

It is worth emphasizing in this connection that Feigl's commitment to private languages is actually a little ambiguous. For when he gives examples of introspective reports he never expresses them in anything resembling a private language—in fact he always uses ordinary English. Thus, on page 403 he remarks that he could assert on the basis of private acquaintance: "Ah, there is that peculiar smell again; I don't know what causes it, I don't even know how to label it; it is so different from any fragrances of flowers, perfumes . . . that I can't even place it in a multidimensional scheme of the rank orders of smells; but I know I have experienced this smell before and I am . . . sure I would recognize it in the future if I were to experience it again." Since this statement is easily understandable by anyone who knows English and yet has all the earmarks of a bona fide introspective report, it is difficult to believe that he is really prepared to deny that we can introspect in the language of everyday life. In the light, moreover, of his occasional remarks about the extreme difficulty of constructing private languages (compare pages 466–468), and of the programmatic air of his talk about their construction, it is very hard to suppress the idea that, his official statements to the contrary, he does not really possess a private language at all but merely thinks that he *could* construct one. But if it is actually his opinion that it is only possible to construct one, that he is not in possession of one now, and that he is presently quite capable of describing his feelings in ordinary English, then the entire complexion of his problem changes: for if he restricts his attention to languages already in existence, he can handle his puzzle about raw feels without any mention of private languages and the difficulties they carry with them.

III

One might therefore ask why he thinks there is any point in constructing private languages, and why he thinks their existence or nonexistence should have any importance for the part of the mind-body problem that mainly concerns him. The answer to such questions, I take it, is that he wants to put his solution of the problem on a secure empirical footing— and for him this means basing it on the data of his immediate experience. But if we recall that there is an important logical difference between *having* a sensation and *thinking about* a sensation, the idea that private, phenomenal statements are necessarily more reliable than statements of other kinds seems extremely doubtful. For what guarantee is there that the private statement I make when I have a certain sensation represents it correctly? How, in point of fact, could I ever rule out the possibility that every time I assert a particular phenomenal sentence I have a radically different sensation—first one that makes me want to laugh, then one that makes me want to scratch my leg, then one that makes me want to scream, and so on? What basis could I possibly have for thinking that such a chaotic situation is even unlikely?

Traditionally, of course, it has been argued that awareness is what guarantees the reliability of one's thoughts about one's own sensations. But what is awareness, and how can it guarantee anything? If we define "being aware of P" as "having P and thinking 'That's P,'" then of course an awareness of P would necessitate the truth of one's thought. But this sort of definition could never remove the difficulty in point, for the question would simply arise: How can one be sure that one is ever really aware of a phenomenal item? The mere thought that one is aware of such an item is not sufficient to show this—any more than one's thinking "That's P" is enough to show that one does indeed have P. The fact is, if awareness is to provide any support for the claims of a private language, it must somehow guarantee the reliability of phenomenal statements generally; and if it is merely described as correct thinking, as it is above, or as a mysterious activity of the mind, as it was by traditional philosophers, then it very definitely fails to do this.

In conversation Feigl once suggested that the "coherence" of private thoughts is perhaps sufficient to show their truth. But this suggestion, though it has been advanced by any number of philosophers, is actually question-begging, for the coherence of one's private thoughts, whatever that is, is presumably just another phenomenal fact itself, and there is no absurdity in the idea that one might think "The thoughts A, B, and C cohere" even when there is no coherence at all. In other words, a thought of this kind is evidently in no better a position to guarantee the accuracy of private thinking than any other private occurrence: they all seem to be in the same doubtful category, and we have no absolute assurance—a priori or empirical—that they could not occasionally be as unrelated to their objects as the word salads of a schizophrenic are unrelated to the world around him.

IV

Now, if it is impossible to establish the superior reliability of introspective reports made within the confines of an essentially private language, it appears that there is no real point in trying to construct such a language,[1] or even in arguing that such things must be possible. Since Feigl himself has no serious doubts about the existence of an "external" world and of other people and the languages they speak, it thus seems fair to disregard private languages entirely and pose his chief mental-physical problem in terms of languages that actually exist.

If we turn, then, to languages actually used, we find that the condition of public confirmability poses certain restrictions on what can meaningfully be said about the thoughts and feelings of human beings. In particular, it requires that "inner processes stand in need of outward criteria."[2] This means that psychological processes must at least be "triangulated," to use Feigl's word, by behavioral indicators. Many behaviorists have of course argued that the connection between the psychical and the behavioral is more intimate than this—and in connection with some psychological states I think they are right. (For example, moods and emotions are mainly dispositional, though some of them, like depression, are in part dispositions to have certain feelings; see my [1], *passim*.) But the idea that feelings, sense impressions, afterimages, and the like are *merely* patterns of behavior or dispositions to behave in certain ways strikes me as exceedingly grotesque. I shall not try to refute the idea here, for I have taken pains to do it elsewhere [1, 2]; but it is worth mentioning that its root mistake is characteristic of phenomenalism, a view that most behaviorists abhor. The mistake here is the contention that anything we can intelligibly speak of must either be observable or else be a logical construction out of observables. For the phenomenalists, of course, the true observables were sense data, and all other things, including persons and physical objects, were logical constructions out of them. For the behaviorists, however, physical objects, persons, and their behavior are observable, and feelings, pangs, and afterimages are given the status of logical constructions. The strategy of both is thus precisely the same;

---

[1] In view of the many recent attacks on private languages, this claim is actually a modest one. For further discussion see [17], Sects. 256ff., [8], and [6].

[2] Cf. [17], Sect. 580. In the following sentence I speak of indicators rather than criteria, because I think the term "criteria" is highly misleading in this connection. Cf. my [1], Sects. X–XIV.

their views diverge mainly because they begin with a different conception of what is truly observable.

Although I emphatically agree with Feigl that the behaviorists' view of feelings and sense impressions is both crude and procrustean, it is useful to consider in a little detail some of the particular difficulties that non-behavioristic views are thought to involve; for behaviorism is still fairly influential, and the cogency of Feigl's contention that sensations (as publicly describable conditions) have the status of central states is perhaps best appraised in the light of dissenting opinion. Three possible objections may be built from the following premises.[3] (1) We do not generally have to *infer* from a person's behavior that he has a certain feeling, for instance pain; in fact we often say that we can simply see, or observe, that he has that feeling. (2) Since the meaning or "use" of mentalistic terms is learned in a social context, where alleged inner feelings are not open to view, these terms must apply to what is observable; and what is observable in the case, say, of a hurt child is his behavior. (3) Reference to unobservable things, events, or processes is unscientific; it is characteristic of the shabbiest metaphysics, and no respectable thinker should ever take it seriously.

V

An objection may arise from (1) as follows. "If Feigl is right in thinking that sensations have the status of central states, then it follows that they are unobservable and that a person's behavior provides at best an indication, a basis for inferring, that he has a certain sensation. But as a matter of fact we seldom have to infer how a person feels from the way he behaves; on the contrary, we often say that we can simply see how he feels. Since these facts suggest that feelings are neither unobservable nor only inferable, Feigl's view seems clearly indefensible."

Two considerations are sufficient to destroy the plausibility of this sort of objection. First, our talk of seeing or observing *that* others have certain feelings does not imply that those feelings are themselves observable. One can see *that* it will rain, *that* a barium atom has just been struck by a neutron in a cloud chamber, and so on, even though, by existing standards, future rainstorms, barium atoms, and neutrons are not considered observable. Second, though we do not always make inferences which lead

---

[3] The third premise is assumed in countless discussions, but for statements of the first and second see [16] and [6], respectively.

us to conclude that other people have certain feelings, it does not follow that their feelings are not, in some sense, "inner states." For while a specific visual stimulus (as of a crying child) may directly elicit a verbal response (such as "He feels pain"), it is not generally true that the response *refers* to the stimulus. The fact of the matter is that we are normally led to think carefully about a man's behavior only when its significance is not immediately obvious: as Dewey used to insist, we begin to think, to infer, only when the situation confronting us is in some way problematic. If, however, we are in a court of law, where we are instructed to relate exactly what we saw, we must ignore our quick decisions and attend to observable behavior; for our opinions about a man's feelings are *justifiable*, in the end, only with reference to the way he acts in a given kind of circumstance. That we must in this way back up our opinions by reference to what we can actually observe (not observe *that*) is especially obvious when it comes to afterimages, hallucinations, or even sense impressions; but if one insists that our frequent lack of inference makes the objects of our assertion observable, then the same status must be awarded to the most recondite of subatomic particles, for experts can come to quick decisions about these, too.

The second argument, that the intersubjective origin of psychological concepts precludes their reference to unobservable "inner" occurrences, is simply a *non sequitur*. For, as I have just pointed out, the fact that we are taught to identify a person's feelings on the basis of observing his behavior does not show that the words we use *refer* to his behavior. Besides, children often learn to say the right thing at the right time, even when they are quite in the dark about the meaning of what they say; and just because a child gains the ability to say "He's in pain" on the appropriate occasions, we are not obliged to agree that he knows just exactly what the word "pain" means. In fact, we might well insist that a person does not fully understand this word until, in a nonparroting way, he can say something to the effect that "pain" refers to a feeling, a covert state or occurrence, that is distinguished from others by its tendency to produce crying, jumping, screaming, or swearing.

Insofar as the public character of learning situations is concerned, it is worth pointing out that the psychologist B. F. Skinner, himself at times a very radical behaviorist, has described [15] at least four ways in which reference to "unobservable stimuli" can readily be learned. I shall not repeat Skinner's arguments here, since they are easily accessible; but it should be emphasized, in view of the third objection listed above, that there is nothing metaphysical about them. The idea that we open the door to metaphysics if we allow reference to what we cannot observe is not only crude but unnecessarily positivistic. For we do not have to purge our ontologies of *all* unobservables in order to avoid the excess baggage of traditional metaphysics; this can be done with far more modest means (compare, for example, [3] and [9]). Moreover, as I believe my discussion of the behaviorists' views about observability has shown, the very distinction between observables and unobservables is far more methodological than ontological, resting largely on what we are willing to call "observable."[4] If, for instance, we are prepared to say that we can observe through an ordinary compound microscope—let alone an electronic one—then microbes and many kinds of molecules become observable entities. Of course, we commonly have no difficulty distinguishing paradigm cases of observables and unobservables, like birds and pi mesons, but there are plenty of borderline cases where indecision is chronic—and this indecision is by no means due to our inability to detect profound ontological differences.

VI

In view of these rebuttals to behavioristic arguments it appears that Feigl's contention, that sense impressions, feelings, and so forth are, like central states, unobservable occurrences defined in relation to a set of behavioral indicators, is not unreasonable. Still, he has little to say about one's ability to introspect in the language of everyday life, and, having already admitted that this is possible, I must now try to square it with his interpretation of feelings and sensations as central states.

The question to be faced, then, concerns the possibility of knowing introspectively that one has a certain sensation, where a sensation is to be interpreted as a central state. Let us therefore suppose that a child has a headache, and that his headache is an unobservable occurrence, or condition, that is identifiable for others by the distinctive behavior, verbal and otherwise, that it occasions. Since a child's headache is normally apparent to those around him, they are able to tell him what he feels as well as teach him to recognize such feelings in other people. As time goes on he gradually gains the ability to say the right things when he is asked "How do you feel?" or "Do you feel pain?" But though he learns to say

[4] For a thorough defense of this point see [9] and [5].

such things, he does not have to base them on some sort of private observation; they are more like conditioned responses, similar to audible responses that even a parrot could be trained to make. As a human being, however, he is capable of learning the conventional significance of the words he utters: he can learn their reference, he can learn to apply them to others, and he can even gain the ability to explain human behavior by the use of them. When he has learned these things, or gained these abilities, he can at least introspect out loud; he can at least identify in audible words the feeling that he has. When he has a headache, he can tell others about it and know that what he says is true.

Now it is obvious that a person can learn to inhibit his overt verbal responses; instead of saying out loud "I have a headache," he can say this to himself *sub voce*. (Silent speech of this sort, which is a species of thinking, is learned as easily as silent reading.) Since these subvocal utterances are made in the language of overt speech, and are the product of the same set of verbal habits, they are every bit as reliable, as correct, as the words he addresses to others. In saying this, I am not claiming that all thought is just subvocal speech—and I am not denying that there is more to speaking than a mere emission of noises and more to thinking than verbal imagery or minute physical movements. In fact I am willing to insist that any true speech, audible or covert, must be more than a blind, parrotish response—must at least be produced when one is in what Ryle [12, page 183] would call a "proper frame of mind," that is, a state of intellectual readiness to re-express or explain what one has just said or thought and to act appropriately when the occasion arises. What I am presently arguing is just that in learning a language one develops a peculiar set of verbal habits, a "reporting mechanism" if you will, that can guarantee, as awareness or direct apprehension cannot, the reliability as well as the reference of what one says or thinks about one's own sensory condition.[5]

If this line of reasoning is sound (as I believe it is), it thus appears that our ability to introspect is not incompatible with the idea that our sensations and feelings have the status of central states. For suppose that a headache is to be understood as a peculiar condition of a person that disposes him to hold his head, blink his eyes, complain about excessive noise, demand aspirin, and so on. He could then be taught to call this

[5] For a more detailed defense of this interpretation of introspection, see [13], [1], and [2].

[27]

condition "a headache" and identify it as such without making an overt verbal response. This sort of silent identification, the correctness of which is justified by the established reliability of his habits of using language, could reasonably be called, I think, "an introspective act."

VII

I have just remarked that my interpretation of introspection appears to be consistent with Feigl's contention that raw feels, as describable in everyday language, have the status of central states. As I shall argue later on, however, this appearance is a little deceptive, for it is possible to show that we can justifiably ascribe properties to our raw feels that are not, in any straightforward way, ascribable to central states. Nevertheless I am convinced that Feigl's view is still very close to the truth, requiring supplementation rather than outright revision; and I shall therefore postpone my criticism until I consider his argument for the identity of raw feels and brain states, which to my mind is the most exciting, promising, and original feature of his essay.

For the moment, however, I want to make a brief comment on how my view of introspection relates to Feigl's empiricist thesis that introspective knowledge constitutes the "deepest level of evidence" for one's views about the world. From what I have said about introspection it should be clear his thesis cannot be correct, for we learn to introspect in a social context and the success of our attempts, as well as the sense of our words, is always to be appraised by social standards. Sensation does, of course, play an important role in perception, and we learn most of what we know about the world by perceiving it. But perceptual knowledge is not to be understood in the traditional way. On the contrary, the basic perceptual statements we learn to make apply not to the sensations that elicit them (as they do in introspection) but to objects in the external world. In the case of perceiving a chair, for instance, one normally has certain visual impressions; but the verbal response or thought elicited by them, e.g., "That's a chair," which might be accompanied by a pointing gesture, applies not to the impressions but to something else, namely a physical object. Of course, we learn to speak of visual impressions too: as Sellars has remarked [13, Section III], this often begins when we say "There's a chair" and we are told that no chair is really there. But because the standard purpose of speech is communication, we tend to respond in perceptual situations with words about public things rather than our impressions of the moment. The fact is, the recognition of one's sense impressions is generally a highly sophisticated accomplishment: in most cases it is far from easy to shift attention from a fascinating and stable world to the fluttering fuzziness of sensory experience.

In order to avoid misunderstanding, a word should also be said about the alleged infallibility of introspective reports. As I have already pointed out, this infallibility was traditionally ascribed to the power of awareness; but many thinkers, finding awareness too mysterious or too tenuous for such an exacting job, have found it sufficient to emphasize the modesty of introspective claims. In introspection, they say, we merely *label* our feelings; and in merely labeling a feeling we do not imply anything about ourselves that could possibly turn out to be false. Yet if we introspect in the language of everyday life, identifying our condition as that of being in pain, for instance, we are surely doing more than merely labeling a feeling. We are in fact ascribing a complicated condition to ourselves, a condition that others are often in; and as I have already shown, such a condition has abundant consequences for our behavior. Besides, our "reporting mechanism," our habits of correct response that add weight to our thoughts and avowals, are as fallible as any other habit, and our words and thoughts about ourselves might conceivably become as wild and chaotic as those of the most disorganized schizophrenic.

It is often argued nowadays, however, that our ability to make the right verbal response when we have a certain feeling constitutes a "criterion" for having the concept of that feeling, and that consequently what counts against the truth of what we seem to be asserting *ipso facto* counts against our having the appropriate concepts, hence against our making the assertion we seem to be making, and a fortiori against our making the false assertion we seem to be making. But it should be clear that this sort of consideration also applies to our assertions about physical objects observed in standard conditions. Thus, if a man looking at a paradigm case of a chair in full daylight in all honesty said "That's a table," we might argue that his remark only shows that he does not know what chairs and tables are, and that he was not therefore *asserting* what he seemed to be asserting. (It might even be argued that he was not really asserting anything at all—only parroting a string of vocables.) This latter point, owing to the vagueness of our criteria for having a concept and making an assertion, is not really strong enough to end all philosophical battles about the fallibility of perceptual knowledge. But it does show—

clearly enough, I think—that any sharp distinction between the fallibility of introspective and observational knowledge is impossible to maintain, and that knowledge of the latter sort provides as secure a "foundation" for empirical knowledge as one could reasonably demand.[6]

VIII

As we turn now to Feigl's view of the relation between raw feels and brain states, it is important to observe that his major argument is based on scientific as well as logical considerations. His "admittedly bold and risky" guess is that progress in neurophysiology will demonstrate an increasingly close correlation between sensations and brain states, and he sets himself the task of showing that there are no serious logical difficulties with the idea that this correlation might turn out to be an actual identity, that is, that purely factual discoveries might eventually entitle one to say that sensations and brain states are identical occurrences. Such an identity would of course be empirical or synthetic, and Feigl accordingly insists that it would therefore be similar to the identity of the morning star and the evening star, not to the identity of say, 5 and 3 + 2.

But while it is easy to see how we came to know that the morning star and the evening star are actually the same planet, it is far from easy to see how we could possibly come to know that sensations are really brain states. Feigl reasons as follows, however. If a comprehensive molar behavior theory, corresponding to our common-sense view of the nature of sensation, were *reducible* to neurophysiology, so that the molar terms corresponding to sensation terms were eliminable from the resulting fused theory, then the occurrences or states denoted by the molar terms would be shown to be identical with occurrences or states denoted by certain neurophysiological terms.[7] That is to say, if a reduction of this sort were carried out, we would then be in a position, Feigl argues, to say that the referents of both the molar and the neurophysiological terms are precisely the same.

[6] I do not mean to suggest here that empirical knowledge really needs a special "foundation." For arguments to the contrary, see [13], [14], and [5].

[7] The word "reduction," as it is used here, can be defined in general terms as follows. If T_1 and T_2 are formalized scientific theories, T_2 is said to be *reduced* to T_1 if, and only if, (a) the vocabulary of T_2 contains terms not in the vocabulary of T_1, (b) any observable data explained by T_2 are also explained by T_1, and (c) T_1 is at least as well systematized as T_2. For further discussion of the notion of reduction, see [11], [7], and [10], Ch. 11.

IX

In order to understand Feigl's reasoning more exactly, let us consider in some detail how the reduction of molar behavior theory to neurophysiology might be accomplished. To simplify matters let us assume that the behavior theory in question is far less complicated than it would actually be: let us assume that it contains just two theoretical terms, "R_T" and "S_T," one theoretical postulate,

(1) $R_T x, t \supset S_T x, t$,

and three so-called correspondence rules,

(2) $R_T x, t \supset D_O x, t$,
(3) $S_O x, t \supset R_T x, t$,
(4) $S_T x, t \supset P_O x, t$,

the subscripts "T" and "O" indicating whether the term is theoretical or observational, respectively. Let us assume that these postulates are to be read as follows, where the observational terms "D_O," "S_O," and "P_O" are presumably familiar:

(1)   If x has the raw feel R_T at t, then the body of x is altered by the unobservable stimulus S_T at t;

(2)   If x has the raw feel R_T at t, then x has the set of behavioral dispositions D_O at t;

(3)   If x is in contact with the observable stimulus S_O at t, then x has the raw feel R_T at t;

(4)   If the body of x is altered by the stimulus S_T at t, the pulse of x assumes the pattern P_O.

If we think of R_T as being something like pain, the theoretical postulate tells us that this raw feel results from some unobservable stimulus, perhaps an alteration in a sense organ, which has a particular effect on x's pulse rate; and the correspondence rules show us how the raw feel is connected with its behavioral indicators.[8] In order to give this simplified model added semblance to a living theory, we might assume that the theoretical postulate (1) was introduced because, at an early stage of the theory's development, R_T was thought to occur occasionally when no S_O was observed, and the unobservable stimulus S_T was then postulated to account for this fact. The postulate (1) would then be similar to our

---

[8] These so-called correspondence rules are highly simplified, and they do not therefore give a fully accurate picture of the connection between raw feels and their behavioral indicators. Some of the qualifications that would have to be made here are pointed out in my [1], Sects. X–XIV.

common-sense assumption that when a person feels pain in the absence of overt stimulation, something unobservable is causing it.

Now suppose that progress in neurophysiology should disclose a cortical state C which always results from S_0 and always in turn produces the set of behavioral dispositions D. Suppose, moreover, that every occurrence of this condition is found to be accompanied by the agent's change in pulse rate P_0, though for special reasons it is asserted that C is quite different from S_T, which elicits P_0 directly. As a moment's scrutiny of the behavior theory—call it BT—will show, the existence of the cortical state C would, under these conditions, explain everything explainable with reference to the central state R_T. Since we may assume that the neurophysiological theory, NT, is as well systematized as BT, the latter would then be reducible to the former, and statements containing "R_T" would no longer be necessary for the scientific explanation of human behavior.

x

But although in the new, fused Theory of Sentient Organisms the term "R_T" would be eliminable in favor of "C," a term far richer in explanatory power, just what is Feigl's justification for concluding that the referents of "R_T" and "C" are the same? Well, if "R_T" is indeed eliminable in favor of "C," some statement must be introduced that warrants this. For Feigl this would be:

(5) $R_T x,t \equiv C x,t.$

Though the terms "R_T" and "C" are not synonymous, and (5) appears to be nothing but a material equivalence, asserting no more than a correlation between R_T and C, Feigl nevertheless contends that (5) may be "interpreted" as showing that the referents of "R_T" and "C" are actually the same (see [3], page 461).

I shall not consider the details of Feigl's argument for this last point, since it is long, discursive, and complicated. Generally speaking, though, it is based on two main considerations, first, that if "$R_T = C$" is true, it is then easy to explain why (5) should hold, and, second, that there are, in view of (5), no good, nonmetaphysical reasons for thinking that "$R_T = C$" is not true; in fact, Occam's Razor positively instructs us to reject the idea that R_T and C are distinct. These considerations, especially the second one, plainly require a good deal of amplification before anything like Feigl's thesis is reasonably secure, and Feigl is accordingly forced to wrestle with many minor difficulties that are generated, for instance by Leibniz's famous principle of *identitas indiscernibilium*. His struggle with difficulties of this sort is what makes his argument so long and difficult to assess.

Fortunately, however, it is possible to defend his thesis with far greater economy of argument. To begin with, we must recall that in Feigl's view sensations and the like are to be construed as publicly unobservable states or conditions, distinguishable from one another (so far as public languages are concerned) by the kind of behavior that they produce and by the kind of stimulation that elicits them. These conditions, moreover, are assumed to be *unique* determinants of human behavior; that is, they are understood to be *the* conditions that result from particular kinds of stimulation and in turn produce distinctive patterns of observable behavior.[9] Pain, for example, is thus definable, in Feigl's view, as *that peculiar condition* of a person which results from cuts, burns, and bruises, and disposes him, in turn, to jump, cry, swear, say "It hurts," and so on.

Now, if sensations are to be understood this way, and if the model theory BT is to represent, even in a highly simplified form, our basic commitments as to the nature of sensations, then BT must contain the added assumption that there is one, and only one, state of a human organism, Φ, such that anyone in contact with the stimulus S_O must be in Φ, and such that anyone in Φ will have the dispositions D_O, probably be affected by the unobservable stimulus S_T, and hence have the characteristic pulse rate P_O. If we express the postulates of BT as

(6) $(R_T x, t \supset : S_T x, t \cdot D_O x, t) \cdot (S_O x, t \supset R_T x, t) \cdot (S_T x, t \supset P_O x, t)$,

the assumption in point will be:

(7) $(E!\Phi)(x)(t)[(\Phi x, t \supset : S_T x, t \cdot D_O x, t) \cdot (S_O x, t \supset \Phi x, t) \cdot (S_T x, t \supset P_O x, t)]$,

which is to say:

(8) $(\exists \Phi)(x)(t)([\Phi x, t \supset : S_T x, t \cdot D_O x, t] \cdot [S_O x, t \supset \Phi x, t] \cdot [S_T x, t \supset P_O x, t] \cdot (\Theta)([\Theta x, t \supset : S_T x, t \cdot D_O x, t] \cdot [S_O x, t \supset \Theta x, t] \cdot [S_T x, t \supset P_O x, t] : \supset \Phi = \Theta))$.

Since from (5) and (6) we can infer

(9) $(C x, t \supset : S_T x, t \cdot D_O x, t) \cdot (S_O x, t \supset C x, t) \cdot (S_T x, t \supset P_O x, t)$,

[9] This is a natural consequence of Feigl's frequent assertion that the raw feels of others are known "by description," known, that is, as *the* conditions such that . . . Cf. [3], pp. 431–435.

it follows from (8) and (6) that

(10) $R_T = C,$

which is a statement of the identity Feigl seeks.

XI

This last argument appears to show that if raw feels do indeed have the status of "central states," so that the intersubjective concept of a raw feel is really an explanatory concept of the theoretical sort, there are then no logical difficulties with Feigl's identity thesis (at least as I have formulated it). Actually, however, certain "type" difficulties remain; for "R_T" refers to a state or condition of a person, while "C" refers to a condition of a person's cerebral cortex. And it is in general not true that a condition of a *part* of a person's body is a condition of the person himself. Thus, to take a very plain example, if a person's hair is black it does not follow that he himself is black, for he might be an albino with dyed hair.

But this difficulty can perhaps be obviated as follows. We might simply say that "Cx,t" means "x is in a C-state at t," where the C-state is to be specified in terms of, say, the pattern of neuron firings on a certain area of x's brain. It might of course seem that this is simply an *ad hoc* device for escaping a serious objection to Feigl's theory; but it must be remembered that if R_T is supposed to be an intrinsically unspecified condition of a person that is posited in order to account for a certain pattern of his behavior, then it need not involve the person as a whole; it might qualify just a part of him. Thus, for example, the condition of Smith which accounts for his proneness to bump into chairs, people, and doors might simply be an eye disease; and this disease might be specified as a particular sort of breakdown of retinal tissue, that is, "as a condition of his eyes, not of him." As this example shows, when we talk of a condition of a person the import of what we say is elastic, or vague, enough to allow a stricter interpretation, namely that the condition is "really" a condition of only a part of a person's body.

XII

If my comments on Feigl's identity thesis are sound, it appears that any serious objection to it must be directed against the assumption that raw feels (as intersubjectively describable occurrences) must have the status of central states, for it is this assumption that makes it possible for Feigl to base his argument for their identity on the possibility of reducing behavior theory to neurophysiology. But although I have already expressed some misgivings about this assumption, I must admit that it is at least close to the truth. For if we take the condition of public confirmability for legitimate assertions seriously, then the behavioristic alternative is apparently avoidable only on the assumption that feelings, sense impressions, and the like are to be understood as publicly unobservable conditions specifiable in relation to a cluster of indicators. This assumption gains plausibility, moreover, from our familiar practice of referring to such conditions in order to *explain* observable behavior. Thus, in answer to the question "Why is he limping?" we might say, not "He has a skeletal disorder," but "He has a very painful, arthritic knee." Explanations of this sort, which have a striking affinity with theoretical explanations generally, add considerable weight to Feigl's view, for they illustrate his point that our everyday (nonprivate) sensation concepts have, to a remarkable extent, the character of typical explanatory concepts.

But while I am not prepared to deny that sensation statements of our ordinary language have an important explanatory force, I cannot agree that they are *merely* a special sort of theoretical statement. It seems clear to me that they have an added dimension of significance, which is due to their role in introspection.[10] For when a properly trained person has a particular feeling or sense impression, he knows it "directly" and is capable of describing it: his access to his own feelings is, after all, every bit as intimate as his access to the observable things around him. Of course, as I have been at pains to stress, a person must be trained to recognize his own feelings; and it is only because we have reason to think his training has been successful in establishing reliable habits of verbal response that we take his words about himself seriously. But when we know that his "reporting mechanism" functions properly, so that what he says about himself and his immediate environment is normally a reliable indicator of how he feels and what his immediate surroundings are like, then the fact that he describes his sense impressions in a certain way gives us reason to think that they are as he says they are. The same, of course, applies to ourselves: if we have been properly trained in the use of our language, we should be confident that our own verbal responses are not wild, and that the descriptions we give, or the analogies we make, in honestly try-

[10] This point is emphasized in [13], p. 321.

ing to convey the *quale* of our experiences to others, are not only informative but even fairly accurate.

The importance of this point comes out more clearly, I think, when we consider sense impressions. If we were concerned to develop a partial behavior theory, designed to account for the fact that a man, Jones, utters sentences like "That's red and triangular" when he is, and sometimes is not, in front of red triangles, we might say that he has an *impression* of a red triangle when the following are true of him [13, Section XVI]: (1) He correctly identifies a red triangle merely by looking at it. (2) He maintains that an object is red and triangular, though it is perhaps a green square. (3) He asserts that there is a red triangle before him, when, say, he is looking at nothing but a blank, gray wall. If we define "having an impression of a red triangle" as a condition of a person common to situations described by (1), (2), and (3) above, then this condition would have pretty much the character of a "central state." But when we realize that Jones's verbal habits are highly developed and hardly ever inaccurate, we have good grounds for taking his remarks seriously when he begins to describe the character of his sense impressions, that is, when he begins to describe what he "sees" when there is no physical object before his eyes. If, of course, we had never had, or thought we had, sense impressions, we might wonder why the man should say such curious things, why he should describe objects that are not really there. But the fact is, we have sense impressions too, and with just a little ingenuity, and perhaps a little reading of the psychology of perception or even the work of "old-fashioned" sense-datum philosophers, we can easily put ourselves in situations, empty of the appropriate physical objects, where we too will describe objects that are not physically there. Indeed, once the mechanism of introspection is understood, there is really no reason to doubt the reports of what people "see," what sense impressions they have, even when they take drugs like mescaline; for if we were to take these drugs, it is actually probable that we should "see" strange shapes too. (It is surely no accident that men like Aldous Huxley have been so interested in the properties of this remarkable drug!)

XIII

Now if, as I believe, raw-feel terms do have this added dimension of meaning, so that they are not explanatory terms pure and simple, then the strategy of Feigl's argument to show that they really denote cortical processes seems highly suspect. Actually, however, his case is considerably better than it might appear. For if raw-feel terms are *in part* explanatory terms, then the theory BT, taken as a highly simplified model, still represents an important *part* of our commitments as to the nature of raw feels. And since, as I have already remarked, it is our assumption that raw feels are *unique* determinants of human behavior, that pain, for example, is *the* condition that disposes a person to exhibit that kind of behavior called "pain behavior," we may assert

(7) $(E!\Phi)[(\Phi x,t \supset : S_T x,t \cdot D_O x,t) \cdot (S_O x,t \supset \Phi x,t) \cdot (S_T x,t \supset P_O x,t)]$,

which, as I have already shown, allows us to conclude that

(10) $R_T = C$.

The last assertion might seem very strange in the light of what I have been saying about introspection. But actually it does not deny that the "phenomenal" properties we apply to R_T on the basis of introspection are quite different from the properties that the neurophysiologist ascribes to C. Indeed, it is plainly true that when we describe a sense impression as being smooth, extended, and lush in color, we are ascribing quite different properties to it from what the neurophysiologist ascribes to C, which he specifies largely in mathematical terms, that is, in terms of the speed of neuron firings, the spike potentials of nerve fibers, the excitation levels of synaptic connections, and so on.[11] On the other hand, the fact that we are not introspectively aware of what the physiologist describes does not show that he is describing a quite different condition, for I cannot see how we could maintain that we are introspectively aware of *all* the properties of the condition we call a "sense impression." In fact, if the reasoning which leads to the statement "$R_T = C$" is sound (as I think it is), we seem committed to the idea that cortical occurrences have phenomenal *as well as* mathematical properties. The reason why the neurophysiologist is not aware of these properties when he examines my head is not that they do not exist, or that they exist only in a nonspatial, Cartesian realm, but that it is characteristic of them that they are apparent only in introspection.

If my conjecture here is correct, the identity Feigl sought to establish,

---

[11] Phenomenal properties, such as being lush in "color," are of course different from properties like *physical* color. But there is still an analogy between them, which explains why people will describe their hallucinations in terms strictly appropriate only to physical things. For a careful discussion of this point, see [13], p. 324.

namely that $R_T = C$, does not strictly identify the mental with the physical. For what we are aware of as mental are *qualities* of R_T (or C, if $R_T = C$); and these qualities, or properties, are no more physical than the mathematical properties I mention are mental. What "$R_T = C$" does show is that the *condition* we might call a "raw feel," because we are introspectively aware of *only* its phenomenal qualities, is really a condition of our nervous system; it does not show that phenomenal qualities are really physical qualities, for as Butler rightly said, "Everything is what it is and not another thing."

XIV

Although my insistence that the phenomenal is not, after all, the physical may prove disturbing to Feigl in his quest of mind-body monism, he can at least rest assured that I have not reopened the door to the traditional parallelism-interactionism disputes. For it is my view, as it is his, that the central occurrences that stand in causal relations to physical movements, of both the stimulating and the responding sort, are cortical processes, not the phenomenal *qualities* of such processes.[12] And once this is accepted, it is plain that there is really no sense to the traditional worries over the differences between, and the relative merits of, the doctrines called "parallelism" and "interactionism," for these views both mistakenly assume that phenomenal qualities are independent objects, capable themselves of holding a position in a causal chain.

REFERENCES

1. Aune, Bruce. "Feelings, Moods, and Introspection," *Mind*, 72:187–207 (1963).
2. Aune, Bruce. "On Thought and Feeling," *Philosophical Quarterly*, 13:1–12 (1963).
3. Feigl, Herbert. "The 'Mental' and the 'Physical,'" in *Minnesota Studies in the Philosophy of Science*, Vol. II, Herbert Feigl, Michael Scriven, and Grover Maxwell, eds., pp. 370–497. Minneapolis: University of Minnesota Press, 1958.
4. Feigl, Herbert. "The Mind-Body Problem in the Development of Logical Empiricism," *Revue Internationale de Philosophie*, 4:64–83 (1950). Reprinted in *Readings in the Philosophy of Science*, Herbert Feigl and May Brodbeck, eds., pp. 612–626. New York: Appleton-Century-Crofts, 1953.
5. Feyerabend, Paul. "An Attempt at a Realistic Interpretation of Experience," *Proceedings of the Aristotelian Society*, 58:143–170 (1959).
6. Garver, Newton. "Wittgenstein on Private Language," *Philosophy and Phenomenological Research*, 20:389–396 (1960).

[12] This remark emphasizes an important similarity between my view and an earlier view of Feigl's, which might be called the "double knowledge view of central occurrences." Cf. his essay [4].

7. Kemeny, John, and Paul Oppenheim. "On Reduction," *Philosophical Studies*, 7:6–19 (1956).
8. Malcolm, Norman. "Wittgenstein's *Philosophical Investigations*," *Philosophical Review*, 43:530–559 (1954).
9. Maxwell, Grover. "The Ontological Status of Theoretical Entities," in *Minnesota Studies in the Philosophy of Science*, Vol. III, Herbert Feigl and Grover Maxwell, eds., pp. 3–27. Minneapolis: University of Minnesota Press, 1962.
10. Nagel, Ernest. *The Structure of Science*. New York: Harcourt, Brace and World, 1961.
11. Oppenheim, Paul, and Hilary Putnam. "Unity of Science as a Working Hypothesis," in *Minnesota Studies in the Philosophy of Science*, Vol. II, Herbert Feigl, Michael Scriven, and Grover Maxwell, eds., pp. 3–36. Minneapolis: University of Minnesota Press, 1958.
12. Ryle, Gilbert. *The Concept of Mind*. London: Hutchinson, 1949.
13. Sellars, Wilfrid. "Empiricism and the Philosophy of Mind," in *Minnesota Studies in the Philosophy of Science*, Vol. I, Herbert Feigl and Michael Scriven, eds., pp. 253–329. Minneapolis: University of Minnesota Press, 1956.
14. Sellars, Wilfrid. "The Language of Theories," in *Current Issues in the Philosophy of Science*, Herbert Feigl and Grover Maxwell, eds., pp. 57–77. New York: Holt, Rinehart, and Winston, 1961.
15. Skinner, B. F. "The Operational Analysis of Psychological Terms," *Psychological Review*, 52:270–277 (1945). Reprinted in *Readings in the Philosophy of Science*, Herbert Feigl and May Brodbeck, eds., pp. 585–594. New York: Appleton-Century-Crofts, 1949.
16. Strawson, P. F. "Persons," in *Minnesota Studies in the Philosophy of Science*, Vol. II, Herbert Feigl, Michael Scriven, and Grover Maxwell, eds., pp. 330–353. Minneapolis: University of Minnesota Press, 1958. Reprinted, with alterations, in Strawson's *Individuals*. London: Methuen, 1959.
17. Wittgenstein, Ludwig. *Philosophical Investigations*. Oxford: Blackwell, 1953.

MAY BRODBECK

\\\()))

Mental and Physical: Identity versus Sameness

Physicists say that the colors of things are identical with certain wave lengths of light rays, that the hotness of a liquid is identical with the rapid motion of certain molecules, and of course they are right. Moreover, it is a reasonable guess, in any and all senses of "reasonable," that the scientists of the future will tell us that the mental and the physical are also identical, that consciousness *is* a state of particles in the brain. In this too, of course, they again will be right. A common argument against either or both identity claims starts from direct experience, that is, the phenomenological description of acts of consciousness and their objects. Others argue instead from language, insisting that both statements about mental states and statements about the sensory qualities of perceptual objects differ in meaning from statements about the mechanical properties of particles. Though the linguistic way has considerable merits, the relevant assertions reflect and express phenomenological experience. The difference, therefore, is more a matter of philosophical technique than one of substance. Either way, from facts or from language, these arguments are quite irrelevant, for they have not the slightest tendency to refute the identity thesis *if that is properly understood*. I shall explain, support, and, in an important respect, qualify this claim.

Since the time of Galileo, three striking statements have been bandied about that demand attention. These are, first, "There are no colors,

NOTE: An earlier version of this paper was presented before the Psychology Colloquium of the University of Iowa in March 1964. In its present and considerably revised form it was read in March 1965 at a University of Pittsburgh Philosophy Department Conference on conceptual and methodological problems in the study of human behavior.

sounds, and the like"; second, "Ordinary perceptual objects, like tables and chairs, are or are identical with clusters of invisible particles"; and third, "Colors and other perceptual characters of things are mental or in the mind." Like many another at first startling scientific pronouncement, these statements have lost their power to shock. But their apparent absorption into common sense differs in an important respect from that of, say, belief in the earth's rotation or even in unconscious human motivation. Whoever accepts these scientific findings denies that the earth is still or that people always know their own motives. On the other hand, we also willingly assent to the contradictories of our three Galilean assertions. "There are of course colors and sounds." "Tables and chairs, their colors, hardness, and temperature, are different from particles in motion." "The table is colored, not my mind; my *seeing* the color is mental, not the color itself." This seeming willingness to acquiesce in both a statement and its negation is paradoxical. Where the paradox lies is evident. We assert the everyday common-sense beliefs with some exasperation as too obvious to need affirming at all. If we acquiesce in their scientific contradictories, however, it is with the sense of reporting an important and far from obvious discovery. This difference is reflected by the fact that though the statement "There are colors" hardly needs explaining, its negation does. This is very odd, and the paradox lies in the denial. We overlook its oddness because we sense, however dimly, that it and our two other statements are not to be taken literally. They don't mean exactly what they say. Analysis is needed to find out what exactly they do mean. It may then turn out that they do not really contradict our everyday or "prescientific" common sense. For the first two Galilean assertions, as I shall try to show, this is in fact the case. However, the third, asserting that colors and such are mental, is beyond repair for it is simply false. I shall also try to explain why it was made and mistakenly believed to be true and consistent with the others.

What is the literal meaning of "There are no colors"? How can we explicate this statement so that it accurately expresses a truth? Rephrasing it provides a cue: "There *really* are no colors." This may mean either that there are no colors *at all* or that there are no colors in the external world, that is, "without the mind." In either case, things are not what they seem. In either case, the force of the term "really" is that ordinary perceptual objects merely appear to be colored, warm, and so on. Appearances deceive. What "really" exist are those entities whose behavior explains the occurrence and behavior of perceptual objects and characters. These entities, the elementary particles of physics, are colorless and soundless, neither hot nor cold, neither hard nor soft. The basic existents of the external world are those things that are mentioned in the ultimate physical theory, that theory which explains everything else, including the behavior of perceptual objects. *That is how "exists" is being used in this context.* The theory contains no terms referring to the perceptual qualities of things. That is the literal meaning of "There are no colors." Thus explicated, the statement is of course true. Moreover, and perhaps more surprisingly, not only colors and sounds, the so-called "qualitative" characters of things, but their length and their mass, the quantitative characters of perceptual objects, also cease to exist. Indeed, the entire perceptual object disappears—or perhaps it merely appears. This consequence follows from the second statement.

"Ordinary perceptual objects, such as shoes, ships, and sealing wax, are identical with clusters of invisible particles." How is "identical" being used here? The perceptual object is our ordinary material object, but in this discussion "material" is patently ambiguous, so I shall avoid it. In what sense, then, are perceptual objects identical with, let us call them, *physical* objects? We say that the morning star is identical with the evening star. We mean that a single perceptual object can be referred to by two different descriptions, in terms of its different position in the heavens at different times. The morning and the evening star have in common a set of characters that so far as we know uniquely specifies the planet Venus. From this independent characterization, together with the laws of astronomy, it follows that "morning star" and "evening star" designate a single object. But a liquid is wet, has a temperature, and may have a color. Molecules and atoms have none of these characters. The perceptual and physical *objects* do not have a set of characters in common and cannot therefore be identical as are the morning star and the evening star. Nor, turning to *characters*, is the heat of an object identical with the rapid motion of molecules as, say, surveyor's length is identical with yardstick length. The latter are two different ways of measuring the same property, namely, length, whether this be the distance between mountain peaks or that between the ends of a table. A perceptual object has a mass, a velocity, and a temperature, three different noninterchangeable characters. Molecules have mass and velocity but no temperature. Molecular kinetic energy, a function of mass and velocity, cannot therefore be identical with temperature as two different measures of one character. Indeed, perceptual and physical objects stand in a special kind of relation to each other. This may be called "identity" only by using that term in a unique way. To explain this special relation and how it controls this use of "identity," I shall employ an analogy which has certain important structural features that also characterize the relation between the perceptual and the physical.

Pure logic and arithmetic are two different formal systems or "languages." Logic contains neither numerals nor arithmetical operations. Yet mathematics is often said to be identical with a part of logic. Numbers and operations upon them are identified with certain logical notions and relations among them. The "identity" is established by coordinating an undefined term, say the numeral two, in the language of arithmetic with a defined term in the language of logic. The result is an *interpretation* of arithmetic such that to every true arithmetical statement there is a corresponding true statement of logic. An interpretation that meets this condition is called a *model*. Logic is thus a model for arithmetic. The relation of Cartesian or analytic geometry to physical geometry is structurally similar. The undefined terms of geometry are coordinated with, or interpreted as, certain defined terms of arithmetic. Arithmetic is a model for geometry. In this case we do not say that a point, for instance, is identical with its coordinated pair of numbers, since, *nota bene*, the language of points and lines is still needed if we are to talk about space. We are, however, tempted to identify the arithmetical and their coordinated logical terms because, among other reasons, the interpretation permits us to say, without using number-words, everything we can say using them. Numerals become expendable. I shall call this use *model-identity*. Accurately speaking, nothing is literally identified with anything else, if only for the very good reason that the language of logic does not contain numerals.[1] Rather, numbers and statements about them are *reconstructed* as certain classes and logical statements about them. That is, talk about the latter replaces talk about the former. This reconstruction is signaled by the phrase "There really are no numbers," or by "Arithmetic is identical with logic."

Though the language of perceptual objects and the language of physical particles are both descriptive systems, the relation between them is

---

[1] See also [5]. For a detailed discussion of the uses of the term "model," see my [3].

structurally analogous to that between arithmetic and logic. The macroscopic theory of gases is about a kind of perceptual object and its properties. Certain primitive terms of this theory, such as temperature, pressure, and volume, are coordinated with certain defined terms of another theory that refer to invisible particles and their properties. The terms of this physical theory provide an interpretation for those of the perceptual theory such that to every true statement about perceptual objects there is a corresponding true statement about particles. The physical theory is thus a model for the perceptual theory, in the mathematical sense of that term. It may or may not also be a model in the further sense that it borrows its terms and the structure of its laws from another theory. Classical kinetic theory of gases, which borrows from macroscopic mechanics, is a model in both senses, but quantum theory is presumably a model only in the mathematical sense. The physical theory or model is confirmed if, via the coordinations, it successfully explains and predicts the behavior of perceptual objects. The confirming perceptual statements, whether about the specific heats of gases, spectral lines, or tracks in a vapor chamber, are not themselves part of the model. Mention of perceptual objects is needed only to answer the question "How do you know what really exists?" To say what is known, such mention is neither necessary nor, indeed, possible, since the model contains no perceptual terms. Talk about physical states replaces talk about perceptual objects. This reconstruction is signaled by the phrase "There really are no perceptual objects," or by "Perceptual objects are identical with invisible particles." Since, roughly speaking, the perceptual object and its corresponding physical objects are "in the same place,"[2] this is a further reason why scientists identify them. Since the particles are much smaller and more numerous than the corresponding perceptual object, it is also a reason they have for saying that perceptual objects consist of particles. Yet a chair does not consist of atoms the way a cake consists of sugar, flour, and shortening. I shall presently analyze further the notion of model-identity implicit in the second Galilean assertion.

To cope adequately with the third statement, "Colors are in the mind," we must ask whether there is any other sense, precise and preferably

---

[2] Since the physical objects replace perceptual ones, they are not literally in the same place. Physical space-time coordinates for physical particles replace perceptual space and time.

literal, in which perceptual and physical objects may be said to be identical. We must ask this about both characters and the things that exemplify them; for characters, whether perceptual or physical, do not occur by themselves but are exemplified by things. The perceptual statement "Something is red" appears in the physical theory only as reconstructed, via the coordinating definitions, as "Something is a light wave with the longest wave length." The perceptual statement and the physical statement each assert that an individual has a certain character. Does the reconstruction of the perceptual by means of the physical permit us to say that the two characters, one perceptual and the other physical, are identical? May we say that the individuals that exemplify them are identical, really one and the same individual?[3] The answers to these questions pave the way for an analysis of the phrase "in the mind." We should then be able to say what is or is not "in" it. A preliminary distinction between primary and nonprimary things will, in turn, help answer the questions about what is identical with what.

There is an old prejudice, with many deep roots in the history of thought, that a defined term is necessarily clearer and better understood than one we can understand without defining it. This notion usually goes with a use of "knowledge" such that we can only really know truths about those entities that are referred to by defined or complex terms. In one version, it follows that we do not really know anything by sense perception, since sense qualities are simple and referred to by undefined terms. Real knowledge is by the mind alone, spinning out the definitions of things. A more moderate version maintains that we can know complex perceptual things, but not simple ones. Or, to put it differently, we can only *know* that for which we use criteria, these criteria being expressed in the definitions or analyses of the terms. (Skeptics reverse the use of "knowing," holding that we can only really know that for which no criteria are necessary.) Thus it is said that I cannot *know* that I am in pain because I do not use any criteria when asserting the fact. Although it is pointless to ask someone how he knows that he has a toothache, it hardly follows that one doesn't really know such things. It is indeed frequently superfluous to assert that we know certain kinds of things. It is superfluous

---

[3] In Professor Feigl's identity theory of mind and body, the individuals are held to be identical: one and the same *physical individual* has both perceptual and physical characters. See his essay [4]. Traditional phenomenalism, on the other hand, identifies perceptual and physical *characters*.

and even fatuous simply because the question of *how* we know them does not arise. It doesn't arise, not because we do *not* in fact know them, but because we know them without criteria. When we learn how to use the words "imagining" and "believing," or "red" and "smooth," or even "mental" and "nonmental," we do not learn what the things referred to *are*, suggesting how these terms are to be analyzed, but only what we *call*, in not further analyzable terms, that which we already know directly. How do I know the difference between a color and a tone or a shape, between red and blue, between thinking and remembering, between imagining my mother and seeing her? How do I know that two simultaneously perceived objects are both red or, indeed, that there are two and not just one of them? All of these questions are queer. They are queer not because they have no answers and even less because I do *not* know these things, but because to know them we need not apply any criteria. We know them by virtue of the fact that they have been presented to us. No other fact is relevant. To be presented with something is to see it, hear it, and so on. A criterion of something is always something to be presented *other* than the thing itself. Being presented with something is not a criterion for it. I shall call whatever we know without criteria, but merely by virtue of being presented with them, *primary* things. All primary things are presented, but not everything with which we are presented is primary. We frequently need criteria that go beyond a single act of perception. In general, ordinary perceptual objects are not primary things, though some of their characters are. Something red exists if, though of course not only if, I see it. The simple sensory qualities are primary things, but not the only ones. The sameness of primary things, such as two instances of the same color, and their difference, as either among colors or between a color and a tone, are also primary. Anything for which we need criteria is nonprimary. *All scientific knowledge is of nonprimary things.* Perhaps this is just another way of saying that all scientific knowledge requires evidence. This does not mean, of course, that knowledge of primary things is unscientific. It means only that such knowledge is taken for granted rather than pursued by science. And indeed why should it be pursued, since the question "How do you know?" is pointless with respect to knowledge of primary things?

Return now to the question about identity. Is there a sense of "identity," stronger than reconstruction or model-identity, by virtue of which the coordinated perceptual and physical characters or individuals may be called identical? By the customary logical definition of "identity," two characters are identical if and only if they are extensionally equivalent, that is, if and only if any individual that exemplifies one also exemplifies the other. Accordingly, being a man and being a featherless biped are in this sense identical characters. If two characters are thus extensionally identical, then one and the same individual exemplifies both of them. Identity of characters presupposes identity of individuals. Literally, identity means sameness, either qualitative or numerical. I shall call this literal use, for either characters or individuals, *sameness* and the technical logical use *identity*. "Model-identity" is still a third notion. It is of course also technical. When do we have one and the same individual? In particular, does one and the same individual exemplify both perceptual and physical characters? If two individuals are logically identical, then any character that one has the other also has. We obviously need an independent explication of what it means for two characters to be the *same* before we can say that the two individuals have all the same characters.[4] Being a man and being a featherless biped are identical but discernibly different characters, hence they are not the same. Identity is weaker than sameness. If two characters are the same, then they are also identical, but not conversely. Primary sameness needs no criteria. Since it is primary, we cannot explicate but only give examples of it. A simple perceptual character is only the same as itself. Two instances of the same shade of red exemplify primary sameness. If two simple characters, such as red and blue or green and C sharp, are different, they are presented as different and this is primary difference. One need not appeal to or know anything about the "grammar" of colors or of tones, that is, the relations of exclusion and inclusion obtaining among them, in order to be acquainted with this difference. Two complex characters are the same (or different) if and only if their definitions contain the same (or different) undefined terms. By this criterion, being a brother is the same as being a male sibling. But the sameness or difference of complex characters is not primary.

Being a light wave of a given wave length is a complex imperceptible character for which we need criteria. It is therefore not the same as the simple perceptual character redness for which no criteria are needed. Are they identical? Being human and being a featherless biped are different though identical characters, since any individual that has one also

---

[4] In other words, "two" individuals that are numerically one and the same must be qualitatively the same, though the converse does not hold.

has the other. But if any particular human is the same individual as a particular featherless biped then "they" also have all their *other* characters in common. But a perceptual individual has a color and a physical individual has none. These individuals therefore cannot be either identical or one and the same. It follows that the perceptual character red and its coordinated physical character, that of being a certain light wave, are not even identical, since it is not true that any individual that has the physical character is also red. Physical entities are colorless. No individual at all has both perceptual and physical characters. Characters of the physical model and characters of the perceptual theory for which it is a model are exemplified by different individuals. These characters, therefore, cannot be identical. Neither perceptual individuals nor their characters are identical with the coordinated physical individuals or characters.

If perceptual characters are not identical with physical ones, are they perhaps identical with *mental* characters? If so, then it would be literally true, as we shall see, that "colors are in the mind." This belief goes back to seventeenth-century science. Locke, the philosopher of Galileo, divided the perceptual characters into primary and secondary qualities. As this distinction has generally been interpreted, the primary qualities, such as solidity, shape, and motion, were really in the external objects. The secondary qualities, however, such as color, heat, and sound, were held to be nothing in the objects themselves, but only effects in us produced by the primary qualities.[5] The atomic theory of matter was still merely speculative. Classical mechanics was macroscopic: its basic terms all referred to complex perceptual characters which, like velocity and distance, were among Locke's primary qualities. The primary and secondary qualities were, therefore, both alike "sensible," since both were perceived by the senses. The difference between size or velocity, on the one hand, and color or warmth, on the other, was in fact a distinction within perceptual characters, between those that were measurable or "quantitative" and those that were nonmeasurable or "qualitative." The ascription of nonmeasurable characters to things, because they were nonmeasurable, varied with the state of the perceiver or with the conditions under which they were

---

[5] Locke's use of "primary" is of course not mine. In my sense of "primary," or known without criteria, all defined perceptual characters—and all measurable or quantitative characters are defined—are nonprimary; no physical characters, whether defined or primitive in particle theory, are primary, since they are never presented to us and therefore require criteria. Moreover, primary characters, as I use the term, may be either perceptual or mental, either objective or subjective.

perceived. Green grass may look brown; hot water may feel lukewarm. The ascription of the measurable characters, because they were measurable, did not thus vary. Measurable versus nonmeasurable was the crest of the slippery slope from primary versus secondary, over objective versus subjective, to reality versus appearance, that ended with ordinary perceptual objects being stripped first of their colors and finally of all perceptual characters. By the assimilation of nonquantitative perceptual characters to sensations, to such things as our *feelings* of pain or of warmth, the whole perceptual object was ultimately to be located in the mind.

Locke's doctrine was not a scientific theory but a philosophical reconstruction prompted by a scientific theory. The development of the kinetic theory, that is, the mechanical particle-model for macroscopic thermodynamics, might superficially appear to support a Lockean metaphysics. The appearance is misleading. In the kinetic theory, the particles of the model have some of the same characters as do perceptual objects. The velocity and mass of a piece of gold leaf, but not its color or texture, may then seem to be in the object itself, since the particles had the former but not the latter characters. However, measurable and nonmeasurable characters of perceptual objects like gold leaves are all equally "qualitative," since they are all descriptive perceptual characters. The perceptual color *and* length of a table are each coordinated with a set of physical characters of the particles. In the classical model these have the same name as the Lockean primary qualities. In the quantum-mechanical model even this is no longer generally true. But, except for the loss of "qualitative" imagery and its heuristic, analogical value, there is no reason why the invisible should be in any way like the visible. Locke's "primary" perceptual qualities are tied to the model just as much and in the same way as are the "secondary" ones. The model provides a scientific reconstruction of the *whole* perceptual object, not just of some of its characters.

The mind is only metaphorically a place. The use of "in" in the phrase "in the mind" is not spatial. My head is not full of thoughts the way it is full of gray stuff. A conscious state is a mental fact; physical and perceptual events are other facts. Facts are expressed by sentences or sentential clauses, not by single words. Facts, thus, are complex. Something is "in" a fact if it is referred to by a word in the sentence expressing that fact. The statement "John is tall" expresses John's being tall. John and tallness are "in" the perceptual fact. Similarly, the ball and redness are "in" the perceptual fact expressed by "The ball is red." Though technical, this use of "in" is clear. With it, we can explicate the phrase "in the mind." A mind is not a substance but a temporal series of conscious states interconnected in various ways. Two people may think the same thought, feel the same pain, or see the same perceptual object. Each is a case of qualitative sameness, that is, of two different instances of the same character. (Only in the object or intention of the perception is there also numerical sameness, that of the object seen.) Jones's believing-that-the-earth-is-round is one fact; Smith's believing the same thing is another. Believing-that-the-earth-is-round is a complex character.[6] Seeing-that-the-ball-is-red or, generally, seeing-that-p is also a character that may have many instances. Particulars, as the bearers of numerical difference, individuate these instances. Let a be the name of one such individual. The sentence "a is a (exemplifies) seeing-that-p" describes a conscious state, or part of one. *Something is "in the mind" if it is referred to by a word in a sentence describing a conscious state.* As the hyphens are meant to suggest, the sentence "p" is not part of this sentence. The ball's being red is not part of the character seeing-that-the-ball-is-red. The roundness of the earth is not part of anyone's conscious state. Neither is the redness of the ball. Colors are not in the mind.

Mental acts are parts of conscious states. So too are pains and joys, itches and tickles. Mental acts, such as perceiving and remembering, are transitive or intentional, that is, they are directed toward an object. The object they are directed toward is the intention of the mental act. When I see a red ball, I see a red ball, not my seeing it. The object of a mental act is never that act itself. How then do I know that I am perceiving? Consciousness requires awareness. Animals see but, unlike men, do not know that they see. Perceiving is a conscious state only because I am aware that I am perceiving. We perceive, that is, see, touch, or hear perceptual objects. Perceiving is not itself a perceptual object. It is the intention of another kind of mental act, a direct awareness. We are directly aware only of our own conscious states. Only some objects of perception, such as the simple sensory qualities, are primary things, that is, known without criteria. *All* objects of direct awareness, the contents of

___

[6] It is a complex mental character, just as being white and square is a complex perceptual one. Being an act of belief and the content of the belief, that-p, are coexemplified characters. The thought referred to by "that-p" has as its object or intentionally means the perceptual state of affairs designated by "p."

our own states of consciousness, are primary things. The question of how we know them never arises. We therefore need never appeal to or, *ipso facto*, even have a firm name in common speech for direct awareness. If, on such grounds, someone claims that he doesn't know what direct awareness is, let him say how he knows without perception, as indeed he *does* know if he is conscious, that he is thinking about or seeing something. Or that he is seeing rather than remembering something. Direct awareness is not a kind of perception or observation, like seeing and hearing, but a mental act of its own kind. By it we know, among other things, the mental acts and the differences among them. By perception, on the other hand, we know the perceptual characters and the differences among them. No criteria are needed to tell the difference between our seeing and what we see. Perceptual characters are not the same as mental ones.

Emotions and feelings are also contents of consciousness, as objects of direct awareness. They, in turn, may themselves be either intentional or nonintentional. Which they are is a matter for phenomenological description of the different kinds of experiences. Some affective states, such as loving and hating, seem clearly intentional; others, like hunger, depression, or "free-floating" anxiety, seem nonintentional. With respect to still others, like toothaches or sensations on the body's surface, decision about their intentionality or nonintentionality may require those subtle phenomenological discriminations that are the concern of another craft. What matters for the philosophical analysis of consciousness is that an emotion or sensation, whether it is or is not itself in turn intentional, is the object of an act of direct awareness. The object of an awareness is not the same as the awareness, any more than the object of a perception is the same as perceiving it. The sentence "a is an awareness-that-the-tooth-aches" describes my conscious state when I know that I have a toothache. Being-a-toothache is part of a conscious state, just as is seeing-that-the-ball-is-red, because the ache and the seeing are each an object of direct awareness. The red ball which I see is not.

Many people may think the same thought or have (be aware of) the same pain. Particulars have or individuate these different instances of the same thing. Perceptual and physical individuals are not identical with each other, since they exemplify different characters. Nor is either identical with mental individuals. Mental individuals are those that exemplify mental characters, such as thinking, perceiving, or feeling a pain. They are therefore part of a conscious state or in a mind. The difference between mental characters, like seeing, and perceptual ones, like redness, is primary. No mental character is the same as a perceptual one. Mental and perceptual individuals cannot be one and the same. An individual cannot both be and not be part of a conscious state, that is, both mental and nonmental. One and the same individual may, of course, have two different perceptual characters, such as red and square. But a single individual cannot instantiate both a seeing, which is "in the mind," and the color seen, which is not. Moreover, perceptual individuals exemplify characters that mental ones do not. Awareness of a toothache may be like seeing an afterimage. The afterimage is not on the wall the way a mirror is. The pain is not in the tooth as a cavity is in the tooth. The difference is not that the pain is private and the cavity is public, but that the toothache or pain-in-the-tooth is part of a conscious state or in a mental fact, as the object or intention of a direct awareness. The cavity is in a perceptual fact which is the intention of an act of perceiving. The constituents of conscious states are not in perceptual space. I can simultaneously have a toothache, see a red ball, and think about going to the dentist. My feeling, seeing, and thinking are not next to one another, as one tooth is next to another. Mental individuals do not exemplify spatial characters, or size, or mass. Perceptual individuals do. By the principle of identity, identical individuals must share all their characters. Mental individuals cannot therefore be identical with perceptual ones. Nor do electrons or photons think and remember, feel pleasures or pains. Physical individuals do not exemplify mental characters. Physical and mental individuals cannot be identical with each other either. Mental, perceptual, and physical individuals each exemplify characters not exemplified by either of the other two kinds. There is therefore no identity or sameness of such individuals. Characters, in turn, are identical if and only if they are exemplified by all the same individuals. If a perceptual character were identical with a mental one, then both would be exemplified by one and the same individual. The perceptual character would therefore also be part of a conscious state or "in a mind." But they are not exemplified by the same individual. Accordingly, the different mental, perceptual, and physical characters are also not even identical. There is no identity of characters or of individuals across these categories. Extensionally identical characters, where they exist, must always be within a category. They must both be mental, both perceptual, or both physical. This follows from the non-identity and difference of their respective individuating particulars.[7]

What can be salvaged of the identity thesis? The logical notion of identity applies to the *constituents* of facts; it holds either between individuals or between characters. But this notion is defined in terms of the extensional equivalence of certain facts. By a natural extension of that notion, we can further explicate the use of "identity" in contexts where two notational systems or languages are so related that one is a model for the other. Something is red if and only if something *else* is a certain light wave. A *fact* expressed by a sentence in one system is "identical" with that expressed by a sentence in the model, if the corresponding sentences are extensionally equivalent. This is what I have referred to as "model-identity." Mere contingent extensional equivalence of statements *within* a single system never signals any kind of identity of the facts they express. When two macroscopic (perceptual) states, such as changes in pressure and in volume under constant temperature, are necessary and sufficient conditions for each other, therefore extensionally equivalent, they are not identified with each other. Nor are two similarly related microscopic (physical) states. Only in the model context, where, by virtue of the coordination rules, extensional equivalence holds between statements in different systems, do we "identify" the corresponding states of affairs. As mentioned earlier with respect to physical and analytical geometry, we do not always do this when one system is a model for another. However, when we do, this is the mark of reconstruction, that is, of the replacement, for purposes that vary with the relevant languages, of one way of speaking about certain things with another way of speaking about them. Just as the language of pure logic replaces that of arithmetic for the purpose of philosophically clarifying the nature of numbers and of mathematical truth, so the language of physical objects replaces that of perceptual objects for the purpose of scientific explanation of the visible by means of the invisible.

Though identity of the constituents of facts, either individuals or char-

---

[7] Bergmann once maintained [1, p. 130] that for any character we can always find another extensionally identical with it and, in particular, that the transcription of an undefined mental predicate in terms of its physiological causes would provide such a character. Bergmann now agrees that this was an error, which he attributes to the residual phenomenalism in his thought at that time. See his [2], especially the essays "Physics and Ontology" and "Realistic Postscript," for discussion of other topics pertinent to this paper.

acters, is always *within* a system or category, model-identity of facts is always *across* categories. In particular, it holds between the perceptual and the physical and, as we shall see, between the mental and the physical, though *not* between the perceptual and the mental. The model-identity of the perceptual and the physical is an identity not of things but of facts expressed by sentences.[8] One sentence asserts that something has a certain perceptual character; another that something else has certain physical characters. These two sentences are extensionally equivalent; whenever one is true, the other is true, and conversely. The water is boiling if and only if a specifiable set of molecules is in rapid motion. There is a green table in the room if and only if there is a corresponding cluster of electrons and photons behaving in certain ways. Model-identity is of states of affairs, not of either things or their characters. If "two" individuals are one and the same or literally identical, then they are also extensionally identical. Defined or complex extensionally identical characters are in some cases also the same. Model-identical facts are never also the same. Model-identity is thus the weakest of these three uses of "identity."

How does consciousness fit into this picture? It will first be useful to say something about causality. The physical reconstruction of perceptual objects implies a reconstruction of our ordinary use of "cause." Facts, not objects, are causes or effects. Causal laws are expressed by conditional sentences asserting that the occurrence of one sort of thing is always accompanied by the occurrence of another sort of thing. Commonsensically, we say that we see a red, hard, moving, spherical object, a perceptual rubber ball, because there *is* such an object. The existence of the red rubber ball is among the causes of our seeing it. But science replaces the occurrence of the ball by its model-identical physical event. Since the physical replaces the perceptual, it cannot be the cause of it. Since, according to the physical-model language game, "There are no perceptual objects," there are none to be caused. The physical event is instead the cause of whatever the replaced perceptual event was said to cause. In particular, it causes our perception-of-the-ball. We see a red ball, not because there is a red ball, but because there is a microscopic state that we do not see. *The scientific world-picture bypasses the perceptual world.* The states of

---

[8] We ordinarily speak of perceptual and physical objects, such as tables and electrons, as things rather than as facts. But something's being a table and something's being an electron are expressed by statements, not by single words. They are therefore logically facts rather than "things."

the particles cause our conscious states. But this is not literally true. We are not left only with particles and minds. Physical causes have only physical effects. For, of course, there are no minds either. Or, rather, in keeping with our enterprise, "There really are no minds." With increasing knowledge of the behavioral and neurophysiological perceptual correlates of consciousness, these correlates will be model-identified with, reconstructed as, or replaced by—the three phrases mean the same—physical states.

The physical states that replace (the perceptual correlates of) consciousness will not be the same ones as those that replace inanimate perceptual objects. Rather, the latter cause the former. We must be clear about this. Under the spell of the formula "There are no perceptual objects," it is sometimes said that physical "redness" or "heat," that is, light waves or molecules in motion, is coordinated with, thus model-identical with, our seeing-red or feeling-heat. If this were so, there would be nothing in the world but minds, which in turn are "really" physical states. Perceptual objects, like chairs and tables, would be in the mind. Accurately, there are two different physical states. One of these is coordinated with, say, an instance of seeing-that-something-is-red or, rather, its correlated behavioral-physiological state. The other is coordinated with the perceptual red object that we see. The causal connection holds between these two different physical states. Once we know all these connections, then talk about physical "cortical" states can replace talk about perceiving and feeling, just as talk about other physical states replaces talk about temperature and light. There will then no more be minds than there are now perceptual bodies. And of course there will no less be minds and bodies than there are now. Mental states are merely model-identical with physical states.

However, by no plausible use of "identity" are mental states identical with perceptual ones. Both mental and perceptual facts, on the one hand, are model-identical with physical facts, on the other. The relation between consciousness and perceptual cortical states, that is, between the mind and the body, is not of this sort. The brain is not a model of the mind, as the atomic theory is a model for the brain. For the purposes of scientific explanation, mental and perceptual facts together form a single system, namely that system which as a whole is replaced by the physical model. Within a system, as mentioned before, contingent extensional equivalence of statements never signals any sort of identity of the facts they express.

Mind-body parallelism is the traditional tag for this extensional equivalence of mental and perceptual facts. The difference between the mental and the perceptual, between my seeing something and what I see, is primary. I am presented with them both and need no criteria for their being different. One sort of primary thing cannot replace another sort. They may, however, be correlated with each other. In particular, mental states are correlated with, that is, they parallel, perceptual states. Perceptual states, in turn, including those correlated with mental states, are replaced by or reconstructed as physical states. The model structure of explanation is such that, for reasons I have tried to bring out, it prompts the assertion that neither minds nor bodies really exist. Among these reasons is a special use of "identity" corresponding to this special explanatory structure. Taken at face value, the Galilean assertion that perceptual objects are identical with physical objects is literally nonsense. The recoverable sense behind it is that perceptual facts are, in the sense explicated, model-identical with physical facts. The physical world is a scientific reconstruction of the perceptual world.

We are aware of our own mental acts and perceive our own and others' behavior. As with every science, the basic terms of behavior theory are abstract or highly defined and become ever more so as the science develops. Scientific terms referring to emotions and personality traits are complex. They refer not only to overt behavior but to items of the past and present social environment, to past learning, and to behavioral dispositions. These complex states are of course not primary, but their constituent or defining perceptual entities are. So are mental states. My seeing red is not the same as saying that I do or behaving appropriately. Scientific knowledge is always of nonprimary things: of those things for which we need criteria or evidence. The job of psychology as a science is to find the causal laws among certain complex behavioral, physiological, and environmental perceptual states. A complete physical reconstruction in terms of invisible particles mentions neither perceptual nor mental objects. The purpose of the physical reconstruction is to explain the objects it does not mention. Why some things are red, physics tells us. That there are red things, we know directly. Why I think certain things, feel certain others, the science of psychology tells me. That I think and feel these things, I know without being told. The psychologist will quickly interject that I by no means always know what I think or feel. He is right, of course. But unconscious thoughts and emotions are not what I am talking about. These are not primary things, let alone primary mental things. They are instead very complex or highly defined perceptual things. As I am using "mental," in its primary sense, the notion of unconscious mental activity is self-contradictory.

Mentalistic terms used in behavior science are nonprimary homonyms of their corresponding primary terms in everyday speech. After fifty years of behaviorism this should be but, as recent literature testifies, is clearly not obvious. Psychologists are ever sensitive to the charge that they neglect the facts of consciousness. Some react to this charge by re-baptizing complex behavioral states with mentalistic terms. This is pseudomentalism or materialism in disguise. I do not mean merely that heuristic use of mentalistic terms that every scientific psychologist makes, knowing very well that it is merely heuristic. But the illusion is abroad that behavioristic psychology can *literally* talk about mental states (see [6]). The genetic fallacy is the instrument of this self-deception. We know now more than ever, perhaps, that the human repertoire of responses is greatly dependent upon learning. Sensation and perception, what we see and feel, as well as our awareness of our seeing and feeling, are heavily conditioned by the social environment. We learn not only to see but to see that we see. We have always known that language is a social product. We know how much more difficult it is to learn to label and describe our inner emotional states and awarenesses than it is to learn the right names for, say, the colors. The more we find out about these processes, the better will we be able to formulate fruitful behavioral concepts. But learning to see or to be aware is one thing; seeing and awareness are different things. To have a feeling and to know how to label it correctly are also different things. The behavior of seeing is not seeing; the behavior of seeing that we see is not direct awareness. Nothing becomes mental by being called so.

Materialism in disguise is no answer to the claim that the science of psychology cannot do without mental terms. Nor is capitulation. Is physical theory incomplete because it does not mention perceptual things? Nor is the science of psychology doomed to incompleteness because it omits mental terms in their literal sense. It is just the other way around. The psychologists' guilt feelings are misplaced. Not the omission but the primary use of mental terms signals scientific incompleteness. Or to put it paradoxically, only when science has reached the stage where it can say "There are no minds" will it have accounted adequately for mind. But of course there is no paradox. Identity is not sameness.

REFERENCES

1. Bergmann, Gustav. "Individuals," *Philosophical Studies*, 9:78–85 (1958). Reprinted in *Meaning and Existence*, pp. 124–131. Madison: University of Wisconsin Press, 1960.
2. Bergmann, Gustav. *Logic and Reality*. Madison: University of Wisconsin Press, 1964.
3. Brodbeck, May. "Models, Meaning, and Theories," in *Symposium on Sociological Theory*, Llewellyn Gross, ed., pp. 373–403. New York: Harper and Row, 1959.
4. Feigl, Herbert. "The 'Mental' and the 'Physical,'" in *Minnesota Studies in the Philosophy of Science*, Vol. II, Herbert Feigl, Michael Scriven, and Grover Maxwell, eds., pp. 370–497. Minneapolis: University of Minnesota Press, 1958.
5. Hochberg, Herbert. "Peano, Russell, and Logicism," *Analysis*, 16:118–120 (1956).
6. Skinner, B. F. "Behaviorism at Fifty," *Science*, 140:951–958 (May 31, 1963).

RUDOLF EKSTEIN

\\\ ))

The Psychoanalyst and His Relationship to the Philosophy of Science

A recent symposium, *Psychoanalysis, Scientific Method, and Philosophy* [15], has not dealt too gently with the analyst's work. Nagel [20] emphasizes there that he certainly acknowledges "the great service Freud and his school have rendered in directing attention to neglected aspects of human behavior, and in contributing a large number of suggestive notions which have leavened and broadened the scope of psychological, medical, and anthropological inquiry. But on the Freudian theory itself, as a body of doctrine for which factual validity can be reasonably claimed, I can only echo the Scottish verdict: Not proven." The psychoanalyst would be ill-advised if he were to imitate the philosopher who turned the logical tool against him, and were now to turn the psychological tool against the philosopher and accuse him as one who "does not use language to express scientific propositions but instead uses it in such a way as to create the illusion of doing so, while in fact he gives expression only to his unconscious fantasies" [19].

It seems to me that the task of the psychoanalyst, rather than attempting to "refute" [6] the philosopher of science, would be to identify with the philosophical task, and see in it one of the functions of his own work, and thus combine clinical and empirical tasks with theoretical and philosophical ones. This task will be easier for him if he can see in the philosophy of science not simply a movement which requires strict standards for a scientific theory, but rather a *method* of work, an *activity* rather than a scientific ideal.

The school of the Wiener Kreis of logical positivism, as Frank [12] has shown, has had a more tolerant attitude toward psychoanalysis. Rather than insisting on a theoretical ideal, on "strictest criteria of admission into the realm of legitimate science," many members of the Vienna Circle have stressed the "indivisible trinity of the logical, the semantic, and the pragmatic components." This identification with *theory as a program of action*, in Bridgman's phrase, has allowed some of the philosophers of science not merely to speak in terms of earlier convictions as to what is to be condemned as unscientific and meaningless but to stress philosophical activity rather than its often elusive goal.

It seems to me that Herbert Feigl, in whose honor this contribution is written, has always expressed an attitude in which he stressed philosophical activity without, however, losing sight of the goal of the process of clarification. In 1958 he stated:

There is little doubt in my mind that psychoanalytic theory (or at least some of its components) has genuine explanatory power, even if any precise identification of repression, ego, superego, id, etc. with neural processes and structures is still a very long way off. I am not in the least disputing the value of theories whose basic concepts are not in any way micro-specified. What I am arguing is that even *before* such specifications become possible, the meaning of scientific terms can be explicated by postulates and correspondence rules . . . and that this meaning may later be greatly enriched, i.e. much more fully specified, by the addition of *further* postulates and correspondence rules.

After the recovery from radical behaviorism and operationism, we need no longer hesitate to distinguish between *evidence* and *reference*, i.e., between manifestations or symptoms on the one hand, and central states on the other; no matter whether or not central states are micro-specified (neurophysiologically identified) [10, pages 394–395].

This comment, which I use as the theme of this communication, identifies both with the goal of the task toward an ideal theory and with the activity which leads toward this task. He thus gives the psychoanalyst a task rather than merely censuring him for working in an area of scientific interest and activity which is as yet not amenable to requirements appropriate for other fields of science.

As Frank pointed out [12], both logical positivism and psychoanalysis grew in the same soil, the same intellectual climate of Vienna in the years before and after the First World War. Both, sociologically considered, were also movements of protest, of a demand for change. Such vigorous demand for change sometimes leads to initially doctrinaire positions in which the classical requirements freeze into orthodoxy. Feigl and I, who both had our early education in this very climate, have maintained a position which aims at a bridge between these two fields which have in common the quest for meaning, the search for clarity, including the obvious question as to the way "meaning" is to be given different meanings in these different contexts. This bridge has become endangered, since the specialty of the philosopher of science and the specialty of the analyst have each led into a kind of overspecialization which does not permit either to remain fully acquainted with the other field. The demand of "unity of science" implies the search for necessary bridges between different fields of inquiry. Most of us, regardless of what special knowledge we have acquired in our own field, have remained no more than educated laymen as far as the other field is concerned. And still, if the analyst wishes to make full use of the contributions of the philosophy of science, he will have to become a philosopher on his own. There cannot be a group of clarifiers on the outside who can do more than point out sweeping, general directions. What is needed as well is philosophical clarification in small segments of our areas of investigation where small advances can be made, not an expectation that global answers can be found, be they overall theoretical blueprints or wholesale condemnations.

I have experienced Feigl's contribution, whenever he has touched upon issues central to the work of the psychoanalyst, as helpful in promoting this task. I hope then that this contribution of mine will confirm his influence on the analyst, not only in creating in him a philosophical conscience but in developing the actual capacity for the carrying out of this task in limited but accessible areas of his total interest.[1]

Nietzsche's remark that "men will believe in God as long as they believe in grammar" was an early insight into the motives for our language habits. It suggests that we invest these habits with much affect, that we always consider them appropriate for communication, and that we seldom examine our language to readjust it for new tasks dictated by additional experience. This holds true for the language of science as well as for everyday language. Einstein's re-examination of the concepts of simultaneity was a readjustment of this kind which led to a revolution in the physical sciences. Einstein analyzed the methods of verification and

---

[1] The following part of this paper is a revised and extended version of an earlier communication of mine [7].

confirmation of statements concerning the simultaneity of events, comparing the methods used with events taking place in close proximity with those used with events in places quite apart from each other, or in places apart from each other and in addition moving toward or away from each other. Attempts at the clarification of the nature of language within a given area of science usually lead to much less spectacular discoveries, but are nevertheless a necessary task for the scientist who wants to retain objectivity toward his conceptual tools. From time to time the scientist will need a specialized approach and he must then turn philosopher of science; his task then will be, if I may use a phrase of Moritz Schlick's, to ask meaningful questions, while it will remain his task as a scientist to answer these questions. In other words, our language induces us at times, as is suggested by Nietzsche's comment, to formulate pseudoquestions (Scheinfragen), the clarification of which will lead us either to give up the attempt or to reformulate our puzzlement in such a way that potential answers can be given.

This task is particularly important in the social sciences, since their conceptual tools are new, change often, and are frequently borrowed from everyday life or other sciences and suffer from overlapping meaning. A young science such as psychoanalysis can especially benefit from philosophical clarification, and the analyst needs to be concerned with this task in spite of his known overinvestment in his conceptual tools, a trait which David Shakow [24] considers particularly characteristic of psychotherapists. Psychoanalysis, in common with the other psychological and social sciences, requires this kind of stocktaking in order to keep us as scientists flexible and capable of constantly growing beyond the limits any language system imposes on our descriptive and explanatory power. Kris [18] has formulated this task as follows:

There is, for instance, a lack of trained clarifiers, who might properly coordinate the various propositions with each other or try to eliminate the inequities of language in psychoanalysis. As examples of such inequities, one may mention that definitions of terms are sometimes unsatisfactory, that even their translation from German into English is not always fortunate; that in psychoanalytic writings, metaphors tend to obscure the meaning of statements; and that such usages are ingrained by the fact that a generation of scientists adopted what now seems understandable as the peculiarity and privilege of one genius.

Thus, Kris appropriately seems to advise us to turn to the philosopher of science for help and to acquaint him with our problems, so that he may lighten for us the process of clarification. Hospers [17] also suggests that we rely on "psychoanalytically trained philosophers of science—rare birds indeed," while I identify with the notion that scientific methods and philosophical clarification of psychoanalytic concepts must become part of psychoanalytic training itself, a position held also by Colby [1, 2]. Shakow [25] has voiced similar views.

I propose then to raise some issues which are likely to be of concern to every psychoanalyst whose interest goes beyond mere practical application of the science, who sees in psychoanalysis a living and growing science, which creates new conceptual as well as empirical problems, and thus frequently makes it difficult for us to differentiate between the two.

Freud was confronted with this very problem early in his career as an analyst. Thanks to Marie Bonaparte, we possess now a remarkable document which offers considerable insight into certain of Freud's problems during the creative process. I am referring to Freud's letters [14] to Fliess in which he describes the origins of psychoanalysis, and which Freud himself never intended to publish. He was opposed to publishing unfinished, tentative material, but the availability of this material gives us access to certain linguistic problems which stood in the way of developing psychoanalytic theory. Kris, in his introduction, describes the intellectual conflict which forced Freud to give up the temptation to describe insights gained by intuition through methods of the kind we are accustomed to having from imaginative writers. Freud never quite yielded to intuitive understanding but aimed at scientific explanation. In 1895 Freud [14] wrote "The Project," in which he attempted to describe the functioning of the psychical apparatus as that of a system of neurons and to regard all the processes concerned as, in the last resort, quantitative changes. He attempted to fuse the theory of neurons with the physiology of the brain. One year later he freed himself from the language of neurophysiology. Under the cloak of brain physiology, "The Project" reveals concrete psychological hypotheses, and these can be found in part in *The Interpretation of Dreams*, and some of them in later works such as *The Ego and the Id*, published almost thirty years after the writing of "The Project." The discussion of the Irma dream in "The Project" and later in *The Interpretation of Dreams* is a clear example of how the limitations of neurophysiological models did not permit Freud to go as far as he could later when he had, at least partly, new language available. The

[63]

well-known fence model of the psychic apparatus, as used in the seventh chapter of *The Interpretation of Dreams* [13] is of course deeply influenced, in its attempt to understand dream perception, by the model of the reflex arc; and of course Freud's new language is also borrowed from other fields, and therefore gives rise frequently to potential misunderstandings. He has maintained certain quantitative notions, an ideal of the natural sciences, but we are at a loss at times to see where the rules of the old concept end and where the rules of the new, psychological conceptualization begin. We speak of *psychic energy* and of *energy principle* in the realm of psychology without making clear whether psychic energy can be measured or not. I am not concerned at this point with the empirical issue but rather with the earlier question of whether any kind of scale can and should be applied to such a concept. One may wish to apply scales which only speak of "more or less," but this would not be completely comparable to the usual scale employed in physical science.

Modern ego psychology speaks of neutralized, of deneutralized, of sexualized and desexualized, of fused and defused energy—and thus maintains the concept of *different qualities of energy, describing quantity*. Do such different energies represent one and the same basic energy, measurable as it were, but seen as different derivatives because of different organizational structures? Is the use of the energy principle a useful analogy, and if so, where is the limit of the analogy? Or does its use represent more than an analogy?

Many of the psychological concepts of psychoanalysis are derived, of course, from *spatial language* [4] as when we speak, for example, of the *model* of the *psychic apparatus*. Is the tripartite model of the psychic apparatus to be understood as a replica—like a small model train which reproduces on a small scale the big train—or do we use the model here in terms of an analogy? How much use is there in scientific analogies and where are their dangers?

Many take such models literally, and much of our descriptive clinical language tends to turn explanatory concepts into descriptive ones, such as when we speak about the Ego being a weak slave driven back and forth by the punitive Superego and the corrupting Id.

Psychoanalysis has undergone constant theoretical changes. Only beginning attempts have been made to bring earlier concepts up to date since the dual instinct theory was introduced. Many analytic communications use side by side different aspects of theories, frequently showing apparent contradictions.

Much of psychoanalytic theory has been developed, of course, because of Freud's original special interest in a specific patient group, representing the different neuroses and in the beginning particularly the hysterical syndrome. As our interest in borderline and psychotic conditions developed, we had to rely on conceptual tools which did not quite fit the new task. In order to meet this new task we have introduced descriptive terms such as that of a brittle, a fluid, or a shifting ego, of weak or nonexistent ego boundaries, of a flooded ego organization, and we find different thoughts expressed by different authors through the same words as well as similar thoughts expressed through different terms. As we study a very small child, an infant, we often project adult conditions into the primitive psychic organization, as seems to be true, I believe, in many of the writings of Melanie Klein and her students. Rapaport [22] once suggested that her writings are id mythology rather than ego psychology.

In the ideological warfare which exists between different analytic subgroups, we find it difficult to agree on how much of our disagreement is semantic, a problem of mere translation, how much of it is empirical in nature, and how much of it depends on our not yet having developed a consistent theoretical frame of reference and clear levels of theory between description and the different levels of explanation leading step by step to high-order, abstract theories, as has been suggested by Feigl [11]. So much investment do we have in our language habits that we suspect—and often correctly so—that he who speaks another language hides behind it different empirical or technical views. In a preliminary study [9], I examined the issue of determinants in psychology, with a special consideration of etiological issues in different psychoanalytic approaches. In that study I indicated that different opinions concerning the etiology of emotional or mental illness can be better understood if they are examined at first as propositions concerning technique toward change rather than as propositions which are to establish the cause of illness.

The early model of classical psychoanalytic technique tempted one not to differentiate between genetic explanation and technical interventions. It seemed as if the cause of illness and the freeing of the patient from his symptoms through interpretive interventions were one and the same. As I examined different "schools" of psychoanalysis I felt that the decision to understand them primarily in terms of technical differences would lead to a way of testing these technical propositions by examining on a laboratory level actual changes in therapy as they related to specific techniques. I thus substituted for "ideological warfare" [3] empirical methods in which predictions were matched with outcome. I continued this line of investigation in another study [8], which examined the nature of interpretation in psychoanalysis, and established upon clarification of the differing uses of this concept in psychoanalytic writings that a main attempt must be made to separate those propositions which aim at explanation and those which are actually technical interventions. To establish the nature of interpretation as a technical intervention, a change proposition, as it were, I paid attention to the nature of "communication" in the psychoanalytic process. The examination of the issue of capacity for communication led me into a discussion of the type of patient who is not capable of such communication, or who is only partly capable of communication, because of certain deficits in his personality which may engulf him in autistic or symbiotic struggles. Such patients are said to be capable occasionally of "communion" rather than of "communication." As the analyst "interprets" something to such a patient, he cannot be said to communicate in the ordinary sense, and we discover then the forerunners of communication and interpretation, the precursors, as it were, which could not be fully understood as long as we were satisfied to subsume all kinds of technical interventions under the terms of interpretation or communication in the conventional sense. This problem of the emergence of the capacity for interpretation and communication, clarified in part through a better understanding of the nature of psychoanalytic interpretation, is treated in a further paper of mine [5], which examines the slow development of the capacity for communication on a symbolic level in a three-year-old autistic child whose only capacity for contact-making, for communion, was expressed in the symptom of echolalia and echopraxia. Children like this little girl, who frequently come to our clinical attention, unfortunately often at higher age levels, would be excellent examples for dealing with Hook's question [16], which he has asked "innumerable times since I read Freud in 1919," as to "what kind of evidence they [the psychoanalysts] were prepared to accept which would lead them to declare in any specific case that a child did not have an Oedipus complex." I don't want to understand his question simply as an attempt to embarrass the analysts, even though he seems to be quite successful at giving that impression, but rather as a reference to the fact that early psychoanalytic theory did not provide the descriptive and theoretical means for answering it. It seems to me that only more current investigations into ego psychology, into the early nature and establishment of object relationships, and into the lack of the capacity for object relationships helped us more fully to understand the conditions that would have to prevail in order to prevent a child from reaching the oedipal phase, which is based on the capacity for object relationships, for object and self experience. Incidentally, the question as to what evidence would indicate in a specific case that a child did not have an Oedipus complex seems to me about as useful as if one were to ask what evidence one would accept in any specific case that a person did not have a skeleton. The latter, too, would be a legitimate question, but would Hook discuss issues of anatomy on that basis?

I offer these recent discussions concerning the nature of the ideological components of psychoanalytic theories, the nature of explanation and interpretation, and the nature of technical intervention and communication as examples in which the psychoanalyst was helped by the types of investigations which the philosophy of science provides, even though they are at best fragmentary beginnings. They must accompany his work and will frequently help him gain insight which he would not have obtained if he had been satisfied with earlier, less clear usages of psychoanalytic language.

Also, it seems to be true that our language is better suited for description of the inner life of a person than it is for interpatient comparison. This problem creates serious difficulties in psychotherapeutic research, in attempts to compare different patient groups, in outcome studies, and in follow-up studies.

It may seem that in raising all these questions I have been castigating myself as well as psychoanalysis, but I actually do not intend to apologize for its language. I prefer rather to speak strongly in its defense, and thus add another problem which should also be of interest to the philosopher of science, since it relates to our methods of discovery.

Oppenheimer [21] has told psychologists how important analogy is in the creative, the scientific process of discovery. He makes a plea for tolerance of inexact language on the part of psychologists. Metaphors, models which are really analogies, thinking in terms of imagery, language nearer to what psychoanalysts call the primary process, have led us to psychological understanding. Without these types of more archaic, intuitive thinking, to which Hook [16] refers as "the work of poetic mythologists," we could never hope to achieve significant insights into our problem areas. Many analytic writings, such as those of Groddeck, are in part intuition-producing metaphors and similes; they accompany the creative process as described so well in Reik's popular simile of "listening with the third ear" [23]. Our clinical skills, our sensitivity, and our creativity would suffer were we to become prematurely puritanical cleaners of our language, our concepts, and our theories.

Nevertheless, the question remains as to how we may develop a way of working which permits us to use the archaic forerunners of thinking, and also imposes on us the responsibility of scientific rigor and of a more adequate scientific methodology. While Hook thinks of Freud as a poetic mythologist, Freud thought of the methodologists as people who clean their eyeglasses constantly without ever looking through them. I feel, with Feigl, that psychoanalysis may do well to develop more and more in its students, as they look through their glasses, a desire to keep them clean and to strengthen in themselves the determination as well as the capacity to know the nature and the limitations of the instrument which they use while they look into the depths of the human mind.

REFERENCES

1. Colby, Kenneth M. *Energy and Structure in Psychoanalysis.* New York: Ronald Press, 1955.
2. Colby, Kenneth M. *An Introduction to Psychoanalytic Research.* New York: Basic Books, 1960.
3. Ekstein, Rudolf. "Ideological Warfare in the Psychological Sciences," *Psychoanalytic Review*, 36:144–151 (1949).
4. Ekstein, Rudolf. "The Language of Psychology and of Everyday Life," *Psychological Review*, 49:182–190 (1942).
5. Ekstein, Rudolf. "On the Acquisition of Speech in the Autistic Child," *Reiss-Davis Clinic Bulletin*, 1:63–79 (1964).
6. Ekstein, Rudolf. "The Philosophical Refutation," *Journal of Philosophy*, 38:57–67 (1941).
7. Ekstein, Rudolf. "Philosophy of Science and Psychoanalysis," *Samiksa*, 11:211–216 (1957).
8. Ekstein, Rudolf. "Thoughts Concerning the Nature of the Interpretive Process," in *Readings in Psychoanalytic Psychology*, Morton Levitt, ed., pp. 221–247. New York: Appleton-Century-Crofts, 1959.
9. Ekstein, Rudolf. "The Tower of Babel in Psychology and in Psychiatry," *American Imago*, 7:78–141 (1950).
10. Feigl, Herbert. "The 'Mental' and the 'Physical,' " in *Minnesota Studies in the Philosophy of Science*, Vol. II, Herbert Feigl, Michael Scriven, and Grover Maxwell, eds., pp. 370–497. Minneapolis: University of Minnesota Press, 1958.
11. Feigl, Herbert, "Some Remarks on the Meaning of Scientific Explanation," in

Readings in Philosophical Analysis, Herbert Feigl and Wilfrid Sellars, eds., pp. 510–514. New York: Appleton-Century-Crofts, 1949.

12. Frank, Philipp. "Psychoanalysis and Logical Positivism," in Hook [15], pp. 308–313.
13. Freud, Sigmund. *The Interpretation of Dreams,* James Strachey, ed. New York: Basic Books, 1955.
14. Freud, Sigmund. *The Origins of Psychoanalysis,* Marie Bonaparte, Anna Freud, and Ernst Kris, eds. New York: Basic Books, 1954.
15. Hook, Sidney, ed. *Psychoanalysis, Scientific Method, and Philosophy.* New York: New York University Press, 1959.
16. Hook, Sidney. "Science and Mythology in Psychoanalysis," in Hook [15], pp. 212–224.
17. Hospers, John. "Philosophy and Psychoanalysis," in Hook [15], pp. 336–357.
18. Kris, Ernst. "The Nature of Psychoanalytic Propositions and Their Validation," in *Freedom and Experience,* Sidney Hook and Milton R. Konvitz, eds. Ithaca, N.Y.: Cornell University Press, 1947.
19. Lazerowitz, Morris. "The Relevance of Psychoanalysis to Philosophy," in Hook [15], pp. 133–156.
20. Nagel, Ernest. "Methodological Issues in Psychoanalytic Theory," in Hook [15], pp. 38–56.
21. Oppenheimer, Robert. "Analogy in Science," *American Psychologist,* 2:127–135 (1956).
22. Rapaport, David. "An Historical Survey of Psychoanalytic Ego Psychology," *Bulletin of the Philadelphia Association for Psychoanalysis,* 8:105–120 (1958).
23. Reik, Theodor. *Listening with the Third Ear.* New York: Farrar, Straus, 1949.
24. Shakow, David. Discussion of Talcott Parsons's "Psychoanalysis and Social Science," in *Twenty Years of Psychoanalysis,* Franz Alexander and Helen Ross, eds. New York: W. W. Norton, 1953.
25. Shakow, David. "Psychoanalytic Education of Behavioral and Social Scientists for Research," in *Science and Psychoanalysis,* Vol. V, Jules Masserman, ed. New York: Grune and Stratton, 1962.

WOLFGANG KÖHLER
\\\ ))/

A Task for Philosophers

At the sixty-sixth annual convention of the American Psychological Association, in 1958, Herbert Feigl delivered an address which he called "Philosophical Embarrassments of Psychology" [4]. Early in this lecture he declared that at the present time an important function of the philosopher in his contacts with the sciences resembles that of a psychotherapist; for, work in a particular discipline is often impeded by disturbing influences, the nature of which a calm philosopher who looks at this discipline from the outside will easily recognize, while those who are deeply immersed in that work may remain utterly unaware of the disturbance itself and of its causes. When applying this principle to psychology Feigl was careful not to offend the psychologists, and therefore restricted his therapeutic suggestions to fairly mild remarks. I have the feeling that present-day psychology may need a more drastic treatment. Could Feigl perhaps visit his patient, psychology, again but now be more outspoken, and discuss her mental troubles more specifically? I will go a bit farther, and ask Feigl whether he would allow me to accompany him on such a visit. I know the patient and her symptoms quite well. Actually, the following paragraphs are written for the purpose of telling him what I discovered when recently watching her once more.

After a short while, I found myself particularly interested in Behaviorism. Since Professor Price of Oxford has recently discussed this school in an interesting article [7], my remarks ought to be compared with his statements. It seems to me that Feigl will not object if occasionally my remarks refer to questions which the philosophers of science are thorough-

[70]

ly accustomed to deal with. The transgression is unavoidable because the Behaviorist's lapses originated in this region when he decided to ignore the only part of the world which is directly accessible to a human being.

In order to avoid misunderstandings, I must now briefly explain what I mean when I call one part of the world directly accessible. At first, this explanation may seem to be superfluous because the same topic has often been discussed by others. Apparently, however, such older statements have not been sufficiently explicit, for even in modern philosophical writings I sometimes find arguments which are at odds with basic facts in this field.

Among the directly accessible parts of the world, perceptual scenes are, on the whole, accessible in a particularly satisfactory fashion. I will begin with these. Perceptual scenes are roughly divided into two regions. One contains the perceptual facts around the self, such as a street, trees, automobiles, and other people; the other contains this self. When understood in one sense, what we call the self is just one more directly accessible percept. Its owner can see, feel, hear, touch it, and so forth. I will call it the "body," a name which, in the following, will always refer to this perceptual entity. When dealing with perception more in detail, we shall find it necessary to distinguish sharply between the self as a percept and the physical organism in question. Apart from the body-percept as a whole, human beings also have a self in a second, less tangible sense. This somewhat elusive entity is perhaps not a part of the directly accessible world in the same sense as is the body-percept, for it appears mainly as a center from which such directed states as attention and related vectors, all as such accessible facts, are felt to issue. The center itself seems generally to be experienced only as a place, the place of origin of such vectors, but not as a place with particular characteristics of its own. Curiously enough, this place is nevertheless fairly well located within the body-percept, namely, in frontal parts of the head-percept, a short distance behind the perceived nose. Obviously, not everything is quite simple in the directly accessible world. I should perhaps add that this location of the self in the narrower sense within a particular region of the body-percept must, of course, be clearly distinguished from the localization which the physiological representation of this self may have in the brain as a physical system.

Before we continue our primitive survey of the directly accessible world, it seems advisable to emphasize the difference between its accessibility in general and another property of this world, which its parts exhibit in varying degrees. This other property is "clearness." Not all perceptual situations, for instance, are equally clear. Thus, when we compare central regions of the visual field with more peripheral regions, we realize at once that the latter are less clear, if not actually "vague." I hope it will be obvious that, when using such terms in the present connection, I am referring to characteristics of the compared perceptual facts themselves rather than to the clearness or vagueness of any cognitive operations that refer to these facts.

Now, the same distinction applies everywhere within the directly accessible world. Everywhere what is accessible as a matter of principle may at the same time be experienced as more or less clear or as relatively vague. On the average, perceptual facts tend to be clearer than are other parts of the accessible scene, for example, than merely remembered scenes that, in the past, may have been clearly perceived. Again, when considering our own planning, thinking, deciding, and making efforts, or our moods and our emotions, we often have every reason for calling such states and activities (or parts of them) directly accessible; but this does not mean that such experiences are always as clear as, say, a simple house perceived on a clear day. Even when extraordinarily intense (as emotions, of course, sometimes are), such facts need not, for this reason, be particularly clear in the present sense. Moods, especially, often make the impression of being fairly vague clouds in our interior.

At this point a word of caution must be added. Most of us, especially the philosophers and scientists, like to deal with clear situations just as we try to keep our own thinking clear. We tend to have a low opinion of facts that look or feel vague. But it is not the philosopher's or the scientist's task to prescribe to any part of the world how it ought to look. Can we be sure that facts that in my present sense look a bit vague are invariably less important than optimally clear-looking facts? This applies also to the parts of the directly accessible world that have no clear outlines or structures. If, because of their intrinsic vagueness, we keep away from such states or events, we project upon them a valuation which is justified so far as human cognitive processes are concerned but cannot be applied to the materials to which such processes refer. The projection is not permissible—even if the scientist's work is sometimes made difficult by lack of clearness of what he wants to investigate. When the psychological world first originated, it was probably not meant to be, first of all, a world which the psychologist could easily study.

Some among the directly accessible facts which I have just mentioned are somewhat vague not only per se. Their *localization* within the directly accessible scene is also seldom as clear as that of many percepts. Where, for instance, are our moods and our emotions experienced? Mostly, it seems, in certain regions of the body-percept; but where precisely within this percept they are located we often find it difficult to tell. Nevertheless, some such states are felt to be fairly clearly related to other parts of the accessible scene. For example, expectations, intentions, fears, and the like are generally experienced as being related to this or that particular object within the scene—just as in physics field-vectors relate one physical object to others. Within the directly accessible world, the "other objects" in question may be percepts; but often they are things or situations of which we are *thinking* at the time. No fact could be more important for the purposes of what we now call physiological psychology than the observation that certain functional relations among psychological facts are not matters of mere inference but rather are directly represented within the directly accessible scene. Why our physiological psychologists do not seem to be impressed by this simple but nevertheless fundamental evidence, I do not know.

I have called one part of the world "directly accessible." Another name of this part is the "phenomenal" world. I have not used this name because it almost sounds as though it referred to mere appearances of other, more substantial, and therefore more important, facts. As I see it, we ought not to introduce value judgments of this kind when we have hardly begun to inspect our material. Moreover, if we *have* to use terms that imply values, I am, with others, inclined to attribute a certain value to the directly accessible facts for the simple reason that they *are* so accessible and, in this special sense, clearly superior to anything that is only *indirectly* accessible.

Actually, our main difficulties tend to arise when we now ask ourselves how the content of the directly accessible scene is related to the parts of the world which are not directly accessible. These parts constitute, of course, what the physicists, chemists, astronomers, biologists, and so forth, call *nature*. So long as Naive Realism was not yet overcome by powerful criticism, and sturdy percepts were simply regarded as parts of an environment that existed independently—that is, whether or not there were perceivers around who "had" these percepts—so long, of course, the physical world did seem to be directly accessible. I need not enumerate the steps that gradually made this original (and most natural) attitude untenable. Suspicions that certain nonperceptual contents of human experience do not also occur in nature probably arose fairly early. Then the secondary qualities of percepts became suspect of being merely "subjective" ingredients of the otherwise objective perceived world, and only their primary qualities survived the attacks of skeptics—until, during the late parts of the nineteenth century and the first decades of the twentieth, some began to doubt whether what is called the extension of perceptual facts in space or time is quite the same thing as the spatial or temporal extension ascribed to facts in the physical world. It was mainly investigations of nature itself, particularly early work in neurophysiology, that led to this radical separation of the perceptual world from an altogether objective nature.

Eventually, of course, the conclusion became inevitable that no property of physical systems is directly accessible to the scientist, and that, therefore, all statements about physical nature must be based on inferences, that is, must be results of constructions in the scientist's thought. Observation of physical facts remained possible only in the sense that certain simple perceptual facts used in the scientist's observations have structural characteristics in common with states or events in nature, and thus give the scientist the foundations on which he can erect his constructions. The assumption that some perceptual, that is, directly accessible, facts share certain structural properties with facts that are not so accessible has never been subjected to serious doubts. The constructional part of the scientist's procedure is, as a matter of principle, also generally accepted; for, its results and consequences are thoroughly examined all the time in further perceptual observations of the kind just mentioned, which either prove or disprove that given constructions are acceptable.

This again is a well-known story. I have to repeat it because occasionally we still find statements in the philosophical literature which do not seem to agree with it. Thus, a philosopher's argument may begin with the words "When I perceive a physical object . . . ." Even if such expressions may merely be used as convenient abbreviations, that is, not as implying a form of Naive Realism, they ought, it seems to me, to be avoided. Otherwise, misunderstandings and errors are almost bound to occur. I do not yet know whether at this point Feigl and I entirely agree; for in a recent article [3] he mentions certain questions which, he says, can quickly be shown "to rest on elementary conceptual confusions." Does Feigl not want us to discuss such questions? Some among those he mentions really deserve no answer. But one example is: "Do we really see physical objects?" I like to answer questions of this kind because only when they are answered will the conceptual confusions to which Feigl rightly refers finally disappear. When we consider the long chain of events that connects physical facts in our physical environment with directly accessible percepts, our answer to this particular question can only be a clear No. It is dangerous to use expressions which imply that in such situations the beginning of a long causal chain may be identified with its end. My doubt as to whether Feigl completely agrees with what I have just said arises from his interpretation of certain everyday expressions. These expressions, he says, combine phenomenal and physical terms, as for instance when one person, referring to another, makes the statement: "Eagerness was written all over his face." I hesitate to admit that, when used in common language, this statement refers to any physical facts in our present sense of the term. Rather, the "face" which is here mentioned is a *percept* that, in the spirit of everyday Naive Realism, is supposed to exist independently of the perceiver; and "eagerness" is a tertiary quality of this percept "face" which, at other times, might be replaced by such qualities of the same class as "fatigue" or "depression" or "haggardness."

My sharp distinction between percepts and corresponding physical objects may be in need of more explicit support. The next paragraphs are meant to give it this support. Unavoidably, I have now to consider what may seem to be mere details in the fields of physical optics and elementary neurophysiology. What is an object or thing in perception? It is a particular area or, because of its possible extension in three dimensions, a kind of block in visual space, in both cases an entity that is, as a whole, segregated from its background and from other things. If somebody were to tell us that this segregation simply follows from the existence of a corresponding image on the retina, he would not be aware of a simple fact. Generally speaking, a physical object affects the retina by the light which its surface reflects. Now, small parts of this surface reflect light independently of one another, and so do the small parts of the physical background and of the surfaces of other physical objects in the neighborhood of the first. Some such locally reflected beams reach the refractive parts of the physical eye, and in this transmission and in their final projection upon the retina the spatial order of the local beams is fairly well preserved according to the laws of optics. As a result, the mosaic of the reflecting physical surface-elements is rather adequately repeated as a corresponding mosaic of the retinal stimuli in the eye. (It does not essentially affect this description that actually retinal stimulations do, to a degree, overlap.) Now, if local retinal stimulations are mutually independent facts, just as the elements of all physical surfaces before the organism reflect light independently, then these stimulations must be regarded as a mere mosaic. Consequently, we use a seriously misleading expression if we refer to what happens on a particular area of the retina as "the image" of this or that physical object. In doing so, we inadvertently ascribe to the retinal projection a segregation of circumscribed molar entities from the rest of the mosaic, for which, up to this point, there are no grounds in the physics of the retinal situation—however clearly such a segregation of particular molar entities may be present in the perceptual field of the owner of the retina.

How does this segregation of visual things arise? It is the outcome of neural interactions which begin within the neural tissue of the retina, continue to occur at higher levels of the neural medium, and seem to be completed in occipital (and perhaps also parietal) parts of the brain. Such interactions mainly depend upon the properties of given local events in the anatomical visual system, or rather upon their distances from each other and upon their similarities and dissimilarities. Now, since these properties are everywhere determined by the nature of the local beams which at each retinal point contribute their local share to the total mosaic of the stimuli, the interactions ultimately depend upon the physical and chemical characteristics of the surface-elements in the physical environment where the beams started. In visual perception the final result is the organized character of the perceived scene, the segregation of circumscribed molar entities from their visual surroundings, the formation of visual groups of such entities, and so forth.

It is this dependence of the interactions involved upon the physical characteristics of surface-elements in the physical environment which often makes the final outcome, the structure of what we see, a more or less adequate representation of the physical objects before our physical eyes. Do the perceptual structures always have this "veridical" character? Of course they do not. Anybody familiar with visual perception can fabricate physical patterns the visual counterparts of which are mild or crude distortions of the physical originals. He can also arrange these physical conditions in such a way that in the resulting visual scene the presence of a particular physical object in physical space is not at all announced by a corresponding segregated percept.

I do not believe that, after this description of certain physical and physiological facts, I need defend the strict distinction between percepts and physical objects any further. But why is it so difficult to convince people that this distinction is necessary? Some philosophers may hesitate to make perfectly clear statements in this respect because they do not wish the content of physical science to be too loosely connected with observational, that is perceptual, evidence. Others may not yet have been able to discard the last remnants of Naive Realism from their philosophy of science. I admit that this is a hard task for all of us. Part of the trouble, I suspect, arises from the fact that even distinguished authors sometimes confuse one particularly important perceptual entity with the corresponding physical object. Since this mistake always causes further errors in the philosophy of science, I must now describe both this error and the way in which it can be corrected by more consistent thinking.

Recently an outstanding philosopher explained his interpretation of the relation between perceptual facts, such as colors, and cortical events. I need not discuss this interpretation. In the present connection, only the way in which he deals with that particularly important percept is relevant. The physical event, he says, which is directly related to a seen color takes place in the organism, namely in the brain. Nevertheless, he continues, this color is, through conditioning, referred to the surface of an object in the environment of the organism. In other words, what is actually "inside" now appears "outside." More generally, he adds, all distance perception, whether visual or auditory, is in this fashion established by conditioning. In evaluating this thesis, I have to refer first to some experimental findings and second to the fact that, when the meanings of the terms "inside," "outside," and "organism" are kept clear, the philosopher's problem disappears immediately. The experimental evidence is that, when the distance-perception of rats reared up to that time in darkness is quantitatively tested in a lighted room, it proves to be highly adequate at once, although these animals have had no opportunity to learn by conditioning that visual contents have to be transferred to the surfaces of distant objects in the physical environment—and what the right distances from the organism are in each case. But, secondly, the philosopher's explanation is quite unnecessary for the following reasons. We have to distinguish between percepts and their physical counterparts not only when the physical objects in question are tables, chairs, and so forth, but also when we consider our physical organism (as investigated by anatomists and physiologists, and not directly accessible) and the directly accessible body-percept that each of us has, that entity combining visual, auditory, tactual, and kinesthetic components, to which I referred when first describing the content of the directly accessible world. Once this distinction between the organism and the body-percept has become clear, and Naive Realism has thereby lost its last stronghold, we realize immediately that the relational terms "inside" and "outside" do not refer to the same facts when we consider the organism and its spatial relations to other physical objects, on the one hand, and the body-percept and its spatial relations to other visual percepts, on the other hand. Suppose the author is not astonished when a chair-percept and a table-percept appear in separate parts of visual space. Why, then, should it surprise him that the surface of a certain visual percept (with its color) and the visual body-percept are separated by a visual distance? He will not, I assume, claim that all visual distances between all visual percepts are products of learning by conditioning. Since the author is interested in cortical events which are directly related to perceptual facts, I should perhaps add that, when visual percepts are clearly separated in visual space, the cortical events directly related to those percepts also generally have separate places in the *brain*—with all the functional consequences that follow from this separation. Therefore, the cortical representation of the body-percept is located in *certain* cortical regions, and the cortical representation of such visual percepts as chairs, etc., in *other* parts of the cortex. Consequently, there is no reason whatsoever why our seeing other percepts outside our body-percept should be regarded as a problem that can only be solved by a reference to learning. The *physical* distance between a *physical* object and our *physical* organism is, of course, a fact that does not, as such, appear in our perceptual field at all—because it is not a directly accessible fact. And also, the further fact that all our percepts and their distances from each other are functionally related to certain events within our physical brain does not appear in what we perceive; for the physical brain and the physical processes in its interior are just as little parts of the directly accessible scene as is the physical distance between the physical organism and, say, a physical table.

The decisive point is, of course, that the body-percept must be clearly distinguished from the physical organism. Does our philosopher doubt that the body-percept really *is* a percept, that is, by no means the physical organism? If he does, there is a simple demonstration experiment that will probably remove his doubt. Suppose that a small object is shown on the surface of a larger object, and that the latter object can be physically moved without moving the former. Actual movement of the larger surface while, physically, the small object remains stationary now causes the small object *as a percept* to move in the opposite direction. Karl Duncker [1] has thoroughly investigated this phenomenon, which is called an "induced movement." Similarly, when wind moves scattered clouds across the moon, the perceived moon performs a visual movement in the opposite direction. Now, precisely the same thing, an induced movement, occurs when a physical person is quietly seated on a physical chair while a pattern of alternately black and white vertical stripes (on a curtain) slowly moves around him. In the perceptual field of this person, his own body-percept now begins to turn in the opposite direction. I can assure the philosopher that this is a most striking and convincing experience—and that it occurs when the physical organism involved does not turn at all. It follows that we *must* distinguish between the physical organism and what I have called the body-percept; in the situation just mentioned, the perceived self behaves exactly as other percepts do under comparable circumstances.

It is only fair to add that our philosopher finds himself in excellent company. For instance, Helmholtz regarded it as a curious fact that "red," "green," and various other sensory qualities seem to cover objects in space "in spite of the fact that such qualities belong to our nervous system, and do not extend into outside space." It is actually simpler to find authors who commit this error than people who have recognized it as an error. The mistake was first corrected a hundred years ago, in 1862, by Ewald Hering—an extraordinary achievement, since in 1862 little was known about the way in which perceptual facts and their spatial relations are represented in the cortex. Characteristically enough, in his publication Hering made a pessimistic remark about the chances that his explanation would be understood by his contemporaries. As a matter of fact, few ever became acquainted with it during the past hundred years, and not very many seem to know about it now. How, under the circumstances, can philosophy give us a clear account of how, in physics, an observer is related to what he is observing?

I have, however, offered my assistance to Feigl not for an application of therapeutic measures to philosophers but, rather, when the patients are psychologists. I will, therefore, now turn to a symptom I have observed in this part of the population. One of my major findings is that psychologists are astonishingly liberal in their use of certain words. At one moment a given term is meant to refer to a certain fact, but the very next moment it may be applied to a different fact. One is seldom told which meaning it is supposed to have in a particular situation. Many examples of such conceptual confusions are available. I will restrict my remarks to a few examples, and begin with the various meanings of the terms "subjective" and "objective." A lack of precision in the use of these words is as dangerous as failure to distinguish between the physical organism and the body-percept has just proved to be.

A psychologist (who has not yet become a Behaviorist, and therefore permits himself at times to inspect the directly accessible world) might be inclined to use the terms "subjective" and "objective" in a purely descriptive or geographical sense. He would call all percepts that look solid, and independent of his own self, "objective," while anything that seems to be part or action of this self he would call "subjective." It would not always be easy to tell whether a certain directly accessible fact belongs to one or the other category, particularly since the self and the "objective" parts of the experienced scene are so often related by experienced vectors (see above, page 71). But then, where does the eastern part of this country stop and the Middle West begin? And yet this distinction is quite useful, since when we have arrived from somewhere else in the "real" Middle West we cannot miss the difference. In the same sense the distinction between "subjective" and "objective" parts of the directly accessible world may also often be convenient. But if our psychologist were actually to use these terms in such a descriptive sense, he would almost surely be misunderstood by other members of the profession. For the words "subjective" and "objective" have long since become imbued with other meanings, meanings which they acquired in the history of natural science.

In physics the term "objective" refers, of course, to the independently existing facts of nature per se, but occasionally also to such *procedures* as give us adequate knowledge of such facts. From this point of view, the physicist once looked with some suspicion at the psychological equipment of man because, research in physics being done by humans, intrusion of such "merely subjective" human factors might have endangered the objectivity of physical science. They "did not belong." Nowadays physicists no longer believe that there is such a danger and therefore look at psychological facts with complete equanimity. But the name "merely subjective" still adheres to whatever is a psychological state or event, and it does so even when we are not concerned with the physicist's business at all. Obviously this use of the term is entirely unrelated to a possible descriptive use of the same word in a description of the directly accessible world. For, however the physicists may *now* feel about psychological facts, their former reserve in this respect implied a distinction of *values*, "objective" facts and operations being *good* facts, and "subjective" influences that might have come from the psychological world being *bad* facts. It is these value-characteristics of the two adjectives which still strongly affect us when we hear one or the other. One has to do with truth, and the other with untruth, or with truth-in-danger. While we cannot object to the former connotations of these terms in physics, it is most unfortunate that they are still being applied in the same sense when now used in a purely psychological context. To a degree, it is true, such selected perceptual facts as the physicist himself uses in his observations seem to be excepted; they are regarded as "less subjective" by those who are sufficiently acquainted with the physicist's actual procedures. But to others the word "subjective" continues to sound bad, particularly when applied to any part of the directly accessible world. Or am I mistaken? According to some philosophers the directly accessible world is perhaps not really dangerous; rather, while it remains bad, it is now bad only because it is in a way *inferior*. Its contents, we hear, are barely discernible phenomena in a remote region, mere shadows, if not simply illusions. Most probably this curious attitude would not have developed if young psychology had advanced more rapidly, and if similar views had not been held within this discipline itself by the Behaviorists.

I have to say a few words about the directly accessible world as a world of thin, subjective shadows. We remember that in everyday life we all are Naive Realists, who regard the more robust percepts before us as independently existing entities—*because that is how they look.* They still look the same even when we have learned that, when considered in a wider scientific context, percepts cannot be identified with the real objects of natural science. And this is, of course, the reason why we remain Naive Realists in everyday life. The periods of sophistication during which we do consider that larger context are rare and short indeed, and so we practically continue to live and to think within the directly accessible scene. Does it consist of mere shadows? To be sure, some parts of the scene actually have the fleeting character of mere shadows as, for instance, weak and moving shadows in the usual sense of the word. But what about the extraordinarily firm ground (-percept) on which I (my body-percept) am now standing? What about the very hard and resistant wall (-percept) against which my hand and arm (-percepts) are now exerting a considerable (felt) pressure? Again, the heavy weight (-percept) which I yesterday tried to lift—does it deserve to be compared with a mere shadow? Such percepts simply look and feel utterly substantial. I do not like to be in (perceived) places where big rock-percepts are just beginning to tumble down a steep slope-percept right above my body-percept. And do not tell me that I have just used expressions which are borrowed from physics, and are now merely projected upon the perceptual world. For the concepts of physics are defined in extraordinarily abstract terms. If, occasionally, such expressions as I just used are applied to facts in physical nature, then just the opposite happens: properties of the perceived world are then projected upon entities and events in physics.

Perhaps the philosophers who tell us that the directly accessible world may practically be ignored will here raise the objection that, when referring to faint and remote phenomena, they mean the moods and feelings of man rather than his percepts. But have they never heard of the terror of extreme fear, or of how people feel who are suffering from a deep depression? Surely the rapture of overwhelming joy cannot have remained entirely unknown to them. And what about the scientist's unshakable insistence on proper procedures in the pursuit of knowledge? Faint phenomena? Clearly, the mere fact that an event occurs within the directly accessible world need not prevent this event from being extremely powerful—even if it is located within the self.

I now turn to Behaviorism, the school that shares the views of such philosophers, and therefore claims that the directly accessible world is not worth a true scientist's attention. Behaviorism originated when students of psychology had just heard about the tremendous achievements of a strictly objective natural science, in which nothing subjective was ever permitted to play a part. Some such students now developed what,

I believe, teen-agers would call a crush. The crush referred to that majestic enterprise "science." I have to add, however, that (just as it is with other crushes) this science-crush grew up with particular ease among people who did not know too much about the actual makeup of the admired being, and also showed little inclination to learn more. Now, one of the outstanding characteristics of a crush is that objects which might otherwise be of interest lose their valences. A neat scale of values is soon established. The more positively something seems related to the idol, the better it is; anything that appears to be at odds with the idol's actions and intentions is obviously bad. The crush that grew up in our particular instance exhibited the same symptoms. Those who were caught lost the ability not only to look carefully at the specific content of natural science but also to consider other enterprises in an impartial fashion. Such enterprises were now good or bad, important or without interest, depending upon their relation to the ideas and procedures of the scientists. Hence, since the scientists of the time wanted to deal only with objective facts, and seemed to have a low opinion of the "merely subjective" psychological facts, those young psychologists decided to become Behaviorists, that is, to study only the objectively observable actions of their subjects, and to do so with methods comparable to those of natural science.

I suggest that the crush which led to this decision be now replaced by a more mature feeling of great respect, by serious efforts to become more familiar with the specific achievements of natural science, and also by a more natural distribution of interests. Do we really know that, in psychology, one may safely ignore certain facts merely because natural science was once afraid of them? Did not the very fears of the scientists imply that some such facts might have fairly important even if (in natural science) undesirable effects?

At first, Behaviorism could be regarded as a special form of Materialism; for some leaders of the new movement virtually denied that there was a directly accessible world in my sense of the term. Most probably, all members of the school would now say that they are simply not interested in this question, and that they prefer to define Behaviorism in purely methodological terms. This means, they would add, that all psychological phenomena as seen from the inside had better be left alone, because no proper way of dealing with such phenomena is available, and that therefore so-called "introspection" ought to be replaced by observation from the outside, i.e., by observation of truly objective behavior, which occurs in a just as objectively given environment. Since, in experiments, the observed behavior mostly consists of responses to particular objects (called "stimuli"), the Behaviorists often call their work a study of stimulus-response connections.

The main advantage of the transition from "introspection" to the observation of behavior is sometimes said to be as follows. Whatever other weaknesses "introspection" may have, the psychological facts observable from the inside are, in each case, accessible only to the one person who does the observing, while facts observable from the outside may always be observed by any number of people, and can thus be established in a strictly reliable fashion.

Sophisticated members of the school may also have been impressed by a further argument against the study of private human experiences, an argument that was first formulated by certain Positivists. Suppose that observations of such experiences are possible. Then we still must ask whether they are really valuable from the point of view of science. To be sure, a person may find in his private world such qualities as "red" and "blue" or "loud" and "soft." But this means no more than that this person becomes *acquainted* with such phenomena; and mere acquaintance with certain data is something quite different from what a physicist or philosopher of science would call "knowledge."

In discussing the Behaviorist's arguments, I will concentrate on the following issue: Do these arguments force us to conclude that psychologists ought to ignore the directly accessible world? My answer will be closely related to this further question: Is the Behaviorist right in claiming that his observations "from the outside" permit him to answer all questions that psychology must be expected to answer?

Once more, the argument that, because of their "subjective" character, psychological events as seen "from the inside" do not deserve our scientific attention suffers from the vague meaning of its main term "subjective." The fact that the objective study of nature once seemed endangered by the operation of factors located in man's interior made caution with regard to such influences a fully justified attitude. But, as an independent discipline, psychology should not primarily be concerned with bad (or good) effects which certain psychological processes might have in other enterprises; its foremost task is that of studying psychological facts as such and of discovering the principles involved in their occurrence. Consequently, those fears of the scientist can no longer be allowed to affect the psychologist's choice of what he will investigate.

Is there any further cause for calling the directly accessible world a collection of merely subjective phenomena? The Behaviorists are quite prepared to answer this question. According to them, we remember, psychological facts as observed "from the inside" are accessible only to the person who observes them. Such psychological phenomena are, therefore, subjective facts in a further sense of the word "subjective," and it is this sense of the term which must be regarded as decisive from the point of view of science. I will not deny that other people are unable to look into the world that is directly accessible to me. But whether it follows that this world should not interest the psychologist is an entirely different question. In order to answer it, we have next to examine the Behaviorist's claim that his own observations can be repeated, and checked, by any number of other persons because all these persons observe precisely the same objective facts. Take my experiments, the Behaviorist would say. There is, for instance, that jumping stand which I am now using, that is, opposite a screen with two doors in it, one platform, and, behind the doors, a second platform. All these are physical objects, accessible to any observer. A rat which I place on the former platform is, of course, also a physical object; and when the rat now jumps against one of the doors, opens it by the impact, and thus lands on the second platform where it begins to eat—these events are again physical facts which everybody can observe.

My answer to this report follows from our earlier considerations. The Behaviorist's account of what he observes in such experiments is a striking example of Naive Realism. For how does he know about platforms, a screen with doors, and a rat? And how about the rat's jump, the opening of a door, and the rat's eating? As he observes these facts, they are without exception accessible to him only as *perceptual* objects and events in his private visual field. Physical objects and physical events as such are just as inaccessible to him as they are to a physicist. I need not repeat the arguments that make the identification of perceptual facts with their physical counterparts impossible. I must therefore conclude that, in all his observations, the Behaviorist relies on facts that appear in his private experience, the only experience in which he can do any observing. Moreover, when other observers are present, and describe what they have seen during his experiment, their descriptions again refer to occurrences within *their* private perceptual worlds. Hence, when the Behaviorist says that the private, "subjective" content of the phenomenal world cannot interest a true scientist, this statement is plainly contradicted by his own procedure. He actually proves that certain contents of the directly accessible world must, and can, be used as reliable tools in his science. Why, then, should they not also be accepted as materials which may be studied by psychologists? If the Behaviorists are convinced that, in a given situation, observations of one Behaviorist tend to agree with those of another, then this holds also for observations within the perceptual scenes of psychologists who believe that such scenes are worth their full attention. Such scenes are accessible to only one person in each case? This may be true; but, then, they are accessible *at least to one*, while the independently existing objects in the sense of physics, including the physical behavior of physical men and animals, are directly accessible to *nobody*.

Behaviorists do not show much interest in perception. Few Naive Realists do. Members of the school might therefore be inclined to raise this objection: "Even if you are right in your interpretation of our observations from the outside, you overlook an important point. All our observations refer to very simple facts such as platforms, screens, doors, rats, and jumping. Under such conditions perceptual facts may practically be regarded as copies of corresponding physical facts so that the former tell us what is also true of the latter." I will answer as follows. In the first place, the Behaviorist does not realize that even the simplest perception of individual molar objects is the outcome of organizational processes in the nervous system. In the mere mosaic of local physical stimuli on the Behaviorist's retina there are no individual molar objects such as platforms, doors, and rats (see above, page 76). If the Behaviorist is not interested in this part of neurophysiology, other psychologists find it a fascinating part. They therefore study not only perceptual facts which have proved to be veridical from the point of view of physics but also others of which this cannot be said. For only when, in this respect, the study of perceptual facts is strictly impartial will the psychologists' investigation of perception give them an adequate view of how the neural processes involved organize themselves, and thus produce our organized perceptual fields. Actually, this study now begins to yield results in which, as admirers of objective science, Behaviorists ought to be intensely interested. Nowhere, it is now generally admitted, are important events in the physical world more closely related to psychological facts than they are in brains. It therefore seems natural to use the characteristics of such psychological facts as evidence concerning the nature of their physiological foundations in the brain. Among the psychological data that might be used for this purpose, the percepts of human beings can be studied with particular ease and accuracy. Indeed, investigations of this kind now seem to give us more adequate information about related brain-processes than even otherwise excellent physiological procedures have so far brought to light. I once more conclude that the Behaviorist's low opinion of the directly accessible world is mistaken. At least from the perceptual part of this world extremely short and reliable paths appear to lead into the most interesting province of physical nature. Nor is this access restricted to those brain-events which are directly related to perception; for, the organizational aspects of brain function which were first revealed by studies in this particular field have now been found to be also relevant to the solution of certain problems in memory, learning, and thinking.

After these remarks, I need not spend much time on a discussion of the thesis that inspection of the directly accessible world makes us merely acquainted with its contents, but cannot yield what is called scientific knowledge. This thesis may have seemed plausible when the examples mentioned in this connection were sensory qualities. But in the meantime Gestalt psychology has taught us that many facts of *organization* are just as directly observable as those simple qualities, and that on this basis knowledge in a very good sense is possible not only within the directly accessible world but also beyond it, namely, in brain-physiology.

How could early Behaviorists develop their radical views, if simple considerations such as those contained in the preceding paragraphs actually show that those views were based on simple misunderstandings? Most probably their mistake was facilitated by a further conceptual confusion. The term "stimulus" (which Behaviorists so often use) now has no fewer than three different meanings; but authors do not always make it clear which of these meanings it is supposed to have in a given case. Psychology first used the term "stimulus" in the sense in which it was then used by physiologists who studied the reactions of sense organs to physical agents such as light waves, sound waves, pressures, electric currents, and certain chemicals. It is these agents as actual stimulants of sensory cells (or of nerve fibers and muscles) which were originally called "stimuli." But in the case of perception such stimulating agents could be regarded as outposts or effects of objects in the physical world. Thus, in order to abbreviate their verbal references to such objects, psychologists began to speak of "stimuli" also when they meant those objects rather than, for instance, the light which they reflected and which actually stimulated retinal cells. For a while it was customary to specify in which sense the term "stimulus" was being used in a given situation by calling the actually operating stimulants *proximal*, and the related physical objects *distal*, stimuli. We no longer hear or read these specifying adjectives very often and as a consequence the term "stimulus" is now being used in an ambiguous fashion. Unfortunately, there is even a third entity to which psychologists give the same name. When studying the formation of associations or conditioned reactions, they call the effects of such connections "responses" and, in referring to the facts with which these responses are being connected, they again use the term "stimuli." The "stimuli" in question may now be the distant physical objects involved, or the proximal stimulating agents such as light waves, or also the *percepts* which finally appear in the subject's psychological scene. Particularly when psychologists speak of "the stimulus-object," the ambiguity begins to be quite disturbing. What, for instance, is being associated with a "second item" in certain experiments on learning, the physical object in question or its perceptual counterpart? What is the "stimulus-object" with which a response is being connected in an experiment on conditioning? We are seldom told. For example, in a recent article that explains what is now called the probabilistic theory of learning, the term "stimulus-object" plays an important role; but the author does not say whether it is the physical or the perceptual object in question to which this expression refers. Combined with the usual lapses into Naive Realism, this ambiguity tends to deprive not only this particular theory of learning but also other theoretical discussions of a sufficiently precise meaning. To what does the Behaviorist refer when he uses the "stimulus-response" formula? Since all his terms are supposed to have strictly "objective" meanings, we must assume that in this formula "stimulus" means to him, say, a physical door with a physical pattern on it as a part of a physical jumping stand. Now, of course, the confusion is complete, and the Behaviorist virtually *must* make the mistakes which I have criticized. Placed at a certain distance from the Behaviorist's physical rat, the door and its pattern do not, as these physical objects, affect the physical rat on its platform. These objects are not, as such, "stimuli." The optical (proximal) stimuli which impinge on the rat's retinal cells *do* deserve this name; but they cannot, as such, explain the rat's behavior. We remember that they produce a mere mosaic of local alterations in those cells, while the Behaviorist tells us that the rat's jumping refers to such circumscribed molar entities as a "door" or a "pattern." Since these entities are actually products of perceptual organization, they should never be called "stimuli."At any rate, the Behaviorist has now equipped the rat with more or less the same perceptual scene as he himself sees. But since he is a good Naive Realist, he will nevertheless continue to call such percepts "stimulus-objects," as though they were the *physical* objects "door" or "pattern." Once this mistake is made, we need not be surprised by other results of the Behaviorist's thinking, particularly not by his thesis that the interior worlds of individual men (or rats) play no role in his work.

While I cannot agree with the Behaviorist's interpretation of his own procedure, I do not, of course, suggest that investigations done in his style should not be undertaken. In certain instances, as for example in animal psychology, no other procedure is available; and some results obtained with this method are obviously important contributions to general psychology. This holds, first of all, for several discoveries made by Skinner; but it is also true of recent investigations in which the interests and techniques of the Behaviorist have been combined with physiological questions and procedures. Still, only if in the future the school decides to use its terms in a less ambiguous way can the full and precise import of such findings become apparent. At the same time the school will naturally have to discard its objections to work which deals with the directly accessible world. Thus at least *one* unnecessary limitation of its studies may at last disappear.

But in the meantime I must mention a further restriction which many Behaviorists impose on their own activities. Not only do they want to deal only with what they regard as "objective" *facts;* the term "objective" is also being used in a second sense in which it refers to certain special *methods.* In the Behaviorist's system, "objective" methods are those which permit him to subject the reliability of his findings to severe statistical tests. These tests are excellent. But at the present time not all forms of behavior permit us to apply these procedures. The Behaviorist, therefore, now restricts his investigations by a further rule. Within his own realm, the study of behavior, he investigates only such aspects of the subject's conduct as can be described in numerical terms, and thus permit the application of those statistical tests. A great many forms of behavior cannot be handled in this fashion and are therefore never investigated by the Behaviorist. Perhaps he does not realize that, when new problems arise and new forms of observation become necessary, it is not always possible to use at once the most satisfying quantitative techniques. At any rate, the Behaviorist is now in danger of imprisoning himself. One understands that life in a small apartment, where familiar furniture can easily be kept in the right places, has its attractions. But neighbors are sometimes surprised to see that the inhabitants pay so little attention to the larger world outside. Why should, at times, details in the field of conditioning be almost the only items of which these retiring people wish to hear? The very meaning of the name "Behaviorism" is now tending to change. Since the school cares only for those few aspects of behavior which happen to fit the requirements of particular procedures, its name is beginning to sound as though it referred to an almost *subjective* trend in psychology. A strictly objective science would hesitate to derive general convictions from a few selected data, particularly when the selection is based on standards of technical approach rather than on the objective importance of the data themselves.

In concluding, I should like to ask Feigl whether he approves of my first, tentative suggestions in the therapeutic field. At the beginning of my remarks I stated that some patients of ours are in need of a firmer treatment than he has applied to them. Does he believe that in what I have just said I have been *too* firm? I hope I have not. For in a few patients I now seem to discover the first indications of a slight spontaneous improvement. It would be unfortunate if my frank discussion of their predicament were to aggravate their symptoms again.

REFERENCES

1. Duncker, Karl. "Ueber induzierte Bewegung (ein Beitrag zur Theorie optisch wahrgenommener Bewegung)," *Psychologische Forschung,* 12:180–259 (1929).
2. Feigl, Herbert. "The 'Mental' and the 'Physical,'" in *Minnesota Studies in the Philosophy of Science,* Vol. II, Herbert Feigl, Michael Scriven, and Grover Maxwell, eds., pp. 370–497. Minneapolis: University of Minnesota Press, 1958.
3. Feigl, Herbert. "Mind-Body, Not a Pseudoproblem," in *Dimensions of Mind,* Sidney Hook, ed., pp. 24–34. New York: New York University Press, 1960.
4. Feigl, Herbert. "Philosophical Embarrassments of Psychology," *American Psychologist,* 14:115–128 (1959).
5. Köhler, Wolfgang. *Gestalt Psychology* (Rev. Ed.). New York: Liveright, 1947.
6. Köhler, Wolfgang. "Gestalt Psychology Today," *American Psychologist,* 14:727–734 (1959).

7. Price, H. H. "Some Objections to Behaviorism," in *Dimensions of Mind*, Sidney Hook, ed., pp. 78–84. New York: New York University Press, 1960.
8. Zener, Karl. "The Significance of Experience of the Individual for the Science of Psychology," in *Minnesota Studies in the Philosophy of Science*, Vol. II, Herbert Feigl, Michael Scriven, and Grover Maxwell, eds., pp. 354–369. Minneapolis: University of Minnesota Press, 1958.

WALLACE I. MATSON

\\(JJ

Why Isn't the Mind-Body Problem Ancient?

What would we have to do to make the ghost of Aristotle understand the mind-body problem?

Any teaching assistant can set up the mind-body problem so that any freshman will be genuinely worried about it. Yet none of the ancients ever dreamed of it, not even the author of *De Anima*. Why didn't they? Was it just a lamentable oversight, like the failure of the Alexandrians to invent the steam engine?

I

Feigl suggests [2, page 451] that the historical origins of the identity theory set forth in "The 'Mental' and the 'Physical' " might be found in Aristotle. Presumably he had passages like these in mind:

Sensation consists in being moved and acted upon. . . . It seems to be a sort of change of state. (*De Anima* 416b33, Hett translation, Loeb Classical Library, modified.)

The affections (*pathê*) of the soul are proportions (*logoi*) expressed in matter. Their definitions therefore must be in harmony with this; for instance, anger must be defined as a movement of a body, or of a part or faculty of a body, in a particular state roused by such a cause, with such an end in view. (*Ibid.*, 403a25.)

The natural philosopher will define anger as a surging of the blood and heat round the heart. (*Ibid.*, 403b1.)

Sensing is a bodily function. (*Ibid.*, 427a27.)

The affections of the soul, such as desire (*thumos*) and fear, are inseparable from the matter of living things in which their nature is manifested, and are not separable like a line or a plane. (*Ibid.*, 403b17.)

[92]

By "separable like a line or a plane" Aristotle means "separable in thought" (see De Anima 403a13). Thus the last passage amounts to a claim that "The affections are inseparable from matter" is analytically true. This stronger version of the identity thesis Feigl himself explicitly repudiates.

However, Aristotle was by no means the originator of these ideas about mind. Here as elsewhere he was codifying opinions commonly held. A century earlier Empedocles had asserted that "mind (noêma) in men is the blood around the heart" (Fragment 105). Not very many explicit statements of this sort are to be found in Greek literature, but that is so because mind-body identity was taken for granted. An elaborate physiology of mind is to be found in Homer (see [5], Part I, Chapters I–IV). Indeed, in the whole classical corpus there exists no denial of the view that sensing is a bodily process throughout.

If, then, one means by "identity theory" simply the contention that what we call mind and its manifestations are not separable from the body, surely Aristotle and his predecessors subscribed to this theory. But in the more correct sense in which use of the word "theory" implies a pre-existent theory-generating puzzlement, the Greeks held neither an identity theory of mind-body nor any other.

Feigl expresses the mind-body problem in the material mode as "How are the raw feels related to behavioral (or neurophysiological) states?" and in the formal mode as "What are the logical relations of raw-feel-talk (phenomenal terms, if not phenomenal language) to the terms and statements in the language of behavior (or of neurophysiology)?" [2, page 372; compare pages 416, 424, 425, 446]. These formulations are superior to the more usual ones, which go approximately "Does the mind affect the body? or body mind? or both? and if so how?" For in order to say anything sensible to the latter type of question, one must first theorize mightily about Mind. In the end the question is either trivialized or rephrased in some way equivalent to Feigl's. Moreover, the question with "affect" in it prejudges the answer, insofar as it is bound to be given in terms of causation.

Even though no Greek could have understood a question stated in terms of neurophysiology, it seems strange nevertheless that the ancients did not ponder questions amounting to the mind-body problem in its Feigelian formulation. If one were told that anger was the boiling of blood around the heart, might one not be expected to point out that, granting the invariable presence of boiling blood in the chests of angry men, still the angry feeling is clearly distinguishable from the boiling blood? And if so, might one not conclude that the way is open for questions of a conceptual sort concerning the logical relations of anger talk to the statements in the language of hematothermodynamics? Nor can we say that the Greeks failed to ask the mind-body question because they had not attained the appropriate level of sophistication. For it is a crucial feature of the mind-body problem that if it is a problem at all, it is a glaringly obvious problem; or at least it can be made so in a few words, to persons uncorrupted by philosophy.

So at any rate we are assured by enthusiasts for the problem such as C. D. Broad. His method for disposing of people who say that the mental is nothing but the physical [1, pages 622–623] can be paraphrased as follows. To the man who says anger is nothing but boiling blood, we point out that there are questions which make sense when asked about boiling blood but are nonsense if raised about anger: Has it changed its color? Is it hotter or colder than boiling water? Is it getting thicker or thinner? Conversely we can ask of anger, but not of boiling blood, whether it could be appeased by an apology, whether it is justifiable or childish, and so on. Therefore "anger" and "boiling blood" cannot be synonymous expressions. What their relation may be is a subject for inquiry.

Broad goes on to say: "It seems to me then that Reductive Materialism in general, and strict Behaviourism in particular, may be rejected. They are instances of the numerous class of theories which are so preposterously silly that only very learned men could have thought of them" (ibid.).

Aristotle was a very learned man. And some of his theories may even deserve to be called preposterously silly. However, Broad has by implication indicted not just Aristotle but the whole Greek nation. Therefore we in our turn are compelled to reject the contention that reductive materialism and strict behaviorism, whether or not preposterously silly, could have been thought of only by very learned men. At least we must do so, if taking-for-granted is to count as thinking-of.

This in itself, however, is only to score a debating point against a turn of Broadian rhetoric. The substantial question remains that of whether reductive materialism and strict behaviorism are indeed preposterously silly. There is nothing unusual about whole nations and cultures holding silly views. In the case before us, however, we are asked to believe not only that the Greeks—not the dullest people who ever lived—held a view that will not stand against a paragraph of criticism, but also, what is far more paradoxical, that none of their philosophers was capable of producing the paragraph.

II

Those who teach the introductory course in philosophy know that it is not hard to set up the mind-body problem. One way is to begin with the question whether a tree falling in a deserted forest makes a sound. Often a freshman will suggest, without being professorially prompted, that the word "sound" is ambiguous: it can mean the motion in the air, or the sensation in the hearer. There is sound in the former sense, not in the latter. This solution seems always to content the students, who through their lives count this bit of semantical sophistication among the treasures that made the Humanities requirement worthwhile.

The distinction having thus been made between vibration in the air and sensation or "raw feel" in the—what?—it is but a short step further for the instructor to convince the students that it makes sense to talk of raw feels separate from all physical processes, actual or hypothetical, in the body of the sentient. If some dullard persists in maintaining that the feel just *is* the neural discharge or the boiling blood, he can be at least silenced, and often convinced, by describing the construction, function, and results hoped to be obtained from the autocerebroscope. "Sensation" and "neural discharge," everybody now admits, are not synonyms. Therefore it is logically possible for what the terms respectively designate to exist apart from each other. Indeed, at this point it looks as if the feels and the transactions at the synapses must be separate items in the inventory of the universe. Yet it is also obvious that somehow they are intimately linked. The question can at last be asked: What is the nature of this linkage? Or to put it only slightly more technically, "How are raw feels related to behavioral (or neurophysiological) states?" A few more lessons in the jargon and the student will even understand "What are the *logical* relations of raw-feel-talk . . . to the terms and statements in the language of behavior (or of neurophysiology)?"

This way of setting up the mind-body problem consists in pointing out to the student that there is something of which he is "immediately" or "directly" aware or which is the "content of his awareness," viz., his sensations or "raw feels"; that the sensations cannot be identical with the

[95]

objects of the external world, such as trees and vibrating air; that for the same reasons, they cannot be identical with certain subcutaneous goings-on—or that, at least at the outset, it looks hopeless to maintain that they are. Whereupon one asks: What is (how are we to conceive) the relation between the sensation and the brain event? The class is now in a position to begin pondering the merits and drawbacks of "materialism, mentalism, mind-body interactionism, evolutionary emergence theories, psychoneurophysiological parallelism (epiphenomenalism, isomorphism, double aspect theories), and neutral monism" [2, page 371].

Yet Aristotle would have been baffled by all this. Why? Do the freshmen really understand it? Do we?

If one is puzzled about how X is related to Y, one must already know, or think one knows, a great deal about X, Y, and the possible sorts of relations between them. If the puzzlement is relieved by an explanation, the terms in the explanation must all be understood; and that means they must all be familiar to the person whose puzzlement has been cleared up.

Let me illustrate these platitudes by referring to a problem the Greeks did consider, the soul-body problem. The question is, How is the soul related to the body? In the formula S R B, the B already is familiar, the R is restricted at the outset to the category of (inter)action, and the S signifies "the vital principle," that is, whatever there is in or about a living being that distinguishes it from a corpse.

Before Aristotle, it was further taken for granted that S must be a "thing," which meant for the Greeks a material object. (As indeed it did and does for everyone, no matter what may be *said*.) Whatever kind of object it might turn out to be, it had to be of a sort that could conceivably affect the body, i.e., move it. And since the only familiar, hence comprehensible, way in which one thing could affect another was that in which the individual Greek affected something else, it followed at once that the soul had to be a double of the individual Greek, wholly or in part. It is not surprising that in Greece, as well as in every other culture that has the concept at all, the soul is initially thought of as an interior double, which both pushes and orders the body around. For the same reason gods are gigantic personages hurling thunderbolts and shooting arrows as well as issuing commands and deceiving men and each other.

For there are only two ways to get something done: do it yourself, by pushing and tugging, or get someone else to do it for you. The latter method, being much preferred, tends to be emphasized as the *modus operandi* of the Ideal. In simple societies the tendency is checked somewhat by the necessity the rulers have to justify their status by being good at handling weapons (see for instance *Iliad*, XII, 310–321). But at length the activity of gods, and of souls, comes to be conceived exclusively on the model of commanding:

There is one god, greatest among gods and men, not like mortals in form nor in thought (*noêma*). All of him sees, all of him thinks (*noei*), and all of him hears. But exempt from labor he sets all things in motion by the force of thought (*noou phreni*). Forever he remains in the same place, not moving at all, nor does it befit him to ramble hither and yon. (Xenophanes, Fragments 23–26.)

For mind (*nous*) is the most rarefied of all things and the purest, and it has complete knowledge (*gnômên*) in regard to everything and the greatest power; . . . and mind ruled the rotation of the whole, so that in the beginning a rotation started. (Anaxagoras, from Fragment 12.)

And God said: Let there be light. And there was light. (Genesis i:3.)

In the beginning was the Word (*logos*). (John i:1.)

This kind of view, though it may be stigmatized as magical, is nevertheless progressive in three ways. It marks the growth of society from petty tribalism, in which the chief is the mightiest warrior, or must pretend to be, to a large and organized state in which the Great King is the fountainhead of administration. It shows some dissatisfaction with, and emancipation from, the sort of pseudoexplanation which merely duplicates the explicandum. And it embodies an application of the principle of parsimony. For if the operative factor is the giving of the order, or even anteriorly the forming of the intent, why require the agent also to execute it? The execution can be put on the side of the effect.

Here we have the genesis of idealist metaphysics. Materialism develops from the other side of the human-action model, the banausic manhandling. This is one reason why materialism through the ages has been unacceptable in the best society.

Refinement of the anthropomorphic soul and god could go no further. The great step, the greatest single step ever taken in thinking on this subject, was made at last by Aristotle, who rejected the notion that the soul is a thing at all, and said instead that it is the kind of organization and functioning that certain pieces of matter have. "If the eye were a living creature, its soul would be its vision." (*De Anima* II, i.) Aristotle's achievement has not been sufficiently recognized and applauded. But that is another story.

Now back to the mind-body problem. Since this also is a puzzlement about a relation, its schema is M R B. B again stands for body or relevant parts or aspects thereof: "neurophysiology," perhaps. M = "raw feels," sensations, or what not—at any rate, things prima facie distinct from anything and everything symbolized by B. R appears again to be the relation of (inter)action.

When now we turn our scrutiny to the R, we see that we are really in no better case than the Greeks. Even today no kinds of action are familiar to us from our experience except push-pull and command. Indeed we are worse off than the Greeks, and even than our early modern predecessors, for we are convinced that command is not a distinct kind of action. The passages in Descartes and Berkeley that tell of how God puts images directly into our minds and brings about various states of affairs by willing them no longer carry conviction or even make sense. Hence the mind-body problem with R interpreted as (inter)action becomes in effect "How does a sensation push or pull, or get pushed or pulled, by a nerve tissue?"; and this problem, not surprisingly, is insoluble. Some philosophers think the way out is to be Humean about causation, but such evasive tactics have nothing to recommend them.

Unless our ideas about body are in need of revision—a possibility I shall ignore—there seem to be only two ways left for progress. One is to question the assumption that R in M R B must be causation or action of some sort. It might be just "=": we should then have the identity theory. This is of course the way out that Feigl has explored. If the mind-body problem is conceded to be a genuine problem, then the Feigelian solution must be correct and definitive. Needless to say, it entails a drastic modification, though not abandonment, of the traditional philosophical notion of "sensation."

But need we concede the genuineness of the problem? Need we concede that "sensation" as it occurs in the statement of the problem must designate some thing?

III

Was anyone ever really puzzled by the hoary puzzle about the tree falling in the uninhabited forest? Did the freshman who came up with the distinction between two senses of "sound" really think it up on the spot? Or had he heard it from a sophomore roommate?

The question "is quickly clarified by the distinction between the sound waves (vibrations in the air) and sounds-as-heard" [2, page 409]. How? Is this the way? One is asked, "If a tree falls in a deserted forest, does it make a sound?" One replies, "First inform me whether you mean by 'sound' sound waves (i.e., vibrations in the air) or sounds-as-heard." The questioner tells us what he meant, after which we can answer his original question Yes or No.

That can't be the way. If the questioner knew which he meant, he wouldn't have asked the question. So he must not have known, and his question was only a picturesque way of asking whether "sound" means "sound waves" or "sounds-as-heard." The same sort of case, it seems, as William James's metaphysician-and-squirrel. "Take your choice," say both Feigl and James.

But do we have the choice? What will people think if we say that when a wheel is revolving, the outer half of a given spoke goes around the inner half of the same spoke? What will be the reaction if we announce that the wind blew the big tree down and we heard the deafening crash-as-heard?

This business entered the philosophical tradition via the second *Dialogue between Hylas and Philonous*. There it was the conveniently moronic Hylas who tried to make a quick clarification by means of a distinction. Philonous would have none of it. Maintaining that it is an evident contradiction to speak of an unheard sound, he insisted that by hypothesis there would be no sound, if indeed it made any sense to suggest that there might be.

Berkeley was right to deny that the word "sound" is ambiguous; but he was wrong as to what it means. "Sound" means "what is heard"; you can define it that way, if you like (as if definitions mattered!). But what is heard—what sound is—is air vibration. This, to be sure, is a fact that had to be discovered, and the word "sound" is older than the discovery. From this it by no means follows, however, that the word ever meant a sensation or "raw feel." The devices whereby "hear a sound" has been construed as parallel to "feel an itch" have been sufficiently anatomized in recent years. Nor is there any parallel between the Jamesian squirrel and the Berkeleyan tree. There are not two senses of "around," but there are, as Austin has pointed out, two requirements for its application, which are usually satisfied simultaneously: roughly, circumnavigation and boxing the compass. Whereas the suppositious second (or even first) sense of "sound" is simply nonexistent. Or if in philosophy a linguistic explanation is demanded for every metaphysical perplexity, perhaps we ought to diagnose this one as arising from taking the tautology "Nothing can be heard but sound" as excluding the possibility of hearing, "in truth and strictness," bells, explosions, and vibrating air on the ground that these are not sounds "by definition" (see [4]).

Perhaps, however, all we need to do about this puzzle is to point out that the initial question was asked in fact not by the worried freshman but by the suave professor. The presumption, among many freshmen, is that all questions put by professors are sensible. The student's train of thought must have been something like this: "Since the question makes sense, both Yes and No answers must at least make sense also. The No answer can make sense only if 'sound' is tied to 'being heard' by definition. Therefore there must be such a meaning of 'sound,' even though I have never run across it before—but after all, I'm here for an education." Exit Freshman to take the Ph.D. and repeat the cycle.

Hence if the mind-body problem had to be introduced via the alleged distinction of two meanings of "sound," it would be based on a sophism. We could then congratulate the Greeks on never having thought of it. But, it will be said, certainly the matter cannot be so simple as that. There are all sorts of other ways to set up the problem.

Here, for example, is Leibniz's:

Perception, and all that it means, is not to be explained by *reasons which hold good in mechanics*. We cannot, that is to say, explain perception by figures and movements. Let us imagine a machine capable of thinking, feeling, and perceiving; let us conceive it magnified, still preserving its proportions, until we can fancy ourselves entering into it as into a mill. On going in we should see the interlocking parts, but we should not see anything which would explain a perception [3, Section 17, page 55].

But what is it to "explain perception"? What would count? Compare: (1) "Long-wave light reflected from the surface of the tomato is focused on the retina. This causes certain dyes to break down, releasing energy which is transmitted through a fiber of the optic nerve to the visual cortex. We understand the process up to this point, but we do not know yet how the firing of the last neuron on the line causes the sensation of perceiving the tomato." (2) "Long-wave light reflected . . . to the visual cortex. That is what seeing a tomato is." What is wrong with (2)? Anything? Which one is entitled to be called "the causal theory of perception"? Either one?

The Greeks did not lack a concept of mind, even of a mind separable from the body. But from Homer to Aristotle, the line between mind and body, when drawn at all, was drawn so as to put the processes of sense perception on the body side. That is one reason why the Greeks had no mind-body problem. Another is that it is difficult, almost impossible, to translate such a sentence as "What is the relation of sensation to mind (or soul)?" into Greek. The difficulty is in finding a Greek equivalent for "sensation" in the sense philosophers make it bear. It is true that in translations of De Anima one finds "sensation" and "perception" used freely where Aristotle has aisthêsis. But this is seldom right. Aisthêsis means "sense" ("the five senses") or "sensing" (a generic term for cases of seeing, hearing, etc., individually or collectively taken). Perceptions and sensations are had, while the word-for-word equivalent in Greek of "to have a sensation," aisthêsin echein, would mean (if it meant anything) "to be sensed," i.e., to have an aisthêsis directed toward one, to be the object of an aisthêsis. Secondly, "perception" and "sensation" are (in their philosophical employments) terms of art, whereas aisthêsis is not. "Sensation" was introduced into philosophy precisely to make it possible to speak of a conscious state without committing oneself as to the nature or even existence of external stimuli. On the other hand, an aisthêsis must have a cause, though it may turn out not to be what it was thought to be at first. It is this open feature of the term, moreover, that makes "perception" an inadequate rendering.

However, the comparatively rare formation aisthêma, "that which is the consequence of the activity in aisthêsis," occurs in Aristotle's writings some ten times, and in three of these cases it is natural and perhaps inevitable to translate it by "sensation," "sense impression," or even "sense datum." All of them, though, occur in the treatise On Dreams (460b2, 461a19, 461b22), and the spooky context, the need for a word to designate a floating image not ascribable to sense perception, explains the usage. On Dreams, being pre-Cartesian, is not an epistemological work.

On the whole, it seems that the Greeks found it no more necessary, or even possible, to talk "phenomenal language" or "raw-feel-talk" than we do, and that their philosophers lacked motives, such as Ryle has catalogued, for exhorting them to do so. And no sensations, no mind-body problem. It does no good to exclaim, with Feigl [2, page 390], to the unbeliever "Don't you want anesthesia if the surgeon is to operate on you? And if so, what you want prevented is the occurrence of the (very!) raw feels of pain, is it not?" For what one wants prevented is the pain, *tout court.*

REFERENCES

1. Broad, C. D. *The Mind and Its Place in Nature.* London: Kegan Paul, 1925.
2. Feigl, Herbert. "The 'Mental' and the 'Physical,'" in *Minnesota Studies in the Philosophy of Science,* Vol. II, Herbert Feigl, Michael Scriven, and Grover Maxwell, eds., pp. 370–497. Minneapolis: University of Minnesota Press, 1958.
3. Leibniz, G. W. *Monadology,* translated by Herbert Wildon Carr. London: Favil Press, 1930.
4. Margolis, Joseph. "Nothing Can Be Heard but Sound," *Analysis,* 20:82–87 (March 1960).
5. Onians, R. B. *Origins of European Thought.* Cambridge: Cambridge University Press, 1951.

PAUL E. MEEHL

\\(\)))

The Compleat Autocerebroscopist:
A Thought-Experiment on Professor Feigl's
Mind-Body Identity Thesis

Professor Feigl's mind-body identity thesis, which may be characterized as a daring hypothesis of "empirical metaphysics," asserts that human raw-feel events are literally and numerically identical with certain physical$_2$ brain-events. By physical$_2$ events he means, adopting the terminology of Meehl and Sellars [17], events which can be exhaustively described in a language sufficient to describe everything that exists and happens in a universe devoid of organic life. Given the set of descriptive terms (predicates and functors) which would be capable of describing without residue all continuants and occurrents in an inorganic world (say, perhaps, our world in the pre-Cambrian period), we need not supplement this conceptual equipment in order to describe everything that exists and happens when a human being experiences a red sensation ("has a red raw feel," is the locus of a red-qualitied phenomenal event).

It is not my purpose here to attack or defend this identity thesis, concerning which I have, in fact, no settled opinion. Rather I hope to clarify its meaning by examining some implications and alternatives presented when we apply it to a plausible thought-experiment involving Professor Feigl's "autocerebroscope" [7, page 456].

I. The Thought-Experiment
The autocerebroscope is an imaginary device, differing only in arrangement and technological development from instruments already used by

psychologists and neurophysiologists, which would enable a subject to receive continuous and nearly instantaneous information regarding the momentary $physical_2$ state of his own brain while he is experiencing raw feels. For simplicity of exposition as well as avoidance of irrelevant substantive problems (e.g., vagueness in the applicability of certain phenomenal predicates), I shall consider the case of two clearly distinguished color qualities, *red* and *green*. The subject is a nonaphasic, nonpsychotic, cooperative, English-speaking neurophysiologist thoroughly pretested for possession of normal color vision. To avoid the terrible difficulties of methodological behaviorism and to highlight his epistemological dilemma, it will be convenient to speak of this subject in the first person; and I invite the reader to read what follows taking himself as the "I" so spoken of.

The apparatus consists of instruments leading directly off my cerebral cortex which convert the pattern of my current brain activity into either of two symbolic patterns, R (for "red") and G (for "green"), presented on a television screen directly in front of me. The apparatus is wired and adjusted so that symbol R appears whenever the $physical_2$ state of my visual-perceptual cortical area is that known (by Utopian neurophysiology) (a) to be produced by retinal inputs of red light waves in persons with normal color vision, and (b) to ordinarily produce a tokening of "red" in cooperative English-speaking subjects. This brain-state we designate by the lower-case italic letter *r*; also by "Φ_r."

The same conditions hold, *mutatis mutandis*, for the television symbol G in relation to the green brain-state ($= g$). It is important to be clear that the apparatus's symbol presentation depends solely upon the *visual-cortical* state, and is not wired so as to be directly influenced by other events. If, while the visual cortex is in state *r*, the cerebral tokening mechanism should happen (for whatever reason) to token "green," or the light waves entering the eye should be in the $physical_2$-green spectral region, these events are without causal influence upon the television symbol presentation.

However, the television system of the apparatus is also (and independently) arranged so as to vary the hue of whatever symbol is being presented, and the symbol (regardless of whether it is R or G in type) is sometimes colored red and sometimes green, this coloration persisting from, say, 5 to 20 seconds before it changes, and the variable interval lengths being randomly determined.

Under these conditions it is psychologically possible for me as subject to attend simultaneously to two rather simple aspects of my momentary visual experience, i.e., the *shape* and the *hue* of the presented symbol. By this arrangement we avoid the old stomach-ache about when introspection is "really" short-term retrospection, and at least minimize the touchy problem of how many things a subject can attend to simultaneously.

What instructions are given to me as subject in this Utopian experiment? We first agree that I am to use the words "red" and "green" to designate *experienced color qualities*. For simplicity and speed of reporting, the single hue-quality word "red" (or "green") will be conventionally taken as elliptical for "I am now experiencing a visual raw feel of red (or green) hue quality," respectively. As a neurophysiologist I am, of course, aware of the fact that I, and other normal English-speakers, have historically acquired our shared color language by a rather complicated process of social learning. Since the thing-predicate "red" is employed ambiguously in vulgar speech, referring indiscriminately to (a) surface physicochemical properties of external objects, (b) the distribution of light waves such objects are disposed to reflect in "standard" illumination conditions, and (c) the raw-feel quality normally produced in persons exposed to such stimulation, a terminological stipulation is required for more exacting experimental purposes. In common life, the ambiguity is not often a source of malcommunication because either the three conditions are simultaneously realized or the context makes the speaker's intention clear. In special cases, as when a person asserts "That's red" in a red-illuminated darkroom, it may be necessary to question him as to his intention, and decide for the truth or falsity of his claim accordingly. In the present context, I as subject am instructed to employ the color predicate "red" in its phenomenal usage, i.e., as a predicate descriptive of the experienced raw-feel hue-quality.

If all goes as expected, I find myself tokening "red" as descriptive of my experienced color whenever the television symbol has the shape R, and tokening "green" when it presents the symbol G. In speaking the phenomenal language, it seems clearly appropriate to token "red" (labeling the experienced hue) and "R" (labeling the experienced sign-shape) quasi-simultaneously. If necessary, I can be instructed to report the experienced hue orally and the experienced sign-shape by depressing one of two keys. In speaking the physical thing-language, with the intention of denoting the external $physical_2$ properties of the distal stimulus, I find myself willing (on the *basis* of my raw feel but with *reference* to the objective television screen) to allege that the screen is displaying a red-colored letter R, or a green-colored letter G, as the case may be. The received laws of psychophysiology seem to be instantiated, and I am so far content with the status of my mental health as well as the soundness of Utopian neurophysiology. Both my brain and the autocerebroscope appear to be functioning satisfactorily.

But now a frightening aberration unexpectedly occurs. One day, after an otherwise "normal" run has gone on for several minutes, I find that I am experiencing green when the (apparently green-hued) symbol is R-shaped. I announce this disparity to my research assistant, who takes a long look himself and embarrassedly informs me that the R symbol looks appropriately red to *him*. Perhaps, he suggests timidly, I am mis-speaking myself? I take stock carefully, and remain very sure that I am at the moment experiencing a green-hued phenomenal event. I find no difficulty articulating the word "red," and by shutting my eyes I find that I am (being an excellent color visualizer) able voluntarily to call up a pretty good red-hued image. But upon opening my eyes, I continue to "feel certain" that the raw-feel predicate "green" is the correct description of what I see when looking at the screen. I am not in the state of a severe compulsive patient who feels involuntarily impelled to utter the "wrong word," nor of the aphasic who hears himself speak a word he knows isn't what he helplessly wants to say. The word "green" seems perfectly appropriate to me, given the instructions to describe my momentary raw-feel experience. The concurrent "inappropriateness" feeling arises not from doubt or vagueness about the phenomenal quality, but solely from my scientific knowledge about the causal network in which I and my experiences are presumably embedded. The autocerebroscope informs me that my visual cortex is in the r-state, which it *should* be because the television screen is (according to my assistant) emitting red light. I can, of course, dispense with the assistant's report and substitute other multiple observers, plus additional physical apparatus, to confirm that my objective retinal input is physically red light.

Suppose now that I carry out detailed and thorough checking and testing of the entire apparatus, as well as gathering the testimony of multiple observers. And suppose that all of the obtainable evidence continues to indicate, via numerous tightly knit nomological relationships and over-determined particulars, that there do occur unpredictable but repeated occasions in which my visual cortex is in physical$_2$ state r, that state being causally determined by objective inputs of physical$_2$-red light from the physical$_2$-red-colored screen, and yet I am, on those occasions, momentarily certain that I am experiencing phenomenal green. Over an extended series of trials, this happens in about 10 per cent of my phenomenal reports. A critical question here is, of course, what precisely this "momentary certainty" amounts to (e.g., is it more than the fact of psychological indubitability?). We shall set this question aside for now, because we can approach it more fruitfully after examining some further ramifications of the autocerebroscopic thought-experiment in its causal-scientific aspect. Proceeding still at a "common-sense" level (Utopian-science common sense, that is), how do I meta-talk about my situation as aberrant autocerebroscopic subject? I want to token "I experience green" in obedience to the instructions, and I do not need to infer this raw-feel proposition from any other propositions. If my colleagues ask me why I persist in saying "I experience green," I can only remind them of their instructions, which require me to describe my phenomenal events, rather than to make causal claims about the apparatus or the physical$_2$ state of my visual cortex. If asked whether I consider "I experience green" to be incorrigible, I reply that all empirical propositions are corrigible—perhaps adding that if I keep my sanity I may end up being forced to correct "I experience green" in particular! However, I confess that I can't cook up a genuine *doubt* that I am now experiencing green. This means that while I sincerely admit corrigibility, I am at the moment unable "seriously to entertain the notion" that the future evidence will, in fact, turn out that way. I know in general what such evidence would consist of, and I firmly believe that it *would* be rational of me, in the face of such evidence, to conclude that my presently tokened "I experience green" was false. I hope that I am a rational enough man so that I *would* at such time find it psychologically possible to abandon the proposition. And if I were not to turn out in the event to be that rational, still I am prepared *now* to say that such a development would prove me to be less rational than I had supposed. Nevertheless, I am not now psychologically able to make myself seriously doubt that I am experiencing green, and hence I don't seriously entertain the notion that the situation will arise. In short, I remain confident that, if we keep looking, we will succeed in locating the "bug" in the autocerebroscope which, I hypothesize, is the true explanation of these crazy events.

Is there any dishonesty, unreasonableness, or inconsistency in this combination of assertions and expectations? If I am a Utopian identity theorist, I consider it physical$_2$-impossible to "experience a green raw feel" while my brain is in state r. To assert such a thing would be like saying "This soup, while very hot, consists of motionless molecules." Such a statement is frame-analytically[1] false within the nomological network of physics; one who holds the kinetic theory of heat might go so far as to call such a statement meaningless.

Suppose that exhaustive tests of all conceivable kinds fail to reveal any defect in the autocerebroscope's structure, function, or brain-attachments. At some point I become convinced that there are times when my visual cortex is in state r but I am simultaneously tokening "I see green," and that this (inner) tokening "seems clearly descriptive of my raw feel." What are the possibilities open to me for making *causal* sense of such a bizarre state of affairs?

We begin with the received doctrine of Utopian neurophysiology, which accepts the identity thesis and which further identifies a particular brain region (or, better, system of related cell-assemblies) as the physical$_2$ locus of events whose occurrence *constitutes* a visual raw-feel event. (I believe that Professor Feigl is clearly committed, although he is not very happy about it, to saying that a raw-feel event is literally, in a physical$_2$ sense, *in the head*—since otherwise he contradicts Leibniz's Principle. See Section IV below.) Presumably Utopian psychophysiology asserts—or, better, for one who accepts its nomological network, "implicitly defines"—a one-many relationship between raw-feel predicates and physical$_2$ brain-state functors. A set of structural assertions about neurons

---

[1] Throughout this paper I use the expression "frame-analytic" to mean, roughly, true by "theoretical definition"; which latter phrase in turn means, roughly, stipulation of meaning (explicit or implicit) in terms of other theoretical constructs which are themselves "defined implicitly" by the accepted nomological network. While such frame-analytic truths therefore rest in one sense upon conventions, these conventions are far from "arbitrary," but are adopted on the basis of our theoretical knowledge —our current best available notion of "how the world is." The deeper issues raised here (e.g., status of so-called conventions in empirical science, clarity and defensibility of the traditional analytic-synthetic distinction) are beyond the scope of this paper and of my competence. Frame-analyticity is closely related to truth by P-rules, by meaning-postulates or A-rules, and the like. See, for example, Carnap [2, 3], Maxwell [14], Sellars [22, 23], Feyerabend [8]. I do presuppose in employing the phrase "frame-analytic" that whatever may be the final resolution of this cluster of technical philosophical problems, some important distinction will be preserved between the kinds of analyticity involved in "bachelor = unmarried male" and "temperature = mean kinetic energy of molecules."

(numbers, positions, and synaptic connections of a very complex kind) identifies the cerebral system which is the *locus* of visual raw-feel events; thus, visual raw-feel events cannot occur in the transverse gyrus of Heschl (auditory projection area), but they can occur in the calcarine cortex (or Brodmann's area 18?). We designate by "V" the cortical region or functional subsystem which is the locus of visual raw-feel events. Given an appropriately structured cerebral subsystem, its momentary state is exhaustively characterized by a set of $physical_2$ functors. These might be simple (e.g., strength of electromagnetic and electrostatic fields), or, more likely, complex (e.g., second time-derivative of a proportion of instantaneously activated synaptic knobs on cells of type X in cell-assemblies of structure S). The received neurophysiological network asserts that a necessary and sufficient condition for experiencing a red raw feel (or, the theoretical *definition*, within this causal framework, of brain-state r) is that a cerebral system of type S must be in a state described by a complex conjunction of $physical_2$ functor inequalities:

P: One-place predicate designating the phenomenal quality,
L: Two-place predicate locating a brain-event in the brain of a person,
Ψ: Two-place predicate designating the internal *Erlebnis*-relation, ". . . experiences phenomenal event . . .,"
Φ: One-place predicate designating the complex $physical_2$ property which a brain-event has when its $physical_2$ functors satisfy certain inequalities (the relation of raw feel to brain-state being, presumably, one-many),
x: Variable ranging over persons,
y: Variable ranging over phenomenal events,
z: Variable ranging over $physical_2$ brain-events.

Reference to time is omitted, taken as quasi-simultaneous.
Then the empirical "psychophysical correlation-laws" are:

$$(x,y)\,\Psi(x,y) \cdot P(y) \to (E!z)\,L(z,x) \cdot \Phi(z)$$
$$(x,z)\,L(z,x) \cdot \Phi(z) \to (E!y)\,\Psi(x,y) \cdot P(y).$$

The Feigl theory consists of conjoining to each of these correlation-laws the identity-assertion

$$(y = z).$$

But we have so far not done justice to the advanced development of Utopian neurophysiology. Although our thought-experiment began by wiring and attaching the autocerebroscope only to provide information about events occurring in the cerebral locus of visual raw-feel events,

Utopian knowledge of brain function includes much besides this. For the "normally functioning brain," we also possess scientific understanding of the causal relations obtaining in other cerebral systems, including the tokening mechanism. This means that certain problems of methodological behaviorism, and certain philosophical difficulties arising from reliance upon vulgar speech, have been "solved"—insofar as empirical knowledge ever solves problems. The differences between raw-feel utterances which are "correct," "false because of lying," "false because of mis-speaking," "false because of being hypnotized," "false because of aphasia," "false because of slovenly language training," "false because of having previously misread an English-German dictionary," etc., are formulable by reference to *where* in the intracerebral causal chain the tokening process and its controls have gone awry. Presumably Utopian neurophysiology will have isolated a cerebral system T (= the tokening system) which is the physical$_2$ locus of events t_r, t_g, etc., these events being the inner tokenings of raw-feel predicates "red," "green," etc. These tokening events are the immediate causal descendants of raw-feel events in the visual system V; and they are the immediate causal ancestors of events in intermediate instrumental systems which arouse, trigger, and monitor subsequent motor-control systems that give rise to families of overt acts of the reporting kind (vocalizing "red" or pressing a red-colored lever). Detailed experimental and clinical analysis will have made clear which system does which, and it will be precisely known how, for example, a red-qualitied visual raw feel gives rise to vocalizations of "red," "rot," or "rouge" in a trilingual subject, depending upon the instructions given him or his perception of the momentary social context. Obviously none of the three cell-assembly systems on the motoric side which control utterances of "red," "rot," or "rouge" would be considered as the primary tokening mechanism, especially for purposes of philosophical discussion. We need not here decide upon the precise conditions necessary for identifying the primary tokening system T, since for our purposes it will suffice to place certain conditions upon it. It must at least undergo states which are physical$_2$-distinguishable, and these distinguishable states must be correlated (in a normal person) on the one side with the raw-feel events, and on the other with "appropriate" states in the first-order motoric system. That is, T is the locus of events t_r and t_g which are the causal descendants of raw-feel states r and g respectively; and the states t_r and t_g are the causal ancestors of events m_r and m_g respectively, these latter being events in the "English-set motor-control system" which—*ceteris paribus*—give rise to differentiated chains continuing through the motor area to effector-organ events (vocalizations of "red" or "green"). In this scheme, the tokening mechanism T is the physical$_2$ locus of tokening *propositions* (= "making judgments"), whereas the events m are tokenings of *sentences*. For present purposes, a subject *tokens* "red" when the primary tokening system T is the locus of physical$_2$-event t_r regardless of whether he utters, or "tends to utter" (by covert laryngeal twitches) the English word "red" or the French word "rouge," or even if the process is for some reason stopped short of affecting any part of the instrumental reporting mechanism.[2] What we require, in short, is that system T must be the locus of physical$_2$-differentiable events t_r and t_g with input and output conditions appropriately correlated. It will not suffice, for example, to find a system which is activated whenever a visual raw-feel event recurs, and whose correlated report is one of mere "familiarity" (e.g., "I have experienced this color before"). When the hue of a raw feel is our subject matter, the primary tokening mechanism must be the locus of distinguishable symbolic events that are hue-correlated.

The nomologicals of Utopian neurophysiology not only assert causal dependencies between raw-feel events in V and tokenings in T (e.g., $r \ggg\!\!\!\to t_r$, $g \ggg\!\!\!\to t_g$) but they also permit these nomologicals to be derived as theorems. That is, the structural statements about how the brain is organized genetically, when combined with more fundamental laws of neurochemistry and physics, suffice to explain neurophysiological laws of such intermediate molarity as ($g \ggg\!\!\!\to t_g$). Gross (and merely stochastic) regularities at the level of molar behavior (e.g., "Normal people almost always report 'red' as an afterimage of green stimulus inputs") are shown to be physical$_2$-deducible from a combination of neurophysiological laws of intermediate level with detailed narration of social learning histories. These intermediate-level laws are themselves deducible from structural laws about how the human brain is wired, together with microlaws expressed in terms of microanatomy, biochemistry, and physics. The sto-

[2] This formulation does not, I would think, prejudice the philosophical issues, and is simpler to talk about for present purposes. If no such mediating judgmental tokening occurs, then for the "propositional," primary tokening event t we would presumably have to substitute some sort of conjunction of (1) an "English-set" superordinate event, elicited by one's perception of the audience as being English-speaking, and (2) the first link in an English-verbalizing event-sequence, which link is activated (instead of French or German) because of the superordinate "English-set" regnancy. These are presently unsettled issues in psycholinguistics.

chastic character of the more molar laws is itself explained within the system, and provides a causal account of the vagueness intrinsic to most ordinary phenomenal predicates.

If Utopian neurophysiology embodies Feigl's identity thesis, it does so on the basis of much more evidence than that available to Feigl in the mid-1960's. Why has Utopian neurophysiology augmented its psychophysical correlation-law with the conjoined identity statement? Why has it not preferred a psychophysical interactionist nomological of form $g \ggg \rightarrow \Psi_g \ggg \rightarrow t_g$ which speaks of a raw-feel event Ψ_g that is not physical$_2$ but only physical$_1$ (belonging in the space-time network)?

I submit that the reason for this scientific decision would not be different from any other option in which the scientist dispenses with a supernumerary event or entity in concocting and corroborating his causal picture of the world. He does not feel under any obligation to "rule out" alleged events Ψ_g, but only to show that they are causally dispensable. His situation is like that of the geneticist, who began with Mendelian "factors" (evidenced on the molar side by certain phenotypic breeding statistics) and ultimately *identifies* them with genes (i.e., with chemical packets found in specific chromosomal loci). We do not ask the geneticist to "prove that there aren't factors 'associated with' genes," once he has shown that the causal role played by factors in explaining the phenotypic statistics is indistinguishable from the causal role assigned to genes in physiological genetics.

I am not here attempting to beg the crucial philosophical question, whether it can even *make sense* to identify a simple phenomenal predicate's intension with the meaning of a complex physical$_2$ expression. Our Utopian neurophysiologist may be guilty of a philosophical mistake, through not seeing that the mind-body problem involves semantic (or epistemological?) issues which are unique. This question we shall examine below. My point here is that if it is philosophically admissible to assert the identity thesis, if it can be considered meaningful at all, then the empirical grounds for embodying it in the network will be of the usual scientific kind. The scientific aim is to concoct a nomological network in which all events find their place; if the causal antecedents and consequences of Ψ_g are indistinguishable from those of g, we have merely two notations for one and the same scientific concept. The abstract possibility that Ψ_g should be retained to designate a kind of event distinct from g which *might conceivably exist* "alongside it," but lacking any causal efficacy, would not impress any scientist. He would properly point out that when *Lactobacillus bulgaricus* was shown to be the causative agent behind the curdling of milk, the lowliest *Hausfrau* ceased to speak of brownies; that geneticists do not hypothesize factors "parallel with" or "mediating the action of" genes; and that caloric has been dropped from physical vocabulary since the kinetic theory of heat. There "could still be" such things as brownies, factors, and caloric; received science may be in error, and one cannot refute an existential proposition. But when the previously assigned causal role of a hypothesized entity is found to be either unnecessary or identical with a more fully known entity, the separate existence of the old one is no longer seriously maintained.

The "possibility" of a parallel event lacking causal efficacy has a special interest in the raw-feel case, which it may be profitable to examine here. It is sometimes argued that psychophysical interactionism, psychophysical parallelism, and epiphenomenalism are meaningless pseudotheories because they could not in principle be distinguished. In the diagram we represent causal connection by the arrow ⟫→, distinguishable mental events by Ψ_i, distinguishable physical$_2$ events by Φ_i, and time relationships by the correlated subscripts i. The issue of simultaneity versus precedence in causation is set aside for present purposes.

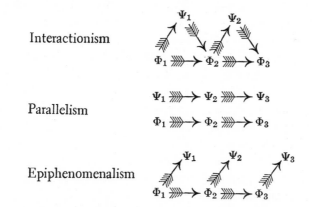

Interactionism	
Parallelism	
Epiphenomenalism	

Critics of these distinctions point out that while the diagrams make it appear that we deal with three theories, they achieve this (misleading) effect by arbitrarily dropping selected arrows which represent perfectly good nomologicals. If Φ_1 is a necessary and sufficient condition for

Φ_2 and also for Ψ_1, then the conjunction $\Phi_1 \cdot \Psi_1$ is necessary and sufficient for Φ_2; and which nomologicals we elect to draw in as "causal arrows" is surely arbitrary. Hence the three theories have indistinguishable content.

In spite of a fairly widespread acceptance of this analysis, I believe it to be mistaken, or at least in need of further justification by invoking an ancillary principle which I see no good reason to adopt. The usual practice in science, when inquiring as to the existence and direction of causal arrows, is to carry out the analysis at all levels. When an experimental separation of confluent factors is technologically (or even physically) precluded, we do not abandon our attempt to unscramble the skein of causality by distinguishing merely correlated from causal relations. The commonest method of doing this is microanalysis, which in advanced sciences is extremely powerful, and often suffices to satisfy any reasonable theoretical interest. In the biological and social sciences, where much of our evidence (especially in "field" and "clinical" studies) consists of correlations within the material as we find it, the only reasonable basis for choice may lie in moving our causal analysis to a lower level of explanation.

In the psychophysical problem, it should not be assumed that the physical$_2$ events designated by the Φ's are incapable of further analysis. If we characterize Φ_1 and Φ_2 by conjunctions of physical$_2$ expressions designating their respective microdetails, so that Φ_1 is written out as a complex conjunction of physical$_2$ functors (limiting case: elementary physical particles, electromagnetic fields), we ask whether the intermediate-level law ($\Phi_1 \ggg\!\!\!\to \Phi_2$) is derivable from the fundamental nomologicals (the structure-dependent features of Φ_1 being now packed into the microconjunction). If ($\Phi_1 \ggg\!\!\!\to \Phi_2$) is microderivable, then our causal account of Φ_2 is complete without the "mental correlate" Ψ_1 being required. The nomological relation between Ψ_1 and Φ_2 is a universal correlation but not a relation of causal dependence. If we retain Ψ_1 in our network, it will have to be for an extrascientific reason, such as a philosophical argument refuting the identity thesis analytically.

Having thus distinguished interactionism from the other two, can we tell *them* apart? Suppose that the phenomenal events themselves have sufficient richness to permit characterizing each of them by, so to speak, crude "phenomenal quasi-functors" (e.g., the color solid, the smell prism). Then we can try to formulate various intraphenomenal causal laws involving these dimensions and their combinatorial laws, and we can ask whether these combinatorial laws are in turn theorems derivable from a more basic set of Φ-Ψ laws. If they are, the usual scientific practice would be to decide for epiphenomenalism, on the ground that parallelism leaves the intraphenomenal combination-laws unexplained. Another approach would, of course, be experimental separation. The Utopian neurophysiologist can induce Φ_2 directly by imposing an artificial intracerebral stimulus, interrupting the immediately preceding events, whereby Φ_2 occurs without Φ_1—or Ψ_1!—having preceded it. If the phenomenal event Ψ_2 then occurs, we conclude that its "regular" phenomenal antecedent Ψ_1 is not part of the causal ancestry. The normal causal role of Φ_1 is unchallenged because the artificial stimulation is physical$_2$-identical with that "normally" imposed by Φ_1.

The ancillary principle alluded to above, which would be needed to defend the indistinguishability of the three psychophysical theories, is that whenever an event is time-place correlated with another, it must be taken to be causative unless shown *not* to be. I see no reason for adopting such a principle in dealing with the mind-body problem, since we do not adopt it anywhere else.

As Utopian neurophysiologist, I have adopted the identity thesis because everything I know about raw-feel events enables me to plug them into the nomological network at the place I have plugged in physical$_2$ brain-states. For ordinary purposes, I continue to use the phenomenal predicates "red" and "green," just as the heating engineer talks to a householder in terms of "winter" and "B.T.U.'s" rather than in the theoretical language of meteorology or kinetic theory. The epistemological peculiarities of raw-feel propositions may be of no interest to me, but if they are, I find it easy to explain them. By "explain," I do not of course mean that all logical and epistemological *concepts* are reducible to physical$_2$ *concepts* (compare [26]). I mean only that, given these philosophical concepts, the fact that they apply in certain unique ways to raw-feel propositions is causally understandable. Why do I have privileged access to my raw feels? Because my tokening mechanism T which tokens propositions descriptive of my raw feels is in my head, wired directly to the locus of my raw-feel events; and this is not true of your tokening mechanism in relation to my raw-feel events (compare [28; 20, pages 225–258]). Why are some raw-feel properties not further analyzable, their predicates not further "definable" in raw-feel language (the "ineffable quale")? Because the physical$_2$ components of certain raw-feel events have not been separately linked to distinguishable reactions of my tokening mechanism, and some of them *cannot* be so linked. Why are my raw-feel predications associated (usually!) with such subjective certainty? Because this special class of tokenings has a history of thousands of reinforcements, with near-zero failures. Why does it seem that raw feels are immediately given, not requiring inference? Because that's how I learned to token raw-feel propositions, by a direct $g \rightarrow t_g$ transition, unmediated by other tokening events linking propositions to other propositions.

Within this causal network, my problem with the aberrant raw feels is pretty clearly defined. *Something has gone wrong between my raw-feel events* (locus in visual-cortical system V) *and my primary tokening events* (locus in tokening mechanism T). We have established by repeated experimentation that the causal sequence is running off as usual up to (and including) events in V. That is, the objectively red television screen is emitting red light which produces the normal photochemical effect in the cones of my retina, which produces the normal pattern of nerve impulses through my second cranial nerve and is relayed normally in my lateral geniculate bodies and back through my optic radiations to my visual cortex. Similarly on the instrumental (output) side, my primary tokening t_g is activating the motoric systems for the utterance "green" and my laryngeal muscles are working satisfactorily. The motivational-affective systems whose activity constitutes a "feeling of appropriateness" between my primary tokening event t_g and my overt utterance are also functioning normally, and I do not feel that I am "unable to express what I experience." In short, each system is functioning normally, in obedience to the received nomologicals, except the linkage system between V and T. The "privileged access" nomological ($r \ggg\!\!\rightarrow t_r$) seems to have broken down.

But we are not stuck with this as a rock-bottom fact. It is a complex fact, a fact with "parts" (the event has literal, physical$_2$ *parts* which constitute it). Since we know that the erstwhile law ($r \ggg\!\!\rightarrow t_r$) is a *theorem*, derivable from the conjunction of *micro*structural and *micro*functional propositions descriptive of a "normal human brain," and of the events r and t_r occurring within such a brain, it follows that my brain must not be a normal brain, assuming that the fundamental nomologicals (physics) are valid.

What sort of abnormality might this be? For our thought-experimental purposes, one kind will do as well as another. If none of my other functions are impaired (e.g., affectivity, verbal reasoning, auditory discrimination, rote memory, motor coordination) it is presumably not a general biochemical defect of single-neuron function, which should produce detectable aberrations in other systems as well. If my verbal learning history has been normal, the enduring microstructural residues of color-tokening activity should be the same as other people's—if the initial microstructure was normal. The best guess is, therefore, that my "visual-associative" system's wiring diagram was initially aberrated microstructurally, so that the imposition of a standard color-learning history upon it has yielded an acquired microstructure such that the control linkage between V and T is stochastic rather than nomological.

To carry the analysis further we must raise the question whether Utopian neurophysiology is strictly deterministic. The stochastic character of nervous activity (e.g., Lorente de No's "optional transmission" at the synapse, or the spontaneous discharge of unstimulated neurons) may be attributable to intracellular events which are intrinsically deterministic but, from the standpoint of the neurophysiologist, essentially random. In addition, it is possible that genuine quantum indeterminacy operates, considering the distances and energies involved at the synaptic interface between a single terminal knob and the cell membrane of the postsynaptic neuron (see [1, pages 116–119; 4; 5, pages 271–286; 6, pages 179–184; 11, pages 108–113; 13; 16, pages 190–191, 214–215, 328–337]). Whether one or both of these factors are responsible, the stochastic character of spontaneous discharge and synaptic transmission may be taken as an empirical fact. Approximation of intersystem stochastic control to nomologicality can be achieved by sufficient overdetermination through involvement of large numbers of elements. Thus it is known that many, perhaps most, synaptically induced discharges are produced by presynaptic activity in excess of that needed to get the cell over threshold. It must not be forgotten, however, that a very great deal of behavior is only stochastically predictable, presumably reflecting the fact that even strong linkages may allow for low but nonzero probabilities of control failure.

The normal brain is so wired that the long-term consequence of social learning is a microstructure yielding complete control between V and T. (Query whether this is literally true. Only, I suspect, if we assume that all mislabeling of pure hues is "Freudian," which is at least debatable.) This must mean that in spite of spontaneous discharge and optional transmission, the number of neurons involved in a simple hue-tokening is so large, given their arrangement, that it yields a quasi-nomological. (We must still prefix "quasi," since if p > 0 for failure to transmit at each synapse, p > 0 for system failure. But this magnitude may be such that neurophysiology pays it no more heed than physicists pay to Eddington's ice cube heating up the warm water.) So we conclude that anyone *might*, theoretically, token "green" when experiencing red, without having anything structurally wrong with his brain. It follows that I *might* be the victim not of a miswired brain but of the binomial theorem. This latter, however, involves such an infinitesimal probability that we determine to accept it only as a last resort.

The obvious next step in investigating my aberrated tokening is to examine the microstructure of my tokening mechanism. My single-cell biophysics (e.g., spike amplitude, speed of transmission, afterpotentials) being established as normal, we already know that the terminal impulses arriving from V are of the appropriate kind. If necessary, this can be checked directly by microleads from these termini, by study of the microfields and transmitter substances there produced, etc. A plausible guess is that the number and spatial distribution of synaptic knobs, either those arriving from V or those linking the neurons into cell-assemblies within T itself, are inadequate to "overdetermine" the tokening events t_r and t_g. By convergence and divergence, a subset of "trigger" neurons in the input subsystem of T, when discharged by presynaptic activity at the termini of V-fugal fibers, normally suffices to determine t_r or t_g in T as a larger system of cell-assemblies. But if this overdetermination is insufficient, the probability becomes nonnegligible that the pattern of optional transmissions and spontaneous firing of the subset of "trigger" elements will result in the "wrong" tokening. In my case this probability has reached, let us suppose, the easily detectable value $p = .10$.

Being a zealous scientist, and considering the low risks attendant upon Utopian neurosurgery, I suggest that a biopsy be performed to corroborate the hypothesis of aberrant synaptic-knob distribution. Previous research has shown what this distribution is in a random sample of normal persons; and theoretical calculations have shown that the density and placement of knobs is such that $p < 10^{-3}$ for the average individual's tokening mechanism to discharge in pattern t_g when receiving input from a modal r-state. It is now noted with interest that, in the researched sample of presumed "normals," individuals lying beyond the 2σ point (some 2–3 per cent of the population) would develop p values as high as 10^{-2}; suggesting that a small but nonnegligible minority of the population are tokening hue predicates erroneously 1 per cent of the time. Since 1 per cent is still quite rare, and since the phenomenon itself is of no clinical interest and each single occurrence likely to go unnoticed or explained away (e.g., "Freudian slip," "I'm tired"), we are not surprised to find that only the autocerebroscopic experiment, performed luckily on an unusually deviant subject, has even called it to anyone's attention.

The biopsy being performed, statistical study of the sections reveals a peculiar "thinning" and "clumping" of synaptic knobs, differing from their normal distribution. Theoretical calculation shows that my T mechanism should be expected to mistoken as between a pure red and a pure green on approximately 12 per cent of occasions under the special condition of continuous, randomly alternated retinal inputs provided by the experiment. This value differs well within combined errors of instrumentation and sampling from the observed 10 per cent in experimental runs on me to date.

Scientifically speaking, everything is again satisfactory. The data are in excellent accord with theory and the particularistic hypothesis about me. If I retain my belief in the identity thesis, I will say: "Because of a structural defect in my tokening mechanism, I token 'green' around 10 per cent of the times when I am experiencing a red raw feel, and conversely. These mistokenings of course 'seem right' at the time, because what T tokens is propositions, not English sentences; and to 'seem wrong' a mistokening must occur farther along the intracerebral causal chain, as when I can't find the right word. In my case, the word-tokening 'green' is the normal one for a primary tokening event t_g in T, so no tendency to feel or report a disparity occurs. It is therefore literally correct to say what many philosophers have considered nonsense, namely, sometimes my raw feels *seem to be green when they are in fact red*."

It is important in contemplating this paradoxical statement to keep in mind that until some sort of tokening-of-a-universal occurs, we cannot properly raise questions of "being right," "being sure," or "knowing." It is extraordinarily tempting to forget this, especially in dealing with raw-feel judgments. Thus, in philosophical conversation, I may imagine myself to be experiencing green, and the impulse is to say exasperatedly, "But surely I couldn't be wrong about *that!*" The trouble is that this imagery of green leads me to think that *if* I were to call *that* imaged green

"green," I could not conceivably be mistaken. And if my image is green, this is certainly true, being tautologous when set forth propositionally; i.e., if I am experiencing green, it cannot be a mistake to call it "green." The trick is in the imagery, whereby I subtly introduce the hypothesis that I *am correctly labeling my experience.* Nor does this tempting error, I think, have any special relation to the identity thesis. A complete metaphysical dualist, for whom phenomenal green is a state of a nonspatial psychoid causally connected to a brain, must also realize this is a mistake and be wary of it. There simply is no necessary connection between "Jones tokens 'green' at *t*" and "Jones experiences green at *t*," regardless of one's Jonesian ontology.

II. Empirical Character of the Identity Thesis

The outcome of our autocerebroscopic studies, while scientifically satisfactory, suggests a disturbing philosophical thought. Professor Feigl insists that his identity thesis, while somewhat speculative and touching on some rather metaphysical questions about the nature of things, is nevertheless a form of *empirical* metaphysics. This means that the identity thesis might, in principle, be discorroborated by scientific evidence. It occurs to us that we imagined the autocerebroscopic thought-experiment to have come out in a particular way, a way compatible with the identity thesis. Was this too easy? What sort of empirical result could have led to our rational abandonment of it? It seems only fair, if we are dreaming up Utopian neurophysiology, to test the allegedly empirical character of the identity thesis by imagining an adverse outcome of the autocerebroscopic research. If we can't do so, something is wrong with viewing the identity thesis as an empirical claim.

To cook up an adverse empirical outcome, let us again proceed in the ordinary scientific way, by postulating a theory contradictory to the received one and deriving its consequences. Suppose there exist psychoids ("minds," "souls," "diathetes") which are substantive entities, not composed of physical$_2$ parts or substances, not space-occupying, and of such nature that most of the predicates and functors appropriate to physical$_2$ occurrents and continuants are inappropriate to them. Thus we can ask about the mass, spin, diameter, charge, etc., of physical$_2$ particles; we study the velocity, amplitude, and wave length of physical$_2$ waves; at the level of ordinary physical things, we treat of their color, shape, volume, temperature, texture, and the like. But if one were to ask about the specific gravity of an angel, we would know he had failed to grasp the idea, as when Haeckel defined God as a "gaseous vertebrate." It will be convenient, however, to adopt the convention that psychoids can be spoken of as being *at* a place in physical$_2$ space, even though they cannot *occupy* a region in the ordinary sense. This convention is perhaps dispensable, although somewhat inconveniently; but it introduces no confusion if we stipulate (as Aquinas did for angels) that "a psychoid is located where it acts" (i.e., where it exerts causal efficacy upon physical$_2$ entities). It goes without saying that psychoids must share *causality* with physical$_2$ entities (i.e., they must be physical$_1$) for us to be able to know about them. A disembodied and causally disconnected psychoid would be unknowable by us humans in the present life, as Professor Feigl has clearly shown ([7; see also 15]). The form of ontological dualism we shall consider makes the further hypothesis that each psychoid is "connected to" an individual human brain, meaning by this that it has a bidirectional causal relation to the physical$_2$ states of one and only one brain. Finally we hypothesize that no physical$_2$ events affect the psychoid except those occurring in the brain to which it is specially connected, nor does it exert any causal influence upon other physical$_2$ events. Thus, for simplicity, we assume that clairvoyance and psychokinesis (as distinguished from telepathy) either do not exist, or are special types of brain-mediated transactions.

The psychoid is conceived to undergo *states*, which change over time and whose occurrences are the causal ancestors and descendants of specific physical$_2$ events in the brain to which each psychoid is coordinated. The existence of a psychoid and its being causally linked to a particular human brain are taken as fundamental facts of the physical$_1$ order, like the fact that there are electrons.

Suppose now that among the transitory "states" into which psychoids get are states of visual experience. When a human brain undergoes state r in its visual cortex system V, the coordinated psychoid ψ_i is causally influenced so as to experience phenomenal state ρ. This state of affairs may be designated by $\rho(\psi_i)$ and the psychophysical correlation-law can only be written properly with use of the psychoid notation. The psychoidal event $\rho(\psi_i)$ is linked by a psychophysical nomological to the physical$_2$ tokening event t_r, and we shall assume that this tokening event occurs upon the confluence of physical$_2$ inputs from V and the concurrent physical$_1$ action upon T by ψ. Diagrammatically,

$$\rho(\psi_1)$$

$$r \ggg\rightarrow t_r$$

Utopian neurophysiology would presumably have considered this theoretical possibility even prior to discovery of the aberrant autocerebroscopic findings, and would have accepted or rejected it depending upon the microderivability of the $(r \ggg\rightarrow t_g)$ quasi-nomological as a physical$_2$ theorem. The theoretically expected departures from strict nomologicality would, of course, be conceptualized as due to the rare confluence of indeterminate microevents having low, but nonzero, joint probability. Prior to the aberrant autocerebroscopic findings, Utopian neurophysiology might have been erroneously (but, on the extant data, quite properly) betting on the identity thesis.

What are the logically available possibilities?

1. $r \ggg\rightarrow t_r$ holds. This, a theoretical consequence of received Utopian neurophysiology, is now refuted by the autocerebroscopic experiment. The putative (raw feel $\ggg\rightarrow$ tokening) "law" was microderivable as a physical$_2$ theorem, so the micropostulates must be modified or *supplemented by postulates concerning additional theoretical entities.*

2. $r \ggg_p\rightarrow t_r$ holds. The (raw feel $\rightarrow$ tokening) law is stochastic, and its low-probability deviations have now been brought to our attention. Under this case, two subcases are distinguishable: a. The incidence and micropatterning of deviations are "random," and microderivable from the physical$_2$ microlaws by applying probability theory to the empirical distribution of initial microconditions. b. The incidence and micropatterning of deviations are "systematic," and cannot be derived as in (a).

This exhausts the possibilities. Clearly (1) and (2a) are both compatible with the identity theory. The former yields a strict deterministic identity theory, the latter an indeterministic one. Neither requires postulation of additional theoretical entities mediating the empirical (raw feel $\rightarrow$ tokening) relation. The first involves strict nomologicals linking the physical$_2$ raw-feel event to the tokening event; the other involves probability linkage only, and the numerical probabilities are derivable from the microconditions.

[122]

It is in case 2a that the psychoids can reveal themselves by exerting causal influence. Suppose it is shown that when a subset of microevents (e.g., synaptic events at individual end-feet) are locally indeterminate, i.e., the physical$_2$ microlaws make k local outcomes quantum-uncertain, the joint probability of a certain outcome pattern is p_1, another such p_2, and so on. Suppose further that the sum of all p's associated with a tokening t_g as intermediately molar outcome is $p(t_g)$. Finally, suppose that $p(t_g)$ is significantly smaller than its observed value over a sufficiently long series. Then we have discorroborated the "random" hypothesis, and may be impelled to concoct a theory embodying a "systematic selection" process determining the locally random microevents. One such theory could be the existence of psychoids, which "select" locally indeterminate outcomes *teleologically* (i.e., the psychoid "throws" a subset of indeterminate events so as to yield a patterned tokening event t_g).

It might be thought that this contradicts our hypothesis of physical$_2$ indeterminacy—that the system is either "random" or "lawful" but we can't have it both ways. This objection, while superficially plausible, is not sound. There is no contradiction between asserting that the individual microevents are "locally random," and that their *Gestalt* is systematic with respect to the molar outcome. A simple example will suffice to demonstrate this, as follows:

Consider a circular arrangement of elements, each of which "fires" on exactly half of the "occasions." Adjacent elements are wired so as to send stimulating termini to common elements in the next system, these latter elements requiring simultaneous stimulation by two inputs in order to be discharged. Hence the next system will be activated only if adjacent elements in the control system fire concurrently, but not if only nonadjacent ones do. Thus firing pattern A will be effective, whereas firing pattern B will not:

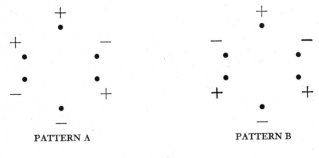

PATTERN A   PATTERN B

It is evident that we can impose "random" requirements upon each individual element, such that it fires exactly half the time and that its firing probability on any occasion is invariant with respect to its preceding firing series, and still be free to select *patterns* which will yield anywhere from zero to 100 per cent activation of the controlee system. A statistical test will tell us whether there is evidence of a "pattern-selection bias," which if found would be evidence for the operation of a "systematic" selector agent, e.g., a psychoid. (For extended discussion see [16, Appendix E].) It is assumed, of course, that the received physical$_2$ nomologicals provide no explanation for the tendency. Whether the $(V \rightarrow \Psi)$ correlation is stochastic or nomological depends upon the level of causal analysis. At the molar level, our autocerebroscopic data discorroborate any $(V \ggg\!\!\rightarrow \Psi)$ nomological, because they show that a red-type cortical state r is sometimes coexistent with phenomenal green. However, since the Φ-Ψ relation is many-one when Φ is microcharacterized, it is logically possible for the aberrated Ψ-occasions to be either nomological or stochastic functions of the V-states when these are subdivided on the basis of their microproperties.

I do not wish to defend such a psychoid theory, which is admittedly rather impoverished in content (although, I think, not empty or frivolous). On the evidence stated, it would seem imparsimonious to postulate such enduring continuants as psychoids. We might better conceive of some sort of "Ψ-field," an occurrent characterized by suitable phenomenal quasi-functors, and acting back upon the physical$_2$ system. Examples like self-induction in physics are helpful in dispelling the anxiety sometimes aroused by the "emergent" features of such psychophysical theories. Of course self-induction is emergence only epistemologically, not ontologically, since Omniscient Jones knows that the field about a coil— its existence and all its quantitative features—is derivable from statements about the fields associated with the elementary particles of which current-in-coil is composed. A scientist who *had* already carried theoretical analysis of electric current to a "deep" enough microlevel would have been able to *predict* the self-induction effect. So we have here emergence in the context of discovery, but not emergence in the "ontological" sense required by the physical$_1$-physical$_2$ distinction. This clarification may itself be helpful in getting clearer about the physical$_1$-physical$_2$ distinction. How could we *know* whether to call a theoretical entity like a "Ψ-field" physical$_1$ or physical$_2$?

The Meehl-Sellars definition of physical$_2$ has the oddity of making a *world-historical* reference in stating the nature of a theoretical construct. "An event or entity is *physical$_2$* if it is definable in terms of theoretical primitives adequate to describe completely the actual states though not necessarily the potentialities of the universe before the appearance of life" [17, page 252]. Suppose Utopian neurophysiology, even after discovery of the aberrant autocerebroscopic effects, is able to provide an adequate causal account of everything that happens by speaking of nothing but elementary particles, electromagnetic and electrostatic fields, etc. The relation of raw feels to "life" might be explicable in terms of certain structural peculiarities of complex carbon molecules, such that the configural relations among elementary physical$_2$ functors needed to render any raw-feel quasi-functor nonzero cannot arise without a kind and order of complexity to which only the carbon atom lends itself chemically. The raw-feel quasi-functor is then a number characterizing certain mathematical features of the physical$_2$ functor *relations*, which is why it is permissible to speak of "identity." That is, the raw-feel event *r* is physically *constituted* or *composed* of the elementary particles with their associated fields and forces. A raw feel is an occurrent, whose physical$_2$ nature is a certain configuration of elementary physical$_2$ continuants; and the "richness" of this configuration presupposes a structural and causal complexity not physical$_2$-possible except with carbon compounds. If it should be technically possible to synthesize organisms built around silicon, such androids [21] would be confidently said to "have experiences," and of course their verbal and other expressive-reportive behavior would be consistent with this. The notion that they might "merely be talking *as if* they 'had experiences' " would not be a theoretically admissible notion, since we constructed them and "a raw feel" would be *constitutively* defined by reference to the configuration of fundamental physical$_2$ functors. Similarly, such classical puzzles as the experiences of dogs or earthworms would be soluble, simply by substituting in the expressions for phenomenal quasi-functors the physical$_2$ functors determined experimentally by studying the brain functions of these creatures.

How could there be any such entity as a physical$_1$ raw-feel event or state which was not physical$_2$ by the Meehl-Sellars criterion? It would have to be an entity not constituted of physical$_1$ entities, an entity not composed of physical$_2$ "phases" or "parts" or "substates," and which literally *comes into being* for the first time when physical$_2$ entities enter into a certain configuration. The occurrence of this requisite physical$_2$ configuration is necessary and sufficient for the existence of the new entity, but the latter is not itself the configuration. It seems that we would have here a truly fundamental nomological, a rock-bottom feature of the world. This brute fact would qualify as one of the "insoluble mysteries of the universe," and DuBois-Reymond would have been vindicated in calling it one of the seven such. I do not know whether there are any comparable cases in current physical$_2$ science; but it is safe to say—as a matter of logic!—that at any given stage of knowledge, even the fictitious "final, Utopian, complete" stage, there will necessarily be some primitive theoretical propositions. One or more of these may be purely dispositional, designating properties whose actualization is contingent within a world-family and "novel" at time t in an actual world. Such a property would be a true emergent in one acceptable sense of that tricky word. Professor Paul Feyerabend has suggested to me the physical$_2$ possibility of a two-particle universe, say a pair of electrons, placed at a distance such that their gravitational attractive force exactly equals their electrostatic repellent force. Stable thus, no electromagnetic field exists; but this universe has the potential to develop one if somehow (e.g., by the finger of God) a relative motion were to occur between them.

These considerations show that a non-physical$_2$ Ψ-field might be similar to what we ordinarily call "mental," or it might not. Suppose all efforts to analyze it failed, and we found it impossible to develop a theory of its fine structure, to break it conceptually into parts or components, to specify any sort of spatial regions or intensity gradients—in short, to say anything about it except its causal role in the physical$_1$ brain-system. Now this would be a very exciting scientific position, because our analysis of case 2a showed a kind of "teleology" in the selective influence exerted by Ψ over the locally indeterminate physical$_2$ outcomes in the tokening mechanism. Crudely put, we could say that "Whatever the nature of Ψ may be, as a causal agent it 'acts purposefully,' it throws the physical$_2$-indeterminate subset of microevents in system T 'so that' the molar outcome is the meaningful tokening t_r, rather than the physical$_2$-probable disjunction of micro-outcomes which would lead to a meaningless pseudo-token (e.g., a neologism), or a jamming of the mechanism, or tokening something inappropriate to the modality (e.g., 'C sharp' when the current physical input is from the visual cortex). All efforts to microanalyze Ψ having thus far failed, all we are able to say about it is that it is a non-extended, homogeneous, unitary, non-space-filling whoozis, which mediates tokenings by teleological selection of subsets of physical$_2$ micro-events." I suggest that it would be quite appropriate to say that such a combination of negative and positive properties and powers is rather like the "mental" of traditional dualism. If I am right in this, it means that a radical ontological dualism must be regarded as having empirical—even "scientific"—meaning, contrary to what was alleged by the Vienna positivists and some of their philosophic descendants.

A philosophically relevant result of this analysis of the scientifically available outcomes of our thought-experiment is that the admissibility of "I seem to be experiencing green but I am really not because my cortex is in state r" hinges upon prior acceptance of a specified nomological network. If case 1 obtains, no one would ever be impelled to say such a thing, but it would be admissible because a person *could* (physical$_2$ possibility) have a structurally defective tokening mechanism. If case 2a obtains, the paradoxical remark might be made, and correctly. If case 2b obtains the remark would be proper or not depending upon whether the net allows for "slippage" between Ψ and T, between r and Ψ, or both. The micronomologicals between r and Ψ (i.e., laws relating phenomenal quasi-functors characterizing Ψ to their determining physical$_2$ functors in r) might be such that "slippage" between the molar r-state and phenomenal qualities is theoretically derivable, whereas the psychophysical correlations relating Ψ and r jointly to the molar tokening events are strict (nomologicals). If that were so, an observer would know (scientifically) that any impulse to token the paradoxical sentence should be resisted, because the object-language "I am experiencing green" will always be correct. (We assume here an autocerebroscopically confirmed *ceteris paribus* regarding other potentially interfering cerebral systems, such as Freudian slips.) Per contra, if the total evidence corroborates a network in which the $(r \Rrightarrow \Psi)$ law is tight and the joint $(\Psi \cdot r \Rrightarrow_p t_r)$ law loose, the paradoxical statement is not only admissible, but mandatory. Intermediate cases (both anchorings of Ψ stochastic) would lead to varying probabilities, the paradoxical statement being sometimes right and sometimes wrong.

III. Some Alleged Metapredicates of Raw-Feel Statements

In the light of this thought-experiment, let us examine some of the metapredicates traditionally attributed to raw-feel statements, together with some of the familiar grounds for attributing them. I shall distinguish (without prejudging their independence) claims that raw-feel statements are (not perhaps always, but sometimes) *noninferential, incorrigible, inerrant, indubitable, private,* and *ineffable.*

1. *Noninferentiality:* Lord Russell, precisely reversing the line of methodological behaviorism, distinguished the physical from the mental by the epistemic criterion that the former is inferred and the latter is not. Both Russell and the (neo)behaviorists are right, inasmuch as the mental events of other people are inferred by me but noninferred by them; and my mental events are inferred by other people but noninferred by me. This is true only if "mental" is taken as synonymous with "phenomenal," a convention which is so inconvenient for clinical psychology that it has been abandoned there. But in the present context, where the mind-body problem is stated in terms of its *raw-feel component* rather than its *intentionality component,* Freud's theories are irrelevant. Our "mental" is—roughly—Freud's "conscious." The intentionality component of the mind-body problem has been solved, in its essentials, by Sellars [26]. While expressions such as "immediately given," "known by acquaintance," "hard data," "true by ostensive definition," and the like have been powerfully criticized as misleading, equivocal, and downright false, still it is generally agreed that these expressions all aim at *something* which is uniquely true of raw-feel statements. Just what that something is remains a matter of controversy, and I have here chosen "noninferential" as the least misleading, least disputed, and most central or "core" component of the explicandum.

It is important that "noninferential" does not mean *noninferable.* If raw-feel events are in the physical$_1$ network, then raw-feel statements are inferable from non-raw-feel statements. I presuppose throughout that phenomenal events, whether physical$_2$ or not, are physical$_1$. If phenomenal events were not even stochastically *correlated* with human speech, writing, or other signals, nor with stimulus events, nor with internal bodily (brain) events, there would be no "mind-body" problem, no identity theory, and no conversation about such matters among philosophers. It is doubtful whether one could even be said to "know about" his own phenomenal events in such a world (see [15]). If Jones tokens "I see red," Smith may infer probabilistically that Jones sees red; Smith's evidence for "Jones sees red" is the statement "Jones tokens 'I see red,' " a statement whose *content* is behavioral (and linguistic), not phenomenal (and nonlinguistic). Smith may alternatively infer "Jones sees red" from other statements, such as "The apparatus is transmitting 7000 Å light waves to Jones's retina," "Jones is fixating a neutral gray wall after having looked for a minute at a green circle," "The neurosurgeon is electrically stimulating Jones's brain (etc.)," "Jones's GSR changes in response to stimulus word 'red.' " These inferences are probabilistic, but they are (probabilistically) valid inferences. Since these other evidential statements are also available to Jones, it follows that he could infer his own phenomenal statement, as Smith does. So we see that the autocerebroscopic situation is not epistemologically unique, but merely tightens the net by providing more "direct" readings from the brain.

We have now put the necessary hedges around the claim that raw-feel statements are noninferential. It does not mean that they cannot be inferred; it does not mean that they are never in fact inferred; it only means that they are sometimes made without being inferred, and typically so by the knower whose raw feels are their subject matter. The familiar sign that a raw-feel statement belongs to the class of noninferred raw-feel statements is, of course, the statement's use of egocentric particulars. Jones may properly say "Jones sees red," and in philosophical or autocerebroscopic contexts he might actually adopt the third-person locution; but normally Jones says "I see red" to designate that state of affairs which Smith would designate by "Jones sees red."

Although other statements might be adduced as evidence for "I see red," and although I may now or later admit evidence against "I see red," it is nevertheless true that knowers sometimes token "I see red" without having antecedently tokened any statements from which "I see red" could be inferred. This fact of descriptive pragmatics is perhaps the minimum content of a claim that raw-feel statements are noninferential; but what is philosophically relevant is our generally accepted belief that such noninferential tokenings are sometimes legitimate moves, so that a knower who tokens "I see red" without antecedently tokening any statements from which it can be inferred is not necessarily tokening illegitimately or irresponsibly. How can such a thing be?

It has sometimes been said that the "evidence" which justifies a raw-feel statement (under the usual noninferential conditions) is "the experience itself." I do not wish to condemn such talk as utterly without merit, since I believe that it intends something true and fundamental. But if we adopt the generally accepted convention that "evidence for . . ."

means "providing a basis for inferring . . ." and remind ourselves that inferability is a relation between statements or propositions, it follows that we cannot properly speak of an experience (something nonpropositional) as being "evidence for" a statement (something propositional). It seems then that noninferential raw-feel tokenings are, strictly speaking, tokenings of statements "in the absence of evidence." On the other hand, we do not ordinarily countenance the tokening of raw-feel statements by a knower who is not concurrently experiencing the raw feel designated by the statement tokened. If Jones makes a practice of tokening "I see red" on occasions when he is not in fact seeing red (a fact which we infer from other evidence, which may include his own subsequent admission that he lied, or mis-spoke, or "just felt like saying it") we consider him irresponsible, because he tends to token illegitimately.

I do not have anything illuminating to add to what others (e.g., Sellars [27]) have said by way of expounding what is involved here. A knower is considered to token egocentric raw-feel statements legitimately when his tokening behavior is rule-regulated, whether or not he antecedently tokens the rule itself (which he normally does not). There is a degenerate, uninformative semantic rule, " 'Red' means red," to which an English-speaking knower's tokenings may or may not conform. It may be viewed, within pure pragmatics, as a language-entry rule, conformity to which legitimates an egocentric raw-feel tokening. We may employ special words like "legitimate" (applied to particular tokenings) and "responsible" (applied to a knower who tokens legitimately) as distinct from the word "rational," since the latter refers to intertokening (intralinguistic) relations, e.g., inferability, conformance to language-transition rules, which we have seen is not at issue for the typical egocentric raw-feel statement. A tokening "I see red" by a knower who is not concurrently the locus of a red-qualitied raw-feel event is false; the act of so tokening is illegitimate (i.e., semantic-rule-violative); knowers who tend to token illegitimately are sense-defective, psychotic, or irresponsible. We need terms other than "irrational" in this context, because we reserve the latter for a disposition to violate language-transition rules, i.e., to token against, or without, (propositional) evidence.

Speaking epistemologically, the legitimacy of tokening egocentric raw-feel statements without antecedently tokening any statements as evidence (and in most cases, without being able to do so upon demand) depends upon the tokening's conformity to the semantic rule. There is in this notion of a legitimate egocentric tokening a small but inescapable element of "psychologism," that amount and kind of reference to the nonlinguistic which is not a philosophic sin because it falls under the heading of pure pragmatics—the coex relationship of Sellars [24, 25]. Speaking psychologically, the English-speaker's overwhelmingly strong impulse to token "red" when experiencing a red-qualitied raw feel has its causal account in intimate wiring plus verbal reinforcement history. We are all trained against tokening non-raw-feel statements without antecedently tokening statements from which they can be inferred, or at least without being able to offer such on demand. "Just because," or "I say what I mean," or "I need no evidence" are childish or neurotic responses to "Why do you say that?" for non-raw-feel statements, and are finally beaten out of all but the most irrational. But we are permitted to token raw-feel statements without evidence, so long as we do it in a rule-regulated way (i.e., in what the reinforcing verbal community takes, on all of *its* evidence, to be conformable to the language-entry rule " 'Q' means Q").

2. *Incorrigibility:* It has been shown above that noninferentiality does not mean noninferability, that while egocentric raw-feel statements are commonly and legitimately tokened without inference, their allocentric equivalents are regularly inferred and even the egocentric ones can sometimes be. Since raw-feel statements can be inferred, it follows directly that their contraries can be discorroborated. Hence a raw-feel statement "Jones sees green" can be argued against by evidence supporting "Jones sees red," given the grammar of these phenomenal color predicates. And while this is clearest in the case of allocentric raw-feel statements, it is true of egocentric ones also. Since evidence supporting "Jones sees red" is evidence against "Jones sees green," and such evidence is also, at times, available to Jones himself, it follows that Jones can have evidence tending to discorroborate his egocentric raw-feel statements. It is puzzling why so many philosophers have doubted this, when it follows rigorously from two universally accepted theses: (a) Raw-feel events have knowable causes and effects (either would do!). (b) Some raw-feel statements are incompatible with others.

Incorrigibility of a raw-feel statement would require that, while counterevidence can unquestionably be brought to bear upon it, the amount and character of such counterevidence could never be sufficient to warrant abandoning it. While this doctrine seems widely held, I have never seen any cogent proof of it. I personally find the autocerebroscopic thought-experiment very helpful in this respect. My dilemma as Utopian neurophysiologist is to decide whether any sufficiently massive and inter-locking evidence could corroborate "I am seeing red" more than all of my evidence corroborates the claim that I always token in obedience to the language-entry rule " 'Green' means green." It cuts no ice at all to "feel sure," since "Meehl feels sure that he always tokens in conformity with the language-entry rules" clearly does not entail that he does in fact so token. The kind of evidence hypothesized in our thought-experi-ment provides an adequate explanation of my aberrated "green" token-ings, as well as of my strong feeling of subjective certainty. Given that other evidence can be *relevant* to the truth of a raw-feel statement, it is hard to see any reason for insisting that it could not conceivably be coun-tervailing against the unevidenced raw-feel statement, unless we accept the metaproposition "All egocentric raw-feel statements are true," a proposition which is surely not analytic. And, if it is itself empirical, it cannot be made untouchable by all amounts of discorroboration.

3. *Inerrancy:* Without making the strong claim of incorrigibility (no egocentric raw-feel statement could, *in principle*, be opposed by evidence sufficient to require its abandonment), it might be hoped that neverthe-less no such statements are *in fact* false. A specious plausibility is lent to this view by the widespread habit of putting "et cetera" after a list of interfering factors which are at present known to produce illegitimate tokenings. Thus a philosopher writes, "An English-speaking plain man, not lying or afflicted with aphasia, etc., cannot err in tokening 'I see red.' " Great danger lies in the innocent-looking "etc.," which has to do duty for all the unlisted sources of mistokening. The statement that one *cannot* token an egocentric raw-feel statement incorrectly without misunder-standing English, being aphasic, having a Freudian slip, being drugged, obeying a posthypnotic suggestion, *and so forth* is analytic only if "and so forth" is short for "any other causal source of mistokening." Can the list be written out, substituting an extensional specification for "etc.," rather than the intensional "causal source of mistokening"? Obviously no such extensional list could be compiled, lacking an admittedly com-plete causal theory of experiencing-and-tokening. Is anyone prepared to say on present evidence that we already *know* all possible sources of mis-tokening? *Could* anyone claim this while the mind-body problem remains *sub judice*? If anyone did so claim, would his claim be incorrigible with respect to the autocerebroscopic experiment? What this argument for

inerrancy really comes down to when explicated is a tautology plus a bow to psychic determinism, namely: "An egocentric raw-feel statement cannot be erroneously tokened unless some disturbing factor leads to the knower's violating the language-entry rule," i.e., an egocentric raw-feel tokening is legitimate unless something causes it to be made illegitimately. This triviality cannot sustain a philosophical claim of inerrancy. Since we already have indisputable evidence that mistokenings do in fact occur, why would we venture on the unsupported empirical claim that the presently known list is exhaustive?

Neither common-sense examples nor philosophical arguments suffice to destroy in some people the conviction that "I just *couldn't* be wrong in 'attentively (etc.)' characterizing the hue-quality of my momentary raw-feel." By way of softening up such a reader, I recommend study of a fascinating experiment by Howells [10] in which he showed that repeated association between a color (red or green) and a tone (low or high, respectively) produced in his subjects a growing disposition to mislabel the colors when presented unsaturated along with the "inappropriate" tone. The experimenter infers (as I do, tentatively) that the subjects came to actually *experience* the wrong color; other psychologists opt for the alternative hypothesis that they came to *token* erroneously. It seems rather implausible that VIIIth-nerve inputs to Heschl's gyrus could acquire such control over the visual-experiencing cortex; but it also seems hard to believe that they began to say "red" when seeing green. The point is that Howells's results are compatible with either interpretation; and reading them should, I think, at least attenuate one's intuitive faith in the "obvious infallibility" of raw-feel statements.[3]

4. *Indubitability:* By this word I mean the psychological inability to doubt our egocentric raw-feel statements at the time we token them. Does this inability, if it in fact obtains, have any philosophic relevance? I think it has none, unless we presuppose that "Jones is psychologically incapable of genuinely doubting p at time *t*" entails, nomologically or analytically, "p is true." I take it that no one will wish to maintain that a knower's psychological lack of power to doubt a proposition implies the latter's truth, the implication being either a law of nature or a truth of logic. I do not myself believe that psychological indubitability is even incompatible with the knower's sincere assertion that p is corrigible. The reader

[3] I am indebted to my colleague Dr. Milton Trapold for calling this experiment to my attention.

will have to judge this for himself, with respect to "sincerity of assertion." But the metalinguistic statement "I know that there could be strong countervailing evidence against p" is surely compatible with "As of this moment, I find myself unable to entertain seriously the notion the p is in fact false." In the autocerebroscopic situation, our Utopian neurophysiologist continued to collect discorroborative evidence against his own raw-feel statements, because he rationally recognized that he *ought*, if such counterevidence were forthcoming, to correct these raw-feel statements. But during the course of this evidence-collecting, he "felt certain" that a bug would be found in the apparatus, because the raw-feel statements were currently indubitable by him. This would be "inconsistent" cognitive activity for one who held that a knower's inability to doubt entails the truth—analytically, in logic or epistemology—of the indubitable statement. But our neurophysiologist holds no such indefensible view.

5. *Privacy* ("privileged access"): It is agreed that no other person is the locus of my raw-feel events. This simple truth can be formulated either epistemically or physiologically, as follows: a. A raw-feel event x which belongs to the class C_1 of events constituting the experiential history of a knower K_1 does not belong to the class C_2 of a different knower K_2. b. The tokening mechanism whose tokenings characterize the raw-feel events of organism K_1 is wired "directly" to K_1's visual cortex, whereas the tokening mechanism of K_2 is not directly wired to the visual cortex of K_1.

It seems that (a), stated in philosophic language, is an analytic truth (but see below), whereas (b), stated in physiological language (except for "tokening"), is synthetic. Query whether the contradictory of the second half of (b), while counterfactual for all historical organism-pairs, is counternomological? Given Utopian neurophysiology, we can at least conceive a procedure whereby the tokening mechanism of K_2 might be wired to the visual cortex of K_1 in such a way that the "causal intimacy" of K_2's tokening events would be as "close" to the events occurring in K_1's visual cortex as are the tokening events of K_1. Or, without such direct anatomical wiring, Utopian neurophysiology could presumably impose a pattern upon K_2's tokening mechanism which was physical$_2$-indistinguishable (within tolerance limits set narrower than those yielding "no difference" reports or discriminations for the single specimen) from the pattern imposed by K_1's visual cortex upon K_1's tokening mechanism. While I don't wish to liquidate any valid philosophical problem by shifting the grounds to biology, it is worth emphasizing that from the standpoint of physical$_2$ causality, the "privacy" of my raw-feel events consists of the rather unexciting fact that "I" ($=$ the person whose body is the locus of the tokening mechanism which tokens the egocentric raw-feel statement in question) am causally related to "my" ($=$ visual-cortical states located within that body) raw-feel events in a close-knit, causally direct way; whereas "you" ($=$ the person whose body is the locus of the tokening mechanism which tokens the allocentric equivalent of the egocentric raw-feel statement in question) are causally related to "my" raw-feel events by a causal chain having more links and therefore, normally, having greater possibility of "slippage" (i.e., of intervening nuisance variables which may prevent complete correspondence). From the physical$_2$ point of view, there is nothing mysterious or special about the fact that Jones knows he has a stomach-ache under circumstances when Smith does not know that Jones has a stomach-ache. Jones's knowing ($=$ tokening) system is linked fairly directly to Jones's stomach; Smith's knowing system is normally linked to Jones's stomach only via Jones's knowing system, thus: Jones's stomach $\rightarrow$ Jones's tokening system $\rightarrow$ Jones's reporting system $\rightarrow$ Smith's receptor system $\rightarrow$ Smith's tokening system. It being a physical$_2$ fact that each of these causal connections is only stochastic, every link involves a further attrition of probabilities: hence the correlation between events in Smith's tokening system and events in Jones's stomach will be lower than that between events in Jones's tokening system and events in Jones's stomach.

Such an analysis of the causal basis of the epistemic situations suggests that, in principle, there could be special physical$_2$ arrangements in which the linkage between Smith's tokening system and Jones's stomach would be more dependable than that between Jones's tokening system and the latter's own stomach. And we already know of such clinical examples, e.g., the recently operated patient who "feels sensations in his leg" when the surgeon knows that the leg has been amputated. Such examples serve to remind us that the "privacy" which is philosophically interesting involves central (brain) events rather than peripheral conditions. The auto-cerebroscopic experiment pushes this "privacy" as far back as it can be taken from the physical$_2$ standpoint, and this extreme is the only stage of causal analysis that is of intrinsic philosophical interest for the mind-body theorizer. Here we have the situation in which two quasi-nomological links are set in (apparent) opposition. The subject's tokening system is considered to be very intimately linked to his visual raw-feel states; and the autocerebroscope is also very intimately linked with them. If the Utopian microanalysis supports Feigl's identity theory, either in form (1) or (2a) above, we must conclude that the usual "privacy" (= privileged access) of raw-feel events merely reflects the usual organic condition of intimate wiring, and the usual lack of an equally tight independent access; but that special physical$_2$ conditions *can* be set up in which the causal linkage between artificial apparatus and raw-feel events is more trustworthy than that provided by nature's cerebral anatomy. The progress of science will merely have carried the "stomach-to-brain" kind of analysis inward, so to speak; and educated Utopians will recognize that scientific instruments are (while fallible) less fallible than the tokening mechanism with its socially learned linkage to events in other cerebral subsystems. Less educated Utopians will absorb this understanding by downward seepage through the Sunday supplement section, and the Utopian "plain man" will feel nothing absurd about such locutions as "Jones thinks he is experiencing a pain, but he's really not."

Given the frame of Utopian identity theory, analytic thesis (a) can also be *stated* physicalistically, but it is no longer clearly analytic. We say, "A raw-feel event occurring in the visual cortex of organism K_1 cannot occur in the visual cortex of organism K_2." (I mean this literally, of course; there is nothing analytic, or even plausible, about a denial that raw-feel events having the *same* properties can occur in two different brains. The statement is about identity of particulars.) This would be frame-analytic given a biological law "A visual cortex V cannot belong to two organisms K_1 and K_2 at the same time," which is contingently true but not clearly nomological, since Utopian neurophysiology may provide surgical techniques whereby two organisms can share their visual cortices. Admittedly such a Siamese-twin brain-fusion would necessitate adoption of a convention as to what "two organisms" will be taken to mean. But it would seem to be a reasonable, nonarbitrary stipulation that if two bodies were so joined as to possess a common visual cortex but shared nothing else (e.g., each has a separate tokening mechanism wired equivalently to the common visual cortex; each has its own motivational cortical subsystems; each retains its own stock of memory-storage and "self-concept" subsystems), Utopian physiology would properly speak of "two organisms having a shared visual cortex." The raw-feel *knowings* of these joined

individuals being conventionally taken as their distinct propositional
($=$ tokening) events, Utopian epistemology would allow the locution
"Knowers K_1 and K_2 share visual raw-feel events," so that (a) not only is
seen to be nonanalytic but is empirically false. It is worth noting that this
Utopian situation is not utterly unlike our present situation, when we say
that "Raw feel x belongs to knower K," even though knower K may be
identifiable over a twenty-year period only by the fact of genidentity
(i.e., most of the matter constituting K's brain has been replaced during
the twenty-year time interval). It is not easy to say precisely why a particular twenty-years-past raw-feel event belongs to "K's set" of raw-feel
events except that it belongs to the set historically associated with a body
genidentical with K's present body. This line of thought may be worth
pursuing on another occasion, because it suggests the possibility that the
inaccessibility of another's mind amounts fundamentally to the same
problem as the reliability of memory in relation to the solipsism of the
present moment; so that he who "resolves" the latter—by whatever means
—will thereby have also resolved the former.

How would the privacy problem shape up if Utopian neurophysiology
were led by the evidence to adopt an ontological dualism of the kind
hinted at in Section II? Surprisingly enough, this does not seem to make
any important difference. It having been shown experimentally that (non-
physical$_2$) raw-feel events are causal descendants of physical$_2$ brain-events
in the visual cortex and that a raw-feel event produced by a state of cortex V_i cannot influence tokening events in tokening system T_j unless T_j
is simultaneously "physical$_2$-close" (and perhaps neurologically wired)
to V_i, we adopt the location-convention that a (non-physical$_2$) raw-feel
event "occurs at (or, even, *in*)" the brain B which contains properly
juxtaposed and wired subsystems V_i and T_i and in which the nomological
subnet

is being instantiated. The physical$_2$ conditions necessary and sufficient
for such instantiation would be known, and it would be a technological
problem to realize them by surgical methods of brain-fusion. Suppose
that somehow, without hopelessly disrupting the general cerebral arrangements needed for preserving minimal "personhood," we could juxtapose

each of the two tokening systems T_1 and T_2 to each of two visual systems V_1 and V_2, so that the surgeon's electrical stimulation of *either* V_1 or V_2 would produce raw-feel events which influence events in *both* T_1 and T_2. Our experimental analysis continues to support the notion that only a single raw-feel event (or short-lived continuant) is produced by such stimulation. Our dualistic network looks like this:

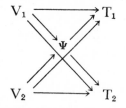

When we stimulate V_1, both subjects token "I see red." Similarly they both token "I see red" when we stimulate V_2. There seems to be no reason, behavioristically, introspectively, or neurophysiologically, for attributing either of these raw-feel events to one of the subjects rather than the other, unless we adopt a convention that the person whose *visual* cortex is causative of (an otherwise shared) raw-feel event is the person who "has" it. Given a Utopian psychophysiology *in dualist form*, such a convention would, I think, be rejected as arbitrary, counterintuitive, and systemically inconvenient. Even adopting such a convention, however, we can modify the situation by reverting to a shared cortex—a third person's, or a chimpanzee's, or even a synthetic one!—and dealing with a setup diagramed thus:

Here everything is symmetrical. The "red" physical$_2$ state Φ_s occurring in (shared) visual cortex V_s produces one raw-feel event Ψ_s ($=$ phenomenal red) which in turn combines with the physical$_2$ neurophysiological links to elicit appropriate tokenings in both T_1 and T_2. Surely we do not want to say, "This raw-feel event occurs, but belongs to no person's experiential history." Unless the now deceased chimpanzee is a candidate, the raw-feel event must be assigned to one of our subjects; and there is not the slightest reason for choosing between them. Note that physicalism and methodological behaviorism are not involved here. The ontology is explicitly dualistic; and if you were either subject, you would indignantly oppose a philosopher's asserting that—because of the oddity of the context—your momentary raw feel "does not really belong to you, but belongs to the other fellow (or the deceased chimpanzee)."

The most fascinating feature of these fantastic thought-experiments, and the feature having most philosophic relevance, is that they force us to re-examine the analyticity of epistemic-pragmatic statements about "I," by bringing out our implicit assumptions concerning the nature and identity of *persons*. Unless a person is a "simple"—an entity without "parts," "regions," "components," "subsystems"—there must be some criteria by which part-events are assigned to their appropriate persons. In phenomenal or dualistic language, we currently take it as analytic that "a particular raw-feel event cannot belong to the class C_i of raw-feel events constituting the *Erlebnis*-history of person I and also to the class C_j constituting the *Erlebnis*-history of a nonidentical person J." But the analyticity of this is not a simple dictionary-analyticity like "No woman x is the wife of any bachelor y." If analytic, it is frame-analytic, involving the nomological network which embodies our received metaphysic of "persons." If a "person" is *defined* by specifying a class of raw-feel events, how is the class to be specified except by reference to the genidentity of a body whose cortical states are the immediate causal ancestors of the raw-feels being classified? And if we do it this way, the statement about persons' raw-feel sets being disjoint hinges upon the supposition that two bodies' cortical states must necessarily be disjoint. This in turn depends upon the alleged impossibility of two brains sharing parts of cortices— namely, the "parts" whose states are the immediate causal ancestors of raw-feel events. I cannot see any clear reason why such a state of affairs is impossible.

One must, of course, beware of the temptation to imagine an inner observer-of-raw-feels, a manikin who is located elsewhere than the visual cortex and who "inspects" the raw feels occurring in the visual cortex. The locus of the phenomenal red quality is the raw-feel event Ψ, and the only "manikin" is the tokening mechanism, which *tokens* but does not *experience*. If someone insists that by "I" he means "whatever subsystem is the raw-feel locus," then there are not two "I"-persons when the brains are conjoined so as to share a visual cortex, but one "I." We have then to remind such a subject that he must avoid token-reflexive discourse about his visual raw feels, because the "I" who *tokens* is not the "I" whose raw feel is being tokened about. Alternatively, if the subject insists that token-reflexive statements be allowed because, he holds, the "I" referred to is not genidentical with that psychophysical system whose tokening mechanism is being used but rather with that psychophysical system which contains the visual cortex genidentical with the experiencing one, then he is committed to saying "I am a (dead) chimpanzee's brain."

The upshot of these considerations seems to be roughly this: If "privacy" means "privileged access," it is a matter of degree as regards the closeness (tightness) of causal connection between a tokening mechanism and a visual raw-feel event. Under ordinary circumstances (lacking autocerebroscopes, supersurgery, and the like) the causal chain connecting a person's raw-feel events to his tokening events is more trustworthy than the chain connecting his raw-feel events to another's tokening events. But this is no absolute principle, for the same reason that a person might sometimes be well advised to accept the autocerebroscopic verdict on his own raw-feel events in preference to the deliverances of his own "direct-line" tokening mechanism.

If "privacy" is taken to mean "absolute noninspectability," in the sense that the nonoverlap of two persons' raw-feel-classes is analytic, I have tried to show that it is at least not dictionary-analytic but, at most, frame-analytic within an (arguable) nomological network about "persons." And I have suggested that this network of constraints about what is possible of persons may really not be nomological but only contingently universal, and perhaps purely technological.

How stands it with the old puzzle about whether my raw-feel qualities are qualitatively the same as yours? If the identity thesis is correct, the problem is solved experimentally, by investigating the physical$_2$ functor conditions present in your brain when you token "red" and in my brain when I token "red." (I hold, as against Professor Feigl, that *if* his identity thesis is correct, he cannot formulate the inverted-spectrum problem in his Utopian theoretical language. It would make no more sense than it would to ask, "Granting the kinetic theory of heat, is the 'hotness' of this bucket of hot soup the same as the 'hotness' of that one, given that their molecules have the same mean kinetic energy?")

What if Utopian psychophysiology is dualistic, along the lines sketched above? We know that English-speaking subjects normally satisfy the causal law network

$$\text{Red surface} \Rrightarrow \rightarrow \text{Red light} \Rrightarrow \rightarrow \ldots \Rrightarrow \rightarrow \Phi_r \Rrightarrow \rightarrow t_r \quad \overset{\Psi_r}{\nwarrow\searrow}$$

in which the *form* of the tokening event t_r is learned but the other connections are nomologically necessitated by the (innate) wiring diagram plus the mysterious fundamental nomologicals which entail the raw-feel event Ψ_r whenever the physical$_2$-"red" cortical state Φ_r occurs in a normally constructed visual cortex. The question is whether the raw-feel event Φ could play this causal role in two brains but be of red quality in one and green quality in another. Concentrating for the moment on the "input" side, a Utopian scientist would probably argue that some such overarching principle as "same cause, same effect" should apply here as elsewhere in scientific thinking. The intersubjective nomological network being well corroborated, we "believe in it" until further notice. It tells us that there are two events Φ_i and Φ_j which occur in the brains of persons I and J, and they have certain common physical$_2$ functor properties which are causative of two events Ψ_i and Ψ_j that also share all known causal properties. If there is a property that is nonefficacious, in the sense that it is only a causal descendant but not a causal ancestor (i.e., a nomological "dangler"), our Utopian scientist would probably feel it imparsimonious to hypothesize that this nonefficacious property was different in the two individuals. He might say, "I find no reason why it *should* differ, being consequent upon similar causal conditions, so I shall assume that it *doesn't*." I must confess that this argument strikes me as convincing, but I don't know what to say if someone challenges the "same cause, same effect" principle.

Perhaps the Utopian thought-experiment can help us gain further insight into this idea of the "phenomenal red quality" as a noncausal property of the raw-feel event Ψ_r. If the phenomenal red quality is noncausal, what can the privileged-access dualist be taken to mean by raising his question? If I am a dualist arguing for absolute, analytic privileged access, how do I frame the question in Utopian physiologese? I say, "While scientific findings may show that my raw feel Ψ_r has causal properties identical with your raw feel Ψ_r, I cannot infer—even in probability—that the noncausal property *red quality* is present in yours, whereas I know that it is present in mine." Since we have agreed that merely experiencing a raw feel cannot be identified with "knowing that it has a certain quality," I as a dualist must be at least claiming that I can token "red" in obedience to the language-entry rule " 'Red' means red." (I do not raise here the incorrigibility or infallibility question, settled above in the negative. All that I claim for the sake of argument is that I "know" in the limited sense of high-confidence probability.) Is my tokening "red" in any way determined by the presence of the red quality in Ψ_r? Not if this quality is taken to be noncausal. If this is true, then my tokening in obedience to the language-entry rule is solely due to the *correlation* between the (causally inefficacious) red quality and the (causally efficacious) physical$_2$ event Φ_r conjoined with the *other* (causally efficacious) properties of Ψ_r. I do not, on such a view, token correctly *because* of the red quality, but because of other factors. *If* I tend to token in obedience to the language-entry rule, it is only because of the nomological dangler which relates the noncausal red quality of Ψ_r to its antecedents. *Consequently I have no stronger ground for trusting my own raw-feel tokenings than for trusting those of others.* In both cases, I must rely upon the "same cause, same effect" principle to infer the noncausal red quality from its *input* conditions. If the phenomenal quality is conceived of as noncausal, as a dangler, I can't know—except by trusting the dangler—that you experience red qualities; but I can't know that I do either!

One way of saying this is that, although a semantic rule and a causal nexus are two very different things, yet in the case of noninferential egocentric raw-feel statements, "legitimated" solely by their obedience to the language-entry rule, *a semantic tie requires a causal tie.* One need not, of course, *assert* the causal tie to "justify" such tokenings as they occur. But if he repudiates the claim that there *is* a causal tie, he cannot maintain in metalinguistic discourse about "privacy" that he trusts the semantic tie and therefore "knows" that he correctly characterizes his own raw-feel events.

There is something at least pragmatically strange—I do not say literally inconsistent—about Professor Feigl's view that phenomenal qualities are not intersubjective, not part of science, not in the public domain. Let us set aside the question as to whether an intersubjective test exists for the inverted-spectrum hypothesis, and consider the broader issue whether the world of science, the causal order, the physical$_1$ network, finds raw-feel qualities theoretically dispensable. Why does Professor Feigl pose the mind-body problem in the first place? What is the "puzzle" which identity theory intends to solve? If you ask him whether there are phenomenal qualities, he says, "Of course there are—this is why we have a mind-body problem." I take this to mean that Professor Feigl would not philosophize about the mind-body problem (nor would he be able to understand the discourse of another who did so) except for his own acquaintance with raw-feel qualities. I conclude from this that raw-feel qualities make a difference (i.e., they influence the verbal behavior of Professor Feigl qua philosopher). Hence they are causally efficacious, the world would be different in both physical$_1$ and physical$_2$ ways without them, and they must find a place in the nomological network. Must they not then be "part of science," like everything else that is causally efficacious?

It would seem so. Yet we must do justice to the claims of a rigorous and consistent epiphenomenalism, such as that defended by Lachs [12]. I am unable to detect any flaw in Lachs's incisive analysis, and feel compelled to retreat to a weaker thesis, namely, "If raw-feel qualities are dispensable from the theoretical entities of physical$_1$ science, as Professor Feigl maintains, then he must also hold that his concern with the mind-body problem does not originate from his own acquaintance with raw feels. Hence, he must hold that he would philosophize about the mind-body problem exactly as he does (compare [15]) if, counterfactually, he experienced no raw feels of any kind whatever." I do not tax Professor Lachs with this consequence, which, I take it, would not disturb him; but I know (personal communication) that Professor Feigl finds it unacceptable. It distresses him—as it does me—to be in the very counterintuitive position of saying, "When I raise the mind-body problem, I am talking about my raw feels and their qualities; the very meaning of the mind-body problem involves the existence of these raw-feel qualities; a being which thinks (computes, ratiocinates, engages in rule-regulated language transitions) but lacks raw feels could not understand the mind-body problem. Nevertheless my raw-feel events have no causal influence upon my tokening behavior." The fascinating question whether, and how, a genuine semantic tie, " 'Red' means red," could exist for a knower, lacking any causal (raw feel $\ggg\!\!\rightarrow$ tokening) tie, I shall not attempt to treat here.[4]

We therefore decide that the phenomenal red quality should be taken

[4] I am indebted to Professor Sellars for bringing home to me, when I was defending epiphenomenalism, the full force of this objection.

as causally efficacious. Hence the tokening event t_r is partially controllable by phenomenal qualities of Ψ_r. (I should perhaps remind the reader, in case "phenomenal qualities of a mental event" seems redundant, that Utopian psychophysiology will have introduced the dualistic entity Ψ_r as a theoretical construct required to make sense of the entire body of evidence, so that Ψ_r might—presumably would—have properties in addition to phenomenal ones.) In short, *whether Ψ_r is phenomenally red or phenomenally green makes a causal (output) difference.*

I have passed over for expository simplicity the fact that the form of t_r, a conventional sign, is learned, as is its connection with the Φ_r-Ψ_r complex. This psychological fact gives rise to the distressing possibility of systematic difference between the "content" of two persons' language-entry habits. Granted that "phenomenal red" and "phenomenal green" are causally differentiable, two persons could have learned to *token* pseudoappropriately if the $(\Phi \rightarrow \Psi)$ links were consistently reversed between red and green. Can Utopian science find this out, given that the phenomenal hue is causally efficacious?

I think that it can. "Mr. Normal" has learned to token "red" according to the chain

$$\text{Red surface} \ggg\!\rightarrow \text{Red light} \ggg\!\rightarrow \ldots \rightarrow \Phi_r \ggg\!\rightarrow t_r$$

with Ψ_r at the apex

and he therefore obeys the language-entry rule " 'Red' means *red*" consistently. "Mr. Funny" has something wrong with his idiographic $(\Phi \rightarrow \Psi)$ "nomologicals" such that he experiences (consistently) phenomenal green when his visual cortex is in the red-state Φ_r. He will, however, *appear* to be normal, since he tokens in accordance with the causal system

$$\text{Red surface} \ggg\!\rightarrow \text{Red light} \rightarrow \ldots \ggg\!\rightarrow \Phi_r \ggg\!\rightarrow t_r \, .$$

with Ψ_g at the apex

If the language-entry rule were " 'Red' means *red-surfaced object*" Mr. Funny would be tokening obediently. And since this is the pragmatic context of verbal learning (see Skinner [28]), he appears all right to the rest of us. When, as a sophisticated adult pursuing philosophy, he intends to shift to the phenomenal language, in which " 'Red' means *red phenomenal quality*" is the language-entry rule, he fails—but he doesn't know it (i.e., he unwittingly tokens disobediently to the rule) and neither do we. This is the inverted-spectrum problem in two colors.

According to the proponents of absolutely privileged access, this fact can never be brought to light, even by Utopian science. Let us see.

We have agreed that the phenomenal qualities must be allowed causal efficacy. That is, Mr. Funny's appropriate tokenings of "red" are causally dependent upon the copresence in his brain of physical$_2$ state Φ_r and the (consistently aberrated) phenomenal event Ψ_g. While this connection has been learned, *once learned, it makes a causal difference.* Suppose we perform the Utopian neurosurgery necessary to bring Mr. Funny's visual cortex into intimate causal connection with Mr. Normal's tokening mechanism, meanwhile disconnecting or functionally suppressing Mr. Normal's visual cortex. Now Mr. Normal's tokening mechanism is controllable by physical$_2$ inputs of type Φ_r and by physical$_1$ influences of type Ψ_r so as to token "red" when these are copresent. What will happen when the novel input $(\Phi_r \cdot \Psi_g)$ "from Mr. Funny's visual cortex" is imposed? Without detail of Utopian microtheory, we can't say. But *something* odd should occur, since Ψ_g is causally differentiable from the usual Ψ_r, and—taken alone—should tend to produce the tokening "green" in Mr. Normal. Better yet, suppose we know from previous research that a somewhat "weakened" or "jammed" physical$_2$ input will not prevent a clear, strong raw-feel event from exerting nonchance discriminative control over a well-learned tokening process. Then we can interfere with the physical$_2$ chain between V and T while allowing the physical$_2$ event Φ_r (and, therefore, the raw-feel event Ψ_g) to occur in full strength and clearness. We might find our subject reporting, "It's a peculiar experience—nothing quite like I'm familiar with—but it *is* a color, and it's green—yet I also feel an impulse to say 'red'—but 'green' is stronger." By ingenious surgical cross-wirings, and well-timed suppressions or chain-interruptions, we could study the tokening consequences of various combinations of physical$_2$ inputs and raw-feel influences upon each subject's several brain-subsystems. The results might very well be so consistent that we would feel confident in saying, "When Mr. Funny normally tokens 'red,' his visual cortex is in the same physical$_2$ state that red light produces in Mr. Normal and the rest of us. But his raw feels are of phenomenal green quality under these circumstances. The rest of us have learned to token 'green' when our tokening mechanisms are under the intimate influence of a green-qualitied raw feel, so when *his* raw feels are allowed to control *our* tokening mechanisms, we token accordingly." But why are they Mr. Funny's raw feels? It's delightfully arbitrary to say *whose* they are. I would say that they are shared, given the Utopian supersurgery cross-wiring.

Of course I do not believe any such circumstance could arise, since I have metaphysical faith in the "same cause, same effect" principle. Another way of saying this, less offensive to modern ears, is that I decide resolutely to pursue the scientific aim of concocting a nomological net which will include everything that happens [18, 19]. If ontological dualism is true, we have the aim to fit our psychoids into the net (i.e., "Everything is physical$_1$, whether it is physical$_2$ or not"). The Utopian physiologist would insist that there can't be two utterly different hue qualities arising from the same brain-condition Φ_r, even though they are in different brains. And he would persist doggedly in searching for the as-yet-undiscovered physical$_2$ functor which makes Mr. Funny have the "wrong hue quality" when his visual cortex is in state Φ_r.

It may be argued against the brain-joining experiment that we *still* do not have any basis for inferring to the "private" raw-feel qualities, because it could be that "everything changes" owing to the special character of such Utopian cerebral rearrangements. This is of course logically possible. My only answer would be to point out that this possibility is always present when we invoke nomologicals to infer to states of affairs only "indirectly known." There is, so far as I can see, nothing peculiar in *this* respect about the mind-body problem. If I infer the chemical constitution of the stars from spectrographic evidence, and cross-check this inference by employing other avenues of inference, it still *could be* that "everything is different" out there—provided it is "different" in a sufficiently systematic way. The "privileged-access" absolutist cannot rely upon the truism "Our postulated nomologicals may not hold, in reality," unless he is willing to concede that the "privacy" of our raw-feel qualities has the same source as does the general fallibility of human knowledge. The philosophically distressing form of the "privacy" problem is not that which merely concedes the possibility of error; it is that which denies the possibility of a human knower's even getting evidence which is relevant to the question about another knower's raw-feel qualities. Since "getting relevant evidence about event Y" is a matter of latching on to other events X and Z to which Y is causally linked, absolute "privacy" means acausality. I have argued that anyone who admits that raw feels are caused has no positive reason for hypothesizing that they differ qualitatively when produced by similar brain-antecedents. And I have further argued that one who admits that raw feels are causally efficacious—in the required sense that the raw-feel quality is causally relevant as a critical determiner of our own raw-feel tokenings, making it possible for each of us to token obediently to even a purely "private" language-entry rule—must allow as logically possible a thought-experiment in which one knower can token responsively to a raw feel which also "belongs to" the experiential history of another knower. If Smith's tokening mechanism is controllable by the phenomenal qualities, making it possible for him to token consistently "red" when a raw-feel event in his brain is of red quality and "green" when it is green, then if we can locate a raw-feel event belonging to Jones's experiential history so as to give it causal control over Smith's tokenings, *what* he tokens will be evidential as to the raw-feel qualities of Jones.

It is worth noting that the inverted spectrum is usually taken by philosophers as an "obviously possible" contingency, whereas the psychological situation is actually far more complicated; and it is very doubtful whether such a concept can be made structurally consistent. Color experience involves more than hue, and hue is not independent of the other phenomenal dimensions of visual experience. When we combine the findings of phenomenologists, classical introspectionists, Gestalt psychologists, and contemporary "eclectic" students of perception, we have to deal with an extraordinarily rich, complex, interknit set of relationships, both "internal" and "external," and we cannot treat of a simple hue dimension that is unrelated to anything else. It would probably be impossible to construct a formal model representing the visual-experience domain with hue order reversed such that the verbal reports and other discrimination behavior exactly matched that of normal-seeing persons in all respects. The same objection holds for C. I. Lewis's stronger hypothesis about interchanging sensory modalities, such that my red hue is your C sharp tone. In this "switched modality" case, things are worse than with intramodality inversions, because here even the dimensionality may not correspond. I think all psychologists would agree that no such switched modalities are possible, given the internal correlations—the phenomenal *structure*—of the several modalities as we know them. This of course does not refute a hypothesis which merely says ". . . some *other* qualities with isomorphic structure . . ." understanding that the "other qualities" cannot be any of those we know (i.e., there must be a radically new modality). With this understanding, the idea becomes rather less interesting; and its abstract possibility is still not obvious. I am not sure just what it means to say, "There *might* be a phenomenal modality different from vision, hearing, taste, touch, kinesthesis, etc.—utterly unlike any sensory qualities we know—whose structure was precisely the same as that of the visual modality." This modality must be related to inputs as vision is; it must be related to the subject's experience of his own movements in objective space as vision is (a very tricky requirement, perhaps impossible to meet); it must possess the appropriate number of phenomenal dimensions; and these must be related to one another (internally) and to light stimulation of the retina (externally) in exactly the way hue, saturation, "grain," brightness, size, distance, interposition, direction, etc., are. I am not prepared to say that there could not be such a modality; I merely wish to enter a psychologist's caveat against the too-easy assumption that it could be worked out. And the familiar form of the idea, in which a phenomenal dimension is simply reversed or two modalities are interchanged, is almost certainly impossible.

6. *Ineffability*: It is commonly said that "the quality of a raw feel cannot be communicated." As it stands, this is ambiguous. One interpretation is, "By tokening a raw-feel predicate, knower K_1 does not inform K_2 as to the quality of K_1's denoted raw feel." Whether this is correct or not depends upon the privacy issue, since if K_1 and K_2 are *in fact* tokening in obedience to the same language-entry rule, each tokening "red" when he experiences the red hue, then K_1 *does* communicate to K_2 by telling him, "Now I am experiencing the red hue." Of course K_1 may at times token erroneously, and on such occasions K_2 will receive misinformation. This kind of mistokening, in which K_1 fails to conform to his own language-entry rules (i.e., he tokens color words inconsistently), is not unique to the raw-feel problem but is also possible when K_1 tokens erroneously in the physical thing-language or in the theoretical language. We do not say that communication is impossible merely because particular communications may (and do) mislead. "Ineffable" means "unspeakable," which is a good deal stronger than "sometimes unspoken" or "sometimes mis-

spoken." If Smith and Jones have each learned to token "red" whenever their visual cortices are in state Φ_r, or their psychoids are in state Ψ_r, then they normally communicate by so tokening. I am not here appealing to the usages of vulgar speech, i.e., what we "ordinarily take as communication," an appeal which is forestalled by the very posing of the inverted-spectrum problem. What I mean here is that if Smith and Jones do in fact obey the *same* language-entry rule, then Jones's token "I see red" communicates *fully* to Smith, and conveys to Smith no less about Jones's raw feel than Smith conveys to himself by his own raw-feel tokenings.

Another unpacking of "ineffability" is "The meaning of raw-feel words can only be conveyed by providing the appropriate raw-feel experience." This is not true for complex raw-feel events, unless we assume the ineffability of simple ones. It is possible for me to explain to you the meaning of "visual image of a centaur" in language permitting you to recognize such a visual image (or even to create one); and this is true for the same reason that "centaur" in physical thing-language is verbally explicable without recourse to ostensive procedures. But I believe we can agree that it is true, in some sense, that certain "elementary" or "simple" raw-feel predicates cannot be thus verbally explained. I could probably convey the meaning of "orange" to a person whose visual history had been rigged so as to exclude any experiences in the (broadly specified) orange region, by telling him "Orange is a color between red and yellow, it's kind of a red-yellow mixture." But I could not do the same for yellow itself (which led some psychologists to reject a trichromatic theory of color on the ground that "yellow is a 'simple,'" although yellow can be matched on the color wheel by a suitable mixture of red and green). While there can be disagreement about many marginal cases, let us here grant for argument's sake that there exist *some* phenomenal predicates which designate raw-feel qualities of this "simple, unanalyzable, rock-bottom" kind. We would find it impossible to formulate in language a definition of the predicate in terms of more elementary concepts, concepts which taken separately are not synonymous (or even near-synonymous) with the predicate in question. A centaur is not simple—it has parts or components, it is "made out of" elements, "centaurhood" is a complex quality. Hence we can translate sentences about centaurs (and, derivatively, about centaur-images) into sentences about hooves, horses, men, etc. But if, say, *red* is a simple quality, we cannot thus reduce the predicate "red" to non-hue-characterizing expressions, enabling a learner to token appropriately in the future.

But even this is not quite true, taken literally as just stated. It would be possible to teach someone to token "red" appropriately, at least under many circumstances, by stating a special kind of semantic rule. We might, for instance, say " 'Red' designates the color of apples"; or " 'Red' designates the color you experience when light waves of wave length λ stimulate your eye." The availability of these verbal meaning-specifications is not philosophically important in the present context, because they will "work" only if the learner then proceeds to *put himself* into the described circumstances (i.e., to look at some apples or have a physicist stimulate his retina with wave length λ). So that our definition of "red" is, in effect, a prescription to him for learning obedience to the language-entry rule. Instead of training him ourselves—the usual way we enable children to acquire color words—we instruct him how to train himself. If we don't permit him to go through this intermediate process of self-tutelage, our definition of "red" will not enable him to token appropriately.

The ineffability of phenomenal simples can be trivialized by saying, "If a person has not been given the opportunity to learn a language, then, of course, he will be unable to speak it." As we discussed above in regard to the noninferential character of egocentric raw-feel statements, such statements are often *inferable* from other statements even though typically they are not, in fact, inferred. When tokened noninferentially, they have no "grounds" or "evidence" or "reasons" or "justification." The tokening occurs "on the basis of" a nonlinguistic occurrence, i.e., the raw-feel event itself. The relation is (a) causal and (b) semantic, but the semantic rule is degenerate and uninformative. We learn to token in obedience to it by training, in the same way a dog learns to sit up or roll over. The required linkage is not intraverbal, as in rational inference or propositionally mediated knowledge; the required linkage is between language and the nonlinguistic. And just as we have to be *trained* to perform intralinguistic transitions, so we have to be *trained* to perform language-entry transitions. From one point of view, since there is nothing philosophically earthshaking about the fact that a person cannot "give the right answer" to ($317 \times 48 = ?$) if he has never learned the multiplication table, why is it considered so very special that a person cannot "correctly name a raw-feel color quality" unless he has learned the color language?

IV. Is "Acquaintance" with a Raw-Feel Quality Cognitive?

This is perhaps an appropriate place to examine briefly what a person "knows" by virtue of having experienced a raw feel. Suppose that knowers K_1 and K_2 share knowledge of the Utopian scientific network, including, of course, the psychophysiology of vision and the psycholinguistics of color language. However, K_2 is congenitally blind and although he has recently undergone a corneal transplant, it is very shortly postsurgery and he has not as yet experienced any visual raw feels. Does K_1 know anything that K_2 does not know?

I have put this question to a number of "plain men" as well as to some not so plain. The natural tendency is to say that K_1 knows something that K_2 does not know, to wit, "what red looks like." Without taking vulgar speech or the theories it embodies as criteria of truth, I must confess that my own instincts in this matter are very like those of the plain man. It is pointed out by Professor Feigl that mere "living-through," "having," "experiencing" is not cognitive. While one might cavil at the persuasive definition of "knowing" presupposed by this exclusion, let us accept it for argument's sake. We may still question the conclusion that K_1 differs from K_2 only as to "mere experiencing." The raw-feel experiences of K_1 have been systematically correlated with color-word token-ings by himself and others during the course of his language-learning history, and he has been thoroughly trained to token "red" in accordance with the language-entry rule " 'Red' means red." He has not merely experienced the red and green hue qualities; rather he has coexperienced the red hue quality with "red"-tokenings and the green hue quality with "green"-tokenings. One reformulation of the plain man's notion that K_1 "knows how red looks, which K_2 does not" might be that K_1 knows how to apply a language-entry rule which K_2 does not. It is true that K_2 knows that there is a language-entry rule " 'Red' means red." He can token the rule itself. He can discuss the pragmatics of the rule (e.g., how people acquire the habit of obeying it, why he himself cannot as yet token in obedience to it, what the physical$_2$ functor values of the visual cortex are for brain-states Φ_r and Φ_g). He can describe precisely what needs to be done by him, or to him, so that he will be rendered capable of tokening in obedience to the rule in the future. Nevertheless he cannot token in obedience to it at present. Is the ability to obey a semantic rule "cognitive"?

There are two related approaches to this question which seem to me to justify at least a tentatively affirmative answer. The first approach asks how it happens that a knower can know a semantic rule and yet be incapable of tokening in obedience to it. We can understand that people lie, make jokes, or mis-speak on a Freudian or other basis. But our knower K_2 cannot token color terms consistently with the semantic rules he "knows" (i.e., rules that he can token, and can fit into Utopian pragmatics). It is all very well to explain this oddity by causal analysis; it may even be somewhat illuminating to trivialize it as we did above by the statement "No one can speak a language he hasn't learned." But these psychological accounts, while perfectly correct as causal explanations, do not remove the oddity in its philosophic aspect. The more strictly philosophical question is: Granted that we can easily explain K_2's status as a psychological consequence of his impoverished visual history, what, precisely, is that status with respect to the semantic rules " 'Red' means red" and " 'Green' means green"? The obvious answer, of course, is that ability to token a semantic rule, and the sincere motivation to emit other tokenings in obedience to it, does not suffice for doing the latter unless one understands what the rule means. Putting this affirmatively, we may say: "A person who understands the meaning of a rule can obey it if he wishes (provided, of course, that the action—in this case, tokening—is physically performable by him)." Therefore, if K_2 wishes to obey the rule but cannot, it must be that he does not understand it. I, like the plain man, am inclined to say that he does not fully understand it. To understand the semantic rule " 'Rouge' means red" one must understand the meaning of "red." When blind K_2 tokens " 'Red' means red" or " 'Rouge' means red" he cannot fully intend all that K_1 intends by this utterance. He cannot, because "red" designates a hue quality and, as our plain man says, a blind person "does not know what red looks like." I am not able to push this argument any further, and I shall simply have to ask Professor Feigl whether he wants to say that a person who has never linked the words "red" and "green" to the hue qualities red and green can fully understand the semantic rules " 'Red' means red" and " 'Green' means green." Surely there is something intended by the seeing who enunciate this rule that is not intended by the blind who enunciate it?

It may be objected that our truism, "A person who understands the meaning of a rule can obey it if he wishes," was insufficiently qualified by the stipulation that the required action be physically performable by him. This way of putting it, focusing entirely upon the *action* (output) side, leaves open the question of his lacking sufficient information, and the latter is equally necessary for rule-obedience. If I am to obey the rule, "The king may not be put into check," it is insufficient that I am physically able to move the chessman; I must also know the position. Any rule which specifies an action appropriate to a condition will normally require for its consistent obedience that the action be physically performable *and* that the condition be knowable at the time of action-choice. And a semantic rule is such a rule—it makes specified tokenings licit conditional upon the occurrence of certain raw-feel events. The truism must be formulated more carefully so as to take this into proper account. A hard-nosed consistent identity theorist (tougher than Professor Feigl—say one like Professor P. K. Feyerabend) might argue thus: In order for K_2 to token in obedience to the rule " 'Red' means *red*," he has to possess the information that he is experiencing a red-hued raw feel. We know (Utopian identity theory) that a red-hued raw feel is (*sic!*) a physical$_2$ state Φ_r in the visual cortex. Hence the semantic rule is " 'Red' means Φ_r," and in order to be rule-obedient, one must token "red" if one's brain is in the Φ_r-state. Now the Φ_r-state is explicitly definable in terms of certain physical$_2$ functor inequalities, the satisfaction of which is ascertainable via the cerebroscope. Further, by means of the autocerebroscope (or an autocerebrophone, since K_2 has not yet learned visual form discrimination, so he couldn't read the television screen's symbols), K_2 can ascertain whether his brain is currently in state Φ_r or Φ_g, and he can do this upon the *first* postoperative occasion that red or green light enters his eyes. We have agreed that K_2 knows all the Utopian psychophysiology and the psycholinguistics that K_1 knows, so he will of course be able to understand the workings of the autocerebrophone and will token "red" (if, say, the instrument's high-pitched tone indicates his brain is in state Φ_r) and "green" (low-pitched tone indicating brain-state Φ_g) appropriately. It is therefore incorrect to say that K_2 "must not understand" the semantic rule, on the ground that he can't token in obedience to it. He can—provided he is given the necessary information.

Now this is an interesting move, and its use by an identity theorist testifies to his theoretical consistency. If the identity theory is taken literally —if a red-hued raw-feel event *is* literally, numerically identical with a physical$_2$ brain-event—then the autocerebrophone (or -scope, or -tact, or whatever) is a perfectly good epistemic avenue to that which is denoted variously in phenomenal, behavioristic, and neurophysiological languages. I rather suspect that this move is some kind of touchstone for an identity theorist's wholeheartedness; and I take note of the biographical fact that (in conversations) Professor Feigl finds the move somewhat distressing, as contrasted with Professor Feyerabend who sees it as the most straightforward approach and employs it aggressively and unapologetically.

Granted that K_2 could, by using the autocerebrophone, enable himself to obey the semantic rules even upon the first postoperative occasions of his experiencing red and green raw feels, what does this prove? Let us recapitulate the argument. We began with the principle that a person can, if he desires, obey a rule whose action-side is physically performable. We argued that just-operated knower K_2 cannot token in obedience to the semantic rule " 'Red' means red," even though he desires to, and even though he is able to perform the tokening act itself (i.e., he has long since learned how to pronounce "red" in the course of studying Utopian science). Therefore, we argued, he must not understand it. To this argument was offered the objection that the possibility of rule-obedience involves knowing the conditions which are to be compared to the rule's conditions, and that if K_2 were permitted to know the conditions (by using the autocerebrophone) then he would be able to token appropriately. Hence it has not been demonstrated that K_2 "does not understand the meaning of the rule."

This brings me to the second approach to "Does K_1 know something which K_2 doesn't?" The reason we—most of us, I mean—are not happy with the autocerebrophonic basis of K_2's rule-obedient tokening is that it is an alternative avenue, one which K_1 can dispense with because he has "more direct access." I do not expect this to disturb a good materialist like Professor Feyerabend, who of course views the situation as symmetrical in two indicator instruments: the tokening mechanism (biologically wired and learning-calibrated) and the autocerebrophone (scientifically built and calibrated), with the latter presumably being more reliable! Perhaps our dissatisfaction points the way to an argument not rebuttable by invoking the autocerebrophone?

Try this one: "If, given a shared system of propositions T and identical momentary physical inputs S_1 and S_2, a knower K_1 can predict a future external event E which K_2 cannot predict, then K_1 understands T more fully than K_2 understands it." Here T refers to the entire system of propositions known to Utopian science and shared by our two subjects, including the semantic rules. (It does not, however, include all particulars concerning the present experiment.) Inputs S_1 and S_2 are red light stimuli which we shine into the eyes of K_1 and K_2 (thereby giving the latter a red-hued raw feel for the first time). As we present this visual stimulus, we also give the following instructions to each subject: "I am going to shine this same light into the eyes of ten normal-visioned English-speaking subjects with the request to 'name the color.' What will they say?"

These instructions augment T somewhat, but equally for both subjects. The momentary stimulus inputs (while not identical) are "relevantly identical" in that they are clearly red (or can be made so by repeatedly stimulating K_2 before presenting the instructions). Yet we know that K_1 will be able to predict the verbal behavior of other subjects, whereas K_2 will not. Since both knowers have the same system T, the same instructions, the same momentary input, but differ in their predictive ability, we conclude that K_1 understands something about T which K_2 does not. (I say "understands something," rather than "knows," because they can both token T's propositions, can both derive portions of T from other portions, can both engage in meta-talk about object-language parts of T, etc.) Of course the reason that poor K_2 cannot predict the verbal behavior of others is that merely being informed in our instructions that they will be stimulated by "this same light" does not entail that he will be informed what color the light is; hence he cannot move within the T-network to reach the semantic rule " 'Red' means *red*" or its pragmatic counterpart "English speakers token 'red' when they experience *red*." He knows these rules, but he—unlike K_1—cannot apply them to solving his cognitive problem. And there is, I submit, a very simple reason for his inability to apply them: *he doesn't fully understand them.* If he fully understood " 'Red' means *red*," he would know that the light entering his own eye was inducing red-qualitied raw feels in him; hence he would infer that "this same light" would have that effect upon others; and hence, finally, that they would token "red" in obedience to the rule.

Unless there is some flaw in this example and argument, it provides a refutation of the view that "knowing how to obey a language-entry rule is not cognitive." Because surely everyone will admit that he who can, by virtue of some extra "know-how," predict an external event which another lacking that "know-how" cannot predict has a genuine *cognitive edge* over the latter. Admittedly there is a considerable element of arbitrariness in where the line is drawn between "knowing that" and "knowing how," so that, whereas "knowing how" to solve physical problems by using calculus would be universally considered equally a "knowing that" and unquestionably cognitive, knowing how to obey linguistic rules is less clearly so. Our example suggests a fairly broad stipulation here, since we have seen that knowing *how* to obey a semantic rule can lead (via linguistic transitions) to a definite surplus of knowing *that*, i.e., rational prediction of a future external event. Knowing a language is conventionally considered cognitive; and we have good reason to follow conventional usage here. Not that anything philosophically critical hangs upon how tolerant a convention we adopt for labeling those marginal "knowings that" which are mainly "knowings how" as "cognitive." If a very narrow convention were adopted, it would still be true that possessing habits of semantic-rule-obedience gives one a cognitive edge, even if the habits themselves are classified as noncognitive. Suppose someone then maintains that raw-feel qualities can be deleted from the scientific world-picture, since that picture deals only with the cognitive, and the having of a raw feel is not cognitive. To this we reply the following:

1. A knower who has never experienced the raw-feel quality designated by a phenomenal predicate Q cannot mediate predictions (in the domain of descriptive pragmatics) which can be mediated by a knower who has experienced this raw-feel quality but who is in all other respects equivalently trained and informed.

2. This is because the inexperienced knower cannot employ the semantic rule " 'Q' means Q" and the pragmatic rule "L-speakers token 'Q' when experiencing Q" to make the necessary derivations.

3. His inability to employ these semantic and pragmatic rules in derivation chains arises not from ignorance of these rules, since he "knows" both of them.

4. Rather he is unable to employ them because he does not fully understand them.

5. Specifically, he does not fully understand " 'Q' means Q" because he is unacquainted with the raw-feel quality Q which "Q" designates.

6. But if there is (exists, occurs) anything designated by "Q"—which must be so, if the inexperienced knower's predictive disadvantage is to be explained—then that something is left out of any world-account which does not include mention of Q.

7. A world-account which does not include "Q" when there is a cog-

nitive edge favoring knowers who understand the meaning of "Q" is cognitively defective.

The basic point of all this, it seems to me, is really quite simple. What makes it seem difficult is our (understandable) phobia about "the given," "knowledge by acquaintance," "incorrigible protocols," and "the ineffable quale." If we shuck off these things (without adopting an untenable dispositionalism or logical behaviorism as our account of raw feels) the matter can be formulated as follows: Part of my knowledge consists of knowing when the people who speak "my" language use its various words. If I don't know this, if I cannot recognize a particular circumstance as being one for which the language has a certain expression, then there is clearly something about the language and its users which I do not know. But what is it about the language that I don't know? I know all of the language-transition rules; I even know—in a sense—the language-entry rules. But in another and critically important sense I do not fully "know" the language-entry rules, because there occur some situations legitimating a language entry in which others are able to make the prescribed entry but I am not. The common-sense explanation of this disability is that I cannot make the entry because I don't fully understand the meaning of some of the words involved. I am skeptical as to whether philosophese can improve fundamentally on this account of the matter.

Some have felt that this line of thought is adverse to the identity theory, but I am unable to see why. The identity theorist may agree that a knower who has experienced red-hued raw feels "knows" something, as shown by his ability to predict events under circumstances such that the prediction can only be mediated by the knower's habit of obedience to the language-entry rule " 'Red' means red." What bearing does this have upon the identity theory? We have adopted a tolerant conception of "the cognitive," and we therefore say that, while mere experiencing of a red-hued raw feel is not cognitive, such experiencing together with an appropriate tokening "red" (by another, or by oneself if thereupon reinforced by another) is a "cognitive" event in the derivative sense that it generates a "cognitive" disposition, to wit, the ability to token in conformity with the semantic rule; and he who knows how to obey the semantic rule "knows" something. Let it be further admitted that if K_1 can perform a rule-regulated language-entry under physical input conditions such that K_2 cannot, K_1 knows more than K_2 knows—in the present case K_1 knows "what quality the word 'red' designates." Does this prove,

[157]

or have any tendency to prove, that "red" does not designate the physical$_2$ cortical state Φ_r? I am not yet raising the question whether (and, if so, how) a hue-quality term can designate a physical$_2$ cortical state (i.e., whether the "meaning" of "red" can *conceivably* be identified with any complex of physical$_2$ functor inequalities). I am only considering the anti-identity argument which arises from the K_1-K_2 cognitive edge. Can anything be inferred about ontological identity from the admission that a knower who is historically acquainted "by direct experience" with raw-feel quality Q can, by virtue of that acquaintance, recognize a new instance of it and token appropriately, whereas a knower who lacks such acquaintance "by direct experience" cannot do so?

How does identity theory handle this? In the reconstructed theoretical language of the identity theory, the semantic rule " 'Red' means *red*" can, of course, still occur; but there is also a more informative semantic rule which provides an explicit definition of "red" in terms of physical$_2$ functor inequalities, i.e., the rule " 'Red' means the brain-state functor condition Φ_r." This semantic rule has been adopted (conventionally but nonarbitrarily) on the basis of a well-corroborated object-linguistic generalization that a red-hued raw-feel event *is* (in fact) a cortical state, characterizable in terms of functor inequalities represented by the explicitly defined symbol Φ_r. Within this revised language, we define *in usu*:

1. "Knower K experiences a raw feel y of red-hued quality at t" means that K's visual cortex is in physical$_2$ state Φ_r at t.

2. "Knower K is directly acquainted with the meaning of 'red' " means that he has experienced a raw feel of red-hued quality concurrently with a tokening of "red." (I neglect here the psychological refinements which would be necessary for completeness, e.g., we would have to distinguish between such "opportunities to become acquainted" and effectively "becoming acquainted.")

Then we have, in descriptive pragmatics, an empirical law which asserts, roughly,

3. A knower cannot token (extra-chance) in conformity with the semantic rule " 'Red' means Φ_r," unless either (a) He is directly acquainted with the meaning of "red," as in (2); in which case he tokens correctly by a language-entry only. Or (b) He is provided with other information as to the state of his brain or its physical$_2$ inputs; in which case he tokens correctly by a combination of *other* language-entries and language-transitions (i.e., he makes rational inferences).

We note in passing that each of these molar-level laws is in turn micro-derivable within the identity theory.

The appropriate tokening of "I see red" can occur so long as the knower's tokening mechanism is somehow brought under the causal control of his visual-cortical events. The causal chain from Φ_r to t_r, the "direct access" link, is available if he has learned the raw-feel language, but otherwise not. "Knowledge by acquaintance" consists, causally analyzed, in having established this intrabrain direct-access linkage.

Dualists often object to the identity theory on the ground that a person can know the meaning of "red" without knowing anything about brain-states. There is, at least to me, a troubling force to this objection if it goes to the intension of "(phenomenal) red," a point to which we shall return later. However, insofar as the objection lays its emphasis—as it commonly does—upon the pragmatic fact that a knower can consistently token in obedience to " 'Red' means red" without knowing anything about brain-states, I believe it has no force against the reconstructed identity theory. In order for this pragmatic fact to speak against the identity theory, we must show that the identity theory itself entails something to the contrary. But this is surely impossible to show in physical$_2$ terms. We would have to prove, within the identity frame, that in order for an organism's tokening mechanism to be differentially responsive (by tokening "red" versus "green") to the physical$_2$ states Φ_r versus Φ_g in the visual cortex, that same organism's tokening mechanism must also respond to the several physical$_2$ component aspects of Φ_r and Φ_g by tokening theoretical physical$_2$-language statements descriptive of these components. There is of course nothing about the laws of learning or the microphysiology of the brain which would even remotely suggest such a consequence. Insofar as the identity theory is, after all, a scientific theory —its substantive content being assertions in the physical$_2$ object-language —a refutation based upon the laws of tokening behavior must proceed within the theory's network and show therefrom that an entailed correlation among tokening dispositions is empirically false. The theory identifies red-hued raw-feel events with Φ_r-states in the visual cortex. A Φ_r-state consists of a conjunction of component conditions, such as, say, "The second time-derivative of the proportion of simultaneously activated termini of the synaptic scales on cells of type M in cell-assemblies of form F lying within Brodmann's area 17 has a value $l_1 \leqq d^2p/dt^2 \leqq l_2$." Nothing within the theory need entail the consequence that a subject whose tokening system has been brought (through learned microconnections) under stochastic control of such a part-condition has also been trained to token so much as the word "derivative," let alone the whole collection of scientific statements involved in Φ_r. The tokening system is itself a complex entity, and its connections (wired-in plus conditioned) with the visual cortex are also complex. Tokening "red" is an event of immensely complex physical$_2$ composition, the components of which are not themselves tokenings. Nor are the microcomponents of the state Φ_r themselves raw feels. (Does anyone imagine, even if he is an identity theorist, that a single neuron "experiences the red quality" when that neuron undergoes a single discharge as part of its sustained firing contribution to the Φ_r-pattern?) There is just no reason to expect, on the identity theory's own grounds, that everyone who is able to token correctly in accordance with " 'Red' means red" should be able to token the theoretical statements contained in the explicit definition of state Φ_r. Given the causal laws and structural statements of the theory, we have no more reason to expect tokenings characterizing the microcomponent events or state-values than we have for expecting in the kinetic theory of heat that our thermometers should provide readings in terms of the mean free path or average velocity of the molecules in a bucket of hot soup. Therefore the fact of descriptive pragmatics that persons can "know what red is" (i.e., can know when they are themselves experiencing red-hued raw feels) without "knowing what a Φ-state is" (i.e., without knowing that their momentary brain-states fulfill certain functor conditions) provides no grounds for rejecting the identity theory *as being an inadequate causal account of raw-feel tokening behavior.*

V. The Identity Theory and Leibniz's Principle

This causal analysis has its more strictly philosophical counterpart in the well-known qualification upon Leibniz's Principle, to wit, that it does not bind in intentional contexts. Actually our attempted refutation of the identity theory proceeds by ignoring this qualification, which in other philosophical disputes is routinely applied. The dualist is here arguing, in effect, that "K knows that he is experiencing a red raw feel," when conjoined with the identity theory's equivalence, "Experiencing a red-hued raw feel *is* having a Φ_r-state in one's visual cortex," entails "K knows that he is having a Φ_r-state in his visual cortex," a conclusion which is factually false (for all contemporary knowers, and for most knowers in Utopia). But the inference proceeds through substitution of the (red-hued raw feel = Φ_r-state) identity into the first statement "K knows . . ." a substitution via Leibniz's Principle in a forbidden intentional context.

Arguments against the identity theory which rely on Leibniz's Principle fall naturally into two classes, depending upon whether the allegedly unshared property is physical or mental. The commonest objection of the first class invokes one of the classic distinctions between the physical and the mental, to wit, that the former is "in space" and the latter is not. (Whether "in space" means space-filling or spatially located I shall not consider, although this refinement may be important in deciding upon a suitable convention for categorizing theories as monistic or dualistic.) Critics of the identity theory point out that physical$_2$ brain-events are literally, anatomically, spatially located in the head; if Professor Feigl means what he says, and a red-hued raw feel is identical with a Φ_r-state, then since the Φ_r-state is in the head, he is committed to asserting that the red-hued raw feel is in the head. And the critic considers this a reductio ad absurdum on the ground that a raw feel is "obviously" not located in the head.

As stated above, I believe Professor Feigl is so committed by his theory, although I know him to feel a bit queasy about asserting "My phenomenal events are in my head." I shall attempt to show that this is an unobjectionable locution, and one which we must adopt if we take the identity theory seriously and literally.

Consider the phenomenal event which occurs in the ordinary negative afterimage experiment. Following upon fixation of a red circle in a booklet, I now fixate the gray wall twenty feet away and I "see there" a large, unsaturated, blue-green circle. While it is true that I do not believe it is "out there" (i.e., I do not assert that the causal ancestor of my current visual experience is a circular object on the wall), the "out there" character of the phenomenal event is strong, involuntary, and quite unmistakable.

Let us designate the color quality of this afterimage by the predicate "P," its apparent size by "Q," and its spatial ("out there") quality by "R." It does not matter whether "R" is 1-place or 2-place, since even if "my body" needs to be put in the second place, this "spatial" relation must of course be understood phenomenally, i.e., the red patch is phenomenally external to my phenomenal body. We use the 2-place predicate "L" as before, to mean ". . . is located (literally, spatially, anatomically) in the head of . . ."

Then when a is experiencing the afterimage we write, in our original notation for the psychophysical correlation-law and conjoining the identity statement:

$$(E!y)\Psi(a,y) \cdot P(y) \cdot Q(y) \cdot R(y) \cdot (E!z)L(a,z)\Phi(z) \cdot (y=z).$$

Which requires us to assert, substituting,

$$(E!y)L(a,y),$$

i.e., "The phenomenal event y is located in a's head," which leaves us asserting the conjunction

$$(E!y)L(a,y) \cdot R(y),$$

i.e., "There is a phenomenal event located in a's head and this event has the phenomenal property of seeming external to a's head." This entailed conjunction is deemed contradictory by the critic, and is therefore taken to refute the identity conjunct $(y=z)$.

But $L(a,y) \cdot R(y)$ is not self-contradictory, because the predicate L characterizes the physical$_2$ location of the phenomenal event, whereas the predicate R characterizes one of the phenomenal event's internal phenomenal properties. It is a phenomenal property of the afterimage to "appear out there," that is, the "externality" is *a quality of the experience.* In simpler notation, if v is a visual raw feel and b a brain-event, the identity theorist says

1. v is "out there (phenomenally)."
2. b is "in the head (anatomically)."
3. v and b are identical.

Spelling these out a bit more,

1'. The visual phenomenal event v possesses as one of its phenomenal properties an "out-there" quality.

2'. The brain-state b occurs in the head.

3'. The phenomenal event is the brain-state.

Hence we are required to say, "There occurs in the head a phenomenal event one of whose phenomenal properties is the 'out-there' quality." This kind of talk seems a bit odd, but what is there actually contradictory about it? R is a phenomenal predicate characterizing an experienced quality *of* the phenomenal event; whereas L is *not* a phenomenal predication and does *not* characterize the event as possessing or lacking experienced locus as a visual quality, but instead tells us where the phenomenal event is in physical$_2$ space. The critic relies on an allegedly clear truth, that

$$(x,y)[L(x,y) \supset {\sim}R(x,y)],$$

i.e., nothing can be "inside" and "outside" a person at the same time. But L means "physically inside" and R means "having the phenomenal quality 'outside,'" so nothing as to the predicability of R is inferable from the identity theory's universal predication of L. It goes without saying that the reconstructed theoretical language of Utopian identity theory will identify the phenomenal "out-there" property with certain physical$_2$ functor conditions in the brain-state, different from those identified with phenomenal hue, size, etc.

VI. Summary as to Nonsemantic Objections

Beginning with the autocerebroscopic thought-experiment, we have examined some of the commoner objections to the identity theory and, I believe, found them answerable. I have tried to show in what sense the theory can be genuinely empirical, by suggesting how Utopian neurophysiology might provide experimental results either corroborative or discorroborative of identity or dualism. In the light of the autocerebroscopic thought-experiment, I have briefly examined (with no claim to exhaustive treatment) several of the more familiar claims regarding raw-feel statements, especially those which are thought to militate against the identity theory. Most, if not all, of these claims would fail as refutations even if true, because they are claims about *knowledge* and therefore do not permit substitution via Leibniz's Principle. But I also tried to show that none of these claims is clearly correct, and that some are clearly incorrect. Raw-feel statements are, if I am right,

1. Noninferential normally, but not always, even when tokened egocentrically;
2. Corrigible;
3. Sometimes errant;
4. Indubitable, normally; but not always;
5. Private, contingently, but not nomologically or analytically;
6. Ineffable, when simple; but not in the sense of "incommunicable."

Finally I have discussed the question whether knowledge of raw feels by direct acquaintance is cognitive (I conclude that it is), and whether the occurrence of such knowledge without knowing the physical$_2$ nature of one's brain-events is ground for rejecting the identity thesis (I conclude that it is not).

The net result of these ruminations is, I think, to leave the identity theory in pretty good shape as an internally consistent hypothesis of "empirical metaphysics." The positive grounds for adopting it have not been discussed, and are too well known to require discussion. It must, I believe, be admitted that the evidence in its support, even within the limitations of current science and common sense, is fairly strong. Further, the purely *conceptual* difficulties we meet in trying to formulate even a sketch of ontological dualism (e.g., in getting clear "where Smith's non-physical$_2$ raw feels are" for purposes of their causally influencing events in Jones's brain) should discourage a scientifically oriented theorizer from working along dualistic lines, at least until the more manageable monism runs into serious scientific difficulties.

VII. The Strongest Objection to Identity Theory: Semantic

I have left to the last the only objection (other than certain parapsychological phenomena) which I find continues to bother me somewhat. It involves the problem of intension—of "what sense-quality words *mean*" —in a way which is, I fear, rather too technical to be usefully discussed by a psychologist lacking the philosopher's union card. I shall therefore treat it only briefly in this place.

As a first approximation to formulating the difficulty, let the dualist advance the following: Your theory says that a red-hued raw feel is literally, numerically identical with a cortical Φ_r-state. According to this view, that which I experience as a red quality is—not "depends upon," "arises from," "correlates with," "corresponds to," "is produced by," but *is*—a complex of electromagnetic and electrostatic fields, alterations in potassium ion concentrations, disarrangements of membrane molecules, and the like. You have explained satisfactorily how it is that I can know when my brain is in this state, and how I can token "I am experiencing a red-hued raw feel" in obedience to the semantic rule " 'Red' means Φ_r," without knowing the physical$_2$ nature of the state Φ_r. You have resolved a paradox in pragmatics by combining a microcausal analysis of my learned tokening dispositions with a philosophical reminder that Leibniz's Principle does not bind in an intentional context. It is, as I now see, a mistake to attack you in the domain of pragmatics. But the problem has also a reflection in semantics. Surely you will concede that "red" and "green" designate raw-feel *qualities*. And these qualities do not appear anywhere in your theoretical reconstruction. When I examine the component expressions in the explicit definition of "Φ_r," I find physical$_2$ predicates and functors, but where are the red and green raw-feel qualities mentioned? They have got lost in the shuffle. I can't help feeling that, whatever you *have* done, you have *not* dealt with the problem we started to worry about, which was the nature of raw feels. Whatever else may be true of raw feels—and you have made it very doubtful whether anything else is uniquely true of them—at least it is true that they have qualities. And this, the sole distinguishing feature of raw feels, has been liquidated in the course of your analysis. I maintain that "red" designates a quality; that the *meaning* of "red" is this quality; and that there occur raw feels *of* this quality, i.e., "red-hued raw feel" denotes as well as designates. These qualities are in the world (if anything is!). But they find no place in your world-account. Therefore I must reject your account.

Professor Feigl himself has apparently some difficulties with the identity theory on this score. It might be said that his view is not entirely consistent, insofar as he takes the inverted-spectrum problem seriously. If the identity theory is correct, there can be no such *philosophical* problem, because Utopian science will presumably find out that your and my tokenings of "red" are correlated with the same kind of state Φ_r and that will settle the matter. If the identity theorist persists in philosophic doubt after that point in science is reached, or if he *adds* some sort of argument from "analogy," or appeals to "induction" or "determinism" or "parsimony" or "same cause, same effect," we know that he does *not* believe that a red-hued raw feel is literally identical with a Φ_r-state, since if it is, then there *is* no "other something" which requires analogy, etc., to infer.

Similarly, one may question Professor Feigl's emphasis upon the intersubjective and causal features of scientific knowledge insofar as this knowledge is contrasted with our "knowledge" of raw feels. If the identity theory is understood literally, raw feels are as much in the nomological network as anything else, and therefore they are part of the "public, intersubjective" world-picture. As I have argued above, it is also necessary for them to be causally efficacious. If a red-hued raw feel *is* a Φ_r-state, and what distinguishes it from a green-hued raw feel is a difference in the physical$_2$ conditions, then the qualities *red* and *green* are represented by physical$_2$ expressions which are not nomologically different from those of nonpsychological science.

Within the frame of identity theory, can it be properly said that the occurrence of phenomenal qualities is "a contingent fact"? If we mean by this that the world could have been otherwise in its fundamental nomologicals, of course. Also if we mean that a different world of our world-family might have produced no living brains, and hence realized no Φ-states of raw-feel complexity. But what the identity theorist may *not* say is that the world could have been "just as it is, except for the absence of raw feels." It is not contingent (granting identity theory) that for every Φ$_r$-state there is a red-hued raw feel. This truth is analytic for an identity theorist. That the world could have contained no Φ$_r$-states is logically (and even nomologically) possible, but any world which *does* contain Φ$_r$-states contains red-hued raw feels. To return again to the kinetic theory analogy, a physicist who believes in kinetic theory can say:

1. Kinetic theory is empirical. It might be false; and, if true, it might have been false.

2. Even if kinetic theory is true, it might have been false that there ever existed such an entity as hot soup.

It is a contingent fact that the world has molecules in it. Given that there are molecules, it is a contingent fact that certain aggregates of molecules exist and have a certain mean kinetic energy. But what a physicist who believes in kinetic theory *cannot* say is:

3. It is a contingent fact that soup is hot when its molecules are moving rapidly.

The physicist who adopts kinetic theory has—until further notice—committed himself to a theory which demands obedience to the semantic rule " 'Hot' means *containing fast-moving molecules*." If subsequent evidence leads him to abandon the theory, he will again revise the semantic rules. But while he continues to hold the theory, statements like "The molecules of this hot soup are motionless" are analytically false. Similarly, for an identity theorist such statements as "Jones is experiencing no visual raw feel and his visual cortex is in state Φ$_r$," are analytically false. While disagreement exists among logicians as to which statements of a scientific theory are implicitly definitional of its constructs and which—if any—remain contingent even after adoption of the theory, I believe it is clear that what we may call *constitutive* statements always belong to the former class. Theoretical reductions in which complex physical$_2$

events are allegedly analyzed into their "parts" or "components," thereby permitting an explicit definition of the complex in terms of other theoretical primitives in the revised language, are constitutive in this sense. So that while one may adopt kinetic theory and (according to some) still view "Hot soup raises the mercury column of a thermometer placed in it" as contingent, as not frame-analytic, one may not adopt kinetic theory and yet view "Hot soup contains fast-moving molecules" as contingent. (I need hardly say that I am here using the phrase "hot soup" as a predicate of the physical thing-language and not as a predicate of a phenomenal sense quality.) The reduction of raw-feel statements to physical$_2$ statements is obviously constitutive within identity theory.

If the experienced properties of a raw feel were taken to *be* the raw feel instead of *properties of it*, the identity thesis could be refuted easily by any knower who was directly acquainted with them. The refutation relies upon what Wilfrid Sellars calls the "difference in grain" between raw feels and physical$_2$ brain-states.[5] Suppose I am experiencing a circular red raw feel, large, clear, saturated, "focusing all my attention" upon its center. Granted that rapid fluctuations in attention can occur, that sensory satiation will take place, that the hue and "clearness" at the circle's edge may differ from those at its center; nevertheless, the most careful and sophisticated introspection will fail to refute the following statement: "There is a finite subregion ΔR of the raw-feel red patch Ψ_r, and a finite time interval Δt, such that during Δt no property of ΔR changes."

The properties of a phenomenal event being the properties it "appears

---

[5] I am not sure that I correctly understand Sellars's use of the term "grain," but I learned the term, and this objection to the identity theory, in discussions with him. Roughly put, "grain" refers to an admittedly vague cluster of properties involving continuity, qualitative homogeneity, unity or lack of discrete parts, spatiotemporal smoothness or flow, and the like, which many raw feels possess in ways that their corresponding physical$_2$ brain-states do not. Thus a small phenomenal red patch is typically experienced as a continuous, homogeneous expanse of red hue. The identity theory makes the phrase "phenomenal red patch," in the revised theoretical language, refer both to this entity and to that "gappy," heterogeneous, discontinuous conglomerate of spatially discrete events that are described in a physical$_2$ account of the brain-state Φ_r. The issue raised is similar to Eddington's problem about "which table is the real table"—the solid object of ordinary experience or the inferred entity of physical theory, mostly empty space sparsely occupied by gyrating electrons? Whereas Eddington's problem is fairly easily dissolved by proper linguistic analysis (both tables are real, being the same table, and the macrodispositions being causally analyzed in terms of the microstructure), its analogue in the identity theory is more refractory. The objection is termed "semantic" because it is, fundamentally, based upon an alleged radical difference in (intensional) meanings (= designata) of phenomenal and physical$_2$ predicates, taken together with Leibniz's Principle.

to have," we state the above in phenomenal object-language and avoid any unnecessary reference to knowing. This is important because the desired refutation utilizes Leibniz's Principle. We say of the physical$_2$ state Φ_r (by substituting Φ_r for Ψ_r as allowed by the theory): "There is a finite region ΔR of the brain-state Φ_r and a finite time interval Δt, such that during Δt no property of ΔR changes." But this, as even pre-Utopian neurophysiology shows us, is factually false. The region ΔR and the interval Δt are not infinitesimals, they are finite values taken small enough to satisfy the raw-feel statement of constancy. Thus, during, say, 500 milliseconds, the 5° region at the center of my phenomenal circle does not change in any property, whereas no region of the physical$_2$ brain-event can be taken small enough such that *none* of its properties changes during a 500-millisecond period.

This "grain" objection cannot, of course, be answered by saying that a property of the brain-state, such as an average value of a certain complex physical$_2$ functor, remains constant during Δt, analogizing to the relation between macrotemperature and molecular motion (compare [9, page 53]). The phenomenal assertion is stronger than this rebuttal can meet, because it says ". . . no property changes . . ." not ". . . some property remains constant . . ."

This "grain" argument seems to me to provide a clear refutation of the identity theory, provided we identify "the raw-feel event" or "the phenomenal entity" with the experienced circular red patch. But we need not do this, and the identity theorist will of course not do it. He will instead speak of the entity as *having the properties* red, circular, saturated, etc. He thinks of the denotatum as a *tertium quid*, whose existence becomes "known" to science either via the internal linkage to a tokening mechanism ("knowledge by acquaintance") or via the external linkage to the cerebroscope (hetero- or auto-, it doesn't matter). From Professor Feigl's standpoint, the identity of a raw-feel event as known "from the inside" with a raw-feel event as known "from the outside" is of the same sort as the identity between the morning star and the evening star. He relies upon the principle that identity of denotata does not imply identity of designata.

Many find this analogy unsatisfying, myself among them. Let me try to say why it bothers me. Since the morning star example involves an individual, it will be preferable to use another of Professor Feigl's own examples, to wit, the diverse indicators of an electric current. Passage of an electric current is associated with several indicators of its occurrence, two among them being a heating effect and an electromagnetic field effect. A temperature rise in the conductor or its vicinity is an "avenue of knowledge" to the *tertium quid*: electric current, as is the deflection of a compass needle near the wire. Professor Feigl wishes to say that the phenomenal quality *red* (known "by acquaintance," "directly," "from inside") and the cerebroscopically indicated neurophysiological facts (known "by description," "indirectly," "from outside") are related to the one brain-event in the same way that thermoelectric and electromagnetic indicators are related to the one electric current.

In critically examining this analogy, I first take note of the fact that a temperature rise and a compass deflection are events (or states) distinct from the denotatum of "electric current." The entity *designated and denoted* by "electric current" is a movement of electrons through the conductor. This entity is nomologically linked to two other sorts of events, but theory does not identify them with *it* any more than with each other. We say that *when* and *because* the electrons move through the conductor, the latter's molecules increase their average velocity (which we detect by means of a thermometer) and an electromagnetic field surrounds the conductor (which we detect by means of a compass). There are *three* designata, and *three* denotata, thus:

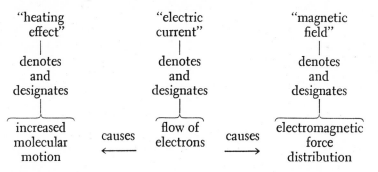

I note also that we do not consider our theory complete unless it provides a theoretical (derivable) answer to the question why the passage of electrons can be detected by thermometers and compass needles, i.e., why the indicators work.

Now if Professor Feigl took the view that the only "inside indicator" was the tokening event itself, his analogy would be strictly accurate. We would have the following:

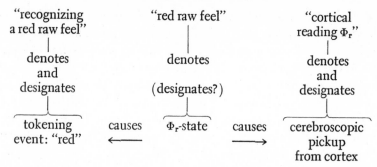

("Red raw feel" only *denotes* the Φ_r-state as tokened egocentrically, although it also *designates* the Φ_r-state as tokened by a sophisticated Utopian believer in the identity theory.) The above diagram represents Professor Feyerabend's view of the identity theory, since he rejects the claim that phenomenal quality words designate anything other than the vaguely understood Φ-states to which they are linked by language-entry habits.

However, the above diagram does not represent Professor Feigl's view of the matter, since he admits—nay, insists—that phenomenal predicates *do* designate something, and that their "meaning" is known to us by acquaintance. That is, the *red quality* is itself an indicator, the tokening "red" being still farther along in the indicator chain. If a person fails to token "red" on certain occasions when he experiences a red raw feel, there nevertheless occurs an instance of the red quality, according to Professor Feigl's view. How is this interpretation to be diagramed? Following the analogy, we have:

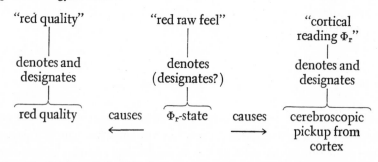

But surely this won't do. We have a something called "red quality" being *produced by* the Φ_r-state. Such an interpretation is objectionable on at least two counts. First, qualities are *of* existents, they do not exist on their own. Secondly, if there is a red quality which is "produced by" the Φ_r-

state, the physical$_2$ reduction sought by the identity theory is endangered. "Red" as a phenomenal predicate is not to be found among the physical$_2$ functors and predicates of physical theory. If there is a property designated and denoted by the quality-word "red" which does not "belong to" (or is not "part of") the physical$_2$ Φ_r-state, then the identity theory is not—literally—an *identity* theory; it is only a weaker claim that all mental events are physical$_1$, i.e., nomologically linked to physical$_2$ occurrents and dispositions. This claim is, of course, quite compatible with dualism (interactionistic or epiphenomenalistic, assuming that the latter can be made consistent).

But if there is no numerically distinct *entity* (even, so to say, a "short-lived continuant") to which the Φ_r-state gives rise, then the quality-word "red" must denote a *property of the* Φ_r-*state itself*. The causal and semantic situation would then be represented thus:

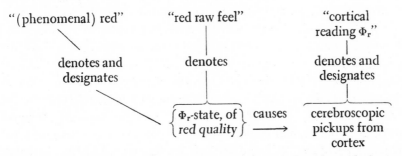

In this interpretation, "red-hued" is a property of the physical$_2$ brain-state Φ_r. But since, as Professor Feigl holds, "red" as a phenomenal predicate is absent from the list of fundamental predicates and functors of theoretical physics—speaking object-linguistically, among the elementary properties and dimensions of the world there is no such thing as a red quality—how is it theoretically possible for *red* to be a property of the physical$_2$ brain-state Φ_r? So far as I can see, the only way this would be possible is if "red-hued" designates a *configural* property of the complex physical$_2$ state Φ_r. That is, "red-hued" designates a complex conjunction of physical$_2$ functor inequalities, analogously to the way in which "hot" (physical thing-language, not phenomenal language!) designates a summary statement about molecular motion, or "charged" designates a configural statement about the distribution of elementary particles on the plates of a condenser.

Such an analysis, forced upon us by our determination to maintain a genuine *identity* thesis, brings us back again to the counterintuitive difference in "grain" between the intension ("by acquaintance") of "red hue" and the intension ("by description") of "Φ_r," formulated in terms of physical$_2$ functors. But in the course of returning full circle to that objection on the basis of meanings, we have, I fear, precluded Professor Feigl from one kind of defense. Initially, he was able to answer the "grain" objection by distinguishing *property* from *entity* and *designatum* from *denotatum*. This rebuttal is no longer available to him because now the "grain" objection is reiterated at the level of *properties* rather than at the level of occurrents or continuants themselves. Can anyone who knows the red quality "by acquaintance" really allow, on the basis of any theoretical reconstruction, that this quality *is* a configural property of physical$_2$ components?

I must confess that I do not know how to put this question in a less "intuitive" form, which leaves me in an unsatisfactory philosophical position vis-à-vis a radical materialist like Professor Feyerabend (who, when I put it to him, looks me right in the eye and answers "Yes"). I am impelled to pursue the argument in terms of "understanding the equivalence," but I do not know how to do this with any philosophic rigor. It strikes me as very odd that I could fully understand the intension of the phenomenal predicate "red-hued," this predicate designating a configural physical$_2$ property, and could also fully understand the intension of the physical$_2$ predicate "Φ_r"; and yet not "understand why" they designate the same *property*. This seems to me radically different from the situation where I can understand two designating expressions without knowing that only one denotatum satisfies them. In the morning star–evening star example, it is easy to see why I can understand the meaning of each expression and yet be uninformed as to the factual identity. We deal there with the difference between propositional functions and the (otherwise unknown) individuals whose names or definite descriptions can be filled into the variable positions; whereas in the present case we are dealing not with values of the variables but with the intension of the predicates. Not to understand that "author of *Waverley*" denotes the same entity as "author of *Rob Roy*" is compatible with understanding both expressions, because understanding the identity involves knowledge of *facts*. Similarly, understanding the meanings of "specific etiology of paresis" and "specific etiology of tabes" is compatible with ignorance that their denotata are identical, again because factual information is involved. But the identity theory—if held consistently—identifies the *property* designated by "red" with the complex physical$_2$ property designated by "Φ_r."[6] I do not see how one can fully understand the intension of two property expressions which designate the same property—one expression being shorthand for the other, which is complex—without understanding their equivalence.

And, be it noted, this lack of understanding can be expected to continue even *after* a claim of identity has been made within the revised theoretical language. Consider a Utopian neurophysiologist who is not blind and who has learned to speak the ordinary color language, but who has *not studied either psycholinguistics or psychophysics* (i.e., he knows all about the fundamental nomologicals—the laws of physics—but he does not know those structure-dependent quasi-nomologicals that are provided by the contingent facts of his verbal culture and the characteristics of organic transducers). He does not, therefore, know *all* of Utopian science, because that corpus includes such disciplines as descriptive pragmatics and the psychophysiology of vision. He does, however, know cortical anatomy and neurophysiology. We provide him with the following information about experimental particulars:

1. *Stimulus*: A bright, saturated red light is made to fall upon his retina.

2. *Proposition*: "A light stimulus, possibly but not necessarily of this kind, was applied to Subject X, a physically normal individual."

3. *Proposition*: "The cerebroscopic reading off X's visual cortex under that stimulation was Φ_r."

Query: "Was X stimulated with the same light you were?"

What will be our Utopian's epistemic situation given these inputs? Having learned the habit of obedience to the language-entry rule (i.e., knowing the meaning of "red" by acquaintance) he can correctly token "I experience red" and, via nomologically legitimated language-transitions, can thereby also token correctly, "If X was stimulated by this same light, X experienced red." He also knows that X's visual cortex was in state Φ_r as a result of whatever light stimulation he received. There is

---

[6] Professor Feigl does not, of course, assert this identification of properties; quite to the contrary, he wishes to deny it. But I hope that my discussion up to this point has shown that a genuine, consistent identity theory cannot escape such an identification of the property *phenomenal red* with the property Φ_r.

nothing about this physical$_2$ description of X's brain-state that he does not "fully understand." Why then can he not tell us whether the state "Φ_r" matches "experienced red"?

The situation here is different from that of our congenitally blind Utopian, who could not solve his cognitive problem because he did not *know the language*. It is also different from that of a non-Utopian, who does not know all about the fundamental nomologicals (or, at least, does not fully understand the microphysiology represented by the physical$_2$ description Φ_r). Our present subject "knows all there is to know" about the state Φ_r which occurred in the brain of X. He "knows all there is to know" about the phenomenal quality *red*, including how to designate it (by "red"). If "red" is a shorthand expression for the physical$_2$ configural property Φ_r, he should be able to say that the states are the same. But, of course, he cannot.

Nor will it do for the identity theorist to complain that we have unfairly rigged the thought-experiment by withholding crucial information, when we disallowed him knowledge of psycholinguistics and the visual-system transducers. It is not relevant to the *nature* of state Φ_r that it is induced by the "usual" (retina $\rightarrow$ . . . $\rightarrow$ lateral geniculate $\rightarrow$ . . .) causal chain. Nor is it relevant to the rule " 'Red' means *red*" that people historically learn it in a certain way. Our subject knows the rule, and he knows that X knows the rule. He knows what "red" *means*; and *he knows that it means the same to X as to himself.* And he knows the configural state of X's brain. If *red* is, literally, nothing but a configural property of the Φ_r-state, it is very strange indeed that he cannot match "red" with "Φ_r" so as to postdict X's stimulus input.

And what about after we inform him? Even *after* he knows that phenomenal red consists of (*sic!*) the physical$_2$ configuration Φ_r, will this seem in any way "appropriate" or "comprehensible" to him? It is always dangerous to anticipate science, especially in the negative. But I cannot conceive that any theoretical reconstruction involving the fundamental physical$_2$ functors would enable me to "see how" the red phenomenal quality *consisted* of such and such a configuration of fields, ions, disrupted neuron membranes, and the like. And I do not believe that Professor Feigl envisages any such possibility either.

I have not been able to formulate the psychophysical correlation-law and, as a separate claim, the identity thesis, by means of a notation essentially different from that of Section I; nor has Professor Feigl suggested any such (personal communication). It would seem not only natural but unavoidable, in meeting Professor Feigl's own conditions on the epistemological status of the identity thesis, that our notation should represent the entities to be identified—the raw-feel event and the brain-state—by bound *variables*; whereas the raw-feel qualities predicated of the former, and the physical$_2$ functor conditions characterizing the latter, should occur in the role of descriptive constants. I think that the notation brings out more clearly than words what is intuitively unsatisfying about the morning-star kind of analogy. It also shows why Professor Feigl's invocation of the designatum-denotatum distinction, while important in forestalling certain alleged refutations relying upon unnecessary puzzles in pragmatics, does not quite succeed in clearing matters up. Consider a critic who attempts to refute the identity thesis by saying, "A psychophysical correlation-law presupposes that there are *two* 'somethings' being correlated; you admit that there is such a law, and that it is empirical. How then can you turn about and assert that there is only *one* 'something' without contradicting these very statements which constitute your main scientific ground for adopting the identity thesis in the first place?" Contemplation of the logical form of our correlation-law provides the answer to this objection. We have

$$(x,y)\Psi(x,y) \cdot P(y) \to (E!z)L(z,x) \cdot \Phi(z)$$
$$(x,z)L(z,x) \cdot \Phi(z) \to (E!y)\Psi(x,y) \cdot P(y)$$

which shows that a raw-feel event y is characterized by phenomenal hue quality P and related (Ψ) to a person x; a brain-state z is characterized by the complex physical$_2$ functor condition Φ and related (L) to the body of that same person. The correlation-law asserts that the necessary and sufficient condition for a person to be the experiential locus of a raw-feel event having property P is that his brain should be in state Φ. Obviously there is nothing about this formally which estops us from a subsequent assertion that the event and the state are identical. The critic cannot complain of a "shift" here from speaking about two entities to speaking about only one, unless he is prepared to maintain that there is something impermissible logically about saying "One individual wrote *Waverley*," and "One individual wrote *Rob Roy*," following these with "And these ('two') individuals are the same ('one')." The psychophysical correlation-law merely informs us that whenever there is an entity satisfying one pair of propositional functions (P,Ψ), there is a unique entity which satisfies another pair of propositional functions (L,Φ); it leaves open the question as to whether one or two numerically distinct entities are involved. So Professor Feigl is correct in answering *this* criticism in terms of the usual distinction between designatum and denotatum.

But the notation also shows clearly why such an attack is misconceived, being aimed at the *variables* instead of at the descriptive constants. If Sellars is right in seeing an insuperable objection to the identity thesis *even on present knowledge* to be the difference in "grain" between phenomenal events and physical$_2$ brain-states, then the proper focus for attack is not the conjoined identity claim "$(y = z)$" itself, but (via Leibniz's Principle) its *consequence*, to wit, that

$$(f)\,(fy \equiv fz)$$

from which we conclude that, given the correlation-laws,

$$(y)\,(Py \supset Pz)$$

i.e., the physical$_2$ brain-state must possess the red hue quality. And since the predicate "P" designating the red hue quality is not to be found among the component physical$_2$ functor conditions $\phi_1, \phi_2, \ldots, \phi_m$ which jointly constitute the explicit definition in our theoretical language of the brain-state property Φ, we must conclude that "P" designates the configural physical$_2$ property Φ itself. Quite apart from the possibility that property P is causally inefficacious (epiphenomenalism), or that "P" does not designate the same quality in Professor Feigl's language and in mine, we have his insistence that "P" does designate something that exists, that there are phenomenal qualities "in the world." Nor does it help him to argue—if indeed he can successfully—that they are not includable within the intersubjective world-network of physical$_1$ science. Be that as it may, he is concerned about the mind-body problem qua philosopher (if not "of science," then "as empirical metaphysician") because he holds that phenomenal predicates have a referent, that they denote something, namely, the raw-feel qualities themselves. He stoutly maintains that he has raw feels and is acquainted with their qualities; he cheerfully admits that others have them too. So we are initially agreed that the phenomenal predicate "P" does refer to an existent quality. Granted that there is such a quality, the identity thesis entails via Leibniz's Principle that it be literally attributable to the brain-state. Hence in the reconstructed theoretical language of identity theory, we should adopt the semantic rule

$$\text{"P" means } \Phi$$

which I, like Sellars, find it quite impossible to make myself genuinely intend.

Can the "grain" objection be restated in terms of properties? Yes, it can, and in a tight, simple form which is unavoidable except by denying its premises. If "Sim(. . .)" is a second-type one-place predicate designating the property *simple* (a property of first-type properties) we assert:

$$\text{Sim}(P)$$
$$\sim \text{Sim}(\Phi)$$
$$\therefore P \neq \Phi$$

by Leibniz's Principle applied to properties. The only trouble with this direct hammerblow is that "Sim(P)" itself is not provable, although it has a strong intuitive obviousness to most (but, alas, not all) thinkers. And while its intuitive claim upon me (and, interestingly, upon Professor Feigl) is compelling, I am hardly prepared to insist that English or epistemologese has a clear language-entry rule about *simplicity* which is violated by a denier of the premise "Sim(P)."

Another approach to rigorous formulation of the "grain" argument, also involving predicates of higher type, relies upon the alleged non-transitivity of the "equal," "nondiffering," "indiscriminable," or "indistinguishable" relation among phenomenal qualities. Some have argued that "indistinguishability" is transitive for physical$_2$ properties but is nontransitive for phenomenal properties. The highly technical issues involved in that allegation are beyond the scope of this paper, and I shall content myself with making two critical observations. First, the commonly assumed nontransitivity of phenomenal "equality" rests upon experimental facts interpreted via an arbitrary definition of the difference threshold (e.g., the old 75 per cent criterion, which is wholly without logical, psychometric, physical, or physiological justification). Secondly, the autocerebroscopic thought-experiment and its attendant theoretical speculations should have made it clear to the reader that it is *not* absurd, meaningless, or self-contradictory to say that two raw feels "seem equal but are not," the reason being that "seeming," when carefully analyzed, invariably turns out to be a matter of tokenings or *other intervening or output events*. I must emphasize that no dispositional or logical-behaviorist analysis of mind is presupposed in saying this; it must be obvious that I reject all such analyses. Nor is the identity thesis or any variant of "materialism" presupposed. I am simply insisting that "seeming equal" is a state, process, event (whether physical$_2$ or not) which, while a causal descendant of the raw-feel event and correlated with the latter's properties, is certainly not to be identified with the raw-feel event or its properties. "These two phenomenal [sic!] greens seem equal to me," which expresses a *judgment about* experience that is numerically distinct from the experience, does *not* entail phenomenal equality. Taking these two considerations jointly into account, I do not believe we are compelled by the available psychological evidence to assert that "equality" is nontransitive for phenomenal properties.

I warned the reader at the start of this concluding section that I was not competent to present a rigorous philosophical objection on purely semantic grounds, and I am acutely conscious of not having done so. It remains my conviction that there is something fishy about the identity thesis when interpreted literally, i.e., as a genuine *identity* thesis. Professor Feigl must, I think, make his mind up as to whether or not there are any raw-feel qualities, i.e., whether phenomenal predicates denote anything. I do not believe that he has solved the basic problem by emphasizing the designatum-denotatum distinction, because this only takes care of the relation between the tokening of phenomenal predicates and the neurophysiological readings off the visual cortex. He—unlike Professor Feyerabend—maintains that the reference of phenomenal predicates is to raw-feel *qualities*. This insistence creates a dilemma for him: if these qualities are other than complex physical$_2$ functor conditions, then the "identity thesis" is misleadingly named; for there is something in the world—and a causally efficacious something at that—which is not reducible to the theoretical entities of physics. Alternatively, if these qualities are *not* other than physical$_2$ functor conditions, they must be configural combinations of the latter. It does not seem to me that they can possibly *be* that, but I leave it to a competent philosopher to prove what to me is only intuitively obvious as a matter of "grain."

If the identity of raw-feel red with a physical$_2$ configural property can be shown impossible upon rigorous *semantic* grounds, the identity theory is demolished; and the outcome of an autocerebroscopic experiment is thereby rendered partly irrelevant and partly predictable. Per contra, if the equivalence of "phenomenal red" and "brain-state Φ_r," is free of semantic difficulty, then I think it must be admitted that the identity theory is in a very strong and easily defensible position. In particular, I have tried to show in this paper that some of the commonly advanced nonsemantic refutations of it are without merit.

REFERENCES

1. Bohr, Niels. *Atomic Theory and the Description of Nature*. New York: Macmillan, 1934.
2. Carnap, Rudolf. "Empiricism, Semantics, and Ontology," *Revue Internationale de Philosophie*, 11:20–40 (1950).
3. Carnap, Rudolf. "Meaning Postulates," *Philosophical Studies*, 3:65–73 (1952).
4. Eccles, J. C. "Hypotheses Relating to the Brain-Mind Problem," *Nature*, 168:53–57 (1951).
5. Eccles, J. C. *The Neurophysiological Basis of Mind*. Oxford: Oxford University Press, 1953.
6. Eddington, A. S. *The Philosophy of Physical Science*. Cambridge: Cambridge University Press, 1939.
7. Feigl, Herbert. "The 'Mental' and the 'Physical,' " in *Minnesota Studies in the Philosophy of Science*, Vol. II, Herbert Feigl, Michael Scriven, and Grover Maxwell, eds., pp. 370–497. Minneapolis: University of Minnesota Press, 1958.
8. Feyerabend, P. K. "Explanation, Reduction, and Empiricism," in *Minnesota Studies in the Philosophy of Science*, Vol. III, Herbert Feigl and Grover Maxwell, eds., pp. 28–97. Minneapolis: University of Minnesota Press, 1962.
9. Feyerabend, P. K. "Materialism and the Mind-Body Problem," *Review of Metaphysics*, 17:49–66 (1963).
10. Howells, T. H. "The Experimental Development of Color-Tone Synesthesia," *Journal of Experimental Psychology*, 34:87–103 (1944).
11. Jordan, Pascual. *Science and the Course of History*. New Haven: Yale University Press, 1955.
12. Lachs, J. "The Impotent Mind," *Review of Metaphysics*, 17:187–199 (1963).
13. London, I. D. "Quantum Biology and Psychology," *Journal of General Psychology*, 46:123–149 (1952).
14. Maxwell, Grover. "Meaning Postulates in Scientific Theories," in *Current Issues in the Philosophy of Science*, Herbert Feigl and Grover Maxwell, eds., pp. 169–183. New York: Holt, Rinehart, and Winston, 1961.
15. Meehl, P. E. "A Most Peculiar Paradox," *Philosophical Studies*, 1:47–48 (1950).
16. Meehl, P. E., H. R. Klann, A. F. Schmieding, K. H. Breimeier, and S. S. Sloman. *What, Then, Is Man?* St. Louis: Concordia Publishing House, 1958.
17. Meehl, P. E., and Wilfrid Sellars. "The Concept of Emergence," in *Minnesota Studies in the Philosophy of Science*, Vol. I, Herbert Feigl and Michael Scriven, eds., pp. 239–252. Minneapolis: University of Minnesota Press, 1956.
18. Popper, Karl R. *Conjectures and Refutations*. New York: Basic Books, 1962.
19. Popper, Karl R. *The Logic of Scientific Discovery*. New York: Basic Books, 1959.
20. Reichenbach, Hans. *Experience and Prediction*. Chicago: University of Chicago Press, 1938.
21. Scriven, Michael. "The Mechanical Concept of Mind," *Mind*, 62:230–240 (1953).
22. Sellars, Wilfrid. "Concepts as Involving Laws and Inconceivable without Them," *Philosophy of Science*, 15:287–315 (1948).
23. Sellars, Wilfrid. "Is There a Synthetic A Priori?" *Philosophy of Science*, 20:121–138 (1953).

24. Sellars, Wilfrid. "Pure Pragmatics and Epistemology," *Philosophy of Science,* 14:181–202 (1947).
25. Sellars, Wilfrid. "Realism and the New Way of Words," *Philosophy and Phenomenological Research,* 8:601–634 (1948). Reprinted in *Readings in Philosophical Analysis,* Herbert Feigl and Wilfrid Sellars, eds., pp. 424–456. New York: Appleton-Century-Crofts, 1949.
26. Sellars, Wilfrid. "A Semantical Solution of the Mind-Body Problem," *Methodos,* 5:45–84 (1953).
27. Sellars, Wilfrid. "Some Reflections on Language Games," *Philosophy of Science,* 21:204–228 (1954).
28. Skinner, B. F. "The Operational Analysis of Psychological Terms," *Psychological Review,* 52:270–277 (1945).

CARROLL C. PRATT

\(\( ))/

Free Will

The language used in modern epistemology and in the philosophy of science is difficult for me to translate without the aid of a dictionary, and even then I am often uncertain of its meaning. It would obviously be painful both for me and the reader if I were to try to write in that language, so I beg leave to fall back on the vernacular and also on frequent use of the first person singular. The idea that I want to tell Herbert Feigl about is certainly not original with me, for I suppose there is nothing new under the philosophical sun; but since I should have trouble knowing whether or not I had found the proper authorities to cite, I shall omit all footnotes as well as bibliography on the assumption that the reader can supply those himself.

The thesis I am going to defend can be very simply stated, although some brief elaboration may serve to lessen the paradox involved in the argument. My thesis is that the belief in free will is so firmly rooted in everyday experience that it is not likely ever to be upset by any discovery of science. Nothing can change the conviction of most people that within certain limits they are free to decide and choose what they will do next. I can stop writing at the end of this sentence or I can go on. And that's that.

For those who may care to attack my support of the doctrine of free will, I shall reveal some of the philosophical assumptions that have become more or less fixed in my way of thinking. Refusal to go along with the doctrine of free will may be the result of different assumptions rather than of any basic disagreement about the facts of experience.

[181]

All knowledge comes from the senses. *Nihil est in intellectu quod non prius fuerit in sensu.* In the present context the senses refer to a far wider range of experience than the sensations of classical psychology. Awareness or consciousness would probably be more appropriate words. It is conscious experience that is the source of knowledge for the individual. When he is dead there is for him no knowledge, no consciousness, so far as we know.

All knowledge began as private experience. It was known only by the person who had it. But there are all kinds of knowledge, large areas of which are placed in the public domain by the gift of language. It is a safe assumption, on the basis of verbal tests and subsequent performance, that the vast majority of people experience red and green in much the same way, not as 650 millimicrons or 530 millimicrons, but as *colors*, otherwise the control of automobile traffic would be much worse than it is. The flurry over an intersubjective language as a necessary basis for an acceptable physicalism might never have arisen had not pontifical behaviorists issued so many encyclicals to the effect that the phenomena of consciousness, the only source of knowledge, should be excommunicated. To bring salvation to these phenomena, a powerful amount of sweat and labor was devoted to the semantics of verbal reports in a fervent effort to show what common sense and the physical sciences had always taken for granted, namely, that words are more than mere lingual twitches and sounds. Words refer to private experiences which the speaker hopes to bring into an intelligible universe of public discourse. The initial data of the "physical" sciences are no more public in origin than are the data of the "mental" sciences. The stars in the heavens or the distribution of iron filings around a magnet do not report themselves any more than do rats in a maze or the flight of colors in an afterimage. Someone has to report those events, and if under controlled conditions several competent observers agree in their verbal reports, then those events acquire the provisional status of fact and become the points of departure for the construction of scientific theory.

All sciences have their points of departure in the same matrix of private experience. The data delivered up and made public out of such experience are neither mental nor physical. Since unresolved and endless disputes as to what they are litter the pages of philosophy, it would be best to regard them as neutral entities for which acceptable labels cannot be found. They are what they are, and for science any inquiry into their nature is unnecessary and would certainly prove unprofitable. For an astronomer color may be a clue as to whether or not the universe is expanding, while for a psychologist color is an item in the construction of visual theory. The differences among the sciences merely indicate divisions of labor. They do not represent differences in subject matter. On the other hand, the differences in the *concepts* developed by the various divisions of scientific labor are enormous, and one man is hardly able to understand the work done outside the narrow segment in which he is interested. Whether the time will ever come when a unified theory will encompass the whole of science is a question for which at present any answer would be no better than a shot in the dark.

To return now to the thesis of this paper, let me restate my conviction that the belief in free will is an inescapable item among the facts of human experience. Countless times a day one is faced with the need or desire to make a decision, and unless he has done some reading in the principles of scientific determinism it probably never occurs to him that he is not free to choose among the alternatives that confront him. He knows of course that he is not completely free, for circumstances often block, influence, or alter his decisions; but freedom within limits he has, for he has exercised it again and again.

The nature or classification of the belief in free choice is not of **any** great importance, if indeed it has any significance at all. An older psychology was almost neurotically concerned as to whether the objects of verbal report were elements, attributes, feelings, percepts, meanings, images, fusions, colligations, or what not, just as a later psychology debated whether a response was a reflex, tropism, habit, instinct, insight, aggression, frustration, paranoia, generalization, etc. The labeling of objects of report may be of some help for purposes of identification, but to split hairs in doing so can be a waste of time, for it is hardly likely that in such matters a mere hair divides the false and true. Description of the way the world appears is for general conversation, and especially for the brush or pen of the artist, not for the scientist. Tolstoi was able to describe human nature far better than any psychologist could ever hope or want to do.

The task of psychology is to probe below the surface in a search for the *conditions* that *determine* human experience and behavior. Red may be a simple attribute, or at times it may carry a complex meaning. Making a choice is probably a complex affair, although at times it may be simplicity itself. The important thing is that both of those events, under variously controlled conditions, can be reported. The verbal report or reaction is the device by which data are made public. In the frantic effort to work out a suitable physicalism for psychology, some writers have been led to identify the datum with the reaction made to it, a strange aberration that is of course sheer nonsense, as the logical positivists used to be fond of saying about doctrines not to their liking. If one presses a key when he sees red, the red and the pressing of the key are plainly not the same thing.

To search for the conditions that determine the nature and course of events implies that objects of investigation are lawful in their behavior. One article of faith in the creed of most men trained in the older sciences is certainly that of determinism, and even psychologists and sociologists are inclined to adopt the same view. A philosophical monism is not likely to be half free and half slave. The universe and everything therein is all of a piece. If it were not so, the task of looking for uniform antecedents and consequents would in certain areas be impossible, for the events of Monday, Wednesday, and Friday might under the same conditions behave quite differently on Tuesday, Thursday, and Saturday, and on Sunday they might not appear at all. An event is the product or correlate of its conditions and cannot escape them merely by deciding to run away. But now comes the paradox.

Freedom of choice is a fact of experience no less than the perception of red, yet there can be no such thing as freedom of choice in a deterministic world. Any seeming choice among alternatives must be an immutable correlate of surrounding and antecedent conditions. Given a certain concatenation of circumstances, William James had to go home by way of Divinity Avenue, although as he started out he was presumably certain in his own mind that he could have gone by way of Oxford Street just as well.

One simple way out of the dilemma of determinism is the refusal to extend the principle beyond the "physical" sciences. The objects of nature are lawful in their behavior, but human nature is another kind of object that can reveal a number of degrees of freedom. Tough-minded thinkers, however, will have no truck with such nonsense. The whole universe, including the behavior of man, is lawful. Any suggestion of indeterminacy, even of the Heisenberg variety, is dismissed as faulty report that will be corrected as soon as observation can be made more precise. Indeterminacy is a private mistake, not a public fact.

There is another way of looking at the problem which I hope Feigl will not regard as wholly futilitarian in character, although I am not sure that it solves anything. I am going to suggest that the paradox of free will is basically no different from dilemmas that occur all the time when a series of antecedents (= conditions) leads to the report of a consequent that has found its way into the brain of a human organism. The consequent (= the event reported) may have nothing whatever in common with any of its antecedents, but this lack of correspondence seems to cause no bewilderment, save in the case of free will. Among all the conditions that produce red, from nuclear explosions in the sun through the radiant energy at the surface of the cornea to the electrical-chemical impulses along the fibers of the optic tract, there is presumably nothing that is red. So in the case of free will, it is reasonable to suppose that among the antecedents that lead to the decision to choose one alternative rather than another (Divinity Avenue rather than Oxford Street) there is no trace of freedom.

In the present context it is important to keep in mind that an event made public by a verbal report may differ drastically from the conditions that produce it. Middle C on the piano does not sound like 256 cycles. The latter have no sound at all until they are well along the VIIIth nerve of the listener. Moving pictures are made up of a succession of motionless photographs. People insist that the moon looks larger near the horizon than at the zenith, although they know perfectly well it has not changed in size. Railroad tracks as seen from the rear platform of a train seem to converge in the distance, and no amount of knowledge that such is not the case has any appreciable effect on the way the tracks appear.

A striking illustration of what I am trying to say is given in Eddington's well-known account of the contrast between the familiar table in his study and the strange physical analysis of the same table. The former is solid, extended, colored, and will support the weight of a man sitting or leaning on it as well as various objects scattered over the top. The scientific table seems to belong in an entirely different world. It is mostly empty and has neither color nor palpable shape. Sparsely scattered in the space of this table are electric charges rushing about with great speed and possessed of a bulk only one-billionth that of the perceived table. The distances between the small particles of the table, relative to their size, are as great as the distances between the stars. Emptiness is the salient characteristic of the scientific table.

What kind of table is that? Well, some would say it is the only real table and that the perceived table is merely some sort of private illusion not worthy of scientific study. Nonsense! For most people, including the physicists themselves, the perceived table is a solid object. They sit on it, place heavy books on it, lean against it, walk around it if it is in their way, all of which they would certainly not do if the table were composed largely of thin air. The scientific table is a logical *construct*, and although as such it may tell us something about ultimate truth, whatever that means, a construct is not an object people respond to in their everyday behavior.

It is odd that so many efforts have been made to exclude the phenomenal world, the world of consciousness, from scientific study when in point of fact that world is the only one to which any science can turn for its initial data of observation. So far do we wander from the main channel when the sirens of metaphysics display their seductive charms.

Free will is present in the experience of everyone when he makes a choice. Freedom of choice is as real as the solidity of the perceived table. Both events are inexorable facts of the phenomenal world, and they are not altered in the least, let alone made to vanish, by the discovery that among the conditions that underlie and produce them there may be no freedom, no solidity. The paradox of free will is a phantom that will probably always bother philosophers and scientists, if not the fortunate man in the street, because the assertion that necessity and freedom may both exist in the same sequence of antecedents and consequents seems like an antinomy beyond any rational solution. Yet it may be argued— at least I am going to argue—that no solution is called for, unless one insists that all dilemmas in the logic of science must be gotten rid of, a task I suspect can never be accomplished.

The knowledge that railroad tracks are parallel does not alter our judgment that they seem to converge in the distance. If an occasional person obsessed by the knowledge of parallelism were to deny convergence, convergence would nevertheless still remain as a fact of visual perception for the vast majority of people. The possibility, on the other hand, that the choice between alternatives may be correlated with necessity leads many who are possessed of that knowledge to deny that there can be any such thing as free will. "There is no such thing as free will," said Spinoza. "The mind is induced to wish this or that by some cause, and that cause is determined by another cause, and so on back to infinity." They are free to make the denial, but the fact of freedom still remains.

Every psychophysical correlation presents a mystery as to why it behaves the way it does, but every sequence of antecedents and consequents in the whole realm of science is equally mysterious. Why does water begin to freeze at 32° Fahrenheit? Why is red rather than blue correlated with 650 millimicrons? These questions are certainly not meaningless, but there is no answer to them, unless the pronouncement that God moves in a mysterious way his wonders to perform constitutes an answer. Whenever the mind of man conjures up an explanation of something, the validity of what he says can only be tested by searching for more information, which means more *what* and *how*. The *why* is always beyond the horizon, and although there may be lovely and alluring colors in that direction, the *Ding an sich* remains forever out of sight. Necessity and freedom apparently work together, and the only thing to do about it is to do a Margaret Fuller, and then to accept freedom as a necessity.

It would be a strange society indeed if every member were convinced that whatever he decided to do had been completely predetermined from the beginning of time. There would be no point in trying to achieve some independence of judgment, no sense in spending time and thought over tough decisions. Yet people do give heed to the future. They make all kinds of moral and political judgments, although they may say that the future has all been mapped out long in advance. A friend of mine in electrical engineering whom I had urged to join a group seeking a way to promote a peace race instead of an arms race refused on the grounds that war and peace are part of a sequence of predetermined events which can in no way be changed, and that the wise man is he who just sits on his rear and waits to see how the cookie crumbles. After a bit of discussion he rushed off with the remark that he had decided to turn his afternoon labs over to his assistants because he had suddenly thought of a good idea he wanted to put into an article he was working on.

The Great Man theory of history is neither better nor worse than Tolstoi's view, so impressively woven into the text of his tremendous novel, that Napoleon and Kutuzov did not shape the course of history, but rather that those "great men" were the consequents of historical necessity. In the epilogue of *War and Peace*, Tolstoi the philosopher is less persuasive than Tolstoi the novelist. Numerous inconsistencies in his argument could be cited. The sentence, for example, in which he speaks of an unreal sense of freedom follows hard on his reference to that unwavering consciousness of freedom recognized by all thinkers and felt by all men without exception. But it is carping criticism to say anything about inconsistency in either Carlyle or Tolstoi, for their great minds could afford not to be bothered by the hobgoblin of consistency, especially in dealing with the seeming inconsistencies of necessity and freedom. It may not be irrational to suggest that perhaps Tolstoi and Carlyle were both right. For all we know, some foreordained destiny may control the events of history, yet man, a creature of that same destiny, feels free on many an occasion to decide what he is going to do. Whether after carrying out his plan he could have done something else can never be known, for time cannot be turned back to find out whether he could have made a different decision.

The searchlight of a glowworm must present a world very different from the one we know. Within that world the worm may feel that he chooses those responses best suited to his needs, but from our lofty position we examine his behavior and announce that we find it lacking in freedom. The little creature is the victim of circumstances over which he has no control. Our own mental searchlight presents to us a world vastly more complex, yet in spite of obvious limitations imposed on our behavior, we seem to move about in our perceived world with many degrees of freedom. Examination of our behavior leads some philosophers and scientists to call our sense of freedom an illusion. From some loftier position of observation it could turn out that they are right; but that position is one that man is never likely to reach. Even if from the angle of eternity it could be proved that every human action is predetermined, the experience of free choice would still remain, just as the perception of convergence persists in spite of our knowledge that convergence is not among the conditions responsible for the perception.

Man lives in a world of appearance and will always continue to do so, no matter how great the discrepancy between appearance and reality may be. Those words I know are dangerous, but in the present context I trust they are harmless enough. By "appearance" I mean the way things look and feel, are remembered and loved or feared, especially as described by competent observers in the psychological laboratory or clinic. By "reality" I mean the conditions found to be correlated with those things when they are subjected to the numerous procedures of scientific analysis and logic.

To call those conditions "reality" is probably an appropriate conditioned verbal response if the meaning is supposed to suggest merely that it is difficult and unwise to try to refute the statements of science. If an astronomer says that a given star is a million light-years away, I am prepared to believe he is right, however impossible it may be to make the star take on such a nonsensical appearance. The word "reality" is bad only if it implies that the world of appearance is an illusion.

The study of illusions has almost disappeared from psychology, or rather, it might better be said that their study is coextensive with the whole of psychology. If an illusion is a perception that does not correspond with the stimuli that produce it, then all psychological events are illusions. Every datum of observation shows some lack of correspondence with its conditions. Is the datum therefore an illusion? Some data were at one time called illusions when the disagreement with their stimuli could easily be shown to the observer, as in the case of the vertical-horizontal illusion. But instances of that kind differ only in degree from all observations in psychology. The studies that led to the formulation of the Weber-Fechner Law were never called illusions, presumably because the observer was not aware of the discrepancies between his just noticeable differences and the corresponding increments of stimulus-differences.

So, freedom of choice may be called an illusion, but by the same token red, middle C, the smell of a rose, the convergence of railway tracks, and the solidity of furniture are all illusions. The way things appear and the conditions for their appearance are not the same. To call appearances illusory merely because they do not correspond exactly with the conditions that produce them implies that we respond all the time to errors in perceiving, which is certainly not the case. We respond to what we perceive, not to reality, and for the most part our responses are surprisingly effective in guiding us on our way. However swift the progress of science, appearances will always remain pretty much the same, so long as man's neural system remains the same.

If some man of great learning and imagination were convinced that the behavior of properly selected people could be so controlled as to create a sort of Utopia like Skinner's Walden Two, there would be no glaring inconsistency if he tried to bring such a community into existence. The scheme could very well be part of the unchangeable course of history, but neither Skinner nor anyone else would have any way of knowing that, and since the time allotted to any one person for putting the scheme into operation is only a brief moment, his decision to make the effort would be timely from his point of view, even if he felt certain that his toil and trouble had been decided upon aeons ago and written into a script that could never be altered even by so little as the dotting of a single *i*. The peculiar charm of such an attitude toward the universe is that those who hold it can believe in necessity and at the same time retain their freedom of action.

For the benefit of my readers I have decided to stop writing at this point. The decision has been all my own, so it seems to me. I cannot believe it was formed when time began, and least of all can I bring myself to think that the English words I picked out to express my thoughts were not my own choosing. I could have said the same thing in German, but the sentences would have been shot through with grammatical blunders —the result of my own bungling free will.

MICHAEL SCRIVEN

\\\(\)\)\)/

The Limitations of the Identity Theory

Introduction.

I am selecting one of Herbert Feigl's great interests to discuss, and hope that these thoughts may provide a little stimulation for him on a topic about which he has stimulated me so much. I set out a number of summary theses, beginning with ones which are now relatively acceptable, often owing to Professor Feigl's telling papers, and proceed to currently still contentious claims which I think we must now accept.

1. *The mind-brain identity is not identity of meaning.*

This claim is now generally acknowledged, and the standard reason for it is that one can perfectly understand the meaning of "X is in pain" or "X is thinking of home," and "X is in brain-state B," without conceding that the two mean the same, whatever specific B is involved.

Other grounds for rejecting identity of meaning involve category differences which will be mentioned in a moment.

2. *The mind-body identity is not a pure empirical identity.*

The identity between "X is a man" and "X is a tailless, featherless biped" is a pure empirical identity, or pure identity of reference, because it is simply a matter of fact, rather than a matter of standard definition or new convention, that the extensions of the two classes coincide.

The identity between brain-states, B, and states of consciousness, C, is not of this kind because the C's either lack certain properties that the B's possess or have incompatible properties. Both have temporal duration; but the B's are properties of an object with certain physical dimensions and location, the brain, whereas the C's must be called states of the whole person (which has much larger and hence incompatible dimensions), or of the mind (which has none), or of parts of the person other than the brain and hence of different dimensions. To illustrate this:

A standard argument here concerns a pain which we identify as *being in the left ankle*. The dualist says that this kind of localized pain shows identity cannot hold, since the ankle is not the brain and hence pain in one cannot be identified, even empirically, with a state of the other. The identity theorist replies that the identity holds, not between the pain and the brain-state, but between the state of *being-in-pain* and the brain-state.

To this the dualist could, I think, reply:

a. The mind-body problem is partly a problem of the relation of sensations, e.g., pain, to bodily states, e.g., brain configurations. It is not very interesting to offer as a solution the argument that the state of *being-in-pain* is a state of the person, hence of the body, hence of the brain, hence identity. The connections are too loose at every stage to make this a valuable identity; it is only a fancy way of saying that the same person has the pain and the brain-state simultaneously. The truth is that *pains* cannot in any way be identified with brain-states; pain, or even the *sensation of pain*, or the *feeling of pain* may be localized in parts of the body other than the head. But it might be argued that pains are not mental states, and that other aspects of the mind-body problem may be more susceptible to the identity solution.

b. Suppose we adjust our conception of the mind-body problem so as to meet point (a), i.e., we take it to refer only to the relation of mental states, M, to bodily states, where C's are not to count as M's. A typical mental state which lacks the peculiar spatial properties of some pains would be "remembering how Carol looked as she said good-bye at the airport." This does not have an obvious claim to any spatial location, apart from poetic options for the heart. And the same might be argued for something we might construct and call *the mental state of being in pain*. It would, therefore, be a harmless *extension* of logical grammar—rather than an infraction—to award it spatial location in the brain, where it would then be possible and natural to identify it with the particular brain-state which is an empirical concomitant of it. This would be identity by fiat, but not by arbitrary fiat; and, it may be said with considerable justice, every case of the identification of concepts in the development of the physical sciences involves some element of logical adjustment like this. Certain important consequences of this strategy will be examined in a moment; first, we should consider another possibility.

c. It may be argued that mental states are states of a *person* and that a person does have a physical aspect, so that the physical dimensions and location of a person are the prime candidates for any election to the office of physical dimensions and location for mental states. These are not the dimensions or location of his brain. This is a different case of incompatible properties from (a). I think it must be regarded as part of the price we pay for the neatness of the identity theory that we must dismiss the claims of (c): it is intrinsically about as plausible as the suggestion in (b), but aesthetically less attractive.

We conclude that the identity theory, although based on the plausible hypothesis of neural correlates, and hence in a sense empirical, plainly involves linguistic legislation to such a degree that a claim or request that would be meaningless or logically false ("Where are your memory experiences?") with respect to our present use of mental-state language is made sensible and true. In particular, some brain-states will acquire the property of intentionality, e.g., they will be said to be about Carol at the airport, and sensations will become more public than they are now, and may even be called physical events.

3. *A semiconventional identity theory cannot replace dualism.*

The great appeal of the identity theory, initially, is that it can handle the puzzles which produce parallelism, epiphenomenalism, and interactionism in a delightfully simple way. Can mental events causally interact with physical events? we ask; and the identity theorist answers, Of course they can, for they are physical events. No mysterious two-substance theory is necessary, no special intersubstantial causal links need be forged.

Unfortunately, if the identity theory is established in the way outlined above, this answer will not serve. For even if we can award sensations a place in the brain without serious confusion, doing this does not settle the question whether, *prior* to this change in their logical grammar, sensations are caused by or cause the usual bona fide kind of brain-events. If the identity theory were a pure discovery or a pure meaning equivalence, such a question would be as confused as the question whether the morning star is larger or smaller than the planet Venus.

In the present circumstances, however, we have had to concede at least the nonspatial (and possibly the spatial but non-brain) characteristics of mental states *as they are now*. And the causal problem of course refers to their present meaning.

The empirico-conventional identity theory thus tells us nothing about the very important problem of the causal relations between mental and physical events, since it is really a (reasonable) linguistic proposal; it appears to me to be compatible with all three traditional dualist positions.

4. *Interactionism is demonstrable.*

4.1. The truth of interactionism implies the falsehood of epiphenomenalism and parallelism;[1] the converse does not hold, on the usual interpretations. But the way in which we hereafter contravene parallelism leaves only interactionism as a possibility.

4.2. We assume the existence of a one-many or one-one M-B correlation, and of complete B-level explanations of overt behavior.

4.3. We use the rather crude definition of a cause as a nonredundant member of a set of conditions that are jointly sufficient for the effect, where

> A is a *sufficient condition* for E $=_{df}$ (A $\cdot \sim$E) is physically impossible, A and $\sim$E being, separately, physically possible $=_{df}$ A $\rightarrow$ E.
> A is *the cause* of X $=_{df}$ A $\ggg\!\!\rightarrow$ X $=$ ($\exists$A$_1$, A$_2$, . . . A$_n$) $\cdot$ $\{$(A $\cdot$ ΠA$_i$) $\rightarrow$ X$\}$ $\cdot \sim\{$$\Pi$A$_i \rightarrow$ X$\}$ $\cdot$ A $\cdot$ ΠA$_i$.

A contextual condition is also required, to distinguish between the several candidates A, A′, A″ . . . which may meet the above formal condition (and may include some of the A$_i$); it presents little difficulty in practice and can be expressed technically by saying that *the* cause or causes are those A's which are not contained in the *implied contrast class*. This definition fails logically because it identifies an inoperative overdetermining condition as a cause, but it provides useful guidance in most cases.

4.4. Parallelism is false. Proposition: Stimulation of the brain by probe or drug (B-state) sometimes causes hallucinations (M-state). We may apply the alleged cause (A) at randomly selected moments during the tenure of the required background conditions (A$_1$ . . .) and we inevitably get the alleged effect (X); and we do not get the effect from

---

[1] I discuss only that part of these views which bears on the claim that B-states cause and are caused by M-states (interactionism), and hence take epiphenomenalism to assert that only the first kind of causation occurs, and parallelism to assert that neither occurs.

those background conditions alone. Thus we have a set A, A_1, . . . , A_n which is jointly sufficient for X, of which A is a nonredundant member; the random application ensures the absence of any factor $\bar{A}$ which is actually responsible and which happens to co-occur with A.

Parallelism is based on a misconception of the notion of cause: it presupposes that some more intimate connection is involved besides those given. Now, given that some B's cause some M's, does the converse ever occur? Epiphenomenalism says No, interactionism Yes.

4.5. Epiphenomenalism is false. Propositions: Having a serious toothache (a C-state) causes me to go to the dentist. Believing the child would be returned (an M-state) caused me to deliver the ransom money without notifying the police. We shall just discuss the toothache case, the other being essentially similar. Under suitable circumstances, e.g., availability of time, money, knowledge, dentist, etc., we can plausibly suppose we get a jointly sufficient condition here. The problem is to show the nonredundancy of the pain-feeling, i.e., to show that the remaining set of conditions will not of themselves produce the dentist-going behavior. If the remaining conditions had to include the concurrent brain-state, this would raise an interesting difficulty. They do not, and hence interactionism is proved.

The interesting difficulty is this: our assumptions in (4.2) assure us of a brain correlate of the pain, and that the brain-story is enough to explain, in a respectable scientific way, the trip to the dentist. This appears to show that we could dispense with the pain, and still get the same overt behavior. This would show the pain is causally inefficacious and hence that epiphenomenalism and not interactionism is true.

That this move is fallacious has, I think, been demonstrated by Professor Baier [1]. The contrary-to-fact supposition involved (that we could dispense with the pain) is contrary-to-hypothesis; that is, the argument shows the logical possibility of epiphenomenalism but not its truth.

Suppose we discovered a drug or an operation which *in fact* cut out the pain but still left a connection such that states of advanced decay in teeth led to our going to the dentist. Wouldn't this show that the pain is an epiphenomenon? Not at all; it would only show that *another* brain-state besides the one correlated with the pain can initiate dentist trips, i.e., it demonstrates plurality of causes, not the inefficacy of an alleged cause. The first assumption of (4.2) guarantees that we can't have the same brain-state both with and without the pain, so a fortiori we can never get the pain-associated brain-state, without the pain, leading to or explaining the dentist-visiting outcome.

But surely constant conjunction is here being confused with causal connection? Surely we are unfairly dismissing epiphenomenalism? Granted the pain is indispensable with respect to the pain-brain-state, ex hypothesi, this doesn't suffice to show that the *pain itself* is the cause of the trip. For else a man's shadow might be said to cause his sunburn; one can't have the sun without the shadow, but it is the sun and not the shadow that produces the burn.

The difference is this. A man's skin does not redden from the shadow, but a man responds directly to pain. The pain, *whether or not* there is an accompanying B-state, would lead us to attempt remedial action; the neural account simply tells us the concurrent physiological story of this process. It is a complementary and not a competitive account. The pain causes the action just as indubitably as recognizing a friend causes us to stop on the street, forgetting the time makes us late, and bright lights make us blink. Science can indeed give another account, but it is just another account of a causal connection, not a potential proof that there is no causal connection.

5. *Psychic Overdetermination and Mechanism.*

A loophole remains. Might not this conclusion depend on the Achilles' heel of the above definition of "cause"; may not the pain be an inoperative overdetermining factor, capable of but not in fact causing action? The entire actual cause is, in this view, the correlated brain-state. The move that refutes parallelism cannot be employed here, because we cannot randomly manipulate C-states except via B-states, and thus we cannot eliminate the possibility that the B-state we use to arouse a C-state itself causes the later B-states. Epiphenomenalism appears to threaten us again.

But there is something **extremely** insubstantial about this possibility. Would it really be *more accurate* to say, not "The angina pain drove me to a doctor, for the first time in twenty years," but "The condition of my heart caused me great pain and also drove me to a doctor," etc.? Isn't it actually true that it *was* the felt pain that affected my actions, indeed dominated my thoughts? I act *to alleviate* that pain, and succeed. The action is deliberate, goal-directed, and determined by the pain; it would certainly not have occurred without the pain. This is a strong basis for calling the pain the cause, for causes do not have to be necessary conditions for their effects, even with respect to certain standing conditions. The case is, I think, now watertight. Of course it entails that states of consciousness (and, in the analogous case, mental states) can be causes of and not just reasons for actions, but no good arguments appear outstanding against that view. Of course, too, it is a view not only consistent with but, I think, a necessary consequence of a completely mechanistic account of human behavior. And perhaps that is the ultimate defense of the identity thesis: there is a single ground of even dualistic being. The Perfect Robot does not necessarily exist—but if it exists it necessarily feels pain [2].

REFERENCES

1. Baier, Kurt. "Pains," *Australasian Journal of Philosophy*, 40:1–23 (May 1962).
2. Scriven, Michael. "The Compleat Robot," in *Dimensions of Mind*, Sidney Hook, ed., pp. 118–142. New York: New York University Press, 1960.

WILFRID SELLARS

\\\)))

The Refutation of Phenomenalism: Prolegomena to a Defense of Scientific Realism

In the following argument I shall assume that there is available for the phenomenalist an account of sense contents which does not rule out his enterprise *ab initio*. I shall turn my attention directly to the exploration of what might be meant by the phrase "possible sense content." Here the essential point can be made quite briefly, though its implications will require careful elaboration. A "possible" sense content in the desired meaning of "possible" would be more aptly referred to as a *conditional* or (to use Mill's term[1]) *contingent* sense content. The logical structure of this concept can best be brought out by an analogy. Suppose we use the phrase "conditional skid" to refer to a skid which *would* take place if a certain driver *were* to do something, e.g., swerve. A beginning driver is constantly aware of the "existence" of conditional skids, collisions, etc., relatively few of which, fortunately, become actualized.

Notice that the contrasting term to "possible skid" in the sense of *conditional* or *contingent skid* will be "actual skid," *not* in the sense of *actually existing skid*, but simply as used to refer to skids *in the ordinary sense of the term* as contrasted with the conditional skids which are contextually defined in terms of them. Thus "actual skid" differs from "skid"

AUTHOR'S NOTE: This paper appeared in my book *Science, Perception and Reality* (pp. 76–90), published in London by Routledge and Kegan Paul in 1963, and is reprinted here with their permission.

[1] [2, third edition], appendix to Chs. XI and XII. This appendix is such a clear formulation and defense of the phenomenalist's position that it fails by a hairsbreadth to refute it along the lines of the following argument.

only by calling attention to the contrast between skids and conditional skids.

Let us, therefore, explore what it would mean to say that at a certain time and place there was a conditional skid. Obviously a conditional skid does not exist merely by virtue of the fact that the statement "Such and such a motion of such and such a car on such and such a surface occurred at this time and place" is both logically and physically self-consistent. "Conditional" involves a reference to *existing circumstances*, to *alternative courses of action* and to the *outcomes* of these courses of action in the existing circumstances. The sense of "possible" ($=$ "conditional") which we are exploring must also be carefully distinguished from the *epistemic* sense of "possible" illustrated by

It is possible that it will rain tomorrow.

This sense, like the one we are defining, is also not simply a matter of the logical and physical self-consistency of the statement "It will rain to-morrow." It is a cousin of "probable," and the above statement has, roughly, the sense of

The presently available evidence is compatible with the idea that it will rain tomorrow.

The sense we have in mind, on the other hand, is, so to speak, ontological rather than epistemic. It says how things stand, not how we stand with respect to evidence about how things stand.

Consider the following statements, where x is a piece of salt:

X is soluble.
It is possible that x will shortly dissolve.
A possible dissolving of x exists.

The first statement says simply that if x were put in water, it would dissolve. It is compatible with the idea that x is in an inaccessible place miles away from water. The second statement, which involves the *epistemic* sense of "possible" claims that the available evidence is compatible with the idea that x will shortly dissolve, and hence rules out the idea that *the evidence points to* the above description of the circumstances. The third statement—a contrived one obviously, *but so is the language of possible sense contents*—claims that the circumstances of x are such as to leave open to us at least one course of action which would eventuate in the dissolving of x, and hence rules out the above description of the circumstances.

Notice that in statements of the kind we are considering agents and circumstances do not come into the picture in the same way. Roughly, circumstances come in as *actualities*, agents come in as *having powers*. Thus, returning to the example of the skid, we have

> The circumstances of the driver are such and his capacities to move his limbs are such that there is at least one move he can make which would result in a skid.

We are clearly in the region of difficult problems pertaining to the conceptual framework of *conduct*. What is an action? What is the scope of "circumstances"? Could a person ever have done something other than what he actually did? etc., etc.[2] Fortunately these problems are tangential to our investigations. For our purposes, the significant feature of the above analysis of a "possible" or "conditional" skid is the implied reference to general principles (laws of nature) about what circumstances are consistent with the performance of what actions and about what would eventuate if the agent were to do an action of a certain kind which he is able to do in his circumstances. For, to bring the matter to a head, to say that E would eventuate if X, who is in circumstances C, were to do A, is to imply that it is a general truth that

> When A is done in C, E eventuates.

This general truth may be either "strictly universal" or "statistical." The important thing is that it is *factual*, i.e., that it is not *logically* true. Thus, if the belief in such a generalization is to be a *reasonable* one, the reasons must be of an inductive character. This points to inductive arguments of the form

> In observed cases of A being done in C, E has invariably (usually) eventuated.
> So (in all probability) doing A in C invariably (usually) eventuates in E.

If we transfer these considerations from the case of the possible skid to the case of the possible sense content, a number of points can be made at once. To begin with, we must distinguish between

---

[2] It is worth noting in this connection that when we say of Jones, who in fact did A, that he could have done otherwise, A', where A and A' are incompatible *minimal* actions (roughly, bodily changes which are under direct bodily control), we mean that though Jones did A, he was able at the time both to do A and to do A' (i.e., if he had willed to do A (A'), he would have done A (A')). Where A and A' are not minimal actions, we mean that there was a minimal action which Jones was able to do (but did not in point of fact do), which, in the circumstances, would have been the initial

(a) the fact that the circumstances of perception are of kind C;
(b) the fact that the perceiver can do A; and
(c) the fact that doing A in C (usually) eventuates in having a sense content of the kind in question.

Now we can readily imagine that someone who, though a friend of sensations and sense contents, is not engaged in defending classical phenomenalism might well illustrate these distinctions by putting himself in a position in which he can truthfully say:

(a') I am standing, eyes closed, facing a fireplace in which a fire is burning.
(b') I am not blind and can open my eyes.
(c') Opening my eyes when facing a fire usually eventuates in my having toothy orange and yellow sense contents.

He might well say in these circumstances that a possible or conditional toothy orange and yellow sense content exists.

Suppose, however, that he undertakes to defend the idea that "physical objects are patterns of actual and conditional sense contents," where "conditional sense content" has the sense we have been explicating. What moves can he be expected to make? The simplest one would be to start with the above model for interpreting the existence of conditional sense contents but claim that each of the three statements, (a'), (b'), and (c'), can be reformulated in terms of sense contents. But what sort of sense contents? Actual? Or both actual and conditional?[3] This question probes to the heart of the matter. For if the presuppositions of statements asserting the existence of conditional sense contents are such as are ordinarily formulated in terms of physical objects, persons, sense organs, etc., as above, then the claim that physical objects are patterns of actual and conditional sense contents implies that when reformulated in terms of sense contents, these presuppositions refer to conditional as well as

stages of a doing of A'. A key confusion often found in this context is that between (1) "It could not have been the case (relative to the preceding state of the universe) that Jones did A' at t," and (2) "Jones could not do A' at t (was unable at t to do A')." Determinism entails (1) but not (2). A related confusion is that between (3) "Circumstances were physically incompatible with the development of relevant minimal actions within Jones's power into a certain nonminimal action A'," and (4) "The antecedent state of the universe was physically incompatible with the occurrence of a Jonesean doing of A'."

[3] See p. 198 above for an explication of the sense of "actual" in the phrase "actual (as contrasted with conditional) sense content." I take it that is obvious from what has been said that the existence of conditional entities presupposes the existence of actual entities.

actual sense contents. But if so, then an obvious difficulty arises. For these conditional sense contents *in their turn* presuppose generalizations, and if these generalizations are also such as are ordinarily formulated in terms of physical objects, persons, sense organs, etc., then we are faced with the absurdity of generalizations which are such that their own truth is presupposed by the very meaning of their terms. This vicious circularity finds its partial expression in the fact that if the reformulation from the language of physical objects to the language of sense contents were carried on step by step, it would not only be an endless regress, but would involve a *circulus in definiendo*, "eye," for example, being explicated in terms of "eye."

The assumption that the general truths presupposed by the existence of conditional sense data are such as are ordinarily formulated in terms of physical objects, eyes, etc., also has the consequence that those generalizations could never be supported by instantial inductions the premises of which referred to actual sense data only. For since the terms of the supported generalizations refer to actual and conditional sense contents, the premises would have to do so as well. Indeed, the truth of the premises for such a generalization would presuppose the truth of such generalizations.

The preceding argument has been based on the assumption that the general truths presupposed by the existence of conditional sense contents are such as are formulated in ordinary language by statements relating sensations to the physical and physiological conditions of perception. This consideration suggests that all the classical phenomenalist need do by way of reply is to insist that there are *independent*[4] general truths about sense contents the terms of which involve no reference to conditional sense contents and which can, therefore, be supported by instantial inductive arguments the premises of which refer to actual sense contents only. To probe more deeply into classical phenomenalism we must examine this new claim. Are there inductively establishable generalizations about the occurrence of sense contents which make no reference to either physical objects or conditional sense contents? Can we, in short, explain conditional sense contents in terms of actual sense contents?

Now there is no contradiction in the idea that there are (perhaps statistical) uniformities which specify the circumstances in which a sense con-

[4] By calling them "independent" I mean simply that they are not supposed to be "translated" counterparts of common-sense or scientific propositions about perception.

tent of a certain kind occurs in terms of actual (i.e., not conditional) sense contents. Are there any such? Here we must be careful to distinguish between two radically different kinds of generalizations.[5] Let me call them *accidentally autobiographical* (A-generalizations) and *essentially autobiographical* (E-generalizations), respectively. If one fails to distinguish between them, the fact that there are true generalizations of one kind may deceive him into thinking that there are true generalizations of the other.

The difference between the two kinds of generalization is that between (1) statements like

> Whenever (or for the most part whenever) I have such and such a pattern of sense contents, I have a sense content of the kind in question

where it makes good sense to suppose that the generalization remains true if "anybody" is substituted for "I," and (2) statements of the same form where it is clear that the generalization would not remain true if the substitution was made. The former are A-generalizations, the latter E-generalizations.

Now it is reasonably clear that there have been uniformities in my immediate sense history. It is notorious that the antecedents must be very complex in order to discount the circumstances (e.g., blinks, getting one's hand in the way, etc., etc.) which upset simple applecarts. But if I am guarded enough in my conception of the antecedent, it will indeed have been followed (for the most part) by the consequent in my past experience. Before we ask ourselves whether such uniformities in a person's sense history can serve as premises for an inductive argument, and whether, if they can, the evidenced generalizations can do the job required of them by the phenomenalist, let us imagine someone, Mr. Realist, to comment on the above as follows:

> I grant that such past uniformities can be discovered, but surely I have come to discover them while conceiving of myself as a person, having a body, and living in an environment consisting of such and such physical objects (my house, this fireplace, the road out front, the wallpaper, etc.). I cannot even imagine what it

[5] For present purposes it is unnecessary to break up the antecedents of these generalizations into a phenomenally characterized circumstance and a (supposed) phenomenal act of the perceiver (e.g., a setting oneself to open one's eyes) which jointly eventuate in the sense content in question.

would be like to discover them without operating within this conceptual framework.

To which we can imagine someone, Mr. Phenomenalist, to reply:

> I grant that in the "context of discovery" your coming to notice these uniformities occurred within the framework you mention; but surely in the "context of justification" these uniformities stand on their own feet as evidence for inductive generalizations about sense contents.

Mr. Realist is likely to retort:

> Surely it is paradoxical to grant that the noticing of the uniformities occurs within the conceptual framework of persons and things in space and time, while insisting that this framework is one in which physical objects are patterns of actual and conditional sense contents. For, ex hypothesi, the notion of a conditional sense content is to be explicated in terms of the kind of uniformity which is discovered while using the framework.

and Mr. Phenomenalist to counter with:

> The *historical* or *genetic* fact that a child is taught the conceptual framework of persons and things in space and time and later uses this framework in the discovery of the complex uniformities which are presupposed by conditional sense contents is not incompatible with the *logical* claim that this framework is reducible to the framework of sense contents, actual and conditional. Surely the common heritage of countless generations can embody a wisdom which the individual must scratch to acquire. . . .

It is at this point that the distinction drawn above between the two kinds of generalizations about actual sense contents becomes relevant. For if we ask, "Are the uniformities we have found to obtain in our past experience such that if they could serve as inductive evidence for sense content generalizations, the conditional sense contents they would make available would serve the phenomenalist's purposes?" the answer must be a simple No. For the uniformities each of us finds are not only autobiographical, they are expressions of the fact that each of us lives among *just these individual physical objects*. The uniformities I find are bound up with the fact that my environment has included wallpaper of such and such a pattern, a squeaky chair, this stone fireplace, etc., etc. My having had *this* pattern of sense contents has usually eventuated in my having had *that* sense content, because having *this* pattern of sense contents guarantees, for example, that I am awake, not drugged, wearing my glasses, and looking at the fireplace. And a generalization which is an expression of the contingencies of my existence can scarcely be one of the generalizations which, in the intersubjective conceptual heritage of the race, support the phenomenally conditional sense contents postulated by the phenomenalist. Thus, even granting that there are inductively warranted generalizations which permit the definition of phenomenally conditional sense contents, the latter will be logically tied to the peculiarities of my environment in such a way that they cannot be transferred to other things in other places.

What the phenomenalist obviously *wants* is generalizations which will serve the same purpose as the familiar principles about what people generally experience in various kinds of circumstance, but which will not lead to circularity or vicious regress when put to phenomenalistic use. But these principles are *impersonal;* with qualifications which allow for individual (but in principle repeatable) differences, they apply to all perceivers. In other words, what the phenomenalist *wants* is generalizations, in sense content terms, which are *accidentally* autobiographical, generalizations in which the antecedent serves to guarantee *not* that I am in the presence of the *this individual* thing, e.,g., my fireplace, but rather that my circumstances of perception are of a certain *kind.* What he *wants* for his antecedents is patterns of sense contents which are the actual sense content counterparts of the kinds of perceptual circumstance which common sense expresses in the language of persons, sense organs, and physical things. The best he can *get,* however, are essentially autobiographical uniformities in which the antecedents, however complex, are the actual sense content counterparts of the presence to *this* perceiver of *these individual things.*

In pinpointing our argument to the effect that the phenomenal uniformities we actually can put our fingers on cannot serve the phenomenalist's purpose, we have had to neglect an equally telling consideration. Thus, we have permitted the phenomenalist to refer to perceivers and their personal identity in stating his phenomenal uniformities, without raising the objection that these concepts are part and parcel of the framework of physical things in space and time. We could do this because it is clear that the phenomenalist would simply retreat to the idea of an actual-phenomenal counterpart of a person, and there would have been no point in criticizing this notion until we had explored his account of the framework of phenomenal possibilities (conditionalities) with which the actual-phenomenal is to be supplemented in the reconstruction of the framework of persons and physical things alike. We are now in a position to press our offensive on a broader front. For if we are correct in asserting that autobiographical generalizations of the sort which could find support in the uniformities which have occurred in our sense histories could not authorize conditional sense contents required by the phenomenalist's analysis, we can now make the stronger point that these uniformities are precluded from serving as instantial evidence for these putative autobiographical generalizations. For these uniformities come, so to speak, with dirty hands. The burden of our argument to date has been that the framework of physical things is not reducible to that of actual and conditional sense contents. This means that the very selection of the complex patterns of actual sense contents in our past experience which are to serve as the antecedents of the generalizations in question presupposes our common-sense knowledge of ourselves as perceivers of the specific physical environment in which we do our perceiving and of the general principles which correlate the occurrence of sensations with bodily and environmental conditions. We select those patterns which go with our being in a certain perceptual relation to a particular object of a certain quality, where we know that being in this relation to an object of that quality normally eventuates in our having the sense content referred to in the consequent. Thus, the very principles in terms of which the uniformities are selected carry with them the knowledge that these uniformities are *dependent* uniformities *which will continue only as long as these particular objects constitute one's environment.* Hence, these principles preclude the credibility of the generalization in sense content terms which abstract consideration might lead us to think of as instantially confirmed by the past uniformities.

The fact that the noticing of complex uniformities within the course of one's sense history presupposes the conceptual picture of oneself as a person having a body and living in a particular environment of physical things will turn out, at a later stage of the argument, to be but a special case of the logical dependence of the framework of private sense contents on the public, intersubjective, logical space of persons and physical things.

One final remark before closing this section. It should be noticed that although the uniformities we have been considering are biographical facts about individual persons, there is a sense in which they imply impersonal truths about all perceivers. For we know that if *anybody* with a similar perceptual equipment were placed in our environment, (roughly) the same uniformities would obtain in his immediate experience. As is made clear by the preceding argument, however, this knowledge is not an induction from uniformities found in our immediate experience, but simply one more consequence of our framework knowledge about persons, physical things, and sense perception.

The New Phenomenalism

The view we have been discussing, and which we have called classical phenomenalism, has fallen from its high estate of a few short years ago. It has been explicitly abandoned by many of its most ardent proponents, including most of those who brought it to its present state of intricate sophistication by their successive attempts to strengthen it against ever more probing criticism. And these defections have by no means been offset by new recruits. One might therefore be tempted to conclude that the above tortuous argument was a waste of time, and that the task of exploring the whys and wherefores of classical phenomenalism should be left to the historian. There might be something to this contention if philosophers had abandoned classical phenomenalism for the right reasons and with clear understanding of its inadequacies. That this is not the case is the burden of the present section.

The point can best be introduced by noting that the decline of the claim that the framework of physical objects is "in principle" *translatable* into the framework of sense contents has been accompanied by the rise of the claim, often by the same philosophers, that even if such a translation is "in principle" impossible, nevertheless there is a sense in which only sense contents *really* exist. This new phenomenalism can best be understood by comparing it with a form of realism which is almost its twin.

In the early years of the century, certain philosophers in the Lockean tradition were wont to argue that the framework of physical objects is analogous to a *theory*. Just as it is reasonable to suppose that there are molecules although we don't *perceive* them, because the hypothesis that there are such things enables us to explain why perceptible things (e.g., balloons) behave as they do, so, they argued, it is reasonable to suppose that physical objects exist although we don't *directly* perceive them, because the hypothesis that there are such things enables us to understand why our sense contents occur in the order in which they do.

This neo-Lockean approach responded to the venerable challenge, "How can evidence in terms of sensations alone provide inductive reasons for supposing that sensations are caused by material things?" by granting that *instantial* induction cannot do the trick and appealing, instead, to that other mode of inductive argument so central to modern physical science, the "hypothetico-deductive method." I shall shortly be arguing that this appeal was in principle misguided, and that, to put the matter in the form of a paradox, a necessary condition of the success of the appeal is the viability of classical phenomenalism. Hypothetico-deductive realism can get off the ground only by granting all the premises of classical phenomenalism, which would mean, of course, that it only *seems* to get off the ground.

But before making a frontal attack on hypothetico-deductive realism, I shall first show how closely it is related to what I have called the new phenomenalism. The point is a simple one. The new phenomenalism can be regarded as that variant of hypothetico-deductive realism which accepts the claim, characteristic of positivistic philosophies of science, that theoretical entities are "calculational devices" and do not exist in the full-blooded sense in which observables exist. Just as certain philosophers of science were prepared to say that

> atoms, electrons, etc. don't really exist. Frameworks of so-called scientific objects are pieces of conceptual machinery which enable us to derive observational conclusions from observational premises. Frameworks of scientific objects cannot be translated into the framework of observable fact, not, however, because they refer to *unobservable* entities, but because the very idea that they refer to *anything* is an illegitimate extension to theoretical terms of semantical distinctions appropriate to the language of observable fact

so there is a current tendency, particularly among ex-phenomenalists of the "classical" variety to argue that

> although the framework of physical objects is not translatable into the framework of sense contents, this is not because it refers to entities over and above sense contents. It is merely a conceptual device which enables us to find our way around in the domain of what we directly observe, in a manner analogous to the

role played by scientific objects with respect to the domain of the observable in a less stringent sense of this word.

It is my purpose to argue that this won't do, *not*, however, on the ground that "real existence" should not be denied to theoretical entities —though, indeed, I agree that it should not[6]—but rather on the ground that the relation of the framework of physical objects to the framework of sense contents cannot be assimilated to that of a microtheory to its observation base. To see that this is so requires no more than a bringing together of certain themes from the preceding section of the paper with the standard account[7] of the relationship between theoretical and observational frameworks.[8]

According to what I have referred to as the "standard" account of the role of theories, a theoretical framework is an uninterpreted deductive system which is coordinated with a certain sector of the framework of observable things in such a way that *to each inductively established generalization in this sector there corresponds a theorem in the calculus, and to no theorem in the calculus does there correspond a disconfirmed inductive generalization in the observation framework.* The coordination is done by "correspondence rules" which are in certain respects analogous to definitions in that they correlate defined expressions in the theoretical framework (e.g., "average momentum of a population of molecules") with empirical constructs in the framework of observation (e.g., "pressure of a gas"). The correspondence rules provide only a partial coordination (a "partial interpretation") in that they are not strong enough to permit the derivation of rules coordinating the primitive expressions of the theory (e.g., "molecule") with observational counterparts.

There are many interesting facets to this account of the tie between theoretical and observational discourse. The one which is directly relevant to our argument, however, is expressed by that part of the above summary statement which has been put in italics, according to which the tie between theoretical and observational discourse is a matter of coordinating *inductive generalizations* in the latter with theorems in the former.

---

[6] I have argued this point most recently and, in my opinion, most effectively in [4].

[7] This "standard" account is the one associated with the names of Norman Campbell, Hans Reichenbach, Rudolf Carnap, and many others. A clear presentation is contained in Carl G. Hempel's monograph [1].

[8] For our purposes it will be sufficient to note certain formal features of the relationship. That the standard philosophical commentary on these formal features involves serious mistakes is the burden of [4], mentioned above.

The significance of this point should be obvious. To claim that the relationship between the framework of sense contents and that of physical objects can be construed on the above model is to commit oneself to the idea that there are inductively confirmable generalizations about sense contents which are "in principle" capable of being formulated without the use of the language of physical things. If the argument of the preceding section was successful, this idea is a mistake.

A few paragraphs ago I made the point that the new phenomenalism can be construed as that form of hypothetico-deductive realism which denies that theoretical entities "really exist." To this it can now be added that the success of the new phenomenalism presupposes the success of the old. Hence the new phenomenalism is either mistaken or superfluous; and if it is mistaken, neither classical phenomenalism nor hypothetico-deductive realism is available as an alternative.

Direct Realism: Causal versus Epistemic Mediation

What, then, is the alternative? Surely to scrap the premises that led to this impasse by affirming that physical objects are really and directly perceived and that there is no more basic form of (visual) knowledge than seeing physical objects[9] and seeing that they are, for example, red and triangular on this side. But to make this affirmation stick, it is essential to realize that it doesn't commit one to the view that the only items in visual experience which can be directly known are physical matters of fact. Thus it is perfectly compatible with the idea that people can directly know that there seems to be a red and triangular physical object in a certain place, and, I shall argue, with the idea that people can directly know that they are having a certain visual impression (e.g., an impression of a red triangle).

What can properly be meant by speaking of a knowing as "direct"? Clearly the use of the modifier is intended to imply that the knower has not inferred what he knows. But this is no mere psychological point. For one only knows what one has a right to think to be the case. Thus to say that someone directly knows that-p is to say that his right to the conviction that-p is not simply a matter of the availability to him of same-level evidence which would justify the inference that-p. The phrase "same-level" is intended to remind the reader that the rightness of some con-

[9] Including public flashes of light and other publicly perceptible visual phenomena.

victions that-p essentially involves the fact that the idea that-p occurred to the knower in a specific way. I shall call this kind of credibility "trans-level credibility," and the inference schema

X's thought that-p occurred in manner M
So (probably) p

to which it refers, as trans-level inference. The problem of spelling out the principles of trans-level inference and explaining their authority is a difficult one which far transcends the scope of this paper. The above remarks are at best an indication of the direction in which a discussion of the "directness" of direct knowledge would move. I cannot pass up the opportunity, however, to emphasize once again the inextricable mutual involvement of trans-level and same-level inference in the justification of empirical statements (matters I have discussed at length in [3]).

The distinction within visual perception between what is directly known and what is not must be carefully drawn if one is not to backslide into representationalism. Thus, although there is a sense in which my knowledge that this is a book and in all probability red and rectangular on the other side is an inference from my perception that this physical object is red and rectangular on this side, this fact must not be confused with the idea that my knowledge that this is a book, etc., is an inference from a "direct seeing" of a red, flat, and rectangular "surface." The perception that this physical object is red, flat, and rectangular on this side is a direct but limited perception of a physical object. Its limitations are characteristic of most visual perception, though they are minimized in such cases as the perception of a cube of pink ice.

Again, the fact that my knowledge that I am having an impression of a red triangle, or that there seems to me to be a red and triangular object over there, is more secure than my perception that this physical object is red and rectangular on this side does not impugn the latter's status as direct knowledge. For, first, the fact that on occasion I can infer that there is a physical object in front of me which is red and triangular on this side from the fact that there seems to me to be a physical object in front of me which is red and triangular on the facing side, or from the fact that I am having an impression of a red triangle, by no means requires that such knowledge is always a conclusion from such premises; and, second, both the framework of qualitative and existential appearings and the framework of sense impressions are parasitical upon discourse concerning physical things. The latter is obvious in the case of the framework of appearings; it is, I have argued elsewhere [3, Sections 60–62], equally true, if less obviously so, in the case of the framework of sense impressions.

On the other hand, while the direct realist rejects the view we have called classical phenomenalism, it is nevertheless phenomenalistic in a broad sense. For it holds that although things frequently appear other than what they are, they are as they appear to be under advantageous circumstances. Thus, to take an example adumbrated above, a pink ice cube is a directly perceived, public, cold, solid, smooth, pink physical object having the familiar thermal and mechanical-causal properties of ice. In advantageous circumstances it

> (a) appears to perceivers to be pink and cubical
> (b) is responsible for the fact that there appears to these perceivers to be a pink and cubical physical object in front of them
> (c) causes these perceivers to have impressions of a pink cube.[10]

Again, the phenomenal world, thus conceived, of public physical objects, sounds, flashes, etc., exhibits a lawfulness which is formulable in phenomenal terms, i.e., in terms of the directly perceptible qualities and relations of these objects. (Generalizations which are in this sense phenomenal must not, of course, be confused with the generalizations in sense content terms which we found to be snares and delusions.) And since there are such generalizations, it is here, rather than at the level of sense contents, that we find a *pou sto* for the apparatus of hypothetico-deductive explanation, the introduction of theoretical entities to explain why observable (phenomenal) objects behave as they do.

At this point it is imperative that our direct realism be sufficiently critical. And to make it so requires three steps which will be seen to be closely related as the argument proceeds. The *first* step is the abandonment of the abstractive theory of concept formation in all its disguises. In its simplest form this theory tells us that we acquire our basic equip-

---

[10] Much can be learned about the grammar of sense-impression talk by reflecting on the fact that we speak of Jones and Smith as having sensations of a red triangle. Could it be the same red triangle? The fact that it doesn't make sense to say that the sensations are of the same red triangle (except as an odd way of saying that they are having sensations of the same kind) is partly responsible for the doctrine of essences. The logical form of sensations is not, to use a crude schematism,

> xRy, i.e. (sensation) R (a red triangle)

but

> fx, i.e. sensation of the *of-a-red-triangle* kind.

ment of concepts from the direct perception of physical objects as determinately red, triangular, etc. Thus, we come to be able to think of an *absent* object as red by virtue of having directly perceived *present* objects as red. Having the concept of red presupposes the direct perception of one or more objects *as red*, the direct perception *that they are red*. This is at best a misleading half-truth. For while one doesn't have the concept of red until one has directly perceived something as red, *to be red*,[11] the coming to see something as red is the culmination of a complicated process which is the slow building up of a multidimensional pattern of linguistic responses (by verbal expressions to things, by verbal expressions to verbal expressions, by nonlinguistic behavior to verbal expressions, by metalinguistic expressions to object-language expressions, etc.), the fruition of which as conceptual occurs when all these dimensions come into play in such direct perceptions as that this physical object (not that one) over here (not over there) is (rather than was) red (not orange, yellow, etc.). Thus, while the coming to be of a basic empirical concept coincides with the coming to be of a direct perception that something is the case, the abstractive theory, as Kant saw, makes the mistake of supposing that the logical space of the concept simply transfers itself from the objects of direct perception to the intellectual order, or, better, is transferred by the mind as Jack Horner transferred the plum. The idea that this logical space is an evolutionary development, culturally inherited, is an adaptation rather than a rejection of Kant's contention that the forms of experience are a priori and innate. We are now able to see that his conception of the forms of experience was too narrow, and that nonformal patterns of inference are as essential to the conceptual order as the patterns explored by formal logic, Aristotelian or mathematical.

To nail down this point, we must take the *second* step toward an adequately critical direct realism. This step consists in the recognition that the direct perception of physical objects is mediated by the occurrence of sense impressions which latter are, in themselves, thoroughly noncognitive. The *third* step consists in stressing that this mediation is *causal* rather than *epistemic*.[12]

But beyond all these steps lies the discovery that the victory of direct

[11] A more careful formulation would add "unless it has appeared *that* there is a red object in front of one": for a child *could* be taught the use of color words by showing him objects of the wrong colors under conditions of abnormal illumination.

[12] For an exploration of historical critical realism, particularly that of the nonessence "wing" represented by Roy Wood Sellars, with an eye to these issues, see my essay [5].

realism, however critical, is a Pyrrhic one. For it is the correct analysis of a framework which doesn't really exist! The world of common-sense objects is a *phenomenon bene fundatum*, a conceptual projection of what there really is, which is of immediate practical utility, but which reveals its inadequacy when pressed into the service of more demanding questions. That *Dinge an sich* are knowable objects of scientific theory rather than unknowable objects of metaphysical theory enables the transformation of Kant's critical idealism into a realism, both critical and scientific, in which the current tension between *analysis* and *reconstruction* finds its proper resolution.

REFERENCES

1. Hempel, Carl G. *Fundamentals of Concept Formation in Empirical Science* (*International Encyclopedia of Unified Science*, Vol. II, No. 7). Chicago: University of Chicago Press, 1952.
2. Mill, John Stuart. *An Examination of Sir William Hamilton's Philosophy* (Third Ed.). London: Longmans, 1866.
3. Sellars, Wilfrid. "Empiricism and the Philosophy of Mind," in *Minnesota Studies in the Philosophy of Science*, Vol. I, Herbert Feigl and Michael Scriven, eds., pp. 253–329. Minneapolis: University of Minnesota Press, 1956.
4. Sellars, Wilfrid. "The Language of Theories," in *Current Issues in the Philosophy of Science*, Herbert Feigl and Grover Maxwell, eds., pp. 57–77. New York: Holt, Rinehart, and Winston, 1961.
5. Sellars, Wilfrid. "Physical Realism, " *Philosophy and Phenomenological Research*, 15:13–32 (1959).

S. S. STEVENS
ιιιιιι

Quantifying the Sensory Experience

Back in the days when I still nursed an on-again, off-again yearning to become a philosopher, one of the accidents that shape our aspirations took me to the third floor of Emerson Hall where E. G. Boring, Harvard's lone professor of psychology, directed a laboratory in what was then the department of philosophy. There I was destined to find a niche and acquire an obstinate interest in sensory psychophysics and the theory of measurement —subjects that are first cousins to epistemology. The philosophers proper dwelt on the first floor of Emerson Hall under lofty ceilings where thought and talk soared upward, as they must when great philosophers engage their students. There we heard lectures by A. N. Whitehead, C. I. Lewis, W. E. Hocking, R. B. Perry, and H. M. Sheffer. Later in the thirties, Emerson Hall played host to a parade of distinguished visitors, some of them bringing word of a new kind of positivism that fitted neatly with the operationism we had learned from P. W. Bridgman, over in the physics laboratory, and which psychologists had tried to adapt to the needs of a behavioristic outlook [15, 16, 17].

Rudolf Carnap joined the staff as visiting professor. Perhaps a little too shy to do the task himself, he suggested one day that I should try to gather a monthly discussion group composed of those whose interests could be said to overflow the fences surrounding their narrow professional specialties. Our strategy was to enlist a small committee of sponsors who would sign the invitation. We selected Herbert Feigl (who was at Harvard on a research fellowship), E. G. Boring, Philipp Frank, W. V. O. Quine, and J. A. Schumpeter, the economist. P. W. Bridgman led off as speaker on the first evening, October 31, 1940, and many sharp discussions followed, for the "science of science," as we called our topic, was an intense concern in the Cambridge of those days. That first evening produced a memorable turnout. As I recall it, Alfred Tarski was there from Warsaw, I. A. Richards from England, and George Polya from Zurich. The local crowd included mathematicians G. D. Birkhoff, E. V. Huntington, and Saunders MacLane. Nelson Goodman was there, along with G. K. Zipf, and several others. I tried to introduce each one to the rest of the assemblage. Amid a certain hilarity, Dr. Feigl was presented as the "chief public-relations counsel of logical positivism." I was only half joking, for even a score of years ago it was obvious that Feigl was a master of clear expression and a gifted expositor of philosophic inquiry.

Some people, I learned, do not nourish their minds by word of mouth. This was the penned response from our most distinguished historian of science:

October 19, 1940

DEAR MR. STEVENS,

I am very sorry not to be able to attend these interesting discussions. I am not the right man for them. I prefer to *read* and *write* than to *listen* and *talk*, and can do the former much better than the latter. It is true I teach, but only because I must; I would prefer not to teach orally but only by example—in cooperative work, even as a master craftsman teaches apprentices. I am sorry that I cannot be of use in your very laudable undertaking. *Vale.*

GEORGE SARTON

With the passing years I have come to value Sarton's point of view, but in those days the excitement of the philosophic ferment produced a heady intoxication, if not addiction. Who would want to miss hearing G. D. Birkhoff on the principle of sufficient reason, or Richard von Mises on the theory of probability, or L. J. Henderson on the hopelessness of social science, or Oskar Morgenstern on the theory of games? I do not recall the full list, but I cannot forget the pervading sense of high intellectual encounter.

The foregoing recollections are admittedly tangential to the theme of this paper, but they try to do two things. They tell how it was that I first met Professor Feigl and they help to explain why I came to regard the study of sensation as first cousin to epistemology. If there is a natural-science approach to epistemology, it probably begins with sensation, which by many accounts is an important source of knowledge.

On the first floor of Emerson Hall in the early thirties, we heard much about the immediate, private experience, exemplified in some discussions by the allegedly simple act: "I see red" (*not* in the figurative sense). We learned that in the beginning was the quale, the inside view of a conscious percept, and from it was said to stem all knowing. On the third floor we also talked about sense qualities, but our talk had the rough accents of natural science. We wanted to relate sensations to the stimuli that caused them, and (loftiest of ambitions!) we wanted to measure the magnitudes of the sensations produced by our lights and our sounds. No doubt more thinking took place on the first floor of Emerson Hall, but more observing took place on the third.

Only in 1934 did psychology get its own separate department. With its hardware, machine shop, and animal colonies, psychology had finally become too awkward a lump for philosophy to contain, even at Harvard, which was one of the last universities to effect this particular parturition. By that time the early behaviorists' denials of sensory contents had become passé, and it was once again admitted that sensations and perceptions can be acceptable objects of study. But for many of us the basic epistemology of behaviorism still retained its validity, if not its vigor, and there was a mounting concern for the formulation of a more sophisticated behaviorism—one that experimental psychophysics could live with. The "operational" approach seemed to provide the answer.

It is easy enough for the philosopher to speculate about immediate experience, the sensory given, the fundamental quale, and to set them apart from knowledge as a system of constructs. He may even try to distinguish between the "language of data" and the "language of constructs," as some of the logical positivists did at first. But the sensory psychologist, trying to work with the input-output functions of a sentient system, is apt to find these distinctions rather slippery, for the sensations he works with are constructs. They get into science by reason of their amenability to experimental manipulation. The psychophysicist really has nothing to say about private experience, and he usually avoids the embarrassment of making public statements about a private subject matter. Less embarrassment faces the physicist, it seems, for Bridgman liked to argue [1] that "in the last analysis science is only my private science." When Bridgman forsook physics and talked about epistemology, he, like many philosophers, tried to do psychology on himself, a procedure that provides a shifty, idiosyncratic basis for a discipline.

Operationism in Psychophysics

The study of sensation divests itself of many tangles, provided the distinction between experimenter and experimentee is carefully preserved. Max Meyer [7] gave us the slogan "the psychology of the other one," a forceful phrase that draws a safe guideline for scientific psychology. Of course, a given experimenter may use himself as a "subject," or as an "observer," but he ought properly to treat his own responses and reactions as he would treat those of any other observer. Controlled and reproducible responses may enter as facts into the scientific list, even though the experimenter was also the experimentee. Under this view, the meaning of sensation rests in a set of operations involving an observer, a set of stimuli, and a repertoire of responses. Sensations are reactions of organisms to energetic configurations in the environment. The study of sensations becomes a science when we undertake to probe their causes, categorize their occurrences, and quantify their magnitudes.

The foregoing assertions, I fear, come perilously close to sounding like the prologue to a "nothing-but" philosophy. Such is not the intent. Admittedly, however, a challenge is implied to those who claim there is "something more" to sensation than can be revealed by operations. We want to be told the evidence for the something more, because if one can point to it, either literally or figuratively, the operational psychologist will know (a) what is meant, and (b) how to start a study of it. I hope, however, that what I am trying to say puts me safely within the bounds of the philosophy made popular by Professor Feigl [3]: the philosophy of "what's what."

Here then are some of the *whats* that are *what* in an operational view of science. They constitute a kind of scientific epistemology.

1. Science, that curious hurly-burly of intellectual probing, makes progress to the extent that its models succeed in mapping the universe on paper. It is useful to distinguish here between the formal, analytic, syntactical statements of logic and mathematics and the empirical statements that result when parts of a formal discipline can be made to parade successfully as representatives of one or another empirical observation. By themselves, logic and mathematics are operationally empty. Wedded to observables by semantic definitions, they become the powerful models by means of which man exerts his scientific dominion.

2. Science is a public enterprise. Although Professor Bridgman and I

never settled our difference on this point, I think that Bridgman's "personal science" becomes science in the wider sense only when there is a degree of public agreement about it. Just as agreements regarding science fluctuate from week to week, so may knowledge or truth be said to exist only in a state of flux. The "true" value of a physical constant that we look up in a handbook is true only to the extent that physicists agree that it is true. When some physicist gets his colleagues to change their opinion about it, a new value becomes true and the old value becomes false.

3. To the extent that science does in fact become a matter agreed upon, we have implicitly accepted as competent the word of some experimenter or other. This seems simple and obvious enough as far as physics is concerned, but in psychology we have that dizzy possibility of making the experimenter himself the object of study. We are landed thereby in what has been called [18] the "experimenter-regress." In principle we can study the experimenter who studies the experimenter who studies . . . ad infinitum. In practice this regress terminates itself when an experimenter appears whom we do not question. Of course, we may question him tomorrow, or the next day, but while the case rests, his is the last word. He stands as the independent experimenter whose conclusions we trust—for the time being. This attitude toward the role of the experimenter accords with "the psychology of the other one," and it provides the escape hatch from the kind of subjectivity that has long frustrated a scientific epistemology. Any one man's assertions about sensory contents can be regarded either as final or as the occasion for instituting a study of the matter.

Fashions change rapidly in science (how else can the excitement hold its heat?), and operationism is some three decades old. It is not quite correct, nevertheless, to say that operationism has given way to something better. Those whom Feigl calls the "radical operationists," who would have a different concept for each operation, and who would thereby dissolve the world of concepts into a vicious particularism, may have run for cover. They have certainly been whipped often enough, but one mystery has long puzzled me. Who were the radical operationists? Who was it who would partition the world into an ever-expanding variety of discrete concepts without interconnection or logical coherence? The only such "radicals" I can find appear to have been liberally stuffed with straw. If the critic distorts the operational view by insisting that operations must be "all hands and no mind," in Bentley's phrase, and that no fabric of interconnected operational concepts can tie the scientific system together, then the critic will find it easy to rout the imaginary radicals. But, as I said, the operationists that have blood in their arteries seem to have no qualms about searching out the generalities, interconnections, and convergencies among their operations. In short, they try to behave like scientists. If they have a vice, it is perhaps an overactive passion for clarity.

The point was made elsewhere that operationism has no precepts about the scientific method, and no prescription for how to become a clever scientific discoverer. Discovery is a matter of human ingenuity. We can say of operationism as James said [5] of pragmatism, "It has no dogmas, and no doctrines save its method." Furthermore, the method is one that is applied after the fact: we inquire about the empirical content of what has been said. In other words, operationism hopes to test the meaning of scientific propositions, but it does not tell how to invent them.

Although operationism has been accused of a withering conservatism because it would presumably fetter the human fancy, this fear rests upon a misconception. Operationism is not opposed to meaningless statements, it merely provides a way of knowing whether they are indeed without meaning. Operationism is not opposed to hypotheses, or speculations, or heuristic models. There is no right or wrong to flights of fancy, whether emotional, religious, or poetic. All we ask in the laboratory is the privilege of trying to disengage the operationally meaningful propositions from those whose empirical content is not readily pinned down. Our freedom to test the meaning of speech must remain as firm as the freedom of speech itself.

Measurement

The study of sensation in the 1930's had more to contend with than purging its discourse of nonoperational meanings. It was important to get clear about the principal terms and their operational significance, but equally pressing was the need for a workable conception of what is meant by measurement. If the acoustical engineers were going to insist on having a scale of subjective loudness [11], it would be well to know what kind of measurement would be involved and how its operations would mesh with the classical dicta of N. R. Campbell [2].

Campbell gave us a liberal definition of measurement—it is the assignment of numerals to objects or events according to a rule of some sort—but his fixation on the empirical operations of addition landed him among the reactionaries when the British committee issued its now famous report [4]. In what sounds like a counsel of despair, Campbell lamented: "Why do not psychologists accept the natural and obvious conclusion that subjective measurements of loudness in numerical terms (like those of length . . .) are mutually inconsistent and cannot be the basis of measurement?"

Sensations cannot be laid end to end like measuring rods, but possibly there is something more basic to measurement than an accidental isomorphism between certain operations with rods and the syntactical manipulations known as mathematical addition. It is indeed possible that if, for one reason or another, no physical operation of addition could be performed, we would still have "ratio" scales of measurement—the kind used for measuring length, weight, density, work, and so forth.

Much as I was devoted to Campbell, the contagious enthusiasm of G. D. Birkhoff for the power inherent in the principle of invariance finally made me do an about-face. Instead of fixing our attention on the operations for measuring length, why not ask what group of transformations on the resulting scale will leave the scale form invariant? In other words, what can we do to the numbers of a scale without losing any of the empirical information on which the scale was based? With scales of length we can only multiply by a constant (as when we change from inches to centimeters); with temperature we can both multiply by a constant and add a constant (as when we turn Celsius into Fahrenheit). Therein lies the clue. Now we extend the principle to other kinds of measurements and forthwith it becomes possible to erect a kind of hierarchy of scales, each defined by a transformation group, as illustrated in Figure 1.

A fuller discussion of these scales will be found elsewhere [12, 14]. Here the point to be made is simply this. He who tries to legislate the admissible operations of measurement will impede matters only temporarily. Just as yesterday's experimenters learned how to change the measurement of temperature from exclusively interval scales (Celsius and Fahrenheit) to ratio scales (Kelvin and Rankine), tomorrow's experimenters will surely devise procedures not yet thought of. The question concerning the kind of measurement that will then have been achieved will rest with the test of invariance. From the point of view of preserving information, which transformations of the scale are permissible, and which are not?

As elsewhere in science, mathematics here provides us with a model—the number system. But we note that each class of scale uses a different

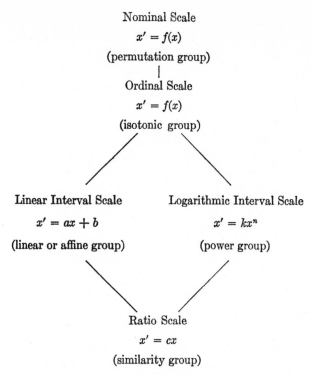

Figure 1. Hierarchy of scales.

selection from among the properties of the mathematical model. The isomorphism between mathematics and matter is never more than partial. In the theory of measurement itself, we neither need nor find the complete isomorphism that was thought to obtain in early times, when, for example, no distinction was recognized between formal number and empirical numerosity. A couple of centuries ago it was generally thought that numbers and pebbles (L. *calculi*) were by natural necessity related one to one, which is why negatives, surds, and imaginaries were so long resisted.

Sensory Measurement

What has all this to do with sensory measurement? Aside from quieting certain needless clashes over pseudoproblems, a clear conception of measurement serves to define the goal of a principal endeavor of psychophysics. We should like, if possible, to generate *ratio* scales of sensory intensity (loudness, brightness, and so forth). Why? Because then we may find out how the sensation grows as a function of various environmental variables, including, of course, the stimulus intensity. Scales less definitive than a ratio scale are not entirely useless, to be sure. We use nominal scales, in effect, when we name and classify the sensory qualities, and we make frequent allusions to the ordinal scale when we comment on degrees of warmth, cold, sweetness, and so forth. Curiously, the empirical evidence shows that the linear interval scale of sensory magnitude is the most difficult one to create experimentally. This need not embarrass us, however, because the interval scales are contained in the ratio scale, as are all the lower (more general) forms of scale.

If the big payoff lies in the ratio scale of sensory magnitude, how do we achieve it? A variety of operations have been employed [13, 19], but here there is space to tell about the results of only two: magnitude estimation and cross-modality matching. First, however, a distinction needs to be made between two kinds of continua.

Prothetic versus Metathetic

The prototypes of the two kinds of continua are exemplified by loudness and pitch. Loudness is an aspect of sound that has degrees of magnitude or quantity. Pitch does not. Pitch varies from high to low; it has a kind of position, and in a sense it is a qualitative continuum. Loudness is a prothetic continuum, and pitch a metathetic one. The criteria that define these two classes of continua reside wholly in how they behave in psychophysical experiments, but the names themselves are suggested by the nature of the physiological processes that appear to underlie each of them.

Sensory discrimination may be mediated by two processes: the one additive, the other substitutive. Additional excitation may be added to an excitation already present, or new excitation may be substituted for excitation that has been removed. An observer can tell, for example, when a light pressure becomes a strong pressure at a given point on the arm, and he can also tell when the stimulus is moved from that point to another location. Different sets of general laws govern these two types of sensory discrimination.

The metathetic, positional, qualitative continua seem to concern *what* and *where* as opposed to *how much*. They include such things as pitch, apparent position, apparent inclination, and apparent proportion. Perhaps they also include visual hue—at least to whatever extent hue may be made to behave as a continuum. All in all, the metathetic continua do not seem to constitute a neat and orderly class of perceptual variables, and as yet they have not been very thoroughly explored.

The prothetic continua, on the other hand, have lately yielded rich rewards for the systematic efforts made to scale their magnitudes. Some two dozen continua have been examined, always with the same outcome: the sensation magnitude ψ grows as a power function of the stimulus magnitude ϕ. In terms of a formula,

$$\psi = k(\phi - \phi_0)^\beta$$

In this equation, the constant k depends on the units of measurement and is not very interesting; ϕ_0 stands for the threshold below which nothing happens; and the value of the exponent β may vary from one sensory continuum to another. As a matter of fact, perhaps the most interesting thing about a sensory continuum is the value of the exponent β.

So rarely does it happen in psychology that a simple quantitative law can be shown to hold under many diverse circumstances, that the widespread invariance of the power law becomes a matter of acute interest. A law of this form seems to govern our reactions to light and sound, taste and smell, warmth and cold, vibration and shock—in fact, every continuum yet explored on which variations in intensity may be said to exist. As a general psychophysical law it provides a new aid to understanding and a new challenge to explanation.

Before we consider it further, a word is in order concerning the antecedent state of affairs.

The Older Psychophysics

G. T. Fechner, the father of psychophysics, had a different idea about the psychophysical law. Although he was aware of conjectures to the effect that the growth of sensation might be governed by a power law, he damned the notion from the start and fought stubbornly to the end for his famous and fallible logarithmic law. So well did he contend, in fact, that for almost a century Fechner's logarithmic law ruled the textbooks and the thinking in psychology and physiology.

Fechner's law, simple though suspect, is founded on the idea that sensation can be measured by counting its constituent units, thought by Fechner to be the just noticeable differences. The just noticeable difference between two stimuli—the resolving power, so to speak—is really a measure of variability or "noise." Since the noise usually turns out to be proportional to the stimulus magnitude itself (compare Weber's Law), it follows that the number of just noticeable differences (Fechner's scale of sensation) grows as the logarithm of the stimulus.

The Fechnerian attack on the problem of sensation was an assault from the rear, an indirect approach via resolving power, or least detectable differences [20]. The idea that measurement must be reducible to counting still prevailed in Fechner's time, and the older psychophysics was looking for something to count. William James objected that a sensation is a unitary thing and is not like a pile of blocks or a congeries of elements. Scarlet, he said, is not a collection of pinks. True enough; but must one necessarily conclude therefrom that sensations have no magnitude?

The new psychophysics takes the stand that sensation is analogous to many other scientific constructs to which measurement is commonly applied. For example, no one hopes to slice temperature into units that can be added or subtracted like measuring rods or counted like beans. We know the temperature of a body only through that body's behavior, which we note by studying the effects the body produces on other systems. It is much the same with sensation: the magnitude of an observer's sensation may be discovered by a systematic study of what the observer does in a controlled experiment in which he operates on other systems. He may, for instance, adjust the loudness in his ears to match the apparent intensity of various amplitudes of vibration applied to his fingertip and thereby tell us the relative rates of growth of loudness and the sense of vibration.

Magnitude Estimation

Perhaps the easiest way to elicit the relevant behavior from an observer is to stimulate his eye, say, with a variety of different light intensities, and to ask him to assign a number proportional to the apparent magnitude of each brightness, as he sees it. Most observers, once they understand the problem, carry out this process (known as magnitude estimation) with reasonable success. Not that all observers make the same estimates, or even feel any great confidence in their reactions, but the geometric mean of the results for a group of normal observers turns out to be remarkably stable and reproducible. After all, it is the reaction of the typical (median) observer that interests us here, for we are not concerned, at least at the out-set, with the fact that people differ, or that some are blind and some are photophobic. Psychophysics wants to know, first of all, the general form of the typical input-output operating characteristics governing the sensory systems.

To date, the observed values of the exponent in the relation $\psi = k(\phi - \phi_0)^\beta$ have ranged from about 0.33 for brightness to about 3.5 for the apparent intensity of electric shock applied to the fingers. The exponent of the power function determines its curvature. If the exponent is exactly 1, the function is a straight line, and the output (reported sensation) varies linearly with the input (stimulus magnitude). But when the exponent is greater than 1, the line representing the function ascends on an ever steeper slope. When it is less than 1, the curvature is the other way and the line becomes ever more horizontal.

These relations are illustrated in Figure 2, which shows examples of three perceptual continua, each having a different exponent. Electric current produces a sensation whose intensity grows more and more rapid-

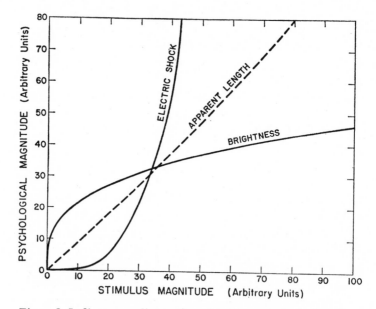

Figure 2. In linear coordinates the subjective-magnitude functions are concave upward or downward depending on whether the power-function exponent is greater or less than 1.0.

ly as the current increases, whereas brightness seems to grow less and less rapidly with increasing physical intensity. As we might expect, the apparent length of a line seems to grow very nearly in direct proportion to the physical length. One foot looks about half as long as two feet—not quite, it seems, but almost.

A felicitous feature of power functions is the form they assume when graphed in log-log coordinates (logarithmic scales on both axes). The plot of a power function then becomes a straight line, and the slope of the line is a direct measure of the exponent. We can see how this works out if we make a log-log plot of the same three functions shown in Figure 2. We find that the differences in curvature in Figure 2 become differences in slope in Figure 3.

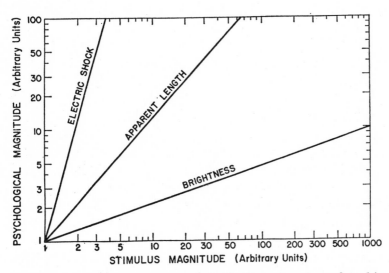

Figure 3. The same three continua shown in Figure 2 are here plotted in log-log coordinates. The slope of the line corresponds to the exponent of the power function that governs the growth of the sensory magnitude.

The nature of these power functions and the universality of their application testify to the existence of a profoundly simple relation between stimulus and sensory response: equal stimulus ratios produce equal subjective ratios. That is the essence of what I have ventured to call the psychophysical law. For example, it requires approximately a ninefold increase in energy to double the apparent brightness of a light, no matter where we start from in the first place. Doubling the apparent intensity of an electric shock requires an increase in current of only about 20 per cent, but this percentage increase is approximately the same all up and down the scale. On all continua governed by the power law, a constant percentage change in the stimulus (the value of $\phi - \phi_0$) produces a constant percentage change in the sensed effect.

Cross-Modality Validation

The curves in Figure 3, and many like them, were determined by asking observers to undertake, by one procedure or another, what amounted to a numerical estimation of relative sensory intensity. A scientist is properly uneasy about procedures that seem to rely on a mere expression of opinion and that seem also to depend on a fairly sophisticated acquaintance with the number system. (Naïveté about numbers is indeed a source of trouble with some observers!) But the question of greatest consequence concerns the issue of validation: Can we confirm the power law without asking observers for numerical estimations, and can we verify the predictions implicit in the type of functions plotted in Figure 3?

The nature of these predictions can most easily be expressed in terms of the lines in the log-log plots. If two sensations, loudness and vibration, grow by different exponents (slopes), then an experiment in which the observer matches loudnesses to vibrations for equal apparent strength should produce a matching function that is a straight line in log-log (or decibel) coordinates. Moreover, the slope of the line should be predictable from the two original slopes, and should, in fact, equal the ratio between the slopes.

An experiment of this kind gave a close approximation to the predicted results. Ten observers matched apparent loudness (which grows as the 0.6 power of the sound pressure) to apparent vibration (which grows as the 0.95 power of the amplitude), and produced a function whose slope was approximately 0.6, i.e., close to the ratio of 0.6 to 0.95. Figure 4 shows a plot of the data [10].

The success of this experiment and several similar ventures led to a bolder undertaking. If cross-modality matches can be made so easily, why not stimulate the observer through a sense organ and allow him to produce a matching sensory magnitude—apparent force—by simply squeezing a hand dynamometer? By exerting force on a precision dynamometer, an observer can produce a sensation of strain, and at the same time activate a dial indicating the physical force exerted. In effect, then, the observer is asked to report the apparent magnitude of brightness, loudness, electric shock, and so forth, by emitting appropriate squeezes instead of numerical estimates.

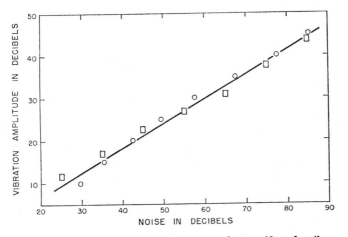

Figure 4. An equal-sensation function relating 60-cycle vibration on the fingertip to the intensity of a band of noise. The observers adjusted the loudness to match the vibration (circles) and the vibration to match the loudness (squares). The stimulus values are measured in terms of logarithmic scales (decibels).

The actual data for nine different prothetic continua, which the observers tried to match by squeezing, are shown in Figure 5. Two features of this plot are especially interesting. All the functions approximate straight lines, as the power law predicts they should, and the slopes vary from steep to flat in the manner expected. The function for electric shock rises most abruptly, proving that its exponent is large, whereas the function for brightness grows relatively slowly, proving that its exponent is much smaller.

So far so good, but a vital question remains. In order to complete the circle of validation and to exhibit all the compelling consistency that might be hoped for, we must ask whether the actual numerical values of the slopes in Figure 5 can be correctly foretold.

First, however, we must ask what happens when observers make numerical estimations of the apparent intensity or subjective force of their

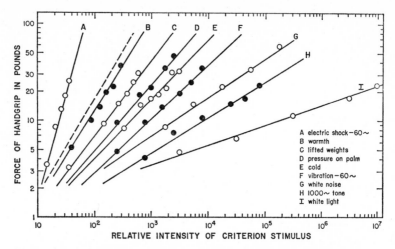

Figure 5. Equal-sensation functions obtained by matching force of hand-grip to various criterion stimuli. Each point stands for the median force exerted by ten or more observers to match the apparent intensity of a criterion stimulus. The relative position of a function along the abscissa is arbitrary. The dashed line shows a slope of 1.0 in these coordinates.

squeezes. In a careful and thorough experiment, my colleagues J. C. Stevens and J. D. Mack [8] found that the apparent force of handgrip grows as the 1.7 power of the physical force applied. With this factor available, we are equipped to pose the decisive question: If the slopes in Figure 5 are multiplied by the factor 1.7, do they then equal the respective values of the slopes obtained by the method of magnitude estimation? It turns out that, within close limits, they do [9]. Conversely, the slopes (exponents) of the lines in Figure 5 are nicely predicted by the magnitude estimations that had been made earlier. These comparisons are shown in Table 1.

Despite the variability of human reaction, despite the lack of high precision with which a given sensory effect can be gauged, and despite the inevitable fact of individual difference, it grows increasingly clear that there is a simple and pervasive law that controls the overall dynamics of sensory intensity. Encouraging and interesting as this may be, we are left, as always, with unanswered questions. Why the power law? Is this a form that is dictated, as R. D. Luce [6] has suggested, by a kind of mathematical necessity? And what about the physiological mechanisms involved

Table 1. The Exponents (Slopes) of Equal-Sensation Functions, as Predicted from
Ratio Scales of Subjective Magnitude, and as Obtained by Matching
with Force of Handgrip

Ratio Scale Continuum, with Exponent of Power Function	Scaling by Means of Handgrip		
	Stimulus Range	Predicted Exponent	Obtained Exponent
Electric shock, 60-cycle current (3.5)	0.29–0.73 milliamp	2.06	2.13
Temperature, warm (1.6)	2.0–14.5°C. above neutral temperature	0.94	0.96
Heaviness of lifted weights (1.45)	28–480 grams	0.85	0.79
Pressure on palm (1.1)	0.5–5.0 pounds	0.65	0.67
Temperature, cold (1.0)	3.3–30.6°C. below neutral temperature	0.59	0.60
60-cycle vibration (0.95)	17–47 db re approximate threshold	0.56	0.56
Loudness of white noise (0.6)	55–95 db re 0.0002 dyne/cm²	0.35	0.41
Loudness of 1000-cycle tone (0.6)	47–87 db re 0.0002 dyne/cm²	0.35	0.35
Brightness of white light (0.33)	56–96 db re 10^{-10} lambert	0.20	0.21

—can we look to them for further explanation of the psychophysical functions? The discovery of a general principle susceptible of confirmation by experimental test has the effect of generating a spiraling sequence of new challenges.

Epilogue

In measuring sensation and establishing for its growth a solid general law, we may ask whether in any sense we have penetrated the privacy of immediate experience—that common retreat of the introspective philosopher. Probably not, for an operation that penetrates privacy is a self-contradiction. Once we can expose a sense datum (which really turns out to be a construct) to the kind of public view that is implicit in performable operations, it no longer remains private. If one objects that there remains "something more" behind it all, and that our experiments have not penetrated the deeper essence, then we must retort with the tiresome query of operationism, "What is meant by this something more?" Point it out, please, and conceivably we may experiment upon it.

This operational attitude, which I think typifies the attitude of the working psychophysicist, resembles behaviorism minus the early phobias. Psychophysics involves the study of behavior, but there need be no forbidden terms. The operationist can be quite happy with so-called subjective notions like conscious experience, mental state, sensory attribute, or memory image, provided some rule can be given to guide him toward the objects or events that must exist in order for these terms to be applicable. Thus, if the phrase "immediate sense datum" turns out to find its application under a semantic rule that prescribes a human being confronted with a stimulus, then we know, to at least a first approximation, what operations are intended. The "bright datum" that my friend and colleague Donald Williams [21] claims to enjoy when he looks at the moon becomes to me a possible object of study and measurement. If Professor Williams could spare the time for the necessary cross-modality matchings, it might be possible to tell him precisely whether his moon datum is as bright as that of the normal (median) viewer of the moon. But this, I am sure, would not soften my colleague's cordial disdain for "positivistic philosophasters." For no matter how fully the scientist may lay hold on what has seemed to be the substance of the philosopher's discourse, there will ever stretch ahead an endless reach for the poetic surmise of metaphysical construction.

REFERENCES

1. Bridgman, P. W. *The Nature of Physical Theory*. Princeton, N.J.: Princeton University Press, 1936.
2. Campbell, N. R. *Physics: The Elements*. Cambridge: Cambridge University Press, 1920.
3. Feigl, Herbert. "Philosophical Embarrassments of Psychology," *American Psychologist*, 14:115–128 (1959).
4. "Final Report," *Advancement of Science*. 1940, No. 2, 331–349.
5. James, William. *Pragmatism*. New York: Longmans, Green, 1907.
6. Luce, R. D. "On the Possible Psychophysical Laws," *Psychological Review*, 66:81–95 (1959).
7. Meyer, M. F. *Psychology of the Other-One*. Columbia, Mo.: Missouri Book Company, 1921.
8. Stevens, J. C., and J. D. Mack. "Scales of Apparent Force," *Journal of Experimental Psychology*, 58:405–413 (1959).
9. Stevens, J. C., J. D. Mack, and S. S. Stevens. "Growth of Sensation on Seven Continua as Measured by Force of Handgrip," *Journal of Experimental Psychology*, 59:60–67 (1960).
10. Stevens, S. S. "Cross-Modality Validation of Subjective Scales for Loudness, Vi-

bration, and Electric Shock," *Journal of Experimental Psychology*, 57:201–209 (1959).

11. Stevens, S. S. "The Measurement of Loudness," *Journal of the Acoustical Society of America*, 27:815–829 (1955).
12. Stevens, S. S. "Measurement, Psychophysics, and Utility," in *Measurement: Definitions and Theories*, C. W. Churchman and P. Ratoosh, eds., pp. 18–64. New York: Wiley, 1959.
13. Stevens, S. S. "On the Psychophysical Law," *Psychological Review*, 64:153–181 (1957).
14. Stevens, S. S. "On the Theory of Scales of Measurement," *Science*, 103:677–680 (1946).
15. Stevens, S. S. "The Operational Basis of Psychology," *American Journal of Psychology*, 47:323–330 (1935).
16. Stevens, S. S. "The Operational Definition of Psychological Concepts," *Psychological Review*, 42:517–527 (1935).
17. Stevens, S. S. "Psychology: The Propaedeutic Science," *Philosophy of Science*, 3:90–103 (1936).
18. Stevens, S. S. "Psychology and the Science of Science," *Psychological Review*, 36:221–263 (1939).
19. Stevens, S. S. "Psychophysics of Sensory Function," in *Sensory Communication*. W. A. Rosenblith, ed., pp. 1–33. New York: M.I.T. Press and Wiley, 1961.
20. Stevens, S. S. "To Honor Fechner and Repeal His Law," *Science*, 133:80–86 (1961).
21. Williams, Donald. "Mind as a Matter of Fact," *Review of Metaphysics*, 13:205–225 (1959).

Part II

INDUCTION, CONFIRMATION, AND PHILOSOPHICAL METHOD

CHARLES E. BURES

\\\(J)J

Contextual Analysis

The central theme of this essay is an explication of the phrase "contextual analysis." This phrase is taken to be the name of a philosophical strategy, a guide both for constructing a philosophy and for philosophizing. An explication, it is assumed, results in a proposal. A proposal concerning a strategy suggests that it is fruitful or useful, perhaps even necessary, to pay attention to certain conceptual and actional landmarks in carrying out the strategy. A philosophical strategy, and it is assumed every intelligible philosophy has a strategy, exhibits under scrutiny certain "joints," or lines of distinction, the most salient of which form contexts. Contexts are problem areas considered important enough to be held distinct in a given philosophy. For example, "logic" and "psychology," "knowledge" and "science," are context-names.

The contexts of a given philosophical strategy are exhibited explicitly or implicitly in the philosophical vocabulary which is used for overt formulations of philosophical matters. The word "implicitly" is meant to suggest that a strategy is seldom fully exhibited. The present explication proposes that in addition to the subject matter referred to when philosophy is called "a formal theory of languages" there are cultural patterns and patterns of individual behavior which also are relevant to contextual analysis as a philosophical strategy. First, there are the patterns of behavior that form the cultural matrix out of which a philosophy is "carved" by assumptive decision and by which it is sustained as a human enterprise. Second, there are the patterns of behavior evoked by and judged relevant to the normative functions of philosophical vocabulary. Contextual analysis, as here explicated, requires one to pay attention both to linguistic and behavioral (presumed nonlinguistic) occurrences in their appropriate roles.

Every philosophy adopts a patterned orientation toward the fundamental conditions of human life. This patterned orientation has its origin in certain basic working decisions that a philosopher strives to make explicit. The most comprehensive of these working decisions are the guiding philosophical beliefs one adopts and uses concerning nature, human nature, and the procedures by which man knows anything reliably about nature and human nature.

As an illustration, a contemporary philosopher recently stated his orientation as follows: "In my conception of it . . . naturalism embraces a generalized account of the cosmic scheme and of man's place in it, as well as a logic of inquiry" [6, page 6]. To use the words of the same philosopher again [6, page 5], the threefold decision framework comprises "the expressed or tacit beliefs . . . concerning the overall nature of things" (that is, a conception of nature), "views on human destiny" (a conception of human nature, with its implications for human living), and "the scope of human reason" (a conception of reliable knowledge and the scope of the cognitive domain).

Philosophical decisions of such moment provide two kinds of functions for philosophical strategy. In the first place, the decisions themselves may be phrased as basic assumptions, or propositions. These assumptions have a primary position in the working domain of the philosopher for they carry the weight and determine the style and course of a philosophical position [6, pages 7–8]. Such assumptions are not empty of information. They arise out of the accumulated intellectual experience of men, and consequently they constitute the general content of a philosophy. For instance, if the decision is made to take scientific knowledge as a working conception of knowledge for one's philosophy, then one function of the decision is to describe the elements, the patterns, and the aim of the working conception.

In the second place, decisions may be viewed as a set of rules, or guiding principles, which underwrite the fundamental strategy for formulating and solving philosophical problems. This means that the basic working decisions prescribe that one is to set up philosophical problems along certain ground lines of organization. For example, when one has decided to use a certain conception of knowledge as a guide, then his philosophical procedure will tend to organize itself according to this conception. This means that problems will be conceived, styled, and carried toward solutions in ways that are conditioned by the guiding conception.

From this view of philosophical strategy, it follows that the decisions that lie at the basis of a philosophy may be viewed as playing two different intellectual roles. They function as assumptions or as guiding principles, depending on the orientation, or context, that is relevant for a given problem. If one is studying the manner in which the philosophy constructs a world view, then the decisions function as basic assumptions with content. If one is working with the philosophy, that is, using its orientation, then the decisions function as guiding principles. They have a normative function. These two interpretations of decisions form the working basis of the philosopher. Which interpretation is uppermost at any time depends on whether the emphasis is on the patterned orientation, the logical status, of the specific philosophy, or on the strategy for seeking, mapping, formulating, and solving philosophical problems.

Philosophical decisions do not originate in a vacuum of belief. They arise partly out of the common experiences of men, mostly out of the accumulated experiences of countless investigators in science and philosophy. It might be said that human nature abhors a cultural vacuum. Each philosopher cuts the warp of the historical-cultural process of his time, as he is acquainted with it. He selects the relevant strands for the texture (or con-texture) of his decisions on pivotal conceptions. Decisions stipulate, in a chosen vocabulary, the structure and the content of each fundamental area, or context.

To return to the historical-cultural process in which the original decision-making partition (or cross section) is made, it may be remarked that the concepts of culture and cultural process are increasingly moving into the area previously dominated almost entirely by the concepts of history and historical process. "Culture" and "history" are two important context-names in philosophy. The notion of culture is of significant aid in forming another important philosophical context, the context of common-sense belief. This context arises out of the fact that all specific cultures provide orientations for their members in all those situations where science and philosophy give no guidance at all as well as providing alternative beliefs and orientations for those situations in which science and philosophy do give guidance.

The definition of culture favored here is that of Ralph Linton. "A culture is the configuration of learned behavior and results of behavior whose component elements are shared and transmitted by the members of a particular society" [5, page 32]. Two aspects of this definition are stressed for present purposes. The first is the emphasis on learned modifications of human orientation and action. (The term "behavior" in the definition can be regarded as open, so that any psychological theory with an adequate account of learned modifications may substitute its own word.) The second emphasis is on sharing. Sharing cultural elements implies some form of transmission or communication. Sharing, communicating, learning, provide the core for the notion of common-sense belief.

A "common-sense belief" is any belief, held by an individual or a group, to which no explicit scientific or philosophical criteria of validity, or justification, have been applied by the carriers of the belief. The reference to "an individual" in this definition is simply instantial reference, that is, idiosyncratic, unshared beliefs held by any individual at a given time are not included as instances of this definition. It is assumed that effective idiosyncratic belief occurs rarely, if ever, as a "cognitive" or "empirical" orientation. If it does so occur, it can be added ad hoc as a singular subclass. The central idea in the notion of common-sense belief is that the holders of the beliefs in question hold them uncritically, and if they were challenged to justify them, they would attribute their status to something other than scientific or philosophical criteria of justification. Since, it is assumed, every individual begins life in such a common-sense context, each individual begins his scientific and philosophical experience in this context. He departs from it only as he espouses the critical apparatus and standards of science and philosophy. The common-sense context is a basic matrix of contextual analysis. (It should be remarked that the reservoir of common-sense belief is gradually changing and being augmented by feedback from scientific and philosophical belief, but innovations in this context are again held uncritically in the aggregate.)

An example of common-sense belief, primarily relative to scientific standards of certified belief, concerns the belief of mothers in a certain Central American culture that when a child is ill, all solid food should be taken from it. This shared belief encountered the protein deficiency condition named kwashiorkor. Removal of all solid food from a child with kwashiorkor tends to remove any remaining protein, with possibly fatal consequences. Scientific practice, represented in this case by an international organization, introduced the critically assessed belief that relatively small amounts of powdered milk would reverse the disease state. This example displays an uncritically held common-sense belief meeting a critically held scientific belief. Of greatest relevance to contextual analysis is the manner in which these classes of beliefs flow, through individual or shared policy, into conception, attitude, orientation, and action.

A scientific or philosophical system, with its elements functioning in either the descriptive or normative role, serves as a set of critical standards which can be applied to such uncritical, common-sense beliefs, for specified purposes. (The definition of "common-sense belief" is deliberately set relative to such cognitive standards.) Application to such a belief or practice of scientific procedures of analysis, reformulation, and inquiry, or of philosophical procedures of explication, contextual assignments, analysis, and justification moves a belief out of the ruck of common sense. More accurately, it moves a belief out for those who share the critical results with insight and understanding. It is possible to hold scientific or philosophical beliefs and share them—uncritically. This happens when such beliefs diffuse through a culture to become common-sense beliefs. Common-sense belief stands at the borderline of the kind of norm-relevant orientation significant for science and philosophy.

It will be assumed here that a philosophical context requires, as one condition of its contextuality, that specific beliefs reach the stage of explicit linguistic formulation, however arrived at. In this sense, when the relevant beliefs are formulated, the domain of common-sense belief becomes a significant philosophical context. John Dewey has commented on the systemic aspect of shared cultural habits, contrasting it with scientific systematizing of language: "While all languages or symbol-meanings are what they are as parts of a system, it does not follow that they have been determined on the basis of their fitness to be such members of a system . . . The system may be simply the language in common use. Its meanings hang together not in virtue of their examined relationship to one another, but because they are current in the same set of group habits and expectations. They hang together because of group activities, group interests, customs and institutions. Scientific language, on the other hand, is subject to a test over and above this criterion. Each meaning that enters into the language is expressly determined in its relation to other members of the language system. In all reasoning or ordered discourse this criterion takes precedence over that instituted by connection with cultural habits" [1, pages 49–50].

The anchoring of common-sense beliefs in cultural settings permits introduction of a working principle called "the range of credibility." The range comprises three categories arranged on a line. At one extreme is located common-sense belief. At the other extreme are located scientific and philosophical beliefs adjudged certified or justified according to shared specified standards of the respective domains. The middle range, which may be called "heuristic belief," recognizes that critical application of the vocabularies and analytic techniques of science or philosophy results in formulations which may be believed by some individuals (and on which they may have to act) before the beliefs are adjudged fully accredited. A reasonable claim can be made that a majority of the beliefs on the basis of which individuals in any culture make decisions and take action are of the common-sense or heuristic type, predominantly the former.

These three kinds of belief status share with all other distinctions of a philosophical order (and in the present case, especially contextual distinctions) the significant normative function of calling attention to features of cognitive material that are ignored under penalty of confusion. Confusion is the antithesis of specificity of contextual orientation.

The anthropologist A. Irving Hallowell has written that man lives in a "culturally constituted behavioral environment." Every individual is born into a specific ongoing culture, and this culture gives him a five-fold set of basic orientations [2, pages 89–110].

The first of these important cultural contributions is self-orientation. Through namings and concrete actions each individual member of a culture is given a manner of relating other persons and other cultural elements to himself. This could not be achieved without some common sociopsychological functions of language. As Hallowell puts it: "A personal existence and sphere of action is defined as a fundamental reference point" [2, page 89]. In a complex culture it is very unlikely that any single individual is aware of (or shares) a major fraction of his culture's significant elements. A second contribution of any culture is orientation to a sorted and varied world of objects. Here too language is indispensable. Third, human action requires orientation in space and time and each culture, in its own way, constitutes these for the individual. The needs of men must be satisfied through oriented actions. This requires patterns of action in relation to surrounding objects. Motivational patterns are the fourth contribution of culture to the orientation of the individual. Finally, all cultures provide their members with values, ideals, standards, norms. Since all things, including self, are appraised in one way or another, these normative orientations are essential to any culture. An understanding of this fivefold endowment reveals that cultures provide working models for living and believing which sustain and support human life, and provide the matrix out of which both science and philosophy do their proper work.

Ernest G. Schachtel has written eloquently about a problem that arises after an individual has undergone cultural orientation. After emerging from the postuterine period of primary autocentricity, the individual develops into his culture's orientative patterns, moving into a stage called "secondary autocentricity" by Schachtel. This way of life is judged necessary for the individual up to a point, but it may develop into a closed, stagnating kind of embeddedness. In Schachtel's words: "The anxiety of the encounter with the unknown springs not only from social pressures toward conformity, i.e. from the fear of transcending the socially accepted views of life and the world. It arises also, perhaps primarily, from the person's fear of letting go of the *attitudes* to which he clings for safety, of the *perspectives* which these attitudes give him on the world, and of the familiar *labels* for what he sees in the world" [7, page 195]. Since this may happen to individuals, and even be shared by groups ("shared autocentricity"), it becomes of interest to the present thesis. One may become embedded in orientations, in particular meanings, attitudes, beliefs, perceptions, actions, and so on. If philosophy (and similarly science) were to admit all norm-relevant behavior, oriented by their cognitive symbols, as a part of their proper domain, then fixity of this type would be of direct concern to them as a negative condition on their progressive, revisionist standpoints.

When an individual philosopher constructs his philosophy, he works within a cultural heritage of which he is a part. He absorbs from this heritage a set of orientations, a belief system. In the long tradition of Western philosophy, a conception of knowledge has always held a primary position. By the same token it will be assumed here that the basic strategy of contextual analysis rests on a conception of knowledge as a primary decision. It is simplest to consider only the case of a unitary conception of knowledge, that is, the claim that there is only one kind of knowledge available to man. However, dualistic conceptions of knowledge have been common in Western thought.

A unitary conception of knowledge, as the first decision, provides three normative functions. First, the conception of knowledge serves as a criterion of selection for both heuristic and certified knowledge. A philosopher is, however, responsible for insight into both sides of this partition, common-sense "knowledge" on one side, heuristic and certified knowledge on the other. Second, one proceeds philosophically to map the groundlines and furniture of the world on this basis. It is assumed that the content of the philosopher's views comes from identifiable sources, and the kinds of information mapped by the range of credibility give content to the matrix. The third main legislative function of the adopted conception of knowledge brings philosophy into a close relation with psychology, namely, a mapping of human nature. Psychology, as presently culturally constituted, is one source of heuristic and certified knowledge for a philosopher's conception of human nature. On the present proposal, the conceptions of nature and human nature so constructed will have both descriptive and normative functions.

With a conception of knowledge, one can proceed to the *primary cognitive context*. To set up this context, one sets up a situation containing a *reference-knower*. As in some forms of traditional epistemology, this reference-knower is any human being considered as a knower in the sense of knowledge adopted. The name "reference" indicates that either a typical or an actual individual is being referred to. Since the individual performing the contextual construction (i.e., the writer or the reader doing the referring) is a philosopher, he will be called an *observer-knower*. It is, then, assumed that the observer-knower is engaged in philosophical construction or inquiry of some kind, and it will be assumed that the reference-knower is either a scientist or a philosopher.

An observer-knower, as philosopher, will map the situation of the reference-knower in some specific vocabulary. A specific symbolism is in this way exhibited. Now the adopted conception of knowledge, with its norm-relevant actions in mind, in principle permits a partition of the reference-knower's behavior into cognitive and noncognitive orientations and actions. Relevance to the normative function of the adopted conception of knowledge is explicit in the name "cognitive orientation." Granted the partition into cognitive and noncognitive sections, if the philosopher (as observer-knower) fastens his attention exclusively on the cognitive side of the partition in his mapping, he is restricting himself to the primary cognitive context. An alternative way of putting the matter is to state that the philosopher is constructing the reference-knower and his situation in terms of cognitive orientations and actions. This approach forces one to consider whether he can map this primary cognitive context entirely in terms of certified knowledge or not. The range of credibility provides the other possibilities.

Contemporary philosophical discussion usually pushes on to the decision that symbolism is indispensable to the conception of knowledge. This decision adds to the primary cognitive context the detail of cognitive symbolism and all relevant formal apparatus and distinctions. The reference-knower mapped in the primary context may be an analytic philosopher who believes that "philosophy" and "analytic philosophy" are synonymous terms. His action arena consists of orientations restricted to a specified technical range of symbol-complexes and their controls (usually other symbol-complexes). The explication of contextual analysis here conceived proposes that the reference-knower's knowledge-relevant actions, ranging from the main partition into cognitive and noncognitive through all norm-relevant actions occasioned by his restricted symbolic domain, be included in the subject matter of contextual analysis. The responsibility of the philosopher in this way extends to whatever he needs to refer to in constructing and working with his philosophical orientations. For example, if he talks of "rational behavior," he should be able to recognize rational behavior if he encounters it.

If the reference-knower is mapped as exclusively oriented to (attending to) his cognitive symbolism, thereby ignoring all behavioral concomitants, this restricted domain is a legitimate concern of the philosopher. It may be called a *frame cognitive context*, where "frame" is a name indicating a contextual restriction to cognitive symbolism. It is short for "frame of reference."

Further detailed construction of contextual analysis will not be attempted in this essay. The name "context" has been reserved for the most general conceptual lines of distinction made in philosophies, whereby the subject matter and the activities are sequestered into patterns. The main point of the essay has been to indicate that philosophical practice does not fruitfully limit itself to abstracted symbolism alone, symbolism carefully and anesthetically stripped even of the behavioral concomitants it orients. Actual practice only rarely and extremely achieves this symbolic chastity.

One important philosophical consequence of the inclusion of norm-relevant actions in contextual analysis is the possibility of *purposive definition*, where "purposive" is used in the sense of contemporary motivational theory. For example, if one selects, following Robert Merton, the extension of certified knowledge as the main aim of science, one can define the range of application of the names "science" and "scientific" in terms of contributions in principle to this end. Similarly, one can give a purposive definition of "cognitive symbol," assuming a cognitive context has been set up, as *any identifiable sign-design possessing an explicitly specifiable function in the relevant context*. The name "purposive definition" is applied to such patterns. Some of the customary difficulties in defining contextual terms like these arise from too narrow a limitation of the materials allowable.

But there are many interesting wider issues also. Recent discussions of creativity, mainly by psychologists or psychoanalysts, such as Koch, Kubie, Fromm, Maslow, Rogers, Schachtel, and Rugg, have clearly shifted the emphasis from creative *product* to creative *process*. Current conceptions of science, for example, even in the educational phases, would hardly include as a proper part of the subject matter of the nonbehavioral sciences Kubie's preconscious process [4] even though it may be conceived as the basis for scientific thinking and creativity. But it is not hard to imagine a steady sociocultural pressure, generated by significant progress in the understanding of such cognition-relevant behavior, which in time might force incorporation of the "psychological conditions" of scientific progress into the purview of a conception of science. This is an example of the type of analogical thinking which has influenced the present explication of contextual analysis. A deeper appreciation of the family of contexts used by the philosopher indicates that he may include human behavior as relevant to the cognitive norms implicit in his contextual distinctions and contents without usurping the proper tasks of the psychologist. The judgment, for example, that certain exhibited behavior fits one's conception of "rational behavior" is a different contextual problem from the customary orientation of the psychologist to the same sample of behavior. The proposal that the philosopher has responsibility for some aspects of actually exhibited behavior is not idle chatter. If one takes seriously the remarks of some psychologists and some anthropologists

CHARLES E. BURES

that they expect to absorb all of man's philosophical orientations into their disciplines, then perhaps the problem is an ecological problem of survival for philosophers!

Koch has referred to the orientation of psychological conceptions and theoretical structure today in these words: "the immense power of those schematisms which at some rock-bottom level regulate psychological thought" [3, page 631]. If the word "philosophical" is substituted for the word "psychological," the resulting statement may stand for the power ascribed to contextual analysis in this essay.

REFERENCES

1. Dewey, John. *Logic: The Theory of Inquiry.* New York: Holt, Rinehart, and Winston, 1938. Quoted by permission.
2. Hallowell, A. Irving. *Culture and Experience.* Philadelphia: University of Pennsylvania Press, 1955.
3. Koch, Sigmund. "Psychological Science versus the Science-Humanism Antinomy: Intimations of a Significant Science of Man," *American Psychologist*, 16:629–639 (1961).
4. Kubie, Lawrence S. *Neurotic Distortion of the Creative Process.* Lawrence, Kans.: University of Kansas Press, 1958.
5. Linton, Ralph. *The Cultural Background of Personality.* New York: Appleton-Century-Crofts, 1945.
6. Nagel, Ernest. *Logic without Metaphysics.* Glencoe, Ill.: The Free Press, 1956.
7. Schachtel, Ernest G. *Metamorphosis.* New York: Basic Books, 1959.

RUDOLF CARNAP

\\(JJ)

Probability and Content Measure

1. On Knowledge and Error

Before I begin the discussion of questions about probability and content measure, in which my views differ from those of Karl Popper, I should like to emphasize that I agree to a large extent with Popper's views on *general* questions of the theory of knowledge and the methodology of science, as represented in his *Logic of Scientific Discovery* [8] and especially in two more recent papers.[1] The picture he draws of a sharp contrast between his conception and that of the "empiricists" (or "positivists," as he frequently says) is not correct as far as my conception is concerned.

First, I agree completely with Popper's criticism of classical rationalism and classical empiricism inasmuch as both regard the source of knowledge in question (reason or senses, respectively) as "authoritative," i.e., as yielding definitive certainty. There was indeed a tendency in this direction in my book *Der logische Aufbau der Welt* (1928, but written in 1924–1925, before I came to Vienna) and later in Schlick's paper "Das Fundament der Erkenntnis." But in the Vienna Circle, I always emphasized, together with Neurath and the majority of the other members, that every factual statement is not certain (in the strict sense of this

---

[1] [9], reprinted as Introduction in [6]; and [10], Sects. I–X (pp. 215–233), and [6], Addenda, Sect. 2, pp. 388–391. Compare also [7], Sect. VI, and my reply in [3], Sect. 31, pp. 995–998.

NOTE: This paper is a revised version of a discussion memorandum which I contributed in December 1962 to the discussions on probability at the Minnesota Center for the Philosophy of Science. The paper was written in a period of work supported by a grant from the National Science Foundation.

word) but may always be subject to re-examination and modification. I further agree with Popper that all knowledge is basically guessing, and that the scientist has the task, not of going beyond guessing in order to come to certainties, but rather of improving his guesses.

In this paper I shall leave aside the question of the nature of the theory which I call "inductive logic." This theory is not, as Popper thinks, in contradiction to my conception in matters of general methodology as indicated above, but, on the contrary, is based on this general conception. In my view, the purpose of inductive logic is precisely to improve our guesses and, what is of even more fundamental importance, to improve our *general* methods for making guesses, and especially for assigning numbers to our guesses according to certain rules. And these rules are likewise regarded as tentative; that is to say, as liable to be replaced later by other rules which then appear preferable to us. We can never claim that our method is perfect. I say all this only in order to make quite clear that inductive logic is compatible with the basic attitude of scientists; namely, the attitude of looking for continuous improvement while rejecting any absolutism. However, in the present context I cannot go into the details of these questions. I believe that my paper [1] gives an exposition of my view on the nature of inductive logic which is clearer and from my present point of view more adequate than that which I gave in my book [2]. This exposition emphasizes especially the application of inductive logic to the choice of a rational, practical decision, e.g., with respect to a bet, a business investment, or any other action whose outcome is uncertain.

2. Probability and Content Measure

In this paper I intend to explain my views on a special problem which Popper has discussed, namely, the question how a good scientist or a reasonable businessman or engineer chooses his hypotheses, i.e., the suppositions on the basis of which he makes his practical decisions; and especially the question how this choice is influenced by taking into consideration the probability or the content measure of a hypothesis. Here I understand the term "probability," like Popper, in the sense of logical probability, either as absolute (Popper's $P(x)$, my m-function) or relative to a given evidence (Popper's $P(x,y)$, my c-function). I use for $P(x)$ sometimes also the term "initial probability of x" (instead of the ambiguous term "a priori probability" in the traditional language). If e is the total evidence which the observer possesses at the present moment, then let us call $P(x,e)$ "the present probability of x."

For the purpose of this paper, it is not essential what we take as the exact definition of "content measure." I shall here, for the sake of simplicity, follow Popper in defining the content measure (for which he uses the term "content") as the reciprocal of the initial probability:[2]

(1) $Ct(x) =_{df} 1/P(x)$.

I wish to emphasize that I use in this definition the *initial* probability $P(x)$. This seems natural because the amount of information conveyed by x is not changed by the evidence e, while the probability *is* changed. (It is also possible to introduce the *relative* measure of content of x with respect to e, as I have done in [4]. But this is not a measure of the content of x itself, but rather of that part of the content of x which is not contained in the content of e.)

Now Popper asserts the following:

(2)   The larger the probability of a statement, the smaller its content measure.

With this I certainly agree, provided that we mean here initial probability. Obviously the definition (1) yields the following:

(3)   If $P(x) > P(z)$, then $Ct(x) < Ct(z)$.

But when a scientist considers a hypothesis x, be it a physical or biological law or a prediction, and in this context speaks of its probability, then he is thinking not of $P(x)$, but of the present probability $P(x,e)$. Therefore he might interpret the thesis (2) as follows:

(2')   If $P(x,e) > P(z,e)$, then $Ct(x) < Ct(z)$.

However, (2') is not generally valid. It is indeed valid in the special case that logical implication holds in one direction between the two hypotheses x and z under comparison:

(4)   If z L-implies x, but x does not L-imply z, then
        (a) $Ct(x) < Ct(z)$,
        (b) $P(x) > P(z)$,
        (c) For any evidence y (not L-false), $P(x,y) \geqq P(z,y)$.

[2] In my terminology I distinguish between "content" and "content measure" (or "measure of information"). A statement specifying the *content* of x is an answer to the question of *what* is said by x (this may be explicated, for example, by the class of the non-L-true sentences which are L-implied by x). A statement giving the content *measure* tells us *how much* is said by x. In [4] I proposed two different explicata for

An implication relation of the kind indicated holds in many of the cases occurring in the discussions on content measure and probability; we shall later give examples of this kind. Therefore, in these cases (2') holds. But it is important to be aware that this is in general not the case. (On the other hand, the assertion (2') would be valid for the *relative* measure of content.)

Now we come to the question which property of a hypothesis makes it preferable if there is a choice among several hypotheses. For the sake of simplicity let us consider a situation where the choice is between just two proposed hypotheses. There are under discussion the following two rules:

(5a)   Choose the hypothesis with the higher content measure.
(5b)   Choose the hypothesis with the higher probability.

On the basis of (2) Popper thinks that these two rules are incompatible. Sometimes he gives the impression of defending rule (5a). At any rate he believes that Keynes, I, and others plead for (5b). Actually I would reject both rules if formulated in this simple form. Elsewhere I have discussed a rule like (5b)[3] which advises choosing among incompatible hypotheses the one with the highest probability. There I show in detail, with the help of examples, why a rule of this kind should be rejected. I think that most of the authors who at the present time use a concept of subjective or personal probability would likewise reject (5b) for similar reasons. I am in agreement with Popper's emphasis on the importance of the content measure for judging hypotheses and for choosing a hypothesis. And it is true that there are special cases in which the simple rule (5a) is valid, e.g., those in which the content measures of the two hypotheses differ but the other relevant factors are equal and among them, in particular, the probabilities. Thus I would agree with the following rule as a modification of (5a):

(6a)   If two hypotheses have different content measures, while their probabilities (and other circumstances) are equal, then choose the hypothesis with the higher content measure.

this concept. I called the first one "content measure" and defined it by $P(\sim x)$ or $1 - P(x)$; the second, under the term "measure of information," was defined as $\log_2 (1/P(x))$. This distinction is not essential for the present discussion. In assimilation to Popper, I shall use here the first term, with a simplified version of the second definition. (The two definitions just given are also mentioned by Popper as alternatives.)

[3] See the discussion of rule R_2 in [2], Sect. 50C.

But then I should like to point out that the counterpart to this rule is likewise valid:

(6b)   If two hypotheses have different probabilities but their content measures (and other circumstances) are equal, then choose the hypothesis with the higher probability.

If (2) were unrestrictedly valid, then obviously the conditions in rule (6a) would be impossible, and likewise those in (6b). Thus each of the two rules would be inapplicable. The same holds if *relative* content measure is used. However, these rules are here to be understood in my sense of the terms as explained above; that is to say, the content measure is understood as constant (not changing with growing evidence), and probability is understood in the sense of present probability. Thus the rules are to be interpreted as follows (for the sake of simplicity I omit reference to other circumstances):

(7a)   If $Ct(x) > Ct(z)$, and $P(x,e) = P(z,e)$, then choose x.
(7b)   If $P(x,e) > P(z,e)$, and $Ct(x) = Ct(z)$, then choose x.

Here in each of the two rules the two conditions are compatible, as we shall see in an example.

3. An Example

I shall now show with the help of a simplified example that higher content measure (in my sense) is not always associated with lower probability, but may also be associated with equal, and even with higher, probability.

When I consider the application of the concept of probability in science then I usually have in mind in the first place the probability of predictions and only secondarily the probability of laws or theories. Once we see clearly which features of predictions are desirable, then we may say that a given theory is preferable to another one if the predictions yielded by the first theory possess on the average more of the desirable features than the predictions yielded by the other theory.

Suppose that a practically acting man X, say an engineer, asks a theoretician (in this case, a meteorologist) for a prediction h of the temperature at this place tomorrow at noon, a prediction to be based on a comprehensive body of evidence e available today. X intends to use the prediction in order to make an adjustment of a certain apparatus which he will leave at this place so that the apparatus will automatically carry out something tomorrow at noon, say, take a photo or register the results of certain measurements. X is aware of the fact that it is impossible for him to obtain information today about the exact temperature for tomorrow noon; what he asks for is merely an interval prediction of the form "the temperature will be between n and m," where n and m are integers interpreted as degrees of the Fahrenheit scale. Let us assume that for the given place and time only temperatures between 0 and 100 are to be expected. Let us further assume that the hundred unit intervals of this total interval have equal initial probability; hence for each hypothesis h for a unit interval $(n, n+1)$, $P(h) = .01$. For any hypothesis h, with an interval (m, n) of the length $l = n - m$, the following holds. First, $P(h) = 1/100$; thus the initial probability is proportional to l. Then we have by (1): $Ct(h) = 100/l$; that is, the content measure is inversely proportional to l. Intervals of equal length have equal initial probabilities and equal content measures. We assume that X knows these values. The evidence

Table 1. Values for Four Hypotheses

Hypothesis (h)	Interval	Length (l)	P(h)	Ct(h)	P(h,e)
h_1.........	(70,71)	1	.01	100	.04
h_2.........	(69,72)	3	.03	33	.12
h_3.........	(86,87)	1	.01	100	.01
h_4.........	(84,89)	5	.05	20	.05

e available today to the theoretician may include many results of previous meteorological observations which are relevant for the hypotheses to be predicted, including the weather situation of today. We assume that the theoretician has rules for the computation of logical probability. With the help of these rules he calculates, on the basis of the given evidence e, a probability density function for the temperature tomorrow at noon. Let us suppose that this is a normal function with the mean 70 and the standard deviation 10. Then the P-density at 70 is 0.04, and at 86.5, 0.01. If h is a hypothesis with an interval of a small length l, with the center point 70 (or 70.5), then $P(h,e)$ is approximately 0.04 l; and similarly, if the center point is 86.5, then $P(h,e) \cong 0.01\ l$. Hence we obtain the values in Table 1 as examples.

Now I shall show—which really should be obvious—that, if X applies either rule (5a) or rule (5b), and thus bases his choice either on content measure alone or on probability alone, he will sometimes be led to choices which are clearly wrong. Since the maximum of the density is at 70, an interval which includes this point is clearly preferable to an interval far away from this point. But each of the rules (5a) and (5b) is in many cases in conflict with this common-sense consideration. Suppose X always follows rule (5a). Thus, when given the choice between the two hypotheses h_2 and h_3, he will prefer h_3 because this is a more precise prediction and therefore has a greater content measure than h_2. (The relative content measure $Ct(h,e) = 1/P(h,e)$ has the value 8 for h_2 and 100 for h_3; thus it would lead even more strongly to the wrong preference.) On the other hand, let us suppose that X always heeds rule (5b). Then, if he has to choose between h_1 and h_4, he will have to choose h_4 because the present probability of h_4 is higher than that of h_1.

We can also easily see now that increase in content measure (in my sense) is not incompatible with increase in present probability. For example, in comparison to h_4, the hypothesis h_2 has both higher content measure and higher present probability.

The most important point is the following. Any prediction with an interval whose center point is at or close to 70 is preferable to any prediction with an interval around 87 or any other point removed from 70. Thus we recognize that the feature which is primarily important is the *location* of the interval; its length is also of interest, but only secondarily. In other words, what is primarily important is the probability density itself (more exactly speaking, the mean density in the interval in question), while the probability and the content measure are only of secondary importance.

4. The Optimum Interval Hypotheses

In view of our preceding considerations, we may now disregard the intervals which do not include the point 70. Then furthermore, among the intervals which include this point, we shall restrict our attention to a still narrower class, namely, that of the *optimum intervals*. We call an interval hypothesis h optimum if there is no other hypothesis h′ which is preferable to h either according to rule (7a) or according to (7b). Thus, for example, the hypothesis with the interval (65,75) is optimum. For if h′ is any other hypothesis with an interval of the same length 10, but with a different (present) probability, e.g., the interval (68,78), then the probability of h' is lower and therefore h is preferable according to rule (7b). And if h'' is any other hypothesis which has the same probability as h (or a nearly equal but somewhat lower probability) but a different content measure (i.e., different length), then the content measure of h'' is smaller than that of h (the interval is longer than that of h) and therefore according to (7a) h is preferable.

In Table 2 I shall give for a few selected values of $P(h,e)$ the length l' of those symmetrical intervals around the mean (here 70) for which the present probability, in other words, the integral of the probability density over the interval, has exactly the value of $P(h,e)$ given in the first column. (These values of l' can be taken from any table for the probability integral, i.e., the integral of the normal density.) These values l' refer to a continuous scale. But in our example we have restricted ourselves to a discrete scale with only integers as values. Therefore we have to take here an interval with integer boundaries and with an integer value l close to the calculated value l', as stated in the table. (Since our scale is discrete, the optimum interval is often not uniquely determined.

Table 2. The Optimum Interval Hypotheses for Some Values
of the Present Probability

$P(h,e)$	l'	l	Optimum Interval
.5	13.4	13	(64,77)
.6	16.8	17	(62,79)
.7	20.8	21	(60,81)
.8	25.6	26	(57,83)
.9	32.8	33	(54,87)
.95	39.2	39	(51,90)
.98	46.6	47	(47,94)
.99	51.6	52	(44,96)

For any odd length l there are two optimum intervals: for example, for $l = 3$, both the interval (69,72) and the interval (68,71); both interval hypotheses have the same content measure and, because of the symmetry of our curve, equal probability. In order to have a unique optimum interval, we make the arbitrary convention that for the length $2n + 1$ we shall take the interval $(70 - n, 70 + n + 1)$.)

Thus we restrict our consideration now to the class of optimum interval hypotheses. In this class (made unique by convention as indicated above) the following holds. Of any two distinct optimum intervals one is included in the other. Therefore of any two distinct optimum interval hypotheses, one of them L-implies the other. Hence, theorem (4) is now applicable. And therefore, within the restricted class, Popper's thesis (2') is valid, since all cases in which (7a) or (7b) would be applicable are now excluded through the restriction to optimum intervals. In this special situation we can thus increase at most one of the two magnitudes, either probability or content measure, but not both. Are now Popper's views here correct, first the view that we have to make a choice between two alternative methods, namely, either aiming at high probability or aiming at high content measure, and second the view that a good scientist would always choose the latter method?

It seems to me that in this situation it would be wrong simply to aim at high content measure; but it would also be wrong to aim at high probability. Both high content measure and high probability are valuable features of a hypothesis. But it is unreasonable to increase as much as possible either the one or the other of the two magnitudes. The reasonable procedure consists in making a compromise solution. To some extent it is good for X to aim at high content measure provided that he does so within reasonable bounds. If X were to disregard bounds, then he would choose the interval (70,70) of length zero and hence with infinite content measure. But clearly this would be unreasonable; the probability would be zero, and that means that it would be almost certain that the chosen prediction is false and that the actual temperature lies outside of the chosen interval and therefore his adjustment would not fulfill its purpose. On the other hand, X might well aim at a high probability, but here again he must be careful to remain within reasonable bounds. Otherwise he would take the total interval, with probability one. But thereby he would disregard the experience collected so far, and that would be clearly unreasonable. In order to act reasonably he must take into consideration the known experiences, and he must make his arrangements in such a way that they take care of the situation as well as possible with respect to the possible temperatures. In the case last described he would adjust also to very high and to very low temperatures, although both of them are practically excluded, and thereby he would make his arrangements inefficient.

5. Utility

The conflict between striving for high content measure and striving for high probability is merely a special case of the following general kind of situation. Frequently in our life we have to make a choice between different things or actions of such a kind that we are motivated by two conflicting tendencies. We find two different features of which each is desirable; but the situation within the given class of cases among which we have to choose is such that, generally speaking, the higher the degree of the first feature, the lower the degree of the second. In situations of this kind, rules which advise us to choose either the maximum degree of the first feature or the maximum degree of the second feature, as rules (5a) and (5b) do, are inappropriate. The reasonable solution consists in trying to find a suitable compromise; that is to say, in choosing a thing which has a fairly high degree of both features. But how shall we determine the exact point at which the two conflicting tendencies are, so to speak, in balance? In those situations where, for any possible action, we know which of the possible outcomes that concern us directly (e.g., gain or loss of money, things, time, health, and the like) will result from the action, the answer can easily be given: we should choose that action whose outcome has the maximum utility. In general, however, the situation is such that for each of the possible actions different outcomes are possible, and we do not know which of these outcomes will actually occur. In a case of this kind we should choose that action for which the expectation value of the utility of the outcome is a maximum. The expectation value is the weighted mean of the utilities of the different outcomes, each utility value of an outcome being multiplied with a factor which is to be taken higher the more reason we have to expect just this outcome to occur. As Ramsey and de Finetti have shown, if we wish to act in a reasonable way, these factors must satisfy the axioms of the calculus of probability (compare my [1], statement 6, pages 307–308). This use of probability values may be regarded as the basic role of the concept of probability (the term "probability" understood, as generally in this paper, in the sense of either logical probability or personal probability).

We must now recognize that the discussions in the preceding sections of this paper concerning the choice of a hypothesis have only a limited validity, because they left utility out of consideration. Suppose that someone asks himself the question: "Shall I accept the hypothesis h that my house will burn down at some time during the next year, or shall I rather accept its negation h'?" If he disregards utility considerations, then he would presumably accept the hypothesis h', because it seems to be a more natural choice than the assumption h that his house will burn down. However, the acceptance of h' would lead him to the decision not to take out fire insurance; and this would clearly be unreasonable.

In our previous example, X must take into account the gains or losses he would have in each of the hundred possible cases with respect to the temperature tomorrow if he were to adjust his apparatus in accordance with one or the other of the interval hypotheses among which he has to choose. For each of these hypotheses X will calculate the expectation value of his gain (counting a loss as a negative gain). Then X should accept as a basis for his adjustment of the apparatus that hypothesis for which the expectation value of the gain is a maximum. (This is my rule R_4 in [2], Section 50E; in Section 51A of the same work I explain in detail a further refinement, rule R_5, which advises maximizing the expectation value not of the gain but of the corresponding utility. For our present discussion we may leave out of consideration the distinction between gain and utility.)

6. Hypotheses of Purely Theoretical Interest

So far I have discussed the problem of the choice of a hypothesis with respect to a practical decision to be taken by the man X, where the decision together with unknown circumstances in the environment of X will lead to a tangible gain or loss. But what about the choice of a hypothesis in the case not of an engineer or another man concerned with practical actions but of a theoretical scientist? For example, X may be an astronomer who considers an astronomical prediction in a situation where he does not intend to base any practical decision on the hypothesis, and therefore there is no tangible gain or loss connected with the acceptance of the hypothesis. In my view it would be advisable not to talk about the acceptance of this or that hypothesis in a situation of this kind, at least not if we wish to make a more exact analysis of the situation. It is true that it is customary to speak in terms of acceptance. But in my view this is an oversimplification which, though in general harmless, should still be avoided if we wish to see the situation more clearly. Instead of saying:

"Among the given hypotheses h_1, h_2, etc., I choose the hypothesis h_1," it would be better to say: "I assign to the hypothesis h_1 a high probability" (and, if possible, in more exact terms: "the probability with the numerical value q_1"), "to the hypothesis h_2 a smaller probability" (and again, if possible: "the numerical value q_2"), and so on. For X to pick out one of the hypotheses and to declare that he accepts it would give only a crude indication of the knowledge that X possesses with respect to the matter in question. A more exact description of his knowledge is given rather by the specification of the probability values, say by a specification of a probability distribution over the values of a certain magnitude (e.g., the probability density of temperature in our previous example). It is frequently said that actual scientists never make such ascriptions of probability values to their hypotheses. But I think that this is not quite correct. It is true that in the period of classical physics this was not frequently done. Today, however, a physicist would very frequently give a probability distribution for a magnitude. (I am speaking here of a probability distribution in the logical sense, characterizing his knowledge with respect to given evidence; I am not speaking of the likewise frequently occurring but quite different case where a physicist gives a probability distribution of a certain magnitude in the statistical, empirical sense, namely, as indicating frequencies to be expected.) He may give the probability distribution either for a particular empirical magnitude, e.g., the length A of the great axis of the orbit of the earth around the sun, or for the value of a general parameter which occurs in one or several basic laws, e.g., the velocity of light c. In cases of this latter kind we have to do with a constant, e.g., A or c. Therefore it makes no sense to speak about frequencies. There is only one value; but the exact value is not known, and for this reason the physicist gives a probability distribution. He does this frequently by a statement of the following form: "$k = 0.356 \pm 0.0012$." This statement is not meant as a declaration of the acceptance of the interval (0.3548, 0.3572) but rather as a specification of a probability distribution (which may for instance be interpreted in the following way: "The probability density for k on the basis of the available evidence is the normal function with mean 0.356 and standard deviation 0.0012"). But even if it were true that at the present time no scientist would ever give a specification of probability values (in the sense indicated) for hypotheses of theoretical science, then I would still say that it is advisable to do so, because this is a better method of formulating the knowledge situation than the formulation in terms of acceptance.[4]

REFERENCES

1. Carnap, Rudolf. "The Aim of Inductive Logic," in *Logic, Methodology, and Philosophy of Science: Proceedings of the 1960 International Congress,* Ernest Nagel, Patrick Suppes, and Alfred Tarski, eds., pp. 303–318. Stanford, Calif.: Stanford University Press, 1962.
2. Carnap, Rudolf. *Logical Foundations of Probability.* Chicago: University of Chicago Press, 1950; second ed., 1962.
3. Carnap, Rudolf. "Replies and Systematic Expositions," in [11], pp. 859–1013.
4. Carnap, Rudolf, and Yehoshua Bar-Hillel. *An Outline of a Theory of Semantic Information.* Cambridge, Mass.: Research Laboratory of Electronics, Massachusetts Institute of Technology, 1952. Reprinted in Bar-Hillel, Yehoshua, *Language and Information: Selected Essays.* Reading, Mass.: Addison-Wesley, 1964.
5. Jeffrey, R. C. "Valuation and Acceptance of Scientific Hypotheses," *Philosophy of Science,* 23:237–246 (1956).
6. Popper, Karl R. *Conjectures and Refutations.* New York: Basic Books, 1962.
7. Popper, Karl R. "The Demarcation between Science and Metaphysics," in [11], pp. 183–226. Also in [6], pp. 253–292.
8. Popper, Karl R. *The Logic of Scientific Discovery.* New York: Basic Books, 1959.
9. Popper, Karl R. "On the Sources of Knowledge and of Ignorance," in [6], pp. 3–30.
10. Popper, Karl R. "Truth, Rationality, and the Growth of Scientific Knowledge," in [6], pp. 215–250.
11. Schilpp, Paul Arthur, ed. *The Philosophy of Rudolf Carnap.* La Salle, Ill.: Open Court, 1964.

---

[4] Elsewhere I have stated my reasons against the view that the end result of an act of inductive reasoning is the acceptance of a hypothesis (see the last paragraph of Sect. 25 in [3]; cf. Jeffrey [5]). And I have tried to show that the changed point of view makes it possible to give an answer to Hume's skeptical objection against induction (see the last two paragraphs of my paper [1]).

ANTONY FLEW

\\(\JJ\)

Again the Paradigm

Herbert Feigl recently collaborated with Grover Maxwell in a typically
forthright and good-humored article, "Why Ordinary Language Needs
Reforming" [11]. On this occasion I do not want to take issue with anything they said there. But that article can serve as excuse for returning
here once again to the questions of the nature, power, and limitations of
the Argument of the Paradigm Case (APC). This argument, even in its
most general form, is only one element in that loose agglomeration of
general ideas, methodological policies, and stock moves which is often
bundled up and labeled the Philosophy of Ordinary Language (POL).
That in turn can be seen as one manifestation of the conception of philosophy as an enquiry concerned essentially, but in its own special way,
with language [6]. It would, therefore, at a superficial level, be a mistake
to think that to explode this argument is necessarily a short way to under-
mine all those general ideas, methodological policies, and stock moves
which together characterize the POL, or even to dispose of "Linguistic
Philosophy" in general. On the other hand, at a deeper level, once it is
appreciated how fundamental are the principles to which the APC appeals, and how immediately it rests upon them, it does become at least
difficult to see how you could reject this particular element without becoming at the same time committed to rejecting not only the whole of
the POL but also the entire generic conception of the nature of philosophy under which that falls as a species. So it was not unreasonable
for Watkins [16], and later Gellner [7], to think that if they could get
rid of the APC they could also say goodbye to a whole lot else besides.

INDUCTION, CONFIRMATION, AND METHOD

What I have to say is very trite and very obvious. The only possible excuse for taking up space with such stale and elementary stuff is that fundamental points have recently been overlooked, confused, or even denied: first, in Watkins's rollicking outburst "Farewell to the Paradigm Case Argument" [16] and also in some of the ensuing controversy in *Analysis*[1]; and, second, in Gellner's sustained and bitter polemic *Words and Things* [7]. This latter work has been very warmly welcomed by many, including the author of its preface, who should have known better. It is always tedious to have to reiterate pedestrian truisms. In the present case it is a partly appropriate consolation to reflect on the First Maxim for Balliol Men: "Even a truism may be true."

1. In the *Analysis* controversy the starting point of most of the participants seems to have been an important article by Urmson [15] and a paragraph or so in two papers of mine [4, 6], all reprinted in 1956. The perspective might with advantage be deepened to include Moore's defense of common sense. This is the classic modern use of paradigm case arguments. So it is as it should be that some of the most important contributions to the discussion of the APC are to be found in that monumental volume *The Philosophy of G. E. Moore* [13]. All the discussions there of Moore's defense of common sense are to some degree relevant and valuable here. But perhaps it would be most useful in the present stage of the argument to look back to Norman Malcolm's "Moore and Ordinary Language" [10].

In this Malcolm starts by listing twelve philosophical paradoxes. This gets us off on the right foot. The APC is peculiarly relevant to the treatment of extreme paradoxes. It is as well to appreciate this from the beginning, especially in view of the peculiar weight of the emphasis in the statement made by Eveling and Leith at the end of the *Analysis* controversy: "If this is so then the PCA [= APC] has *some* force. It does present a valid argument against a *paradoxical* thesis" [2, page 152]. The emphasis is peculiar, though the statement is otherwise unexceptionable, because it is precisely against paradoxical theses that the APC has in fact been deployed.

---

[1] In addition to the paper by Watkins, there was a reply by me [5] and a rejoinder by Watkins [17], all in the same issue. These were followed in numbers 4, 5, and 6 of the same volume by contributions from R. Harré [8], H. G. Alexander [1], and H. S. Eveling and G. O. M. Leith [2]. R. J. Richman's 1961 article [12] was originally read at the Christmas meeting of the Pacific Division of the American Philosophical Association at the University of Oregon in 1958, and so belongs to the same controversy.

Malcolm's list of such theses includes many old favorites: "There are no material things," "Time is unreal," "No one ever perceives a material thing," and "All that one ever sees when he looks at a thing is part of his own brain." In each case Malcolm suggests the type of disproof which Moore might have offered. Thus to the first of those cited the reply comes: "You are certainly wrong, for here's one hand and here's another; and so there are at least two material things." To the second the reply is: "If you mean that no event ever follows or precedes another event, you are certainly wrong; for after lunch I went for a walk, and after that I took a bath, and after that I had tea." And so it goes on; right through the full dozen.

Malcolm's thesis is "that what Moore says in reply to the philosophical statements in our list is in each case perfectly true; and . . . that what he says is in each case a good refutation, a refutation that shows the falsity of the statement in question." In each case, Malcolm maintains, Moore is in effect reminding us of the ordinary and everyday uses of the key words and expressions. Thus in one instance Malcolm says: "What his reply does is to give us a *paradigm* . . . just as in the case previously discussed his reply gave us a paradigm of seeing something not a part of one's brain" [10, pages 349 and 354]. But what is the purpose of this reminder?

2. The first value of an appeal to the standard example—the paradigm case—is purely elucidatory. In this aspect it could scarcely be impugned by any serious philosopher. But in this aspect it could hardly be called an argument either. However, when one is dealing with extreme paradoxes the elucidatory appeal to the standard example cannot in practice be separated from the argumentative APC.

When confronted with some apparently bizarre assertion, what could be more elementary and more prudent than to begin by probing its meaning with instances? And in such a case obviously the more central, the more standard, the instances the better. The protagonist of the paradox is thus challenged to make clear, both to others and to himself, what he is really up to. The chances are that, when forced in this way to face the issue squarely, he will no longer be so willing to commit himself unequivocally and without reservation to the full implications of his original words, construed in their ordinary acceptation. The philosophical hero prepared to try to take the full logical consequences of his paradoxes with his eyes open is largely a figure of legend. The man of our ordinary human clay will usually begin to hedge or to haver. He may explain that, actually, he means something different: perhaps it is not the existence of hands and furniture and suchlike which, really, he wants to deny, but only some fellow philosopher's analysis of material thing propositions. Or, again, he may admit that the implications of what he said are intolerably paradoxical, but insist nevertheless that the arguments which led him to say it seem to him ineluctable and compulsive. But in all such cases, assuming that the first paradoxical assertion was not the product of mere carelessness or linguistic incompetence, the elucidatory appeal to standard examples has been tacitly construed as an APC and accepted as a refutation.

3. The logical form of the appeal to standard examples, considered as an argument, consists in two steps. The first is a matter of insisting on some plain matter of fact: that there are chairs and tables in the universe around us; that things do happen one after another, or simultaneously; that so far from its being the case that we never see anything but our own brains, the fact is that few of us ever have seen or ever will see any part of our own brains even in a mirror; and so on. The second consists in the assertion that the examples presented just are paradigm cases of whatever it is which is required to show the paradox in question to be false. As that famous Broadway philosopher Mr. Damon Runyon might have said: "If this is not a so and so it will at least do until a so and so comes along."

Obviously this sort of refutation must be quite decisive: provided, of course, that the plain matters of fact are indeed matters of fact; and provided that they do indeed constitute paradigm cases of whatever it was that the original paradox denied. Nevertheless it may be felt to be as a philosophical argument unsatisfactory and incomplete. Certainly it would be most unsatisfactory to leave the matter there. No philosopher worthy of the name would be content to leave it at that. We must go on to examine the intellectual sources of the paradox, to seek out the false assumptions and the invalid arguments which have misled reasonable men to preposterous conclusions. Through doing this we may expect to make philosophical discoveries: thus by studying the arguments which suggested the extreme paradox of the unreality of time we can hope to find out something, less exciting but true, about the logic of time expressions. Yet to point out, what in fact no "keen PCA-man" seems ever to have denied, that the application of an APC is only a begin-all and not a be-all and end-all of a satisfactory treatment of such paradoxes is in no way to diminish its vital importance as a begin-all [8, page 96].

It may also be thought that there is something wrong or insufficient about this sort of refutation unless it is possible to provide some informative general account of the occasions on which an APC is or is not applicable. But there is no reason at all why there should be any general account, beyond the uninformative statement that an APC will be appropriate wherever the two provisos can in fact be met. To speak here of common sense would not be very helpful, unless all that was meant was that judgment is required. Insofar as the expression *common sense* is used to refer to collections of beliefs it will take no tricks for us. Since it is certainly used in this sense by different people, in different places, and at different periods to cover very different ideas, some of them certainly mistaken, it would not be clear what was being defended or on what grounds the common sense of any particular time and group was to be taken as immaculate.

Talk of common sense in this context might also seem to give some ground for the suspicion that to believe in the value of an APC on occasion is necessarily to be committed to an indiscriminate philosophical complacency, prejudging every possible question in the conservative sense. Probably it was this rather than any restriction of interest to the metaphysically sensational which led Watkins to complain: "As I understand it, the Paradigm-Case Argument is a knock-down recipe for killing every interesting philosophical thesis stone dead" [16, page 26]. Certainly this is one of Gellner's main charges against his straw monster "Linguistic Philosophy," which he defines in terms of commitment to the APC and three other pillars.

4. Though the employment of an APC as a refutation on any occasion where the two preconditions of its decisiveness are satisfied is not a move which demands any further justification, Malcolm offers an illuminating supplementary rationale for one very important subclass of those occasions. His contention is that the philosophers putting forward the paradoxes which Moore challenged were all in effect urging that some ordinary forms of speech must always be inapplicable; presumably because these were supposed to presuppose or to embody a self-contradiction. The reason why these philosophers were able to deny, and to deny so confidently, the reality of time, matter, or what have you was that they thought they had shown that the very ideas were self-contradictory. Now,

Malcolm argues, Moore's response to this sort of thing is, as far as it goes, on the right lines. But it is, he urges, incomplete, in that it does not go to the roots of the trouble by tackling the sources of the paradoxes. And it is unsatisfactory in that it does not bring out the nature of the error involved. "His reply does not make it clear that what the paradox does is to attack an ordinary form of speech as an incorrect form of speech, *without disagreeing as to what the empirical facts are*, on any occasion on which that ordinary form of speech is used" [10, page 367].

Malcolm is careful to underline that he is not denying that on occasion everyone may happen to be mistaken about a matter of fact. It is wryly distressing to notice that the first illustration he gives is the very one which has since become a favorite with those hoping for a quick and easy triumph over the POL in general and the APC in particular. He considers the objection: "At one time everyone said that the earth was flat, when it was actually round. Everyone was mistaken; and there is no reason why in these philosophical cases the philosophers should not be right and everyone else wrong." His answer is: "The way in which their statement was wrong was that they were making a mistake about the facts, not that they were using incorrect language, they were using perfectly correct language to describe what they thought to be the case. In the sense in which they said what was wrong, it is perfectly possible for *everyone* to say what is wrong" [10, page 356].

Malcolm's point is that it is not similarly possible for everyone to be mistaken about the correct use of words. If an expression is the one customarily employed to describe a certain recognized state of affairs then it must *ipso facto* be the correct one to use: "ordinary language *is* correct language" [10, page 357]. To this Malcolm adds two further observations. The first is: "One thing which has led philosophers to attack ordinary language, has been their supposing that certain expressions of ordinary language are self-contradictory." In a footnote he is bolder: "I think that this is really behind *all* attacks upon ordinary language" [page 358]. Attacks on this ground are egregiously misguided: "The proposition that no ordinary expression is self-contradictory is a tautology . . . We do not *call* an expression which has a descriptive use a self-contradictory expression." The point is developed around the example of "It is and it isn't," used as an answer to the question "Is it raining?" The moral drawn is: "Whenever a philosopher claims that an ordinary expression is self-contradictory, he has misinterpreted the meaning of that ordinary expression" [page 359].

The second observation is made in answer to the earlier objection that "it does not follow from the fact that a certain expression is used in ordinary language that, on any occasion when people use that expression, what they say is true" [page 360]. Certainly there are plenty of expressions where this applies. But there are also other "expressions the meanings of which must be *shown* and cannot be explained . . . it follows, from the fact that they are ordinary expressions in the language, that there have been many situations of the kind which they describe; otherwise so many people could not have learned the correct use of those expressions" [page 361]. Although the key expressions in several of the paradoxes in his initial list pretty clearly belong to the class of those the meanings of which have to be shown, Malcolm is cautious not to claim that the same holds wherever a philosopher launches a paradoxical attack upon the alleged impropriety of some expression for which ordinary language provides a use.

(It is worth noticing that in his Wittgensteinian emphasis on the question of what people could and could not have learnt Malcolm is making the traditional empiricist assumption—which is, presumably, empirically true—that all our knowledge of the meanings of words is in fact the acquired result of learning. This assumption is not strictly essential for reaching Malcolm's conclusions. Regardless of how a person in fact acquired his present capacity to use the expressions, he could not truly be said now to know their meanings unless he was now able to recognize as such at least some standard cases of their correct applicability. But this he could not be able to do, as he in fact can, were they indeed self-contradictory. This point, which we cannot develop here, is obviously important: for instance, in dealing with an extreme Cartesian skepticism about the external world. For it would seem that such a skepticism can only be formulated and expressed at the price of in some way making assumptions incompatible with itself. If the skeptic can understand what he is saying he must be in a position to know what he is saying he does not know.)

5a. If Malcolm's insistence that "ordinary language *is* correct language" is to be rendered defensible the qualification *descriptive* has to be inserted, and heavily emphasized. What he says holds good only of descriptive as opposed to evaluative language. For it is certainly not legitimate to infer from "This is what everyone who knows the facts calls good" to the conclusion "This is good." This is a point which Malcolm seems not to have seized. He applies the same treatment without discrimination to both evaluative and nonevaluative paradoxes. Thus one of his specimens is: "We do not know for *certain* the truth of any statement about material things." He cites Ayer as arguing "that the notion of certainty does not apply to propositions of this kind," on the grounds that the achievement of certainty here would require us "to have completed an infinite series of verifications; and it is an analytic proposition that one cannot run through all the members of an infinite series." Malcolm tries to dispose of Ayer's contention by a straight appeal to "how we ordinarily use the expressions 'know for certain' and 'highly probable' "; and urges that there are really two different ordinary, and hence legitimate, senses of "certainty." "The truth is, not that the phrase 'I know for certain' has no proper application to empirical statements, but that the sense which it has in its application to empirical statements is *different* from the sense which it has in its application to *a priori* statements" [pages 353 and 355].

This will not do. In the first place, as Urmson has indicated, in the case of wholly or partly gerundive or diploma concepts such as "know for certain" an appeal to ordinary language is insufficient; there is here a further question whether the evidential standards embodied in this usage can be passed as satisfactory. In the second place, once it is recognized that this is a question of standards there seems to be no call for any multiplication of senses of "know for certain." The difference between the two cases is not in the nature of the diploma but in the conditions of the award. Those who claim that the phrase "I know for certain" has no proper application to empirical statements are in effect urging that the award would be justifiable here only on conditions which cannot be satisfied. To the extent that they are making a recommendation for a change of standards, rather than an assertion, their suggestion cannot be rebutted by a mere reminder that present standards are less exacting.

Richman, commenting on Urmson, urges "that if this restriction is necessary then . . . the APC is rendered of little philosophical importance." His main reason is that "I should wish to assert that, generally, key philosophical terms are used evaluatively" [12, pages 80 and 81]. Now it is certainly true that the key terms of several of the paradoxes in Malcolm's list are evaluative. It is possible to go further and to argue with Lazerowitz that they all *might* be construed as disguised proposals to change "the language of Common Sense" [9, page 393]. But none of this is sufficient to render the APC of little philosophical importance. Paradoxes of this sort obtain most of their apparent force from the way in which they are represented as if they expressed the rather startling findings of enquiry. As such they would just have to be accepted. Once they are reformulated to make it clear that they embody only recommendations, the question inevitably arises whether there is any good reason for acceptance.

It is one thing to be told that philosophical analysis has revealed that the notion of certainty cannot apply to empirical propositions. It is quite another to be asked to accept a recommendation to change our standards for knowledge in such a way that no amount of evidence could ever be allowed to be sufficient to justify a claim to know any empirical proposition for certain. In the cases where the key term in the paradox is not ostensibly evaluative the same applies, perhaps with even greater force. For while it might be possible to make out a fairly presentable independent case for a tightening up of our standards of certainty, without recourse to the argument that the notion cannot conceivably have any application in an empirical context, it is very hard to discern any room at all for a case for jettisoning temporal terms, except on the ground that the whole notion of time is self-contradictory. Yet the moment you suggest that some expression which has a descriptive use in ordinary language is really self-contradictory, you are again within range of the APC.

5b. So far we have been emphasizing that Malcolm's claim that "ordinary language *is* correct language" only applies to the purely descriptive as opposed to the evaluative aspects of ordinary usage. It is also necessary to repeat that it concerns only the purely descriptive as opposed to the theoretical. This is not a qualification which Malcolm made in exactly these terms, for his interest was only in those cases where there was no disagreement about the empirical facts. But in his very emphasis on this as characteristic of his sort of paradox he made it quite clear that he was not arguing that any theory which may happen to be encapsulated in ordinary discourse must on that account be correct. On the contrary, as we have seen, Malcolm employed the very example which has since become such a favorite with the opponents of the POL and the APC. He labors to explain how the fact that at one time everyone said that the earth is flat is not inconsistent with his claim. "Everyone believed that if you got into a ship and sailed west you would finally come to the edge and fall off. They did not believe that if you kept on sailing west you would come back to where you started from. When they said that the earth was flat, they were wrong. The way in which their statement was wrong was that they were making a mistake about the facts . . . they were using perfectly correct language to describe what they thought to be the case" [page 356].

Alexander, having recognized the present qualification, argues that it implies "that the PCA [= APC] is applicable only if the predicate corresponds to what Locke would have called a simple idea, that is a predicate which can only be learned through ostensive definition. And the only cases in which it can be shown clearly that this condition holds are comparatively trivial ones such as red." Alexander goes on to urge that "in so far as a term figures in any type of deductive theory, it cannot be a simple predicate whose meaning can be *completely* conveyed by ostensive definition and *only* conveyed by ostensive definition." He concludes: "The PCA is therefore either trivial or inapplicable" [1, pages 119–120]. But this surely will not do. For how could spatial or temporal expressions be taught at all without reference to actual examples of things standing in spatial or temporal relationships? These two cases alone are quite sufficient to upset Alexander's depreciatory conclusion. The argument certainly applies here, and space and time are certainly not philosophically trivial.

6. The members of that important subclass of philosophical paradoxes which Malcolm was considering, and which he was inclined to identify with the entire class, all spring from the idea that expressions having a descriptive use in ordinary language can nevertheless be self-contradictory. But there are other paradoxes against which the APC can be and has been used and to which Malcolm's account does not apply. Urmson, and later Watkins and Richman, refer to a chapter in Susan Stebbing's *Philosophy and the Physicists* [14, Part II, Chapter III]. Whereas Malcolm's interest is in paradoxes supported by purely a priori arguments, Stebbing is concerned with equally paradoxical contentions put forward by scientists, appealing to the authority of modern physics. At this particular point she is dealing with Eddington's thesis that furniture and floorboards, and all the other things which he and she and we and everybody else would ordinarily describe as solid, are not really solid at all. It would have been quite irrelevant for her to urge that a descriptive term like *solid*, which has ordinary uses, cannot be self-contradictory. Eddington had

never disputed this. His bizarre conclusions were supposed to be the consequences not of logical analyses but of factual discoveries.

Typically the same is true of the suggestion that perhaps, or really, no one ever acts of his own free will. This is not usually supported by any claim that the very notion is self-contradictory. It is normally based on the idea that either science or religion either has presented or might in the future present us with factual evidence showing that free will was nothing but a chimera. In these two cases, of solidity and of free will, and in many others besides, the APC consists simply and essentially in making the two steps described already (see (3) above): the first is to bring to mind certain very familiar facts, and the second is to insist that these are paradigm exemplars of the concepts in question. It is simply in hopes of underlining this second point that Stebbing appealed to what has since been named the principle of nonvacuous contrast: "If these objects are not solid what would *solid* mean?" The point of appealing to how one does, or would, or could, teach expression such as "could have helped it" or "of his own free will" is the same. It is no more essential here than it is in the cases discussed by Malcolm that the key expression should be one which has to be taught by reference to examples [see 6, pages 37–38].

Of course, in these "empirical" cases, as in the earlier "a priori" ones, the refutation provided by the APC is only a first step. That and that alone is precisely what it is supposed to be. Gellner was just having his fun with his Aunt Sally when he ridiculed, in an engaging phrase, the notion that: "The Argument from Smiling Bridegrooms solves it all" [7, page 31; compare 16, page 26]. Once we have recognized and become reconciled to the possibly disappointing truth that even our modern atomic thaumaturges are not able to show that solid things are not solid, then we can proceed, with Stebbing, to the difficult but pedestrian question of the relations between the concepts of physical theory and those of common sense and common experience. Again, and similarly, to get it clear that in ordinary untechnical discourse freedom is opposed not to predictability but to compulsion is only one early, albeit essential, stage in the extended and laborious businesses of assessing both the true implications of predestinarian theism and those of certain theories in psychological science. It was for this reason that the considerations about paradigm cases of acting of one's own free will, which Gellner and Watkins picked out for the whirlwind treatment, occupied so small a place in the articles in which they appeared ([4]; compare on the other theme my [3]).

7. This is all very much less exciting than the fine flashing paradoxes which the paradigms kill stone-dead. But that is not necessarily a philosophical fault. To coin a Feigelian phrase: "Philosophers must be journeymen, not journalists!"

REFERENCES

1. Alexander, H. G. "More about the Paradigm-Case Argument," *Analysis*, 18:117–120 (April 1958).
2. Eveling, H. S., and G. O. M. Leith. "When to Use the Paradigm-Case Argument," *Analysis*, 18:150–152 (June 1958).
3. Flew, Antony G. N. "Crime or Disease," *British Journal of Sociology*, 5:49–62 (1954).
4. Flew, Antony. "Divine Omnipotence and Human Freedom," in *New Essays in Philosophical Theology*, Antony Flew and Alasdair MacIntyre, eds., pp. 144–169. London: SCM Press, 1955.
5. Flew, A. G. N. " 'Farewell to the Paradigm-Case Argument': A Comment," *Analysis*, 18:34–40 (December 1957).
6. Flew, A. G. N. "Philosophy and Language," in *Essays in Conceptual Analysis*, Antony Flew, ed., pp. 1–20. London: Macmillan, 1956.
7. Gellner, Ernest. *Words and Things: A Critical Account of Linguistic Philosophy and a Study in Ideology*. London: Gollancz, 1959; Boston: Beacon Press, 1960.
8. Harré, R. "Tautologies and the Paradigm-Case Argument," *Analysis*, 18:94–96 (March 1958).
9. Lazerowitz, Morris. "Moore's Paradox," in [13], pp. 369–393.
10. Malcolm, Norman. "Moore and Ordinary Language," in [13], pp. 343–368.
11. Maxwell, Grover, and Herbert Feigl. "Why Ordinary Language Needs Reforming," *Journal of Philosophy*, 58:488–497 (August 31, 1961).
12. Richman, Robert J. "On the Argument of the Paradigm Case," *Australasian Journal of Philosophy*, 39:75–81 (1961).
13. Schilpp, Paul Arthur, ed. *The Philosophy of G. E. Moore*. Evanston and Chicago: Northwestern University, 1942.
14. Stebbing, L. Susan. *Philosophy and the Physicists*. London: Methuen, 1937; New York: Dover Books, 1958.
15. Urmson, J. O. "Some Questions Concerning Validity," in *Essays in Conceptual Analysis*, Antony Flew, ed., pp. 120–133. London: Macmillan, 1956.
16. Watkins, J. W. N. "Farewell to the Paradigm-Case Argument," *Analysis*, 18:25–33 (December 1957).
17. Watkins, J. W. N. "A Reply to Professor Flew's Comment," *Analysis*, 18:41–42 (December 1957).

ADOLF GRÜNBAUM

\(\(J\)\)

The Falsifiability of a Component of a
Theoretical System

Introduction

In his book *The Aim and Structure of Physical Theory*, the physicist, historian of science, and philosopher of science Pierre Duhem denied the feasibility of crucial experiments in physics. Said he [3, page 187]: ". . . the physicist can never subject an isolated hypothesis to experimental test, but only a whole group of hypotheses; when the experiment is in disagreement with his predictions, what he learns is that at least one of the hypotheses constituting this group is unacceptable and ought to be modified; *but the experiment does not designate which one should be changed*" (my italics). Duhem illustrates and elaborates this contention by means of examples from the history of optics. And in each of these cases, he maintains that "If physicists had attached some value to this task" [3, page 187] any one component hypothesis of optical theory such as the corpuscular hypothesis (or so-called emission hypothesis) could be preserved in the face of seemingly refuting experimental results such as those yielded by Foucault's experiment. According to Duhem, this continued espousal of the component hypothesis could be justified by "shifting the

NOTE: Portions of the Introduction and of Sections I and II are drawn by permission from a prior essay of mine in *Boston Studies in the Philosophy of Science*, M. Wartofsky, ed. (Dordrecht: Reidel, 1963); most of Section III is reprinted from my paper by the same title in *Philosophical Studies*, 15:71–79 (1964). Sections I and II, which present a significantly revised form of my earlier critique of the philosophical legacy of Pierre Duhem, are here combined with Section III into a single essay because of their common focus on issues in the logic of falsifiability.

weight of the experimental contradiction to some other proposition of the commonly accepted optics" [3, page 186].

In contemporary philosophy of science, a generalized version of this thesis with its ramifications has been attributed to Duhem and has been highly influential. I shall refer to this elaboration of Duhem's philosophical legacy in present-day philosophy of science as Duhem's thesis. But in doing so, my principal concern is with the philosophical credentials of this legacy, *not* with whether this attribution to Duhem himself can be uniquely sustained exegetically as against rival interpretations given by Duhem scholars. However, one such interpretation which is due to Mr. Laurens Laudan is of *logical* importance. A statement of it will therefore be given at the end of Part A of Section II as part of my critical examination of the Duhemian legacy in Sections I and II. This examination will amplify the critique of Duhem which I have given in earlier publications and will deal with some objections to it.

My overall aim in Sections I and II is to demonstrate the unsoundness of Duhem's presumed *general* categorical denial of the *separate falsifiability* (i.e., *refutability*) of any one component hypothesis within a theoretical system. Thus, I shall reject Duhem's presumed claim that the *separate* falsification of a component hypothesis is *never* feasible. But my rejection of this claim does allow, of course, that some one individual hypothesis or other might be inherently *nonfalsifiable as such* in virtue of being physically meaningless in the context of a particular theoretical system, when introduced as an added component of that system. The hypothesis that everything has doubled overnight has been held to be an example of such a *nonfalsifiable* individual proposition in the literature. Since this assertion of inherent nonfalsifiability of that hypothesis has recently been contested by some authors, I shall devote Section III of this paper to a clarification of the falsifiability status of the hypothesis of universal nocturnal doubling. It will turn out that this hypothesis can be understood in *at least two* quite different senses and that one, but only one, of these two versions of the hypothesis is inherently nonfalsifiable within the framework of a certain kind of physical theory.

I now turn to the precise statement and critique of Duhem's philosophical legacy.

It has been maintained that there is an important *asymmetry* between the *verification* and the *refutation* of a theory in empirical science. Refutation has been said to be conclusive or decisive while verification was claimed to be irremediably inconclusive in the following sense: If a theory T_1 entails observational consequences O, then the *truth* of T_1 does *not*, of course, follow *deductively* from the truth of the conjunction

$$(T_1 \rightarrow O) \cdot O.$$

On the other hand, the *falsity* of T_1 is indeed *deductively inferable* by *modus tollens* from the truth of the conjunction

$$(T_1 \rightarrow O) \cdot \sim O.$$

Thus, F. S. C. Northrop writes: "We find ourselves, therefore, in this somewhat shocking situation: the method which natural science uses to check the postulationally prescribed theories . . . is absolutely trustworthy when the proposed theory is not confirmed and logically inconclusive when the theory is experimentally confirmed" [10, page 146].

Under the influence of Duhem, this thesis of asymmetry of conclusiveness between verification and refutation has been strongly denied as follows (compare [3], Part II, Chapter VI, especially pages 183–190): If "T_1" denotes the kind of individual or *isolated* hypothesis H whose verification or refutation is at issue in the conduct of particular scientific experiments, then Northrop's formal schema is a misleading oversimplification. Upon taking cognizance of the fact that the observational consequences O are deduced *not* from H alone but rather from the conjunction of H and the relevant body of *auxiliary* assumptions A, the refutability of H is seen to be no more conclusive than its verifiability. For now it appears that Northrop's formal schema must be replaced by the following:

(1) $[(H \cdot A) \rightarrow O] \cdot O$ (verification)

and

(2) $[(H \cdot A) \rightarrow O] \cdot \sim O.$ (refutation)

The recognition of the presence of the auxiliary assumptions A in both the verification and refutation of H now makes apparent that the *refutation of H itself* by *adverse* empirical evidence $\sim O$ can be no more decisive than its *verification* (confirmation) by *favorable* evidence O. What can be inferred deductively from the refutational premise (2) is *not* the falsity of H itself but only the much weaker conclusion that H and A cannot both be true. It is immaterial here that the *falsity of the conjunction* of H and A can be inferred *deductively* from the refutational premise (2) while the *truth* of that conjunction can be inferred only *inductively* from the verificational premise (1). For this does *not* detract from the fact that there is parity between the refutation of *H itself* and the verification of *H itself* in the following sense: (2) does *not* entail (deductively) the falsity of *H* itself, just as (1) does not entail the truth of *H* by itself. In short, isolated component hypotheses of far-flung theoretical systems are not separately refutable but only contextually disconfirmable. And Northrop's schema is an adequate representation of the actual logical situation only if "T_1" in his schema refers to the entire theoretical *system* of premises which enters into the deduction of O rather than to such mere *components H* as are at issue in specific scientific inquiries.

Under the influence of Duhem's emphasis on the confrontation of an entire theoretical system by the tribunal of evidence, writers such as W. V. O. Quine have gone further to make what I take to be the following claim: No matter what the specific content O' of the prima facie adverse empirical evidence ~O, we can always justifiably affirm the truth of *H* as part of the theoretical *explanans* of O' by doing two things: (1) blaming the falsity of O on the falsity of A rather than on the falsity of *H*, and (2) so modifying A that the conjunction of *H* and the *revised* version A' of A does entail (explain) the actual findings O'. Thus, in his "Two Dogmas of Empiricism," Quine writes ([13], page 43; compare also page 41n): "Any statement can be held true come what may, if we make drastic enough adjustments elsewhere in the system." And one of Quine's arguments in that provocative essay against the tenability of the analytic-synthetic distinction is that a supposedly synthetic statement, no less than a supposedly analytic one, can be claimed to be true "come what may" on Duhemian grounds.

The aim of Sections I and II of my present paper is to establish two main conclusions:

I. Quine's formulation of Duhem's thesis—hereafter called the *D*-thesis—is true *only* in various *trivial* senses of what Quine calls "drastic enough adjustments elsewhere in the system." And no one would wish to contest any of these thoroughly uninteresting versions of the *D*-thesis, while granting that Quine's critique of one version of the analytic-synthetic distinction itself requires only the *trivial* correctness of the *D*-thesis.

II. In its *nontrivial*, exciting form, the *D*-thesis is untenable in the following fundamental respects:

A. *Logically*, it is a *non sequitur*. For independently of the particular empirical context to which the hypothesis H pertains, there is no logical guarantee at all of the existence of the *required* kind of revised set A' of auxiliary assumptions such that

$$(H \cdot A') \to O'$$

for any one component hypothesis H and any O'. Instead of being guaranteed logically, the existence of the required set A' needs *separate* and concrete demonstration for each particular context. In the absence of the latter kind of *empirical* support for Quine's unrestricted Duhemian claim, that claim is an unempirical dogma or article of faith which the pragmatist Quine is no more entitled to espouse than an empiricist would be.

B. The D-thesis is not only a *non sequitur* but is actually false, as shown by an important pair of counterexamples in which a particular component hypothesis H is *separately* falsifiable.

To forestall misunderstanding, let it be noted that my rejection of the very strong assertion made by the nontrivial form of Quine's D-thesis is *not* at all intended as a repudiation of the following far weaker contention, which I believe to be eminently sound: the logic of every disconfirmation, no less than of every confirmation, of an isolated scientific hypothesis H is such as to *involve at some stage or other* an entire network of interwoven hypotheses in which H is ingredient rather than in *every* stage merely the separate hypothesis H. Furthermore, it is to be understood that the issue before us is the *logical* one whether *in principle* every component H is unrestrictedly preservable by a suitable A', *not* the psychological one whether scientists possess sufficient ingenuity at every turn to propound the required set A', *if it exists*. Of course, *if* there are cases in which the requisite A' simply *does not even exist logically*, then surely no amount of ingenuity on the part of scientists will enable them to ferret out the nonexistent required A' in such cases.

I shall devote Section III of this essay to a clarification of the nonfalsifiability status of the hypothesis of a universal nocturnal expansion.

I. The Trivial Validity of the D-Thesis

It can be made evident at once that unless Quine restricts in very specific ways what he understands by "drastic enough adjustments elsewhere in the [theoretical] system" the D-thesis is a thoroughly unenlightening truism. For if someone were to put forward the false empirical hypothesis H that "Ordinary buttermilk is highly toxic to humans," this hypothesis could be saved from refutation in the face of the observed wholesomeness of ordinary buttermilk by making the following "drastic enough" adjustment in our system: changing the rules of English usage so that the intension of the term "ordinary buttermilk" is that of the term "arsenic" in its customary usage. Hence a necessary condition for the nontriviality of Duhem's thesis is that the theoretical language be semantically stable in the relevant respects.

Furthermore, it is clear that if one were to countenance that O' itself qualifies as A', Duhem's affirmation of the existence of an A' such that

$$(H \cdot A') \rightarrow O'$$

would hold trivially, and H would not even be needed to deduce O'. Moreover, the D-thesis can hold trivially even in cases in which H is required in addition to A' to deduce the explanandum O'; an A' of the trivial form

$$\sim H \vee O'$$

requires H for the deduction of O', but no one will find it enlightening to be told that the D-thesis can thus be sustained.

I am unable to give a formal and completely general sufficient condition for the nontriviality of A'. And, so far as I know, neither the originator nor any of the advocates of the D-thesis have even shown any awareness of the need to circumscribe the class of nontrivial revised auxiliary hypotheses A' so as to render the D-thesis interesting. I shall therefore assume that the proponents of the D-thesis intend it to stand or fall on the kind of A' which we would all recognize as nontrivial in any given case, a kind of A' which I shall symbolize by A'_{nt}. And I shall endeavor to show that such a nontrivial form of the D-thesis is indeed untenable, after first commenting on the attempt to sustain the D-thesis by resorting to the use of a nonstandard logic.

The species of drastic adjustment consisting in recourse to a nonstandard logic is specifically mentioned by Quine. Citing a hypothesis such as "There are brick houses on Elm Street," he claims that even a statement so "germane to sense experience . . . can be held true in the face of recalcitrant experience by pleading hallucination or by amending certain statements of the kind called logical laws" [13, page 43]. I disregard for now the argument from hallucination. In the absence of specifics as to the ways in which alterations of logical laws will enable Quine to hold in the face of recalcitrant experience that a statement H like "There are brick houses on Elm Street" is *true*, I must conclude the following: the invocation of nonstandard logics either makes the *D*-thesis *trivially* true or turns it into an interesting claim which is an unfounded dogma. For suppose that the nonstandard logic used is a three-valued one. Then even if it were otherwise feasible to assert within the framework of such a logic that the particular statement *H* is "true," the term "true" would no longer have the meaning associated with the two-valued framework of logic within which the *D*-thesis was enunciated to begin with. It is not to be overlooked that a form of the *D*-thesis which allows itself to be sustained by alterations in the meaning of "true" is no less trivial *in the context of the expectations raised by the D-thesis* than one which rests its case on calling arsenic "buttermilk." And this triviality obtains *in this* context, notwithstanding the fact that the two-valued and three-valued usages of the word "true" share what Hilary Putnam has usefully termed a common "core meaning" [12, page 74]. For suppose we had two particular substances I_1 and I_2 which are isomeric with each other. That is to say, these substances are composed of the same elements in the same proportions and with the same molecular weight but the arrangement of the atoms within the molecule is different. Suppose further that I_1 is not at all toxic while I_2 is highly toxic, as in the case of two isomers of trinitrobenzene.[1] Then if we were to call I_1 "aposteriorine" and asserted that "aposteriorine is highly toxic," this statement *H* could also be trivially saved from refutation in the face of the evidence of the wholesomeness of I_1 by the following device: only *partially* changing the meaning of "aposteriorine" so that its intension is the second, highly toxic isomer I_2, thereby leaving the chemical "core meaning" of "aposteriorine" intact. To avoid misunderstanding of my charge of triviality, let me point out precisely what I regard as trivial here. The preservation of *H* from refutation in the face of the evidence by a *partial* change in the meaning of "aposteriorine" is trivial in the sense of being only a *trivial* fulfillment of *the expectations raised by the D-thesis*. But, in my view, the possibility *as such of preserving H by this particular kind of change in meaning* is not at all trivial. For this possibility as such reflects a fact about the world:

---

[1] Cf. H. L. Alexander [1, p. 14]. Alexander writes: "It is true that drugs with closely related chemical structures do not always behave clinically in a similar manner, for antigenicity of simple chemical compounds may be changed by minor alterations of molecular structures. . . . 1,2,4-trinitrobenzene . . . is a highly antigenic compound. . . . 1,3,5 . . . trinitrobenzene is allergenically inert." (I am indebted to Dr. A. I. Braude for this reference.)

the existence of isomeric substances of radically different degrees of toxicity (allergenicity)!

Even if one ignores the change in the meaning of "true" inherent in the resort to a three-valued logic, there is no reason to think that the D-thesis can be successfully upheld in such an altered logical framework: the arguments which I shall present against the nontrivial form of the D-thesis within the framework of the standard logic apply just as much, so far as I can see, in the three-valued and other nonstandard logics of which I am aware. And if the reply is that there are other nonstandard logics which are viable for the purposes of science and to which my impending polemic against the nontrivial form of the D-thesis does not apply, then I retort: As it stands, Quine's assertion of the feasibility of a change in the laws of logic which would thus sustain the D-thesis is an unempirical dogma or at best a promissory note. And until the requisite collateral is supplied, it is not incumbent upon anyone to accept that promissory note.

II. The Untenability of the Nontrivial D-Thesis

A. The Nontrivial D-Thesis Is a Non Sequitur

The nontrivial D-thesis is that for every component hypothesis H of any domain of empirical knowledge and for any observational findings O',

$$(\exists A'_{nt})[(H \cdot A'_{nt}) \rightarrow O'].$$

But this claim does not follow from the fact that the falsity of H is not deductively inferable from premise (2) above, i.e., from

$$[(H \cdot A) \rightarrow O] \cdot \sim O.$$

For the latter premise utilizes not the full empirical information given by O' but only the part of that information which tells us that O' is logically incompatible with O. Thus, for example, O' might be the true statement that an ammeter reads 10 amperes, while O would assert that the amperage is 3. Clearly, O' asserts more than $\sim O$, since O' entails $\sim O$, but not conversely. In conjunction with A'_{nt}, H must permit the deduction that the amperage is 10 rather than merely the deduction of the weaker claim that it is not 3. Hence the failure of $\sim O$ to permit the deduction of $\sim H$ does not justify the assertion of the D-thesis that there always exists a nontrivial A' such that the conjunction of H and that A' entails

O'. In other words, the fact that the falsity of H is *not* deducible (by *modus tollens*) from premise (2) is quite insufficient to show that H can be preserved nontrivially as part of an *explanans* of *any* potential empirical findings O'. I conclude, therefore, from the analysis given so far that in its nontrivial form, Quine's D-thesis is *gratuitous* and that the existence of the required nontrivial A' would require *separate* demonstration for each particular case.

So far, I have argued that the nontrivial D-thesis is a *non sequitur*. But I maintain that the D-thesis is not only unfounded but also *false*. And I rest this claim of falsity on geometric counterexamples, the details of which I am about to set forth. Let me first clarify, however, in what precise sense I regard my geometric counterexamples as proving the falsity of the nontrivial D-thesis.

In the case of each of them, I shall adduce logically possible empirical findings O' for which every nontrivial A' that is capable of preserving H in the face of O' is empirically false. Hence I claim that my counterexamples show the D-thesis to be false in virtue of each being such that there exists *no true* nontrivial A' which would preserve H by explaining O' in conjunction with H. Since every A'_{nt} that yields the true O' is false in the case of these two counterexamples, the conjunction of H with any true auxiliary hypothesis denying such an A'_{nt} entails observational consequences which are *incompatible* with the assumedly true O' and hence *false*. But since the conjunction of H with any *true* A'_{nt} entails a false observational conclusion $\sim O'$ of one kind or other in these examples, H is *separately falsified*. It is inconsequential here that *some* false observational claims incompatible with O' may be deducible from *false* A'_{nt} in conjunction with H. For what matters is that the falsity of an observational conclusion $\sim O'$ deduced from H in conjunction with an A'_{nt} *cannot always* be blamed *solely* on the falsity of the auxiliary hypotheses, since the conjunction of H with any true A'_{nt} is known to entail a *false* observational conclusion $\sim O'$. In short, the force of my geometric counterexamples to the D-thesis is the following: If H were true *and* explanatory of O', then there should exist a *true* A'_{nt} enabling H to entail the correct observational finding O'. But no such A'_{nt} exists, since every A'_{nt} which yields the true O' is false. Consequently, the conjunction of H with any true A'_{nt} entails a false result. Hence H itself is false.

On the alternative interpretation of Duhem's writings given by Mr. Laurens Laudan, these examples of separate falsifiability would be compatible with Duhem's views on the logic of falsifiability of a component hypothesis. He calls attention to Duhem's argument for the impossibility of crucial experiments in physics in Section 3 of Chapter VI, Part II of *The Aim and Structure of Physical Theory*. And Laudan maintains that Duhem's text there and elsewhere admits of the following alternative interpretation.

Duhem is concerned primarily to show that the refutation of a component hypothesis is *usually* no more conclusive than its verification. He is claiming that we can rarely, if at all, know that there does not exist some set of tenable assumptions A'_{nt} which would enable an allegedly falsified H to explain O'. In this way, he is not committed to the claim that such a set A'_{nt} always exists. Instead, he is claiming that the separate falsification of a component hypothesis H depends on a proof that no such set A'_{nt} exists. Thus, the *onus probandi* is not on Duhem to show that such a set A'_{nt} exists in every case; instead, the demonstration of the non-existence of such a set is obligatory upon anyone claiming the separate falsification of H. On this construal, Duhem's argument is not a *non sequitur* but rather a charge of *non sequitur* against those others who assert that H has been separately falsified without first having established the nonexistence of a suitable set of A'_{nt}.

Laudan believes that if Duhem himself had actually been an exponent of the thesis usually attributed to him, then Duhem's reasoning in support of the impossibility of crucial experiments would have been different from what, in fact, it was. Specifically, he points to Duhem's reason for *rejecting* the possibility that an experiment could decide crucially in favor of a hypothesis H_2 as against its rival H_1. Duhem's reason is *not* that H_1 can always be preserved by a suitable A'_{nt} in the face of any evidence; instead, his reason is that though H_1 might indeed be falsified, we cannot infer the truth of H_2, because there may well be at least one other hypothesis H_3 capable of explaining the phenomena but overlooked by the scientist. Laudan argues that if Duhem had believed in the strong claim usually ascribed to him, he would not have appealed to the possible existence of an overlooked alternative hypothesis H_3, when denying that an experiment can decide crucially in favor of H_2 as against H_1. For an exponent of the *D*-thesis would have rested the denial of the feasibility of such a crucial experiment on the assertion that H_1 cannot be falsified but can rather always be upheld in the face of any evidence whatever.

B. Physical Geometry as a Counterexample to the Nontrivial D-Thesis

Einstein has articulated Duhem's claim by reference to the special case of testing a hypothesis of physical geometry. In opposition to the Carnap-Reichenbach conception, Einstein maintains [4, pages 676–678] that no hypothesis of physical geometry by itself is falsifiable even though all of the terms in the vocabulary of the geometrical theory, including the term "congruent" for line segments and angles, have been given a specific physical interpretation. And the substance of his argument is briefly the following: in order to follow the practice of ordinary physics and use rigid solid rods as the physical standard of congruence in the determination of the geometry, it is essential to make computational allowances for the thermal, elastic, electromagnetic, and other deformations exhibited by solid rods. The introduction of these corrections is an essential part of the logic of testing a physical geometry. For the presence of inhomogeneous thermal and other such influences issues in a dependence of the coincidence behavior of transported solid rods on the latter's *chemical composition*. Now, Einstein argues that the geometry itself can never be accessible to experimental falsification *in isolation from* those other laws of physics which enter into the calculation of the corrections compensating for the distortions of the rod. And from this he then concludes that you can always preserve any geometry you like by suitable adjustments in the associated correctional physical laws. Specifically, he states his case in the form of a dialogue in which he attributes his own Duhemian view to Poincaré and offers that view in opposition to Hans Reichenbach's conception. But I submit that Poincaré's text will *not* bear Einstein's interpretation. For in speaking of the variations which solids exhibit under distorting influences, Poincaré says "we neglect these variations in laying the foundations of geometry, because, besides their being very slight, they are irregular and consequently seem to us accidental" [11, page 76]. I am therefore taking the liberty of replacing the name "Poincaré" in Einstein's dialogue by the term "Duhem and Einstein." With this modification, the dialogue reads as follows:

Duhem and Einstein: The empirically given bodies are not rigid, and consequently can not be used for the embodiment of geometric intervals. Therefore, the theorems of geometry are not verifiable.

Reichenbach: I admit that there are no bodies which can be *immediately* adduced for the "real definition" [i.e., physical definition] of the interval. Nevertheless, this real definition can be achieved by taking the thermal volume-dependence, elasticity, electro- and magneto-striction, etc., into consideration. That this is really [and] without contradiction possible, classical physics has surely demonstrated.

Duhem and Einstein: In gaining the real definition improved by yourself you have made use of physical laws, the formulation of which presupposes (in this case) Euclidean geometry. The verification, of which you have spoken, refers, therefore, not merely to geometry but to the entire system of physical laws which constitute its foundation. An examination of geometry by itself is consequently not thinkable.—Why should it consequently not be entirely up to me to choose geometry according to my own convenience (i.e., Euclidean) and to fit the remaining (in the usual sense "physical") laws to this choice in such manner that there can arise no contradiction of the whole with experience? [4, page 677.]

By speaking here of the "real definition" (i.e., the coordinative definition) of "congruent intervals" by the corrected transported rod, Einstein is ignoring the fact that the actual and potential physical meaning of congruence in physics *cannot* be given exhaustively by any *one* physical criterion or test condition. But here we can safely ignore this open cluster character of the concept of congruence. For our concern as well as Einstein's is merely to single out *one* particular congruence class from among an infinitude of such alternative classes. And as long as our specification of that one chosen class is unambiguous, it is wholly immaterial that there are also *other* physical criteria (or test conditions) by which it could be specified. (For details relevant here, see [4], pages 11 and 14–15.)

Einstein is making two major points here: (1) In obtaining a physical geometry by giving a physical interpretation of the postulates of a formal geometric axiom system, the specification of the physical meaning of such theoretical terms as "congruent," "length," or "distance" is *not* at all simply a matter of giving an operational definition in the strict sense. Instead, what has been variously called a "rule of correspondence" (Margenau and Carnap), a "coordinative definition" (Reichenbach), an "epistemic correlation" (Northrop), or a "dictionary" (N. R. Campbell) is provided here *through the mediation of hypotheses and laws* which are collateral to the geometric theory whose physical meaning is being specified. Einstein's point that the physical meaning of congruence is given by the transported rod *as corrected theoretically* for idiosyncratic distortions is an illuminating one and has an abundance of analogues throughout physical theory, thus showing, incidentally, that strictly operational definitions are a rather simplified and limiting species of rules of correspondence. In particular, we see that the physical interpretation of the term "length," which is often adduced as the prototype of all "operational" definitions in Bridgman's sense, is *not* given operationally in any *distinctive* sense of that ritually invoked term. (2) Einstein's second claim, which is the cardinal one for our purposes, is that the role of collateral theory in the physical definition of congruence is such as to issue in the following *circularity*, from which there is no escape, he maintains, short of acknowledging the existence of an a priori element *in the sense of the Duhemian ambiguity*: the rigid body is not even defined without first decreeing the validity of Euclidean geometry (or of some other particular geometry). For *before* the *corrected* rod can be used to make an empirical determination of the *de facto* geometry, the required corrections must be computed via laws, such as those of elasticity, which involve Euclideanly calculated areas and volumes (compare [15] and [16]). But clearly the warrant for thus introducing Euclidean geometry *at this stage* cannot be empirical.

In the same vein, Hermann Weyl endorses Duhem's position as follows: "Geometry, Mechanics, and Physics form an inseparable theoretical whole . . ." [17, page 67]. "Philosophers have put forward the thesis that the validity or non-validity of Euclidean geometry cannot be proved by empirical observations. It must in fact be granted that in all such observations essentially physical assumptions, such as the statement that the path of a ray of light is a straight line and other similar statements, play a prominent part. This merely bears out the remark already made above that it is only the whole composed of geometry and physics that may be tested empirically" [page 93].

I now wish to set forth my doubts regarding the soundness of Einstein's geometrical form of the D-thesis.[2] And I shall do so in two parts, the first of which deals with the special case in which no deforming influences are effectively present in a certain region whose geometry is to be ascertained.

Suppose we are confronted with the problem of falsifying the hypothesis H which employs the customary congruence and ascribes a geometry G to a region which is actually effectively free from substance-specific deforming influences. In that case the correctional physical laws play no role as auxiliary assumptions, and the latter reduce to the claim A that the

---

[2] I elaborate here on some parts of my earlier treatment of this and related issues [8, pp. 135–144] so as to deal with objections that have been raised against it.

region in question is, in fact, effectively free from substance-specific deforming influences. And if compelling reasons can be given against postulating such deforming influences under these circumstances, then A
could not be warrantedly denied. In that case, the geometric hypothesis
H, which is predicated on the customary congruence, would be *separately*
falsifiable by metrical observations O' that H must explain and which are
incompatible with the conjunction $H \cdot A$. By contrast, if, under the
posited circumstances, A might be warrantedly or reasonably denied in
favor of a rival assumption A' of *specific* deformations, then Duhem and
Einstein could maintain that H is not separately falsifiable, because A'
would enable H to explain the specific metrical findings O'.

Hence we must ask: What considerations would warrant the assertion
of A under the posited circumstances and what is the character of the
assumptions made by the denial of A? Freedom from deforming influences can be asserted and ascertained independently of the theoretical
elaboration of any of the various metrical magnitudes (e.g., temperature)
whose constancy collectively constitutes such freedom. For the very existence of a physical geometry relatively to the standard congruence entails
that such freedom is certifiable for the region by the following: *any* two
solid rods, however different in qualitative appearance, which coincide
at one place in the region will also coincide everywhere else in it independently of their paths of transport. The mere determination that a
rod is solid, as contrasted with being liquid or gaseous, does *not* presuppose a spatial metric or a metric geometry. Neither does the visual and
tactile certification of the topological relation of coincidence (as opposed
to noncoincidence) among rods involve the assumption of a geometry,
although its accuracy is not, of course, unlimited. And at the level of
qualitative perceptual judgment required here, no distinctively *metrical*
discriminations are needed in regard to the characterization of solids as
chemically *different*. The dispensability of metrical specifications which
I am affirming here is entirely compatible with the fact that the chemical
identification of any particular solid body as being a piece of wood or iron
may make reference to properties like density or molecular weight which
do presuppose geometrical attributes. Thus, suppose that each of two
differently colored bodies feels hard and that only one of them floats on a
given lake. Then these two bodies could be held to be chemically different and certified as exhibiting concordance of coincidence under transport without identifying these bodies as wood and iron respectively and

the liquid in the lake as being water. And if *all* hard-feeling bodies whatever of otherwise diverse qualitative appearance exhibit concordance of coincidences under transport in the specified region, the region can be inductively held to be free from deforming influences without presupposing any metric geometry. For the very conception of the existence of a physical geometry as independent of the chemical composition of solids entails that the observed concordance of coincidence under transport inductively assures freedom from deforming influences whose effects would destroy this concordance.

It is of decisive importance to be clear here that the issue between the Duhemian and myself is *not* whether the observational certification of two solids as coinciding under transport and as (quite) different chemically is theory-laden; instead, the issue is whether this observational certification—theory-laden though it be—*is theory-laden to an extent precluding the separate falsifiability of H*! We shall now see that the theory-involvement in the claim A that there is freedom from deforming influences is *not* such as to allow the assertion of the kind of A' needed to deny the separate falsifiability of H by O'. To see this, we shall now state and assess the kinds of assumptions ingredient in any denial A' of A which would be capable of preserving H as an *explanans* of O'.

Any particular denial A' of freedom from deforming influences which is to save H in the face of O' *despite the observably concordant coincidences* must postulate quantitative substance-specific deformations relatively to the customary congruence as follows:

1. Although there is no *independent* evidence supporting the existence of any physical sources (e.g., thermal sources) for the alleged presence of deforming influences, A' must assert that the region is, in fact, inhomogeneous in one or more specified respects (e.g., thermally);

2. To account for the concordance of coincidence under transport, A' must assert that all coinciding solid rods present in the region are sustaining specified *like* deformations relatively to the customary congruence in accord with stated correctional laws;

3. Therefore A' must assert that all of the prima facie chemically different solids are chemically of the *same* kind, and indeed are of *one specified kind* with which particular values of the various substance-specific correctional coefficients can be associated;

4. A' must assert that the like deformations produced by the alleged

sources are such as to explain that there is *unfailing* concordance in the rod-coincidences *independently* of the paths of rod transport; and

5. *A'* must be such as to enable *H* to explain the metrical findings *O'* in conjunction with *A'*.

I submit that the theory-involvement in the observational certification of freedom from deforming influences does *not* provide sufficient latitude for the kind of rival *A'* required to preclude the separate falsifiability of *H*. Theory-laden though they be, the observational findings of the unfailing concordance of the rod-coincidences contain enough *relatively stubborn fact* to *disallow* the assumption of such an *A'*. Indeed, if the Duhemian is to maintain, as he does, that a *total theoretical system* is falsifiable by observations, then surely he must assume that the relevant falsifying observations present us with sufficient *relatively* stubborn fact to be falsifying. Could the Duhemian maintain consistently that the relatively rudimentary kinds of observations supporting A (e.g., coincidence and qualitative difference of solids) are sufficiently ambiguous to permit the alternative assertion of the rival *A'*? If the Duhemian were to maintain this, then how could *any* observation ever possess the univocity which he must ascribe to it in order to qualify it for falsifying a total theoretical system? And if there were no relatively stubborn fact with which a total theoretical system could be confronted in a particular context, how could the Duhemian avoid the following conclusion: "Observational findings are always so unrestrictedly ambiguous as not to permit even the refutation of any given total theoretical system." But such a result would be tantamount to the absurdity that any total theoretical system can be espoused as true a priori.

By the same token, incidentally, I cannot see what methodological safeguards would prevent Quine from having to countenance such an outcome within the framework of his *D*-thesis. In view of his avowed willingness to "plead hallucination" to deal with observations not conforming to the hypothesis "There are brick houses on Elm Street," one wonders whether he would be prepared to say that *all* human observers who make disconfirming observations on Elm Street are hallucinating. And, if so, why not discount all observations incompatible with any total theoretical system as hallucinatory? Thus, it would seem that if Duhem is to maintain, as he does, that a total theoretical *system* is refutable by confrontation with observational results, then he must allow that the coincidence of diverse kinds of rods at different places in the region (independently of their paths of transport) is an observationally certifiable finding.

Accordingly, the absence of deforming influences is ascertainable *independently* of any assumptions as to the geometry. Let us now employ our earlier notation and denote the geometry by "H" and the assertion concerning the freedom from perturbations by "A." Then, once we have laid down the congruence definition and the remaining semantical rules, the physical geometry H becomes *separately* falsifiable as an *explanans* of the posited empirical findings O'. It is true, of course, that A is only more or less highly confirmed by the ubiquitous coincidence of chemically different kinds of solid rods. But the inductive risk thus inherent in affirming A does not arise from the alleged inseparability of H and A, and that risk can be made exceedingly small without any involvement of H. Accordingly, the actual logical situation is characterized not by the Duhemian schema but instead by the schema

$$[\{(H \cdot A) \to O\} \cdot \sim O \cdot A] \to \sim H.$$

The force of this counterexample to the D-thesis lies in the fact that H is *separately falsifiable* for the following reason: in conjunction with an evidentially *true* auxiliary hypothesis A, H entails *false* observational consequences O, and the (posited) actual observational findings O' are such that *every* nontrivial A' capable of preserving H in the face of O' is known to be empirically false. For every such A' falsely asserts the existence of deformations operating according to some set or other of correctional laws.

We now turn to the critique of Einstein's Duhemian argument as applied to the empirical determination of the geometry of a region which is subject to deforming influences.

There can be no question that when deforming influences are present, the laws used to make the corrections for deformations involve areas and volumes in a fundamental way (e.g., in the definitions of the elastic stresses and strains) and that this involvement presupposes a geometry, as is evident from the area and volume formulas of differential geometry, which contain the square root of the determinant of the components g_{ik} of the metric tensor [5, page 177]. Thus, the empirical determination of the geometry involves the joint assumption of a geometry and certain collateral hypotheses. But we see already that this assumption *cannot* be adequately represented by the conjunction $H \cdot A$ of the Duhemian schema, where H represents the geometry, a symbolization which fails to exhibit the logical ingredience of H in A.

Now suppose that we begin with a set of Euclideanly formulated physical laws P_0 in correcting for the distortions induced by perturbations and then use the thus Euclideanly corrected congruence standard for *empirically* exploring the geometry of space by determining the metric tensor. *The initial stipulational affirmation of the Euclidean geometry G_0 in the physical laws P_0 used to compute the corrections in no way assures that the geometry obtained by the corrected rods will be Euclidean!* If it is *non*-Euclidean, then the question is: What will be required by Einstein's fitting of the physical laws to preserve Euclideanism and avoid a contradiction of the theoretical system with experience? Will the adjustments in P_0 necessitated by the retention of Euclidean geometry entail merely a change in the dependence of the length assigned to the transported rod on such *nonpositional* parameters as temperature, pressure, and magnetic field? Or could the putative empirical findings compel that the length of the transported rod be likewise made a nonconstant function of its *position* and *orientation* as *independent* variables in order to square the coincidence findings with the requirement of Euclideanism? The possibility of obtaining *non*-Euclidean results by measurements carried out in a spatial region uniformly characterized by standard conditions of temperature, pressure, electric and magnetic field strength, etc., shows it to be *extremely doubtful*, as we shall now demonstrate, that the preservation of Euclideanism could *always* be accomplished short of introducing *the dependence of the rod's length on the independent variables of position or orientation.*

But the introduction of the latter dependence is so radical a change in the meaning of the word "congruent" that the extension of this term is now a class of classes of intervals *different* from the original congruence class denoted by it. And such tampering with the semantical anchorage of the word "congruent" violates the requirement of semantical stability, which is a necessary condition for the *nontriviality* of the *D*-thesis, as we saw above.

Suppose that, relatively to the customary congruence standard, the geometry prevailing in a given region when *free* from perturbational influences is that of a strongly *non*-Euclidean space of spatially and temporally constant curvature. Then what would be the character of the alterations in the *customary* correctional laws which Einstein's thesis would require to assure the *Euclideanism* of that region relatively to the customary congruence standard under *perturbational* conditions? The required alterations would be *independently falsifiable*, as will now be demonstrated, because they would involve affirming that such coefficients as those of linear thermal expansion *depend on the independent variables of spatial position*. That such a space dependence of the correctional coefficients might well be necessitated by the exigencies of Einstein's Duhemian thesis can be seen as follows by reference to the law of linear thermal expansion. In the usual version of physical theory, the first approximation of that law[3] is given by

$$L = L_0 \, (1 + a \cdot \Delta T).$$

If Einstein is to guarantee the Euclideanism of the region under discussion by means of logical devices that are consonant with his thesis, and if our region is subject only to *thermal* perturbations for some time, then we are confronted with the following situation: unlike the customary law of linear thermal expansion, the revised form of that law needed by Einstein will have to bear the twin burden of effecting *both* of the following two kinds of superposed corrections: (1) the *changes in the lengths* ascribed to the transported rod in different positions or orientations which would be required even if our region *were* everywhere at the standard temperature, merely for the sake of rendering Euclidean its otherwise non-Euclidean geometry, and (2) corrections compensating for the effects of the *de facto* deviations from the standard temperature, these corrections being the sole onus of the *usual* version of the law of linear thermal expansion. What will be the consequences of requiring the *revised* version of the law of thermal elongation to implement the *first* of these two kinds of corrections in a context in which the deviation ΔT from the standard temperature is the *same* at *different* points of the region, that temperature deviation having been measured in the manner chosen by the Duhemian? Specifically, what will be the character of the

---

[3] This law is only the first approximation, because the rate of thermal expansion varies with the temperature. The general equation giving the magnitude m_t (length or volume) at a temperature t, where m_0 is the magnitude at $0°C$, is

$$m_t = m_0(1 + at + bt^2 + \gamma t^3 + \ldots),$$

where a, b, γ, etc. are empirically determined coefficients (compare *Handbook of Chemistry and Physics*, Cleveland: Chemical Rubber Publishing Co., 1941, p. 2194). The argument which is about to be given by reference to the approximate form of the law can be readily generalized to forms of the law involving more than one coefficient of expansion.

coefficients a of the *revised* law of thermal elongation under the posited circumstances, if Einstein's thesis is to be implemented by effecting the *first* set of corrections? Since the new version of the law of thermal expansion will then have to guarantee that the lengths L assigned to the rod at the various points of *equal* temperature T *differ* appropriately, it would seem clear that logically possible empirical findings could compel Einstein to make the coefficients a of solids *depend* on the *space coordinates*.

But such a spatial dependence is *independently falsifiable*: comparison of the thermal elongations of an aluminum rod, for example, with an invar rod of essentially zero a by, say, the Fizeau method *might* well show that the a of the aluminum rod is a characteristic of aluminum which is *not* dependent on the space coordinates. And even if it *were* the case that the a's are found to be space-dependent, how could Duhem and Einstein assure that this space dependence would have one of the particular functional forms required for the success of their thesis? More decisively, at points for which $\Delta T = O$, even the assumption of the space-dependence of the a's cannot possibly yield the variation required in the length L of the rod, since the formula shows that L has the *constant* value L_0 at all such points independently of what a is assumed to be.

We see that the required resort to the introduction of a spatial dependence of the thermal coefficients might well *not* be open to Einstein. And in order to retain Euclideanism, it might well be necessary to *remetrize* the space in the sense of abandoning the customary definition of congruence, entirely apart from any consideration of idiosyncratic distortions and even after correcting for these in some way or other. But this kind of remetrization, though entirely admissible in *other* contexts, does *not* provide the requisite support for Einstein's Duhemian thesis! For Einstein offered it as a criticism of Reichenbach's conception. And hence it is the *avowed onus* of that thesis to show that the geometry by *itself* cannot be held to be empirical, i.e., separately falsifiable, even when, with Reichenbach, we have sought to assure its empirical character by choosing and then adhering to the usual (standard) definition of spatial congruence, which *excludes* resorting to such remetrization.

Thus, there may well obtain observational findings O', expressed in terms of a particular definition of congruence (e.g., the customary one), which are such that there does *not* exist any nontrivial set A' of auxiliary assumptions capable of preserving the Euclidean H in the face of O'. And this result alone suffices to invalidate the Einsteinian version of Duhem's thesis to the effect that any geometry, such as Euclid's, can be preserved in the face of any experimental findings which are expressed in terms of the customary definition of congruence.

It might appear that my geometric counterexample to the Duhemian thesis of unavoidably contextual falsifiability of an *explanans* is vulnerable to the following criticism: "To be sure, Einstein's geometric articulation of that thesis does not leave room for saving it by resorting to a remetrization in the sense of making the length of the rod vary with position or orientation even after it has been corrected for idiosyncratic distortions. But why saddle the Duhemian thesis as such with a restriction peculiar to Einstein's particular version of it? And thus why not allow Duhem to save his thesis by countenancing those *alterations in the congruence definition* which are *remetrizations?*"

My reply is that to deny the Duhemian the invocation of such an alteration of the congruence definition *in this context* is not a matter of gratuitously requiring him to justify his thesis within the confines of Einstein's particular version of that thesis; instead, the imposition of this restriction is entirely legitimate here, and the Duhemian could hardly wish to reject it as unwarranted. For it is of the essence of Duhem's contention that H (in this case, Euclidean geometry) can always be preserved *not* by tampering with the principal semantical rules (interpretive sentences) linking H to the observational base (i.e., specifying a particular congruence class of intervals, etc.), but rather by availing oneself of the alleged *inductive latitude* afforded by the ambiguity of the experimental evidence to do the following: (a) leave the factual commitments of H *essentially unaltered* by retaining both the statement of H and the *principal* semantical rules linking its terms to the observational base, and (b) replace the set A by A' such that A and A' are logically incompatible under the hypothesis H. The qualifying words "principal" and "essential" are needed here in order to obviate the possible objection that it may not be logically possible to supplant the auxiliary assumptions A by A' without also changing the factual content of H in some respect. Suppose, for example, that one were to abandon the optical hypothesis A that light will require equal times to traverse *congruent* closed paths in an inertial system in favor of some rival hypothesis. Then the semantical linkage of the term "congruent space intervals" to the observational base is changed to the extent that this term no longer denotes intervals traversed by light in equal round-trip times. But such a change in the semantics of the word "congruent" is innocuous in this context, since it leaves wholly intact the membership of the class of spatial intervals that is referred to as a "congruence class." In this sense, then, the modification of the optical hypothesis leaves intact both the "*principal*" semantical rules governing the term "congruent" *and* the "*essential*" factual content of the geometric hypothesis H, which is predicated on a particular congruence class of intervals. That "essential" factual content is the following: relatively to the congruence specified by unperturbed transported rods—*among other things*—the geometry is Euclidean.

Now, the essential factual content of a geometrical hypothesis can be changed either by preserving the original statement of the hypothesis while changing one or more of the principal semantical rules or by keeping all of the semantical rules intact and suitably changing the statement of the hypothesis. We can see, therefore, that the retention of a Euclidean H by the device of changing through remetrization the semantical rule governing the meaning of "congruent" (for line segments) effects a retention *not* of the essential *factual commitments* of the original Euclidean H but only of its *linguistic trappings*. That the thus "preserved" Euclidean H actually repudiates the essential factual commitments of the original one is clear from the following: the *original* Euclidean H had asserted that the coincidence behavior common to all kinds of solid rods is Euclidean, *if* such transported rods are taken as the physical realization of congruent intervals; but the Euclidean H which survived the confrontation with the posited empirical findings only by dint of a *remetrization* is predicated on a denial of the very assertion that was made by the original Euclidean H, which it was to "preserve." It is as if a physician were to endeavor to "preserve" an a priori diagnosis that a patient has acute appendicitis in the face of a negative finding (yielded by an exploratory operation) as follows: he would redefine "acute appendicitis" to denote the healthy state of the appendix!

Hence, the confines within which the Duhemian must make good his claim of the preservability of a Euclidean H do *not* admit of the kind of change in the congruence definition which alone would render his claim tenable under the assumed empirical conditions. Accordingly, the geometrical critique of Duhem's thesis given in this paper does *not* depend for its validity on restrictions peculiar to Einstein's version of it.

Even apart from the fact that Duhem's thesis precludes resorting to an alternative metrization to save it from refutation in our geometrical context, the very feasibility of alternative metrizations is vouchsafed not by any general Duhemian considerations pertaining to the logic of falsifiability but by a property characteristic of the subject matter of geometry (and chronometry): the latitude for *convention* in the ascription of the spatial (or temporal) *equality* relation to intervals in the continuous manifolds of physical space (or time).

It would seem that the least we can conclude from the analysis of Einstein's geometrical *D*-thesis given in this paper is the following: since empirical findings can greatly narrow down the range of uncertainty as to the prevailing geometry, there is no assurance of the *latitude* for the choice of a geometry which Einstein takes for granted in the manner of the *D*-thesis.

III. Is a Universal Nocturnal Expansion Falsifiable or Physically Vacuous?

As noted in the Introduction, my contention that there is at least one isolated hypothesis *H* which *is* separately falsifiable allows that there be some other *H* which, *taken by itself*, is intrinsically nonfalsifiable within a given theory in virtue of being physically vacuous or meaningless in that theory. My next problem is to determine whether the hypothesis of universal nocturnal doubling is nonfalsifiable in this sense.

G. Schlesinger has maintained that "a set of circumstances can be conceived under which one would have to conclude that overnight everything has doubled in size" and that "in the absence of these circumstances we are entitled to claim that it is *false* that overnight everything has doubled in size."[4] And Schlesinger went on to contend that the only way of actually rendering the hypothesis of nocturnal doubling physically vacuous is as follows: construe this hypothesis so as to make it a singular instance of the tautology that no unverifiable proposition can be verifiable, a triviality which does not qualify as an interesting ascription of physical vacuousness to the *particular* hypothesis of nocturnal doubling.

In order to appraise Schlesinger's contention, we must note at the

---

[4] [14], p. 68. Similar views were put forward earlier by B. Ellis [6]. The views which I attribute to Schlesinger are not found in their entirety in his own paper but were partly set forth by him in oral discussion at the meeting of Section L of the AAAS in December 1963, and also in a departmental colloquium at the University of Pittsburgh. The stimulus of Schlesinger's remarks was very helpful to me in articulating my views.

outset that he takes quite insufficient cognizance of two relevant facts: (1) the hypothesis of nocturnal doubling—hereafter called the "ND-hypothesis"—can be construed in several different ways, and (2) the charge of physical meaninglessness, inherent nonfalsifiability, and unverifiability has been leveled against the ND-hypothesis in the philosophical literature on a number of quite distinct grounds.

For my part, I have always construed the ND-hypothesis as being predicated on the kind of conception of spatial and temporal congruence which is set forth by Newton in the Scholium of his *Principia*.[5] On this kind of conception, container-space (and, *mutatis mutandis*, container-time) exhibits congruence relations which are *intrinsic* in the following sense: its structure is such that the *existence*—as distinct from the epistemic ascertainment—of congruence relations between nonoverlapping intervals does *not* depend at all on the *transport* of any kind of material congruence standard and therefore cannot depend in any way on the particular behavior of any kind of physical object under transport. This *transport-independence* of all congruence relations existing among intervals in principle permits the invocation of these intrinsic congruences to *authenticate* as a congruence standard any standard which is "operational" in the following *special* sense: the "operational" standard's performance of its metrical function is *transport-dependent* either because the standard is constituted by a transported physical object or because its application depends logically in some way on physical transport of a body or bodies. And, by the same token, once a unit of length is chosen, metrical equality and inequality of nonoverlapping intervals could be authenticated on the basis of the intrinsic congruences. Given the context of the Newtonian assumption of the existence of a container-space having intrinsic congruences between different intervals at the same time and between a given interval and itself at different times, it was therefore possible to construe the ND-hypothesis as asserting the following: relatively to the congruences intrinsic to container-space there has been a nocturnal doubling of all extended physical objects contained in space, and *also* a doubling of *all* "operational," i.e., transport-dependent, congruence standards. Because of the legacy of Newton's metrical philosophy, it was this nontrivial version of the ND-hypothesis which I appraised logically in my recent book ([8], Chapter 1, especially pages 42–43). And

[5] Cf. the edition by Florian Cajori [2], pp. 6–12.

when I denied the falsifiability of this interpretation of the hypothesis, I did *not* rest my denial on Schlesinger's triviality that no unverifiable proposition is verifiable; instead, my denial was based on the following weighty presumed fact: the *actual failure* of physical space to possess the kind of structure which is endowed with intrinsic congruences. For this (presumed) failure deprives space of the very type of metric on whose existence the ND-hypothesis depends for its physical significance and hence falsifiability. But, one might ask: Is it *logically* possible that there be a world whose space does have a structure which exhibits intrinsic congruences?

I shall answer this question in the affirmative by giving an adumbration of such a world. First I wish to point out, however, that Newtonian mechanics and the nineteenth-century aether theory of light propagation each cut the ground from under their own thesis that their absolute space possesses intrinsic congruences, and they did so by postulating the mathematical *continuity* of their absolute space. For, as Riemann pointed out in his Inaugural Lecture, if physical space is mathematically continuous, the *very existence* and not merely the epistemic ascertainment of congruences among its intervals is transport-dependent, *and nothing in the continuous structure of space can vouch for the rigidity (self-congruence) of the congruence standard under transport.*[6] Thus, if physical space is continuous, it is devoid of intrinsic congruences, since the very existence of its congruences derives *solely* from the behavior of conventional standards *all of which* are "operational" in the above special sense: the performance of the metrical function by each and every standard is transport-dependent, because either the congruence standard is itself a transported body or its application depends logically on the physical transport of a body or bodies. This Riemannian account of the status of the metric in continuous physical space can be summarized by saying that this space itself is metrically amorphous. Given, therefore, that the continuous absolute space of Newtonian mechanics and nineteenth-century wave optics cannot be adduced to prove the *logical* possibility of a space endowed with intrinsic congruences, can a kind of world be imagined which is such as to establish this logical possibility?

[6] For details and references, see my [8], pp. 8–16, 45, and 404–405. Mr. Peter Woodruff has pointed out to me that David Hume anticipated Riemann's insight in his *Treatise of Human Nature*, Part II, Sect. IV. It should be noted, however, that Riemann's thesis of the intrinsic metrical amorphousness of the continua of space and time does *not* apply to *all* kinds of continuous manifolds: cf. [8], pp. 16–18.

In now confronting this question, rigorous care must be exercised lest the challenge to furnish this proof of logical possibility be turned into the following very different second challenge: to specify empirical conditions which would justify that we *reinterpret* our present information about the physical space of our *actual* world so as to attribute a structure endowed with intrinsic congruences to that space. This second challenge has to be faced *not* by my impending characterization of an appropriate imaginary world, but rather by contemporary speculations of space and time *quantization* going back, according to at least one historian, to Democritus's *mathematical* atomism, a kind of atomism which must be distinguished from his much better known physical atomism.[7] Moreover, we must guard against being victimized by the tacit acceptance of a challenger's implicit question-begging requirement as follows: his implicit demand that the spatial vocabulary in which I couch my compliance with the *first* of these challenges be assigned meanings which are predicated on the assumption of spatial continuity ingredient in present-day confirmed physical theories. For the acceptance of that question-begging requirement would indeed import into the description of the sought-after imaginary world inconsistencies which could then be adduced to maintain that a physical space endowed with intrinsic congruences is logically impossible. And this conclusion would then, in turn, enable Schlesinger to uphold his contention that my version of the ND-hypothesis cannot be falsified in any logically possible world and hence is only trivially meaningless.

Having cautioned against these pitfalls, I now maintain that just as the three-dimensionality of actual physical space cannot be vouchsafed on a priori grounds, so also it cannot be guaranteed a priori that in every kind of spatial world the congruences would be transport-dependent rather than intrinsic. For imagine a world whose space has elements (space-atoms, lumps, or granules) such that (1) for any one space-atom, there are a fixed finite number of space-atoms which are next to it or contiguous with it (the magnitude of this finite number will determine the granulo-"dimensionality" of the atomic space by being two in the case of one-space, eight for two-space, etc.), (2) there are only a finite (though large) number of distinct space-atoms all told, and (3) there are no

---

[7] For details on this distinction, cf. S. Luria: "Die Infinitesimaltheorie der antiken Atomisten," *Quellen und Studien zur Geschichte der Mathematik, Astronomie, und Physik*, Abteilung B: Studien, II (Berlin: J. Springer, 1933).

physical foundations whatever for mathematically attributing proper (nonempty) parts to the space-atoms, as attested by the existence of only finitely many rest positions for any object. It is clear that the structure of this granular space is such as to endow it with a transport-independent metric: the congruences and metrical attributes of "intervals" are intrinsic, being based on the cardinal number of space-atoms, although it is, of course, trivially possible to introduce various other units each of which is some fixed multiple of one space-atom. To be an extended object in this kind of granular space is to comprise more than one space-atom. And the metric intrinsic to the space permits the factual determination of the rigidity under transport of any object which is thereby to qualify as an "operational" congruence standard. By the same token, the sudden nocturnal doubling of all "operational" (i.e., transport-dependent) metric standards along with all extended physical objects could be said to obtain in such a granular space, if on some morning they each suddenly occupied or corresponded to twice as many space-atoms as before. Accordingly, the ND-hypothesis formulated above is indeed falsifiable in the context of an atomic theory of space. But it is not falsifiable within the framework of any of the confirmed modern physical theories pertaining to our actual world: their affirmation of the mathematical continuity of physical space precludes that there be an intrinsic kind of metric, which is the very kind on whose existence the ND-hypothesis depends for its physical significance and hence falsifiability. Thus, we note that the content of the theory to which the ND-hypothesis is adjoined is relevant to its falsifiability. But this relevance of the remainder of the theoretical system does not detract from the fact that within the latter theoretical system the ND-hypothesis is separately inherently nonfalsifiable.

Ellis and Schlesinger mistakenly believe that they have corrected all previous treatments of the ND-hypothesis in the philosophical literature, because they have completely overlooked a fundamental logical fact which is an immediate corollary of my Riemannian justification for making alternative choices from among incompatible spatial and temporal congruences (compare [8], pages 22–23; Chapter 2, and Chapter 3, Part B). This logical fact is that Riemann's doctrine of the intrinsic metrical amorphousness of the spatial continuum permits the deduction both of the nonfalsifiability of the ND-hypothesis and of the falsifiability of a certain modified version of the ND-hypothesis which I shall call the "ND-conjecture." The ND-conjecture differs from the ND-hypothesis by not attributing the doubling to *all* operational standards of length measurement but only to one of them, while exempting the others from the doubling. In order to demonstrate the falsifiability of the ND-*conjecture* on the basis of Riemann's metrical doctrine, I must first clarify the logical relation of that doctrine to the view that the physical concepts of congruence and of length are each multiple-criteria concepts or open cluster concepts rather than single-criterion concepts.

Riemann's thesis that the spatial and temporal continua are each intrinsically amorphous metrically sanctions a choice among alternative metrizations of these continua corresponding to *incompatible* congruence classes of intervals and thus to incompatible congruence relations. By thus espousing the *conventionality* both of the *self*-congruence of a given interval *at different times* and of the equality of two different intervals at the same time, Riemann denies that the obtaining or nonobtaining of these congruence relations is a matter of factual truth or falsity. But clearly, Riemann's conception of congruence fully allows that any one set of congruence relations be specified physically by each of several different operational criteria rather than by merely one such criterion! For example, this conception countenances the specification of one and the same congruence class of intervals in inertial systems by the equality of of the travel times required by light to traverse these intervals no less than by the possibility of their coincidence with an unperturbed transported solid rod. Thus, as I have pointed out elsewhere [8, pages 14–15], Riemann's conventionalist conception allows that congruence (and length) is an open, multiple-criteria concept in the following sense: no one physical criterion, such as the one based on the solid rod, can exhaustively render the actual and potential physical meaning of congruence or length in physics, there being a potentially growing multiplicity of compatible physical criteria rather than only one criterion by which any one spatial congruence class can be specified to the exclusion of every other congruence class. And hence the conventionalist conception of congruence is not at all committed to the crude operationist claim that some *one* physical criterion renders "*the* meaning" of spatial congruence in physical theory.

A whole cluster of physical congruence criteria can be accepted by the proponent of Riemann's conventionalist view during a given time period, provided that the members of this cluster form a *compatible* family during this time period in the following twofold sense: (1) the various criteria yield *concordant* findings during the time period in question as to the self-congruence or rigidity of any one interval at different times, and (2) one and the same congruence class of separated spatial intervals must be specified by each member of the cluster of congruence criteria. It is a matter of empirical fact whether the concordance required for the compatibility and interchangeable use of the members of the cluster obtains during a given time period or not.

Now imagine a hypothetical empirical situation relevant to the falsifiability of the ND-*conjecture*: up to one fine morning, there has been concordance among the various congruence criteria in regard to the self-congruence of particular space intervals in time, but after that particular morning, that concordance gives way to the following kind of *discordance*: intervals which, *in the metric furnished by metersticks*, remain spatially congruent to those states of themselves that antedated the momentous morning, thereafter have *twice* their pre-morning sizes in the metric furnished by *all the other* congruence (length) criteria, such as the travel times of light. In that case, the requirement of logical consistency precludes our continuing to use metersticks interchangeably with the other congruence criteria after the fateful morning to certify continuing self-congruence in time. And it is perfectly clear that in the hypothetical eventuality of a sudden discordance between previously concordant criteria of self-congruence, the thesis of the intrinsic metrical amorphousness of the spatial continuum sanctions our choosing *either one* of the two incompatible congruences as follows: *either* we discard the meterstick from the cluster of criteria for self-congruence of space intervals in time *or* we retain the meterstick as a criterion of self-congruence to the exclusion of all the other criteria which had been interchangeable with it prior to the fateful morning.

The two alternatives of this choice give rise to the following two physical descriptions of nature, the *first* of which states the ND-*conjecture*:

Description I: Since the fateful morning, all metersticks and extended bodies have doubled in size relatively to all the *other* length criteria belonging to the original cluster, which are being retained after the fateful morning, and the laws of nature are unchanged, provided that the lengths l ingredient in these laws are understood as referring to the latter retained length criteria; or

Description II: Relatively to the retention of the meterstick as a length standard after the fateful morning and the discarding of all other previously used length criteria, there is the following *unitary* change in those functional dependencies or laws of nature which involve variables ranging over lengths: all magnitudes which were correlated with and hence measures of a length *l* prior to the fateful morning will be functionally correlated with the new length *l/2 after* the fateful morning. Given that the lengths symbolized by *l* are referred to and measured by metersticks after the fateful morning no less than before, this mathematical change in the equations means *physically* that after the fateful morning, the same lengths will no longer correspond to the previous values of other magnitudes but to new values specified by the new laws. Thus, if L is the length of a path traversed by light, and c the velocity of light, then the time T required by light for the traversal of the distance L before the momentous morning is given by

$$T = L/c,$$

whereas the time T' which corresponds to the *same* length L after the fateful morning is

$$T' = 2L/c.$$

Again, if L is the length of a simple pendulum (of small amplitude) and g the acceleration of gravity, then the period P corresponding to L before the fateful morning is given by

$$P = 2\pi \sqrt{L/g},$$

whereas the period P' which corresponds to the *same* length L after the momentous morning is

$$P' = 2\sqrt{2}\pi \sqrt{L/g}$$

It should be noted that the nocturnal change from P to P', which Description II characterizes as a change in the law relating the period to the given length L, is described equivalently in Description I as a nocturnal doubling of the length of the pendulum *not* involving any change in the *law* relating the period to the length.

A number of important points need to be noted regarding the two descriptions I and II.

1. I and II are *logically equivalent* in the context of the physical theory in which they function. And, contrary to Schlesinger's allegation, they incontestably have the same explanatory and predictive import or scientific legitimacy. I and II each enunciate an unexplained regularity in the form of a time-dependence: I asserts the unexplained new fact that all

metersticks and extended bodies have expanded by doubling, while II enunciates an unexplained change in a certain set of equations or laws according to a unitary principle.

2. Schlesinger mistakenly believes that he has shown on methodological grounds that the doubling of the metersticks asserted by I is the uniquely correct account as contrasted with the change in the laws of nature affirmed by II. Specifically, he supposes that he can disqualify II as a valid equivalent alternative to I on the grounds that I explains all the phenomena under consideration by the *single* assumption of doubling, whereas II allegedly can claim no comparable methodological merit but is a linguistically unfortunate and futile attempt to evade admitting I. And he derives this supposition from the fact that in Description II, the laws describing nature after the fateful morning can be derived from the previously valid *different* laws by the mathematical device of replacing the length *l* in the original laws by 2*l*. But the error of Schlesinger's inference lies in having misconstrued the mere computational strategem of replacing *l* by 2*l* as a warrant for claiming that the only *physically admissible* account of the phenomena is that all metersticks have doubled. For he overlooks the fact that the alternative metrizability of the spatial continuum allows us to *retain* the meterstick as our congruence standard after the fateful morning to the exclusion of the other criteria in the original cluster, no less than it alternatively permits us to preserve the others while jettisoning the meterstick. Thus, Description II is based on the convention that the meterstick does not change but is itself the standard to which changes are referred, since the lengths *l* are measured by the meterstick after the fateful morning just as they were before then.

In this connection, I should remark that I find Schlesinger's own computations misguided. What is at issue here in the context of the assumed continuity of physical space is only the *logical* rather than the physical possibility of an observational falsification (refutation) of the ND-conjecture. It therefore strikes me as ill-advised on Schlesinger's part to use the *actual known laws of nature* (e.g., the conservation laws for angular momentum, etc.) as a basis for calculating whether the hypothetical changes postulated by the ND-conjecture would be accompanied by other compensatory changes so as to render the detection of the hypothetical changes *physically* impossible. All that is at issue is whether we can specify logically possible observable occurrences relevant to the falsifiability of the

ND-conjecture, not the compatibility of such occurrences with the time-invariance of the actual laws of nature.

3. The sudden discordance between previously concordant criteria of self-congruence in time is indeed falsifiable. Being a proponent of Riemann's view of congruence, I countenance Description I no less than Description II to formulate that hypothetical discordance. And I therefore maintain that if the language of Description I is used, the falsifiability of the discordance assures the falsifiability of the ND-conjecture. By contrast, suppose that a narrowly operationist defender of the single-criterion conception of length were to declare that he is wedded to the meterstick once and for all even in the event of our hypothetical discordance. The putative defender of such a position would then have to insist on Description II while rejecting I as meaningless, thereby denying the falsifiability of the ND-conjecture.

4. Schlesinger is not at all entitled to claim that II is false while I is true on the basis of the following argument: if one were to countenance II as veridically equivalent to I as a description of our hypothetical nocturnal changes, then one would have no reason to reject analogously equivalent descriptions of phenomena of temperature change and of other kinds of change. This argument will not do. For suppose that one could construct analogues of my Riemannian justification of the equivalence of Descriptions I and II and thus could show that temperature changes also lend themselves to equivalent descriptions. How could this result then serve to detract from either the truth or the interest of my contention that II is no less true than I?

As is shown by the treatment of nocturnal expansion in my book [8, pages 42–43], I have not denied the physical meaningfulness of the kind of doubling (expansion) which results from a sudden discordance between previously concordant criteria of self-congruence in time. And it is puzzling to me that Reichenbach's writings and mine both failed to convey our awareness to Ellis and Schlesinger that the very considerations which serve to exhibit the physical vacuousness of the ND-hypothesis also allow the deduction of the falsifiability of the ND-conjecture. It is with regard to the ND-hypothesis but not with respect to the ND-conjecture that I have maintained and continue to maintain the following: on the assumption of the continuity of physical space, this hypothesis can have no more empirical import than a trivial change of units consisting in abandoning the Paris meter in favor of a new unit, to be called a "napoleon," which corresponds to a semi-meter.

REFERENCES

1. Alexander, H. L. *Reactions with Drug Therapy*. Philadelphia: Saunders, 1955.
2. Cajori, Florian, ed. *Sir Isaac Newton's Mathematical Principles of Natural Philosophy and His System of the World*. Berkeley: University of California Press, 1947.
3. Duhem, Pierre. *The Aim and Structure of Physical Theory*. Princeton, N.J.: Princeton University Press, 1954.
4. Einstein, Albert. "Reply to Criticisms," in *Albert Einstein: Philosopher-Scientist*, P. A. Schilpp, ed., pp. 663–688. Evanston, Ill.: Library of Living Philosophers, 1949.
5. Eisenhart, L. P. *Riemannian Geometry*. Princeton, N.J.: Princeton University Press, 1949.
6. Ellis, B. "Universal and Differential Forces," *British Journal for the Philosophy of Science*, 14:189–193 (1963).
7. Grünbaum, Adolf. "Geometry, Chronometry, and Empiricism," in *Minnesota Studies in the Philosophy of Science*, Vol. III, Herbert Feigl and Grover Maxwell, eds., pp. 405–526. Minneapolis: University of Minnesota Press, 1962.
8. Grünbaum, Adolf. *Philosophical Problems of Space and Time*. New York: Knopf, 1963.
9. Hempel, Carl G., and Paul Oppenheim. "Studies in the Logic of Explanation," *Philosophy of Science*, 15:135–175 (1948).
10. Northrop, F. S. C. *The Logic of the Sciences and the Humanities*. New York: Macmillan, 1947.
11. Poincaré, Henri. *The Foundations of Science*. Lancaster, Pa.: Science Press, 1946.
12. Putnam, Hilary. "Three-Valued Logic," *Philosophical Studies*, 8:73–80 (1957).
13. Quine, Willard Van Orman. *From a Logical Point of View* (Revised ed.). Cambridge, Mass.: Harvard University Press, 1961.
14. Schlesinger, G. "It Is False That Overnight Everything Has Doubled in Size," *Philosophical Studies*, 15:65–71 (1964).
15. Sokolnikoff, I. S. *Mathematical Theory of Elasticity*. New York: McGraw-Hill, 1946.
16. Timoshenko, Stephen, and Goodier, J. N. *Theory of Elasticity*. New York: McGraw-Hill, 1951.
17. Weyl, Hermann. *Space—Time—Matter*. New York: Dover, 1950.

VICTOR KRAFT

\\\(///

The Problem of Induction

1. That there is no theoretical justification for induction was explained very clearly by Feigl in 1934 [6]. (My own reasons were explained in 1925 [10].) However, the epistemological consequences of this situation have not been generally recognized, and it is also necessary to clarify them in greater detail. Such clarification will have to deal with the argument that without induction we end up in skepticism [1]; it will have to analyze the still existing attempts to find a basis for induction as a theoretical procedure (compare [14], [2], and [4]); and it will have to consider the more recent attempts to justify it at least practically as was first done by Feigl [5; 11, Section 39]. The absence of clarity in these matters is my motive for once more dealing with the problem of induction in a comprehensive fashion.

The reason for trying to retain induction is the wish to construct a firm foundation for our knowledge of nature. Such a foundation cannot be obtained deductively. For this one would need general major premises. Premises of this kind are not given a priori in the form of factual statements. They can only be gained from experience—this after all is the most basic principle of empiricism. However, all that is given by experience is single facts. It is from them that general statements of fact and laws of nature are to be derived. For knowledge aims at general insights, both in the sciences which are *primarily* concerned with laws and also in the sciences dealing with individuals, which are not exhausted by an enumeration of the single facts pertaining to these individuals.

NOTE: This paper was written in German for this volume. The translation is by Paul K. Feyerabend.

Now the experienced single facts are viewed as the foundation of our knowledge of reality. Immediately given perceptions are supposed to be such facts which can be obtained without the use of further presuppositions. Using them one thinks it will be possible to obtain a secure foundation for our knowledge of reality, a foundation, moreover, which does not involve any presuppositions and which is completely *ab ovo*. It is for this reason that the derivation of all our knowledge from the given facts of experience appears to be necessary, and induction is regarded as the procedure which achieves such derivation. This elucidates the fundamental importance of induction, and this is the reason why it appears to be irreplaceable and unavoidable and a necessary condition of all our knowledge [11, pages 357–360].

Induction, as we have said, has above all the task of making legitimate generalizations from our experience of singular states of affairs. It is not sufficient to "infer" one such singular state of affairs from another one that is already known. For generality cannot be dispensed with, as has just been shown.

2. Induction must be a *specific* procedure of generalization. For if it is built up as a special kind of deductive procedure, then it cannot achieve what it is supposed to achieve; namely, finding a basis for general facts in singular facts. Such a procedure would require a general principle in order to prove the generalization itself. But in this case generalities are already *presupposed* and not *established* on the basis of singular facts. Hence, induction must consist in a separate nondeductive procedure.

3. For quite some time, and up to the present, attempts have been made to develop such a procedure with the help of the theory of probability (see [11] and [14], among others). As we must not presuppose anything but observed singular cases, a large number of them, a body of statistics, is regarded as the proper starting point of the procedure. It is to such a collection that the theory of probability is applied in order to determine the so-called probability a posteriori. This probability concerns the relative frequency of cases exhibiting a certain property in an infinite sequence which approaches a limit. In this fashion a basis is found for the assumption that the relative frequency observed in a statistical sequence will be approximately valid in each prolongation of the sequence.[1]

But we cannot be sure of this. For when applying the theory of proba-

---

[1] Thus Reichenbach [11, page 340]: ". . . the relative frequency observed statistically is assumed to hold approximately for any future prolongation of the series."

bility to an empirical statistical sequence we leave unsatisfied a very essential presupposition. The theory of probability deals with infinite sequences for which a limit is assumed, and the approach to the limit takes place *within these very same sequences.* Experience, however, can give us only finite sequences which are always extremely short in comparison with an infinite sequence. And if one prolongs such a finite sequence, then the limit is approached within a new sequence; the original sequence is continued by different sequences of different length. Even if each of those new sequences were to show convergence toward the same limit, it would still always remain uncertain whether this limit would persist in the new sequences which are obtained by adding further observed members (compare [1]). They are different sequences, and therefore their limits, too, can be different. Nor can one use the argument that the prolongation of a statistical sequence must show whether it converges toward a limit and what the limit is, and that such prolongation is therefore self-correcting [5, page 137; 11, pages 319–348; 12]. For to each prolongation of the statistical sequence applies what we said of the original sequence: we can never be certain that the limit will retain its value, and we cannot even be certain that the sequence will remain convergent. The inductive principle that a convergent relative frequency in a finite statistical sequence must lead to a probability for similar cases *outside* the sequence cannot therefore be based on the theory of probability.

4. It is essential for induction that it transcend the statistical basis and be applicable to new cases. Enumerative induction on the basis of simple counting concerns a closed class and doesn't go beyond it; it has no major importance for our knowledge (this was already stated by Francis Bacon). All it achieves is a comprehensive report of what is contained in the observed singular cases. However, induction is supposed to bring about an extension of what has been observed; it is supposed to work in an open class. Extrapolation is essential for induction. What has become known in a restricted domain of cases is to be applied to cases which are as yet unknown.

However, we have no right to proceed in this fashion. What is known does not tell us anything about what is unknown; the latter is a new element. We would have to know a relation which connects the known with the unknown. And in order to be of use this relation would again have to be known, which leads to a contradiction. There is no theoretical justification for the process of extrapolation. Hence, the "expanding" induction cannot be justified as a specific procedure, a point which has been frequently emphasized by Feigl and which is no doubt true [6, pages 135–136].

5. But empiricists think they cannot do without induction. For induction is supposed to help them build up their knowledge of reality on the basis of experience. Hence, attempts were made to find a "pragmatic justification" instead of a theoretical justification of induction. Such a pragmatic justification of induction had been proclaimed by Feigl as early as 1932 and was developed in detail by him later [5, pages 123–139; 7]. Reichenbach developed similar ideas [11, pages 356–357; 12]. Since then these ideas have spread [8, 13], and they are now under discussion [1, 3]. A theoretical "justification" of induction is contrasted with its practical "vindication." The former has to do with the validity of an assertion; the latter doesn't concern an assertion, but the maxim of a course of action [6, page 302]. The practical justification of this course of action lies in its being a suitable means for an existing purpose. The purpose is to be able to make valid predictions and general statements about reality. Induction is a means for this purpose, and it is a course of action, a certain behavior, guided by a rule of operation. This rule says [6, page 303]: "Seek to achieve a maximum of order by logical operations upon elementary propositions. Generalize this order (whatever its form: causal, statistical or other), with a minimum of arbitrariness, that is, according to the principle of simplicity." This rule of induction does not give any guarantee for the validity of the generalization obtained. We do not know whether the world is orderly. The rule of induction does not contain any assertion concerning the regularity of what happens in the world. If there is no such regularity, then induction cannot be successful; it will then be unable to discover order. However, *if* regularity obtains, then induction is the safe means of discovering this order. This line of reasoning is supposed to constitute a practical justification of induction. The principle of induction does not tell us anything about reality; however, it has a pragmatic meaning, it guides our actions [5, page 138; 6, page 304; 11, pages 319–357].

Now this practical justification of induction is in need of a thorough examination. The principle of induction, as Feigl formulates it, consists in the instruction: Try to achieve a probable order. The justification for this instruction lies in its being a suitable means, and the only means, for reaching the aim of knowledge, namely, order. This can be shown deductively [5, page 137; 6, page 303]. However, concerning the procedure by means of which the desired order is to be achieved, the instruction only makes the following quite general pronouncement: "Seek to achieve a maximum of order by logical operations upon elementary propositions" [6, page 303]. Even the additional remark that this is to be done on the broadest possible basis and in the simplest fashion [6, page 303; 5, page 134] leaves it completely open how to proceed. One thing is certain: this sort of induction cannot be a nondeductive procedure, for the construction of order is supposed to take place *with the help of logical operations*. However, induction as it was introduced originally and as it is used by empiricism is a method in its own right, a genuine counterpart of the deductive method. One even tries still to retain this status of induction by connecting it with the theory of probability. Such an attitude toward induction can be found in Feigl, too, and this despite his talk of logical operations. For he sees the task of induction explicitly as providing "successful prediction, more generally, true conclusions of nondemonstrative inference" [5, page 136]. And he regards the ascription of a probability to predictions and hypotheses on the basis of a statistical relative frequency as a procedure of exactly this kind [5, page 134]. But the application of the rule of induction does not guarantee success, namely, the construction of order. We do not know whether the world is actually orderly. We can only try to find such order.

6. Induction, therefore, is seen to consist of two components. If we interpret it as the procedure of generalization on the basis of given facts, as the determination of what is unknown on the basis of what is known (the "principle of straightforward extrapolation in sequences of frequency ratios" [5, page 135], then it is on the one side extrapolation, unjustifiable extension beyond the domain of what has in fact been observed. This side of it is nothing but an attempt, a mere trial and error procedure, to show whether the extrapolation leads to success. Such attempts, and the instructions concerning them, can only be justified in a practical manner. They can be justified by pointing out that if we want to go beyond a mere description of existing experience and if we want to determine in a rational fashion what is to be expected, we must venture some generalizations. All this, expectation and tentative generalization, belongs to the pragmatic domain. It is a matter of action, of practical behavior.

But induction is on the other side more than mere extrapolation. If it were simply to consist in the instruction: If you want to find order, then try to bring about order—then it would be completely trivial and empty.

It is not sufficient just to extrapolate and to generalize; one must not extrapolate blindly and arbitrarily. A blind procedure would lead much more frequently to disaster than it would to success. We want to obtain *probable* predictions and generalizations. We must therefore first *select* those features of experience which we may generalize. Only some constituents of experience are suitable for determining the features of what has not yet been observed. We must know conditions which make an extrapolation reliable. It is only then that the attempt to extrapolate is not a blind trial and error process but a rationally guided procedure. This methodical recognition of what can be extrapolated has also to be done by induction. It is for this reason that it essentially contains a theoretical function. Induction is not exhausted in the practical function of extrapolating; it cannot be exhausted in a mere trial procedure. Induction must also be a theoretical method.

7. In accordance with this, John Stuart Mill formulated rules for induction, and others have also used the theory of probability or the quotient of the converging relative frequencies for the same purpose. To find the conditions for *probable* extrapolation—that is the function of induction. Induction has therefore not simply the task of extrapolating, it has also the task of finding what can be extrapolated. Whatever choice is made must be justified. Induction must make legitimate *what is* extrapolated even if it cannot legitimize the fact that *one does* extrapolate. Insofar as induction is extrapolation it can only be a practical attempt without any justification of its validity. But as a procedure for determining what can be extrapolated, it must give results which are theoretically sound, and it must be a method which justifies validity. It is in this fashion that the apparent opposition between the "practicalists" and those who want to justify induction in theoretical fashion can be resolved. Each of the parties holds an acceptable point of view in a one-sided manner.

The method for determining what can be extrapolated has been sought in a specific nondeductive procedure. Feigl, too, has explicitly characterized it as such [5, page 136]. But what kind of nondeductive method is to be taken into consideration? What method is available? Induction is nondeductive only if it is extrapolation, and if it is mere extrapolation, then it cannot provide any foundation for validity. Regarded as extrapolation it is not a theoretical procedure at all; it is just a practical mode of behavior. Yet the method by means of which those features which can be extrapolated are selected must be capable of making its results at least probable; it must provide a theoretical foundation for them. We must now find out whether this is possible in a nondeductive fashion—whether it is possible at all. Only such clarification will lead to a complete analysis of the problem of induction.

What the inductive method is supposed to achieve is this: it is supposed to determine those features which can be extrapolated with probability. When generalizing from observed singular cases, one argues from a part to a whole; one assumes that a feature which has been found in some cases applies to a whole class. However, this can only be the case if the part has the same structure as the whole and doesn't differ from it in essential points. An institute for public opinion asks people concerning their candidate in the next election. A proper picture of the general situation at the election is obtained only if the people are selected properly. They must not be selected in a one-sided manner, but must form a representative section of the whole; they must form a fair sample. The chosen part of the class must show roughly the same distribution of relevant properties as does the domain to be determined. It must not contain an accidental abundance or an exceptional lack of the cases possessing those properties. Now such proper choice can be guaranteed only if one has knowledge of a different kind which makes it probable that equal distribution has been achieved. If such knowledge is not available, then one can only try to discover whether the extrapolation will work out. And this, then, is no longer a rational procedure, a procedure that is guided by knowledge. One must possess criteria for the choice of what can be extrapolated; it is only then that a probability for the correctness of a generalization is obtained.

8. Such criteria are given in Mill's rules of induction. These rules concern only the finding of causal laws. The criteria for distinguishing between those relations between phenomena which can be generalized into causal laws and those which cannot be generalized are regular connection for the one, independent variability for the other. These criteria are an analytical consequence of the definition of causal laws as laws which assert exceptionless conjunction or, formulated as a general implication, whenever A then B. Mill's rules have the purpose in each single case of separating lawlike connections from accidental ones. It is in this, in the separation of lawlike relations from accidental relations, that the criteria for what can be extrapolated must consist in the case of induction in general. Induction is not only concerned with causal laws, it is concerned with any

type of generalization. Such generalizations are supposed to be confirmed; it should at least be probable that the new cases which are determined by expanding what is known to them do in fact possess the extrapolated property. In the case of statistical induction, this is guaranteed by showing that the property to be extrapolated does not occur just accidentally. And this is shown by the fact that the relative frequency in a statistical sequence will converge with an increasing number of cases. That this is the criterion for the possibility of extrapolation and the probability of the phenomenon extrapolated follows from the definition of chance and law. Lawfulness obtains when there is a relation between phenomena of two classes which always repeats itself. Chance prevails when occurrences in two different classes are sometimes related to each other, sometimes not. If we are dealing with only a small number of cases, then an accidental relation between two kinds of occurrences may repeat itself relatively frequently and thereby simulate a law. With an increasing number of cases, however, such an accumulation of coincidences will cease to exist. Chance therefore introduces a more even distribution of changing relations. The so-called "law of large numbers" is a consequence of this definition of chance. When the relative frequency in a statistical sequence converges, when the fluctuations become smaller and smaller as it is continued, then this contradicts chance; the sequence is thereby shown to be a not-chancelike sequence. And this gives us a justification; it gives us a probability concerning the proposition that the extrapolation of this frequency will also apply to new cases. Here, too, the distinction between chance and regularity in the domain of the known cases forms the foundation for determining what can be extrapolated. It is for this reason that the separation of what is not due to chance forms the task of the inductive method.

9. There are two ways of doing this. One is experiment. This completely satisfies the demand to find general conditions and laws on the basis of sometimes very few single cases of observation. In our experiments we always distinguish between lawlike and accidental relations. In order to be able to do this we must know the relevant conditions of the experiment, and this presupposes knowledge of natural laws on whose basis the conditions are brought into effect. Both these things are done deductively. In this fashion we can obtain a new law of nature only on the basis of laws which are already known, of course. A fundament for our knowledge of reality, its reconstruction *ab ovo* which is supposed to be

the task of induction, cannot be thus achieved. For such a reconstruction must be without presuppositions. Experiment, however, already presupposes general knowledge.

The second way is statistics. This method for determining what can and what cannot be extrapolated does not seem to be in need of any presuppositions. All it requires is a series of observed single cases in which the relative frequency of cases of a specific kind is noted. And we then inquire whether this relative frequency converges. The convergence gives us a criterion for deciding whether or not the relative frequency will remain constant in each prolongation of the sequence.

If it remains constant, then we obtain a probability for predictions concerning the prolongation of the series. This probability says that their truth will have a frequency identical with the relative frequency in the statistical sequence; it concerns a relation between true and false predictions within a class of predictions. It doesn't tell us anything about the single case. What will happen in the next single case remains a completely open matter. The true predictions are only part of all predictions considered; they occur together with false predictions in accordance with the quotient of relative frequencies. When this quotient equals one, then the predictions are true without exception. We can therefore supply laws in this fashion [11, page 350]. The statistical procedure is therefore a universal procedure.

But a statistical series even with converging relative frequencies does not suffice. For this relative frequency may apply only to the sequence as far as it has been constructed, and it may change when the sequence is continued. Even if the sequence should turn out to be convergent with an ever increasing number of its members, we still cannot be certain that further prolongation will not completely change the situation. We must have a guarantee that the sequence will remain convergent. Such a guarantee can only be obtained from the conditions under which the statistical sequence has come into existence. We must know whether these conditions are stable. Everything that is known about the conditions of a statistical sequence must be taken into consideration; we must make inductions on the broadest possible basis as is demanded in the rule of induction [6, page 303; 5, page 134]. This means, however, that additional knowledge will have to be used, especially laws of nature which allow us deductively to infer the conditions of a sequence and their stability. We therefore need presuppositions in addition to a statistical sequence if we want to be able to extrapolate its relative frequency. These presuppositions cannot be justified by other sequences of pure factual observation, for these too must be shown to be stable in the very same fashion. It follows that general statements about reality cannot be shown to be probable on the basis of that mere accumulation of observations which was thought to be the original and characteristic foundation of induction. Statistical induction too is unable to give an observational foundation for our knowledge which is entirely without any presuppositions.

10. Both the experimental method and the statistical method share a further presupposition which is easily overlooked, as it appears to be obvious. It can be demonstrated with the help of an example used by Feigl as a paradigm case of statistical induction [7, page 214–215]. The example is the eleven-year period of the frequency of sunspots. We do not need to concern ourselves with the question whether the knowledge of this period is based only on (centuries of) observation (a circumstance which obviously does not apply to the additional argument that the changing thickness of the year-rings of old trees is caused by a periodical variation of precipitation and this again by the changing frequency of the sunspots). It is a presupposition which is contained in the facts of observation themselves with which we are here concerned.

For what is actually given in the astronomical observation is a subjective visual image; solar spots, however, are objective material processes. That we perceive solar spots when these images are given has its reason in the fact that the images are taken as indications for sunspots.[2] Presuppositions of a very special kind are therefore added to what is actually observed: the sun regarded as a celestial *body*, changes of the solar *surface*, the telescope and its function as well as the laws governing this function. It is for this reason that only the expert recognizes the images as sunspots; what the layman sees is simply images. Now the elements of a statistical sequence and also those of an experiment are objective things and processes. They are very different indeed from subjective perceptions, and the latter, too, are not simply sense impressions, but sense impressions which have received an objective interpretation. These objects cannot be resolved into lawful relations between sense impressions. It is assumed that they exist continually, and that their shape, their magnitude, and their properties too remain and obey laws of their own. They are obtained by adding

[2] As regards this and what follows, compare [9], Chapter 5.

constructive assumptions to the sense impressions, assumptions which go far beyond anything which can be directly observed. The whole procedure of selection is therefore carried out within the framework of a realistic theory. This theory forms its most essential presupposition. If we wanted to avoid this presupposition, then we would have to restrict ourselves to lawful relations between subjective data of experience. Such data, however, could only be constituted by one's sense impressions. One would then have to be content with solipsism.

11. The procedure that is claimed to be induction possesses, as has been shown, a twofold function: on the one hand it consists in an extrapolation from known cases to new cases as yet unknown. This extrapolation cannot be justified theoretically, either as certain or as probable. It is a mere trial. On the other hand, induction is supposed to give us at least a probability for the validity of the extrapolation. This it can do only if the extrapolation is from features which are not accidental to the known cases, and which are therefore lawful. Induction must therefore in addition contain a procedure for the connection of these lawful features. It is in *this* procedure that the selection is shown to be valid. Induction so conceived is therefore a theoretical procedure, a method, and not a mere trial. However, this method is not specifically "inductive"; it is not a nondeductive procedure as it was thought to be in the beginning. It is purely deductive.

The proof of regularity is achieved with the help of observation and deduction. As regards experimental procedure, this does not need to be shown any more. Even in those cases where the nonaccidental character of a process is shown on the basis of converging relative frequencies in a a statistical sequence this is done by observation and deduction only. That convergence of a relative frequency shows its nonchancelike character follows deductively from a definition of law and chance. According to this definition accidental accumulations will disappear as the number increases; persistence of an accumulation shows it to be nonaccidental. It indicates a law or at least it indicates that a law is at work. And if the conditions of a statistical sequence make the persistence of the convergence probable, then this is inferred from laws of nature and single facts. This, too, is done deductively. The statistical method is therefore not a special nondeductive method. It proceeds only by deduction. This is the only procedure used to show validity.

[316]

Deduction, however, already presupposes general major premises. What is the foundation for these premises? What about the justification of the presuppositions used insofar as they are not definitions? What about the justification of the laws of nature and of the realistic theory? Laws of nature cannot be deduced from singular cases which are all that is given. They are extrapolations from them and, as such, unjustifiable if justification is to be absolute and without presuppositions. Judged theoretically an extrapolation is an assumption, the assumption of the existence of a law which connects the known with the unknown cases. This assumption is confirmed by the fact that new cases are in agreement with it. However, because of its unrestricted generality and because of our ignorance concerning new cases, it is impossible to verify it completely. All we can do is again and again to assume lawfulness. This assumption will always remain tentative. It lies at the bottom of all special knowledge of reality, and it is its necessary presupposition. It is therefore the fundamental principle of a theory of reality. Knowledge of reality does not come about by induction, for such a procedure does not exist. Such knowledge is developed in the form of a theory.

REFERENCES

1. Black, Max. "Can Induction Be Vindicated?" *Philosophical Studies*, 10:5–16 (1959).
2. Black, Max. "The Justification of Induction," in his *Language and Philosophy*, pp. 59–88. Ithaca, N.Y.: Cornell University Press, 1949.
3. Black, Max. " 'Pragmatic' Justifications of Induction," in his *Problems of Analysis*, pp. 157–190. Ithaca, N.Y.: Cornell University Press, 1954.
4. Churchman, C. West. *Theory of Experimental Inference*. New York: Macmillan, 1948.
5. Feigl, Herbert. "De Principiis Non Disputandum . . .?" in *Philosophical Analysis*, Max Black, ed., pp. 119–156. Ithaca, N.Y.: Cornell University Press, 1950. Reissued (New York: Prentice-Hall, 1963); in the reissue the pages are 113–147. Page references here are to the 1950 edition.
6. Feigl, Herbert. "The Logical Character of the Principle of Induction," *Philosophy of Science*, 1:20–29 (1934). Reprinted in *Readings in Philosophical Analysis*, Herbert Feigl and Wilfrid Sellars, eds., pp. 297–304. New York: Appleton-Century-Crofts, 1949.
7. Feigl, Herbert. "On the Vindication of Induction," *Philosophy of Science*, 28: 212–216 (1961).
8. Kneale, William. *Probability and Induction*. Oxford: Clarendon Press, 1949; New York: Oxford University Press, 1949.
9. Kraft, Victor. *Erkenntnislehre*. Vienna: Springer Verlag, 1960.
10. Kraft, Victor. *Die Grundformen der wissenschaftlichen Methoden*. S.-B. d. Oesterreich. Akademie d. Wissenschaften. Bd. 203/3. Vienna: Hölder, 1925.
11. Reichenbach, Hans. *Experience and Prediction*. Chicago: University of Chicago Press, 1938.

12. Reichenbach, Hans. "On the Justification of Induction," in *Readings in Philosophical Analysis*, Herbert Feigl and Wilfrid Sellars, eds., pp. 324–329. New York: Appleton-Century-Crofts, 1949.
13. Salmon, Wesley C. "Should We Attempt to Justify Induction?" *Philosophical Studies*, 8:33–48 (1957).
14. Williams, Donald C. *The Ground of Induction*. Cambridge, Mass.: Harvard University Press, 1947.

GROVER MAXWELL
\\\(\)///

Criteria of Meaning and of Demarcation

A brief personal note should be permitted in a *Festschrift* essay for a dear friend and colleague. I have, without doubt, learned more of whatever philosophy I know from Herbert Feigl than from any other source. Of the same order of magnitude, however, is my debt to Karl Popper and to Rudolf Carnap. In this essay, I criticize a family of ideas some member of which has been advocated, defended and, perhaps, even given its original formulation by each of these philosophers. However, it seems to me that, far from indulging patricidal impulses in so doing, I am treading in the most select subset of their footsteps. For theirs have been the voices of sanity in a philosophical milieu where extremism of one sort or another has run rampant, unfettered by self-examination or self-criticism. In particular, I am trying to continue along the lines exemplified by their efforts to stem the abuses and excesses, however well-intentioned, committed in the name of empiricism.

The thesis I shall attempt to defend is that the aim of contemporary empiricists to develop clear-cut, significant criteria for meaningfulness (or scientific status) is bound to be frustrated, and furthermore, that this can be shown to follow from the very principles defining contemporary empiricism, along with certain other principles which seem to me incontrovertible. I do not deny that there may be meaningless concatenations of symbols, nor that helpful rules (of thumb, probably) for detecting them may be developed. But such rules, I contend, will not use criteria based on verifiability, falsifiability, or even confirmability, unless the latter is defined in a very broad, loose manner *and* (circularly) *in* terms of *meaningfulness*. Nor can such rules require as necessary or sufficient conditions deductive or even statistical connections with observation or sense experience.

I shall deal first with empiricist criteria of meaning and later with Popper's criterion of demarcation for separating scientific, empirical statements from metaphysical ones. For the purposes of this discussion I shall grant (and use) the following two assumptions made by most contemporary empiricists (although, personally, I have grave doubts about both of them). (1) A viable, reasonably sharp distinction can be drawn between observation terms (or "the observation language," or "the observation vocabulary," etc.) on the one hand, and nonobservational, that is, *theoretical*, terms (. . . etc.) on the other. (2) Every theoretical term obtains any meaning it may have from the postulates of the theory in which it functions and from the "correspondence rules" *and from these alone*.

Today almost all empiricists agree that early meaning criteria formulated in terms of *verifiability* were much too narrow. Most would agree, even insist, that only *confirmability* or something similar is required. As is well known, most attempts (notably those by Ayer in *Language, Truth and Logic*, first *and* second editions) to give satisfactory formal criteria for confirmability (or direct or indirect connection with observation) have failed; for, if certain very trivial conditions are satisfied, then according to the proposed criteria any statement whatever is meaningful (see, for example, [4]). One point needs to be made here, and a brief consideration of Ayer's first attempt will serve its purpose. According to it, a sentence is meaningful if and only if there is an observation sentence which may be derived from it and other sentence(s) S_K, but which cannot be derived from S_K alone. The story, of course, is well known: Let S_M be any sentence whatever. We then take S_K to be $S_M \supset S_O$, where S_O is some observation sentence. So the criterion admits S_M and, thus, any sentence whatever as significant. Now at this point, some empiricists became impatient, taking something like the following position. "It is true that the criterion will not do as it stands; but what is intended is quite clear. Let us modify it to read something like, 'Some observation sentence must be derivable from S_M and S_K, and S_M must function nontrivially and in an uncontrived manner in the derivation.' It is true," this position continues, "that we may not be able to give formal criteria for triviality and for contrivedness—criteria which will meet all of the logicians' trick cases. Nevertheless, we know what is meant and will be able to recognize triviality, etc. (in this sense) when we see instances of it." Now I would certainly subscribe to the principle that we can sometimes have a criterion of something without having a formal criterion. But, as I shall try to show, triviality (in this sense) and contrivedness turn out to be matters of degree, so that the position sketched above cannot provide a means of delineating a sharp *meaningful-meaningless* dichotomy.

The failures of the attempts by Ayer and others led some empiricists, notably Hempel [5], to adopt what Carnap [3] termed a "skeptical" position to the effect that the question of meaningfulness cannot be raised for single terms or statements but only for *theories* and that, moreover, no sharp distinction can be drawn because, he holds, meaningfulness is a matter of degree.

Carnap was more optimistic and in 1956 [3] proposed a new criterion of empirical significance. It consists of three definitions, in which L is the language of science, which is divided into two parts, L_o, the observation language and L_T, the theoretical language. V_T is the theoretical vocabulary, T is the conjunction of the postulates of a theory, and C is the conjunction of the theory's correspondence postulates. The definitions, $D1$, $D2$, and $D3$, follow [3, pages 51, 60]:

$D1$. A term "M" is *significant relative to the class K of terms*, with respect to L_T, L_o, T, and $C =_{Df}$ the terms of K belong to V_T, "M" belongs to V_T but not to K, and there are three sentences, S_M and S_K in L_T and S_o in L_o, such that the following conditions are fulfilled:

(a) S_M contains "M" as the only descriptive term.
(b) The descriptive terms in S_K belong to K.
(c) The conjunction $S_M.S_K.T.C$ is consistent (i.e., not logically false).
(d) S_o is logically implied by the conjunction $S_M.S_K.T.C$.
(e) S_o is not logically implied by $S_K.T.C$. . . .

$D2$. A term "M_n" is *significant* with respect to L_T, L_o, T and $C =_{Df}$ there is a sequence of terms "M_1", . . ., "M_n" of V_T, such that every term "M_i" $(i = 1, . . ., n)$ is significant relative to the class of those terms which precede it in the sequence, with respect to L_T, L_o, T, and C. . . .

$D3$. An expression A of L_T is a *significant sentence of L_T* $=_{Df}$
(a) A satisfies the rules of formation of L_T,
(b) every descriptive constant in A is a significant term (in the sense of $D2$).

The criterion is striking in several respects, some of which have not been sufficiently noted:

1. It is basically a meaning criterion for terms (and only derivatively one for statements).

2. It is thus a step away from the *judgment empiricism* currently in vogue back toward the more old-fashioned *concept empiricism*. (Obviously, it is markedly different from a narrow Humean *concept empiricism*, however.)

3. The criterion is extremely liberal, as Carnap himself emphasizes, especially as regards the significance of *sentences* or *statements*; as he says (page 61), ". . . it includes [as significant] certain sentences for which no observational evidence can ever be relevant, e.g., the sentence: 'The value of the magnitude M at a certain space-time point is a rational number,' where 'M' is significant."

4. In fact, the criterion admits not only such "useful" statements as the one above, but, as M. B. Hesse and George Schlesinger have independently pointed out, such so-called "category mistakes" as "The cosmic mind dislikes cheese" and "The average velocity of anger is 30 cm. per second." Here I must defend Carnap. Such statements seem to be merely outrageously false (some of them, perhaps, necessarily false, i.e., A-false—inconsistent with some meaning postulate of the theory —see my [6]).

5. It seems not to have been noticed that statements like the following are also admitted: "Last night everything doubled in length" and "At time t electron e has the position $x \pm \Delta x$ and momentum of $p \pm \Delta p$, and $\Delta x\, \Delta p << h/2\pi$." Again, I would hold such statements to be meaningful, although they may be false, or inconsistent with theory, or even self-contradictory in a broad sense, i.e., A-false.

6. The stipulation that any descriptive non-observation term obtains any meaning it has from T and C and from these alone takes much of the sting out of criticisms such as those of Stephen Barker [2, pages 136–142]. (See Salmon's comments on Barker [8], and also Achinstein [1].)

Achinstein's "counterexample" also fails for another reason; he forgets or fails to note that the C-postulates are required to be universal postulates—or at least statistical laws (see Carnap [3, page 49]). However, it suggests an example which is instructive. Consider the heretofore meaningless term "masiquity," and let T.C be any good theory-cum-C-postulates. We then "enrich" the theory by adding the C-postulate: "For any space-time region, if its masiquity is 12 or greater, then it is red." Let S_M be a sentence asserting that the masiquity of a certain space-time region has the value 12. (Because of a device of Carnap's, the exact nature of which need not concern us, S_M can do this and still contain "masiquity" as its only descriptive term.) In this case, we may let S_K be some L-true statement. The observation sentence S_O asserting that the space-time region in question is red will then be derivable from $S_M.S_K.T.C$ but not from $S_K.T.C$. Hence, "masiquity" is a meaningful term and S_M a meaningful sentence. Carnap, however, has already considered a possibility almost identical with this [3, pages 57–58]. So his reaction to our example would presumably be the same, i.e., that our additional C-postulate is "stated as holding with physical necessity; therefore it conveys some empirical meaning on ['masiquity']" (page 58). We can agree with Carnap that *some* meaning is conveyed but must hasten to add, "Not much!" Furthermore, our additional C-postulate and S_M function not quite but *almost* as trivially in the derivation of S_O as did the contrived additions in the counterexamples to the older criteria. (As, in the older Ayer criterion, any sentence S_M could be shown to be meaningful by adding the sentence $S_M \supset S_O$.)

Suppose then, however, we added to T.C another C-rule, and perhaps one or two T-postulates, containing "masiquity." We might then have a "theory" of masiquity on about the same level as Barker's "theory of the Absolute"—still pretty trivial and nonsensical (in a nontechnical sense of "nonsense") but not as bad as previously. If we continued this process in an appropriate manner (and were lucky in our scientific speculations), the notion of masiquity might begin to acquire considerable explanatory and predictive power—considerable "theoretical fruitfulness."

This brings us, of course, to the heart of the matter and also returns us to something like Hempel's "skeptical" position of 1951. The meaningfulness, to any nontrivial, interesting, important degree, of a (non-observation) term is inextricably linked to the fruitfulness—or scientific satisfactoriness, etc.—of the T- and C-postulates which contain the term; and as Carnap himself has said (page 62), "There is no sharp boundary line between fruitful and useless hypotheses or theories: this is rather a matter of degree. It seems even doubtful whether it is possible to formulate in a completely general way a definition of a quantitative degree of fruitfulness of a scientific theory."

Since most empiricists today agree that all non-observation terms are wholly dependent on the C-rules and T-postulates for their (descriptive) meaning, it would seem that all future empiricist meaning criteria must be constructed along the same lines as that of Carnap and that they must be subject to virtually the same limitations.

It seems then that we should be concerned less about meaningfulness and meaninglessness and more about what is *meant*, and even more concerned about what is true or false, confirmed or disconfirmed, justified or unjustified. For the considerations above indicate that each theory, or portion of a theory, must be examined in some detail and on its own merits, that there are no simple, blanket criteria permitting us to make any interesting pronouncements on its "meaningfulness."

Let us turn now to Popper's "criterion of demarcation" [7]. According to it a system of statements is scientific (or empirical) if and only if it is falsifiable; the potential falsifiers are singular observation statements of a certain kind, the exact nature of which need not concern us here. Systems which do not fulfill this requirement are nonscientific, nonempirical or metaphysical. (Popper is emphatic in denying that he is proposing a *meaning criterion*; according to him, nonscientific or metaphysical statements may be meaningful and may even play a useful role in science.)

Note that his criterion is applicable to statements (or sentences) rather than to terms. Furthermore, the falsifiability requirement obviously requires that the statement (or system of statements) function nontrivially in the logical implication of some singular observation statement. Thus it will encounter difficulties analogous to those met by the putative confirmability criteria of Ayer and others; either the criterion will be so broad that any statement whatever must be admitted as scientific, or scientific status will be a matter of degree so that there will not be any *scientific-metaphysical dichotomy*.

But if Popper's criterion taken purely formally is so broad that it admits any statement whatever as scientific, it will become too narrow if we add a nontriviality-uncontrivedness condition and interpret this in an intuitively acceptable manner. Before trying to show this, let us note that Carnap's meaning criterion is much less restrictive than the demarcation criterion. For, as we have noted, it admits as scientific sentences which are not only nonfalsifiable by observation but for or against which no observation could ever be relevant as evidence.

Perhaps the most obvious objection is one of which Popper is well aware and which he has discussed at some length: any purely existential statement (even if all its descriptive terms are observational) is nonfalsifiable and, thus, nonempirical. I have not been convinced by Popper's answers to this objection, but I am not concerned to press it here, for I believe that there are more important ones. These involve nonfalsifiable statements containing both universal and existential quantifiers. Many such statements play a crucial role in science and many of them are so basic and so taken for granted that they are rarely stated, such as, "For every pure solid at a given external pressure there is a temperature (melting point) above which it becomes liquid." A case of some recent interest: "For every beta particle emitted in radioactive decay there is emitted a neutrino." Popper has already indicated [7] at least two lines of defense against such objections. He might say that before the enunciation of hypotheses such as the ones whereby the neutrino was "detected" experimentally in 1956, the neutrino hypothesis was, indeed, metaphysical, and that he admits, indeed *insists*, that nonempirical ("metaphysical") statements may play roles of great importance in empirical science. Why then, we may ask him, should we place such statements on the "wrong" side of a line separating empirical science from "metaphysics"? If they play roles of great importance in science, why are they not scientific? Or second, he might reply that he has often pointed out that his criterion should, in general, be applied to *systems* of statements or theories as wholes rather than to isolated statements and that, since the statements in question are parts of a scientific system the whole of which *is* falsifiable, they thereby attain scientific status. This will not do at all as it stands, for we could give any statement whatever scientific status simply by conjoining it with some falsifiable theory. Popper's answer would presumably be along the same lines as the one he gives concerning some purely existential statements [7, page 70n]. Such a statement ". . . if taken *in a context* with other statements . . . may *in some cases* [all italics are Popper's] add to the empirical content of the whole context: it may enrich the theory to which it belongs, and may add to its degree of falsifiability or testability. In this case, the theoretical system including the existential statement in question is to be described as scientific rather than metaphysical." But is it not clear that the statements in the examples above as well as any nonfalsifiable statement not derivable from the other statements of the theory will not increase the degree of falsifiability but will, in general, make the system, as a whole, less falsifiable?

Although Popper has been, perhaps, even more instrumental in removing many of the excesses of contemporary empiricism than Carnap and Feigl, it seems to me that his criterion of demarcation is worse off in both directions (too broad and too narrow) than empiricist meaning criteria.

It may be objected that some of my judgments against this family of criteria have been too harsh. For example, are there not cases where something like Carnap's criterion can be of service? How about terms for which no C-postulates exist, and how about sentences containing such terms? Do such cases ever arise? Occasionally, I believe, but in a rather devious fashion. These are the cases which Feigl sometimes calls "giving with one hand and taking away with another." (See, for example, his presidential address at the 1963 meeting of the Western Division of the American Philosophical Association.) Two of his examples are the demythologizing theologian and the last-ditch defenders of theories of the ether. These miscreants begin with terms which *had* perfectly good meanings, such as "God" and "ether"; then, when they encounter difficulties they begin discarding C-postulates, continuing when pressed further, until *none* remain. Two remarks: (1) Such slippery characters would probably discard *any* and *all* meaning rules, empirical or otherwise, if it suited their purposes. It is somewhat loading the situation in favor of empiricism to speak in terms of C-rules only here. (2) Rather than a formal or semantical criterion, the main consideration here seems pragmatic, even psychological: we attribute to such persons the behavioral disposition to so equivocate and otherwise mutilate the meanings of some of the terms they use that we just don't know what they are talking about. (Although we suspect that, in order to retain the old, favorable emotive, etc., overtones, they wish, *inconsistently*, also to retain some of the very meaning rules they discard—the old trick of "persuasive definition.")

We can sympathize with the motives of many of those who have propounded the various criteria under discussion. Surely *some* "speculative metaphysicians" and others have been guilty of spouting nonsense (at least in a nontechnical sense). But it seems to me, although I have not the space to argue for it here, that such cases do not require criteria based on observation or experience (however important these may be for a general theory of knowledge) but that they can almost always be handled by pointing out tacit equivocations and inconsistencies (or, sometimes, disguised analyticity) as indicated above.

[326]

GROVER MAXWELL

REFERENCES

1. Achinstein, Peter. "Theoretical Terms and Partial Interpretation," *British Journal for the Philosophy of Science*, 14:89–105 (1963).
2. Barker, Stephen F. *Induction and Hypothesis*. Ithaca, N.Y.: Cornell University Press, 1957.
3. Carnap, Rudolf. "The Methodological Character of Theoretical Concepts," in *Minnesota Studies in the Philosophy of Science*, Vol. I, Herbert Feigl and Michael Scriven, eds., pp. 38–76. Minneapolis: University of Minnesota Press, 1956.
4. Church, Alonzo. Review of A. J. Ayer, *Language, Truth and Logic* (2nd ed.), *Journal of Symbolic Logic*, 14:52–53 (1949).
5. Hempel, Carl G. "The Concept of Cognitive Significance: A Reconsideration," *Contributions to the Analysis and Synthesis of Knowledge*, Proceedings of the American Academy of Arts and Sciences, 80:61–77 (July 1951).
6. Maxwell, Grover. "Meaning Postulates in Scientific Theories," in *Current Issues in the Philosophy of Science*, Herbert Feigl and Grover Maxwell, eds., pp. 169–183. New York: Holt, Rinehart, and Winston, 1961.
7. Popper, Karl R. *The Logic of Scientific Discovery*. New York: Basic Books, 1959.
8. Salmon, Wesley C. "Barker's Theory of the Absolute," *Philosophical Studies*, 10: 50–53 (1959).

STEPHEN C. PEPPER

))(())))

On Knowledge of Values

In this paper I wish to consider the justification of value judgments. This has become a more than ordinarily heated issue since the advent of the emotivists and their extreme position that value judgments are cognitively meaningless. Feigl exhibits a qualified agreement with their view. I wish to look into the tenability of his stand.

His approach is by way of an analysis of justification in general. He makes a fruitful distinction between justification of a knowledge claim (*justificatio cognitionis*) and justification of an action (*justificatio actionis*). The first he calls "validation," the second "vindication." "The rules of deductive and inductive inference," he writes, "serve as the justifying principles in validation; purposes together with (inductively confirmed or at least confirmable) empirical knowledge concerning means-ends relations, or in the extreme degenerate case with purely logical truths, serve as the basis of vindication" [3, page 674]. In an article, "De Principiis Non Disputandum . . .?" [1], Feigl takes up validation and vindication in the four areas (1) of formal logic, (2) of factual knowledge or inductive method, (3) of factual meaningfulness, and (4) of ethics (or more generally values).

In his analysis of justification in these four areas, the first three fall into a homogeneous group different from the fourth. The difference, in Feigl's view, arises in that the first three deal with propositions, analytic or synthetic, whereas the fourth deals mainly with "value judgments" in the nature of prescriptions, which are neither true nor false. It will be found relevant to go briefly over his analysis of the first three areas before launching into the fourth, the area with which this paper is chiefly concerned.

Feigl points out that in the area of formal logic any instance of valid reasoning such as a valid syllogism is validated by reference to the formal rules that cover the procedure, in this instance the rules of the syllogism. These in turn are validated by reference to definitions and more fundamental principles such as the rules of substitution and inference. But how are these ultimate principles of formal logic to be justified? Feigl rejects an appeal to self-evidence as involving "psychologism." He rejects several other traditional suggestions, and finally concludes that ultimate formal principles of logic cannot be validated at all, but only vindicated. They cannot be validated because there are no further rules of formal reasoning to which these ultimate rules could conform. But they can be vindicated in terms of a purposive aim—namely, that of reaching true conclusions from true premises, or rational consistency. The vindication is in the form: If anyone wishes to avoid the discomforts of ambiguity and inconsistency, and to reach true conclusions from true premises, he will conform to the rules validated by the ultimate principles of formal logic. These principles cannot be validated, for they are themselves the conditions of validation, but they can be vindicated in terms of the human purposive demand for consistent reasoning.

Feigl analyzes the justification of factual knowledge similarly. We justify any particular prediction by reference to some empirical generalization or law. If this is questioned, we justify it by reference to some more general and inclusive law. But ultimately we reach a terminus for these references and this terminus turns out to be the principle of induction itself, the principle of procedure by which we justify all our correlations, laws, and hypotheses about factual structures and relationships. The process by which we justify inductive conclusions by reference to higher inductive principles is one of validation all the way up to the ultimate principle of induction. For these are justifications of knowledge claims. But how justify the ultimate inductive principle which validates all these claims? Just as Feigl rejects an appeal to self-evidence as a rationally acceptable validation of ultimate principles of formal logic, so he rejects an appeal to immediate incorrigible data as a kind of ultimate knowledge that might validate inductive conclusions. It is not that Feigl rejects all claims of immediacy, but that he finds these claims justifiable only in references "to the data of the present moment of a stream of experience" [1, page

130], and such data are far removed from the "observation statements" used to verify or confirm inductive laws and hypotheses. "Observation statements" must be corrigible enough to be subject to confirmation on their own account in terms of other "observation statements" and an extensive system of natural laws. Again Feigl's conclusion is that the principle of induction, which validates other inductive conclusions, is not itself eligible for validation. Its justification can only be a vindication. The form of the vindication is: If anyone wishes to find such order as there may be in nature, the principle of induction will bring it out. "For this method is according to its very definition so designed as to disclose whatever order or regularity may be present to be disclosed. Furthermore, since the inductive method is self-corrective, it is the most flexible device conceivable for the adaptation and readaptation of our expectations" [1, page 138].

The justification of the area of factual meaningfulness resolves itself, if I read Feigl aright, into a special application of factual justification or of factual combined with logical justification. For the meaningfulness of statements, even those derived from epistemological and metaphysical sources, is in the ultimate analysis hypothetical. And the meaningfulness of a hypothesis is ultimately determined through the principle of confirmability by factual evidence. Meanings of statements can be validated by reference to the meaning of more and more widely confirmed systems of knowledge, but ultimately the principle of confirmability itself comes up for validation. As the ultimate validating principle, it cannot obtain validation for itself. But it can be vindicated in the form: If anyone wishes to be clear in his thinking and free from confusions as to which of the statements he uses have factual meaning and which have not, he will conform to the principle of confirmation.

This brings us to Feigl's treatment of the justification of ethical principles. Here he introduces a serious alteration. One way of bringing this out is to show that in the three previous systems there is a single principle or set of principles which validates all subordinate items (rules, generalizations, meanings) in the area. This single set is then justified by a vindication. But in the ethical area there appear several independent principles (ultimate moral ideals, norms) mutually contrary in their validations, so that there is no single system of principles which can validate all subordinate items. The different moral systems are vindicated separately.

The reason at the bottom of this sudden shift in the mode of analysis is that Feigl allowed himself to accept a prescriptive interpretation of value judgments. The typical conclusion of the emotivist school of ethics is thus drawn that there can be rational discussion of means-ends relationship, but not of ends. A statement that an act or an object serves as a means to an end is a descriptive statement of fact, true or false, an instance of knowledge, and so capable of validation. But an expression of an end or ideal is a normative sentence, a prescription or an imperative, and as such neither true nor false, and so capable not of validation but only of vindication. Thus cognitive justification of ethical judgments is not possible in the way it is for the deductive propositions in formal logic or the inductive statements of science. This is the position of Feigl's that I am questioning.

Here is not the place to examine the mistakes of analysis which I believe have led to the theory that value judgments (other than means-end judgments) are neither true nor false.[1] All I wish to do here is to show that if a prescriptive interpretation of ethical judgments is not assumed, then there is as much validation of propositions to be found in the ethical area as in the other three.

I am suggesting that a thoroughgoing naturalistic ethics is possible. If so, it will have the status of a scientific hypothesis, descriptive of a special area of human and perhaps animal activity, and open to confirmation like any other scientific hypothesis. Of course, the truth of a naturalistic hypothesis of ethical activity would not be irrefutably established any more than the ultimate truth of any descriptive hypothesis. But it could be rendered more and more probable. Also alternative hypotheses could be put forward and their relative adequacy tested in the light of available evidence. One can go further and point out that even a prescriptive interpretation of ethics cannot exclude itself from competition with alternative naturalistic ethical hypotheses. For unless the prescriptive interpretation of ethical judgments is offered as a priori or in some other way privileged to an immunity from cognitive examination, it presents itself as just one of a number of hypotheses to account for the activity of men called ethical.

Feigl, at least, should not object to this treatment of prescriptive ethical theory in view of his general attitude toward incorrigible judgments as

---

[1] Such an examination may be found in Chapter 12, "Emotive and Prescriptive Theories," of my *Ethics* [4].

unjustified beyond "the data of the present moment of a stream of experience" [1, page 130]. For if prescriptions (neither true nor false) are offered as the central subject matter of an ethical system, this is tantamount to using them as incorrigible judgments not open to cognitive criticism. Any naturalistic moralist will, nevertheless, whether forbidden to do so or not, subject these judgments and the hypothesis that utilizes them to cognitive criticism. One is surprised in view of his strong naturalistic interest that Feigl allows himself to accept an ethical approach based on incorrigible value judgments. He is careful to dismiss "divine commandments" and "intuitive self-evidence" [1, pages 142–143] as validating criteria. How does he allow himself to accept the self-validation of prescriptive judgments for a prescriptive theory of ethics to the extent of permitting them to invalidate corresponding descriptive judgments in an alternative descriptive theory of ethics?

My point here is that without resort to devices of dogmatism by which elements in a theory are marked as immune to cognitive criticism, a prescriptive ethical theory cannot escape comparison with any descriptive ethical theory covering the same subject matter. Imperatives, prescriptions, recommendations, etc., have been used by emotive and prescriptive moralists essentially as dogmatic devices. I am quite sure Feigl would not intentionally do this. If he does not, then there is a fair and open competition between prescriptive and descriptive hypotheses about ethics as to their comparative adequacy in consistently covering the field.

If that step is accepted, all that remains to be done to show that validation in the ethical field need not be different from validation in, say, physiology, is to demonstrate that a descriptive account of ethical normative activity can be given with a respectable prospect of confirmation. This definitely can be done.

It is admitted even by the prescriptivists that judgments about means to ends are open to validation in Feigl's terms, and Feigl explicitly admits this. Why is this admitted? If one examines the structure of an instrumental (means-end) act, one finds that the correctness of the choice of a means is determined by its achieving its end, and the verification of the means for this achievement consists in the discovery *by inductive procedures* of a causal agent for attaining the end. The determination of a means is thus (in the vocabulary of the prescriptivists) a "scientific procedure," and may be properly expressed in a declarative statement, true or false.

[332]

The first comment I want to make is right at this point. I want to stress the fact that here is one value judgment (the judgment of the value of a means for the attainment of an end) which is admitted even by the prescriptivists to be a declarative statement, true or false.

The reply will be made that the value derives from the value felt in the end, and that the scientific procedure for finding a causal agent to attain the end is a purely cognitive affair entirely neutral to any value accruing to the situation. This reply is put forward as a true statement, of course. It sounds very plausible. But it contains an implicit inference which when made explicit is not valid.

There are three statements condensed within this sort of reply: (1) A statement about the behavior of values in a means-end situation, to the effect that the value of a means is derived from the value of the end. This is an empirically well-confirmed statement. (2) A statement that the cognitive procedure for finding cause and effect relations is independent of the presence of values in the cause, the effect, or the relation between them. This is also a well-confirmed statement. (3) An implicit conclusion that the cause and effect relation, and, indeed, cognitive procedures generally, have no bearing on values. This conclusion I find false. It immediately leads to the further statement typical of the prescriptivists that value judgments are neither true nor false, and to their device of identifying value judgments with imperatives and the like which *linguistically* are indeed neither true nor false.

The third statement, the implicit conclusion, does not follow from the first two statements taken as premises. It is, in fact, contrary to the first statement, which would ordinarily be taken to affirm that a means has a value which is derived from the value of an end by way of a judgment concerning the causal relation of the means to the end. The justifiable conclusion would be that whenever a cause and effect relation is applied to a behavior situation in which value is attributed to the effect then value will be attributed to the cause. In other words, though cognitive procedures for determining cause and effect relations are often neutral to values, yet whenever values do enter into a cause and effect relationship these values are cognitively relevant. The usual indication of such relevancy is to refer to such a cause and effect relationship as a means-end relationship. In short, some cause and effect relationships are means-end relationships, and all means-end relationships are cause and effect relationships.

These last statements would need some qualification for their full empirical validation, but they are adequate to block off any sweeping assumption that no value judgments are cognitive statements, or scientific, or true or false.

It is still possible, however, for a prescriptivist to rule out instrumental judgments from the class of value judgments by definition, to identify value judgments with judgments of value ends, and then assert that judgments of ends cannot be validated but only vindicated.

If I interpret Feigl correctly, he would not go so far as to say that instrumental judgments are not about values or to deny that these may be validated through an extensive hierarchy of means justified by further means up to a final end. But the ends, he would maintain, can only be vindicated emotively. For the sphere of values does not move up to a terminal set of rules such as those of logic for guaranteeing consistency, or of empirical induction for discovering such order in nature as there is. There may even be highly organized cultures in which values culminate in a set of recognized principles of morality for all persons acculturated to them. But as between cultures, principles will differ and there is no higher principle by which to validate them.

Feigl seems to be anxious to validate values and ethical principles by purely valuative means. Why not validate them by cognitive means? When people are making ethical decisions what they desire is to *know* what the correct decision is, the one that is *cognitively* validated. There are many ethical principles but the principle that a man *ought* to follow is, according to a long tradition, the one *cognitively* most fully justified. Why should Feigl seek to break away from this tradition?

In a short article on "The Difference between Knowledge and Valuation" [2], he presents his reasons clearly. He first states what he regards as the unbridgeable difference between cognitive and value judgments in terms of a typical prescriptive theory of ethics. "It is one thing," he writes, "to *study* evaluations, their conditions and consequences; it is another thing to *make* evaluations and in this manner to influence the course of events . . . It is one thing to describe by means of declarative sentences what *is* the case . . . it is another thing to prescribe by means of overtly or covertly imperative sentences . . . what *ought* to be done" [2, page 39]. "What I do dispute here is the claim that a science of valuations *ipso veritate* provides a validation of valuations" [2, page 40]. He disputes this claim for two reasons, of which the second he regards as the more important.

His first reason is "that there is nothing in the nature of evaluation that ensures its intersubjectivity" (page 41), nothing to ensure the kind of agreement on which the validation of scientific statements is grounded. "Since any application of scientific knowledge presupposes purposes and since it is in the light of such purposes that we evaluate means," he writes, ". . . we cannot ignore the actuality (or at least the possibility) of cognitively irremediable disagreements in regard to purposes" (page 41). He admits that empirical research can in principle offer a "cognitive basis for determining which means lead to the attainment of which ends," but "it remains possible that no matter how complete the information of each party to a dispute over ends, no agreement on these ends may be attainable."

His second reason is that "scientific knowledge, even if its [sic] concerns the conditions and consequences of valuations, is in a perfectly clear sense value-free or value-neutral" (page 41). "Scientific statements can by their very nature not contain such words as 'advisable,' 'desirable,' 'should,' 'ought,' or 'must'" (pages 41–42). And he repeats the typical maxim of a prescriptive theory of ethics, "indicatives never imply imperatives" (page 43).

The first reason, as he observes, is the weaker of the two. The demand for agreement as the basis of scientific validation holds only when highly qualified. It is only agreement among experts that counts, and even then agreement on principle rather than in actuality. And as regards evaluation, Feigl admits in the quotation above that evaluation of means is open to the kind of agreement demanded for scientific validation. So, Feigl must either exclude by definition evaluations of means as valuations, or admit that at least in this area valuation and knowledge overlap, and that here at least there is cognitive validation of values.

As to disagreement about ends, there is a question of fact involved and possibly an ambiguity as to the meaning of the phrase. There are, of course, plenty of disagreements about means. But these disagreements do not bother Feigl, because, like other scientific disagreements, they are in principle resolvable by experts. Not all disagreements about ends, then, are relevant to Feigl's criterion, but only those not resolvable in principle by experts when theoretically all the information is in. Notice that this qualification takes the issue out of the hands (or rather the feelings) of the agents posing the ends in disagreement. It will require experts in the relevant information about ends as values to determine whether the disagreement is not resolvable.

The difference between ends and means in this issue is probably greatly exaggerated. An agent is often mistaken as to what he thinks is his end. This mistake may not even be available to the intelligence of the agent—not simply because of lack of information but because of repressions which conceal from him important elements of his motivation. More significant still, there are hierarchies of ends, some of which take precedence over others. Lastly, in a general theory of value (and any special theory is by its limited scope inevitably not final in its conclusions) social values and group survival values may take precedence *empirically* over the personal values of an individual. These considerations on the bearing of ends in relation to one another are not transparent to any ordinary man. Only a science of the subject conducted by experts whose cognitive disagreements are resolvable in principle would be competent to give judgments on the matter.

Exponents of the prescriptive theory of ethics have been prone to view ethics on a limited individualistic basis. The background has been that of the traditional hedonistic ethics, often biased toward egoistic hedonism with the assumption that there is no empirically justifiable value appeal beyond the impulse of the individual, sometimes modified, however, by a *definition* of moral values requiring that the impulse be "universalizable" by the individual, though sometimes also allowing for the acculturation of individual impulses yielding an ethical theory close to that of cultural relativism. There is a sentence in the article quoted above in which Feigl seems to accept this last modification. "In the give and take of interpersonal relations, in the claims and counter-claims made by man upon fellow-man, certain ideal standards, e.g., of equity and benevolence could not fail to arise" (page 42). But the pivot on which the prescriptive theory rests is that there is no evaluative appeal from an end served by means values. An emotionally charged end initiates an "ought," which for the strange reason that it is emotional, is regarded as not susceptible to scientific investigation and description. And if such descriptions are discovered, they are promptly dismissed as merely "psychological" or "sociological" and not ethical. And at this point regularly appears the maxim: "It is one thing to study evaluations, another thing to make them." Likewise, of course, "It is one thing to study breathing, another thing to breathe." The latter in each instance is the subject matter studied, the former the study of it. "Don't confuse fact with theory" is a sound maxim. But when, until emotivists and prescriptivists came along, have *empirical* philosophers taken the position that descriptions of facts were not to be regarded as relevant to the facts described and true of them to the best of human knowledge?

One more point as regards Feigl's first reason. Suppose it should appear in the empirical investigation of human activities and their expression interpreted as imperatives, prescriptions, wishes, and ideals that there were no empirical sanctions or regulations or "justifications" of these beyond the goals desired by individuals or the cultural patterns of various societies, would not this be the most significant information we could have about human values? That is, suppose that through cognitive validation, and the agreement in principle among the experts in the subject, we were assured that individual relativism, or cultural relativism, was the rational conclusion from the evidence on ethical behavior, what better basis for future ethical action on our part would there be? If the scientific conclusion was that of individual relativism, we would know just at what point further argument with a man or attempts at rehabilitation were useless, and could deal with him firmly and decisively. Similarly in our relations with diverse cultures, we should *cognitively* need to investigate no further if we had full assurance that the evidence indicated that cultural relativism was the true theory of ethical activity. In short, disagreements in emotive and obligatory cultural behavior are as irrelevant to a cognitively validated knowledge of emotive demands and human obligations as biological competition is to an understanding of the evolutionary principle among living organisms. It is not necessary to have emotive agreement among ethical principles in order to have cognitively validated agreement about them. This last sort of agreement is the important kind to have for the intelligent determination of human policy and action.

Feigl's first reason thus seems to me irrelevant to the basic issue, and one lending confusion rather than clarity to its solution.

The second reason, as he says, is the crucial one. For this amounts to the assertion that an empirical treatment of the "ought" is impossible in its very nature, because no scientific description can contain an "ought." An empirical statement may describe anything that "is," but it cannot describe something that "ought" to be.

This seems to me, as it does to any exponent of a naturalistic ethics, sheer dogma. One way to answer it is to trace the history of the dogma and analyze the ambiguities and confusions it contains.[2] The more decisive way is to present some descriptions of "oughts" among natural events. This I shall seek to do very sketchily in the next few paragraphs. Detailed descriptions of "natural norms" and their interrelations can be found, however, in my *The Sources of Value* [5].[3]

One of the assumptions that have made it difficult to discriminate norms in natural processes is that of an atomic conception of experience and behavior. As long as pleasures and desires were thought of as disconnected simples and behavior conceived as sequences of reflexes, there was not much opportunity to observe normative activities in these areas. Actually, however, pleasures, desires, and responses occur in experiential and behavior structures, and some of these structures are laminated so that certain elements of these structures overlap and control others.

One of the most elementary of these structures is that of a goal-seeking purpose. This is the structure that yields instrumental and achievement value. The normative action of this structure is so obvious that even the prescriptivists could not miss it. And, as we have noticed, they manage to exclude it from their concern only by *defining* the area of genuine values as beginning with ends.

The structure of a purposive act consists of a dynamic element (often called the drive) and a terminal goal (or consummatory act) which "reduces" or satisfies the drive. If there is a gap between the emergence of the drive and its consummation, subordinate or instrumental acts have to be introduced to bridge the gap. These subordinate acts are motivated by the very drive that motivates the aim for the consummatory goal. The drives for these subordinate acts are directed through anticipatory sets or judgments for subordinate goals which are expected to produce the attainment of the consummatory goal. The drive is thus split between its aim for the terminal goal and its aims through successive anticipatory sets for a succession of subordinate goal objects expected to be the means of attaining the final goal. This split dynamics which ties the subordinate acts to the overarching drive for the terminal consummatory goal is the

[2] This I have sought to do in my *Ethics* [4] in Ch. 12, "Emotive and Prescriptive Theories."

[3] In a somewhat different form, such descriptions are presented in the chapters on each of the traditional naturalistic ethical theories and in the terminal chapter of my *Ethics* [4].

defining character of a behavior system of this sort; such a behavior system I call a *selective system*. And it functions as a natural norm. For the drive for the terminal consummatory goal determines the *correctness* of the anticipatory sets and the goal objects of the subordinate acts. If the subordinate acts fail to produce the terminal goal for the original drive which is also the drive that motivates them, this drive will cease to charge these incorrect acts, and will try other subordinate acts till it obtains a correct one. These acts are thus dropped as *wrong* and as not the acts that *ought* to be performed in order to attain the terminal consummatory goal. As we say, "That is the *wrong* key for this lock; you *ought* to have used the other one on your key ring."

So, here is an "ought" imbedded in a natural process clearly evident for anyone to see. Just *describe* what actually goes on in detail, and a structure is revealed in the process itself which *prescribes* a correct act and rejects an incorrect one. The values that emerge from the selective action of the purposive structure are cognitively validated by the description as truly selected in furtherance of the norm.

The same sort of normative selection happens in a personal situation where a number of distinct purposes are all pressing for satisfaction in the shortest possible time. Such a situation also constitutes a selective system. The dynamics of such a situation is the joint dynamics of the several drives. Notice here we are dealing with *ends* and with what a person *ought* to do with a number of competing purposes. A simple instance of such a situation would be a lady's shopping trip to the town. She has food purchases to make, a new hat to buy, a dentist's appointment, a defective headlight to be fixed on her car, and a visit to a friend in the hospital. There are better and worse ways of getting all these purposes satisfied, and the situation itself determines the way she *ought* to arrange her time in town to get these all done most satisfactorily. Part of the situation has to do with the streets of the town and how the shops and offices she must visit are distributed, and part with the relative urgency of the various purposes, supposing she cannot get them all done or runs into delays on some of the items. Alternative plans of action will go through her mind and the structure of the situation is the norm of her selection, and will punish a wrong choice of plan by frustrating her desires and limiting her satisfaction. She will learn to plan more carefully next time.

The same natural normative action arises in social situations where the dynamics comes from the desires of a number of different persons. When the persons involved are few and the mutual satisfactions desired are limited in the period provided (as, for instance, for a number of strangers traveling together on a bus to a certain destination) the normative action of the situation is as clearly visible as that of the lady planning her day in town. If the complexity of a situation makes the discovery of the correct act exceedingly difficult, that in no way evades the normative action of the situation, and in retrospect a wrong act is often but too obviously apparent.

Another natural norm not always recognized as such is that of a cultural pattern. Because this is a human artifact it is easily interpreted as unnatural. But the institution of a culture and the action of acculturation are as natural to man as a social animal as inborn social behavior is to social insects such as ants and bees. As a vertebrate animal whose adaptation and survival depend on the capacity of learning, man could achieve social solidarity only through learning, and that means through acculturation to a cultural pattern. The normative action of a culture through tradition and the powerful sanctions of operating social institutions is as obvious to the common man as the normative action of a purposive goal over the means to attain it. It remains only to show that this action follows the form of a selective system. The dynamics of a social institution is to be found in its sanctions enforcing conformity. Just consider the operation of the institution of law in a community. The force of the law comes out of the acculturated drives of the community to demand obedience to the law. These same drives, by inattention or inadequate acculturation or rebellion against a convention, from time to time break through the institutional rules and are sooner or later corrected and brought into conformity. As long as a culture is vital, and that means as long as it maintains its dynamics for conformity, it functions as a selective system, a natural norm, determining what is right or wrong and what ought or ought not to be done under its institutions. And the description of its prescriptive operations states in declarative sentences just what people in the community ought to do and what corrective sanctions are set in motion if they do not do what they ought. A careful study of a culture cognitively validates the cultural norms selecting values there by proving that the norms do in fact operate.

And now let me make a final observation regarding the cognitive validations of ethical principles. This has to do with the possibility of a unified ethical system organized under certain ultimate ethical principles. It will be recalled that Feigl sought to validate ethical principles by higher ethical principles which emotive agreement among men would admit to be legitimate. In such agreement among men on ethical principles he found himself balked by the diversity of men's purposes and men's cultures, whence human agreement on a universal basis of evaluation, comparable to agreement in principle about the rules of logic and the method of induction, appeared impossible.

I have already in replying to Feigl's first reason shown that disagreement among men was not important for the areas of logic and science, but only disagreement among experts in a subject and even that only on the assumption that agreement was possible on principle even if difficult in practice. For consistency Feigl should insist on no different criterion of agreement in the ethical field. In short, the issue is not over actual disagreements but over the basis of disagreements.

Now let me point out that when expert observation and description of the natural norms is seriously considered, it appears that the norms themselves are subject to natural normative action. At least there is considerable evidence that they are. For instance, what is the ethical significance of acculturation except that, over a large area of individual human action, the natural purposive impulses of an individual child are overruled by the dynamics of the natural norm of the cultural pattern within which he happens to be born? Discretely considered, it would seem as if that could be no justification for the subservience of a moral principle calling for the maximum of individual satisfaction to another calling for cultural conformity. But the subservience of the one to the other at least during the upbringing of a child is clearly indicated by a descriptive observation of how these two ethical principles are related to each other in the early years of a child's life.

The same sort of observations of the relations of natural norms to one another may well bring out in the end a general set of evaluative principles regulative among all norms and over all human action. I have ventured to suggest that such a set of evaluative principles might be confirmably made out in what I have called the ethics of the adjustable society. This hypothesis is presented in the final chapter of my *Ethics* and also of *The Sources of Value*. But my contention in this paper is not that the hypothesis there suggested is fully confirmable, but only that such a hypothesis might be confirmable, and that, if it was, the unifying validation of ethical principles would be brought about not by one ethical principle being emotively regarded as validated by another ethical principle, but quite differently by a cognitive validation which through the agreement of experts determines that in fact one ethical principle is observed under certain conditions to be subservient to another. That is to say the validation of ethical principles in relation to one another can well be discovered through *cognitive* validation.

The notion of emotive ethical validation—such as that of validation by emotive agreement about emotive attitudes—is a phantom. Feigl found that out. But he failed to observe that cognitive validation is applicable to ethical norms, and might well bring to light even a hypothesis for a universal system of ethical principles confirmable in cognitive terms. Ethical principles would then have the same sort of validation as physical laws. The key to an understanding of this possibility lies in noticing that value norms are embedded in those highly structured processes of nature which I am calling selective systems. It will then appear that dynamic (not merely verbal) prescriptions lie embedded in the structures of selective systems. And these are open to description and validated by the selective action of the selective systems described. Thus the range and validation of a *prescription* becomes subject to what is confirmable through a *description* of its mode of operation within its selective system.

But whether a universal ethical system of interlocking natural norms could be cognitively validated or not, a considerable amount of legislative sanction for some natural norms over others seems factually observable. The cognitive confirmation of these dynamically sanctioned evaluative relationships would be of enormous practical assistance to men for private planning and public policy. For knowledge of values is essential for intelligent value acts.

REFERENCES

1. Feigl, Herbert. "De Principiis Non Disputandum . . .?" in *Philosophical Analysis*, Max Black, ed., pp. 119–156. Ithaca, N.Y.: Cornell University Press, 1950. Reissued (New York: Prentice-Hall, 1963); in the reissue the pages are 113–147. Page references here are to the 1950 edition.
2. Feigl, Herbert. "The Difference between Knowledge and Valuation," *Journal of Social Issues*, 6(4):39–44 (1950).
3. Feigl, Herbert. "Validation and Vindication," in *Readings in Ethical Theory*, Wilfrid Sellars and John Hospers, eds., pp. 667–680. New York: Appleton-Century-Crofts, 1952.
4. Pepper, Stephen C. *Ethics*. New York: Appleton-Century-Crofts, 1960.
5. Pepper, Stephen C. *The Sources of Value*. Berkeley: University of California Press, 1958.

KARL R. POPPER
\\(\\)//

A Theorem on Truth-Content

Herbert Feigl and I are almost the same age: I am the elder by about five months. But when we first met in Vienna more than thirty years ago, Herbert was already a philosopher of international renown, having been lately appointed to a professorship in an American university, while I had just been appointed to my first teaching job—at a lower secondary school in Vienna. I had then been working on philosophical problems for thirteen years; but though I had written much, I had published hardly anything.

Prior to meeting Herbert I had known three philosophers on terms which permitted prolonged personal discussions: Julius Kraft, who was about four or five years my senior, and Victor Kraft and Heinrich Gomperz, both belonging to an older generation. Herbert was the first philosopher who was ready to meet me on terms of complete personal equality and personal friendship, who took my criticism of positivism and the Vienna Circle seriously, and who encouraged me to publish what I had written. On our first meeting we spent a whole night in a most exciting discussion, and we have remained fast friends ever since. My debt to him is very great: I do not think that I should have published my *Logic of Scientific Discovery* without his encouragement.

Herbert's most important work, I believe, is on the body-mind problem (see particularly his [1]); and for this reason I had intended to use as my contribution to this volume a longish paper on the history of this problem written some years ago. But I found that this paper was in an unfinished state; and so I ultimately decided that, rather than trying to

[343]

revise a long old paper, I should write a new short paper on a problem which holds my present interest, and of which I could hope, judging from discussions with Herbert, that it would be of interest for him too.

My problem here is one of mathematical logic, but it arises out of a problem of the methodology of the natural sciences.

I proceed in this paper as follows. In Section I, I explain briefly some of the fundamental ideas of Tarski's calculus of deductive systems. In Section II, those ideas are combined with the idea of T, that is to say, *the class of true statements* (which is a complete deductive system). The idea of T in the form here used is, of course, also due to Tarski; but he does not seem to have introduced it into his calculus of systems; at any rate the main fruit of this combination, the idea of a *truth-content*, does not seem to have occurred to Tarski.

In Section III, I state my methodological problem and the logical problems connected with it; in Section IV, I state my main theorem and prove it; and in Section V, I indicate some extensions and some applications.

I

Let a be a statement—for example, a scientific hypothesis; we shall denote its negation by "$-a$". Let A be the set of statements which follow logically from a, or in Tarski's terminology ([2], pp. 30ff., and especially pp. 342ff.) *the set of all consequences of a, or the consequence class of a.* I write, with Tarski, "$Cn(X)$" for *the consequence class of the set of statements X*. Accordingly we write "$Cn(\{a\})$" for the consequence class of the set of statements whose only member is a, so that we have for our class A mentioned above

$$A = Cn(\{a\}).$$

I shall write, in general, "B" for $Cn(\{b\})$, etc., up to say the letters "C" and "c".

"A", "B", "C", denote *deductive systems*, that is to say, sets X of statements for which quite generally the formula

$$X = Cn(X)$$

holds, and therefore also

$$X = Cn(X) = Cn(Cn(X)).$$

But I reserve the letters from the beginning of the alphabet, "A",

"B", "C", for a special kind of deductive system, that is to say, for the (finitely) *axiomatizable systems*. The axiomatizable systems are those systems A for which there exists at least one statement x such that $A = Cn(\{x\})$; for we may interpret such an x as *the logical conjunction of a system of axioms* for A.

Not all deductive systems are axiomatizable: we know, for example, that no consistent deductive system containing all true statements of number theory is axiomatizable. Thus there exist deductive systems X,

$$X = Cn(X)$$

for which *no* statement x exists such that X is the consequence class of $\{x\}$.

I shall use the letters "X", "Y", "Z", for systems which are either axiomatizable or nonaxiomatizable, while the letters "R", "S", and especially the letter "T" (see below) will be reserved for systems which are non-axiomatizable.

The complement of the class X is designated by "X'". Finally, because of typesetting exigencies, the following symbols have been chosen instead of the more usual ones: "$\smallsmile$" for class union, "$\smallfrown$" for class intersection (this is to distinguish the ordinary operations class union and class intersection from the corresponding but different operations performed on deductive systems, which will be denoted by "+" and "×"; see below). We further use "$\leqq$" for subclass and "$<$" for proper subclass.

In addition to variables I shall use some constants. The set of statements which we accept as *logically true* will be denoted by "L"; and the universal set of all statements under consideration by "U". The subset of *true statements* of our system I shall denote by "T" and the set of *false statements* by "F".

We have therefore, for all deductive systems X,

(1) $L \leqq X \leqq U$
(2) $U = Cn(\{x \cdot -x\})$ (1)
(3) $L = Cn(\{x \vee -x\})$ (1)
(4) $T \smallsmile F = U$

Symbols not previously explained here are used in their traditional senses.

In his famous paper "Foundations of the Calculus of Systems" ([2], Paper XII), Tarski shows that a calculus somewhat like a Boolean algebra (it is an extension of a Boolean algebra) holds for *systems in general*, and that the set of *axiomatizable systems* is, in fact, a Boolean algebra.

The main operations of the *general calculus of systems* are:

(a) Complementation: X' is the deductive system complementary to X and defined ([2], p. 351) by

(5) $X' = \Pi\, Cn(\{-x\})$,   (Definition)

where the product (intersection) is that of all those $Cn(\{-x\})$ for which $x \in X$ holds.

That is to say, X' is the greatest deductive system small enough to be part of every system $Cn(\{-x\})$ such that x is a statement belonging to X.

(b) The formation of the union-system $X + Y$ of the two systems X and Y defined by

(6) $X + Y = Cn(X \cup Y)$ (Definition)

That is to say, $X + Y$ is the smallest deductive system containing all the consequences of the class of all statements belonging either to X or to Y. We have, by (1) and [2], pages 350–351, Theorem 5 and Definition 6,

(7) $X + L = X.$

(c) The formation of the intersection system $X \times Y$ of X and Y, defined by

(8) $X \times Y = X \cap Y = Cn(X \cap Y).$ (Definition)

This formula indicates that the *ordinary* set-theoretical intersection of the two deductive systems is always a deductive system. As opposed to this, the formula $X + Y = X \cup Y$ is *not* generally valid—not even for axiomatizable systems—although

(9) $X \cup Y \leqq X + Y$

is of course generally valid.

We can use as diagrammatic illustrations of deductive systems angles which are open at the bottom.

FIGURE 1

If we wish to indicate that the system in question is axiomatizable, we can do so by adding to the diagram a letter indicating the axiom:

FIGURE 2

On the other hand, if we wish to indicate that the system in question is nonaxiomatizable, we can do so by the diagram:

FIGURE 3

The union system of two axiomatizable systems, $A + B$, may be represented by

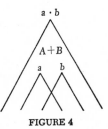

FIGURE 4

The intersection system $A \times B$ may be represented by

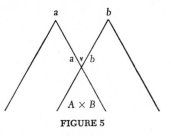

FIGURE 5

We have, clearly, for axiomatizable systems:

(10) $A + B = Cn(\{a \cdot b\})$,
(11) $A \times B = Cn(\{a \vee b\})$.

We also have, as Tarski shows, for the complement A' of an axiomatizable system A

(12) $A' = Cn(\{-a\})$.

Thus the Boolean algebra of axiomatizable systems may be said to be dual to the Boolean algebra (the Lindenbaum algebra) of their axioms ([2], p. 355).

Apart from the sets of *axiomatizable* (and nonaxiomatizable) *systems*, Tarski introduces the equally important sets of *irreducible* (and nonirreducible), and of *complete* (and noncomplete), *systems*.[1]

A system X is called *"irreducible"* if, and only if, $X \neq L$ and for all its subsystems $Y \leq X$, $Y \neq X$ implies $Y = L$. Or in other words, X is irreducible if *its only proper subsystem is the system L of all logically true statements.*

Similarly a system X is called *complete* (that is to say, more fully, *complete and consistent*) if and only if *its only proper supersystem is U*, the inconsistent system of all statements.

II

I now proceed to explain the *methodological setting* which gives rise to my logical problem.

In the natural sciences we are engaged in the critical discussion of *competing hypotheses* and their merits, such as, for example, their explanatory power or their *verisimilitude*.[2]

Let a be a *scientific hypothesis*. Then the deductive system $A = Cn$ $(\{a\})$ which corresponds to a may be called the *theory* corresponding to a; or if we have in mind questions connected, say, with the *explanatory power* of a, A may be called the (*informative*) *content* of a.

These terms are unimportant (as is all terminology), but they give a hint of the intuitive ideas which may be associated with $A = Cn(\{a\})$.

Now every a, whether true or false, has among its consequences some *true* statements. (And unless A is irreducible *and* false, a has among its consequences even some statements which are true but not L-true; that is, some statements for which $x \in T$ but not $x \in L$.) For example, the statement

$a = $ all the planets move in square orbits

has among its consequences the true statements

---

[1] [2], pp. 364–365. Tarski also introduces the important sets of *convergent* (and nonconvergent) *systems*; but I shall dispense with these here, making implicit use of the fact (p. 366, Theorem 36) that the *complete* systems (as well as *axiomatizable* ones) are *convergent*.

[2] See my [3], especially Ch. 10 and the Addenda.

$b =$ some planets move in orbits
$c =$ there are planets

and many other statements which, for all we know, are factually true.

I have called the set of the true statements which belong to $A = Cn(\{a\})$ the *truth-content of a* ([3], *loc. cit.*) and I shall denote it by Ct_T (a). The definition is:

(13) $Ct_T(a) = A \times T.$

The truth content of a is, obviously, a deductive system; that is to say, we have

(14) $Ct_T(\{a\}) = Cn(Ct_T(a)).$

We might therefore denote it here by "A_T"; but before doing so we have to agree that our convention that we use the letters $A, B, \ldots$, exclusively for *axiomatizable* systems does not apply to letters with subscripts, such as A_T, B_T, etc.; for we must allow for the possibility that

(15) $A_T = Ct_T(a) = Cn(Ct_T(a)) = A \times T$

may *not*, in general, be an axiomatizable system.

It is, of course, axiomatizable if a is true; for

(16)   If $a \in T$ then $A_T = A = Cn(\{a\}).$

But if $a \in F$ then A_T will not be axiomatizable unless T, the system of true propositions, is axiomatizable. But this will not be the case if, for example, our universal system U contains all number-theoretical statements, so that T contains all number-theoretical *true* statements.

In what follows I shall assume:

(17) T is nonaxiomatizable.   (Assumption)

Yet the system T will always be complete; that is to say, we have:

(18) T is complete.

Proof: Let x be a statement outside T. Then $x \in F$ and $-x \in T$. So if we extend T by adding to it one statement, calling the new set "T^*", we shall have a couple of contradictory statements in T^*, so that $Cn(T^*) = U$. Thus the conditions for completeness are satisfied (since T is obviously consistent).

III

Now we can formulate our *methodological problem*. Let us consider the following diagram (Figure 6).

Here a is a (false) hypothesis, and b one of its consequences. The fol-

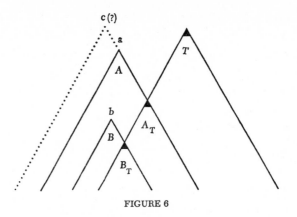

FIGURE 6

lowing important questions arise, bearing on the adequacy of the diagrammatical representation.

(1) Is $b \in A$ (or $B \leqq A$) a sufficient condition for $B_T \leqq A_T$, as the diagram (Figure 6) suggests?

(2) Are, more especially, $B \leqq A$ and $B \neq A$ sufficient conditions for $B_T \leqq A_T$ and $B_T \neq A_T$?

These questions are very important for the discussion of the relative merits of competing hypotheses. For let us assume that we have a hypothesis b, and that $b \in A$ such that $A \neq B$ and $A_T = B_T$. Then, b would clearly be preferable to A because it has the same *truth-content*, although its *total* content is smaller than that of a so that it contains less false information than a.

If we consider the position of $c(?)$ in our diagram, then we should expect at first sight that a c so placed might indeed exist: $c(?)$ seems to have the same truth-content as a though its position indicates that $a \in C$ and $A \neq C$, so that c is logically stronger than a; and a seems to contain a lesser number of false statements than c (its "falsity content" appears to be "smaller"). But can such a c exist?

IV

Now a theorem whose proof is very easy (since we have Tarski's calculus of systems at our disposal) says that all this cannot happen: there can be no such c in the position suggested by our diagram. For we have:

Theorem 1.
$$\begin{cases} A_T = B_T \text{ if and only if } A = B; \text{ and also} \\ A_T < B_T \text{ if and only if } A < B. \end{cases}$$

[350]

We consider first the equalities ($=$).

That $A = B$ entails $A_T = B_T$ is trivial; we have only to show that

$$A_T = B_T \text{ entails } A = B.$$

Proof.

(P.1) $X_T = X \times T$.   (13, 15)

(P.2)   If either Y or Z is axiomatizable (and thus "convergent") or complete (and thus "convergent") then

$\qquad (Y \times Z)' = Y' + Z'$.   ([2], Theorem 26, page 363)

(P.3)   If Z is complete and nonaxiomatizable then

$\qquad Z' = L$.   ([2], Theorem 34, page 366)

(P.4) $X + L = X$.   (7)

(P.5) T is complete.   (18)

(P.6) T is nonaxiomatizable. (Assumption about number theory.) (17)

(P.7) $X_T = Y_T$ entails $X' = Y'$, for all systems X and Y.   (P.1 to P.6)

(P.8) $X_T = Y_T$ entails $X'' = Y''$.   (P.7)

It is clear that a corresponding theorem must hold for every system S which, like T, is complete and nonaxiomatizable.

(P.9)   If X is axiomatizable then $X = X''$.   ([2], Theorem 16, page 356)

(P.10) $A_T = B_T$ entails $A = B$.   (P.8, P.9)

This completes the proof of our theorem as far as the equalities ($=$) are concerned. In order to prove the theorem for the inequalities ($<$) we first show that:

(P.11) $A < B$ entails $A_T \leqq B_T$

which is a consequence of

(P.11.1) $A = A \times B$ entails $A \times X = A \times B \times X$.

$\qquad\qquad\qquad\qquad\qquad\qquad\qquad\qquad$ (Definition 8 above)

Since according to (P.10) $A \neq B$ entails $A_T \neq B_T$, we get from (P.11)

(P.12) $A < B$ entails $A_T < B_T$.   (P.10, P.11)

Thus we have only to prove

(P.13) $A_T < B_T$ entails $A < B$;

or what is the same,

(P.14) $A \times T = A \times B \times T$ entails $A = A \times B$.

It is clear that the proof of (P.14) follows from (P.10) by substitution.
This concludes the proof of our theorem.

It will be seen that, thanks to the foundations laid by Tarski, the proof of our theorem is very simple. Nevertheless the theorem is far from trivial, as may be seen from the fact that the completeness *and* the nonaxiomatizability of T enter the proof essentially.

Thus we have here a nontrivial theorem of mathematical logic which is of very considerable significance for understanding the critical discussion of hypotheses or theories, which in turn constitutes the method of science.

v

If we consider the various steps of our proof, then we may generalize our theorem as follows:

Theorem 2.

Let X be any complete *and* nonaxiomatizable system. Then
$$\begin{cases} A \times X = B \times X \text{ if and only if } A = B; \text{ and also} \\ A \times B < B \times X \text{ if and only if } A < B. \end{cases}$$

The system T is undoubtedly the most important of these systems, but to any "possible" world or "model" M there corresponds a system T_M ("true in M") of those statements which would be true if this possible world M were the actual world. This shows that our theorem has wider methodological implications than may appear at first sight.

One not quite uninteresting way of putting our theorem is the following.

Let X be again a complete and nonaxiomatizable system. Let $Y \leqq X$. Then there exists *at most* one axiomatizable extension A of Y such that:

(a) $Y \leqq A$
(b) $A \times X \leqq Y$.

This holds for $X = Y$, in which case $A = U$. (I have so far been unable to prove—or disprove—that an axiomatizable extension A with the properties (a) and (b) exists for every $Y \leqq X$.)

Our theorem establishes a *one-to-one correspondence* between the *truth-content* of a theory and its *content*. It shows further that for any two hypotheses a and b whose contents or truth-contents are comparable, contents and truth-contents will be comparable; and that the comparison of their contents will always produce the same ordering of a and b as the comparison of their truth-contents.

One application of this is that any *measure of the content* can be used, for many purposes of comparison, as a *measure of the truth-content*; and vice versa.

[352]

This makes it possible to simplify the measure for verisimilitude which I have given in the *Addenda* to [3]. In fact, for *most purposes* of mere comparison, $vs(a)$, that is, my measure of the verisimilitude of a,

$$vs(a) = (p(A,A_T) - p(A_T))/(p(A,A_T) + p(A_T))$$

can be replaced by

$$vs^*(a) = (p(A,A_T) - p(A))/(p(A,A_T) + p(A)) = (1 - p(A_T))/(1 + p(A_T)) = ct_T(a)/(2 - ct_T(a)).$$

The phrase *"for most purposes"* is intended here to exclude such cases as $A_T = T$. But if we exclude such cases we may even replace $vs^*(a)$ by a further simplification,

$$ct(a)/(2 - ct(a)).$$

Replacing $vs(a)$ by $vs^*(a)$ amounts, in effect, to saying that we can measure verisimilitude approximately by *content minus falsity-content* (instead of *truth-content minus falsity-content*).

This indicates that, for most cases of competing (and consistent) theories, *the comparison of their contents* will provide a *rough first comparison of their verisimilitude*. The roughness of the measure makes crucial empirical tests necessary for further comparison; yet our considerations explain, by and large, why only hypotheses whose content exceeds that of their predecessors have much chance of being considered as promising lines of progress in science—as hypotheses that may lead to an increase in verisimilitude.

REFERENCES

1. Feigl, Herbert. "The 'Mental' and the 'Physical' ", in *Minnesota Studies in the Philosophy of Science*, Vol. II, Herbert Feigl, Michael Scriven, and Grover Maxwell, eds., pp. 370–497. Minneapolis: University of Minnesota Press, 1958.
2. Tarski, Alfred. *Logic, Semantics, Metamathematics*, tr. by J. H. Woodger. New York: Oxford University Press, 1956.
3. Popper, Karl R. *Conjectures and Refutations*. New York: Basic Books, 1963. London: Routledge and Kegan Paul, 1963; revised second edition, 1965.

WESLEY C. SALMON

)))(((

Verifiability and Logic

Herbert Feigl has long been one of the ablest and most devoted champions of logical empiricism. On this occasion I should like to re-examine a complex of issues which lie at the heart of this doctrine. They center around the verifiability criterion of cognitive meaning.

Until 1949 it could have been said that the verifiability criterion was one of the cornerstones of logical empiricism. The criterion had been hotly debated and had undergone numerous reformulations. By that time it was quite generally recognized that the criterion had to be formulated in terms of verifiability in principle rather than actual verification and that verifiability itself had to be understood as the possibility of partial verification instead of the possibility of complete and conclusive verification. Nevertheless, the notion that cognitive meaningfulness was to be explicated in terms of empirical verifiability remained a fundamental principle. The history of the criterion up to that time has been well recounted by Hempel [9].

In 1949 an apparent disaster struck in the form of Church's critique [3] of Ayer's second formulation [1]. Shortly thereafter Hempel expressed grave doubts about the possibility of giving any satisfactory formulation of the verifiability criterion [8]. The view that the verifiability criterion faces insuperable difficulties has subsequently spread. In the past fifteen years the number of its defenders and the amount of attention it has received have dwindled considerably. Feigl has remained an exception to this general trend [4, 5, 6, 7]. Writing in 1956 [7] he referred to the "serious doubts" of Hempel and others "as to the adequacy of all [formulations] thus far suggested, or even as to any conceivable formulations of the meaning criterion." He goes on to say, "I admit that an all-around satisfactory and fully precise explication is difficult, but I am confident that confirmability-in-principle (for statements) or logical connectibility with the terms of a suitably chosen observation basis (for concepts) is the explicandum of at least a necessary condition for factual meaningfulness. Understood in this way, the meaning criterion still provides a sharp delimitation between sense and nonsense" [7, page 15].

The present essay will not offer any direct defense of the verifiability criterion. Instead it will attempt to diagnose and assess some of the major difficulties which have stood in the way of an adequate formulation. It is my view that certain difficulties, though familiar, are not sufficiently understood, and that other difficulties, though not much discussed, are of fundamental importance. My own attitude toward the verifiability criterion is, like Feigl's, optimistic. I hope that the present essay will clarify certain basic issues, thereby facilitating judgment as to whether such optimism is well grounded.

I

In order to achieve some degree of terminological clarity I shall construe the verifiability criterion to consist of the following series of explications:

1. A sentence (or statement) has factual meaning if and only if it is empirically verifiable (or confirmable).

2. A sentence (or statement) has formal meaning if and only if it is either analytic or self-contradictory.

3. A sentence (or statement) has cognitive (or literal) meaning if and only if it has either formal meaning or factual meaning.

4. A sentence (or statement) is either true or false if and only if it has cognitive (or literal) meaning.

These explications identify cognitive meaningfulness with the possibility of being either true or false, and they reduce these properties to empirical verifiability and analyticity (or self-contradiction). There remain, however, the tasks of explicating empirical verifiability and analyticity. Ayer undertook to provide an explication of empirical verifiability. A statement is empirically verifiable if and only if it is either directly or indirectly verifiable, where these latter concepts are explained as follows:

I propose to say that a statement is directly verifiable if it is either itself an observation-statement, or is such that in conjunction with one or more observation-statements it entails at least one observation-statement which is not deducible from these other premises alone; and I propose to say that a statement is indirectly verifiable if it satisfies the following conditions: first, that in conjunction with certain other premises it entails one or more directly verifiable statements which are not deducible from these other premises alone; and secondly, that these other premises do not include any statement that is not either analytic, or directly verifiable, or capable of being independently established as indirectly verifiable [1, page 13].

This explication is intended as an account of what Ayer calls "weak" verifiability, that is, confirmability or verifiability to some degree. It is meant to explain what is involved in the possibility of having empirical or scientific evidence for or against a statement, recognizing that such evidence is often partial and inconclusive.

The inadequacy of this explication of empirical verifiability was shown by Church as follows:

. . . let O_1, O_2, O_3 be three "observation-statements" . . . such that no one of the three taken alone entails any of the others. Then using these we may show of any statement S whatever that either it or its negation is verifiable, as follows. Let $\bar{O}_1$ and $\bar{S}$ be the negations of O_1 and S respectively. Then (under Ayer's definition) $\bar{O}_1O_2 \mathbf{v} O_3\bar{S}$ is directly verifiable, because with O_1 it entails O_3. Moreover S and $\bar{O}_1O_2 \mathbf{v} O_3\bar{S}$ together entail O_2. Therefore (under Ayer's definition) S is indirectly verifiable—unless it happens that $\bar{O}_1O_2 \mathbf{v} O_3\bar{S}$ alone entails O_2, in which case $\bar{S}$ and O_3 together entail O_2, so that $\bar{S}$ is directly verifiable [3].

It is evident that Church's criticism has no bearing upon the verifiability criterion (see explications 1–4 above); it shows only that Ayer's explication of empirical verifiability is faulty. Church did not claim to have proved more.

Church's criticism also raises problems for the explication of empirical verification. With respect to Ayer's explication of empirical verifiability there seems only one plausible way of construing empirical verification. A statement is empirically verifiable according to Ayer's definition if, in conjunction with certain verifiable premises, it has a verifiable consequence. Presumably, then, that statement is verified to some degree if the verifiable premises and conclusion have been verified to some degree. With this understanding of empirical verification, Church's criticism translates immediately into a recipe for verifying any hypothesis whatever by a trivial and obviously irrelevant procedure. For example, to verify the hypothesis

$H: E = mc^2$

formulate the auxiliary hypothesis

H': Either there is no ink bottle on my desk and I am sitting in a chair, or my copy of *Language, Truth and Logic* has a red cover and it is not the case that $E = mc^2$.

This hypothesis H' in conjunction with

O_1: There is an ink bottle on my desk,

which I find by observation to be true, entails

O_3: My copy of *Language, Truth and Logic* has a red cover.

I observe that my copy of *Language, Truth and Logic* does have a red cover, so H' is verified. From H' and H we can deduce

O_2: I am sitting in a chair.

I observe that I am sitting in a chair; hence, H is verified. Anyone who objects to my use of physical-object statements as observation statements may substitute three logically independent protocol statements for them.

Ayer's account of empirical verifiability and the related account of empirical verification are in many ways fairly typical of what is often said about scientific verification (or confirmation) and scientific verifiability (or confirmability). These matters fall within what may broadly be called inductive logic. Church's criticism raises fundamental difficulties concerning these basic concepts. In this respect it is analogous to Hempel's paradox of confirmation and Goodman's grue-bleen paradox. Any satisfactory theory of scientific verification (or confirmation) must avoid such paradoxical consequences.

It is of greatest importance to distinguish between the problem of explicating cognitive meaningfulness and the problem of explicating empirical verifiability. The problem of the meaning criterion is the problem of the propriety or desirability of explicating cognitive meaningfulness in terms of empirical verifiability. Leaving this problem entirely aside, there remains the problem of explicating empirical verifiability. This latter problem is surely an extremely important and fundamental one whether or not a verifiability criterion of meaning is to be adopted. This is the problem Church's criticism bears upon. It did not show Ayer's explication of cognitive meaningfulness to be inadequate; it showed that

Ayer did not have an adequate conception of empirical confirmation. Considering the extreme difficulty of confirmation theory and the fact that there is no theory of confirmation which is generally accepted as satisfactory, this result is not too surprising.

The only way in which Church's criticism can be taken as a critique of the verifiability criterion is by construing it as an indication that the concept of empirical verifiability is inexplicable in principle. This seems like a harsh conclusion to draw from Ayer's failure to provide a satisfactory explication of empirical verifiability. It is my personal suspicion that many philosophers who have had little hesitation in dismissing the possibility of formulating an unobjectionable explication of cognitive meaningfulness in terms of empirical verifiability would be far more hesitant to conclude that the concepts of scientific confirmation and confirmability are inexplicable in principle.

It might be said that the problem of the verifiability criterion cannot be dealt with until the concept of empirical verifiability has been satisfactorily explicated. This, I think, would be a mistake. Even if we have no precise explicatum of the concept of empirical verifiability, it seems to me that we have a sufficiently clear notion of the explicandum to be able sensibly to consider the merits of explicating cognitive meaningfulness in terms of empirical verifiability. Feigl [4, 5, 7], Reichenbach [12, Chapter I], and many others have made amply clear the import of a *vindication* [4] of the verifiability criterion, whatever explication of empirical verifiability is ultimately accepted. It is not my purpose to add further arguments for the verifiability criterion. Instead I propose to examine certain consequences of accepting the verifiability criterion, and in the course of so doing I shall try to show how some alleged difficulties can be avoided.

II

If we ask what went wrong with Ayer's account of empirical verifiability, there is an obvious and in some respects easy answer. Ayer did not sufficiently restrict the kinds of statements which are directly and indirectly verifiable. In particular, he neglected to stipulate that to be verifiable a non-observation-statement must be a lawlike statement. If we look at the alleged verification of $E = mc^2$ in the relativity-made-easy example of the preceding section, it is apparent that one source of trouble lies in the use of the unlawlike auxiliary hypothesis H'. Leaving aside the difficulties in explicating the concept of a lawlike statement, we could perhaps patch up Ayer's explication of empirical verifiability by inserting the condition of lawlikeness at the appropriate places:

. . . a statement is directly verifiable if it is either an observation-statement, or is a *lawlike statement* such that . . .

. . . a statement is indirectly verifiable if it satisfies the following conditions: first, *that it is lawlike and* that in conjunction with certain other premises . . .

This emendation will block the exact form of the refutation presented by Church, but there is no assurance that a similar type of objection could not be formulated. In any case, it seems to me that the root of the problem goes much deeper.

Ayer's account of cognitive meaningfulness is ultimately question-begging. Very briefly, the situation is this. Cognitive statements are taken to be just those statements which are either true or false. Statements which are either true or false are the admissible substituends for the variables of truth-functional logic. But, for those statements which are neither analytic nor self-contradictory, a statement is cognitive if and only if it is empirically verifiable. The test for empirical verifiability involves using a statement as a substituend for a truth-functional variable (or larger expression involving variables) in the premise of a deductive argument. This procedure is logically permissible only if the statement in question is either true or false, which is precisely the question at issue. Although making no explicit reference to Ayer, Quine has expressed the point very cogently in a passing remark:

As an empiricist I consider that the cognitive synonymy of statements should consist in sameness of the empirical conditions of their confirmation. A statement is analytic when its operational condition of verification is, so to speak, the null condition. But I am using terms here which we cannot pretend to understand until we have made substantial progress in the theory of confirmation. Considering what good hands the problem of confirmation is in, it may seem that optimism is in order. However, if synonymy and analyticity and the rest are to be made sense of only in terms of an eventual account of confirmation, I think philosophers are tending to be insufficiently chary of the circularity involved in resting their eventual account of confirmation upon such concepts as synonymy and analyticity [10, page 92].

One striking feature which Ayer's explication of factual meaningfulness has in common with many others is that the meaningfulness of a statement is determined by its consequences and not by what it is a consequence of. There is something extremely misleading in supposing that any kind of argument from conclusions to premises is at issue. To say that a statement is verified is to say that it is supported by evidence. To say that a statement is verifiable is to say that it could be supported by evidence. The evidence (actual or possible) plays the role of a premise—more exactly, the statement of the evidence is a premise—and the verified or verifiable statement is the conclusion. Of course, in many important instances the conclusion is not a deductive consequence of the premise but is inductively supported by it. Strangely enough, Ayer's explication of empirical verifiability makes no reference to inductive relations. Empirical verifiability is explained entirely in terms of the deducibility of observation-consequences.

Ayer apparently held that inductive inference is simply the converse of deductive inference. According to this view (which is, unfortunately, widely held) a valid deductive argument becomes a correct inductive argument merely by interchanging the conclusion with one of the premises. Any number of considerations show that this characterization of induction is untenable; in fact, this is precisely what Church's criticism shows. The alleged verification of H' in the preceding section is obviously a counterexample to the view that induction is the converse of deduction. Furthermore, even assuming that H' has somehow been satisfactorily verified, the alleged verification of H is another counterexample. Again it might be tempting to have recourse to restrictions involving lawlikeness. This would amount to a view that certain kinds of valid deductive arguments have correct inductive arguments as converses while other kinds of valid deductions do not. Under this view serious questions would arise concerning the grounds for deciding which kinds of deductions have correct inductive arguments as converses. In any case it is an abandonment of the thesis that inductive correctness is simply a converse of deductive validity.

A more straightforward approach, it seems to me, is to admit inductive relations explicitly into the explication of empirical verifiability. On this approach we might say, roughly, that a statement which is neither analytic nor self-contradictory is empirically verifiable if and only if it is either an observation-statement or the conclusion of a correct inductive or deductive argument from verifiable premises. Such a formulation leaves many problems unsolved, but it is a step in the right direction. In the first place, it places appropriate emphasis upon the role of inductive relations in the explication of empirical verifiability. It calls attention to the need to specify (and possibly justify) the rules of inductive inference. In the second place, it escapes the question-begging procedure of using a statement whose cognitive status is at issue as a premise in any argument, inductive or deductive.

Let us re-evaluate the situation now that the statement whose cognitive status is at issue has been shifted from the position of premise to the position of conclusion. Consider deduction first. A fundamental requirement of a satisfactory deductive logic is that it shall be truth-preserving. Such a logic will also be "verifiability-preserving"; that is, if a conclusion C is derivable from premises $P_1, \ldots, P_n$ and the conjunction of these premises is verifiable, then the conclusion C is ipso facto verifiable. One way to put this is to say that whatever is evidence for a statement is evidence for anything entailed by that statement. Another way to put it is to cite the theorem of the probability calculus to the effect that the degree of confirmation of C on any evidence e is at least as great as the degree of confirmation of P on e if C is derivable from P. This condition is so basic to the notion of evidence that it might well be listed as a condition of adequacy for an explication of degree of confirmation. Unfortunately for Ayer's attempted explication of empirical verifiability, the converse relation does not hold. Given that P entails C, it is not generally true that whatever is evidence for C is evidence for P. Just as one cannot argue legitimately from the truth of the conclusion to the truth of the premises, so one cannot argue from the verifiability of the conclusion to the verifiability of the premises.

The situation with respect to induction cannot be spelled out fully in the absence of a completed inductive logic and it goes almost without saying that no inductive logic is at present widely accepted as reasonably complete and satisfactory. Nevertheless, there are certain general considerations which would seem to hold regardless of the precise character of inductive logic. Two cases, which correspond closely to Ayer's direct and indirect verifiability, need to be distinguished.

First, a statement may be the conclusion of an inductive argument which has no premises which are not observation-statements. Let us say that such conclusions are directly inductively verifiable. This case presents no particular difficulty, for the conclusion is directly supported by empirical evidence. Admitting that the inductive rule which governs the argument is correct is tantamount to admitting that the observation-premises constitute inductive evidence for the conclusion.

Second, a statement may be the conclusion of an inductive argument which has among its premises at least one non-observation-statement which is the conclusion of another inductive argument. Let us say that such conclusions are indirectly inductively verifiable. In this case, the situation is more complex because the relation of inductive support, unlike the relation of deductive entailment, is not transitive. Even if P inductively supports Q and Q inductively supports R, P may not inductively support R. A simple example will illustrate this point. Consider a population known to consist of ninety white stones, nine white gumdrops, and one black gumdrop. All of the gumdrops are soft and all of the stones are hard. Let P be the statement that some particular randomly selected member of the population is a gumdrop, Q the statement that it is white, and R the statement that it is hard. P strongly supports Q and Q strongly supports R (each to about the degree 9/10), but P and R are incompatible by hypothesis.

Suppose H is indirectly inductively verifiable. It is the conclusion of an inductive argument which has at least one non-observation-premise D. For the sake of simplicity, let D be the only non-observation-premise and let D be directly inductively verifiable. This means that D is the conclusion of an inductive argument which has only observation-premises O. These premises provide inductive support for D. H is the conclusion of an inductive argument which has D as a premise and which might have other observation-premises O'. Do O and O' inductively support H? Not necessarily.

We must be careful not to be misled into attempting to answer the wrong question. Our problem is not whether H is inductively supported by the observation-statements given; rather, the question is whether the characteristic of empirical verifiability is transferred from O to D and thence from D and O' to H. The question is this. Given that H is the conclusion of an inductive argument of the kind specified, does it follow that there exist observation statements which would support H? No decisive answer can be given in the absence of a precisely specified inductive logic. Nevertheless, an affirmative answer is to be expected; indeed, this affirmative answer might be considered a condition of adequacy for an inductive logic. The reason is as follows. With what is given it is impossible to assess the support of H by O and O', but added information would make the assessment possible. We need to know the degree to which H would be supported by the conjunction of D and O and the degree to which H would be supported by the conjunction of *not-D* and O. For statements of the kind we are considering, it is not unreasonable to suppose that this added information is obtainable in principle. If so, the support of H by O can be established. It would follow that indirectly inductively verifiable statements are empirically verifiable and that inductive arguments have the property of "verifiability preservation." These considerations show, I believe, that the prospects of satisfactorily explicating verifiability improve when we regard a statement as empirically verifiable if and only if it is either an observation-statement or the *conclusion* of an argument of a specified type.

III

It might seem that the only remaining task is to construct an inductive logic and choose an appropriate observation basis. Then, with deductive logic, inductive logic, and the observation basis we could, in principle, determine unambiguously which statements are verifiable and which ones are not. We could then decide, if we had not already done so, whether we want to identify factual meaningfulness with empirical verifiability. Unfortunately, there are further complications, as a simple example will show. Consider the following two deductive arguments:

(i) Jack is lazy.

Jack is lazy or the Absolute is lazy.

(ii) Jack is lazy or the Absolute is lazy.
Jack is not lazy.

The Absolute is lazy.

Let us agree that "Jack is lazy" is a verifiable statement. If we allow that (i) is a valid argument, then its conclusion is verifiable, for whatever evidence supports its premise also supports its conclusion. We would also maintain that the negation of any verifiable statement is verifiable. Thus (ii) has two verifiable premises, so its conclusion must be verifiable. But let us agree that "The Absolute is lazy" is not verifiable. Therefore, something has gone wrong. If we allow such proofs of verifiability, then it is trivial to show that every statement is verifiable.

However, we might question the validity of (i). The form of (i) seems to be

(iii) P.
$$\frac{}{P \vee Q.}$$

which is certainly valid, but the statement "Jack is lazy or the Absolute is lazy" may be ruled an improper disjunction because of its noncognitive component. The trouble seems to stem from the fact that (iii) is an argument form which permits the addition of an arbitrary disjunct in the conclusion. Everything is all right if the addition is a cognitive statement, but we get into trouble if the addition is a noncognitive statement. Unfortunately, it seems that we have to know whether a conclusion is cognitive before we can tell whether it actually follows validly from verifiable premises. Under these circumstances we can hardly use the fact that a statement is a conclusion of verifiable premises as a criterion of verifiability. We are back in a circle again.

There is a very easy way of handling (iii) and the problem of arbitrary additions to conclusions. It is a well-known fact that truth-functional logic can be formalized using a finite set of axioms, a rule of substitution, and the rule of detachment. Rules like (iii) are then derived rules. For purposes of our criterion we could eliminate all derived rules. Substitution and detachment will not permit arbitrary additions to conclusions. Form (iii) would then become

(iv) P.
  $P \supset P \vee Q.$
$$\frac{}{P \vee Q.}$$

where the second premise is taken as a logical truth. The problem of the noncognitive part is now referred to the premises; it is the question of whether "If Jack is lazy then Jack is lazy or the Absolute is lazy" is admissible as a premise in (iv). If not, of course, we cannot get the unwanted conclusion "Jack is lazy or the Absolute is lazy."

Arguments like (i) and the general problem of compound statements having noncognitive components played a conspicuous part in the considerations which led to Hempel's abandonment of hope for a satisfactory formulation of the verifiability criterion. Hempel laid down a condition of adequacy for meaning criteria which merits careful consideration:

. . . any general criterion of cognitive significance will have to meet certain requirements if it is to be at all acceptable. Of these, we note one, which we shall consider here as expressing a necessary, though by no means sufficient, *"condition of adequacy"* for criteria of cognitive significance.

(A) If under a given criterion of cognitive significance, a sentence N is non-significant, then so must be all truth-functional compound sentences in which N occurs non-vacuously as a component. For if N cannot be significantly assigned a truth value, then it is impossible to assign truth values to the compound sentences containing N; hence, they should be qualified as non-significant as well [8, page 62].

While Hempel's criterion seems rather straightforward, it is essential to distinguish between its application to sentences constructed within formal logic and its application to sentences of a natural language. A sentence of formal logic cannot have a nonsignificant component, whether occurring vacuously or nonvacuously, for the sentences of formal logic are all either true or false, and this includes component sentences as well as complete sentences. It is inadmissible to interpret any formula of truth-functional logic as a sentence which is neither true nor false.

The conjunctions of natural language are not, however, truth-functional in the same way. There are restrictions upon logical operations which do not apply to ordinary conjunctions. In particular, while it is meaningless to join sentences which are neither true nor false with truth-functional connectives, it is patently admissible from the point of view of English grammar to join them with the conjunctions of English. For example, "Shut up *and* eat your dinner," "Alas *and* alack," and "Be sure to lock the door *if* you leave," are all perfectly grammatical. Nevertheless, "Shut up," "Eat your dinner," "Alas," "Alack," and "Be sure to lock the door," are all sentences which are neither true nor false. Furthermore, it is not clear that the following two sentences must be devoid of cognitive meaning:

(v) If Jack is lazy then the Absolute is lazy.

(vi) Jack is lazy and the Absolute is lazy.

Since "The Absolute is lazy" is (by hypothesis) noncognitive, it follows that sentences (v) and (vi) cannot be schematized in truth-functional logic as $S \supset N$ and $S \cdot N$ respectively. We need not conclude, however, that there is no correct way of schematizing them truth-functionally. If Hempel's criterion were applied directly to sentences like (v) and (vi), the result would be that the presence of any noncognitive part takes the cognitive content away from the cognitive parts of a compound sentence. It seems more reasonable to say that the cognitive parts render the compounds cognitive to some extent and that the noncognitive parts do not add to the cognitive content but do not detract from it either. One might adopt something like the following rules of thumb:

> Let S be a cognitive sentence and N a noncognitive sentence; then:
> a. *Not-N* is noncognitive.
> b. *S and N* has the same cognitive meaning as S.
> c. *S or N* has the same cognitive meaning as S.
> d. *If S then N* has the same cognitive meaning as *not-S*.

It is essential, of course, that these rules be stated in terms of conjunctions of English rather than truth-functional connectives.

The foregoing rules are not to be regarded as hard and fast; they may, however, be somewhat indicative of the manner in which compound sentences with noncognitive parts may be treated. The intuitive rationale is simple. We treat the conjunction as false if and only if some component is false and the disjunction as true if and only if some component is true. Since the noncognitive part has no truth value, the conjunctive and disjunctive compounds have the same truth value as their cognitive parts. It is as if to say that by adding conjunctively or disjunctively the noncognitive sentence, "The Absolute is lazy," to the cognitive sentence, "Jack is lazy," no cognitive content is added or taken away. To preserve some analogy with truth functions, the hypothetical is translated into a disjunction and treated by the appropriate rule. Another way to look at it is this. Sentence (v) says that it is true that the Absolute is lazy if it is true that Jack is lazy. Since "The Absolute is lazy" cannot be true, Jack cannot be lazy. Sentence (v) says that Jack is not lazy much as "If Jack is lazy the moon is made of green cheese" does, except that "The moon is made of green cheese" is not true because it is false while "The Absolute is lazy" is not true because it is noncognitive. However, all of this is only intuitive. Because English is informal and imprecise it is impossible to have formal rules to deal with all cases of compound sentences with noncognitive parts.

As Reichenbach long maintained [12, 13], the verifiability criterion of cognitive meaningfulness needs to be supplemented with a verifiability criterion of sameness of cognitive meaning. Sentences with noncognitive parts can be handled by means of this additional criterion. The problem is to find other sentences which have the same cognitive meaning but which have no noncognitive parts. After this has been done we are in a position to schematize compound sentences in truth-functional notation. Sentences (v) and (vi) would be schematized as $\sim S$ and S respectively. Arguments (i) and (ii) would come out as follows:

(vii) Jack is lazy.   P.

     Jack is lazy or the Absolute is lazy.   Q.

(viii) Jack is lazy or the Absolute is lazy.   Q.
       Jack is not lazy. $\sim$P.

     The Absolute is lazy.

Because of the equivalence in meaning between "Jack is lazy" and "Jack is lazy or the Absolute is lazy" (vii) must be considered valid, but the nearest we could come to (viii) would be to conclude "It is not the case that Jack is lazy or the Absolute is lazy," which is equivalent to "Jack is not lazy." We have blocked the proof of the cognitive meaningfulness of "The Absolute is lazy" without denying the validity of (i).

A similar approach will dispose of certain problems concerning the meaningfulness of theoretical systems. Hempel, after characterizing an *isolated sentence* as one which is neither logically true nor logically false and whose "omission from the theoretical system would have no effect on its explanatory and predictive power in regard to potentially observable phenomena," asks, "Should we not, therefore, require that a cognitively significant system contain no isolated sentences?" [8, page 70]. Hempel answers his own question in the negative and so would I, but for very different reasons. Applying the verifiability criterion of sameness of cognitive meaning, I should say that a theoretical system containing an isolated sentence has precisely the same cognitive meaning as the system which would result from the deletion of the isolated sentence. Suppose that G is a physical (interpreted) geometry and that G′ is the system which results when "The Absolute is lazy" is added to that system as another postulate. G′ clearly is not lacking in cognitive significance; it has the same cognitive content as G. It is worth noting that a nonindependent postulate is, under Hempel's definition, an isolated sentence. Let T be a theorem of the system G and let G* be the system which results by making T a postulate. We would certainly, under these circumstances, want to say that the systems G and G* have the same cognitive meaning even though G* has an isolated sentence, especially in view of the logical truth:

$$(ix) \ (P \supset Q) \equiv (P \equiv P \cdot Q).$$

In large measure, the approach via a criterion of sameness of cognitive meaning circumvents Hempel's objections to a verifiability criterion.

A verifiability criterion of sameness of cognitive meaning would be the sort of thing suggested by Quine:

. . . the cognitive synonymy of statements should consist in sameness of the empirical conditions of their confirmation [10, page 92].

This amounts, I take it, to saying that two statements have the same cognitive meaning if and only if every observation-statement has equal inductive relevance to both. Reichenbach has formulated this criterion as follows:

Two sentences have the same [cognitive] meaning if they obtain the same weight, or degree of probability, by every possible observation [12, page 54].

The criterion of cognitive equisignificance is, I believe, an essential part of the verifiability criterion. Indeed, it may be regarded as basic, for we may define "noncognitive" in terms of it:

A statement is noncognitive if and only if it has the same cognitive meaning as its denial.

This formulation expresses the general idea that there is no empirical difference between the assertion and denial of a noncognitive sentence.

IV

We have not yet faced squarely enough the problem of the relation between truth-functional logic and the verifiability criterion of cognitive meaning. It is a familiar fact that logical systems can be treated in two distinct ways. On the one hand, a system can be regarded as an uninterpreted formal calculus consisting of meaningless marks which are manipulated by formal rules. From this standpoint, only the syntactical properties of the system are considered. On the other hand, a system may be regarded as an interpreted calculus which is endowed with semantical properties by virtue of semantical rules. From this standpoint, the system is one whose marks are meaningful symbols with some kind of reference.

Standard two-valued truth-functional logic (as found, for instance, in

Principia Mathematica) is a system of this sort. There are many alternative formalizations of this logic; in fact, it can be handled either axiomatically or by truth-tables. All of these treatments are formally equivalent. Although some approaches may have certain formal advantages, the philosophical problems of interpretation will be the same for all of them. We shall consider the truth-table treatment as the most perspicuous for our purposes.

Truth-tables themselves can be regarded either syntactically or semantically. From the purely syntactical point of view, either the "T" and "F" are dissociated from the semantical concepts of truth and falsity, or else marks such as "1" and "0" which are already dissociated are used. One of the important interpretations of this system (the only one which shall interest us) is designed to provide a logic of deduction. For this interpretation it is required that the theorems be necessarily true and that the derivations be truth-preserving. Accordingly, the "T" and "F" of the truth-table are to be associated with truth and falsity.

The formulas of the system are constructed from two types of symbols, proper and improper. The proper symbols can be taken as variables or constants; for the sake of definiteness let us regard them as variables, for the philosophical problems we are dealing with will be the same in any case. The improper symbols will include one or more truth-functional operation symbols. The first problem of interpretation is to choose a domain of interpretation, that is, a range for the variables of our system. The elements of the domain of interpretation must be entities which can be associated with truth and falsity. Again, there are various alternatives available, but for the sake of definiteness let us agree to let the variables range over whatever it is that sentences which are either true or false denote—propositions, truth values, or whatever you like. With this choice made, the substituends for truth-functional variables are sentences which are either true or false. Those who dislike "entities" like propositions or truth values can let the variables range over sentences which are either true or false and make names of such sentences the substituends for truth-functional variables. In any case, we cannot avoid the problem of deciding which sentences are true or false and how they are to be distinguished from those which are neither true nor false. The verifiability criterion has been proposed to fulfill this function.

There is a further complication. In order to provide an admissible interpretation for the propositional calculus, we must satisfy a *closure condition*:

The result of applying an n-ary operation of the system to an n-tuple of elements of the domain of interpretation is an element of the domain of interpretation.

In other words, the negation of a sentence which is either true or false must be a sentence which is either true or false, the conjunction of two sentences which are either true or false must be a sentence which is either true or false, etc. Now this condition can be satisfied by fiat; we can define the class of sentences which are either true or false so that it includes the negation, conjunction, etc., of sentences which are either true or false. However, there might be good reasons to reject such a definition. Consider, for example, the following trivial argument form which is valid in ordinary logic:

$$(x) \quad \frac{\begin{array}{l} P. \\ Q. \end{array}}{P \cdot Q.}$$

Is it reasonable to say that the conjunction $P \cdot Q$ is verifiable if the conjuncts P and Q are separately verifiable? If P and Q are statements about conjugate parameters of a quantum-mechanical system, we might want to deny it. It is well known that quantum mechanics imposes severe limitations upon the possibility of verification. Even though we might define possibility of verification in such a way as to automatically satisfy the condition of closure with respect to ordinary two-valued truth-functional logic, the fact would remain that it is physically impossible to verify certain statements (though we shall see that the difficulties attach more directly to negations and disjunctions than to conjunctions).

Before going into a more concrete discussion of the situation in quantum mechanics, it is important to note that the difficulties being considered arise out of an ambiguity in the term "verifiability." Possibility of verification may mean logical possibility or it may mean physical possibility. The impossibilities of verification imposed by quantum mechanics are physical impossibilities. There is, as far as anyone knows, no logical impossibility in a universe something like the Newtonian in which there are no incompatible parameters and hence no restriction on the verifiability of compound statements involving different parameters. If we accept physical possibility of verification as a criterion of factual meaningfulness, then we are committed to the consequence that empirical matters of fact to some extent determine our deductive logic. This would result in a rather subtle relationship between the a priori and the a posteriori. Whether two-valued truth-functional logic is acceptable becomes, in some sense, an empirical question.

There are some philosophers, I am sure, who would regard the foregoing reasoning (if correct) as a conclusive argument against interpreting verifiability in terms of physical as opposed to logical possibility. However, there are strong reasons for adopting the physical sense of possibility. In the first place, physical impossibility is impossibility of an insurmountable kind; to speak of mere physical impossibility would surely be a solecism.[1] In the second place, the logical analysis of modern physics seems to require the interpretation of verifiability in terms of physical possibility. Reichenbach, who has given this problem considerable attention [12, 13], has put the point as follows:

Schlick, and with him most members of the Vienna circle, have used logical possibility. But a definition of meaning in terms of logical possibility of verification makes the definition of meaning too wide, at least, when the interpretation of physics is concerned. For instance, Einstein's principle of equivalence, according to which being in accelerated motion means the same as being in a gravitational field, presupposes a definition of verifiability based on physical possibility. For these reasons I have advocated a definition of meaning in terms of the physical possibility of verification [13, page 53].

Without further argument as to which sense of possibility should be selected, let us consider the situation which results in quantum mechanics from adopting physical possibility of verification as a criterion of factual meaningfulness.

A classic discussion of the adoption of an alternative propositional logic for quantum mechanics is that of Birkhoff and von Neumann [2]. The present brief discussion is based upon their treatment. In classical and quantum mechanics a phase-space Σ can be associated with a given physical system S in such a way that the state of the system at any instant is represented by a point of Σ. Given that S is at t_0 in a state represented by

---

[1] Physical impossibility is, of course, to be sharply distinguished from technical impossibility; this latter sort of impossibility can be overcome by increased knowledge and improved technology. Until recently it was technically impossible to obtain photographs of the opposite side of the moon, but now it is technically possible. It was never physically impossible to do so. See Reichenbach [12, 13].

the point x_0, the physical laws governing the system determine what point x_1 will represent the state of S at a later time t_1. The laws of physics constitute, so to speak, the laws of motion of the points in phase-space. In classical mechanics the phase-space is a region of $2n$-dimensional Euclidean space (i.e., n position coordinates and n momentum coordinates); in quantum mechanics the phase-space is taken to be Hilbert space. In order to provide physical significance for the phase-space, its subsets must be made to correspond with "experimental propositions." (This, I take it, amounts to the verifiability criterion with possibility interpreted in the physical sense.) Even in classical mechanics it is unrealistic to identify each subset of phase-space with an experimental proposition, but it does seem reasonable "to assume that it is the *Lebesgue-measurable* subsets of a phase-space which correspond to experimental propositions, two subsets being identified, if their difference has *Lebesgue-measure* 0" [2, page 825]. In any case it turns out that set-sums, set-products, and set-complements of subsets corresponding to experimental propositions are themselves subsets corresponding to experimental propositions. Because of its Boolean character, ordinary two-valued truth-functional logic is adequate for the experimental propositions of classical mechanics. The closure condition will not be violated because the subsets corresponding to experimental propositions constitute a field of subsets.

Owing to the existence of incompatible parameters in quantum mechanics, not every measurable subset of phase-space corresponds to an experimental proposition. The experimental propositions are associated instead with the closed linear subspaces of Σ. These do not constitute a field of subsets; although the set-product of two closed linear subspaces is a closed linear subspace, the set-sum of two closed linear subspaces and the set-complement of one closed linear subspace do not in general constitute closed linear subspaces. The closed linear subspaces form a lattice with respect to which the analogues of negation, conjunction, and disjunction are definable. The negation of an experimental proposition is represented by the *orthogonal complement* of the closed linear subspace which represents that proposition. Conjunction coincides with set-product. Disjunction is defined in terms of negation and conjunction by means of the De Morgan relation; thus defined it differs from set-sum. With these definitions the closure condition is satisfied because negations, conjunctions, and disjunctions of experimental propositions are experimental propositions. The resulting logic is not a Boolean logic. The basic difference is that it fails to satisfy the distributive laws:

(xi) $P \cdot (Q \vee R) \equiv P \cdot Q \vee P \cdot R.$
$P \vee Q \cdot R \equiv (P \vee Q) \cdot (P \vee R).$

In their place the "modular identity" is proposed which, though not satisfied by every lattice, seems plausible for quantum mechanics:

(xii) If P implies Q, then
$P \vee R \cdot Q \equiv (P \vee R) \cdot Q.$

It is interesting to note that the paper concludes with the following two suggested questions:

(xiii) What experimental meaning can one attach to the meet [conjunction] and join [disjunction] of two given experimental propositions?

(xiv) What simple and plausible physical motivation is there for condition L5 [(xii) above]?

Question (xiii) is a question about the *physical* significance of *logical* connectives; question (xiv) is a question of *physical* grounds for adopting an axiom of *logic*. These authors are certainly not guilty of a naive failure to grasp the distinction between logical necessity and empirical fact; they are to be credited, in my opinion, with a deep insight into the fact that the adoption of a criterion of significance in terms of physical possibility of verification makes the selection of a propositional logic contingent upon physical theory. As they say near the close of their discussion, "The above heuristic considerations suggest in particular that the *physically significant* statements in quantum mechanics actually constitute a sort of projective geometry, while the *physically significant* statements concerning a given system in classical dynamics constitute a Boolean algebra" ([2], page 836, italics added).

There is, I think, a germ of truth in the view, often attributed to Mill, that the laws of logic are extremely highly confirmed empirical generalizations. Empirical fact does not determine the formal validity of any logic. The empirical question is this: If we choose a certain domain of interpretation and assign meanings to the improper symbols in a certain way, is the interpretation an admissible one? There seems to be ample empirical evidence that the physically verifiable statements about the macrocosm constitute a Boolean algebra and hence an admissible interpretation of ordinary two-valued truth-functional logic. The situation seems different for the microcosm. The importance of this point depends in no way upon the truth of quantum-mechanical theory. In the first place, even if the theory undergoes drastic modification, as it probably will, the same logical considerations will apply as long as the new theory involves incompatible parameters. More importantly, in the second place, as long as quantum-mechanical theory cannot be shown to be false a priori, there is no reason to rule out a priori the possibility that a logic different from the ordinary two-valued truth-functional variety may be required to satisfy the closure condition in the presence of the meaning criterion.

If this account of the situation is correct, then the syntactical features of a logical system are strictly a priori matters, but any application of the system involves empirical considerations. This means that any use of a logical system to determine whether a given English sentence is analytic, contingent, or self-contradictory, and any use of a system to determine whether one English sentence is a logical consequence of other English sentences, involve empirical considerations. Such applications of logic depend upon the admissibility of a given interpretation.

The point I have been arguing is, perhaps, similar to one expressed figuratively but forcefully by Quine as follows:

The totality of our so-called knowledge or beliefs, from the most casual matters of geography and history to the profoundest laws of atomic physics or even of pure mathematics and logic, is a man-made fabric which impinges on experience only along the edges. Or, to change the figure, total science is like a field of force whose boundary conditions are experience. A conflict with experience at the periphery occasions readjustments in the interior of the field. Truth values have to be redistributed over some of our statements. Reëvaluation of some statements entails reëvaluation of others, because of their logical interconnections—the logical laws being in turn simply certain further statements of the system, certain further elements of the field. Having reëvaluated one statement we must reëvaluate some others, which may be statements logically connected with the first or may be the statements of logical connections themselves [11, page 42].

Perhaps it amounts to the same thing to say that the interpretation of a formal logical system is always an empirical matter, the statement that an interpretation is admissible being an empirical generalization.

V

The main points I have been arguing may be summarized as follows. First, it is essential to distinguish the problem of explicating cognitive meaningfulness from the problem of explicating empirical verifiability. Second, empirical verifiability must be explicated in terms of inductive relations and not exclusively in terms of deductive relations. Induction is not simply the converse of deduction. If the explication of empirical verifiability is merged with the explication of cognitive meaningfulness, the joint explication must not be given solely in terms of the existence of observational consequences. Third, any criterion of cognitive meaningfulness needs to be supplemented with a criterion of cognitive equisignificance. Equisignificance must be explicated in terms of equal inductive support, not in terms of equal observational consequences. Fourth, if verifiability is to be understood as physical possibility of verification (as I think it should), then applications of deductive logic depend for their admissibility upon empirical considerations.

Where does all of this leave us? First, it reaffirms the fundamental importance of two old philosophical problems, the problem of specifying an observation-basis and the problem of constructing (and possibly justifying) an inductive logic. These two problems are intimately related, as is shown, for example, by Goodman's grue-bleen paradox. Second, it leads, I believe, to what might be called a formalistic theory of logic. Logical calculi are on a par with other uninterpreted formal systems; they admit physical interpretations but the question of admissibility is an empirical question. If such a view is correct it raises difficult problems concerning the status of logical truth. There is surely a question as to whether it is possible in a nonarbitrary manner to distinguish logical calculi from other fully formalized calculi or, given what would be regarded as a nonlogical calculus, to distinguish its logical from its nonlogical parts. Furthermore, the serviceability of the distinction between analytic and synthetic statements is again called into question.

I think it would be overly hasty to conclude, however, that the distinction between analytic and synthetic statements breaks down entirely or becomes perniciously relativized. Given a fully formalized system and a metalanguage adequate to discuss it, it still makes good sense to describe its syntax. If the system is interpreted, it still makes good sense to discuss its semantics. I do not think that the concepts of definition, linguistic convention, and semantic rule dissolve. There may remain a sufficient basis for a distinction between logical (or linguistic) truth and factual truth. These are problems which deserve further careful consideration.

REFERENCES

1. Ayer, Alfred Jules. *Language, Truth and Logic*, 2nd ed. New York: Dover, 1946.
2. Birkhoff, Garrett, and John von Neumann. "The Logic of Quantum Mechanics," *Annals of Mathematics*, 37:823–843 (October 1936).
3. Church, Alonzo. Review of Ayer's *Language, Truth and Logic*, in *Journal of Symbolic Logic*, 14:52–53 (1949).
4. Feigl, Herbert. "De Principiis Non Disputandum . . .?" in *Philosophical Analysis*, Max Black, ed. Ithaca, N.Y.: Cornell University Press, 1950; Englewood Cliffs, N.J.: Prentice-Hall, 1963.
5. Feigl, Herbert. "Logical Empiricism," in *Readings in Philosophical Analysis*, Herbert Feigl and Wilfrid Sellars, eds., pp. 3–26. New York: Appleton-Century-Crofts, 1949.
6. Feigl, Herbert. "Philosophical Tangents of Science," in *Current Issues in the Philosophy of Science*, Herbert Feigl and Grover Maxwell, eds., pp. 1–17. New York: Holt, Rinehart, and Winston, 1961.
7. Feigl, Herbert. "Some Major Issues and Developments in the Philosophy of Science of Logical Empiricism," in *Minnesota Studies in the Philosophy of Science*, Vol. I, Herbert Feigl and Michael Scriven, eds., pp. 3–37. Minneapolis: University of Minnesota Press, 1956.
8. Hempel, Carl G. "The Concept of Cognitive Significance: A Reconsideration," *Contributions to the Analysis and Synthesis of Knowledge*, Proceedings of the American Academy of Arts and Sciences, 80:61–77 (July 1951).
9. Hempel, Carl G. "Problems and Changes in the Empiricist Criterion of Meaning," in *Semantics and the Philosophy of Language*, Leonard Linsky, ed. Urbana, Ill.: University of Illinois Press, 1952. Originally published in *Revue Internationale de Philosophie*, 11 (1950).
10. Quine, Willard Van Orman. "Semantics and Abstract Objects," *Contributions to the Analysis and Synthesis of Knowledge*, Proceedings of the American Academy of Arts and Sciences, 80:90–96 (July 1951).
11. Quine, Willard Van Orman. "Two Dogmas of Empiricism," in *From a Logical Point of View*, pp. 20–46. Cambridge, Mass.: Harvard University Press, 1953. Originally published in *Philosophical Review*, 60, 1 (January 1951).
12. Reichenbach, Hans. *Experience and Prediction*. Chicago: University of Chicago Press, 1938.
13. Reichenbach, Hans. "The Verifiability Theory of Meaning," *Contributions to the Analysis and Synthesis of Knowledge*, Proceedings of the American Academy of Arts and Sciences, 80:46–60 (July 1951).

J. J. C. SMART

\\\(\))\)

Philosophy and Scientific Plausibility

I

In the *Tractatus*, 4.1122, Wittgenstein said: "Darwin's theory has no more to do with philosophy than any other hypothesis in natural science."[1] It is clear that Wittgenstein held that the results of scientific investigation have no bearing whatever on our philosophical investigations. On his view the sciences can be no more than the *object* of philosophical activity, which is the delimitation of sense from nonsense. This view of Wittgenstein's has become pretty orthodox in much contemporary philosophy, and I wish to challenge it in this paper. This seems an appropriate topic for a contribution to Professor Feigl's *Festschrift*, since especially in his writings on the relations between mind and body he has shown a willingness to consider the bearings of contemporary science on his problems. Moreover I have found his conception of a "nomological dangler" of great interest in the present connection, and in Section II I intend to expatiate a little on this theme. In Section III I shall use the philosophical problem of free will as an example to show that science is relevant to philosophy. Indeed, contrary to Wittgenstein's remark quoted above, I shall try to show that the Darwinian theory, or more properly the modern theory of evolution which combines the theory of natural selection with the ideas of recent genetics, is particularly relevant. In Section IV I shall try to defend my position by arguing against a too narrow con-

[1] [24, p. 49]. Since writing the first draft of this article I have seen that Ernest Gellner opens his review of T. A. Goudge's *Ascent of Life* (*Inquiry*, 5:85–90, 1962) with this same quotation from Wittgenstein, and like me he rejects Wittgenstein's point of view here.

ception of philosophical method, such as, for example, relying on an analogy with mathematics.[2]

It is necessary first of all to clear up a possible misunderstanding. In appealing to modern scientific ideas I do not wish to imply that the body of our scientific knowledge is something inviolable and immune from drastic modifications, or that some such drastic modifications may not be inspired by philosophical speculation. The traffic between science and philosophy can go in both directions. In some of his recent papers P. K. Feyerabend [10, 11, 12] has spoken up against the self-perpetuating character of scientific orthodoxy, and in particular has argued persuasively for the legitimacy of such attempts as those of D. Bohm and J.-P. Vigier to work out theories of microphysics alternative to those currently accepted. He has pointed out that dogmatic acceptance of a current theory may indeed make it impossible to discover facts which would refute it, since these facts could be satisfactorily understood only in the light of a novel and at present speculative theory. It is therefore important to work out *in detail* new theories which are capable of explaining all the facts which are explicable by the orthodox theory and which may lead us to new unascertained facts. While a theory is still in the metaphysical stage, that is, while it has no empirical advantage over the orthodox one, it is of course unknown whether it will ever be more than a merely speculative system. Perhaps it never will be, but we must not be afraid to try out new ideas.

While, however, we must remain alive to the possibility of radical changes in our scientific outlook, we must not exaggerate this possibility either. Consider a corridor which gives access to a number of rooms, in each of which there is a scientist engaged in fundamental research. In room number one there is a nuclear physicist, in room number two an atomic physicist, in room number three a classical physicist. In room number four there is a physical chemist and in room number five there is an inorganic or an organic chemist. In room number six there is a biochemist, in room number seven a cytologist, and in room number eight there is a physiologist. It is likely that revolutionary changes made in room n will usually have very little practical effect on room $n + 1$, and will probably

---

[2] I should like to thank Professor D. A. T. Gasking of the University of Melbourne, who read an earlier draft of this paper and made helpful comments, without which it would have been very much worse than it is.

have no practical effect at all on rooms $n + 2$, $n + 3$, etc.[3] (I say *practical* effect, because I do not wish to deny that the changes in earlier rooms may have some effect on how the scientists in later rooms look at the world.) This relative independence of the various rooms from one another obtains because it is usually only the *approximate* correctness of the results got in room n that are needed by the man in room $n + 1$, and an approximation to the results got in room n will pretty certainly be enough for the man in room $n + 2$. Now a revolutionary theory will clearly have to predict, within the limits of experimental error, the results which constitute the evidence for the theory that it is meant to replace. Consider, for example, the general theory of relativity in its relation to the Newtonian theory of gravitation. Only in exceptional cases will the two theories predict different results, over and above the limits of experimental error. Most of the results that the man in room $n + 1$ wants from the man in room n can be got from a rather old-fashioned theory on the n level, and in the case of room $n + 2$ it is probable that all can. Still more is this so with rooms $n + 3$, $n + 4$, etc. It is, for example, extremely unlikely that revolutionary discoveries in nuclear physics will lead to any substantial modification of our beliefs about the physiology of respiration.

In any case I hope to make it plausible that the bare possibility of radical changes in our scientific beliefs does not furnish any reason for ignoring these beliefs, such as they are, in dealing with philosophical problems.

II

As I have mentioned above, Professor Feigl has introduced a particularly important concept, that of a "nomological dangler." As he defines it, a nomological dangler is a law which purports to "connect intersubjectively confirmable events with events which *ex hypothesi* are in principle not intersubjectively and independently confirmable."[4] There are perhaps difficulties in this definition, but it is implied in it that nomological danglers would have to be ultimate laws, which are not further explicable, and which nevertheless have a minimal explanatory function. At best a nomological dangler would merely subsume a lot of A's that are

---

[3] I think that this vivid example of the rooms along the corridor was suggested to me in conversation by Professor C. A. Hurst, of the mathematical physics department of the University of Adelaide.

[4] See [6], especially p. 428. In an article "Sensations and Brain Processes" [21] I made use of Feigl's concept, but inadvertently used the term "nomological dangler" for the psychical entity that is supposed to dangle from the psychophysical law rather than for the psychophysical law itself. In this paper I have reverted to Feigl's usage.

associated with B's under the generalization "All A's are B's." The reason for this is that the nomological danglers would be laws purporting to connect physical events, in fact neurophysiological ones, with allegedly nonphysical ones, conscious experiences. These laws would therefore be ultimate ones, not explicable within neurophysiology or any other physical science. (There is the bare logical possibility that they might be deducible from the laws of some very general science which straddled the physical and nonphysical, but this does not, in the present state of our knowledge, seem to be one that we can take very seriously.) It is supposed to be just a fact, inexplicable by neurophysiology or any other science, that when a certain complex neurophysiological event occurs there also occurs a certain psychical event, such as the having of a green sense datum.

I wish now to point out that these nomological danglers have a further property which should make us view them with very great suspicion. This is that they purport to relate very complex neurophysiological processes to other things, which may or may not be simple, namely conscious experiences, and they relate those two classes of events in respect of the *fine structure* of the neurophysiological processes. For it is known that, in virtue of rather subtle differences between them, two neurophysiological processes which are roughly comparable in their complexity may be related to quite different experiences. Perhaps something of the order 10^{10} neurons are importantly involved in the having of a green sense datum. (This is an uninformed guess on my part, but if the number is 10^7 or even 10^5 that is still a big enough number.) Moreover if these neurons had been hooked up together in a different way there would not have been the experience. For example, however the neurons in the auditory area of the brain are stimulated there will not be a visual experience. It is clear, therefore, that a law which relates a neural process to the having of a green sense datum must take account of the structure of the visual area of the brain which distinguishes it from the auditory area. Indeed it will have to go much further than this: it will have to take account of the fine structure of a visual neural process which ensures that it goes with the experience of having a green sense datum and not with, say, that of having a red sense datum. I wish now to suggest that since a nomological dangler has this feature, that of relating to something very complex in terms of its fine structure, then it is a bad candidate for an ultimate law of nature. In science as it has developed hitherto there has been a tendency for the more complex to be explained in terms of the more simple.

For some purposes, of course, the human brain can be regarded as a simple entity. For example, a brain might be dropped out of an airplane and we might calculate the velocity with which it hit the earth. There would be no more difficulty in calculating the velocity of the brain than there would be in the case of a stone. We could treat the brain as a homogeneous solid to which the laws of gravity and air resistance could be applied. (Even so, the law of gravity in the first instance applies to particles or point masses and has to be applied to sizable bodies by integration. It was in fact this problem of integration that held Newton up for some time.) The unacceptable thing about the nomological danglers which purport to relate neurological events to psychical ones is that they would be ultimate laws and yet would have to be stated in terms of complex and nonhomogeneous fine structure.

Various writers, including Herbert Feigl [6, 7, 9], U. T. Place [14, 15, 16], and myself [18, 19, 21, 22], have recently tried to argue for the view that experiences just are brain processes. The arguments largely consist in attempts to rebut philosophical arguments which are commonly thought to put such a view quite out of court. For if such arguments can be refuted the brain-process theory enables us to do without the suspect nomological danglers. Even so it would still be *logically* possible that the danglers and the purely psychical experiences should exist. The dualist simply says that there are two entities that always occur together, where the physicalist says that there is only one entity. No observation or experiment could, I think, refute the dualist. In the absence of positive reason to the contrary, this should not go to support dualism. Equally it is logically possible that the world should have begun ten minutes ago just as it was ten minutes ago, and no experiment or observation could refute this hypothesis (see [17], pp. 159–160). (Only the most hardened positivist can deny that there is a difference in meaning between the sentences "The universe began ten minutes ago" and "The universe has existed for many thousands of millions of years.") The ten-minutes-ago hypothesis is much too much an *ad hoc* one, leaving countless facts (describing how the world was ten minutes ago) as quite inexplicable. In short it is an unnecessarily untidy and complex hypothesis. Similarly if the view that experiences just are brain processes can be defended against a priori objections it should be preferred, as against dualism, as a more simple, elegant, and economical hypothesis.

It is worth noting how widespread are the forms of dualism of which I am suggesting we should be wary. My objections do not apply only to full-fledged Cartesian dualism. Even so restrained a dualism as that of Strawson in his recent book [23] will be affected. For according to Strawson's account, conscious experiences are ontologically distinguishable from bodies, even though they are epistemologically dependent on them. This is made obvious by Strawson's contention that disembodied existence is consistent with his point of view. In the case of ordinary, not disembodied persons we therefore have brain events on the one hand and experiences on the other hand. No less than Descartes, Strawson surely needs nomological danglers.

III

In case the foregoing illustration of the relevance of scientific plausibility to philosophy is not found convincing, I shall try to drive home my point by means of another one. Directly contrary to Wittgenstein's remark which was quoted at the beginning of this paper, I wish to consider the relevance of the theory of evolution to a philosophical problem—the problem of free will.

Modern evolutionary theory is extremely mechanistic. In the case of bisexual organisms the variety on which natural selection gets to work is achieved partly through recombination and crossing over of chromosomes. These, however, merely shuffle the pool of genes in a species, and radical innovation is dependent on mutations, or changes in the genes themselves. The genes are thought to be DNA molecules. These are very stable self-replicating macromolecules. In spite of this great stability there will very occasionally be a change in the structure of a gene, perhaps on account of heat or of ionizing radiation. For our present purposes it is not important to speculate on exactly how such changes occur. The important thing to notice is that it would be a wonder if they did not occur and that they occur by chance: perhaps an alpha particle happens to bump into a certain part of a DNA molecule. The genes are believed to determine the production of enzymes, or organic catalysts, and hence the development of the organism. A mutation is therefore nearly always deleterious: the cell in which a mutated gene occurs, or the organism from which the cell develops, will nearly always fail to be viable or will be less able to cope with its environment. (There are more ways of spoiling a mechanism than of improving it.) Very occasionally, however, a mutation will be advantageous, and as the generations pass the process of natural selection will increase the proportion of members of the species in question which carry the mutated gene.

In the light of these ideas, of which only a rough and crude outline has been given, let us take a look at the libertarian theory of free will. The libertarian believes that there is a "self" or "will" which is capable of "contra-causal freedom" [4] and which is able to interfere with the usual processes in the central nervous system. How is it possible to reconcile this with the mechanistic conceptions of modern biology? It is quite possible to see how mutations may cause radical new types of neuronal hookup to occur: the "wiring diagram" of the brain is determined by the biochemical processes in the cells of the embryo, and these themselves are determined by the chemistry of the genes. A change in the brain, such as the increase of the visual areas, could well come about in this sort of way. But how could there come about, not just a change in circuitry or perhaps a change in the structure or biochemistry of the individual neurons themselves, but the production of a contracausal "self" or "will"? Such a thing could not be explained in terms of biochemistry. Yet somewhere or other a "self" or "will" must have emerged; it would be fantastic to attribute such a thing to an amoeba, and still more fantastic to attribute it to the complex systems of organic molecules which presumably preceded true living cells. In any case any sort of "self" or "will" would apparently have to depend on special psychophysical laws, which would be nomological danglers. This would also be the case if the libertarian did not think of the self or will as a separate nonphysical entity but nevertheless thought of the brain as itself operating in accordance with nonphysical or "vitalistic" laws. The emergence of such laws would be quite inexplicable within any mechanistic account of evolution in terms of changes in the chemistry of the nucleic acids.

The notion of emergence used to be supported by an analogy which the development of science has shown to be based on an error. It used to be said, for example, that however much we knew of the properties of sodium and however much we knew of the properties of chlorine, we could not predict the properties of salt (sodium chloride). To find out the chemical properties of salt, it was said, we should have to experiment with salt itself, and the properties we should find would therefore be emergent, not deducible from those of sodium and chlorine taken separately. By this it was meant not simply that the chemical properties of salt could not be deduced from the physical properties of the elements because the calculation would be too difficult, but that it was in principle impossible that there should be any such calculation. It was then commonly suggested that just as chemical properties were supposed to be emergent relative to physical ones, so there were properties of life and mind which were emergent relative to the chemical and the physical. This analogical argument, however, contains a false premise. In fact it is, in simple cases, quite possible to deduce the chemical properties (the chemical bonds) from purely physical (spectroscopically ascertained) properties of the elements. This is done by means of the quantum theory of the chemical bond. In cases where this can not be done in practice, the failure can be put down partly to plain ignorance of the physical assumptions that would be needed and partly to the complexities of the calculations that would have to be carried out. Simplifying assumptions have to be made, and these can easily lead to gross inaccuracies in prediction. Such difficulties do not in themselves lend support to a doctrine of emergent laws.

There is, of course, a trivial sense in which new qualities emerge when we move toward more complex structures. Consider a number of point masses, such as were envisaged by Boscovich. A cloud of such point masses could have a shape, roughly spherical or cubical, say. Four such point masses could determine a tetrahedron. In this context the properties of shape and of determining a tetrahedron could be said to be emergent, in the sense that they could not belong to individual point masses. This *trivial* sense of "emergence" is clearly quite compatible with the most completely mechanistic of theories. Again, consider a wireless set. If you like to say that the property of being able to receive wireless signals is an emergent property of the set, since it is not possessed by the individual components of the apparatus, then you can. Nevertheless, if you do say this, then you must by no means imply that from a knowledge of the parts and the way they are put together we cannot deduce the behavior of the hookup as a whole.[5]

In spite of its evolutionary inspiration, the metaphysical idea of emergent evolution is in spirit alien to the modern genetical theory of natural selection. About all they have in common is the word "evolution." There is no mystery about the fact that genes mutate, incomplete though our

[5] For criticism of the notion of emergence, see [2] and [13, pp. 366–380].

knowledge of what happens may be in detail. Then, since the biochemistry of the cells of an embryo is determined in part by the genes and in part by the topographical relationship between the cells, a change in the chemical structure of a gene or genes may lead to a snub nose instead of a straight one or to a more complex piece of neurophysiological circuitry. But how could such chemical changes lead to a nonphysical self or will, or even to vitalistic laws of functioning?

In science we sometimes come across a certain type of irresponsibility. For example, consider some of those writers who think that they see difficulties in special relativity and the clock paradox, and in consequence try to establish a new and nonrelativistic kinematics. In some cases, though not always, such writers do not seem to recognize an obligation to show how their unorthodox ideas can be worked out in such a way as to deal with various secure and important branches of physics, e.g., electromagnetism and the study of fast-moving particles in microphysics. Unless they recognize this obligation and show that they can fulfill it in an *acceptable* way there is clearly no hope of their unorthodox kinematics being taken very seriously, especially since most physicists, in my opinion rightly, see no difficulties in orthodox relativistic ideas. In short, in physics a new theory not only must work in a limited field but must be shown to work in as many fields as does the orthodox theory which it is supposed to replace. This obligation to consider the wider ramifications of a physical theory has, I suggest, its parallel in philosophy. It is not at all satisfactory to produce a libertarian theory of free will as a solution to a limited set of puzzles and paradoxes if one cannot show how it can be reconciled with our biological knowledge.

In this respect the libertarian is in a worse position than his rivals. Those philosophers, such as David Hume, R. E. Hobart, and P. H. Nowell-Smith (to name but three), who maintain that free will is perfectly compatible with determinism (with or without a bit of pure chance thrown in at the quantum-mechanical level) have no such problem. Their position is patently quite compatible with mechanistic biology. The libertarian is in a much more difficult position since, as I have suggested, his position is hard to reconcile with the modern biological picture of man. The libertarian has a responsibility to consider how such a synthesis of ideas could be carried out, but he commonly fails to discuss the matter adequately. Usually his interest lies in quite another direction. For example, Sir Isaiah Berlin, in his *Historical Inevitability* [3, especially pages

30–34], holds that determinism would entail a drastic change in our ordinary moral concepts. Berlin seems to think that this contention, that determinism is incompatible with our ordinary moral notions, provides a good reason for coming down on the libertarian side. Berlin is thinking here not of moral judgments themselves but of the common-sense metaphysical beliefs on which these moral judgments are (partly) based. (If a philosopher were to argue directly from moral judgments themselves to a metaphysical conclusion we could accuse him of committing the naturalistic fallacy in reverse.) Now when Berlin says that determinism would entail a drastic change in our common moral thinking he does so on slight grounds and without sufficiently considering the arguments of R. E. Hobart and others to the contrary. I myself would argue that determinism (with or without a bit of pure chance thrown in) does entail a slight modification in our ordinary moral thinking, but not a drastic one such as Berlin envisages. But even if it did, why be so solicitous of common sense, which especially in matters relating to human conduct is heavily loaded with archaic traditional and theological ideas? What evidential value can such an appeal to common-sense beliefs have?

IV

I have tried to argue that considerations of scientific plausibility are relevant to philosophy. It may be said in reply that they can be so in at best a heuristic way.[6] That is, they may lead us to re-examine philosophical arguments, for example those for psychophysical dualism, to see whether they are as cogent as they have hitherto seemed, but if we do examine them carefully we may have to recognize their validity, however implausible their conclusions may be. (I do not admit that the philosophical arguments for psychophysical dualism or for libertarianism are able to survive close examination, but let us for the sake of argument grant that they do.) It may be said that to pit considerations of plausibility against philosophical reasonings is like trying to cut glass with paper. Philosophical reasoning, it will be said, is either demonstrative or nothing, and no considerations of plausibility can affect a demonstrative argument.

This objection confuses demonstrability with certainty. A theorem in mathematics may be demonstrable and indeed demonstrated, but I may not be sure that I have not made a slip in checking the validity of the

[6] In a note [20] I argued for the heuristic importance of plausibility considerations. I now wish to go further than this.

proof. Even in adding a column of figures I may be uncertain whether I have got the right answer, and even if I get some of my friends to check too there is the faint possibility that we may all have made the same slip. Of course in practice I am quite reassured when my calculations check with those of others, but this sort of reassurance is not so easily got in philosophy, since philosophical arguments are notoriously slippery, and philosophers are rarely unanimous. It therefore seems to me to be optimistic of philosophers to suppose that their a priori arguments give a higher order of certainty than do considerations of scientific plausibility. Even if we ourselves have so far not perceived any fault in our apparently demonstrative arguments, we can be pretty sure that some other philosophers will, though of course we may continue to disagree with their diagnoses.

In any case can we be sure that a philosophical argument can ever give the sort of demonstrative certainty that we can get in mathematics? Mathematicians commonly agree with one another on their assumptions and on the rules of proof. The difficulty in mathematical proof lies in the discovery of the appropriate chains of sentences which yield proofs; there is usually agreement on whether or not such a chain of sentences constitutes a correct proof. Sometimes, however, mathematicians do disagree on the methods of proof which are acceptable to them. The most important case is the disagreement between those who do and those who do not accept nonconstructive methods of proof. The majority of mathematicians accept such methods, mainly, I suppose, because they can do so much more with them, but a minority reject these methods as not sufficiently perspicuous. Other mathematicians again adopt a neutralist attitude and are interested in seeing both what can be and what can not be got by constructive and nonconstructive methods. If there is a serious controversy between constructivists and nonconstructivists it takes on all the undecidability of a philosophical dispute. It follows that an analogy between philosophy and mathematics will not necessarily lead us to suppose that philosophy can yield unquestionable demonstrations.

Someone who has been much influenced by Wittgenstein may wish to say that philosophical disputes are due to lack of clarity about the functioning of our language, and that if we work hard enough we shall resolve our disputes. The last part of this contention seems to be either a tautology or an empirical falsehood. If "hard enough" means "hard enough to resolve our disputes," then it is a tautology to say that if we work hard enough we shall resolve our disputes. The question still remains whether it is possible to work hard enough in this sense. On any other criterion of "hard enough" it is probably an empirical falsehood that if we work hard enough we shall resolve our disputes, since there is scarcely a philosophical issue on which all competent philosophers agree. There is therefore no adequate empirical evidence that all, or even many, philosophical issues are simply a matter of "showing the fly the way out of the fly bottle," to use Wittgenstein's metaphor.

Our Wittgensteinian philosopher may now say that he has no theory of philosophical method; he just gets on with the job. The way in which he gets on with the job is by drawing attention to similarities and dissimilarities in the ways in which words are used. This sort of investigation of "logical grammar" is a very good way of getting on with philosophy, and I should be one of the last to decry it. But what I do want to say at this stage is that if you do not lay claim to a theory of philosophical method then you are not in a position to object to me when I use considerations of scientific plausibility as part of my philosophical armory.

After all, there will be some philosophers who will resist the procedures of the logical grammarian even in those cases where most of us believe them to be fruitful. A philosopher may object to the whole way of thinking about language which is implicit in this approach. For example, he may assert that meanings are apprehended by means of intellectual intuition. It is partly because a philosopher may question anything, including the theory of meaning and the psychology of knowledge, that it is always possible that he may be able to evade any contradiction in which you may think you have trapped him. Another difficulty is that one philosophical controversy may lead on to another, and this to yet another, and so on, without prospect of reaching finality. Thus in the dispute about free will we may give the libertarian two mutually exclusive alternatives: acting in a deterministic way and acting by pure chance. We point out that neither of these are what the libertarian wants. The libertarian may reply by questioning our assumption that determinism and pure chance are contradictories (see [1] and [5]). He may argue that we have here begged the question, and that a subspecies of what we call "pure chance" is "free action," and that he can give a sense, perhaps by appealing to inner experience, which distinguishes free action from what he is willing to call "pure chance." This will pretty certainly shift the issue to yet another philosophical controversy, and it does not seem to be evident that a really determined libertarian need ever allow himself to be finally caught. That at any rate is borne out by the seemingly interminable literature on the subject. Even what seems to one lot of philosophers to be an absolutely knockdown argument does not seem to be so to another lot of philosophers. There is, even so, another way in which our philosophical opponent may be attacked. He may be committed to a far less simple system of total science than we are. For example it is the difficulty of fitting intellectual intuitions into our biological and psychological conceptual schemes which makes them unacceptable to some of us, even though talk about them should perhaps be rendered free from contradiction. Of course our opponent may question this approach too: he may repudiate the ideal of simplicity and economy of explanation. Philosophical disputes may still be intractable. Nevertheless, the appeal to scientific plausibility may carry weight with those who accept the ideals of simplicity and economy of explanation, and if so it may help to settle some arguments among some philosophers.

I hope that I have done something in this paper to support the contention that considerations of scientific plausibility have some part to play in philosophy. It is true of course that what appears to be a plausible conceptual scheme may in future turn out to be false, and an implausible one may after all be true. We must certainly not discourage the production of metaphysical speculations which may foreshadow the testable science of the future. Nevertheless, if we want to find out what, on our present knowledge, is the most probable view about some philosophical question, such as that of free will or of the relations between mind and body, then we should be foolish to neglect the direction in which our present scientific knowledge points. Indeed, part of this paper may be looked at in another light, not so much as an attempt to discourage the speculations of the dualist or of the libertarian, but as itself part of a speculative attempt to advocate a materialist or a physicalist metaphysics. In doing this we need not be dogmatic, for we can recognize fully that our present scientific beliefs have always to be tested against the facts, and so may have to be replaced by other beliefs in the future. In this way, therefore, I hope that I can avoid the suggestion that this essay is, to use the title of one of Professor Feigl's recent papers [8], no more than a dogmatic and undesirable "philosophical tangent of science."

REFERENCES

1. Acworth, Richard. "Smart on Free Will," Mind, 72:271–272 (1963).
2. Berenda, C. W. "On Emergence and Prediction," Journal of Philosophy, 50:269–274 (1953).
3. Berlin, Isaiah. Historical Inevitability. London: Oxford University Press, 1954.
4. Campbell, C. A. "Is 'Free-Will' a Pseudo-Problem?" Mind, 60:441–465 (1951).
5. Campbell, C. A. "Professor Smart on Free-Will, Praise and Blame: A Reply," Mind, 72:400–405 (1963).
6. Feigl, Herbert. "The 'Mental' and the 'Physical,'" in Minnesota Studies in the Philosophy of Science, Vol. II, Herbert Feigl, Michael Scriven, and Grover Maxwell, eds., pp. 370–497. Minneapolis: University of Minnesota Press, 1958.
7. Feigl, Herbert. "Mind-Body, Not a Pseudoproblem," in Dimensions of Mind, Sidney Hook, ed., pp. 24–36. New York: New York University Press, 1960.
8. Feigl, Herbert. "Philosophical Tangents of Science," in Current Issues in the Philosophy of Science, Herbert Feigl and Grover Maxwell, eds., pp. 1–17. New York: Holt, Rinehart, and Winston, 1961.
9. Feigl, Herbert. "Physicalism, Unity of Science and the Foundations of Psychology," in The Philosophy of Rudolf Carnap, Paul Arthur Schilpp, ed., pp. 227–267. La Salle, Ill.: Open Court, 1964.
10. Feyerabend, Paul K. "Explanation, Reduction, and Empiricism," in Minnesota Studies in the Philosophy of Science, Vol. III, Herbert Feigl and Grover Maxwell, eds., pp. 28–97. Minneapolis: University of Minnesota Press, 1962.
11. Feyerabend, Paul K. "How to Be a Good Empiricist—A Plea for Tolerance in Matters Epistemological," in Philosophy of Science: The Delaware Seminar, Vol. 2, 1962–1963, Bernard Baumrin, ed., pp. 3–39. New York: Interscience, 1963.
12. Feyerabend, Paul K. "Problems of Microphysics," in Frontiers of Science and Philosophy, R. G. Colodny, ed., pp. 189–283. Pittsburgh: University of Pittsburgh Press, 1962.
13. Nagel, Ernest. The Structure of Science. New York: Harcourt, Brace, and World, 1961.
14. Place, U. T. "Is Consciousness a Brain Process?" British Journal of Psychology, 47:44–50 (1956).
15. Place, U. T. "Materialism as a Scientific Hypothesis," Philosophical Review, 69:101–104 (1960).
16. Place, U. T. "The 'Phenomenological Fallacy': a Reply to J. R. Smythies," British Journal of Psychology, 50:72–73 (1959).
17. Russell, Bertrand. Analysis of Mind. London: Allen and Unwin, 1921.
18. Smart, J. J. C. "Brain Processes and Incorrigibility," Australasian Journal of Philosophy, 40:68–70 (1962).
19. Smart, J. J. C. "Further Remarks on Sensations and Brain Processes," Philosophical Review, 70:406–407 (1961).
20. Smart, J. J. C. "Plausible Reasoning in Philosophy," Mind, 66:75–78 (1957).
21. Smart, J. J. C. "Sensations and Brain Processes," Philosophical Review, 68:141–156 (1959).
22. Smart, J. J. C. "Sensations and Brain Processes, A Rejoinder to Dr. Pitcher and Mr. Joske," Australasian Journal of Philosophy, 38:252–254 (1960).
23. Strawson, P. F. Individuals. London: Macmillan, 1959.
24. Wittgenstein, Ludwig. Tractatus Logico-Philosophicus. Translation by D. F. Pears and B. F. McGuinness. London: Routledge and Kegan Paul, 1961.

HENRY B. VEATCH

\\\(\)///

A Case for Transempirical and Supernaturalistic Knowledge Claims

Is it insult or irony that a contributor to a volume of essays honoring Herbert Feigl should set himself the task of trying to defend some of the traditional arguments for God's existence? It is neither insult nor irony. If anything, it is sheer folly. For the day is long gone when men were wont to shake their heads and remark, "The fool hath said in his heart, 'There is no God.'" Rather the situation is now one in which all would agree that the fool is precisely he who takes it into his head to say "There is a God."

At the risk, then, of seeming only to speak in praise of folly, I should like in this paper to direct attention to certain logical features of the so-called cosmological argument for God's existence. Or rather, it is not so much the logic of this argument itself that seems to me to deserve re-examination, as it is the logic of certain characteristic criticisms that have been made and still continue to be made of this argument.

So to specify my objective is, unfortunately, hardly likely to make the undertaking seem any less egregious or far-fetched. For it goes almost without saying that if any benighted philosopher nowadays feels a compulsion to talk about the traditional proofs for God's existence, he had better occupy himself with the ontological argument. This is the argument that has been attracting a certain amount of attention in the last couple of years—such attention, in fact, that while few would concede that the argument has thereby been rendered credible, there is some evidence that it has at least been made halfway respectable. But the cosmological argument—surely that is beyond the pale! Having once been consigned to oblivion, in oblivion is where it should be allowed to remain—at least, so everyone seems to think.

What, though, is it about the cosmological argument that renders it so suspect? Admittedly, it does involve what Herbert Feigl, in another connection, has most happily termed "trans-empirical or 'supernaturalistic' knowledge-claims."[1] And to any dogmatic empiricist this would doubtless be sufficient to justify ruling the argument summarily out of court: "Our ideas reach no farther than our experience: We have no experience of divine attributes and operations [and presumably Hume might have added divine existence as well]: I need not conclude my syllogism . . ." [5, Part II, pages 142–143].

But it is not from any such uncritical empiricism that the interesting criticisms of the cosmological argument arise. Instead, it is the criticisms that strike directly at the logic of the argument that are especially significant and deserving of scrutiny. Thus on the one hand there is the criticism, made famous by Kant and still generally accepted, that the cosmological argument is quite lacking in cogency so long as it attempts to stand alone; it is obliged to fall back on the ontological argument to make up for the deficiencies in its own logic. And on the other hand there is the criticism, once more happily articulated by Herbert Feigl, though again not in just this particular context, that "the justification of knowledge-claims in this type of metaphysics or theology [must be] conceived in analogy to the 'transcendent' hypotheses in scientific theories" [2, page 12]. But since the hypothesis of God's existence is not subject to either verification or falsification in the usually accepted senses, the cosmological argument, it is thought, must be rejected, because while pretending to proceed by analogy with the hypothetico-deductive method, it quite fails to bring off any such demonstration as it claims to. Let us look at the first criticism first. It was this line of criticism which only a few years ago was most confidently exploited in several of the pieces appearing in the volume entitled *New Essays in Philosophical Theology* [4]. And what is particularly noteworthy about this recent attempt at dismissing the cosmological argument as being no more than the ontological argument in disguise is that at least some of the contributors to the volume would appear to be unimpressed

---

[1] [2, p. 12]. It is true that Feigl in this article is not considering the specific sort of knowledge claim involved in such an argument as the cosmological argument; instead, he is considering such knowledge claims as are often made on behalf of mystical intuition. Nevertheless, many of the criticisms which Feigl makes with respect to the latter would certainly apply, *mutatis mutandis*, to the former.

with the particular reasons that Kant originally gave for holding the cosmological argument to depend upon the ontological (see especially [7], pages 36–37). Instead, these authors propose some rather different and much more interesting reasons to the same effect. Here is Mr. Smart's account of them:

The trouble comes in the first stage of the argument. For the first stage of the argument purports to argue to the existence of a necessary being. And by "a necessary being" the cosmological argument means "a *logically* necessary being," i.e. "a being whose non-existence is inconceivable in the sort of way that a triangle's having four sides is inconceivable." The trouble is, however, that the concept of a logically necessary being is a self-contradictory concept, like the concept of a round square. For in the first place "necessary" is a predicate of *propositions*, not of things. That is, we can contrast *necessary* propositions such as "3 + 2 = 5," "a thing cannot be red and green all over," "either it is raining or it is not raining," with *contingent* propositions, such as "Mr. Menzies is Prime Minister of Australia," "the earth is slightly flattened at the poles," and "sugar is soluble in water." The propositions in the first class are guaranteed solely by the rules for the use of the symbols they contain. In the case of the propositions of the second class a genuine possibility of agreeing or not agreeing with reality is left open; whether they are true or false depends not on the conventions of our language but on reality. . . . So no informative proposition can be logically necessary. Now since "necessary" is a word which applies primarily to propositions, we shall have to interpret "God is a necessary being" as "The proposition 'God exists' is logically necessary." But this is the principle of the ontological argument . . . No existential proposition can be logically necessary, for we saw that the truth of a logically necessary proposition depends only on our symbolism, or to put the same thing in another way, on the relationship of concepts [7, page 38].

Now what about this contention of Mr. Smart's that any statement about a necessary being must itself be a necessary statement, or better and more generally, any assertion of what is necessarily the case can only be a logically necessary assertion? This does seem a bit far-fetched, at least on the surface, and it is not surprising that Mr. Geach should appear to be nothing if not scornful:

It may be objected that there is simply no sense to the word "necessary," or none that can be coherently explained, apart from the logical necessity of statements. This thesis is upheld with great confidence in some recent essays on "philosophical theology"; one author actually says concerning it: "I have no space to demonstrate this here, and indeed I do not think that it is any longer in need of demonstration." It may well be wondered how much study of modal logic—whether, indeed, any knowledge of there being such a discipline—lies at the bottom of such confidence. Anyhow, since what is "necessary" is what "cannot" not be, to say that "necessary" can only refer to logical necessity is equivalent to saying that whatever cannot be so, *logically* cannot be so—e.g. that since I cannot speak Russian, my speaking Russian is logically impossible: which is absurd [1, page 114].

Apparently, if the cosmological argument is to be shown to be dependent for its validity upon the ontological argument, then it will be necessary to avail oneself of more cogent reasons than the mere dogmatic pronouncement that "God is a necessary being" must be interpreted as meaning "The proposition 'God exists' is logically necessary."

Besides, a further criticism might be leveled against Mr. Smart simply on the ground that he has seriously misconstrued the very cosmological argument which he is attacking, at least as that argument is presented by St. Thomas Aquinas. For Smart seems to suppose not merely that a statement about a necessary being must be understood as being itself a necessary statement; in addition, he suggests that this is the way the conclusion of the cosmological argument always has been understood—indeed, that if it had not been so understood the argument itself would not have had any semblance of cogency in the first place. To quote him again: "If we cast our minds back, we recall that the argument was as follows: that if we explain why something exists and is what it is, we must explain it by reference to something else, and we must explain that thing's being what it is by reference to yet another thing, and so on, back and back." And then Smart readies himself for the kill. He continues: "It is then suggested that unless we can go back to a logically necessary first cause we shall remain intellectually unsatisfied" [page 39]. Immediately, the hunter pounces on his quarry: a logically necessary being, why, that's an impossibility, and not just a physical impossibility, but a logical impossibility! And then for nearly half a page he has some delightful sport with the poor old cosmological argument: its attempt at the impossible is really so ridiculous as not even to merit comparison with the crazy business of asking for the moon; rather the only proper comparison is with the still crazier attempts at squaring the circle.

Nevertheless, although all of this affords excellent entertainment, it does not have much to do with the cosmological argument. For so far from this argument being one in which we say that "unless we can go back to a logically necessary first cause, we shall remain intellectually unsatisfied," it is an argument in which any attempt at reaching a logically necessary first cause is explicitly repudiated. As Aquinas sees it, statements such as "God exists," "A necessary being exists," etc., are not logically necessary statements at all.[2] Indeed, if they were logically necessary, then they would not be conclusions of a cosmological type of argument but rather self-evident truths (per se nota). And to maintain that God's existence is self-evident or logically necessary, Aquinas would say, is simply to invoke the ontological argument, which is the very thing that he (Aquinas) is most scrupulously avoiding. In other words, the statement "God exists" or "A necessary being exists," taken as the conclusion of a cosmological type of argument, is a contingent truth; it is not a logically necessary one.[3]

Moreover, if one asks for the specific reasons Aquinas would give for saying that the existence of God or of a necessary being is only a contingent truth, the answer is simple: it is perfectly conceivable that God or a necessary being might not exist at all; there is nothing in the least self-contradictory or logically impossible about such a supposition [9, I, 2, 1,

[2] Needless to say, we are taking considerable liberties with terminology here. So far as I know, Aquinas has no term, and not even any concept, that exactly corresponds to the contemporary notion of a logically necessary statement. Nevertheless, Aquinas's notion of a proposition that is per se notum seems to have many of the characteristics of a logically necessary proposition. For one thing, a self-evident proposition is one in which it suffices to know only the meanings of the terms of the proposition to know the truth of the proposition. (Cf. Summa Theologiae, I, 2, article 1, 2nd objection.) For another thing, such a self-evident proposition is one the opposite of which is inconceivable (ibid., sed contra).

[3] For Aquinas's discussion of the issue, see Summa Theologiae, I, 2, 1. Sometimes one cannot help suspecting that modern writers have occasionally been misled in the way Hume seems to have been with respect to the conclusions of arguments purporting to demonstrate God's existence. Thus Hume apparently thinks that because such a conclusion is supposed to follow necessarily from the premises, it must therefore itself be a necessary truth. Although one can hardly believe that Hume really meant what he seems to be saying, the following is what he actually says: "I shall begin with observing, that there is an evident absurdity in pretending to demonstrate a matter of fact, or to prove it by any arguments a priori. Nothing is demonstrable, unless the contrary implies a contradiction. Nothing, that is distinctly conceivable, implies a contradiction. Whatever we conceive as existent, we can also conceive as non-existent. There is no Being, therefore, whose non-existence implies a contradiction. Consequently there is no Being, whose existence is demonstrable" [5, Part IX, p. 189]. Just what does Hume mean by the statement "Nothing is demonstrable, unless the contrary implies a contradiction"? Of course, if one accepts the premises of a valid argument, one cannot deny the conclusion without contradiction. But does this mean that the conclusion, taken just in itself, is such a proposition that the contrary implies a contradiction?

sed contra]. Not only that, but even if it could be shown that the statement "God exists" was logically necessary, that still would not prove that God really existed. And the reasons Aquinas would give [ad 2] for this latter contention would be not unlike the reasons Smart would give. Indeed if we were to paraphrase Aquinas, using the contemporary lingo (see footnote 2), we might say that in his eyes a "logically necessary proposition" can scarcely be taken to be "an existential proposition," since "the truth of a logically necessary proposition depends only . . . on the relationship of concepts." In other words, so far from such observations as Smart's being devastating with respect to the cosmological argument, they are the very things that any intelligent defender of that argument would be the first to insist upon.

This is not to say, of course, that there are no differences between Smart's understanding of such things as "necessary truth," "logical necessity," "self-evident propositions," etc., and Aquinas's.[4] But the question is as to the relevance of such differences in the present context. Thus, to cite one obvious example, Smart declares categorically that no logically necessary proposition can be an existential proposition. In contrast, with respect to God's existence, it is well known that Aquinas maintained that although such a thing was not self-evident (sc. logically necessary) to us, it presumably would be self-evident (sc. logically necessary) to God Himself [9, I, 2, 1]. In the latter case—i.e., in the case of God's knowledge of His own existence—one would have an example of a knowledge that was at once logically necessary and at the same time existential and informative.

Now perhaps it is just as well that we not speak with too much confidence about the divine knowledge, it being something that all parties to the dispute would agree was either nonexistent or else inaccessible to us. And yet for our present purposes it can at least be pointed out that the putative example of God's knowledge of His own existence being both logically necessary and existential is hardly a case in point, so far as the present issue is concerned. For God's self-knowledge, however much it might constitute an exception to Smart's principle that no logically necessary truth can be existential, is certainly not to be taken as evidence of the validity of the ontological argument. In God's case, there can be no

---

[4] I have touched on some of these differences in a paper entitled "Matrix, Matter, and Method in Metaphysics" [10]. I have discussed them more at length in another paper entitled "On Trying to Say and to Know What's What" [11].

question of His using a supposedly logically necessary truth about His own existence in order to infer His own existence![5]

Accordingly, the example of divine self-knowledge constitutes no exception to our present thesis, viz., that with respect to any attempted proof of God's existence Aquinas would be just as insistent as Smart that the logical necessity of a proposition asserting God's existence would not warrant our making any assumptions as to the existential import of that proposition. Hence for Smart to introduce into a discussion of the cosmological argument considerations about the lack of existential import of logically necessary truths is nothing but a red herring.

To return, then, to the central issue of this part of the paper: the cosmological argument is an argument that does involve "trans-empirical or 'supernaturalistic' knowledge-claims"; does this, however, mean that it is an argument which cannot itself make good such claims but must fall back on the supposedly far more dubious ontological argument? In the light of the foregoing discussions I believe that the answer that can now be given to this question is No. At least, that most recent attempt which was made in the *New Essays in Philosophical Theology* to make out a case for the dependence of the cosmological argument upon the ontological must be pronounced "not proven." For one thing, the case as there made out turned largely on a dogmatically asserted principle that any statement about necessity must itself be a necessary statement. For an-

---

[5] It must be admitted that some recent defenders of Aquinas's arguments, in trying to meet the sort of criticism that Smart makes, have at least seemed to fall into the compromising position of wanting to have their cake and eat it too. Thus, on the one hand, in seeking to dispose of the criticism that the cosmological argument depends on the ontological, they have made the quite general assertion that for Aquinas no necessary truth (i.e., one depending merely on the meaning of concepts) ever has existential import. Yet on the other hand, these same thinkers have had to recognize that Aquinas himself explicitly declares that the statement "God exists" is, for God, both necessarily true and existentially true, although it is not so for us.

This apparent inconsistency has been very acutely pointed out by Alan Donagan in a review of *The Essentials of Theism* by D. J. B. Hawkins in *The Australasian Journal of Philosophy*, 28:125–131 (September 1950); see especially pp. 128–129. However, Donagan himself, having pointed out this inconsistency, would appear for his part to fall into error, when he suggests that if God's existence is seen to be a necessary truth by God Himself, then that would be at least one exception to the rule that the defenders of Thomas are so insistent upon, viz., that "It is impossible by beginning with mere concepts to end with anything save mere concepts." However, I don't think this would be an exception at all. For in the case of God's knowledge of Himself, it can hardly be supposed that He begins with mere concepts and ends with something other than mere concepts, viz., existence. It is just a bit far-fetched to suppose that God ever undertakes to prove His own existence by resorting to the ontological argument!

other thing, it was simply assumed that in the traditional formulations of the cosmological argument the conclusion "God exists" or "A necessary being exists" is taken to be a logically necessary truth, whereas in point of fact the entire thrust of the cosmological argument is just that such a conclusion is to be regarded as no more than a contingent truth. Finally, although defenders of the cosmological argument may very well hold views about necessary truths and logical necessity that are somewhat at variance with the currently accepted interpretations of these notions, it remains to be shown that such variations and deviations have any bearing at all on the specific issue of the validity of the cosmological argument as traditionally conceived and understood.

And now for that second line of criticism, which, as we suggested earlier, would seem to be both peculiarly contemporary and peculiarly telling against the cosmological argument. For supposing that one cannot challenge the transempirical knowledge claims of this argument merely on the grounds that any such claims must involve a surreptitious reliance upon the ontological argument, then perhaps one can strike at the argument by showing that the logic of such an argument can only be conceived in analogy to the transcendent hypotheses in scientific theories. Yet, when put to the test, there would appear to be no way in which hypotheses such as that of the existence of God or of a first cause or of a necessary being could ever be justified after the manner of so-called transcendent hypotheses in science.

Superficially, at least, it does seem plausible to consider that the use of the cosmological argument to prove God's existence is logically comparable to the use of the hypothetico-deductive method in science. For one thing, the starting point of the cosmological argument is always some given fact that needs to be explained—e.g., the fact of motion, or of contingent being, or of the conditioned, or of beings in which essence and existence are distinct. Further, it might be supposed that the thesis of God's existence or of the existence of a necessary being or of a first cause is nothing but an explanatory hypothesis, one set up as a means of explaining the given facts from which the argument started and which were held to stand in need of explanation in the first place. Finally, to entertain an hypothesis such as that of a God or of a necessary being or of a being in whom essence and existence are not distinct does seem to have at least some of the earmarks of a so-called transcendent hypothesis.

To confirm the point, let us recall Kneale's way of characterizing an hypothesis of this sort. He says that such a theory will be one which

explains laws by means of postulates which are not themselves established by direct induction from experience and cannot, indeed, be tested directly in any way. These postulates are hypotheses about the existence of objects which must, from the nature of the case, be imperceptible. . . . I can see a wave passing over the surface of a pond, but it is merely senseless to speak of seeing or observing in any other way an electro-magnetic wave. It is even impossible to imagine these things, for if we try to imagine them we must attribute to them qualities such as colour or perceptible hardness which they cannot possess. I propose to call hypotheses about things of this kind transcendent . . . [6, page 93].

Now I suggest that what Kneale here says about the hypothesis of electromagnetic waves could be repeated, point for point, about the hypothesis of a necessary being or a first cause.

Nevertheless, beyond this the analogy between the cosmological argument and the use of transcendent hypotheses in science simply cannot be carried. For in the sciences the justification for the setting up of hypotheses lies in the fact that from such hypotheses consequences may be deduced, in terms of which the hypothesis may be either verified or falsified. But is anything of the sort possible in the case of the hypothesis of God's existence?

Suppose, just to simplify the case, we confine our attention to Popper's celebrated contention that it is falsifiability rather than verifiability that should be taken as the criterion of a properly scientific hypothesis. Following this line, one would insist that the idea of verifying a hypothesis is simply futile: it involves all the difficulties of induction, and specifically it commits the fallacy of affirming the consequent. In contrast, falsifying a hypothesis involves no dubious inductive procedures but instead operates solely with the logically impeccable procedure of modus tollens.

But so far as the hypothesis of a necessary being is concerned, what possible observable consequences could ever falsify a hypothesis such as this? And if it is inconceivable that such a hypothesis could ever be falsified,[6] then one has crossed Popper's famous line of demarcation separating the domain of scientific hypotheses from that of the necessary truths of mathematics, of logic, and (if there are any) of metaphysics. But when this

---

[6] I'm not sure but that this is extreme: perhaps there might be a way in which one could make out a case for the possibility of falsifying a hypothesis such as that of God's existence. But for purposes of argument, let us simply waive this possibility altogether.

line has been crossed the cosmological argument ceases to be the kind of argument it pretends to be. For having masqueraded as an argument that proceeds according to the hypothetico-deductive method, it is now seen to involve no such procedure: the conclusion of the argument being in principle not falsifiable, what the conclusion asserts, viz., that God exists, can make no claim to being a scientific hypothesis at all, not even a transcendent hypothesis.

I believe, however, that so to conceive the cosmological argument as being analogous to the use of transcendent hypotheses in science is radically mistaken. The cosmological argument just isn't that kind of argument at all, and this for two reasons.

In the first place, in any use of the hypothetico-deductive method, the particular fact or the law that is to be explained by a certain hypothesis is explained through being logically deducible from, or a necessary consequence of, that hypothesis. And yet in this sense a necessary being does not explain a contingent being, or the unconditioned the conditioned. Oh, it's true that speaking rather loosely one does say that only through a necessary being is it possible adequately to explain or account for the existence of a contingent being, or only through a being whose essence simply is its existence can the existence of a being whose nature does not imply its existence be ultimately explained and accounted for. But this is surely to use "explain" and "account for" in a somewhat different sense from that which is pertinent so far as the hypothetico-deductive method is concerned. One does not deduce the existence of contingent beings from a necessary being, or the conditioned from the unconditioned. Or to use a slightly different idiom, the created world does not follow logically from God.

To be sure, there are types of metaphysics other than the one proper to the cosmological argument. Thus for Plotinus or for Spinoza there might well be a sense in which one could speak of the universe as proceeding necessarily and perhaps even logically from God or from the One: "From the necessity of the divine nature infinite numbers of things in infinite ways . . . must follow" [8, Part I, Proposition XVI].

But this sort of metaphysical context is not the one into which the cosmological argument—at least as this is exemplified, say, in the five ways of Aquinas—is to be fitted. Quite the contrary; from the latter standpoint there is no way in which the contingent may be deduced from the necessary. Or, to put it a little differently, given the hypothesis of a necessary being or a being in whom essence and existence are not distinct, it does not follow logically that there must be contingent beings, or that the existence of beings in whom essence and existence are distinct must be a necessary consequence of the existence of a being in whom they are not distinct.

Moreover, there is a second reason why the cosmological argument just does not fit into the model of the hypothetico-deductive method. For not only would it seem to be the case that, so far as the cosmological argument is concerned, the explicans does not logically imply the explicandum, but also it would appear that the explicandum does necessarily—or at least it is supposed necessarily to—imply the explicans. But there can be no talk of this sort of thing in the context of the hypothetico-deductive method. Indeed, to judge from the usual expositions of this method, one of the salient features of this method lies just in the fact that there is no logical connection whatever, either deductive or inductive, which enables one to get from the fact or law to be explained to the hypothesis that is designed to explain it. Sometimes it is suggested that getting from the explicandum to the explanatory hypothesis is to be accounted for only psychologically and not logically. At other times it is suggested that while the transition from the one to the other is not to be accounted for either deductively or inductively, it may be accounted for by a special logical process to which Peirce's term "retroduction" might be most properly applied.[7]

But whatever may be the eventual resolution of this dispute, the interesting thing from the point of view of the present discussion is that the entire issue is simply irrelevant so far as the cosmological argument is concerned. In this argument one moves from the conditioned to the unconditioned, or from the contingent to the necessary, presumably in virtue of the fact that the former necessarily implies the latter.

Thus, to paraphrase the argument briefly, conditioned beings or dependent beings necessarily imply the existence of the conditions on which their being depends and without which they would not be. But these conditions, in turn, cannot be dependent on other conditions, and these on still others, and so on ad infinitum. For if the conditions of a thing's being were held to be infinite, that would be tantamount to saying that

---

[7] This latter alternative is one which is being vigorously expounded and defended by my former colleague at Indiana University, Professor Norwood Russell Hanson.

the conditions of that thing's being were insufficient to account for its being. (By "infinite conditions" one means conditions without end, such that however many conditions there might actually be or actually exist, these would never be all of them.) However, it having already been admitted that the actual existence of a conditioned or dependent being implies the existence of such conditions as are necessary for that thing's existence, the conclusion must be that sufficient conditions for that thing's existence must actually be or exist. In other words, an unconditioned or independent being must exist. Q.E.D.

From this, then, is it not clear that if one tries to interpret the cosmological argument as if the existence of God were some sort of hypothesis designed to account for the existence of the world, then one must concede that the argument is so structured that that which is put forward as requiring explanation—viz., the world, or contingent being, or dependent being, etc.—is held to imply necessarily the hypothesis that is put forward to explain it—viz., God, or necessary being, or a being whose essence it is to exist, etc.? To concede this, however, is to shatter completely the analogy which was said to hold between the cosmological argument and the hypothetico-deductive method of proof.

But, then, if the cosmological argument is not to be conceived of on the analogy of a hypothetico-deductive method of argument, it presumably cannot claim to proceed along the lines of a *modus tollens* argument. Yet it is just this process of *modus tollens* which in Popper's eyes gives such superior cogency to the hypothetico-deductive method when the latter is employed in the particular manner which he recommends. Does this mean, then, that the cosmological argument is to be construed according to the other alternative, in which the process of proof will consist not in a falsification of a hypothesis but rather in an attempted verification of it? If so, though, the cosmological argument would amount to no more than a kind of inductive procedure, which, formally considered, would be but an affirming of the consequent.

Not at all! Instead, the cosmological argument is not to be thought of as involving the hypothetico-deductive method in any sense, either in the sense of falsifying or in the sense of verifying a hypothesis. What, then, is the logical character of this argument? I suggest that it is a straight *modus ponens* argument. In fact, the contrast between the *modus ponens* form of the cosmological argument and the form of a hypothetico-deductive method of argument might be simply, if crudely, exhibited in the following way:

(a) On the hypothetico-deductive model, the argument would have the form

> If there is a necessary being, then there are contingent beings.
> There are (or there are not) contingent beings.
> There is (or there is not) a necessary being.

(b) On the correct model, the argument has the form

> If there are contingent beings, there is a necessary being.
> There are contingent beings.
> There is a necessary being.

What, then, is the upshot of all this with respect to the philosophical significance and validity of the cosmological argument? Simply this. If, following Popper, we say that the use of transcendent hypotheses is entirely proper and justifiable when such hypotheses are susceptible of falsification through a *modus tollens* argument, then why would not the use of transcendent hypotheses be equally proper and justifiable when they are susceptible not of falsification through *modus tollens* but rather, *mutatis mutandis*, of actual demonstration through *modus ponens*?

"Oh," but someone may retort, "to use a *modus ponens* argument in order to go from the observed to the unobservable can only be done through invoking, somewhere along the line, the ontological argument." This kind of retort, however, I hope that I have effectively scotched as a result of what I tried to show in the first part of this paper: that the usual considerations that have been advanced to show that the cosmological argument is dependent upon the ontological are considerations that will not bear close scrutiny.

Still, the prejudice remains: how, by means of a mere process of inference, can one get from the observed to the unobservable? What, though, is one to say about the use of transcendent hypotheses in science? Does not this largely invalidate the prejudice against passing from the observed to the unobservable? Thus on the basis of the hypothetico-deductive method, while it is not supposed that one can infer the unobservable from the observed, it is at least considered entirely justifiable that one should use a hypothesis of that which is in principle unobservable in order to explain that which is observed. Very well, then, if in certain instances the observed can be shown to imply that which is unobservable, why is it not perfectly proper in such cases to use a straight *modus ponens* argument to infer the existence of such an unobservable? If *modus tollens* justifies our entertaining unobservable entities in the one context, why should not *modus ponens* provide equal justification for our inferring the existence of unobservables in the other context?

And with this, I would conclude by turning the question to Herbert Feigl: what is wrong with the admission of unobservable entities in metaphysics? To be sure, an old-fashioned, uncompromising positivist can give an old-fashioned, uncompromising answer to such a question: "There are no such entities!" Moreover, such a positivistic answer is just as uncompromising with respect to the unobservables that are introduced via the transcendent hypotheses in science as it is with respect to an unobservable such as God, introduced via the cosmological argument in traditional metaphysics.

But so far as Herbert Feigl is concerned, he has repudiated this sort of positivism (see [3], pages 4–7; [2], pages 9–12). He has even gone so far as to say that "as long as one has a 'foothold' somewhere in direct experience, any sort of existent may well be accessible through knowledge by description. This, after all, is the only epistemological view which renders plausible our knowledge of unobserved and unobservable entities, as, e.g., in modern physics" [2, pages 10–11].

Very well, then, my dear Herbert, must you not recognize that what is sauce for the goose is sauce for the gander? If all it takes is a mere foothold in experience to make any existent at least in principle accessible so far as modern physics is concerned, why would not the same be true so far as metaphysics is concerned? And specifically, is not this just what the cosmological argument does: from a foothold in experience, it reaches to a knowledge by description of no less an existent than a necessary being or God Himself?

REFERENCES

1. Anscombe, G. E. M., and P. T. Geach. *Three Philosophers.* Ithaca, N.Y.: Cornell University Press, 1961.
2. Feigl, Herbert. "Critique of Intuition According to Scientific Empiricism," *Philosophy East and West,* 8(1–2):1–16 (April, July 1958).
3. Feigl, Herbert. "Philosophical Tangents of Science," in *Current Issues in the Philosophy of Science,* Herbert Feigl and Grover Maxwell, eds., pp. 1–17. New York: Holt, Rinehart, and Winston, 1961.
4. Flew, Antony, and Alasdair MacIntyre, eds. *New Essays in Philosophical Theology.* London: SCM Press, 1955.
5. Hume, David. *Dialogues Concerning Natural Religion,* ed. by N. Kemp Smith, 2nd ed. London: Nelson, 1947.

6. Kneale, William. *Probability and Induction*. Oxford: Clarendon Press, 1949.
7. Smart, J. J. C. "The Existence of God," in [4], pp. 28–46.
8. Spinoza, Baruch. *Ethics*.
9. Thomas Aquinas, Saint. *Summa Theologiae*.
10. Veatch, Henry B. "Matrix, Matter, and Method in Metaphysics," *Review of Metaphysics*, 4:581–600 (June 1961).
11. Veatch, Henry B. "On Trying to Say and to Know What's What," *Philosophy and Phenomenological Research*, 24:83–96 (September 1963).

Part III

PHILOSOPHY OF THE PHYSICAL SCIENCES

PAUL K. FEYERABEND

)))((

On the Possibility of a Perpetuum Mobile
of the Second Kind

1. In one of his by now classic papers on the kinetic theory of matter von Smoluchowski admits that the second law "in the usual formulation of Clausius and Thomson certainly is in need of revision." Yet he denies that the fluctuations might constitute "a perpetual source of income" (in terms of readily available work). His argument is that one-way valves, lids, and, for that matter, *all* mechanical contraptions designed for transforming fluctuations into such a "perpetual source of income" are themselves subject to fluctuations. "These machines work in normal circumstances because they must remain in a position of equilibrium which corresponds to a minimum of potential energy. Yet in the case of molecular fluctuations all other positions are possible in addition to the position of minimal energy and they are distributed in accordance with the magnitude of total work. The valve has its own tendency of fluctuation; either the spring is so strong that it does not open at all, or it is so weak that it fluctuates all the time and is bound to remain ineffective. A perpetuum mobile would therefore seem to be possible only if one could construct a valve of a quite different kind, and without the tendency to fluctuate, and to do this we see not the slightest possibility today" [4, page 248; translation by P. K. F.].

Smoluchowski adds that a human observer who like a *deus ex machina* "always knows the exact state of nature and who can start or stop macroscopic processes at any arbitrary moment without having to spend any work" might perhaps be capable of establishing those correlations be-

[409]

tween microphenomena and macrophenomena which are needed for a perpetual and systematic violation of the second law [4, page 396].

2. It is well known how the last remark has led, via the investigations of Szilard, Brillouin, and others, to a rather subjectivistic account of thermodynamic properties. The steps may be briefly characterized as follows: (i) Szilard tried to show that the process of obtaining the information necessary for establishing the needed correlations was accompanied by an increase of entropy that exactly balanced the decrease brought about by utilizing that information. A general proof of such equivalence was not given by Szilard, who restricted himself to the analysis of a particular and rather complicated example. (ii) A general "proof" appeared only much later. It was based on a *definition* of information that ascribed to it exactly the value needed for bringing about the compensation. It is hardly possible to regard such a procedure as the required general proof. It is *not* shown, on the basis of a physical analysis of the process of measurement, that it will always lead to entropy changes which guarantee the validity of the second law. Quite the contrary; the validity of this law is *taken for granted* and used for defining the entropy changes connected with the information obtained. (iii) This circular definition was itself misunderstood in a subjectivistic sense. *Originally* the "information" that a particle P dwells in part V′ of a larger volume means that it is *physically re-*

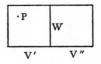

stricted to V′. "Loss of information" after removal of the wall W means that this physical restriction is no longer present, and that new possibilities of behavior have been introduced. Now "information" means knowledge where the particle is and *not* what occupational possibilities are open to it. In the original version the entropy of a system may increase although our knowledge concerning its ingredients remains unchanged (P moves over a larger volume, though we still know where it is). In the more recent version such knowledge *prevents* the entropy from increasing. It is interesting to consider some of the double-talk resulting from the mixture of both versions: "Entropy," writes Leon Brillouin, "*measures the lack of information* about the actual structure of the system. This lack of information introduces the possibility of a great variety of microscopically distinct structures, which we are . . . unable to distinguish from one another" [1, page 160]. This means that there are states of the system which we cannot distinguish from one another (second version). These states can therefore be equally occupied by the system (first version). Lack of knowledge on our part conveniently removes all physical barriers in the world! (and therefore is not really lack of knowledge at all).

3. Continuation of this kind of attack is more entertaining than enlightening. A much more fruitful line of approach would seem to consist in pointing out that the general proof in the form in which it was originally envisaged by Szilard cannot be given and that its circular substitutes are therefore pointless. It *is* possible to correlate fluctuations with devices in such a fashion that a "perpetual source of income" is obtained. We shall of course have to assume frictionless devices. They are used by von Smoluchowski and Szilard and may therefore also be used here. The *Höllenmaschine* I am going to introduce is a modification of a machine used by J. R. Pierce [2, pages 200–201] to establish the exact opposite, namely, that "we use up all the output of the machine in transmitting enough information to make [it] run." A cylindrical vessel Z contains a piston P,

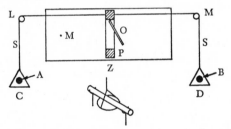

whose center piece O can be removed, and a single molecule M. The piston is held in balance by a string S leading via two wheels, L and M, to the pans C and D. On top of each pan a stick, A and B respectively, is kept suspended on two forks (see top view below Z). The whole arrangement is kept at temperature T. We start the machine by opening O and allowing M to wander freely through Z. We then close O. Now if M is to the left of O, then it will press to the right, lift C, lift A off the fork, and transport it to a higher level. If it is to the right of O, then the same will happen to D and B. The process can be repeated indefinitely without loss of entropy from observing M. We have here a "perpetual source of income" of the kind von Smoluchowski did not think to be possible. Where lies the weakness of his argument?

4. Consider for that purpose a one-way valve V whose upward move-

ment is connected with a mechanism similar to the one mentioned in Section 1. According to von Smoluchowski the arrangement cannot work because it is bound to fluctuate between 1 and 2, and because correlation between 2 and activity of the machine would presuppose knowl-

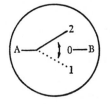

edge accessible to a *deus ex machina* only. (It is *this* feature of the case, the random motion of V between 1 and 2, which led to the intrusion of knowledge into physics and started the trend toward subjectivism.) But if V can be fastened to A at all, then it can also be prevented, say by a ring AB, from moving down to 1. Of course, it will still fluctuate back and forth between 0 and 2, but it will not fluctuate in this manner because of its "own tendency" as von Smoluchowski seems to believe,[1] but because of the impact of fast moving particles.[2] It will move in this way because it takes over the motion of particles moving in a privileged direction, because it is acting as a "perpetual source of income."

5. To sum up: the attempt to save the second law from systematic deviations, apart from being circular and based upon an ambiguous use of the term "information," is also ill-conceived, for such deviations are in principle possible.[3]

REFERENCES

1. Brillouin, Leon. *Science and Information Theory.* New York: Academic Press, 1956.
2. Pierce, John R. *Symbols, Signals and Noise.* New York: Harper, 1961.
3. Popper, Karl R. "Irreversibility; or, Entropy since 1905," *British Journal for the Philosophy of Science,* 8:151–155 (1957).
4. Smoluchowski, Maryan von. *Oeuvres,* Vol. II. Cracow, 1928.

[1] [4], p. 395. Cf. the quotation in Section 1 above.
[2] Cf. Smoluchowski's account of a similar mistake in the case of diffusion, in [4], p. 536.
[3] The present note is to be read as an addendum to Karl R. Popper's [3], and especially to Section 4 of that paper.

NORWOOD RUSSELL HANSON

\\\(JJ)

Equivalence: The Paradox of Theoretical Analysis

In an earlier paper [4] I addressed myself to the concept of equivalence between theories. Indeed, it was Professor Feigl himself who encouraged me to undertake that exploration; the present essay is a development of this earlier work, and a lengthy emendation of some of its shortcomings.

I

That theory Θ_1 entails theory Θ_2 *means* that Θ_2 follows from, or is deducible from, Θ_1. That theory Θ_1 is equivalent to theory Θ_2 therefore *means* that Θ_2 is deducible from Θ_1, *and* that Θ_1 is deducible from Θ_2. Now, is this always the case? The theories in question, of course, are physical theories, not mathematical or logical theories; that is, they are not "closed" or necessary, they are "open-ended" and ultimately contingent. Further observations may always be relevant to their truth. The closest approximation of our Θ_1 and Θ_2 to being deductive theories will be when they are rigorously "hypothetico-deductive."

To quote from the earlier paper:

A physical theory is, at least, a contingently interpreted formalism—a delicate trinity of algorithm, physical interpretation, and correspondence rules.

A *single* algorithm, given two different physical interpretations, results in two different physical theories. . . . In contrast, two *different* algorithms, given the same physical interpretation may result in equivalent physical theories; "equivalent, with respect to suitably defined subsets of their consequences" [4, pages 405–406].

A leading distinction of this present paper is embodied in the forego-

[413]

ing quotation. We are concerned here with the equivalence of *physical theories*; hence we will focus upon just such conspiracies of algorithm-and-physical-interpretation. There may be examples of Θ_1 and Θ_2 between which we will note an algorithmic equivalence in the absence of any corresponding equivalence in their physical interpretations. In other cases algorithmic equivalence may be lacking, while an operational equivalence obtains with respect to subsets of the physically interpretable consequences of Θ_1 and Θ_2. In either case we may remain uncertain about the nature of the equivalence between Θ_1 and Θ_2.

Any physical theory Θ can be represented as an algorithm a, plus physical interpretation ϕ: physical geometry (Θ) can thus be represented as Euclidean geometry (a), and a physical interpretation (ϕ, in which "straight line" may be interpreted as "pencil of light"). It appears then that the possible ways in which two theories Θ_1 and Θ_2 may compare vis-à-vis their equivalence (logical and operational) are as follows:

$$(1) \qquad \Theta_1 \left\{ \begin{array}{l} a_1 =_{\log.} a_2 \\ \phi_1 =_{\text{oper.}} \phi_2 \end{array} \right\} \Theta_2$$

$$(2) \qquad \Theta_1 \left\{ \begin{array}{l} a_1 \neq_{\log.} a_2 \\ \phi_1 =_{\text{oper.}} \phi_2 \end{array} \right\} \Theta_2$$

$$(3) \qquad \Theta_1 \left\{ \begin{array}{l} a_1 =_{\log.} a_2 \\ \phi_1 \neq_{\text{oper.}} \phi_2 \end{array} \right\} \Theta_2$$

$$(4) \qquad \Theta_1 \left\{ \begin{array}{l} a_1 \neq_{\log.} a_2 \\ \phi_1 \neq_{\text{oper.}} \phi_2 \end{array} \right\} \Theta_2$$

This much constitutes the analytical structure into which we will now project an ancient perplexity.

II

To paraphrase Wittgenstein (*Tractatus*, 5.122): "If Θ_2 follows from Θ_1, then the *sense* of Θ_2 is contained in that of Θ_1." Thus, if any one theory may be said to entail another one, then the second one may be merely "unpacked" from out of the semantical content of the first. When Θ_1 entails Θ_2, Θ_2 may be "deductively detached" from Θ_1, just as one might remove a small jigsaw puzzlet from its position within a larger, more complex jigsaw puzzle. Indeed, in 5.141 (to paraphrase again) it is suggested that "if Θ_2 follows from Θ_1, and Θ_1 also follows from Θ_2, then they are one and the same theory." In short, if Θ_1 and Θ_2 are *equivalent* theories, then they are one and the same theory. Actually, in 5.122 and 5.141 Wittgenstein is concerned with propositions, not theories. But since every theory can be represented as a conjunction of all its constituent propositions (can it not?)—what he says can be extended, as we have just done, to a characterization of equivalence between theories.

At this point in my earlier paper a further distinction was sought. The following argument was tendered:

It is a degenerate semantical point that for two physical theories to be equivalent they must be *different*—substantially so. If two theories differed not at all, they would not be equivalent, but identical. They would be one theory. The expressions ". . . are identical" and ". . . are equivalent" do distinct semantical work. . . . Indeed, how could any two genuinely different physical theories be "proven" equivalent at all? [4, pages 401, 402].

My point was that a proof of *identity* and a proof of *equivalence* are distinguishable: Θ_1 and Θ_2 might not be identical, but nonetheless be equivalent. Indeed, I urged that they *must not* be identical for an equivalence proof even to be possible. If Wittgenstein were correct in characterizing Θ_1 and Θ_2 as being but one and the same theory, then there could be nothing left for one to establish equivalence *between*. Identity proofs succeed by disposing of the individuating uniqueness of one theory, showing that its apparent differences from some other theory are merely illusory. This seems to be Wittgenstein's model for equivalence. It controlled my earlier argument. But there *must* be an alternative way of viewing the matter, despite the fact that we will return later to a modified form of the Wittgenstein thesis.

Moore opts for such an alternative. He would argue that it is possible for Θ_1 and Θ_2 to be genuinely different (i.e., nonidentical), while yet being equivalent in that they mutually entail each other (compare [10], pages 276 ff.). It seems clear to Moore that two different theories can remain two theories, that is, not collapse into being one and the same theory, while yet being such that the one entails the other, and the other entails the one. If the very *concept* of theoretical equivalence is not to disappear into that of theoretical identity, then there must be a sense in which Θ_1 and Θ_2 remain logically distinguishable, yet mutually entailing.

Thus Wittgenstein on the one hand, and Moore (and myself in the earlier paper; please pardon the conjunction) would adopt fundamentally different approaches to the notion of equivalence between theories. For Wittgenstein entailment is no more than "semantical unpacking"; mutual entailment (i.e., equivalence) between Θ_1 and Θ_2, therefore, is *all* of Θ_1

being unpackable from Θ_2, and all of Θ_2 being unpackable from Θ_1. Since here the entailment relationship holds both ways, the individualities of each theory merge into a single conglomerate of both. Moore, however, stresses the uniqueness of both Θ_1 and Θ_2, for how else could they be two theories? He then asks how they can mutually entail each other while still maintaining their own self-identities. (The analogies with the "paradox of analysis" are obvious.)

In short, one side argues that if two theories are really equivalent then they are not two, but one. The other side argues that if they are genuinely two, then their equivalence (i.e., mutual entailment) requires some more complex analysis than that of "semantical unpacking." To follow up a point once made by Norman Malcolm [9], one position is that if Θ_1 and Θ_2 are equivalent, then they mean the same thing, are the same theory. The alternative view is that Θ_1 and Θ_2 may be equivalent, but still not mean the same thing, i.e., not be the same theory. This requires exploration in light of the remarks in Section I of this paper.

III

It might be argued that Θ_1 and Θ_2 would not mean the same (i.e., would be different theories) if one of them contained expressions not synonymous with any expressions to be found in the other. Does this mean only that some one expression in Θ_2 may require six expressions in Θ_1 to generate the same meaning? No: that might constitute no more than a *notational* dissimilarity (compare [4], Section A). It means rather that some expression within Θ_2 is such that no combination of expressions in Θ_1 can possibly generate the same meaning. If this could be demonstrated with respect to Θ_1 and Θ_2, even though Θ_1 entails Θ_2 and Θ_2 entails Θ_1, then the intuition of Moore (and myself in 1961) would be confirmed, to wit, that two genuinely nonidentical theories may yet be equivalent. (But the "if" may be unfulfillable.) The specific example to which I addressed myself earlier was that involving the equivalence of matrix mechanics and wave mechanics, as these theories were understood in 1926. I sought there to establish that certain parts of Θ_1 could not be derived from, were not synonymous with, Θ_2; and vice versa. But I felt it as in principle possible that some Θ pairs could be such that, although nonsynonymous, they might yet be mutually entailing—this latter being denied only in the specific case of wave and matrix mechanics. Let us move to some simpler examples which may sharpen the issue.

[416]

Let Θ_1 consist in the following claim (and logical developments thereupon): *The moon describes a circumterrestrial orbit every point on which is equidistant from a given point.*

Θ_2 reads: *The moon describes a circumterrestrial orbit which encloses a maximum area for that length perimeter.* In fact Θ_1 and Θ_2 are false. But this does not matter. Are they equivalent? Within what might be called "Euclidean astronomy" Θ_2 certainly follows from Θ_1, and Θ_1 from Θ_2. It may be said then that the two make the same claim(s). They describe the same state(s) of affairs. They mean the same thing(s). Are they, à la Wittgenstein, identical? Are Θ_1 and Θ_2 one and the same; or are they logically distinguishable yet mutually entailing?

According to our first criterion above, Θ_1 and Θ_2 remain distinguishable. There are expressions in the one which are synonymous with no expressions in the other. Claims about the loci of points are not synonymous with claims more typical of area theory. One could know the meaning of "point," "locus," and "equidistant" without also knowing the meaning of "area" and "perimeter"; and vice versa. On one account then, Θ_1 and Θ_2 do *not* mean the same thing. They are not the same identical theory, although they remain equivalent in that, within "Euclidean astronomy," one can deductively move from Θ_2 to Θ_1 and back again.

Another example, which is historically somewhat more alive, is this one: Apollonios, Hipparchos, Ptolemy, and Copernicus were all well aware that an elliptical orbit could be generated from combinations of uniform, circular motions in two distinct ways. One (Θ_1) was to have an epicycle moving uniformly on a deferential circle such that the planetary point on the epicycle moves with the same angular velocity on the epicycle as the epicycle center moves on the deferent—but in the opposite direction. That will generate a resultant ellipse as the planetary orbit, but so will Θ_2: if one simply puts the planetary point right on the deferential circle and moves it uniformly in that path, but has the center of the deferential circle itself move in the opposite direction, through a circle the same size as the ellipse in Θ_1, the result here will also be an elliptical orbit for the planet. Indeed, the orbit will be absolutely congruent with that generated as a result of the technique in Θ_1 [6].

Now, are Θ_1 and Θ_2 equivalent? Are they identical? They are equivalent in the sense that every geometrical figure generable from the technique set out in Θ_1 is also generable from the technique set out in Θ_2. The rule is: Simply take the epicycle from the construction in Θ_1 and have the center of the deferent in Θ_2 move on that path. But Θ_1 and Θ_2 are not *identical* in the sense outlined; because it is certainly conceivable that an individual may be a master of the technique set out in Θ_2 and yet not have the faintest idea what "epicycle" means. Indeed, there probably was a time, historically, when the geometrical equivalence of these two representations was not known: at least Ptolemy and Copernicus set out their "proofs" of this equivalence as if some of their contemporaries needed persuasion.

So it might be said of the lunar orbit example above, and the epicycle-excentric example here, that they direct our attention to theory pairs which are "equivalent," in the sense that they are mutually entailing but not "identical," inasmuch as one could easily indicate terms within the one which are in no way synonymous with corresponding terms, or sets of terms, in the other.

There are other criteria which distinguish theories. Suppose one argues that when he is guided by Θ_1 he does not "think of the same things" as he does with Θ_2. This criterion is often invoked to distinguish wave mechanics and matrix mechanics, despite the "proofs" (by Eckart and Schrödinger) of the "mathematical equivalence" (i.e., identity) of the two. Thinking of scattered particles seems to be quite different from thinking about propagations of electromagnetic wave interference maxima. If any Θ_1 and Θ_2 make us "think of things" so different, they cannot be one and the same theory, despite their mutually entailing each other. And if thinking about the lunar orbit as a locus of points equidistant from a given point really is different from thinking of it as the perimeter of a maximum area, then here too, despite the two-way entailment, Θ_1 and Θ_2 are not identical. The same point is obviously true in the epicycle-excentric case. Indeed, precisely because ancient astronomers did "think of different things" when using epicycle and excentric constructions, they did, for certain problems, largely prefer one to the exclusion of the other. (Copernicus uses the excentric technique *everywhere* except for his lunar theory. Ptolemy preferred the epicyclical representation for the inferior planets but the excentric representation for the superior planets.)

To approach "equivalence between nonidenticals" in another way, one could *know* the meaning of Θ_1 and not know the meaning of Θ_2; this point is related to, although different from, the earlier one concerning synonymity. An individual could understand "The moon's orbit is a locus of all points equidistant from a given point" and not understand "The moon's

orbit is the perimeter of a maximum area." This is, indeed, true of many
a novice in geometry, logic, or mathematics. One often *learns*, of two un-
familiar expressions, that they *mean* the same thing, e.g., "syzygy" and
"any rectilinear configuration of earth, moon and sun." Hence one could
know the meaning of one of them without comprehending the other;
one could be familiar with Θ_1 while not understanding Θ_2, or vice versa.
One could understand "excentric" and not understand "epicycle." So
they cannot mean the same; otherwise knowing the meaning of Θ_1 *would
be* to know the meaning of Θ_2.

This leads into the conceptual thicket noted by John Wisdom and
explored later by Norman Malcolm. As suggested in my earlier paper, one
seems to have two different theories, dealing (presumably) with nonidentical subject matters, which are yet mysteriously connected via the
entailment relation. How can disparate factual subject matters be necessarily connected by logical equivalence? How, by inference alone, can
one pass from one characterization of a subject matter to a different characterization of a (presumably) distinguishable subject matter, and then
back again? Speaking of Θ_1 and Θ_2 as "different" suggests that there is
some sort of logical gap between them, a gap closed by necessity. This
latter bridge, if it exists, would be supported by two conceptual piers:

1. *that two equivalent physical theories must remain two (and not fuse
into one)*, and

2. *that two such equivalent physical theories must yet be bound by a
necessity unencountered elsewhere in factual subject matters.*

Consider two further criteria. Our earlier three were these:

a. that two theories are not identical if one contains expressions not
synonymous with any in the other;

b. that two theories are not identical if one need not "think of the same
things" with one as against the other;

c. that two theories are not identical if a person could understand the
first while not knowing the meaning of the second.

In our lunar orbit example, and the epicycle-excentric one too, it was
seen to be possible, by these criteria, for one to insist that Θ_1 and Θ_2 were
different (nonidentical), despite their being equivalent (mutually entailing).

Θ_1 and Θ_2, as we have considered them, have the same *verification*. But
this is already saying something slightly different from what has been
said before. Since both Θ_1 and Θ_2 claim that the lunar orbit is circular (a

reference we have subdued until this moment) their entailments are identical. Anything which tends to establish Θ_1 will also establish Θ_2. Any observation which disconfirms Θ_1 will have the same effect on Θ_2. This much alone proves little. It might be termed an "operational consequence" of Θ_1 and Θ_2 being logically equivalent, i.e., mutually deducible. But here is the thin end of a Wittgensteinian wedge which could grow into a slippery slope for Moore vis-à-vis propositional equivalence, and for Hanson (*circa* 1961) vis-à-vis theoretical equivalence. For, once tempted to characterize theoretical equivalence in operational terms, one is soon inclined to ask, "And just what *factual claim* does Θ_1 make that Θ_2 does not make, and vice versa?" Saying that Θ_1 and Θ_2 are different physical theories suggests that we are somehow committed to factual claims with one to which we are not committed with the other. But this is precisely what a proof of the operational equivalence of Θ_1 and Θ_2 reveals not to be the case. Θ_2 in our lunar example is not vulnerable to evidence irrelevant to Θ_1. And vice versa. However much a physicist's expectations, dispositions, and familiarity may make him partial to Θ_1, if Θ_2 makes no factual assertions beyond those of Θ_1, and Θ_1 none beyond those of Θ_2, then the differences between the two are not operationally significant. That physicists think of different things in the Θ_1 case as compared with the Θ_2 case is not operationally important. That they know one theory well, but not the other, is not operationally relevant. That there are terms in Θ_1 not synonymous with any in Θ_2 is somewhat more significant, and will lead us back to the distinctions of Section I (compare my [7]). A somewhat cryptic aphorism of Professor Wilfrid Sellars' is relevant here: he has pronounced that "the meaning of a proposition is identical with the total set of its consequences." For the Θ_1's and Θ_2's we have considered here, their consequence sets are identical—therefore, by Sellars' observation, they mean the same thing. And if they mean the same thing it is difficult to see what precisely was being used to distinguish them other than psychological word associations.

According to our first three criteria, Θ_1 (that the lunar orbit is a locus of all points equidistant from a given point) and Θ_2 (that the lunar orbit is a perimeter for a maximum enclosed area) are *equivalent but not identical*—in some sense. Θ_1 entails and is entailed by Θ_2. But (a) Θ_1 and Θ_2 contain expressions which are not synonymous (are not intertheoretically definable), (b) Θ_1 and Θ_2 may lead one to think of different things in each case, and (c) Θ_1 and Θ_2 may be such that a person may know and assert the one without knowing or asserting the other. This much might incline us to say, with Moore, that Θ_1 and Θ_2 are not identical; they are logically different. But they are equivalent; they are mutually entailing. The same goes for our other two Θ's. The claim that one can generate an elliptical orbit by epicyclical planetary motion (Θ_1) is equivalent to the claim that one can generate an elliptical orbit by excentric planetary motion (Θ_2). However, because of (a), (b), and (c) above, these Θ's are not logically identical.

Our "operational" criteria, however, will lead us to quite a different conclusion. Since anything that confirms Θ_1 will do exactly the same for Θ_2, it follows that there can be no factual claim made either by Θ_1 or by Θ_2 that is not also made by the other theory. This much would incline us to say, with Wittgenstein, that Θ_1 and Θ_2 are equivalent; they are claim-identical. Therefore they are not really different in any sense that matters logically. This might be twisted yet another turn by saying that since the consequence sets of Θ_1 and Θ_2 are indistinguishable, the differences between them are indiscernible. Hence Θ_1 and Θ_2 are logically identical—because they are logically equivalent. But this is not to say that they are therefore identical in every conceivable sense. They may remain notationally dissimilar (e.g., Newton's and Leibniz's calculi; Russell's and Sheffer's logics). They may remain psychologically dissimilar (e.g., as wave mechanics and matrix mechanics remained in the late 1930's even after the 1926 "proof" of their "mathematical identity"). And they may remain also sequentially dissimilar, in the sense that they may be structured quite differently as algorithms (e.g., as Euclid's and Hilbert's geometries are sequentially different, although they express the same geometrical theory; they describe the same space).

IV

Establishing that two theories Θ_1 and Θ_2 are equivalent in any operationally significant sense, however, although it will lead to a *conclusio contra* Moore, may nonetheless be a remarkably complex undertaking. Consider again the matrix of possibilities set out in Section I of this paper:

(1) $\quad \Theta_1 \begin{cases} a_1 =_{\text{log.}} a_2 \\ \phi_1 =_{\text{oper.}} \phi_2 \end{cases} \Theta_2$

(2) $\quad \Theta_1 \begin{cases} a_1 \neq_{\text{log.}} a_2 \\ \phi_1 =_{\text{oper.}} \phi_2 \end{cases} \Theta_2$

$$(3) \qquad \Theta_1 \begin{Bmatrix} a_1 =_{\log.} a_2 \\ \phi_1 \mp_{\text{oper.}} \phi_2 \end{Bmatrix} \Theta_2$$

$$(4) \qquad \Theta_1 \begin{Bmatrix} a_1 \mp_{\log.} a_2 \\ \phi_1 \mp_{\text{oper.}} \phi_2 \end{Bmatrix} \Theta_2$$

Let us consider these possibilities against the background of the discussion we have just gone through. In possibility 1 above, Θ_1 and Θ_2 will certainly be equivalent in some logically binding sense, for a_1 and a_2 are logically equivalent (i.e., mutually entailing) and ϕ_1 and ϕ_2 are such that every observational consequence of Θ_1 will have precisely the same content as some corresponding consequence within Θ_2. There may still be differences between Θ_1 and Θ_2, of course. a_1 and a_2 may be nonsynonymous; notationally, psychologically, and sequentially dissimilar; one could know everything about a_1 and yet be totally ignorant of a_2. There must be some such differences between a_1 and a_2, otherwise why designate them differently? But Wittgenstein certainly shows the way here; such differences are not of fundamental logical importance. They no more affect the claim-content analysis appropriate to a_1 and a_2 than would the fact that these algorithms were written down in different-colored inks. If there is any reason to distinguish a_1 from a_2 (and being written in different-colored inks is almost certainly not enough) then designating them differently is defensible. We usually do designate algorithms differently because of some verbal, notational, psychological, or sequential differences among them. But this much alone is insufficient as an analysis of their logical content. If, however, such an analysis discloses that a_1 and a_2 have every consequence in common, then Moore's considerations must be logically irrelevant. This, of course, leads to the trenchant conclusion that, logically speaking, Θ_1 and Θ_2 can be equivalent (in the strongest sense) only if they are logically identical. This means that for any two physical theories to be strictly equivalent, mathematically equivalent, formally equivalent, they must be logically identical; they must be one and the same theory. This runs directly counter to Moore's sentiments. It also points out that the "degenerate semantical point" to which I referred in my earlier paper (see above) is of no logical moment.

As physical theories, however, there is another way in which Θ_1 and Θ_2 might be said to be equivalent. Possibility 2 above sets this out graphically. Here we must suppose that the two constituent algorithms, a_1 and a_2, are not mutually entailing. They are not logically identical. Their consequence sets are not the same. They are not formally equivalent. It may still be the case that, by some suitable set of physical interpretations, ϕ_1 and ϕ_2 may render every *observational* consequence of Θ_1 and of Θ_2 indistinguishable from each other with respect to claim content and with respect to operations undertaken to verify those claims. Thus, for example, in the eighteenth century Newton's corpuscular theory of light and Huygens' undulatory theory of light were observationally equivalent. They were not formally equivalent. One of the ultimate consequences of Newton's theory was that a ray of light would accelerate on entering a denser medium. This is the negation of an important consequence within Huygens' theory—that light will *decelerate* on entering a denser medium. But in the eighteenth century this difference was not testable, not only in the sense that it had not yet been put to the test, but in the stronger sense that no one then knew exactly what it would be like to design an experiment which could distinguish the two claims. In this it was rather like distinguishing a $1/r^2$ law today from a $1/r^{2.0000001}$ law. Hence, in the eighteenth century, this Θ_1 and this Θ_2 were observationally equivalent. Everything then observable was accounted for equally well in terms of either theory; and this applied also to every possible observation then articulable.

So possibility 1 above sets out everything that could be meant by "strict equivalence" between two physical theories. Possibility 2 sets out an equally important equivalence between physical theories—operational equivalence. In the first case "equivalence" = "identical in algorithm and interpretation," Moore's views (and Hanson's) notwithstanding. In the second case "equivalence" means "although not identical algorithmically, the physical interpretation generates consequence sets which are claim-identical." Moore would not have settled for either alternative. The first reduces strict equivalence between theories to logical and interpretative *identity*; apparent differences between Θ_1 and Θ_2 are of no logical importance. In the second possibility Θ_1 and Θ_2 are indeed logically distinct. But so much so that they are not mutually entailing *in toto*. Their equivalence obtains only with respect to a limited subset of all their possible consequences.

Concerning alternatives 3 and 4 above, the question of the equivalence of Θ_1 and Θ_2 as physical theories does not arise. Although algorithmically equivalent in the third possibility, the physical interpretations of Θ_1 and

Θ_2 are so different that one would look for entirely different phenomena to confirm or disconfirm these two theories. An example would be the use of a single geometry in theoretical cosmology on the one hand, and in nuclear shell theory on the other. Although the formal algorithms here may be logically identical, the physical theories resulting from their employment will be different.

In the fourth possibility above, Θ_1 and Θ_2 would be nonequivalent in every conceivable sense.

V

It is necessary to have achieved some such clarity to understand recent confusions amongst historians of science vis-à-vis the ways in which certain physical theories may be said to be equivalent. In particular, possibilities 1 and 2, above, have been seriously confused. Thus for example, Professor A. R. Hall writes:

The *geometrical equivalence* of the geostatic and heliostatic methods of representing the apparent motions of the celestial bodies, adopted by Ptolemy and Copernicus respectively, is not often clearly emphasized . . . ([2], page 370, my italics).

Professor Derek Price argues similarly:

It follows from this principle [of geometrical relativity] that the use in Ptolemaic theory of a geostatic deferent with epicycle is *strictly equivalent* to a heliostatic system in which the epicycle, transferred to a central position, becomes a second "orbit" ([11], page 203, my italics).

Professor Thomas Kuhn refers to the "*geometrical equivalence* of the Tychonic and the Copernican systems" ([8], page 204, my italics).

Hall, again, writes: "[Tycho's] system is at once both as simple and as complex as the Copernican system, to which it is *mathematically equivalent* . . ." ([3], page 254, my italics).

And J. L. E. Dreyer writes: "This [Tychonic] system is in reality *absolutely identical* with the system of Copernicus . . ." ([1], page 363, my italics).

Each of these distinguished scholars has confused possibilities 1 and 2, set out earlier. It is well known that, although the predictions of Ptolemaic astronomy, Copernican astronomy, and Tychonic astronomy concerning *lines of sight* from earth to planet are identical, these observational predictions constitute but a small subset of the total number of possible consequences within these three theories. Thus, if one considers not just the direction in which each theory instructs us to look in order to see Mars, for example, at a particular time, but also the actual physical orbits which these theories generate, one could hardly conclude that every consequence of Θ_1 corresponded to some analogous consequence in Θ_2 and Θ_3; indeed, this is not even true of the subset of *observational* consequences. If in the Copernican system (Θ_2) Mars moves in an excentric circle around the sun, while the earth does too, the resultant orbit plotted for Mars in "absolute space" must be very different from that predicted within the Tychonic system (Θ_3) wherein Mars also moves excentrically around the sun, while the sun itself describes an orbit around the fixed earth. The *relative* relations between earth and Mars are exactly the same in both accounts. But if the earth moves in Θ_2 and is fixed stationary in Θ_3, it follows that in physical space Mars will not be accorded the same orbit in Θ_2 and Θ_3. This difference is potentially observable. So there are *some* observational consequences of Θ_2 and Θ_3 which are totally dissimilar, although they are not *the* observational consequences which Kuhn, Dreyer, and Hall have in mind when they describe these two astronomical theories as being "geometrically equivalent," "mathematically equivalent," and even "absolutely identical." Rather, Θ_2 and Θ_3 are equivalent only with respect to a *specially selected* subset out of the total set of observational consequences. They may be said to have a restricted observational equivalence. That is very different from what these authors claim.

Concerning the relationship between Ptolemaic astronomy (Θ_1) and Copernican (Θ_2), it must also be denied that these two are, in any sense, either "geometrically equivalent" or "strictly equivalent"—such as is contended by Hall and Price. No proponent of Θ_1 ever projected the twisting, epicyclical resultant orbits of, say, Mars, into physical space—for geostatic astronomers were interested solely in predicting lines of sight, no matter where along such lines the planet had to be placed in order to effect "apparentias salvare." Still, it certainly remains as a geometrical consequence of Θ_1 that the orbit of Mars is going to be representable as having epicyclical twists and backloops, which correspond to nothing whatever in either Θ_2 or Θ_3. So, again, the most that can be claimed for Θ_1 and Θ_2 is that they are *observationally equivalent* in a restricted way; some selected observational consequences in Θ_1 exactly correspond with other selected observational consequences in Θ_2. This does not even constitute the beginning of an argument that Θ_1 and Θ_2 are "strictly" or "geometrically" equivalent.[1]

The analytical point of this paper, therefore, is important in order for us even to understand certain aspects of the history of astronomy: in what sense were the epicyclical and excentric techniques equivalent, and in what different sense were the geostatic and geocentric techniques equivalent; and in what still different sense were the corpuscular and undulatory theories of light equivalent? Historians of science too often describe all three, quite indifferently, as being "equivalent." This is not good enough.

VI

Establishing that two physical theories, Θ_1 and Θ_2, are equivalent "with respect to specific subsets of all their observational consequences" raises an interesting logical point. One *could* show that every known member of an observational subset within Θ_1 "corresponds to" some knowable observational consequence within a subset of Θ_2. This might be shown by way of some "translation-function," by the application of which any observational consequence in Θ_1 will transform into some corresponding observational consequences within a corresponding subset of Θ_2. A proof of this is difficult to imagine, however. How could one know of a particular translation-function that it is sufficiently powerful to couple every one of a possible infinitude of observational consequences within Θ_1 with some corresponding consequence in Θ_2? What usually happens is that one takes selected observational consequences in the Θ_1 subset and considers them seriatim. It is noted what would verify or falsify some "corresponding" observational claim within Θ_2, and then the two theories will be said to be, to that extent, operationally equivalent. Further to show that no observational consequence is generable anywhere within Θ_1 which is not also generable within Θ_2—this would constitute a proof of theoretical equivalence in the strongest possible sense, à la our first possibility set out earlier. It would constitute a proof of mathematical identity within the algorithms associated with Θ_1 and Θ_2.

The example in recent history of science which has been offered most often as an illustration of equivalent physical theories is that involving

---

[1] When $hawk_1$ circles $hunter_1$ while $hunter_2$ circles $hawk_2$, the *lines of sight* from hunters to hawks may be identical. This does not render their paths of attack, or their strategies, equivalent or identical in anything but our limited sense [5].

wave mechanics and matrix mechanics, *circa* 1926. In my earlier paper I demonstrated that, despite almost universal feeling to the contrary, these two physical theories (at that time) were not equivalent in any of the senses set out here.[2] Thus, (a) there are certainly terms in the one synonymous with nothing in the other; (b) few "think of the same things" when dealing with the one as against dealing with the other; (c) many individuals were in fact conversant with the one while being almost totally uninformed about the other (Schrödinger and Heisenberg were themselves the first examples of this situation). The fact that Born's physical reinterpretation of both these 1926 Θs—wherein he replaced the original ϕs with a single ϕ applicable to both—rendered Θ_1 and Θ_2 equivalent "with respect to most observational consequences" is not relevant to the original issue. What Born really did was to introject the same physical interpretation, ϕ_3, into both theories, thereby rendering Θ_1' and Θ_2' (although *not* logically equivalent) observationally equivalent vis-à-vis certain subsets of their consequences. The fact that still later Dirac's powerful operator calculus disclosed new ways of generating observationally testable conclusions as solutions either in wave-theoretic or matrix-theoretic form—this also is irrelevant to the major issue here. Almost anyone can *change* Θ_1 and Θ_2 into a Θ_3 and Θ_4, these latter being then demonstrably equivalent either as algorithms or as genuine physical theories. This is quite different from showing the original Θ_1 and Θ_2 to be either algorithmically equivalent or observationally (or operationally) equivalent. Both Born and Dirac were working with Θ_3's and Θ_4's—a new physical interpretation (the statistical) in the former case, and a new algebra (the noncommutative operator calculus) in the latter case.

A major mistake in my earlier paper is analogous to the mistake made by Moore in his 1922 analysis of the equivalence of propositions. I assumed that the relation of strict equivalence between physical theories was a logically necessary connection between two *logically different* physical theories. It is, in fact, simply a demonstration that two *apparently* dif-

---

[2] In lectures delivered in the U.S.A. during 1964–1965, Professor P. A. M. Dirac has, to my delight, not only made this same point but has extended it far beyond my original historical restriction. How arresting to hear *the* proponent of the thesis that wave mechanics and matrix mechanics are formally equivalent now denying precisely that equivalence! His argument is that "the Schrödinger picture" and "the Heisenberg picture" are different, so much so that any amalgamation of the two must be conceptually superficial, however satisfying formally. This was the claim I sought to establish in 1959 in my paper at the Chicago meeting of the American Association for the Advancement of Science [4].

ferent theories are fundamentally one and the same theory—notational, psychological, and sequential dissimilarities notwithstanding. This, of course, Wittgenstein would have seen immediately. To speak of two theories, or two propositions, as being logically equivalent, therefore, is not to *relate* them in some mysterious and peculiar way. It is, rather, to reveal that *there is no logical relation BETWEEN them at all*. To quote Berkeley: ". . . there cannot be any relation, if there are no terms to be related" [*De Motu*]. A theory (or proposition) cannot be logically related to itself via any principle other than that of identity, a relation to be distinguished from others like disjunction and implication. Proofs of strict equivalence between physical theories look as if they are going to establish some dyadic relationship between two genuinely different, wholly distinguishable entities Θ_1 and Θ_2. They end up revealing only the monadic relationship of self-identity to hold "between" what were just *apparently* different entities: the result is one (logically) nondistinguishable entity. This is not to say that distinctions between theories made along the lines of nonsynonymity, notational dissimilarity, sequential dissimilarity, and psychological dissimilarity are of no conceptual significance. Quite the contrary! In some sense of "logical," distinctions of this latter kind between physical theories can be of the utmost logical significance. Nonetheless, if the two theories are mutually entailing, then, in a stricter sense of "logic," Θ_1 and Θ_2 will be logically one and the same theory. To say of Θ_1 and Θ_2 that they are mutually entailing is to deny that they are two theories at all.

Physical theories that are strictly equivalent may be conceptually distinguishable (as Moore perceived) despite the fact that they are logically identical (as Wittgenstein argued).

Concerning observational equivalence, however—much the more usual variety when considering physical theories—the situation is more flexible, as we have seen. But one thing should be clear from the foregoing analysis: it is always a mistake to characterize the observational equivalence between two physical theories in terms which suggest that they might be algorithmically equivalent, or formally equivalent. Establishing that the former situation obtains will usually be done in an inductive manner. The latter always requires a rigorous formal proof. Writings in the history of science and the logic of science have not been uniformly clear about this cluster of related issues.

NORWOOD RUSSELL HANSON

REFERENCES

1. Dreyer, J. L. E. *History of Astronomy from Thales to Kepler.* New York: Dover, 1953.
2. Hall, A. R. *The Scientific Revolution, 1500–1800.* Boston: Beacon Press, 1956.
3. Hall, A. R. "Tycho Brahe's System of the World," *Occasional Notes of the Royal Astronomical Society,* 3:253–263 (1959).
4. Hanson, Norwood Russell. "Are Wave Mechanics and Matrix Mechanics Equivalent Theories?" in *Current Issues in the Philosophy of Science,* Herbert Feigl and Grover Maxwell, eds., pp. 401–425. New York: Holt, Rinehart, and Winston, 1961.
5. Hanson, Norwood Russell. "Contra-Equivalence," *Isis,* 55:308–325 (September 1964).
6. Hanson, Norwood Russell. "The Mathematical Power of Epicyclical Astronomy," *Isis,* 51:150–158 (June 1960).
7. Hanson, Norwood Russell. "Mr. Pap on Synonymity," *Mind,* 60:548–549 (October 1951).
8. Kuhn, Thomas S. *The Copernican Revolution.* Cambridge: Harvard University Press, 1957.
9. Malcolm, Norman. "The Nature of Entailment," *Mind,* 49:333–347 (July 1940).
10. Moore, G. E. *Philosophical Studies.* New York: Harcourt Brace, 1922.
11. Price, Derek. "Contra-Copernicus," in *Critical Problems in the History of Science,* Marshall Clagett, ed., pp. 197–218. Madison: University of Wisconsin Press, 1959.

E. L. HILL

))((

Classical Mechanics as a Limiting Form
of Quantum Mechanics

Introduction

Many centuries of observation of natural phenomena have led to the recognition of two major elements underlying the structure of the physical universe—that of matter as composed of particulate entities (electrons, protons, neutrons, and so on), and that of continuously distributed fields such as the electromagnetic and gravitational fields. Until recent years these were regarded as distinct modes of existence of energy, itself the all-embracing concept of the natural world.

The discovery of many processes by which energy is transformed from one of these forms to the other has given rise to determined efforts by physicists to unite the concepts of matter and field into a single theory. These attempts have been made on several levels of sophistication. Even when creation and annihilation processes for elementary particles are disregarded one still must face the problem of existence of wave properties of matter. At this level of thought a major difficulty is that of reconciling our kinematical and dynamical theories of matter with those appropriate to a field description. Inclusion of creation processes only complicates an already troublesome situation by requiring an explanation of the modes of transition of matter into radiation, and vice versa.

In this paper we limit ourselves to systems in which creation and annihilation processes do not occur. For most of our purposes it will suffice to consider a system consisting of a single particle, since the most serious logical problems which arise are evident even at this stage.

[430]

There exists among physicists a widely held belief that in some sense classical mechanics is embedded in quantum mechanics as a limiting case. In its most intuitive form this belief is based on the assumption that the analogy between wave mechanics and Newtonian mechanics is similar to that between physical and geometrical optics. If the de Broglie wave length of the wave field of a particle is sufficiently small the particle is expected to follow the orbit which would be determined for it by Newtonian mechanics under the action of the prescribed forces.

Since the formula for the de Broglie wave length of a particle having linear momentum p is $\lambda = h/p$ where h is Planck's constant, it is evident that λ can be made small by making p large. That is, wave mechanics should merge into classical mechanics in the limit of high kinetic energies for the particles. In this form the principle of equivalence of the two theories is used constantly in the construction and operation of high-energy accelerators for charged particles.

But it is evident also that λ can be made small, for a fixed value of p, if the numerical value of Planck's constant is considered variable and if it is treated as an infinitesimal. Although this possibility does not correspond to anything which can be achieved in the laboratory, it is open to our mathematical skill to examine how the equations of wave-mechanical theory would behave if we were to examine the limiting case $h \to 0$. In this sense the problem is one of pure mathematics.

These two procedures are by no means identical from a logical point of view. Neither implies the other unless one has reason to feel confident that the numerical value of the de Broglie wave length is the only determinative variable in the problem. For this reason it is necessary to examine more deeply the comparisons and contrasts to be drawn between the two theories and so attempt to determine the conditions under which they can be expected to merge into each other.

Our primary concern will be to stress the intuitive bases of wave mechanics and classical mechanics as descriptions of position and motion of particles and to draw what inferences we can concerning their similarities and differences. Not unexpectedly we will find it easier to notice points of contrast than of similarity. Purely mathematical results will be stated and explained where needed, but proofs will be omitted. It is hoped that our discussion will be of interest to philosophers who are willing to read the text even when they have no wish to study the formulas.

[431]

PHILOSOPHY OF THE PHYSICAL SCIENCES

The Nature of the Problem

The most basic postulate underlying Newtonian mechanics is that matter can be divided into particles (mass particles) which can be identified and followed in their motions in space and time. Each such mass particle has a definite position in space at every instant of time, so that its position vector with respect to a given reference system can be specified by its three coordinates as functions of time

$$\mathbf{r}(t) = x(t)\,\mathbf{i} + y(t)\,\mathbf{j} + z(t)\,\mathbf{k}.$$

In order to connect the motions of the particles with the forces acting on them Newton made the assumption that the coordinate functions have derivatives of at least the second order with respect to the time, and that the second-order derivatives can be related to the physical forces acting on the particles. If at a given time t the force acting on a particle of mass m is $\mathbf{F}(t)$, Newton's equation of motion for that particle is

$$m\,d^2\mathbf{r}/dt^2 = \mathbf{F}(t).$$

In words, for each particle *mass* $\times$ *acceleration* = *applied force*.

We observe that this pattern of thought is divided into two distinct steps. The first is the purely kinematical concept that a particle necessarily has a definite position, velocity, acceleration, and perhaps higher-ordered derivatives of its motion, at each instant of time. In the second step one introduces the formulation of the actual equations of motion, these equations expressing connections between the kinematical characteristics of the motion and the applied forces.

The description of a particle given in quantum-mechanical theory proceeds along quite different lines. For the moment we confine our attention to kinematical questions, deferring dynamical considerations to a later point of the discussion.

In wave mechanics one starts with a mathematical quantity called the wave function, $\psi(x,y,z,t)$, which is allowed to assume complex values. The physical interpretation of the wave function is based on the following axiom [1].

Axiom A. If D is any fixed region of space of nonvanishing volume the probability that at time t the particle will be in D is given by the expression

$$\Pi(D;t) = \iiint_{(D)} |\psi(x,y,z,t)|^2 \, dx \, dy \, dz.$$

It is natural to extend this axiom at once by the statement that the particle has unit probability of existing somewhere in space at every instant of time. That is, if we let D_∞ represent all of space, and if we omit consideration of creation and annihilation processes, which have no analogs in classical mechanics, we require

Axiom A*. $\Pi(D_\infty;t) = 1$.

These properties justify the designation of the real-valued function

$$\rho(x,y,z,t) = |\psi(x,y,z,t)|^2$$

as the *probability density*. The wave function itself is referred to frequently as the *probability amplitude*.

Axiom A by itself would give us little information about the possible motions of the particle. We complement it by another axiom which carries the implication that if the probability of finding the particle in a given region of space varies with time, this must be because the particle moves across the closed bounding surface of this region.

Axiom B. There exists a real-valued vector function, $j(x,y,z,t)$, called the *probability flux vector*, which is expressible in terms of the wave function, and possibly also of the quantities determining the force field in which the particle is placed, such that the equation of conservation of probability

$$\frac{\partial}{\partial t}\rho(x,y,z,t) + \operatorname{div} j(x,y,z,t) = 0$$

is satisfied.

This last equation is equivalent to the formula

$$\frac{d}{dt}\Pi(D;t) = \iint_{S(D)} j \cdot dS$$

where $S(D)$ is the closed surface bounding the region D. In this form the connection between probability of position and of motion becomes geometrically obvious.

These axioms express the essential kinematic content of the wave-mechanical description of a particle. It is to be emphasized that the space variables (x,y,z) which appear in the wave function, the probability density, and the probability flux vector are not intended to represent the actual position occupied by the particle. Position and motion for the particle are to be described only in the sense of probability concepts.

It is not immediately evident whether these axioms are in conflict with the kinematical concepts of classical mechanics. Several interpretations suggest themselves. On the one hand, we can assume that classical ideas are valid, but that for some reason the wave-mechanical description of a particle is not as explicit as is classical theory. One such reason might be that even if a particle has a position and motion of classical type the laws of nature, as expressed by quantum-mechanical theory, do not allow us to determine these quantities. But to assume this would be to put ourselves in the difficult position of asserting the existence of physical quantities which admittedly could neither be determined by experimental means nor be defined theoretically.

On the other hand, it could be admitted at once that the axioms of wave mechanics give an incomplete description of the real situation. In this case one naturally would conclude that in due time it should be possible to replace wave mechanics by a more complete theory which would restore the full kinematical description given by classical kinematics, even though in a dynamical sense it might differ substantially from Newton's theory.

A third, and possibly more radical, view would be to argue that quantum mechanics is a complete theory and that it is the kinematical basis of classical mechanics which is at fault. To put the point more strongly, we could draw the conclusion that position, velocity, and acceleration are concepts which are applicable, at least to a degree of accuracy sufficient for practical purposes, to bodies of macroscopic size, but which have no validity in principle, and which lead to incorrect results when applied to particles of atomic and nuclear size. In this sense it would be denied that it is a logical necessity that the mere idea of a particle (considered as an ideal entity and not necessarily as a real physical object such as an electron or a proton) implies that it must be identified with some point of space at each instant of time. This point of view could be supported further by the argument that the kinematics of classical mechanics is based on the unprovable assumption that the real space in which physical phenomena are observed is to be identified with the mathematically defined four-dimensional continuum of space and time variables which is used in the theory, so that Newtonian kinematics provides only a particular mathematical model of position and motion which may well have no exact counterpart in the world of real events.

Undoubtedly the failure of physicists to be explicit in the interpretation of this aspect of wave mechanics has contributed materially to the confusion which many logical-minded people feel concerning the theory.

In fact, it is not easy to determine what ideas physicists hold on this point. If one is to believe that the literature expresses correctly the intuitive ideas to which they subscribe, the conclusion seems to be inescapable that a majority believe that particles such as electrons, protons, mesons, and so on actually do have definite positions and motions of Newtonian type, but that the laws of nature are such that these quantities can not be determined completely by direct measurement. The effort to bolster up this position has given rise to a very extensive literature concerning their measurement by various types of idealized experiments. Further comments on this viewpoint will be made in our discussion of the uncertainty principle.

An escape from this difficulty seems to require the adoption of a sharper attitude than is customary concerning the relationship between experiment and theory. In my view the situation is the following. Experimentalists measure what they can in the complex real world as it exists, making use of the techniques available to them. Theory provides a model of this world which corresponds more or less closely to it, but which always is inadequate in some respects. Any physical theory that makes pretensions to completeness should provide at least theoretical means of defining the quantities which it supposes to exist. If it is not able to do so one is forced to suppose either that these quantities do not exist, or that the theory must be denied its claim to completeness. If we maintain that quantum mechanics is a complete theory, and if it fails to provide a technique for defining positions and motions of particles in the sense of classical kinematics, then these things must be considered not to exist. If, on the contrary, we choose to believe in their existence, even though they may not be measurable in the laboratory, then quantum mechanics must be admitted to be an incomplete theory. To do otherwise is to allow in physical theory the use of concepts which can be defined neither experimentally nor theoretically.

As matters stand at present, quantum mechanics has tremendous successes to its credit as a mode of description of the properties of atomic, molecular, and nuclear matter. In some respects the conflict with classical ideas is so deep-seated that no presently conceivable change in the older theory is likely to bridge the gap. Under these conditions it appears to be mandatory to claim a range of validity for the ideas underlying quantum mechanics which is not to be duplicated by classical theory. However, in doing so one is constrained at the same time to admit that since the axioms of wave mechanics do not allow the full kinematical interpretation of classical theory, the latter should be discarded as unnecessary, provided only that we can show that the newer methods are adequate to cover those phenomena of motion which can be tested experimentally. In this way we will at least be relieved of blame for present logical inconsistencies, and if the future should bring a revival of theories based on classical kinematics we need only rejoice in the fact at that time.

The Linearity Axiom of Quantum Mechanics

Before we can study the dynamical content of wave mechanics it is necessary to consider a further postulate of the theory which enforces the divergence from Newtonian laws immeasurably.

Axiom C. The possible wave functions of a particle form a linear system with complex numbers as multipliers. That is, if $\psi_1(x,y,z,t)$ and $\psi_2(x,y,z,t)$ are any two allowable wave functions,

$$\psi(x,y,z,t) = c_1\psi_1(x,y,z,t) + c_2\psi_2(x,y,z,t)$$

is also an allowable wave function, provided the complex constants c_1 and c_2 are so restricted that this function satisfies the normalization axiom A*.

The historical background of this axiom is somewhat ambiguous, but its dominating influence on applications of the theory is unquestioned. From an intuitive point of view it seems at first sight to be demanded by the simple fact that matter exhibits wavelike properties. However, this is not a definitive conclusion since wavelike properties can easily be simulated by nonlinear systems, both physically and mathematically. The belief in the linearity axiom is substantiated most fully by the manner in which it is used in the theory; for example, in the interpretation of the Pauli exclusion principle.

Ehrenfest's Theorem

The most significant attempt which physicists have made to arrive at a description of the motion of a particle which is compatible with wave-mechanical theory is that based on the concept of a *wave packet*. Let it be supposed known that at some particular instant, t_0, the wave function vanishes identically outside a region of space, D_0, of very small linear dimensions. We conclude from axioms A and A* that the particle certainly must be in D_0 at time t_0. This argument suggests the intuitive idea

[436]

that a wave function which is concentrated strongly in some definite region of space, and which has a very small amplitude outside this region, is suitable for the approximate description of a particle which is known with a high degree of accuracy to be in the region of space concerned. Such a wave function is designated commonly as a wave packet. The construction of such wave functions by the methods of Fourier analysis, in which the linearity axiom of quantum mechanics plays a fundamental role, is a commonplace of mathematical theory.

The reader will note, however, that we have neither stated nor implied that "the position of the particle is known to a high degree of accuracy." Indeed, for us this statement is semantically meaningless since we have determined not to admit the reality of the concept "position of the particle."

If it proves feasible to follow the subsequent behavior of the wave packet it will give us an intuitive picture of the motion of the particle insofar as we can think of the latter as remaining within the region of maximum amplitude of the wave packet.

In order to investigate the behavior of a wave packet in time we must make use of the quantum-mechanical analog of Newton's equations of motion. If the particle is in a conservative field of force which in classical terms has an associated potential energy function, $V(x,y,z)$, this is supplied by the Schrödinger equation

$$(1) \qquad \left(-\frac{h^2}{8\pi^2 m}\nabla^2 + V(x,y,z) \right)\psi = \frac{ih}{2\pi}\frac{\partial \psi}{\partial t}$$

where m is the mass of the particle.

Naturally this equation is known to be compatible with axioms A, A*, B, and C. The appropriate form of the probability current density function is

$$(2) \qquad j(x,y,z,t) = -\frac{ih}{4\pi m}(\psi^* \operatorname{grad} \psi - \psi \operatorname{grad} \psi^*).$$

This expression is related intimately to the well-known argument which associates the linear momentum of the particle with the derivatives of the wave function by the operator association

$$(3) \qquad p \sim -\frac{ih}{2\pi}\operatorname{grad}.$$

Ehrenfest [4, 15] has shown that the Schrödinger equation leads to a partial answer to the problem of movement of a wave packet which is

[437]

not dependent on the initial form of the packet. To give his result we define the following expressions

(4) $\mathbf{R}(t) = \iiint \psi^* \mathbf{r}\psi \, dx \, dy \, dz,$

(5) $\mathbf{P}(t) = \iiint \psi^* \left(-\dfrac{ih}{2\pi} \mathrm{grad} \right) \psi \, dx \, dy \, dz,$

(6) $\mathbf{F}(t) = \iiint \psi^* \left(-\mathrm{grad}\, V \right) \psi \, dx \, dy \, dz.$

Each of these integrals is to be extended over all space.

Inspection of these expressions suggests that $\mathbf{R}(t)$ might be identified with the "statistical mean position" of the particle, while $\mathbf{P}(t)$ is its "mean linear momentum." Similarly, $\mathbf{F}(t)$ plays the role of the "mean force acting on the particle." However, these terms should be used with care, for while they are analogous to the corresponding terms used in Newtonian mechanics they clearly are not identical with them in the light of our rejection of classical kinematics.

Ehrenfest's analysis shows that if the wave function satisfies Schrödinger's equation, and is normalized according to axiom A*, these quantities satisfy the differential equations

(7) $d\mathbf{R}(t)/dt = \mathbf{P}(t)/m, \ d\mathbf{P}(t)/dt = \mathbf{F}(t).$

These equations are identical with Newton's equations of motion of a single particle in the given force field, provided we accept the corresponding classical interpretation of the functions $\mathbf{R}(t)$, $\mathbf{P}(t)$, and $\mathbf{F}(t)$.

The great virtue of Ehrenfest's theorem is that it shows how Newton's equations of motion can be given an interpretation in wave mechanics by resorting to mean-value properties of the wave function, even though we have rejected Newtonian kinematics as applied to the particle itself. Many physicists find this reduction of wave-mechanical ideas to Newtonian concepts completely satisfying as a statement of the connection between the two theories.

The major weakness of Ehrenfest's theorem as a description of position and motion for a particle stems from its very generality. It has been noted that the proof of the equations of motion (7) requires only that the wave function satisfy the Schrödinger equation and that it be normalized according to axiom A*. These conditions do not demand that it be localized in any particular region of space, as would be suggested by the idea of a wave packet. Ehrenfest's theorem therefore is only a very weak form of the wave packet theory, and is satisfactory as an intuitive description of the behavior of a particle only if it can be shown that a wave packet retains its property of concentration in some (moving) region of space for a reasonably long time after its formation.

Detailed studies based on the Schrödinger equation show that the rate of spreading of a wave packet depends on its initial form as well as on the field of force in which the particle is placed [3, 15]. Such a study would take us beyond the limitations of this paper. However, a fairly realistic idea of the results can be had by consideration of a simple type of wave packet which moves freely in one direction in space (one-dimensional wave packet).

We define a wave packet which at time $t = 0$ has the form

$$\psi(x,0) = \frac{1}{b^{1/2}\,\pi^{1/4}}\exp(-x^2/2b^2)\cdot e^{-i2\pi px/h}.$$

The associated probability density is the simple Gaussian function

$$\rho(x,0) = \frac{1}{b\,\pi^{1/2}}\exp(-x^2/b^2).$$

The concentration of this wave packet in space is determined by the constant b, while its initial momentum is fixed by the constant p.

A straightforward analysis based on the Schrödinger equation shows that at any time $t \geq 0$ the probability density function has the form

$$\rho(x,t) = \frac{1}{b(t)\cdot\pi^{1/2}}\exp\left[-\frac{(x-pt/m)^2}{(b(t))^2}\right]$$

where

$$b(t) = b\cdot[1 + (ht/2\pi m b^2)^2]^{1/2}.$$

The density function retains its Gaussian form but the position of maximum amplitude moves uniformly to larger values of x with speed $v = p/m$. This is exactly the Newtonian value for the speed of a particle of mass m and momentum p. At the same time the width of the packet increases steadily with time. The time required for the packet to double its initial width is given by the formula

$$T = 3^{1/2}\cdot 2\pi mb^2/h.$$

The following table shows a few pertinent numerical values calculated from this formula ($h = 6.63 \times 10^{-27}$ erg-sec).

m (grams)	b (cm)	T
1	0.1	6×10^{17} years
1.6×10^{-24}	0.1	28 sec
0.9×10^{-27}	0.1	0.02 sec
0.9×10^{-27}	10^{-8}	2×10^{-16} sec

The first line refers to a particle of macroscopic mass, with an initial wave packet width of macroscopic dimensions. The corresponding rate of spreading of the wave packet is extremely slow even when compared with the age of the solar system.

The second entry refers to a proton with a packet width comparable to those used in high-energy accelerators. Here again the spreading of the packet is very slow compared with the time spent by the proton in the acceleration process, which is of the order of a small fraction of a second.

The last two lines refer to a particle of electronic mass. When the width of the packet is of macroscopic dimensions the rate of spreading is appreciable on the scale of everyday events, but still is very slow compared with the time normally required for laboratory experiments involving free electrons. In the last case the initial width of the packet is of the order of atomic dimensions. Here the rate of spreading is so great that it would make little sense to think of the electron as being localized at all.

These results illustrate clearly the empirical basis for the use of classical kinematics in modern physics. Under no circumstances do we apply Newtonian kinematics directly to the particle. But under macroscopic conditions, and also under usual laboratory conditions dealing with free atomic particles, the classical theory is sufficiently applicable to the motion of wave packets so that we can avoid entirely any direct statement of how the particle moves, if we wish to do so. Normally one allows himself to be careless in this matter and identifies the motion of the wave packet with that of the particle. Naturally one would not attempt to extend the classical theory of motion to collision processes between particles of atomic or nuclear character, or to the interaction of such particles with macroscopic matter.

While these arguments go far to justify the use of classical mechanics in the design of experimental equipment, they show conversely that the resulting experiments can yield information of value for quantum-mechanical theory only when interpreted by means of that theory. This gives rise to the troublesome situation that experiments in high-energy physics usually must be designed for the express purpose of testing one or another aspect of a given theoretical model. As a consequence it is becoming more and more difficult to be certain which features of our models have definite empirical support and which are only theoretical inferences. In my opinion this is a cloud on the horizon portending danger in the progress of high-energy physics.

E. L. HILL

The Uncertainty Principle

Much effort has been devoted in the literature to the consideration of the uncertainty principle. It is not my intention to review this subject here but it is necessary to take up some points which are pertinent to our discussion.

The mean position and mean linear momentum associated with a wave packet have been defined by formulas (4) and (5). If we restrict our attention to one coordinate direction (x-axis), for simplicity, the statistical dispersions in position and momentum along this direction are defined as the nonnegative quantities Δx and Δp_x given by the formulas

$$(\Delta x)^2 = \iiint \psi^* (x - X)^2 \, \psi \, dx \, dy \, dz$$

$$(\Delta p_x)^2 = \iiint \psi^* (- \frac{ih}{2\pi} \frac{\partial}{\partial x} - P_x)^2 \, \psi \, dx \, dy \, dz.$$

Here X and P_x are the mean position and momentum components along the x-axis as defined in equations (4) and (5) respectively.

It can be shown [18, pages 77 and 393] that if the wave function is normalized according to axiom A* the minimum possible values of Δx and Δp_x are restricted by an inequality of the form

(8) $\Delta x \cdot \Delta p_x \geqq h/4\pi$.

It is important to observe that this result does not depend on the fact that the wave function is a solution of Schrödinger's equation, so that (8) has no specific quantum-mechanical content beyond the fact that Δx and Δp_x presumably are to be assigned some physical meaning. For this reason we will refer to mathematical relations of type (8) as the *weak form of the uncertainty principle*.

In Heisenberg's hands [9] the uncertainty principle has been given a much more extended form as a restriction on empirical measurements. It is argued that, owing to the atomic structure of matter and the photon structure of light, measurements on the position and momentum of a particle will be subject to uncontrollable statistical fluctuations of which the magnitude is limited by inequalities which also have the general form (8). When these relations are interpreted in Heisenberg's sense they will be referred to as the *strong form of the uncertainty principle*, or as *Heisenberg's uncertainty principle*.

Heisenberg's theory of measurement rests on his clearly stated assumption [9, page 20] that the concepts of position and momentum have meaning as applied to a particle, and that quantum mechanics imposes no restrictions on the determination of either of these quantities by itself. The limitation imposed by quantum mechanics is to restrict the accuracy of simultaneous measurements of both position and momentum. This point of view has been generally reaffirmed by later commentators on the subject.

This ineffectiveness of empirical techniques in simultaneous measurements of position and momentum is usually regarded as a direct consequence of the quantum-mechanical commutation relations, of which the equation

(9) $p_x x - x p_x = - ih/2\pi$

is representative. But if p_x is interpreted as a quantum-mechanical differential operator defined by the usual formula

$$p_x = - \frac{ih}{2\pi} \frac{\partial}{\partial x}$$

it is obvious that (9) is a mathematical identity following from the definition of differentiation. One may find it strange that such an important consequence of experimental physics can be inferred from a mathematical identity.

The answer seems to be that Heisenberg's uncertainty relations do not follow directly from the commutation relations but imply also the use of the normalization axiom A*, just as do the mathematical uncertainty relations (8). The importance of this axiom to the whole structure of quantum mechanics, in particular to the theory of measurement, has been emphasized by von Neumann, who made it a central pillar of his exposition of the theory [17]. On the other hand, its significance has not been sufficiently appreciated by physicists. Many of the apparent difficulties which arise in applications of quantum mechanics can be traced directly to this source [10, 11].

The usual practice in the literature for justifying Heisenberg's assumption that position and momentum are valid concepts as applied to a particle is to fall back on the argument that the uncertainty relations (8) still hold in the limiting cases

(a) $\Delta x \to 0, \Delta p_x \to \infty$,
(b) $\Delta x \to \infty, \Delta p_x \to 0$.

In case (a) one can make an exact measurement of position but with an arbitrarily large error in the determination of momentum. In case (b) one can measure momentum exactly but with an arbitrary error in position.

However, the use of such limiting cases must be regarded as a physical postulate which is without justification in a strict mathematical formulation of the theory based on axiom A*. To test its validity in other formulations would require a theory of measurement of more profound character than is presently available. The conclusion which we draw is that the theory of measurement which is usually associated with quantum mechanics is too idealized from the point of view of actual experimental techniques to be definitive.

The Asymptotic Expansion (WKB) Method and Hamilton-Jacobi Dynamics

Our discussion to this point has been concentrated on the concepts of position and momentum of a particle. A seemingly different approach can be found in a comparison of wave mechanics with the form in which classical mechanics was cast by W. R. Hamilton (1805–1865) and C. G. J. Jacobi (1804–1851). Their ideas, which made use of the analogy between physical and geometrical optics, exerted a strong influence on de Broglie and Schrödinger in their initial studies on wave mechanics. This method is interesting also for the light which it throws on the mathematical structure of quantum-mechanical theory.

The typical problem in Hamilton-Jacobi dynamics runs as follows. Let there be given a conservative field of force with a potential energy function $V(x,y,z)$. Construct an arbitrary oriented surface, S_0, in the field and imagine that from each point of the positive side of this surface a particle of mass m is started moving in the direction of the normal with a momentum such that all particles have the same fixed total energy E. The particles are to move under the action of the external field alone, without mutual interactions.

Each particle will trace out a particular trajectory in space. Since the field is conservative the numerical value of the momentum of a particle which reaches a point $P(x,y,z)$ can be found from the formula

$$p(x,y,z) = [2m(E - V(x,y,z))]^{1/2}.$$

The momentum vector is tangent to the trajectory followed by the particle and is directed in the positive sense of the motion. These definitions

[443]

permit intersections of trajectories to occur, but at crossing points the trajectories involved must have different directions. As an exceptional case trajectories can meet tangentially on caustic surfaces.

One of the most striking results of Hamilton-Jacobi dynamics is that such a family of trajectories, considered merely as lines in space, possesses a family of orthogonal surfaces. The differential equation for these surfaces is

$$\operatorname{grad} S(x,y,z) = p(x,y,z).$$

The surface S_0 is a member of the family by its definition. Once the trajectories have been found, the orthogonal surfaces can be determined by integration of this equation. If a trajectory starts from a point P_0 on S_0 and passes through the point $P(x,y,z)$ the explicit formula for $S(x,y,z)$ is

$$S(x,y,z) = S_0 + \int_{P_0}^{P} p \, ds$$

where the line integral is to be extended along the trajectory connecting P_0 with P.

It is important to note that it is not true that if a set of particles were to be started from the surface S_0 at a particular instant t_0, they would all arrive simultaneously on a surface of this family at a given later instant. For the time required for a particle to go from P_0 to P along its trajectory is given by the expression

$$t(P_0,P) = \int_{P_0}^{P} dt = m \int_{P_0}^{P} ds/p$$

which involves a different line integral from that which determines the orthogonal surfaces. For this reason it is most convenient to drop the interpretation of Hamilton-Jacobi dynamics in terms of the motions of isolated particles and to look at it in the sense of a flow problem for a continuous medium.

The adoption of this point of view allows us to go beyond Newtonian concepts by the construction from classical quantities of a kind of wave function which can be compared with the wave function of quantum-mechanical theory. For this purpose it is convenient to imagine that the surface S_0 is divided in some way into a network of small areas. All of the trajectories starting from some particular region on S_0 will form a tube of trajectories in space. Since our hypothetical flow represents particles which are not subject to creation and annihilation processes, we can treat the flow in any such tube as conserved at every point. This allows us to write the flow at a given point $P(x,y,z)$ as the product of a nonnegative density function, $\rho(x,y,z)$, and a velocity function, $\mathbf{v}(x,y,z)$, such that the flux density has the form

$$\mathbf{j}(x,y,z) = \rho(x,y,z)\mathbf{v}(x,y,z).$$

We identify the velocity function with the velocity which a particle would have at this point, so that

$$\mathbf{v}(x,y,z) = \frac{1}{m}\,\mathbf{p}(x,y,z) = \frac{1}{m}\,\text{grad } S.$$

The conservation property of the flow is expressed by the equation

$$\text{div}(\rho\mathbf{v}) = \rho\,\text{div } \mathbf{v} + \mathbf{v}\cdot\text{grad } \rho = 0$$

which acts as a differential equation for the density function. This relation is equivalent to the statement that at any point on the trajectory

$$\frac{\partial}{\partial s}(\ln \rho) = -\frac{1}{v}\,\text{div } \mathbf{v}$$

where the symbol $\partial/\partial s$ indicates differentiation along the arc of the trajectory.

This way of writing the conservation equation makes it evident that the density function is constrained only in its variation along a trajectory, but not in directions transverse to it. It is an immediate deduction that this function can be specified arbitrarily over any one of the family of orthogonal surfaces, say over S_0. In this way it becomes a measure function for the trajectories leaving S_0. The introduction of such a measure function is an example of the use of integral invariants in classical mechanics.

The network of areas on S_0 can be arranged in such a way that the tubes of trajectories are described as a one-parameter family of surfaces

$$g(x,y,z) = a$$

where a is a real parameter which ranges over some suitable set of values. The fact that these surfaces meet the S-surfaces orthogonally is expressed by the condition

$$\text{grad } g(x,y,z) \cdot \text{grad } S(x,y,z) = 0.$$

These definitions can now be put together in the construction of the *semiclassical wave function*

(10) $\phi(x,y,z,t) = M(x,y,z) \, e^{i2\pi S/h} \, e^{-i2\pi Et/h}$

where

$$M(x,y,z) = [\rho(x,y,z)]^{1/2} \, e^{ig(x,y,z)}.$$

It is not to be expected that this function will be an exact solution of the Schrödinger equation. On the other hand, our belief that classical mechanics is a kind of limiting case of quantum mechanics might well lead us to anticipate the existence of a solution of Schrödinger's equation which has the asymptotic form (10) for very small values of Planck's constant. Unfortunately few exact results are known concerning asymptotic properties of wave functions in two- and three-dimensional problems [16]. In the one-dimensional case, which is sufficiently simple to be mathematically manageable, the semiclassical, or WKB, function is known to give a reasonable approximation to the exact solution in this limit [5, 13].

In any event it is not difficult to see that the linearity axiom of quantum mechanics puts a severe limitation on this connection with classical mechanics. For suppose that there exist two exact solutions of the Schrödinger equation, each of which has an asymptotic form like (10). For example, let them correspond to motion in the same field of force but with different choices of S-surfaces. The additivity property of quantum mechanics would allow us to construct from them another exact solution having an asymptotic form with no corresponding classical representation.

We see from this argument that the set of solutions of the Schrödinger equation which have asymptotic forms of classical type is much smaller than the manifold of all solutions. Whether it is sufficiently extensive to serve as a basis for the linear space of all allowable wave functions (for example, for the space of L_2-functions) is an open question.

This result can be stated in another way. The limiting process by which one tries to pass from quantum mechanics to classical theory is not such as to destroy the linearity of the theory. It is to be expected, therefore, that if there exists a well-defined limiting case it should also admit the linearity axiom. But if we exclude such idealized cases as the theory of small vibrations, classical mechanics is not a linear theory and consequently can not be expected to act in such a limiting capacity.

[446]

Some Extensions of the Argument

It remains only to mention briefly certain attempts of a more sophisticated nature which have been made at connecting classical and quantum mechanics. It was suggested some years ago by Feynman [6] that the theory of the last section should be replaced by the assumption that particles can move from point to point in space along all possible paths. In the limit h → 0 it would be most probable that they would follow the paths prescribed by classical mechanics. This picture leads to a method of construction of the wave function by an integration process over all continuous curves. This in turn requires the existence of a measure function for such paths. Recently Gel'fand and Yaglom [8] have proposed a mathematical formulation of such a measure function, but it has been shown by Cameron [2] that their argument is in error. It is clear, of course, that Feynman's concept is nonrelativistic in character and that any attempt to put it into relativistic form would encounter great difficulties.

For certain important special problems it has been found that connections of a group-theoretical nature can be established between the two theories [12, 14]. For example, in the case of motion under the inverse-square law of force (planetary motion, hydrogen atom), this method has led to a complete explanation of the fact that the energy is independent of the eccentricity of the orbit in the classical case and of the azimuthal quantum number in the quantal case [7]. However, the linearity axiom of quantum mechanics again intrudes itself to make this only an analogy and not a true equivalence so far as the physical interpretation is concerned.

Conclusion

What can be concluded concerning the relationship of classical and quantum mechanics? Certainly it is not to be questioned that there exist strong mathematical analogies between the two theories, but at no point do we find real equivalence. Each theory exhibits a logical structure of its own which admits comparisons with the other but defies the attempt to find close bonds between them.

Fortunately, at least for practical purposes, it is possible to give a real measure of justification for the use of classical mechanics in important applications by the use of wave packets. On the other hand, this method itself is a source of conceptual weakness. For as yet we have not learned how to understand our laboratory apparatus in a thoroughgoing quantum-mechanical sense. Until it becomes possible to understand how our experiments define the wave packets representing such things as particle beams, the physical literature will necessarily be written in a hodgepodge of ideas from both theories.

REFERENCES

1. Born, Max. "Quantenmechanik der Stossvorgänge," Zeitschrift für Physik, 38: 803–827 (1926).
2. Cameron, R. H. "A Family of Integrals Serving to Connect the Wiener and Feynman Integrals," Journal of Mathematics and Physics, 39:126–140 (1960).
3. Darwin, C. G. "Free Motion in the Wave Mechanics," Proceedings of the Royal Society of London, Series A, 117:258–293 (1927).
4. Ehrenfest, P. "Bemerkung über die angenäherte Gültigkeit der klassischen Mechanik innerhalb der Quantenmechanik," Zeitschrift für Physik, 45:455–457 (1927).
5. Erdélyi, A. "Asymptotic Solutions of Differential Equations with Transition Points or Singularities," Journal of Mathematical Physics, 1:16–26 (1960).
6. Feynman, R. P. "Space-Time Approach to Non-Relativistic Quantum Mechanics," Reviews of Modern Physics, 20:367–387 (1948).
7. Fock, V. "Zur Theorie des Wasserstoffatoms," Zeitschrift für Physik, 98:145–154 (1935–1936).
8. Gel'fand, I. M., and A. M. Yaglom. "Integration in Functional Spaces and Its Application in Quantum Physics," Uspekhi Matematicheskikh Nauk, 11:77–114 (1956). An English translation with the above title has been published in Journal of Mathematical Physics, 1:48–69 (1960).
9. Heisenberg, Werner. The Physical Principles of the Quantum Theory. Chicago: University of Chicago Press, 1930.
10. Hill, E. L. "Function Spaces in Quantum-Mechanical Theory," Physical Review, 104:1173–1178 (1956).
11. Hill, E. L. "State Spaces in Scattering Theory," Physical Review, 107:877–883 (1957).
12. Jauch, J. M., and E. L. Hill. "On the Problem of Degeneracy in Quantum Mechanics," Physical Review, 57:641–645 (1940).
13. Jeffreys, Bertha Swirles. "The Asymptotic Approximation (AA) Method," in Quantum Theory, Vol. I, ed. by D. R. Bates, pp. 229–249. New York: Academic Press, 1961.
14. McIntosh, Harold V. "On Accidental Degeneracy in Classical and Quantum Mechanics," American Journal of Physics, 27:620–625 (1959).
15. Pauli, Wolfgang. "Die allgemeinen Prinzipien der Wellenmechanik," in Handbuch der Physik, new edition, Vol. 5, Part 1, S. Flügge, ed., pp. 1–168. Berlin: Springer-Verlag, 1958.
16. Van Vleck, J. H. "The Correspondence Principle in the Statistical Interpretation of Quantum Mechanics," Proceedings of the National Academy of Sciences, 14: 178–188 (1928).
17. Von Neumann, John. Mathematical Foundations of Quantum Mechanics. Princeton: Princeton University Press, 1955.
18. Weyl, Hermann. The Theory of Groups and Quantum Mechanics. London: Methuen, 1931.

HENRYK MEHLBERG

\\\(JJJ)

Relativity and the Atom

I. THE NEW ROLE OF RELATIVITY IN QUANTIZED THEORIES

I.1. *Lorentz covariance in the macro- and the microworld*

The special theory of relativity originated in 1905 as an attempt to reconcile an indubitable experimental fact with two basic, well-entrenched theories: Michelson's experiment [51, page 626] was incompatible with Newtonian mechanics and Maxwellian electrodynamics. The reconciliation was effected by Einstein's first theory of relativity [14]. However, the subsequent development of this theory detracted much from the importance of Michelson's finding, which became simply a particular, historical item in the evolution of special relativity rather than an essential component of the latter. For a while, relativistic mechanics and relativistic electrodynamics, which superseded the two corresponding pre-Einsteinian theories and could be construed as a mere outgrowth of special relativity, occupied the central place on the ever changing scientific scene. The single most spectacular result of special relativity was no longer related to the speed of light but to the newly discovered equivalence of matter and energy. This discovery unified the entire scientific outlook and was destined to usher in, four decades later, a new era in man's history. Then general relativity came into the picture and revolutionized the cosmological outlook, perhaps for centuries to come. All these developments occurred during the first two decades following Einstein's breakthrough in 1905.

NOTE: I wish to express my real appreciation of relevant discussions with V. Bargmann, S. Chandrasekhar, F. J. Dyson, E. L. Hill, G. Wentzel, and E. P. Wigner.
The research summarized in this paper was conducted under a grant from the National Science Foundation.

[449]

The philosophical problems affected or raised by relativistic ideas during these two decades were concerned with the epistemological foundations and ontological implications of the new concepts of space and time inherent in the special and the general theories of relativity. More specifically, the merger of space and time into a single cosmic medium, the dependency of basic spatiotemporal relations upon the frame of reference chosen by the observer, the utilization of empirical, cosmological evidence in support of a non-Euclidean structure of cosmic space, preoccupied the leading philosophers of the period. However, the next, third decade of physical relativity witnessed the emergence of a nonrelativistic and non-Newtonian quantum mechanics, followed, throughout the last three decades, by several relativistic quantum theories, and, even more importantly, by relativistic theories involving second quantization. Relativistic or Lorentz covariant theories which involve but one quantization are typified by Dirac's spinorial theory of electrons [3, pages 120–128]. Relativistic theories with a twofold quantization, significantly different in many philosophical respects from the relativistic theories exemplified by Dirac's theory of electrons, are best illustrated by the relativistic quantum theory of the electromagnetic field due mainly to Dyson, Feynman, and Schwinger [43]. In accordance with the well-known historical pattern of interdependence between theory and experiment, the growth of quantum physics, or, more exactly, of physical, chemical, and biological quantum theory, was paralleled by an ever increasing volume of observational discoveries. The entire process is now in full swing and, historically speaking, it should be considered at this juncture as barely started. Actually, only quantum field theory and in particular quantum electrodynamics evolved enough to become susceptible to a rigorous axiomatization [30] and to the establishment of the logical equivalence of its distinct versions [9].

There is, however, one common aspect which seems characteristic of most quantal theories that came into being during this dramatic period of the history of science. I have in mind the new role which special relativity has now come to play in the life of science. In the last three decades, Einstein's first theory of relativity has served neither as a tool for reconciling recalcitrant experimental findings with well-established theories (as it did in providing a solution to Michelson's paradox) nor as a device for modifying and adjusting such theories to the growing supply of organized scientific knowledge (as illustrated by the emergence of relativistic mechanics and relativistic electrodynamics in the preceding period). Actually, the new quantal theories were created to meet the imperative need of systematizing, explaining, predicting, and controlling [29, page 165] an immense volume of essentially new experimental facts. As for special relativity, it has served during these three decades and is still serving as a yardstick of theoretical progress and as a fundamental principle of theory formation. Thus, Einstein's dual theory of light, an early forerunner of subsequent developments, involved light particles devoid of mass but endowed with momentum. It was incompatible with Newtonian mechanics but perfectly consistent with special relativity, including the validity of the Lorentz transformation group for space-time coordinates and of the Lorentz covariance of the relevant physical equations. The fact that the validity of the Lorentz transformation group need not entail the Lorentz covariance of the equations involving space-time coordinates which transform under the Lorentz group was established in the last decade of these sixty years of relativistic history [19, page 271]. Similarly, de Broglie's dual theory of matter was entirely due to an application of the principle of Lorentz covariance to Planck's equation connecting the energy and frequency of a quantum of radiation, in conjunction with the example set by Einstein's dual theory of photons. Dirac's aforementioned spinorial mechanics led to the revelatory concept of antimatter and to the prediction of the creation and annihilation of pairs of elementary particles. Pauli's explanation of the interrelatedness of the statistical behavior and the spin values of quantum-theoretical entities was based on the requirement of Lorentz covariance. Generally speaking, atomic physics has kept striving to become relativistic ever since the emergence of nonrelativistic quantum mechanics and has actually achieved this goal in the most significant cases. The formal, algebraic expression of the new role of special relativity is the requirement of Lorentz covariance, which the assumptions and laws of all the new quantal theories are trying to meet.

The philosophical aspects of special relativity which became apparent during these last decades are significantly different from those which had once attracted the attention of, and often fascinated, men like Bertrand Russell, A. N. Whitehead, C. D. Broad, Henri Bergson, Émile Meyerson, Ernst Cassirer, Moritz Schlick, Rudolf Carnap, and P. W. Bridgman. The main philosophical problem concerning Einstein's first relativity theory consists now in establishing the new meaning, the new epistemology and ontology, of a presently valid interpretation of the Lorentz covariance of laws of nature and the transformability of the space-time coordinates of pointlike events relative to inertial systems of reference under the Lorentz group. It goes without saying that the conventional, macrophysical interpretation of special relativity, traceable to Einstein himself, is presently inadequate [30]. For Albert Einstein construed his first theory of relativity as dealing with conventionally defined, inertial frames of reference, i.e., with a threefold infinity of rigid bodies each equipped with a set of rigid yardsticks and of natural clocks at rest in it, all of them in a state of rectilinear uniform motion relative to each other. The macrophysical concept of physical rigidity is obviously inherent in all three strategic concepts: conventionally defined inertial frames of reference, rigid yardsticks, and natural clocks. The relevance of the concept of rigidity to the ideas of rigid frames of reference and of rigid yardsticks is self-evident. The fact that the idea of a natural clock also presupposes the concept of rigidity is made apparent by Einstein's illuminating construction of an ideal light clock [6]. Consequently, since the first theory of relativity has been interpreted by Einstein as asserting the covariance of all laws of nature in this threefold infinity of conventionally defined, inertial frames of reference and as accurately describing the actual behavior of conventionally defined yardsticks and clocks which are respectively at rest in various frames of reference, the theory so interpreted loses its literal applicability in the quantum-theoretical universe of discourse, because the latter consists of elementary particles coupled with the appropriate fields and does not provide for any rigid bodies whatsoever. The philosophical issue corresponding to Einstein's original interpretation of special relativity was concerned with the impact of the double claim of invariance of physical laws under any transformation from one inertial frame of reference to another and of the truthful description of the behavior of physically acceptable yardsticks and clocks upon our idea of space and time. The situation has completely changed by now, since it is no longer possible to use the conventional interpretation of special relativity once this theory has come to be applied to the realm of quantal phenomena. For at the atomic and the subatomic level there are neither inertial frames of reference nor the rigid bodies required for yardsticks and clocks.

Hence the meaning, the epistemological foundations and the ontological implications, of Lorentz covariance and of the validity of the Lorentz group of transformations for space-time coordinates must be re-examined from a new vantage point, independently of inherently macrophysical concepts. Needless to say, the validity of the covariance requirement and of the transformation group must be established in an extended domain which includes both the quantum-theoretical realm and the macrophysical universe. Moreover, the relativistic world geometry (in Minkowski's parlance [33]) which underlies the double claim of covariance and of Lorentz transformability should be construed in the same empirical spirit as it was in the preceding period; in other words, it must be viewed as a body of assumptions and laws susceptible to empirical verification and open to observational tests. However, in view of the peculiar nature of the newly extended universe of discourse of special relativity, the interpretation of the latter must now be established independently of concepts which are inherently foreign to atomic and subatomic phenomena.

I.2. Time symmetry in a reinterpreted special relativity

Moreover, several new ideas about the structure of time and space which have originated in connection with the physical developments of the last three decades must be taken into account in any investigation into the new, contemporary philosophical aspects of what is technically referred to as the Lorentz covariance of laws of nature and the Lorentz transformability of systems of space-time coordinates associated with inertial frames of reference. Three of these ideas may be mentioned at the outset. First, the accumulating empirical evidence of this period has come strongly to support the view that all *cosmic laws* are invariant under time reversal. A cosmic law is construed, in this context, as synonymous with a nonvacuously universal physical law, the latter being by definition any true statement which is expressible in terms of physical concepts definable without recourse to constant values of spatiotemporal variables and which refers to physically pervasive processes, i.e., processes which go on always and everywhere [30]. Newton's and Einstein's gravitational laws and Maxwell's electromagnetic laws are cosmic in this sense. Laws describing violations of space parity, which came to be established a few years ago, and laws implying violations of Wigner time invariance [55, page 325] (or what may be termed violations of time parity—I do not recommend the expression "time parity" since Professor E. P. Wigner has recently opposed it in an informal discussion; he also prefers the locution "invariance under time reversal" to "Wigner time invariance," but this preference is hardly justifiable since, in the relevant literature, "Wigner time invariance" is frequently used and other time symmetries are often considered) are not cosmic, on the understanding that the violations of Wigner time invariance are conditional on the validity of what is sometimes referred to as Lüders' Theorem, or, more appropriately, as the Time Reversal-Charge Conjugation-Space-Parity Theorem due to Schwinger, Lüders, and Pauli [21].[1]

At this juncture I would like to point out several reasons for suggesting the above definition of cosmic laws, at variance with all the abortive attempts by many investigators in the last two decades at defining the concept of lawlikeness. (The attempts were abortive either because of a "common language" bias of the Oxford variety or because of failure to restrict "lawlikeness" to use in scientific parlance.)

1. The very need for a precise and "operational" (effective) [4] definition of scientific lawlikeness is made apparent by the occurrence of the concept of lawlikeness in fundamental physical principles. Thus, the principle of special relativity requires that physical *laws* be invariant under Lorentz transformations. The principle of general relativity stipulates the invariance of physical *laws* under any (continuous and bi-unique) transformation. The equivalence principle of general relativity states that *laws* describing any local process in gravitational fields are synonymous with *laws* describing the same process in a system of coordinates associated with an appropriate noninertial frame of reference. I shall show shortly that P. W. Bridgman's objection that the concept of physical law, as used in general relativity, is not operational [12] is taken care of by the proposed definition of cosmic laws (which could easily be extended so as to apply to all "conceptually" [29, page 158] universal laws).

2. Moreover, the concept of cosmic law as defined above is both ontologically and scientifically significant. From an *ontological* point of view, it is important to bring relief to "the man in the street"—this expression applies, of course, to all those interested in the philosophy of science—whose perennial worry about "the origin of things" ("Where does the world come from?") proves unwarranted and physically vacuous in the face of the invariance of cosmic laws under time reversal, or time isotropy (see below), since the distinction between Genesis and eschatology turns out to lack observer-independent meaning if time isotropy obtains. Or, to put it otherwise, the distinction between the "origins" and the "ultimate fate of things" is as devoid of an intrinsic scientific meaning and as dependent on man's particular place in terrestrial biological evolution as

---

[1] S. Chandrasekhar called my attention, a few years ago, to the possible relevance of the *TCP* Theorem to Wigner time invariance.

would be the distinction between the (pointlike) event occurring "first to the left" of a practically pointlike spot I am presently looking at and the practically pointlike event now occurring as the "last event to the right" of the spot now stared at by me. Obviously, the spatial distinction between the figurative spatial "origins" and "ultimate fate" can be made validly, on the assumption that the space we live in is Euclidean, and that "points at infinity" are legitimately taken into consideration. However, a fellow-observer watching the same spot from a vantage point such that the spot was between him and myself would have to interchange "origins" and "ultimate fate." Since his spatial distinction is as good or valid as mine, both distinctions must be considered devoid of intrinsic physical meaning and relative to the respective spatial positions of the two observers. I feel that relieving man of his primeval puzzlement by recourse to time isotropy presupposing the concept of cosmic law is ontologically significant.[2]

3. The *physical* significance of the concept of cosmic law as defined above is made apparent by the fact that the idea of dual time introduced by Milne [32] into science and involving one time variety endowed with a "beginning," while the other variety does its best as far as the scientist's well-known needs are concerned and runs from minus to plus infinity, proves vacuous and physically indefinable.

Needless to say, the above considerations concerning the ontological and scientific significance of the concept of cosmic law as defined in the preceding paragraph and involved in the invariance of cosmic laws under time reversal are valid only on the assumption that the above definition of lawlikeness proves invulnerable to the well-known objections to which all the definitions of lawlikeness proposed until the present moment by several philosophers of science are open. The above explanation of the expression "cosmic law" may not seem watertight to that extent. However, in conjunction both with restricting the concept of lawlikeness to a minimal language capable of expressing physical theories (the *minimum* requirement applies to the extra-logical vocabulary of the language and to its extensionality [7]) and with applying the distinction between statements universal in the conceptual, or the quantificational or the nonvacuously cosmic, i.e., the spatiotemporal sense, the explanation can ac-

---

[2] Time isotropy may require readjustment on the part of certain major religions just as Darwinian evolution did. The newer readjustment raises no insuperable difficulties. Neither did the older.

tually be tightened up to a sufficient degree. This definition will be systematically developed, on the basis of a logically or rather metamathematically novel approach needed to meet the extensionality requirement (and hence to avoid the familiar difficulties of "counterfactual conditionals" which have been troubling philosophers of science because of their unwillingness to take advantage of uncontroversial metamathematical findings) in a forthcoming work of mine. The definition of lawlikeness I have in mind involves only syntactical and semantic concepts, or, alternatively, only syntactical concepts if couched in an appropriate metalanguage [47], and is therefore "operational." The objection to the scientific use of the concept of lawlikeness raised by the late P. W. Bridgman is therefore unwarranted. It may be worthwhile to point out, at this juncture, that quite a few pseudoproblems raised by philosophers of science, even if they happen to be leading physicists like the aforementioned Nobel prize winner of Harvard, are due to their reluctance to make use of a mathematical tool presently indispensable in physical philosophy (and, for that matter, in several advanced theories belonging in physics proper), viz., mathematical logic (of the von Neumann-Birkhoff [50, page 131] variety rather than that of Février [15], von Weizsäcker [50A], and Reichenbach [38]), and, more importantly, the thriving theory of metamathematics [25].

I.3. *The role of collisions in quantum measurement, in quantum field theory, and in relativity*

Another development which took place in physical science during the period under consideration is due to the striking and hardly ever noticed parallelism of Einstein's views on spatiotemporal *coincidence* and the central role of the quantum theory of *measurement* (basically creditable to von Neumann) in atomic theory. Einstein's emphasis on the unique importance of the concept of space-time coincidence of physical events was probably due to the invariance of this dyadic physical relation under any continuous and bi-unique transformation of world coordinates and may have been responsible for Sir Arthur Eddington's [10] slightly overemphasized evaluation of the physical role of "pointer readings" in physical science. Sir Arthur considered these mensural events as coextensive with the entire subject matter of the immense body of scientific knowledge labeled "physics." On the other hand, the emphasis on the quantum-theoretical role of measurements performed on quantal entities originated probably with Heisenberg's discovery of the quantum-mechanical uncertainty principle [22] over three decades ago. The emphasis was then strengthened by von Neumann's pioneering treatise on the mathematical foundations of quantum mechanics published in 1932. A substantial part of this treatise [50] develops von Neumann's own quantum theory of measurement, which constitutes the single most important contribution to date to our understanding of quantal measurements. The *tertium comparationis* between the relativistic emphasis on space-time coincidence and the quantum-theoretical emphasis on quantal measurement is the frequently observed fact [42] that quantal measurements amount to quantal *collisions* of quantal particles and macrophysical measurement instruments while space-time coincidence is obviously an idealization of corpuscular *collisions*. Consequently, it seems advisable in any attempt at reinterpreting, in terms of physically significant concepts, the theory of relativity so as to make it applicable both in the macrocosmos and the microcosmos, to grant a central role to the concept of collision which is clearly applicable in "both worlds."

Finally, a third aspect of recent developments in physical science which affect our present ideas of space and time is illustrated by the fact that the concept of collision involving quantum-theoretical entities is not only fundamental with regard to the crucial issue of quantal measurements but actually plays a dominant role in the impressive volume of successful research that has been carried out during the last decade or so, most frequently under the heading of relativistic quantum field theory. Accordingly, there is hardly any reason for doubting the advisability of making the concept of corpuscular collision central in an up-to-date reinterpretation of relativistic world geometry, since the latter underlies both quantal and prequantal relativistic theories. Hence, the question arises as to what procedure should be adopted in order to make sure that the concept of corpuscular collision will really be central in the proposed reinterpretation of world geometry, and also to succeed in establishing this new interpretation. It seems to me that this twofold objective of extending the scope of the conventional interpretation of world geometry by establishing an appropriate new interpretation can best be achieved by reaxiomatizing world geometry in terms of corpuscular collisions. An axiomatic system of this sort will be outlined in the latter part of this paper and will include a single undefined physical concept, that of collision-connectibility. The physical meaning to be associated with this dyadic relation obtaining between both macro- and microevents cannot be spelled out within the proposed axiomatic system where this relation belongs in the undefined part of the vocabulary. But this meaning can easily be explained in an extrasystemic or metasystemic way by means of what is often referred to as an extrasystemic definitional criterion [29] of an intrasystemic defined or undefined term of the system under consideration.

The definitional, extrasystemic criterion for collision-connectibility can be formulated as follows: The dyadic relation of collision-connectibility is construed as obtaining between two physical pointlike events E_1 and E_n, occurring in two particles P_1 and P_n, respectively, whenever a finite sequence of particles P_j $(j = 2, 3, \ldots, n - 1)$ can be selected in such a way as to make sure that for every j a collision of P_{j-1} and P_j takes place.[3] From the point of view of physical world geometry, event E is collision-connectible with event E' if E' occurs either in the upper or in the lower light cone of event E. Pre-quantum-theoretically, collision-connectibility by a single pair of collisions (i.e., for n = 3 in the above formula) is coextensive with collision-connectibility by any finite number of pairs of collisions. This, however, is not the case in relativistic theories involving second quantization. Accordingly, we shall propose to use the more general relation of collision-connectibility (with n being equal to any finite integer larger than or equal to 3) as the only undefined physical term of the proposed axiomatic system for a relativistic world geometry intended to be meaningful both in the macrocosmos and the microcosmos. Two collision-connectible events will often be simply said, in the latter part of this paper, to be *connected* with each other.

The choice of collision-connectibility as the only undefined physical term of the proposed set of world-geometrical axioms has some additional advantages and is also likely to raise some objections. To make the reading of this paper somewhat enjoyable to philosophers of science who may not appreciate the mathematical and physical technicalities that proved unavoidable, let me first point out the advantages which the axiomatic approach to be developed later is likely to provide. To begin with, it may be noticed that the overall meaningfulness derived from the use of collision-connectibility is reinforced, if I may put it in this way, by the essential circumstance that empirical, extrasystemic meaning criteria are provided not only for the sole physical primitive term of the axiomatic

[3] To make this definition safe, nonorthochronous chains of collisions would have to be excluded. This is easily expressible in terms of a single pair of collisions.

system but also for several of its crucial defined terms, e.g., for the twelve terms defined in Definitions 1–12 of the system. These additional meaning criteria are relevant to the empiricalness of the system. It goes without saying that no upper limit can be set to the number of available extra-systemic definitional criteria in view of the fact I have established elsewhere [29] that any law involving a term endowed with some definitional meaning criteria provides a new definitional criterion for this term. Since the number of lawlike contexts for any given physical term has no upper limit, such a limit cannot be set, either, to the number of definitional criteria associated with this term. Some of these additional meaning criteria for terms definable within the proposed set of world-geometrical axioms will be spelled out below.

I.4. *The monopoly of the Lorentz group as a consequence of the proposed axioms*

Another, more significant circumstance supporting the proposed set of axioms is related to the fact that attempts at deriving the validity of the Lorentz transformation group for spatiotemporal coordinates from a set of axioms which describe observable physical relations among observable physical objects have been made several times, both in the initial and in the present, atomic phase of special relativity. Owing to the particular, Einsteinian interpretation of relativistic world geometry which justifiably prevailed in the prequantum theoretical phase and has unjustifiably been maintained in theories involving second quantization, the axiomatic basis of the legitimacy and uniqueness of the Lorentz transformation group has usually been identified with the fundamental properties of one type of physical signals, viz., light signals. The epistemological reason for these attempts at deriving relativistic world geometry (or, equivalently, the validity of the Lorentz transformation group for space-time coordinates in inertial frames of reference) from observable properties of light signals is obvious. Should such attempts prove successful then the legitimacy of the Lorentz group, and of the theory of special relativity in its prequantum theoretical applications, would be shown to be susceptible to an empirical corroboration; there would be no need to derive this strategic scientific theory from a purely postulational basis. This epistemological reason for choosing intuitive properties of light signals as an axiomatic basis of relativistic world geometry is quite obvious and has even been spelled out in great detail by some writers, e.g., Hans Reichenbach [37]. But there is little

doubt that a similar motivation has been responsible for axiomatic investigations carried out much more competently by many other men,
e.g., C. Carathéodory [6]. His set of axioms for special relativity was presented by Albert Einstein on February 14, 1924 (hence independently of,
and possibly somewhat prior to, Reichenbach's book on the axiomatic
foundations of relativity). In the relevant proceedings of the Prussian
Academy of Sciences, Division of Mathematical and Physical Sciences,
Carathéodory's work was characterized by Einstein as follows: "Es wird
eine axiomatische Darstellung der Raum-Zeit-Lehre der speziellen Relativitätstheorie gegeben, welche nur auf Voraussetzungen über das Verhalten
des Lichtes gegründet ist, von der Idee des starren Körpers aber nicht un-
mittelbar Gebrauch macht." Needless to say, this light-theoretical approach to axiomatic special relativity is actually traceable to Einstein's
pioneering work back in 1905 when he suggested deriving his first theory
of relativity from two postulates, viz., the invariance of electrodynamical
laws in transitions from one inertial frame of reference to another and
one particular property of light, i.e., the constancy of its velocity in all
inertial frames of reference. The task of establishing special relativity on
an observationally accessible basis was then undertaken by men like
Carathéodory in continuation of the Einsteinian approach in a way which
would have naturally occurred to any competent theoretician both interested in a physically meaningful postulational foundation for Einstein's first relativity theory and not devoid of mathematical insight: to
use, instead of the *single* property of light (the constancy of the velocity
of light, resorted to in Einstein's 1905 deductive approach and probably
suggested to him by the Michelson paradox which must have then been
on the minds of leading physicists), that is, the value of its speed as measured with regard to an inertial frame of reference, *several* properties of
light, which may suffice jointly for the establishment of the entire special
theory of relativity.

In connection with this purely optical approach to axiomatic special
relativity, I would like to point out an important result due to H. P. Robertson [40] and then discuss the basic question whether or not the problem of establishing special relativity on a purely optical basis is solvable
at all. Robertson's finding can be described as follows: In 1949, this
physicist succeeded in proving that the purely postulational basis of the
Lorentz group (and, consequently, the justification of the requirement
of Lorentz covariance with regard to theories which do not involve second

quantization) can be drastically reduced and that the validity of this transformation group can be "almost" entirely derived from observational, optical findings if, in addition to Michelson's experiment, two other, more recent optical findings are used. In 1932 Kennedy and Thorndike and in 1938 Ives and Stilwell successfully carried out optical experiments designed to test aspects of the Lorentz transformation group which are insensitive to the Michelson experiment. However, Robertson's nonaxiomatic approach is both inherently incapable of sharply circumscribing the admissible reduction of the postulational basis which is rendered possible by the two post-Michelsonian optical experiments and inherently restricted to the macrophysical domain.

Let us now explore the more basic issue as to whether the construction of an axiomatic system for special relativity on a purely optical basis is at all possible. This question was answered by E. Cunningham [8] and H. Bateman [2] although their result did not prevent several theoreticians, e.g., Milne [32] and Reichenbach [37], from mistakenly assuming that they had constructed an axiomatic system which meets the twofold requirement of involving optical postulates only and of sufficing for the foundation of special relativity. The common mistake made by these two men, and also by A. A. Robb [39], was recently pointed out by L. L. Whyte [54]. It is too bad that Whyte has himself made the mistake of attributing the above mistake to C. Carathéodory, too: the great mathematician refers explicitly to the Cunningham-Bateman result in the opening paragraphs of his 1924 paper and he does not try at all to derive the entire theory of special relativity from a purely optical basis. We shall see shortly, however, that Carathéodory's axiomatic approach is not unobjectionable either, for a different reason.[4]

Cunningham and Bateman proved in 1910 that Maxwell's electromagnetic equations (and the basic equations of optics which follow from them) are invariant under two distinct transformation groups of spatiotemporal coordinates determined in any inertial frame of reference: the linear Lorentz group and the nonlinear group of transformations generated by an inversion of a Minkowski radius in the relativistic Minkowski world. Consequently, it is impossible to characterize the metric properties of space and time in an unambiguous way in terms of light signals only, because the propagation of such signals is governed by physical laws

---

[4] Einstein's apparent approval of a purely optical approach, quoted a few paragraphs earlier, should be construed as on pp. 479–482 below.

which are invariant under two different groups of transformations, only one of which is compatible with the theory of special relativity. The transformations by reciprocal four-dimensional radii are not consistent with this theory since they change inertial frames of reference into frames of reference that are not inertial. The above group-theoretical fact, incompatible with the monopoly of the Lorentz group in the area of Maxwell's electrodynamics, is often referred to in the literature as "Bateman's Theorem" because Wolfgang Pauli used this expression in his monograph on relativity theory published in a German encyclopedia [34]. For the sake of brevity, I shall sometimes use this expression of Pauli's in what follows. Ostensibly at least, Bateman's Theorem seems to entail the impossibility of deriving the validity and the uniqueness of the Lorentz group for inertial frames of reference from axioms susceptible to an interpretation in optical, or, more generally, in electromagnetic terms. But does such impossibility really follow from the Cunningham-Bateman result?

In the latter part of this paper, I shall outline a deductive system which is both meaningful within and without the quantal world and susceptible, outside of theories involving second quantization, to an optical interpretation, in spite of the system's ability to provide a proof for the validity and uniqueness of the Lorentz transformation group for space-time coordinates in inertial frames of reference.[5] However, before proceeding with this outline, I shall briefly discuss two unwarranted misgivings which may arise in connection with reaxiomatizing relativistic geometry in terms of collision-connectibility and, subsequently, prior to this outline, evaluate the most significant attempts at deriving the validity and monopoly of the Lorentz group, which are due to Einstein, Broad, Weyl, Carathéodory, Pauli, Fock, Stiegler, von Ignatowsky, and Frank and Rothe.

I.5. Mathematical rigor versus physical vigor in axioms A1–A7; causality in A1–A7

The first objection to an attempt at reaxiomatizing relativistic geometry in terms of collision-connectibility in order to establish the meaningfulness of such geometry both in the macrocosmos and the microcosmos is connected with the circumstance that such a reaxiomatization would be

---

[5] I would like to thank F. J. Dyson for a recent discussion of the compatibility of the aforementioned axioms with Bateman's Theorem.

intended to provide a novel interpretation of world geometry, whereas a reaxiomatization of any mathematical formalism seems to be inherently incapable of yielding any novel result. After Euclid made what was apparently the first successful attempt to axiomatize geometry, Euclidean geometry was reaxiomatized several times, e.g., by Pieri [36], Peano [35], Hilbert [23], and Veblen [48]. Nobody expects these four variations on a single theme, these constructions of deductive systems for the single mathematical formalism referred to as Euclidean geometry, to yield any new result, either in point of the scope of provable results or in point of the admissible interpretations of the latter. After all, a mathematical formalism inherent in a cluster of physical theories is simply an enumerably infinite set of statements involving an enumerably infinite set of terms. An axiomatization of such a formalism amounts to the choice of a finite or recursively infinite subset of the set of statements and of a finite subset of the set of terms on the understanding that the second subset includes all the terms essentially involved in the statements of the first set and suffices for defining, relative to the first set [44], all the geometrical terms, and, moreover, that the first subset, in conjunction with the definitions, suffices for the construction of proofs of finite length for all the statements included in the formalism. Hence, any formalism common to all possible axiomatizations and reaxiomatizations thereof seems to remain always the same and could not possibly be changed by the choice of some special axiomatization.

This reasoning, however, disregards two important facts. First, the formalisms inherent in a physical theory are not always of the mathematical type. They may also be of the logical and of what can be referred to as the metaphysical type. The existence of these three kinds of formalisms inherent in physical theories was shown in another publication of mine [31]. Moreover, and more significantly in this context, the formalism underlying a physical theory, no matter whether mathematical, logical, or metaphysical, never constitutes the entire physical theory. A physical interpretation must still be put on the formalism in order to promote the latter to the rank of a physical theory. This circumstance seems to have been appreciated for the first time, perhaps, by Albert Einstein [11], although he was hardly aware of the scope of the supplementary "definitional criteria" (which I have explored mainly in [29]). A reaxiomatization of a physically interpreted mathematical formalism, e.g., the conventional formalism of relativistic world geometry, can therefore yield a physically novel theory with regard either to the universe of discourse of the latter theory or to its experimental potentialities (i.e., the experimental consequences derivable from the theory, the experimental "fit" the theory provides, and, finally, the theory's suitability for being readjusted to novel experimental situations, which may call, for instance, for a generalization of the requirement of Lorentz covariance). Accordingly, I am not concerned over the possibility of establishing a *novel* interpretation of relativistic world geometry on the basis of the axioms to be proposed later in this paper. Nor do I feel that the increased mathematical rigor of a reaxiomatized and physically interpreted formalism is incompatible with some physical vigor being creditable to such reaxiomatization. Granted, more rigor than vigor is noticeable in many axiomatizations of physically significant formalisms, e.g., in the single most important axiomatic system for nonrelativistic quantum mechanics due to von Neumann. But there is no incompatibility between rigor and vigor in this field. Nor is there any shortage of historically significant cases where the change of definitional criteria associated with a given formalism has yielded or corresponded to a new physical theory. Thus, the analogy established by W. R. Hamilton [51, page 129] between wave optics and analytical mechanics provides for the intertranslatability of the two formalisms involved in these physical theories. But the two theories remain obviously distinct, in spite of their intertranslatability. The potentialities of this Hamiltonian analogy are clearly shown by the role it played in the emergence of wave mechanics in 1926 owing to Schrödinger's ability to combine Hamilton's mathematical discovery with de Broglie's tentative application, in 1924, of Einstein's dual theory of light, to matter.

A second objection which might possibly be made to a reaxiomatization of world geometry in a way that would provide for the applicability of the reaxiomatized geometry to the quantal realm is connected with the fact that von Neumann succeeded in showing [50, page 170] that the principle of causality[6] is tantamount to the existence, in the system S, of so-called "hidden variables" on the understanding that the existence of such variables is incompatible with the theory of quantum mechanics as axiomatized rigorously in von Neumann's pioneering treatise. Accord-

[6] Or the principle of the exact predictability of the value V which any magnitude ("observable") M will take on at any future instant t' for any isolated quantal system S, on the basis of our knowledge of the "state" of S at the initial instant t and of the relevant quantum-mechanical laws.

ingly, the principle of causality had to be surrendered in all extant quantal theories, whether or not they are relativistic, and whether or not they are doubly quantized. The so-called "principle of microcausality" [3, page 204] proposed or discussed by several authors involves a much weaker idea of causality, that of signal-connectibility, or of collision-connectibility, or of unpredictable disturbance of one microevent by the occurrence of another microevent; consequently, this misleadingly labeled principle of microcausality is compatible with the pervasive surrender of the full principle of causality throughout the sum total of well-established quantal theories. One may therefore wonder whether it is sound to reinterpret world geometry for quantum-theoretical use in terms of collision-connectibility, which looks like a causal relation among the relevant collision-connectible events. We did notice that the world-geometrical equivalent of the collision-connectibility of the events E and E' is the fact that E' occurs either in the upper or in the lower light cone of E. This world-geometrical relation between E and E' has usually been identified with the existence of a causal relation between both events. Thus, reinterpreting relativistic world geometry in terms of collision-connectibility may seem to imply the assumption of the pervasiveness of causal relations in the quantum-theoretical universe. But the import of the world-geometrical relation between E and E' is no longer the same.

To reassure those gloomy readers who might be annoyed by the allegedly causal nature of quantal collisions, I would like to point out that quantal collisions are not causal in the sense of involving full predictability of the values of all the observables for all the quantal systems in the collision. As for those few observables which, like the total linear momentum or the total energy, are governed by conservation laws and remain unchanged during a quantal collision, their future values obviously are exactly predictable on the basis of their present values on the assumption that the quantal systems involved enjoy a global splendid isolation. But only a few observables are known to be governed by such conservative laws. Most observables are not that badly off. They enjoy more freedom and their future values are not predictable on the basis of the present condition of the physical systems in which they may come to be "observed." This applies in particular to spatial position, which, for a pointlike quantal system not subject to constraints, is simply a trio of observables usually labeled "positional coordinates."

II.1. *Einstein*

In this section, I propose to survey and to evaluate some of the most significant attempts which have been made with a view to establishing the validity and uniqueness of Lorentz transformations. Needless to say, all of these investigations were carried out within the framework of special relativity. However, in view of the present situation in special relativity, I shall concentrate on determining the extent to which these investigations can establish the monopoly of the Lorentz transformation in the domain of atomic physics. It is natural to start this critical survey with an account of how Einstein himself viewed the structure of special relativity and tried to derive from this theory the validity and uniqueness of the Lorentz group.

In his pioneering paper [14], Einstein characterized his first theory of relativity as a conjunction of two postulates capable of justifying the monopoly of the Lorentz group. These two postulates are the (special) principle of relativity and the principle of the constancy of the velocity of light. He formulated the principle of relativity as follows: "The same laws of electrodynamics and optics will be valid for all frames of reference for which the equations of mechanics hold good." At the time of his writing, the only available system of mechanics was Newtonian mechanics. The principle of relativity would therefore require the invariance of electrodynamical equations in all frames of reference which insure the invariance of Newton's mechanical equations. However, Newton's mechanics was precisely shown to be literally untenable by the special theory of relativity and was subsequently superseded by a new, relativistic mechanics. Consequently, according to the theory of relativity, Newton's mechanical equations do not hold in any frame of reference, and the characterization of the admissible class of frames of reference in terms of the validity of Newtonian mechanics is therefore vacuous.

Einstein must have realized the difficulty inherent in his first formulation of the principle of relativity, since he added in a footnote that the invariance of electrodynamical equations should be claimed for those frames of reference in which Newton's equations "hold to the first approximation" [14]. This, however, is hardly a sharp and precise formulation of the principle of relativity. No wonder that in another paper [13] published in the same momentous year of 1905, Einstein gives a formula-

tion of the principle of relativity which not only is independent of Newtonian mechanics but actually applies to mechanics as well as to electrodynamics: "The laws by which the states of physical systems alter are
independent of the alternative, to which of two systems of coordinates,
in uniform motion of parallel translation relatively to each other, these
alterations of state are referred (principle of relativity)."

This formulation is not unobjectionable either because, apart from
the family of frames of reference which are not accelerated relatively to
each other and in which all laws of nature should be invariant, there may
be another family of frames of reference all of which are both rotating
relatively to any frame of the first family and also moving in regard to
each other in a rectilinear and uniform way. As presented in the second
Einsteinian formulation, the principle of relativity would not enable us
to choose between the two competing families of frames of reference.

Accordingly, in a paper written eleven years later [12], Einstein again
changed his wording of the principle of relativity. His third formulation
reads as follows: "If a system of coordinates K is chosen so that, in relation
to it, physical laws hold good in their simplest forms, the same laws also
hold good in relation to any other system of coordinates K' moving in
uniform translation relatively to K." This principle we call "the special
principle of relativity." Obviously, the difficulty I have indicated in connection with the second formulation does not apply to the third one. But
the latter refers instead to frames of reference in relation to which physical
laws hold in their *simplest* form, and nobody who is familiar with the discussions which have taken place regarding the simplicity of scientific laws,
especially after Hermann Weyl's devastating criticism of this concept, can
help feeling that the new formulation of the special principle of relativity
again raises serious difficulties.

To avoid these controversies over the content of the principle of restricted relativity, let us assume that the gist of the principle consists in
the claim that there exists an explicitly undefined, though ostensively
definable, maximal family of frames of reference called inertial or Galilean,
with the understanding that these frames are in a state of uniform rectilinear motion relatively to one another and are such that all the laws of nature
take on the same shape when expressed in any one of these frames. The
new objection which then arises is that the postulational basis of special
relativity construed as the conjunction of the principle of relativity and
the principle of the constancy of the velocity of light is conspicuously

redundant. For the constancy of the velocity of light and its independence of the velocity of the emitting body in all inertial frames of reference certainly correspond to a law of nature. Consequently, this law must be invariant in all inertial frames of reference according to the principle of relativity. The principle of the constancy of light would thus be a simple corollary and not an independent assumption. If Einstein derives the Lorentz group from both postulates in conjunction, he can achieve the same result by using the first postulate only.

II.2. Broad's support for Einstein's argument

C. D. Broad has tried to defend the dual basis of special relativity by the following argument: "It is important to be quite clear as to the connexion between this principle (of relativity) and the invariance of the measured velocity of light with respect to all observers who move relatively to each other in straight lines with uniform velocities. The latter fact neither implies nor is implied by the physical principle . . . The physical principle only implies that the measured velocities of light with respect to all observers will be the same function of their respective measurements of distance and time-lapse. It does not imply that all these measured relative velocities will have the same numerical value" [5, page 152].

This view taken by Broad seems to rest on a confusion of local and universal physical constants. Granted that no physical law can tell the present speed of the Nautilus because the speed of this submarine is expressed by a local numerical constant and can be ascertained in a factlike statement rather than in a lawlike statement. But the question whether any particular number expresses a local or a universal constant is, of course, not settled by this example. The statement that space has three dimensions involves the particular number "3" in the capacity of a universal constant, and the statement is therefore lawlike rather than factlike. This obviously holds also for the numerical value of the speed of light since this value is universal. Hence, the statement ascribing a constant, definite numerical value to the velocity of light in vacuo is a physical law whose formulation should be invariant in all inertial frames of reference, according to the principle of relativity. There seems to be no need for a second postulate in the foundations of special relativity. The invariance of all laws of nature in an ostensively defined equivalence class of frames of reference which move relatively to one another without acceleration, i.e., a slightly modified version of Einstein's principle of restricted relativity, apparently suffices as a basis for his first theory.

II.3. *Weyl*

The formulations of the special principle of relativity proposed by some of the most authoritative expositors and continuators of Einstein differ, often appreciably, from his wording. In his classic work *Space—Time—Matter*, Hermann Weyl reformulates the principle of restricted relativity as follows: "The world is a four-dimensional affine space whose metric is determined by a nondefinite quadratic form $Q(x)$ which has one negative and three positive dimensions. All physical quantities are scalars and tensors of this four-dimensional world, and all physical laws express invariant relations among them . . . By introducing an appropriate "normal" coordinate system consisting of the zero point and the fundamental vectors E_i, we may bring $Q(x)$ into the normal form $-x^2_0 + x^2_1 + x^2_2 + x^2_3$. It is impossible to narrow down the selection from these normal coordinate systems any farther; that is, none is especially favored; they are all equivalent" [52, page 173].

Thus, in following Minkowski, Weyl does not split the foundations of special relativity into the postulates of relativity and the constancy of the speed of light. He admits instead the postulate of a four-dimensional world metricized in a pseudo-Euclidean way and notices that the task of physical science is to establish the laws governing invariant connections among vectorial and tensorial quantities observable in this world. On closer analysis, Weyl's double claim that the world geometry is metricized by an indefinite quadratic form and that physical science is confined to vectorial and tensorial laws governing the world proves to be equivalent to Einstein's claim that the validity and the uniqueness of the Lorentz group follow from the double assumption that all the laws of nature have the same form in all inertial frames of reference and that the velocity of light has the same value in all these frames. For Weyl's first claim restricts the class of all admissible space-time transformations to the two aforementioned groups while his second claim entails (in view of the fact that vectors and tensors are subject to linear transformations only) that all the admissible transformations are linear. For if all vectors and tensors are subject to linear transformations only, then this will also hold of positional vectors in space and time. Since a positional vector is indistinguishable from the set of spatial coordinates of its end points, the linearity

[469]

applies as well to spatiotemporal coordinates. This suffices, of course, to eliminate the undesirable nonlinear inversions, to establish the monopoly of the Lorentz transformations, and, indirectly, to support the requirement that all laws of nature are Lorentz invariant.

II.4. *Three types of laws relevant to Lorentz covariance*

There are serious doubts, however, as to whether Lorentz invariance can be meaningfully required of all laws of nature. I am not referring here to the need or the desirability of making the laws of nature invariant in every frame of reference regardless of whether or not it is inertial, according to the program of Einstein's second theory of relativity. The difficulty I have in mind relates to a vast class of essential laws of nature which could not possibly be invariant under *any* group of transformations. Thus, the principle of restricted relativity implies a law of nature to the effect that the spatiotemporal coordinates of any event in an inertial frame of reference are connected with the spatiotemporal coordinates of this event in any other inertial frame of reference by a Lorentz transformation. However, it would make no sense to ask whether this law itself is Lorentz invariant. The point is simply that we have to distinguish at least three types of laws of nature:

1. Laws which deal with various physical systems but can all be expressed within a single frame of reference. We shall call them *intrasystemic laws*. Newton's laws of motion and Maxwell's electrodynamical laws are cases in point.

2. Laws which deal with the interrelations of spatiotemporal coordinates of any event in different frames of reference, with the understanding that the latter either belong to a specifiable class of frames of reference (e.g., in special relativity) or are simply members of the totality of conceivable frames of reference (as in general relativity). The validity of Lorentz transformations for coordinate systems associated with inertial frames is a case in point. We shall call such laws *intersystemic*.

3. Laws governing physical systems, which are often expressible without any frame of reference being involved, e.g., the laws concerning the atomistic structure of electricity and matter (say, that every electrical charge is an integral multiple of the charge either of an electron or of a positron). Laws falling under this heading will be classified as *extrasystemic*.

Now it goes without saying that any requirement of invariance under a specifiable group of transformations can be meaningfully applied to intrasystemic laws only; since such laws are expressible within a single frame of reference, it is both meaningful and important to inquire how their expression in a system of coordinates associated with a given frame will change when the relevant frame is replaced with another frame. However, laws of the second and third category could not be meaningfully asserted to remain, or not to remain, invariant under any specifiable group of transformations. Consequently, the restricted principle of relativity could not possibly assert that *all* laws of nature are Lorentz invariant. Such a claim would make sense only in regard to intrasystemic laws of nature.

An important class of intersystemic laws deals with the proper groups of transformations for various kinds of physical quantities. That momentum and energy can be lumped together into a four-vector under the Lorentz group, that action, electrical charge, and the Minkowski interval are invariant under this group, and that Dirac's multicomponent quantum-theoretical state-function transforms like a spinor under the same group are typical examples of the intersystemic laws I have in mind. The classification of physical quantities into scalars and pseudoscalars, tensors and pseudotensors, and spinors of various kinds and rank falls under the same heading. Needless to say, the law of the Lorentz invariance of electrical charge could not meaningfully be said itself to be, or not to be, invariant under this group of transformations. This holds also of those crucially important laws of the quantum theory of fields, the quantum theory of elementary particles, quantum electrodynamics, and the quantum theory of nuclear phenomena, which claim that a given class of physical quantities is transformed according to some unitary, irreducible representation of the Lorentz group or of any other group. Accordingly, the restricted principle of relativity could not conceivably encompass all the laws of nature; it is inherently limited to intrasystemic laws. This remark will provide the main support for the thesis to be developed in the last part of this paper.

II.5. Carathéodory, Pauli, and Fock

Of course, the requirement that all the intrasystemic physical laws be Lorentz invariant in all inertial frames of reference is nevertheless the crucial tenet of special relativity. How could this requirement be justified? Historically speaking, the unexpected and striking experimental finding of the invariance of one electrodynamical law, the law dealing with the velocity of light *in vacuo*, induced Einstein himself and several of his expositors and continuators to justify the requirement of Lorentz invariance by the experimental fact of the constancy of the velocity of light. However, as already pointed out, the constancy of the velocity of light, or, for that matter, the Lorentz invariance of all electrodynamical laws, does not entail the monopoly of the Lorentz group in respect to all laws of Maxwell, let alone to all intrasystemic laws of nature. Only the invariance under a wider group of four-dimensional similarity-transformations, which includes nonlinear transformations by inversion apart from Lorentz transformations, follows directly from the experiments relative to the speed of light. This is precisely Bateman's Theorem. The monopoly of the Lorentz transformations could be established if the nonlinear transformations of the similarity group were eliminated on some additional, physical grounds.

In Einstein's original paper, the nonlinear transformations are rejected because of their incompatibility with the "homogeneity of space and time" [14]. This argument, however, lacks mathematical precision. Carathéodory rules out the nonlinear transformations because Newton's laws of motion would otherwise not be covariant, and, more specifically, because frames of reference moving in straight lines with constant speed relatively to each other could otherwise become accelerated with regard to one another [6]. Incidentally, this remark of Carathéodory's shows clearly that he does not dismiss nonlinear transformations as "trivial," as one of his critics has objected: the great mathematician points out simply that it is only by recourse to mechanics, and by transcending electrodynamics, that the undesirable nonlinear transformations can be eliminated. Granted, the precise reason he adduces to support this elimination is questionable, since Newton's laws, the covariance of which he would like to secure by eliminating inversions, are rejected in special relativity and replaced with the corresponding laws of relativistic mechanics. Obviously, the objection against using Newtonian mechanics in support of the Lorentz group would not apply to a similar use of relativistic mechanics. Ostensibly, the possibility of a purely mechanical, relativistic approach to an axiomatic foundation of Minkowski's world geometry follows from the central role of the concept of collision in the set of axioms proposed in the present paper. However, a closer study of the quantal theory of collisions shows clearly that this theory essentially transcends any conceivable mechanical framework [33A].

A somewhat similar device for eliminating inversions is also proposed by Wolfgang Pauli [34], who remarks that the coordinate systems associated respectively with two inertial frames of reference K and K' must be connected with each other by a linear transformation to guarantee that a uniform rectilinear motion in K is also rectilinear and uniform in K'. An exact proof that Pauli's kinematical requirement, in conjunction with the constancy of the velocity of light, suffices to establish the linearity of the relevant transformations has recently been constructed by Fock [16]. The Pauli argument was also generalized in certain group-theoretical derivations of the Lorentz transformations proposed by von Ignatowsky [49] and, independently, by Frank and Rothe [17]. However, a closer study of the three arguments shows that the nonlinear transformations have not been rejected because of their incompatibility with the principle of relativity but rather in view of their clash with what may be termed the principle of reciprocity in physics.

The distinction I have in mind can be explained as follows: Any principle of relativity states that the intrasystemic laws of nature are the same in a specifiable class of frames of reference, say, in inertial frames. A principle of reciprocity, implicit in several discussions of relativity although hardly ever formulated with any precision, requires that whenever a law of nature asserts a relation R between the frame K and the frame K' (both members of a specifiable class of frames of reference) there must be a companion law to the effect that the very same relation R obtains also between K' and K. Thus, according to the special theory of relativity, if a physical object is a sphere in one inertial frame K, it will in general be an ellipsoid in any other frame K'. The principle of reciprocity states then, in addition, that a physical object whose shape is a sphere in K' will have the shape of an ellipsoid in K. The numerous consequences of the Lorentz transformation, concerning, for example, the fact that an observer at rest in K will notice the shrinking of rods and the slowing down of clocks at rest in K' are always duplicated by reciprocal laws to the effect that clocks and rods at rest in K slow down or shrink if compared with those at rest in K'. In his attempt to extend the restricted principle of relativity, E. Cunningham [8] emphasized that a transformation by inversion applied to coordinate systems associated with K and K' entails a complete reciprocity of the transformations which connect the main electromagnetic quantities as measured in K and K', respectively.

It goes without saying that the principle of reciprocity does not coincide with the principle of relativity since the latter applies only to intra-

[473]

systemic laws whereas the former is primarily relevant to intersystemic laws. Consequently, the attempts made by Pauli and by followers of the group-theoretical approach cannot be considered successful. As for the principle of reciprocity, obviously distinct from the principle of relativity, this is hardly the place to evaluate its merits. The only question of interest at this juncture is an evaluation of the attempts made with a view to establishing the validity and uniqueness of the Lorentz group and to eliminating the nonlinear inversions, on the basis of the principle of relativity, including its corollary, the constancy of the velocity of light.

I think that the critical analysis just outlined leaves little doubt as to the failure of the relevant efforts. It may be granted that both the invariance of laws of nature in an ostensively defined equivalence class of frames of reference (say, for brevity, "admissible frames") and the lack of such invariance in any larger assembly of frames of reference may be considered as a reasonably established empirical generalization which can serve as the major postulate of special relativity in an axiomatic reconstruction of this theory. To put it otherwise, it is a fundamental claim of special relativity that all intrasystemic laws of nature are the same in an ostensively defined equivalence class of frames of reference which move relatively to each other in straight lines with uniform speed. This postulate, however, must not be confused with the stronger requirement of the Lorentz invariance of all laws of nature in coordinate systems associated with every equivalence class of admissible frames of reference. This stronger requirement cannot be derived either from the invariance of electrodynamical laws in transitions leading from one admissible frame to another (in view of Bateman's Theorem) or from the requirement of invariance of Newtonian mechanics, since the latter is incompatible with the theory of special relativity. It remains to be seen whether intersystemic laws can bridge the gap between the major postulate of special relativity and the stronger requirement of Lorentz invariance.

III. AN AXIOMATIC WORLD GEOMETRY FOR QUANTUM PHYSICS

III.1. *The undefined concept of collision-connectibility*

Let us therefore proceed with a sketch of the proposed axiomatic system and first characterize its vocabulary. This vocabulary includes, apart from the logical and the mathematical terminology, one undefined physical term derived from a dyadic relation between any two events E and E' which obtains whenever a particle a'', distinct from the particles a and a'

in which the events E and E' occur, respectively, collides at different times with the particles a and a'.[7] I shall refer to this dyadic relation between the events E and E' as their connectibility by one pair of collisions.

For the sake of simplicity, it is preferable to replace the concept of connectibility of two events by a single pair of collisions with the more general concept of the connectibility of the events E and E' by any finite number of collisions. The concept of "collision-connectibility" of two events construed in this more general way will actually serve as the only undefined physical term of the proposed set of axioms and will be designated by the letter C. Geometrically speaking, the formula "event E is collision-connectible with event E' " is equivalent to stating that event E is either in the upper or in the lower light cone of the event E'. Should the proposed axiomatic system be applied to macrophysical phenomena only, then stating that E bears the relation C to E' is tantamount to stating that one of these events coincides with the dispatch and the other with the arrival of a light signal. Instead of stating that E and E' are collision-connectible, we shall often simply say that E and E' are connected.

We now come to the principal defined terms in the proposed set of axioms.

III.2. *Definitions*

Definition 1. *Spacelike betweenness.* The event E occurs spatially between the unconnected events E' and E'' if every event connected with both E' and E'' is also connected with E.

Definition 2. *Collinearity.* The events E, E', and E'' are collinear if one of them occurs spatially between the other two events.

Definition 3. *Inertial frames of reference.* By definition, an inertial frame of reference F is any exhaustive partition of all events into mutually exclusive classes which satisfies the following three conditions:

a. If the events E and E' belong to the same class of the frame F then E and E' are unconnected.

b. If the event E is not a member of a class t of the frame F then E is connected with an event belonging to t.

c. If the events E and E' both belong to the class t of the frame F then every event E'' collinear with the aforementioned two events also belongs to t.

[7] With the understanding that E (or E') occurs on a (or on a') when a (or a') collides with a''.

It should be noticed that the above definition of an inertial frame of reference does not involve any term applicable only to macrophysical events. The reason for identifying the partitions of the set of events which meet the three aforementioned conditions with inertial frames of reference will be made obvious by the remaining definitions.

Definition 4. *Meaning of timelike instants.* The timelike instants associated with an inertial frame of reference F, are, by definition, the classes determining the partition which constitutes F. Any instant associated with F will be denoted by the symbol t_F.

Definition 5. *Temporal coincidence (simultaneity) relative to a frame F.* The events E and E' are simultaneous relative to a frame F if both belong to the same instant t_F.

Definition 6. *Spatial coincidence relative to a frame F.* The events E and E' occur at the same place relative to F if both are collision-connectible with the same events at some instant t_F.

Definition 7. *Spatiotemporal coincidence.* The events E and E' coincide in time and space if both are connected with the same events.

Definition 8. *Asymptotic collision-connectibility.* Events E and E' are asymptotically connected if they are connected but do not coincide spatially relative to any frame of reference.

Obviously, asymptotic connectibility is coextensive with connectibility by a light-beam which travels *in vacuo*.

Definition 9. *Spatial congruence of two pairs of events relative to a frame F.* The pair of events (E_1, E_2) is spatially congruent with the pair (E_3, E_4) in F if these four events are simultaneous in F, and, moreover, if every pair of events simultaneous in F, e.g. (E, E'), satisfies the condition that the spatial coincidence in F of E with E_1 in conjunction with the asymptotic connectibility of E with E_2 is equivalent to the spatial coincidence in F of E' with E_3 in conjunction with the asymptotic connectibility of E' with E_4.

Definition 10.[8] *Temporal congruence of two pairs of events relative to a frame of reference F.* The pairs of events (E_1, E_2) and (E_3, E_4) are temporally congruent in a frame of reference F if the events E_k $(k = 1,2,3,4)$ coincide spatially in F with the events E'_k $(k = 1,2,3,4)$, the four events

---

[8] Definition 10 applies only if the events E_j, E_{j+1} (where either $j = 1$ or $j = 3$) are asymptotically connected. The extension of Definition 10 to cases involving no twofold asymptotic connection is obvious.

E'_k being all simultaneous in F and the pairs (E'_1, E'_2) and (E'_3, E'_4) being spatially congruent in F.

Definition 11. *Association of an orthogonal system of coordinates with an inertial frame of reference.* An orthogonal system of coordinates $[X_k]$ ($k = 1,2,3,4$) is said to be associated with an inertial frame of reference F by a bi-unique relation R if X is the class of all ordered quadruples of real numbers and R satisfies the following conditions:

a. The domain of R is the class of all events and its converse domain is X.

b. The spatial coincidence of any two events E and E' relative to F is equivalent to the existence of two quadruples X_k and X'_k such that X_k bears the relation R to E if and only if this relation also obtains between X'_k and E', provided that $X_j = X'_j$. The variable j varies here over the first three values of k.

c. The temporal coincidence in F of any two events E and E' is equivalent to the existence of two quadruples X_k and X'_k such that R obtains both between E, X_k and E', X'_k, provided that the last number in these quadruples is the same.

d. If the four events E_1, E_2, E_3, and E_4 are simultaneous in F then the spatial congruence of the pairs (E_1, E_2) and (E_3, E_4) relative to F is equivalent to the following two conditions:

a'. There are four quadruples of real numbers $\chi^m{}_k$ (k, m varying from 1 to 4) such that the relation R obtains between E_k and the quadruple $\chi^m{}_k$.

b'.
$$\sum_{j=1}^{3} (\chi^1{}_j - \chi^2{}_j)^2 = \sum_{j=1}^{3} (\chi^3{}_j - \chi^4{}_j)^2.$$

Definition 12. *Euclidicity.* Geometry is said to be Euclidean at the instant t_F of the inertial frame F if there is a bi-unique relation R whose domain includes all ordered triples of real numbers, whose converse domain is t_F, and which satisfies the requirement that the spatial congruence, relative to F, of the pairs (E_1, E_2) and (E_3, E_4) is equivalent to the following two conditions:

a. $\chi^m{}_j \epsilon D(R)$ and $j = 1,2,3, m = 1,2,3,4$.

b. There is a coordinate system $[X_i]$ associated with F by $\chi^m{}_j R E_m$ entailing
$$\sum_{j=1}^{3} (\chi^1{}_j - \chi^2{}_j)^2 = \sum_{j=1}^{3} (\chi^3{}_j - \chi^4{}_j)^2.$$

[477]

III.3. *Axioms*

A1. There is at least one inertial frame of reference.

A2. If two unconnected events are not simultaneous relative to F then, at every instant t_F of F which does not include either of these events, a third event is collinear with both.

A3. Given any instant t_F of a frame F and any event E, there is an event at t_F which coincides spatially, relative to F, with E.

A4. If the four events E_k spatially coincide, relative to F, with four events E'_k then the spatial congruence in F of the pairs (E_1, E_2) and (E_3, E_4) is equivalent to the spatial congruence in F of the pairs (E'_1, E'_2) and (E'_3, E'_4).

A5. Relative to any inertial frame F there is at least one instant t_F when geometry is Euclidean.

A6. If event E connected with E' is not asymptotically connected with E' then E' occurs between two events which are both asymptotically connected with E.

A7. If event E is simultaneous with E' relative to the frame F there are at least two events asymptotically connected with E which also spatially coincide with E' relative to F.

To characterize the scope of axioms 1–7, I am going to point out a few significant consequences of these axioms without quoting the available rigorous proofs:

1. Two events are connected with each other if they are not simultaneous with each other in any inertial frame of reference.

2. If geometry is Euclidean in any instant t_F of F, it remains Euclidean in every t_F.

3. An event which spatially coincides in F with event E is connected with E.

4. The frames of reference F and F' are numerically identical if there are at least two events which spatially coincide in either frame.

5. If the coordinate systems $[X_k]$ and $[X'_k]$ are respectively associated with F and F', then the transformation taking $[X_k]$ into $[X'_k]$ is a Lorentz transformation.

6. If the coordinate system $[X_k]$ associated with a frame F undergoes a Lorentz transformation then the resulting system $[X'_k]$ is associated with another inertial frame.

The theorems 1–6, the proofs of which cannot be reproduced here because of shortage of space, show that a condition both necessary and sufficient for the transformation of a coordinate system associated with a given inertial frame of reference into another system which is also associated with some inertial frame of reference is that the transformation should involve, apart from auxiliary substitutions, only substitutions included in the Lorentz group. This can also be shown by an indirect procedure. Suppose that a coordinate system $[X_k]$ associated with the inertial frame is subjected to a four-dimensional transformation by inversion. The system $[X_k]$ involves a bi-unique relation R which maps all conceivable quadruples $(x_i, i = 1,2,3,4)$ of real numbers into all the events. Let the transformation by inversion be defined by the following equations:

$$x'_i = \frac{x_1}{x^2_1 - x^2_2 - x^2_3 - x^2_4} \ (i = 1,2,3,4).$$

If we choose x_i so as to have $x^2_1 - x^2_2 - x^2_3 - x^2_4 = 1$ by putting $x_1 = \sqrt{1 + x^2_4}$, $x_2 = x_3 = 0$, then $x'_i = x_i$.

Similarly, for $X_1 = \sqrt{1 + x^2_4}$, $X_2 = X_3 = 0$, we obtain $X'_i = X_i$.

Hence, two events simultaneous in F, both located on the axis X_1 of F, are also simultaneous in F'. For reasons of symmetry, there will also be two events located on the X_2-axis of F, and two more on the X_3-axis of F all of which are simultaneous both in F and F'. However, all the events simultaneous in F with the six events just mentioned and filling the three axes of $[X_k]$ could not possibly remain simultaneous in $[X'_k]$ because the inversion above would then transform a three-dimensional linear subspace into a similar subspace, contrary to the fact that inversions always transform linear subspaces into curved hypersurfaces. It follows that not every event collinear with two events simultaneous in F will also be simultaneous with these two events relative to $[X'_k]$. Hence, in view of the definition of inertial frames, the coordinate system $[X'_k]$ is not associated with any frame.

We thus see that the axioms A1–A7 eliminate the nonlinear four-dimensional inversions and admit only the Lorentz group, apart from trivial auxiliary substitutions. Yet the only undefined extra-logical concept involved in A1–A7, the dyadic relation of collision-connectibility, is susceptible to an optical interpretation, since to assert that this relation obtains between the events x and y comes to asserting that y is either in the upper or in the lower light cone of x. How does the set of axioms A1–A7 escape the implications of Bateman's Theorem, which apparently entails that ordinary measures of time and space are not definable in optical terms?

The obvious answer is that Bateman's Theorem applies meaningfully to intrasystemic laws only. But several axioms of the groups A1–A7 on closer analysis turn out to be intersystemic. Consequently, although any law which is entirely expressed in spatiotemporal coordinates defined by electrodynamical measurements only is invariant under inversions and cannot eliminate inversions, intersystemic laws, even if dealing with the class of all systems of electrodynamically definable coordinates, cannot be meaningfully granted or denied invariance under inversions. Thus, a statement about Lorentz transformations may happen to be true of this group and false when applied to any more comprehensive group but this statement cannot be meaningfully examined with a view to finding out whether or not it is itself Lorentz invariant.

The intersystemic nature of some of the axioms A1–A7 can be illustrated by the use of the concept of asymptotic causal connection made therein. Two connected events have been defined as being asymptotically connected if they do not coincide spatially in any inertial frame. The sum total of inertial frames of reference involves, of course, the sum total of the associated coordinate systems. It is not surprising, therefore, that an axiomatic assumption involving all conceivable inertial frames, and consequently all the coordinate systems of a specifiable class, cannot be meaningfully classified depending upon whether or not this law remains invariant in all the systems of this class. Accordingly, any axiom in A1–A7 which is concerned with the entire class of inertial frames falls under the category of intersystemic rather than intrasystemic laws and is not meaningfully classifiable in terms of invariance under the class of transformations corresponding to the class of all inertial frames.

A somewhat artificial example may help illustrate the situation. Suppose that the class of inversions is defined as consisting of those transformations which leave the electrodynamical equations unaltered and possess a pointlike singularity. Any statement about singularity-free transformations preserving the electrodynamical equations would then rule out in advance the substitutions by inversion. Granted, no use was made in the axioms A1–A7 of this particular feature of inversions because I have been anxious to save the empirical testability of the axioms while having serious doubts as to whether a difference between two groups of transformations which hinges upon the existence of a single pointlike singularity would be empirically testable. No empirical test has been devised so far, nor could it possibly be devised, in order to check the preferability of assumptions which differ from one another only relatively to a single spatial point. Points are unobservable in principle, and any assumption about a single point is bound to be empirically unverifiable.

However, the status of collision-connectibility, although hardly controversial in view of the extrasystemic empirical criteria associated with this concept, does not seem to be shared by other concepts of the set A1–A7 which are introduced by explicit definitions. Thus, being asymptotically connected with an event x has been defined as tantamount to being connected with x without spatially coinciding with x in any inertial frame. This definition may be construed as a stipulation that, in order to decide whether one event is asymptotically connected with another event, I would have to examine all conceivable inertial frames and find out whether the two events occur at the same place in any of these frames. This difficulty would be insuperable if the extrasystemic empirical criteria available for the only undefined term of the set of axioms A1–A7 were the only available extrasystemic criteria. However, the student of the methodological structure of axiomatized or axiomatizable scientific theories is well aware of the fact that the availability of extrasystemic empirical criteria for concepts involved in a scientific theory does not depend at all on whether the concept under consideration is defined or undefined within the theory. As a matter of fact, a scientific theory gets in touch with experiment and observation because extrasystemic empirical criteria are provided for all its major concepts regardless of whether or not they are intrasystemically defined.

In the case of the group of axioms A1–A7, it is clear that all the relevant major concepts are provided with extrasystemic criteria. Thus, betweenness defined intrasystemically in terms of collision-connectibility, is directly observable for any group of events simultaneous in the observer's frame of reference and close to the frame's origin. Simultaneity in an inertial frame of reference is also directly observable whenever the frame of reference is the one at which the observer is at rest while the two relevant events take place in the observer's vicinity and involve but small velocities. Under similar circumstances, the spatial coincidence of two events in a given inertial frame is also accessible to direct observation. The fact that events x and y are asymptotically connected can be easily ascertained if one of them coincides with the dispatch of a luminous signal, and the other with its arrival. The spatial congruence of two pairs of pointlike events simultaneous in the observer's frame of reference can be established for local events by carrying out the relevant conventional measurements. An inertial frame is uniquely determined by the spatial coincidence of a pair of events and becomes therefore accessible to a direct observational test whenever spatial (local) coincidence is so accessible.

The availability of extrasystemic empirical criteria for all the major concepts involved in a scientific theory shows clearly that the theory gets in touch with experiment and observation not only through the empirical interpretation of its intrasystemically undefined terms but through the entire supply of extrasystemic empirical criteria for all the major concepts of the theory. This is why the proposed axiomatic foundation for the relativistic world geometry at the quantum-theoretical level is susceptible to an empirical verification. It is neither desirable nor possible to provide extrasystemic empirical criteria only for the single undefined term of the theory. Accordingly, we cannot attach any importance to the fact that the intrasystemic definition of some major theoretical term would prevent the empirical verification of any context involving this term, should the relevant intrasystemic definitions be the only clue to such a verification. The point is that no intrasystemic definition is the only clue to an empirical verification of the propositional contexts involving the defined term. The extrasystemic definitional criteria are always available when there is a need for bringing the concept and its uses within the reach of observational tests.

IV. ONTOLOGICAL IMPLICATIONS OF AXIOMS A1–A7

IV.1. *The distinction between Genesis and eschatology reconsidered*

In Section I.2 the major developments in physical science which have taken place in the interval between 1905 and the present and are relevant to the axioms proposed in this paper have been summarized. Apart from the need for reinterpreting relativistic world geometry so as to make it applicable to both macro- and microphysics, three such developments have been touched upon. The first was related to the considerable amount of new evidence that became available in support of the time invariance of cosmic laws, as distinct both from Wigner time invariance and from some other, physically definable time symmetries, e.g., Wigner time invariance considered in conjunction with "charge conjugation." It is worth pointing out, in this final section of the present paper, that the ontologically significant statement to the effect that no physically meaningful or observer-independent distinction can be drawn between the "origins" and the "ultimate fate" of things is actually established by the set of axioms A1–A7 regardless of whether physical time has any or all of the symmetry properties that are referred to as Wigner time invariance, or time invariance of cosmic laws, or any similar type of time symmetry; it is obvious that the number of physically definable time symmetries is considerable. The point is that all scientifically available information about the time component of the cosmic medium in which physical processes are going on, or, in short, about physical time, can be entirely derived, to the extent to which special relativity is valid (this restriction to special relativity is not inherent in the axiomatic approach outlined in the present paper; it is made in view of the current situation in quantum physics) from the axioms A1–A7, the latter being entirely expressible in terms of the time-symmetrical relation of collision-connectibility.

Consequently, if, in addition to the time properties derivable from the seven axioms, any other properties of the temporal component of the pervasive cosmic medium came to be established, with the understanding that these properties endow time with an "arrow"—to use Eddington's metaphor once again—then these arrow-dispensing properties would be attributable to physical time only on the basis of some *temporally* extraneous physical laws, e.g., laws concerning meson decay which seem to be suggested by recent experiments in such a way as to constitute violations of Wigner time invariance. In this context, a temporally extraneous or extrinsic physical law is to be construed as any physical law which is not expressible in world-geometrical terms but involves, in addition, terms foreign to world geometry, e.g., the terms "meson" and "decay." On the other hand, all temporally intrinsic laws, i.e., laws pertaining to the geometry of Minkowski's space-time, fail to provide any clue to time's arrow. I suggest referring to this circumstance as the "intrinsic nondirectionality" of time. Accordingly, the intrinsic nondirectionality of time is established by the fact that the axioms A1–A7 both suffice to determine the physical structure of time and involve only one undefined and time-symmetrical, physical term.

In view of the ontological significance of the intrinsic nondirectionality of time it may be of interest to make the following points:

Intrinsic nondirectionality of time is neither synonymous with nor known to be equivalent to time isotropy. The latter concept involves the

[483]

idea of a cosmic law and of a spatiotemporally pervasive process. Intrinsic nondirectionality of time does not involve any idea of process. Granted that violations of Wigner time invariance are neither violations of time isotropy nor of time nondirectionality. But the point we are now interested in is time nondirectionality inherent in relativistic world geometry. This four-dimensional geometry involves only spatiotemporal concepts. It could not possibly be trimmed so as to involve temporal concepts only. This is incompatible with the relativistic merger of space and time as first realized by Minkowski. Nor is the objection valid that, in view of the fact that axioms A1–A7 contain the concept of collision-connectibility, the connotation of which transcends the realm of world-geometrical concepts, the idea of intrinsic time properties should be considered self-contradictory. Collision-connectibility is undefined in the context of A1–A7. The explanation of collision-connectibility in corpuscular terms which I have suggested at the outset is, obviously, an extrasystemic definitional criterion, not an intrasystemic definition. From an intrasystemic point of view, collision-connectibility may be simply construed as invariant nonsimultaneity.

IV.2. *Incompatibility of Leibniz's "relational" time theory with physical relativity*

My emphasis on the idea of the time component of the pervasive cosmic four-dimensional medium implies the rejection of the so-called relational view of time and space in favor of a field-theoretical view. On a previous occasion I advocated the relational view of time [28] expressed by Leibniz and defended mainly in his correspondence with a follower of Isaac Newton's. This Leibnizian idea of a relational time (which must not be confused with Einsteinian relativistic time, as already pointed out in my earlier work) may be expressed as follows: There is no reason for assuming the existence of a self-contained cosmic medium, like the one Sir Isaac thought of, with the understanding that this nonrelational or "absolute" time may keep flowing over a part thereof even if nothing happens in the relevant interval, or, as the saying goes, if no "event occurs" in this interval. This relational view of time is usually supported by the following argument: Any statement reliably known to be true on the basis of relevant empirical evidence and dealing ostensibly with time (e.g., "time has no beginning" or "between any two time-instants there is another time-instant") is self-evidently equivalent to a statement concerned with temporal relations among events or processes, viz., the relations of simultaneity or succession of two events and the relation of temporal congruence of two pairs of events. Hence, all statements ostensibly concerned with physical time and adequately supported by empirical evidence can be construed as actually dealing only with temporal relations among events or processes. The universe of discourse of a language capable of expressing the sum total of well-established physical theories would then consist of either events or processes but would not include an entity named "time."

This relational view of time (and space) proves, on closer analysis, to be incompatible with the well-established special theory of relativity and with the main assumptions of general relativity. For the four-dimensional continuum described in special relativity by Minkowski's world geometry, and inherent in the general relativistic conception of a manifold that is metricizable by the distribution of gravitating masses over this manifold, is obviously presupposed in the electromagnetic equations describing the values of electric and magnetic field strength in conjunction with the magnitudes of electric charges and the vectorial magnitudes of electric current densities. The electromagnetic field vectors and the corresponding electric charges and currents are conceived of in special and general relativity theories as defined for every individual "point" of the four-dimensional cosmic continuum. This holds also of the spatiotemporal distribution of gravitating masses described in the equations of general relativity. Accordingly, this field-theoretical outlook which Einstein credited to Faraday in the particular case of the electromagnetic field and which is actually, in its general version, creditable to Einstein, implies the logical and ontological independence of spatiotemporal concepts with regard to the concepts of (electromagnetic, or gravitational, or any other) processes or events describable by relativistic equations. In a more pedantic and conventional formulation, the ontological and logical autonomy of field-theoretical space-time concepts comes to the rejection of the "relational" view of space and time in favor of an alternative view. The latter can be misleadingly labeled the "absolutist" view of space and time; it is not "absolutist" because it is relativistic. It seems more proper to state that the special and general theories of relativity are incompatible with a relational "theory" of space and time. More accurately, relativistic theories are not expressible in a language or formalism whose universe of discourse consists of electromagnetic, or gravitational, or any other processes governed by physical laws provided by well-established physical theories. Relativistic theories are expressible only in formalisms or languages the universe of discourse of which is either field-theoretical or includes a field-theoretical component.

IV.3. Infinitist extensions of relativistic world geometry

Let me point out that identifying the sum total of world-geometrical laws with the sum total of statements derivable from the axioms A1–A7 by applying the standard proof procedures would give a false idea of world geometry. The standard proof procedures applied in what is often referred to as "classical mathematics," either "pure" or "applied" (whatever the latter dichotomy may mean), involve the entire mathematical output of civilized mankind until the publication, in 1931, of Kurt Gödel's metamathematical paper [20]. This standard proof procedure was analyzed and clearly described by Gottlob Frege [18] and then elaborated upon and put on sturdier foundations by Bertrand Russell and A. N. Whitehead [53]. The procedure consists basically of the formation and transformation rules of the propositional and functional calculi of mathematical logic, with the understanding that the formation rules of the functional calculus include a classification of the "parts of speech" pertaining to the language (symbolical, of necessity) in which these two calculi are couched. The parts of speech involved in the two logical calculi are usually referred to as "logical types" [53] or "semantical categories" [1]. There are many versions presently available of languages capable of expressing the two basic logical calculi and differing from one another with regard to the parts of speech pertaining to any particular language adequate for the aforementioned logical use. An elementary and elegant presentation of the propositional calculus and the "first order functional calculus" is available in the Hilbert-Ackermann classical outline [24]. An equally elegant extension to functional calculi of any finite order was suggested, independently, by Gödel [20] and Alfred Tarski [47].

Gödel's metamathematical finding of 1931 showed that a statement derivable from axioms A1–A7 or from a similar finite or recursively infinite set of axioms [25] by the standard proof procedure cannot account for all those statements which are "logical consequences" of the set of axioms under consideration. A logical consequence of a set of axioms may be intuitively though vaguely explained as being any statement which could not possibly be false should all the relevant axioms be true. A precise semantic definition of the concept of logical consequence was provided by Tarski [46].

His definition transcends, of necessity, the morphological or "syntactical" vocabulary of the metalanguage associated with the language in which A1–A7 are couched. He resorts, instead, to a "semantic" or model-theoretical language and suggests construing the statement "The sentence S, couched in the indicative mood and possessed, accordingly, of a truth-value, is a logical consequence of the class C of sentences endowed with these two properties" as synonymous with the statement "Every model of all the elements of C is also a model of S." The concept of "model" occurring in this definition is given, independently, a precise meaning, although Tarski's definition of "model" cannot be reproduced here, because of shortage of space. Given this model-theoretical definition of the concept of logical consequence, we can define world geometry as the class of statements each of which is a logical consequence of A1–A7. This takes care of several shortcomings of the concept of derivability by standard proof procedures discovered by Gödel and provides a more reasonable idea of world geometry.

It might seem simpler to define world geometry as the class of all true statements which are expressible within the language that just suffices for the formulation of A1–A7 and of definitions 1–12. However, the class of statements expressible in this language includes a substantial subset of extra-logical statements, i.e., of statements which are not a logical consequence of an appropriately defined set of postulates for logic and pure mathematics nor a substitution-instance of any such consequence. It was shown, however, in a work of mine in 1958 [29], that such extra-logical statements need not possess a definite truth-value although they play an essential part in the basic assumptions of the main physical theories. Consequently, we cannot use the concept of truth in defining the deductive system of world geometry.

In any event, regardless of whether world geometry is construed as the class of statements derivable from A1–A7 by standard proof procedures, or as constituting the class of logical consequences of A1–A7, or even as the class of true statements expressible in a minimal language used to formulate the axioms A1–A7, it is obvious that the occurrence of a sole undefined physical relation, that of a time-symmetrical collision-connectibility, in the axioms A1–A7, prevents the occurrence, in world geometry, of any statement pointing to temporal unidirectionality.

IV.4. *The Lindenbaum-Tarski finding*

Finally, a brief comment is called for at this juncture regarding the type of knowledge of physical time which an axiomatic system of the type here proposed can provide. The inherent limitations of such knowledge follow from the Lindenbaum-Tarski model-theoretical theorem [26]. In our case the finding comes roughly to the assertion that if M is a model of A1–A7 and M' is isomorphic [7A, pages 76 ff.] with M with regard to the relation of collision-connectibility then M' is also a model of A1–A7. Since any two isomorphic models have the same structure (in the Russellian sense), the axioms A1–A7 can, by themselves, only provide a knowledge of the structure common to the cosmic four-dimensional medium and to the infinity of other entities isomorphic with the space-time continuum. No information applying to space-time only is provided by the axioms A1–A7 if they are not supplemented by an additional data.

This epistemological aspect of the axioms A1–A7 is obviously due to the fact that, in applying the Lindenbaum-Tarski metamathematical finding to the axioms, we have taken into consideration only the formalism involved in the deductive system under consideration. However, the availability of extrasystemic definitional criteria for the major undefined and defined terms of the system narrows down significantly the class of isomorphic models for which the axioms hold. Ultimately, the definitional criteria just mentioned will involve "ostensively defined" terms and will, therefore, exclude from the "structure" described by the axioms A1–A7 all models which do not include the individual entities involved in the perceptual processes which underlie the aforementioned ostensive definitions. However, the recourse to ostensive definitional criteria and to the corresponding perceptual processes only restricts the models of A1–A7 without transforming the class of such models into a unit class. This follows clearly from the fact that the physical interpretation of the axiomatic system under consideration is provided by extrasystemic definitional criteria and not by extrasystemic genuine definitions. The epistemological, inherent limitation here described does not affect our knowledge of physical space-time only. Any physical knowledge provided by axiomatizable formalisms in conjunction with sets of extrasystemic definitional criteria is similarly limited. In the particular case of relativistic space-time, this unavoidable shortcoming of scientific knowledge can be described as our inability ever to get hold cognitively of a unique entity constituted by the four-dimensional cosmic medium.

Another issue related to A1–A7 and affecting specific epistemological aspects of quantal theories is discussed in my companion work [29]. This issue arises in connection with Bohr's Copenhagen interpretation, which he has tried to associate with the von Neumann quantum theory of measurement. The result of the discussion implies the independence of von Neumann's theory with regard to the Copenhagen interpretation proper. Accordingly, there is no need to abandon this theory, although the subjectivist epistemology underlying the Copenhagen interpretation proves incompatible with the assumptions of relativistic theories involving second quantization.

REFERENCES

1. Ajdukiewicz, Kazimierz. "Die syntaktische Konnexität," in *Studia Philosophica: Commentarii Societatis Philosophicae Polonorum*, K. Ajdukiewicz, R. Ingarden, and K. Twardowski, eds., Vol. I, pp. 1–27. Lvov: A. Mazzucato, 1935.
2. Bateman, H. "The Transformation of the Electrodynamical Equations," *Proceedings of the London Mathematical Society*, series 2, 8:223–264 (1910).
3. Bogoliubov, N. N., and D. V. Shirkov. *Introduction to the Theory of Quantized Fields.* New York: Interscience, 1959.
4. Bridgman, P. W. "Einstein's Theories and the Operational Point of View," in *Albert Einstein: Philosopher-Scientist*, Paul Arthur Schilpp, ed., pp. 333–354. Evanston, Ill.: Library of Living Philosophers, 1949.
5. Broad, C. D. *Scientific Thought.* London: Routledge and Kegan Paul, 1923.
6. Carathéodory, C. "Zur Axiomatik der Speziellen Relativitätstheorie," *Sitzungsberichte der Preussischen Akademie der Wissenschaften, Physische und Mathematische Klasse*, 1924, 12–27.
7. Carnap, Rudolf. *The Logical Syntax of Language.* New York: Harcourt Brace, 1937.
7A. Carnap, Rudolf. *Introduction to Symbolic Logic.* New York: Dover, 1958.
8. Cunningham, E. "The Principle of Relativity in Electrodynamics and an Extension Thereof," *Proceedings of the London Mathematical Society*, series 2, 8:77–98 (1910).
9. Dyson, F. J. "The Radiation Theories of Tomonaga, Schwinger, and Feynman," *Physical Review*, 75:486–502 (1949). Also in [43].
10. Eddington, A. S. *The Nature of the Physical World.* New York: Macmillan, 1928.
11. Einstein, Albert. *Geometrie und Erfahrung.* Berlin: Springer, 1921. An English translation, entitled "Geometry and Experience," was published in Einstein, Albert, *Sidelights on Relativity*, New York: Dutton, 1923.
12. Einstein, Albert. "Die Grundlage der allgemeinen Relativitätstheorie," *Annalen der Physik*, series 4, 49:769–822 (1916). An English translation, under the title "The Foundations of the General Theory of Relativity," appears in [27], pp. 109–164.
13. Einstein, Albert. "Ist die Trägheit eines Körpers von seinem Energiegehalt abhängig?" *Annalen der Physik*, series 4, 17:639–641 (1905). An English translation, under the title "Does the Inertia of a Body Depend upon Its Energy-Content?" appears in [27], pp. 67–71.

14. Einstein, Albert. "Zur Elektrodynamik bewegter Körper," *Annalen der Physik*, series 4, 17:891–921 (1905). An English translation, under the title "On the Electrodynamics of Moving Bodies," appears in [27], pp. 35–65.

15. Février, Paulette. "Les relations d'incertitude de Heisenberg et la logique," *Comptes Rendus Hebdomadaires des Séances de l'Académie des Sciences*, 204: 481–483 (1937).

16. Fock, V. A. *The Theory of Space, Time and Gravitation*, 2nd rev. ed. New York: Macmillan, 1964.

17. Frank, Philipp, and H. Rothe. "Zur Herleitung der Lorentz Transformation," *Physikalische Zeitschrift*, 13:750–753 (1912).

18. Frege, Gottlob. *Begriffsschrift*. Halle: Nebert, 1879.

19. Gel'fand, I. M., R. A. Minlos, and Z. Ya. Shapiro. *Representations of the Rotation and Lorentz Groups and Their Application*. New York: Macmillan, 1963.

20. Gödel, Kurt. "Ueber formal unentscheidbare Sätze der Principia Mathematica und verwandter Systeme I," *Monatshefte für Mathematik und Physik*, 38:173–198 (1931).

21. Grawert, G., G. Lüders, and H. Rollnik. "The *TCP* Theorem and Its Applications," *Fortschritte der Physik*, 7:291–328 (1959).

22. Heisenberg, Werner. *The Physical Principles of Quantum Mechanics*. Chicago: University of Chicago Press, 1930.

23. Hilbert, David. *Grundlagen der Geometrie*. Leipzig: Teubner, 1899. An English translation is published by Open Court under the title *Foundations of Geometry*.

24. Hilbert, David, and Wilhelm Ackermann. *Principles of Mathematical Logic*. New York: Chelsea, 1959.

25. Kleene, S. C. *Introduction to Metamathematics*. Princeton, N.J.: Van Nostrand, 1962.

26. Lindenbaum, Adolf, and Alfred Tarski. "Ueber die Beschränkheit der Ausdrucksmittel deduktiver Theorien," *Ergebnisse eines mathematischen Kolloquiums*, Fascicle 7:15–22 (1934–1935). An English translation, "On the Limitations of the Means of Expression of Deductive Theories," appears in [45], pp. 384–392.

27. Lorentz, H. A., A. Einstein, H. Minkowski, and H. Weyl. *The Principle of Relativity*. Translated by W. Perrett and G. B. Jeffery. London: Methuen, 1923; New York: Dover, n.d.

28. Mehlberg, Henryk. "Essai sur la théorie causale du temps," in *Studia Philosophica: Commentarii Societatis Philosophicae Polonorum*, K. Ajdukiewicz, R. Ingarden, and K. Twardowski, eds., Vol. I, pp. 119–260; Vol. II, pp. 111–231. Lvov: A. Mazzucato, 1935, 1937.

29. Mehlberg, Henryk. *The Reach of Science*. Toronto: University of Toronto Press, 1958.

30. Mehlberg, Henryk. "Space, Time, Relativity," in *Proceedings of the 1964 International Congress of Logic, Methodology, and Philosophy of Science*, pp. 363–380. Amsterdam: North-Holland Publishing Co., forthcoming.

31. Mehlberg, Henryk. "The Theoretical and Empirical Aspects of Science," in *Logic, Methodology, and Philosophy of Science: Proceedings of the 1960 International Congress*, Ernest Nagel, Patrick Suppes, and Alfred Tarski, eds., pp. 275–284. Stanford: Stanford University Press, 1962.

32. Milne, E. A. *Kinematic Relativity*. Oxford: Clarendon Press, 1948.

33. Minkowski, Hermann. "Space and Time," in [27], pp. 73–91.

33A. Mott, N. F., and H. S. W. Massey. *The Theory of Atomic Collisions*. Oxford: Clarendon Press, 1949.

34. Pauli, Wolfgang. "Relativitätstheorie," in *Encyklopädie der mathematischen Wissenschaften*, Vol. V, part 2: 539–775. Leipzig: Teubner, 1922.

35. Peano, Giuseppe. "Analisi della teoria dei vettori," *Atti Accademia delle Scienze di Torino*, 33:513–534 (1898).

36. Pieri, Mario. "Della geometria elementare come sistema ipotetico deduttivo. Monografia del punto e del moto," *Memorie della Reale Accademia delle Scienze di Torino*, second series, 49:173–222 (1900).
37. Reichenbach, Hans. *Axiomatik der relativistischen Raum-Zeit-Lehre*. Braunschweig: Vieweg, 1924.
38. Reichenbach, Hans. *Philosophic Foundations of Quantum Mechanics*. Berkeley: University of California Press, 1946.
39. Robb, Alfred A. *A Theory of Time and Space*. Cambridge: Cambridge University Press, 1914.
40. Robertson, H. P. "Postulate versus Observation in the Special Theory of Relativity," *Reviews of Modern Physics*, 21:378–382 (1949).
42. Schweber, Silvan S. *Introduction to Relativistic Quantum Field Theory*. Evanston, Ill.: Row, Peterson, 1961.
43. Schwinger, Julian, ed. *Selected Papers on Quantum Electrodynamics*. New York: Dover, 1958.
44. Tarski, Alfred. "Einige methodologische Untersuchungen über die Definierbarkeit der Begriffe," *Erkenntnis*, 5:80–100 (1935). Translated by J. H. Woodger in [45], pp. 296–319, as "Some Methodological Investigations on the Definability of Concepts."
45. Tarski, Alfred. *Logic, Semantics, Metamathematics: Papers from 1923 to 1938*, translated and edited by J. H. Woodger. Oxford: Clarendon Press, 1956.
46. Tarski, Alfred. "O pojeciu wynikania logicznego," *Przeglad Filozoficzny*, 39:58–68 (1936). Translated by J. H. Woodger in [45], pp. 409–420, as "On the Concept of Logical Consequence."
47. Tarski, Alfred. "Der Wahrheitsbegriff in den formalisierten Sprachen," in *Studia Philosophica: Commentarii Societatis Philosophicae Polonorum*, K. Ajdukiewicz, R. Ingarden, and K. Twardowski, eds., Vol. I, pp. 261–405. Lvov: A. Mazzucato, 1935. Translated by J. H. Woodger in [45], pp. 152–278, as "The Concept of Truth in Formalized Languages."
48. Veblen, Oswald. "A System of Axioms for Geometry," *Transactions of the American Mathematical Society*, 5:343–384 (1904).
49. Von Ignatowsky, W. "Einige allgemeine Bemerkungen zum Relativitätsprinzip," *Physikalische Zeitschrift*, 9:972–976 (1910).
50. Von Neumann, John. *Die mathematischen Grundlagen der Quantenmechanik*. Berlin: Springer, 1932; New York: Dover, 1943.
50A. Von Weizsäcker, C. F. *Zum Weltbild der Physik*. Leipzig: S. Hirzel, 1945.
51. Weizel, W. *Lehrbuch der theoretischen Physik*. Berlin: Springer, 1955.
52. Weyl, Hermann. *Space—Time—Matter*. New York: Dover, 1950.
53. Whitehead, Alfred North, and Bertrand Russell. *Principia Mathematica*, 3 vols. Cambridge: Cambridge University Press, 1910–1912.
54. Whyte, L. L. "Light Signal Kinematics," *British Journal for the Philosophy of Science*, 4:160–161 (1953).
55. Wigner, E. P. *Group Theory and Its Application to the Quantum Mechanics of Atomic Spectra*. New York: Academic Press, 1959.

WOLFGANG YOURGRAU

\\\ ⌣ ///

Language, Spatial Concepts, and Physics

Montaigne remarked that no one is exempt from talking nonsense; the misfortune is to do it solemnly. I shall therefore avoid being solemn in the hope that no argument need be entirely useless—even the worst one might serve a didactic purpose and be cited as wrong or invalid.

We live in an age of definitions; it began at the dawn of geometry and has now affected most disciplines of systematic reasoning. A few centuries ago the Jesuit Gropius Bacanus of Antwerp "proved," from definitions, that Adam and Eve spoke Dutch in Paradise. This claim may not be a flagrant absurdity, yet it is highly improbable that it can be upheld. Euclid defined a point as that which has no parts, that which has position but no magnitude. It took mathematics roughly 2300 years to arrive at the insight that there cannot be definitions of some ultimate primitive notions, such as point, line, and plane. Indeed, it required the genius of a Hilbert to repair the logical damage mathematics and physics have suffered through Euclid's wrong conception of rigor. It is a truism that when reason and tradition clash, it is not always reason that wins.

This little excursion should in no way encourage us to give up definitions altogether. Let us review some basic, very general, and favored definitions of ourselves, of man. Of course, there is no sure way of telling what animals think about themselves! It seems safe to say that the human being spends, or wastes, more thought than any other animal on himself—to wit, our diaries, cosmetics, mirrors, and the psychoanalyst's couch. Man moralizes, writes poetry, reasons, theorizes. We designate man therefore *homo sapiens* or *animal rationale*. However, man has also been defined as *homo faber*: man is ingenious, skillful; or as *homo ridens*: man can laugh, smile, be humorous; we know man as *homo ludens*: man can play games, flirt, mimic; and finally man has been dubbed *homo symbolicus*: man creates language, art, science, law, philosophy, religion—in short, a symbolic universe.

I propose to conceive of man as *homo spatifex*, that is, man is able to imagine, construct, and shape space. Now, space has been defined as a frame or system of reference, as the "negative" of matter, which is "positive"; as an empty receptacle; as the totality of all places whose interrelations generate the formal structure of space; as a field in which phenomena take place. Further, we have physical space, empirical, conceptual, representational, haptic, Euclidean and non-Euclidean space, phase space, configuration space, Hilbert space, and many, many other spaces. Some of the definitions of these various spaces are circular; others are, if not inconsistent, then decidedly so heterogeneous that it might be commendable to eschew an explicit definition of space—of space as such, as it were. Kant's faulty proofs for the aprioristic particularity of space were convincingly demolished by Gauss, and it is a commonplace that Newton's doctrine of absolute space was cogently repudiated by Einstein. In parentheses: Henry More actually anticipated Newton's notion of absolute space.

Why bother? After all, we get results in physics, in any applied science, without uniform interpretation of the term "space." Can't we become fine chess players without any knowledge of the basic mathematical principles underlying an axiomatized theory of chess? The philosopher might never dispense with reflective searches and deep cogitations, but the physicist is able to find workable data without delving into the whirlpool of explicit analysis concerning some fundamental concepts he mechanically employs.

Yet it is exactly the current crisis in physics which compels us to investigate the nature of space afresh. And this crisis, though not due to unexpected barriers protruding in our language, is nevertheless conspicuous in the limitations of the vernacular. Despite the incessant coinage of new technical terms or expressions, linguistic restrictions prevent us from expressing ourselves in regard to regions very far beyond common experience. It is a sad fact that we cannot "talk" mathematics, but merely communicate mathematical formalism. Philosophers of science have, at some time or other, encountered the fetters of anthropomorphism and become resigned to this inexorable biopsychological shortcoming, so to speak. In other words, there are situations, events, "interphenomena," on all levels of experience, to which our language, whether ordinary or technical, no longer applies. In such states we are content with internal consistency and coherence, with plausible or good reasons for believing that a certain event took place. Yet we are fully aware that talk about microphenomena and submicrophenomena can easily lead to vacuous assertions. Hence the question arises: How can our poor, relentlessly flogged language make any sense when we venture to describe events or situations in the microcosm? The answer is simple: through surrogates like analogies, models, idealizations.

When mathematicians—Menger, for instance [4]—attribute current deadlocks in theoretical physics to the lack of a new mathematical technique dealing with "lumps," not just with sets and aggregates, one can be almost assured that mathematicians will sooner or later remedy that defect. My argument touches upon a different domain, namely, the hard fact that there is no counterpart in the realm of ordinary language for certain physical states of affairs. That we persist in our scientific pursuits by resorting increasingly to symbols and refined mathematical techniques in no way helps us in our quandary. Abstract mathematical formalism can easily cope with a physics that seems forever to escape a formulation in common-sense language.

All troubles of western civilization have been imputed to Socrates, who was supposed to have poisoned our minds with logicality, rationalism, and critical reasoning. I do not share this prejudice—I have my own: all our troubles in current physical theory stem from Euclid. And now I shall illustrate why I consider Euclidean dogmatism responsible for much that went wrong in theoretical physics.

Euclid and many of his precursors and coevals held that we live and move in Euclidean space, that space is infinite and three-dimensional. This sounds harmless enough, but it is not, for nobody can possibly conceive of infinite space. For reasons too involved to elaborate in this brief paper, we have succumbed to the illusion that space is three-dimensional, and Minkowski's (or, if you wish, Einstein's) four-dimensional space-time continuum, which superseded Euclidean three-dimensional space, does not coincide with common sense, which urges us to regard length, breadth, and height as the "natural" framework of the world. It can be shown that the Euclidean myth reaches back to some Greek thinkers of the three centuries between Thales and Euclid, *but no farther*. It is, therefore, not true that the doctrine of an infinite space in three dimensions can be traced back through all recorded history into the darkness of the Stone Age. And since Euclidean space did not exist in nature, it could not be observed or copied by the geometers. Did they simply develop, in a logical manner, the inherent common-sense dispositions of the average Greek citizen? Cornford [1] apprised us of the highly probable existence of a pre-Euclidean common sense, whose conception of space had to be deliberately and artificially transformed into a Euclidean structure—just as our so-called Euclidean common sense has now to be adapted to the post-Euclidean pattern of relativity theory.

Unfortunately, the atomists made things worse by endowing Euclidean abstract space with unashamed physical existence. They decreed that there is an unlimited Void akin to the infinite space of the geometers. It sounds incredible, but the Pythagoreans, too, were consumed with that mysterious notion of space being the Void, even in arithmetic. We recall that they represented numbers by dots arranged in regular figures such as triangles and squares. The empty intervals between these units or dots, these gaps, were regarded as the Void. We still use the expressions "square numbers" and "cubes." Indeed, it can be established that the Pythagoreans conceived of numbers as points or "particles" in physical space.

As was to be expected, the resistance against the unholy alliance of Euclidean geometry and atomism, though solely confined to the postulate of an unlimited Void and infinite, continuous, geometrical space, was powerful and multitudinous: Parmenides, Empedocles, Aristotle, to mention only a few thinkers who believed in a spherical universe, finite, without Void. Anaximander speaks of the Boundless or Non-Limited, and it is tempting to equate this with Euclidean infinite space. However, when Aeschylus described women standing round an altar "in a boundless company," he meant nothing more than a circular arrangement!

This brief digression into Greek philosophy reminds us that the Einsteinian finite but unbounded space is close to the pre-Euclidean finite but boundless sphere of certain Greek thinkers; nor had the Homeric or pre-Homeric Greek any Euclidean "common sense." Hence, rigid Euclidean space with its infinite extensions and implicit inference of a

Void, as well as Euclidean physical space, is an artifact and not firmly anchored in man's historical development. We may liken Euclidean space to a steel framework and Einsteinian, non-Euclidean space to a lump of india rubber which can be twisted, kneaded, crumpled, and distorted as we wish. A legendary astronomer approved of the model of a spherical, finite universe because he was sure that he would eventually see the back of his head through "a sufficiently powerful telescope."

These remarks were merely to show that Euclidean space was not a constant property of the Greek mind or pre-Greek common sense. But one may suspect that this is all conjecture, biased selection, arbitrary speculation. (After all, college professors only too often have their feet firmly planted in the air.) Let us therefore try another avenue: an inquiry into the behavior pattern of the last survivors of man's rudimentary past—of infants, from the age of eight days up to eight years. These highly primitive "tribes," our children, provide excellent material for the study of initial space perception. During the last few years, some exciting work has been done in this field, in particular by the late Geza Révész [7], a Hungarian who taught at the University of Amsterdam. He investigated the nature of "haptic perception," i.e., perception of an object by means of the sense of touch, in the absence of visual stimulation. Tactile recognition of solids (which must be unseen objects) is haptic perception. Révész's original studies of the psychology of the blind were comprehensively pursued by Piaget and Inhelder [5, pages 3–193], de Planta, Morf, and Demitriades. The outcome of these observations and experiments is most illuminating, for it corroborates the view expressed here before, that Euclidean space is not innate—in fact, it has to be conquered the hard way.

During the period of pure reflexes and when primary habits are gradually acquired—in other words, in the stage of primitive and rudimentary perception—the child is capable of grasping only the most elementary spatial relationships, such as proximity, separation, order (that is, spatial succession, in particular symmetry), enclosure (or surrounding), and continuity. We may thus speak of a "haptic space," a space based upon these primitive perceptions which are definitely prior to visual perception and therefore to representational space. Objects might appear to the infant as global or syncretic wholes, by which we mean unanalyzed wholes whose elements are not yet related to each other in an operational manner, but soon the child becomes aware of the properties "bounded" or "connected."

The mathematically trained reader will have noted at once that I was just enumerating some characteristic features of topology, the study of the qualities of geometrical figures, that persist "even when the figures are subjected to deformations so drastic that all their metric and projective properties are lost" [2, page 235]. As we know, in topology there are no distinctions between circles, ellipses, and polygons, or between cubes and spheres. When two spaces are equivalent topologically, we call them homeomorphic; we mean by this that their points are in bicontinuous one-to-one correspondence. Obviously, all simple closed curves are homeomorphic with one another and also with all closed Euclidean figures (e.g., triangles, squares, and circles). Now, precise experiments with children at all ages prove that rigid shapes, distances, angles, projective relations, the constancy of shape and size, do not derive directly from rudimentary, that is, haptic, perception.

That recognition precedes cognition may sound illogical, but it depicts a true state of affairs. Even adults are prone to misconceptions concerning spatial orientation, as most of us know from not always amusing experience.

Révész found that thirty-five spatial illusions have their counterpart in optical illusions, but he nevertheless insisted upon the independence of haptic from optic function. Piaget and his team recorded that children at the age of 3½ to 6 years always readily recognized topological shapes, and only with some effort Euclidean figures. Circle and square could not be distinguished, for both are closed forms, but they were told apart from open forms. It is only during the ages of 6 to 8 years that geometrical Euclidean figures become increasingly differentiable. The process of translating tactile-kinesthetic perceptions into visual images poses further interesting questions. Does drawing express the child's haptic perception enriched by exploratory movements or does drawing belong to the domain of visual perception? We note that the tested children showed a distinct preference for curved shapes, in keeping with the topological propensity mentioned earlier.

A most perplexing result was registered when children were given a cut-out swastika. They had already acquired the habit of operation. In this context, operation means an action which can return to a starting point and, combined with other actions, is equally capable of reversibility. The operational phase is regarded as comparatively advanced, not to say sophisticated. Now, the children were able to draw some highly complicated geometrical figures, usually after many infelicitous attempts. But no child could reproduce correctly the swastika, which represents a perfectly respectable geometric figure. Of course, none of the children was acquainted with the emotional or political significance of this pattern.

It is not surprising that Révész indulged in some rather too distant, uncontrolled extrapolations concerning his original theory of haptic perception. Perhaps he was right in rejecting the view that visual perception can be regarded as the paradigm *Gestalt* as such, and certainly with respect to space. But he stipulated a somewhat foggy, amorphous basic function—some kind of primordial, protodisposition or instinct—from which all space-perceiving properties, tactile-kinesthetic as well as visual, are supposedly derived. There is not an iota of evidence for such a claim! I think we are more justified in maintaining that the construction of space begins on the haptic level, is followed by the visual level, and that these two levels form the perceptual layer of space-awareness; this phase is succeeded by the representational level with its pictorial space, until we finally reach the heights of conceptual space.

Let me repeat: topological relations are grasped much earlier and more easily than Euclidean shapes. Our education and our environment make us believe that there is a smooth, natural continuity between perceptual and representational relationships. The researches of Piaget and Inhelder have furnished invaluable and profound insight into this whole domain and have proved beyond doubt that such belief is untenable. It seems to me that the predominance of Euclidean geometry in our training has created deeply entrenched misorientations. There is a tremendous gap between haptic perception and mental representation, since the latter invokes the existence of objects in their physical absence. Semantic relations, image, thought, differentiation of diverse signs or symbols not only occur *after* haptic experience, but they differ fundamentally from it.

What are our conclusions from this swift excursion into the haptic region? Topology, a science of comparatively young age but becoming more and more applicable to the natural sciences, corresponds in many essential traits to man's most primitive, elementary experience. Mathematicians and logicians are familiar with the fact that chronological order does not always dovetail with logical order. Throughout the ages the mis-

conception that our adult spatial notions are immanent in our biopsychological makeup—in spite of some opposition by thinkers like Gauss and
especially Poincaré—has been cultivated and dogmatized with such success that Euclidean (I mean metric and projective) concepts have been
considered identical with intrinsic perceptual *Gestalten.*

Poincaré repeatedly stressed that experience does not prove the three-
dimensionality of space; he observed that it was merely convenient to assign three dimensions to space [6, pages 21–31]. But being foremost a
mathematician, he demonstrated that the qualities of the physical continuum do not match the exactitude of the mathematical continuum.

Physical continuum: $A = B, B = C, A < C$
Mathematical continuum: $A < B, B < C, A < C$

The term "physical continuum" was not a felicitous choice. Poincaré
was referring to some ingenious experimental results recorded by the
psychologists Weber and Fechner. They showed that the *psychophysical*
continuum, based on sensations, does not coincide with the mathematical
continuum. Poincaré concluded that in the physical realm equality is an
intransitive relation, whereas in mathematics equality is (trivially) a
transitive relation. Hence, in order to prove his case for conventionalism,
he pointed to the unreliable properties of the physical continuum. Still,
Révész has corrected this issue by drawing our attention to the *haptic
continuum* which conspicuously and drastically differs from and precedes
the physical continuum. Poincaré was nevertheless right, though for the
wrong reasons: our tactile perception is geometrically inferior to the Euclidean organization of projective and metrical relationships. On the
other hand, shortly before his death Révész made an extraordinary claim.
He argued that haptic perception is based upon structure, and this structure is the result of an analytic process; in contrast, visual perception is
based upon *Gestalt* and synthetically conditioned.

To relate the most elementary type of perception to something analytic
seems almost absurd. Moreover, he urges us to endow the haptic sense
with a cognitive function, while he relegates the optical sense to a mere
pictorially perceiving status. This is the way we are supposed to proceed:
first we touch a thing, grip it, explore its nature step by step and are simultaneously involved in a process of conceptualization. To call this procedure "analytic" indicates a somewhat unorthodox usage of our ordinary vocabulary. On the other hand, when we look at an object, we

first absorb it in its totality, and after that begin to determine the individual features. Again, to call this approach "synthetic" is slightly confusing. To top it all, not Euclidean geometry but the haptic sense alone is associated with metric properties.

These remarks were here presented to show that we move in a maze of very difficult notions, partly explored, partly conjectured, but perhaps suggesting an entirely novel attitude as regards language and consequently, if indirectly, as regards the terminology and conceptual approach of theoretical physics.

To summarize a few key points of the discussion:

1. Historical researches prove that Euclidean space is an artifact, in some respects even in conflict with common sense. Its simplicity made it appear to reflect ordinary experience. The objections to Euclidean space were proffered by metaphysicians whose assertions were often more "estranged" than those of the geometers.

2. Recent researches in experimental child psychology give us an insight into the role of the haptic sense, or haptic perception. It can be demonstrated that Euclidean concepts are *acquired*, are the outcome of operations such as movement, leading to systematic (!) exploration. The transition from haptic and later from visual perception to mental representations is affected by the language we use in our communication with the child, by toys, books, kindergarten environment, and most energetically by our school curricula—and thus we are reared in Euclidean terms, Euclidean relations, and finally in Euclidean dimensions of space.

3. Schrödinger advised us fellow-scientists to return to an "assiduous study of Greek thought" [8, page 16], in the obvious hope of thus discovering some "inveterate errors at the source." And the observation of little children's behavior patterns suggests that the "india-rubber" world of the topologist and of Einstein, though highly abstract to the uninitiated, and the haptic perception of the child are much closer to one another than haptic perception is to Euclidean shapes and spaces with their rigid properties. We saw that the child recognizes objects haptically at an early age. But once the level of representation is reached, the aid of speech is invoked and thereby all doors opened to Euclidean commitment.

So far we have illuminated a hitherto neglected aspect of our sensory experience, and thus of our language, with a few bright flashes. We ought now to direct some sharp and steady beams of light toward our initial problem, the oft-maligned incapacity of ordinary language to express the physical content of recent findings in nuclear and theoretical physics.

Language, as was shown by Waismann [10, pages 128–129], has definite distinguishable strata. In our motley account we found, not quite unexpectedly, that the stratum in which one deals with space and an adequate description of certain physical objects or events is vitiated by rigid, improper, almost incorrigible habits that were acquired between the sixth and third centuries B.C. The obnoxiously persevering and seemingly unshatterable idol of Euclidean space still haunts our scientific temples, because it boasts of being the incarnation of common sense. However, once we fall under the sway of an Einsteinian universe where matter is responsible for the manner in which we shape our own space, we can escape the fatal clutches of Euclidean space and find sanity in the salutary "india-rubber" world. In the model of such a universe the influence of Euclidean geometry shrinks to naught: topology and some abstract algebra take over. Whenever we employ evocative words like "close," "open," "near," "remote," "deep," "round," "behind," "after," "across," and so forth, we have entered, via the haptic sense, the promising plains of topology. Gradually one can detect "budding" haptic terms in algebra, terms which will sooner or later become incorporated in the language stratum that struggles with the findings of atomic and theoretical physics. I hope I am not guilty of non sequiturs of reasoning or perverse distortion of data when I maintain that the affinity of haptic experience with topological notions can indisputably be established.

It has been claimed by Waismann that "each stratum has a logic of its own and that logic determines the meaning of certain basic terms" [9, page 30]. I cannot subscribe to this alleged fact. Suppose there existed among us a neo-Cartesian searching for his identity who would formulate the following profundity (which I read somewhere): "I cannot think and do not know, therefore I am—or am I?" Well, if logic were no more than "an organized procedure for going wrong with confidence and certainty," we might take even such a weird concoction seriously. Our goal is a less eccentric one: not to contribute to any wallowing in verbiage, but to increase and intensify those expressions which link haptic-topological-algebraic "naive" terms with the corresponding mathematical formalism in future physical theory.

We need not be concerned any longer as to the fate of relativity theory, special and general. The days have passed when Lenard, Gehrcke, Fricke, O. Kraus, Mohorovičić, and similar crudely confused thinkers could ruthlessly fight Einstein's views in the name of so-called common sense or sane experience. Today the tribunal of scientifically and philosophically competent peers has arrived at its verdict without dissenting opinions: it is for Einstein and against (Euclidean) common sense. Besides, our common sense is definitely not Euclidean; moreover, one could with Poincaré contend that experience can neither confirm nor confute any geometry whatsoever; and finally, Menger has shown that Euclidean geometry does not even possess the virtue of logical simplicity.

The reader may be puzzled about this attempt to connect relativity theory with haptic perception and dismiss the arguments here submitted as signs of facile generalization, of a too "distant extrapolation." I cannot but admit that my conclusions are far from unassailable and that neither haptic exploration nor topology deserves to be extolled as the omnipotent nostrum for all our aches and pains in current physics. I am not certain that it is probable for anyone to find a topological counterpart for the line element

$$ds^2 = \sum_{i,j=1}^{4} g_{ij} \, d\,\xi^i \, d\,\xi^j,$$

where ds^2 is an invariant and the g_{ij} are the components of the so-called fundamental tensor. To form a measure, a "metric" (?) free from measurement in terms of rigidified elementary geometry and expressible in the protean language of analysis situs might prove an unactualizable enterprise. None the less, there seem to exist sufficient worthwhile intimations to vindicate the efforts of a protagonist, or apologist, in this unexplored field.

By contrast, the chances of utilizing haptic or rather topological considerations rewardingly in atomic physics, and especially in quantum field theory, must not, at present at least, be judged too optimistically as portending positive results. And yet rotation and Lorentz groups, and even permutation groups, occupy a prominent role in quantum physics, despite several not merely aesthetic flaws which prevented a truly blissful marriage of group theory and quantum mechanics. By the same token, a topological approach might, or might not, produce some valuable results where more orthodox means have failed.

At immediate hearing, the clangor of this proposal has indeed a hollow ring. It can be argued that some of our physical models possess heuristic value. It is, for instance, still permissible to picture an electron as a kind of very tiny sphere, with a determinable diameter. Are not spheres solid Euclidean figures? Practically all models in spatio-physical language are borrowed from Euclidean geometry. But this is exactly my point: we shall never be able to extricate ourselves from the turbid situation in which we are ensnared as long as we do not re-educate ourselves to reason in terms of topology and abstract algebra, and consider Euclidean geometry as no more than an obsolete abstraction, remote both from our haptic perception and from topological methods. If theoretically *conceptual* statements remain in contiguity with *experiential* propositions, however informal that contact may be, then the newly gained insight of the physicist will be translatable into a language that will satisfy the mandatory criterion of universal intersubjectivity.

Schrödinger never became completely reconciled to the particle concept, his occasional concession to atomistic views notwithstanding. He tried to preserve a minimum of pictorial perspicuity or picturability, that is, the three-dimensionality of the wave, by means of second quantization. This brilliant "trick" is theoretically profitable, but alas! the intended contact with "ordinary" space, and thus the desired picturability, is not attained at all. A topological treatment of this question might enable us to escape the dichotomy of three-dimensional versus multidimensional spaces and thus to interpret the wave function in a novel manner; also, the physical calamity of infinities may thereby cease to disturb us.

Failing proof to the contrary, it is safe to assume that atomicity will be upheld, in one way or another. By the latter remark I mean that hitherto we were confronted with naive atomism (to use L. L. Whyte's expression [12]) as propounded by the classical atomists from Leucippus to Rutherford; with a *puncta* atomism as conceived by Boscovich, who advocated the existence of quasi-material point particles; and with current atomism of elementary particles. Heisenberg's flight into a purely abstract, idealistic exegesis of the nature of atomism has "enriched" our kaleidoscope of atomisms. "The elementary particles are . . . the fundamental forms that the substance energy must take in order to become matter . . ." and are ". . . related rather more closely to the Platonic bodies than to the atoms of Democritus" [3, pages 16, 19]. To dispel some untoward effects of any one of these atomic theories, Schrödinger understandably pines for continuity in contrast to any kind of atomism, to the extent that he regards micro-interaction as a continuous phenomenon. Moreover, it is a source of constant uneasiness that (discontinuous) quantum theory is impaired by the occurrence of divergent integrals. On the other hand, the physical arguments in favor of atomicity are so persuasive that it almost looks as if one may have to relinquish the notion of the continuous field altogether. I personally believe that Schrödinger's eagerness to advocate the legitimacy of a continuity viewpoint as more realistic has led him astray: the fact that continuity is successful as far as mathematical formalism is concerned cannot compensate for the strong confluence of numerous convincing arguments in favor of atomicity.

In relativity theory Riemann's conception of space admits topological ideas which are not merely different from those given in Euclidean space. A topological "reading" of the discontinuity in quantum physics—energy levels are discrete sets of states—and of the genuine atomicity of fundamental particles is facilitated by the existence of discrete manifolds. Besides, Weyl [11, pages 90–91] has already emphasized that the so-called continua are in reality only vaguely presented, whereas the discontinuity of discrete aggregates allows for absolute accuracy in dealing with an individual case.

The foregoing remarks do not claim any spectacular originality and cover, to some extent, familiar ground. Certain recent studies have established the pristine authority of haptic perception and discovered the dependence of Euclidean geometry upon the visual sense. The relation between haptic experience and topology can easily be shown. Haptic perception is also compatible with the spatial notions of relativity theory. It remains to be seen whether one can apply topological reasoning, in particular the principles and methods of anschauliche topology, to quantum physics. Mathematicians conceive of topology as the study of continuity. However, certain topological spaces, homology groups, and homotopic mappings might permit us to treat the discrete manifolds and individual cases in elementary particle physics. Field theory (continuous) is amenable to satisfactory mathematization, but leads to severe difficulties in its combination with atomistic particle concepts. There are, however, some grounds for dimming any gleam of hope that topological methods will furnish fruitful results in wave mechanics and the physics of elementary particles.

Qui nimium probat nihil probat. The truth of this saying should not prevent us from exploring an exciting avenue. After all, negative results could mean no more than that someone has made a fool of himself; in the history of science greater risks have been taken.

REFERENCES

1. Cornford, F. M. "The Invention of Space," in *Essays in Honour of Gilbert Murray,* pp. 215–235. London: Allen and Unwin, 1936.
2. Courant, Richard, and Herbert Robbins. *What Is Mathematics?* New York: Oxford University Press, 1941.
3. Heisenberg, Werner. "Planck's Discovery and the Philosophical Problems of Atomic Physics," in *On Modern Physics,* by Werner Heisenberg and others, pp. 3–19. New York: Clarkson Potter, 1961.
4. Menger, Karl. "The Theory of Relativity and Geometry," in *Albert Einstein: Philosopher-Scientist,* Paul A. Schilpp, ed., pp. 457–474. Evanston, Ill.: Library of Living Philosophers, 1949. See especially Parts 4 and 5, pp. 469–474.
5. Piaget, Jean, and Bärbel Inhelder. *The Child's Conception of Space.* London: Routledge and Kegan Paul, 1956.
6. Poincaré, Henri. *Science and Hypothesis.* New York: Dover, 1952.
7. Révész, Geza. "Optik und Haptik," *Studium Generale,* 6:374–379 (1957).
8. Schrödinger, Erwin. *Nature and the Greeks.* Cambridge: Cambridge University Press, 1954.
9. Waismann, Friedrich. "Language Strata," in *Logic and Language,* second series, Antony Flew, ed., pp. 11–31. Oxford: Blackwell, 1953.
10. Waismann, Friedrich. "Verifiability," in *Logic and Language,* first series, Antony Flew, ed., pp. 117–144. Oxford: Blackwell, 1951.
11. Weyl, Hermann. *Philosophy of Mathematics and Natural Science.* Princeton: Princeton University Press, 1949.
12. Whyte, L. L. "Boscovich's Atomism," in *Roger Joseph Boscovich,* L. L. Whyte, ed., pp. 102–126. London: Allen and Unwin, 1961.

GENERAL SOURCES

Alexandroff, P. *Einfachste Grundbegriffe der Topologie.* Berlin: Julius Springer, 1932.
Broad, C. D. *Scientific Thought.* London: Routledge and Kegan Paul, 1923.
Brotman, H. "Could Space be Four Dimensional?" in *Essays in Conceptual Analysis,* Antony Flew, ed., pp. 253–265. London: Macmillan, 1956.
Fierz, M. "Isaac Newtons Lehre vom absoluten Raum," *Studium Generale,* 8:464–470 (1957).
Hesse, Mary. *Forces and Fields.* London: Thomas Nelson, 1961.
Jammer, Max. *Concepts of Space.* Cambridge: Harvard University Press, 1954.
Lietzmann, W. *Anschauliche Topologie.* Munich: R. Oldenbourg, 1955.
Linschotten, J. "Anthropologische Fragen zur Raumproblematik," *Studium Generale,* 2:86–99 (1958).
Mohorovičić, S. *Die Einsteinsche Relativitätstheorie und ihr mathematischer, physikalischer und philosophischer Charakter.* Berlin: Walter de Gruyter, 1923.
Niemeyer, L. "Das Wesen der Geometrie," *Studium Generale,* 5:292–295 (1957).
Patterson, E. M. *Topology.* Edinburgh: Oliver and Boyd, 1956.

ABOUT THE CONTRIBUTORS

About the Contributors

BRUCE AUNE is an associate professor of philosophy at the University of Pittsburgh. He has published papers in scholarly journals and has contributed to *Philosophy in America*, edited by Max Black. A book by him on epistemology and the philosophy of mind will appear in 1966.

MAY BRODBECK is a professor of philosophy at the University of Minnesota. She has written numerous articles for journals and books on the philosophy of science and is a member of the editorial board of the journal *Philosophy of Science*. She is co-editor with Herbert Feigl of *Readings in the Philosophy of Science*.

CHARLES E. BURES is an associate professor of philosophy at the California Institute of Technology, and teaches both philosophy and psychology. He has contributed to various journals, including *Philosophy of Science* and *Journal of Philosophy*.

RUDOLF CARNAP, professor emeritus of philosophy of the University of California in Los Angeles, previously taught at Vienna, Prague, and Chicago. Among his books are *The Logical Syntax of Language*, *Logical Foundations of Probability*, *Introduction to Semantics*, and *Meaning and Necessity*.

RUDOLF EKSTEIN (Ph.D., Vienna) is a training analyst at the Los Angeles Institute for Psychoanalysis and director of the Project on Childhood Psychosis at the Reiss-Davis Clinic. He has published a number of psychological and psychoanalytic papers and, with R. S. Wallerstein, a book, *The Teaching and Learning of Psychotherapy*.

PAUL K. FEYERABEND (Ph.D., Vienna) is a professor of philosophy at the University of California, Berkeley. He has published numerous papers on philosophy, science, and the philosophy of science in journals and books.

[509]

He has engaged in research and teaching in Vienna, Copenhagen, London, Minneapolis, and other places.

ANTONY FLEW is a professor of philosophy at the University of Keele, Staffordshire, England, and has also taught and lectured in the United States. He is the author of *Hume's Philosophy of Belief* and *Body, Mind and Death*, and the editor of other books.

ADOLF GRÜNBAUM is a professor of philosophy and director of the Center for Philosophy of Science at the University of Pittsburgh. He is the author of *Philosophical Problems of Space and Time* and has contributed to journals of philosophy and science and to anthologies. He is president of the Philosophy of Science Association for 1965–1968, and a member of the board of editors of *Philosophy of Science*, *American Philosophical Quarterly*, and *The Encyclopedia of Philosophy*.

NORWOOD RUSSELL HANSON is a professor of philosophy at Yale, having previously taught at Indiana University. He is the author of *Patterns of Discovery* and *The Concept of the Positron: A Philosophical Analysis*, as well as articles on the history and philosophy of science.

E. L. HILL is a professor of physics and mathematics at the University of Minnesota. He has published articles in his field in *Physical Review*, *Journal of Geophysical Research*, *Reviews of Modern Physics*, and other journals, and was managing editor of *Physical Review* in 1950. He has also contributed to books on the philosophy of science.

WOLFGANG KÖHLER is a professor of psychology at Dartmouth College. From 1913 to 1920 he was director of an anthropoid station in the Canary Islands, from 1920 to 1935 head of the psychology department of the University of Berlin, and from 1935 to 1957 professor at Swarthmore College. In 1958–1959 he was president of the American Psychological Association. His books include *The Mentality of Apes*, *Gestalt Psychology*, *The Place of Values in a World of Facts*, and *Dynamics in Psychology*.

VICTOR KRAFT succeeded Moritz Schlick as professor of philosophy at the University of Vienna. He is the author of *Die Grundformen der wissenschaftlichen Methoden*, *Erkenntnislehre*, and (in English translation) *The Vienna Circle: The Origin of Neo-Positivism*, a history and analysis of the movement with which he has been associated since its beginnings.

WALLACE I. MATSON is a professor of philosophy at the University of California, Berkeley, and has also taught at the University of Hawaii. He is the author of *The Existence of God* and articles in philosophical journals.

GROVER MAXWELL is a professor of philosophy at the University of Minnesota and in the Minnesota Center for Philosophy of Science. He is co-editor with Herbert Feigl of Volumes II and III of the *Minnesota Studies in the Philosophy of Science* and *Current Issues in the Philosophy of Science*, and has published articles in philosophical periodicals and books.

PAUL E. MEEHL is a professor of psychology and clinical psychology at the University of Minnesota. He is the author of *Clinical versus Statistical Prediction*, as well as of many articles on psychology, psychotherapy, and the philosophy of mind. Besides teaching, he is engaged in psychiatric research and the private practice of psychotherapy.

HENRYK MEHLBERG is a professor of philosophy at the University of Chicago. He has also taught at the Universities of Lodz and Wroclaw in Poland, at Toronto, and at Princeton. He is the author of *La théorie causale du temps*, *Science et positivisme*, and *The Reach of Science*, as well as journal and book contributions in the philosophy of science.

STEPHEN C. PEPPER, professor emeritus of art and philosophy at the University of California, Berkeley, was chairman of each department successively. His books include *Aesthetic Quality*, *World Hypotheses*, *The Basis of Criticism in the Arts*, *The Sources of Value*, and *Ethics*.

SIR KARL R. POPPER is a professor of logic and scientific method at the London School of Economics and Political Science (University of London). Among his books are *The Open Society and Its Enemies*, *The Poverty of Historicism*, *The Logic of Scientific Discovery*, and *Conjectures and Refutations*.

CARROLL C. PRATT, emeritus professor of psychology, Princeton University, previously taught at Harvard, Rutgers, and Ankara. He is the author of *The Meaning of Music*, *The Logic of Modern Psychology*, and *Psychology: The Third Dimension of War*.

WESLEY C. SALMON is a professor of philosophy of science at Indiana University. He is the author of *Logic* in the *Foundations of Philosophy* series and of many articles in philosophical journals, and co-editor of the *Contemporary Perspectives in Philosophy* series. He is chairman of the United States National Committee of the International Union for the History and Philosophy of Science.

MICHAEL SCRIVEN is a professor of the history and philosophy of science at Indiana University, before which he was at Swarthmore College and the University of Minnesota. He is consulting editor of the *International Journal of Psychiatry* and has published in books and journals in philosophy, philosophy of science, philosophy of history, and psychology.

WILFRID SELLARS is a professor of philosophy and research professor at the Center for Philosophy of Science at the University of Pittsburgh. He had previously taught at Iowa, Minnesota, and Yale. He was a founding member of the Minnesota Center for Philosophy of Science and, with Her-

ABOUT THE CONTRIBUTORS

bert Feigl, is co-editor of *Philosophical Studies*. He is the author of *Science, Perception and Reality* and many articles and essays in philosophical journals and books.

J. J. C. SMART is a professor of philosophy at the University of Adelaide, Australia. He is the author of *An Outline of a System of Utilitarian Ethics, Philosophy and Scientific Realism*, and articles and essays, and editor of *Problems of Space and Time*.

S. S. STEVENS is a professor of psychophysics and director of the Laboratory of Psychophysics at Harvard University, where he has taught since 1936. He is the author of *Hearing: Its Psychology and Physiology* and other books in psychology and audiology, and has written numerous articles for scientific journals. He edited the *Handbook of Experimental Psychology*.

HENRY B. VEATCH is a professor of philosophy at Northwestern University and was formerly Distinguished Service Professor at Indiana University. He is the author of *Intentional Logic, Realism and Nominalism Revisited, Logic as a Human Instrument* (with Francis H. Parker), and *Rational Man*.

WOLFGANG YOURGRAU is a professor of philosophy of science at the University of Denver. Previously he taught at Berlin, Jerusalem, Capetown, Johannesburg, Natal, Carleton, Smith, Amherst, and Mt. Holyoke. He is the co-author of two books in theoretical physics and has published a number of papers in physical and philosophical journals.

THE WRITINGS OF HERBERT FEIGL

Bibliography of the
Writings of Herbert Feigl, to December 1965

1. "Zufall und Gesetz," in *Wissenschaftlicher Jahresbericht der Philosophischen Gesellschaft an der Universität zu Wien.* 1927/28. (A summary of H. Feigl's doctoral dissertation. Manuscript available at University of Vienna.)
2. *Theorie und Erfahrung in der Physik.* Karlsruhe: G. Braun, 1929.
3. "Wahrscheinlichkeit und Erfahrung," *Erkenntnis*, 1:249–259 (1930).
4. "Logical Positivism" (with A. E. Blumberg), *Journal of Philosophy*, 28:281–296 (1931).
5. "The Logical Character of the Principle of Induction," *Philosophy of Science*, 1:20–29 (1934). Also in H. Feigl and W. Sellars, eds., *Readings in Philosophical Analysis*. New York: Appleton-Century-Crofts, 1949.
6. "Logical Analysis of the Psycho-Physical Problem," *Philosophy of Science*, 1:420–445 (1934).
7. Discussion "The Principle of Induction" (letter replying to Professor Homer H. Dubs), *Philosophy of Science*, 1:484–486 (1945).
8. Discussion "Spatial Location and the Psychophysical Problem" (a reply to V. C. Aldrich), *Philosophy of Science*, 2:257–261 (1935).
9. "Sense and Nonsense in 'Scientific' Realism," *Actes du Congrès International de Philosophie Scientifique*. Paris: Sorbonne, 1936.
10. "Moritz Schlick," *Erkenntnis*, 7:393–419 (1939).
11. "The Significance of Physics in Man's Philosophy," *American Physics Teacher*, 7:324–327 (1939).
12. "The Meaning of Freedom," *The Interpreter* (University of Minnesota), 17:1–2 (December 1942).
13. "Logical Empiricism," in D. D. Runes, ed., *Twentieth Century Philosophy*. New York: Philosophical Library, 1943. Reprinted with omissions in H. Feigl and W. Sellars, eds., *Readings in Philosophical Analysis*. New York: Appleton-Century-Crofts, 1949. Also reprinted with omissions in M. Mandelbaum, F. W. Gramlich, A. R. Anderson, eds., *Philosophic Problems*. New York: Macmillan, 1957. See also Nos. 35 and 57 below for partial reprintings under new titles.
14. "Operationism and Scientific Method," *Psychological Review*, 52:250–259 (1945). Also in H. Feigl and W. Sellars, eds., *Readings in Philosophical Analysis*. New York: Appleton-Century-Crofts, 1949.
15. "Rejoinders and Second Thoughts" (on the Meaning of Scientific Explanation),

Psychological Review, 52:284–288 (1945). Reprinted with slight alterations in H. Feigl and W. Sellars, eds., *Readings in Philosophical Analysis*. New York: Appleton-Century-Crofts, 1949.

16. "Naturalism and Humanism: An Essay on Some Issues of General Education and a Critique of Current Misconceptions Regarding Scientific Method and the Scientific Outlook in Philosophy," *American Quarterly*, 1:135–148 (1949). See No. 33 below for reprinting under new title.

17. *Readings in Philosophical Analysis* (co-editor with Wilfrid Sellars). New York: Appleton-Century-Crofts, 1949.

18. "De Principiis non Disputandum . . . ? On the Meaning and the Limits of Justification," in Max Black, ed., *Philosophical Analysis*. Ithaca, N.Y.: Cornell University Press, 1950; Englewood Cliffs, N.J., Prentice-Hall, 1963. Reprinted in part in Y. H. Krikorian and A. Edel, eds., *Contemporary Philosophic Problems*. New York: Macmillan, 1959.

19. "Existential Hypotheses: Realistic versus Phenomenalistic Interpretations," *Philosophy of Science*, 17:35–62 (1950).

20. "Logical Reconstruction, Realism and Pure Semiotic," *Philosophy of Science*, 17: 186–195 (1950).

21. "The Mind-Body Problem in the Development of Logical Empiricism," *Revue Internationale de Philosophie*, 4:64–83 (1950). Reprinted in H. Feigl and May Brodbeck, eds., *Readings in the Philosophy of Science*. New York: Appleton-Century-Crofts, 1953.

22. "Bibliography of Logical Empiricism," *Revue Internationale de Philosophie*, 4:95–102 (1950).

23. "Felix Kaufmann's Conception of Philosophy as Clarification," *Twelfth Street*, 3:12–13 (1950).

24. Review of K. R. Popper's "A Note on Natural Laws and Contrary to Fact Conditionals," *Journal of Symbolic Logic*, 15:144–145 (1950).

25. "The Difference between Knowledge and Valuation," *Journal of Social Issues*, 6:39–44 (1950).

26. "Logical Positivism," in *Collier's Encyclopedia*, 1950.

27. "Confirmability and Confirmation," *Revue Internationale de Philosophie*, 5:268–279 (1951). Reprinted in P. P. Wiener, ed., *Readings in Philosophy of Science*. New York: Charles Scribner's Sons, 1953.

28. "Principles and Problems of Theory Construction in Psychology," in W. Dennis, ed., *Current Trends in Psychological Theory*. Pittsburgh: University of Pittsburgh Press, 1951.

29. "Validation and Vindication: An Analysis of the Nature and the Limits of Ethical Arguments," in W. Sellars and J. Hospers, eds., *Readings in Ethical Theory*. New York: Appleton-Century-Crofts, 1952.

30. *Readings in the Philosophy of Science* (co-editor with May Brodbeck). New York: Appleton-Century-Crofts, 1953.

31. "Unity of Science and Unitary Science," in H. Feigl and May Brodbeck, eds., *Readings in the Philosophy of Science*. New York: Appleton-Century-Crofts, 1953.

32. "Notes on Causality," in H. Feigl and May Brodbeck, eds., *Readings in the Philosophy of Science*. New York: Appleton-Century-Crofts, 1953 .

33. "The Scientific Outlook: Naturalism and Humanism," in H. Feigl and May Brodbeck, eds., *Readings in the Philosophy of Science*. New York: Appleton-Century-Crofts, 1953.

34. "Scientific Method without Metaphysical Presuppositions," *Philosophical Studies*, 5:17–31 (1954).

35. "Meanings in Ethical Discourse" (reprint in part of No. 13 above), in J. L. Jarrett and S. M. McMurrin, eds., *Contemporary Philosophy*. New York: Henry Holt, 1954.

36. "Physicalism and the Foundations of Psychology" (résumé), in *Proceedings of the*

Second International Congress of the International Union for the Philosophy of Science. Zurich, 1954.

37. "Aims of Education for Our Age of Science: Reflections of a Logical Empiricist," in *The Fifty-Fourth Yearbook of the National Society for the Study of Education,* Part I, pp. 304–341. Chicago: University of Chicago Press, 1955. Reprinted in part in *American Physics Teacher,* 2:295–296 (1964).

38. "Functionalism, Psychological Theory, and the Uniting Sciences," *Psychological Review,* 62:232–235 (1955).

39. "Major Issues and Developments in the Philosophy of Science of Logical Empiricism," *Proceedings of the International Congress for Philosophy of Science.* Zurich, 1955. Reprinted in H. Feigl and M. Scriven, eds., *Minnesota Studies in the Philosophy of Science, Volume I: The Foundations of Science and the Concepts of Psychology and Psychoanalysis.* Minneapolis: University of Minnesota Press, 1956.

40. Review of J. R. Newman, ed., *What Is Science?* in *Contemporary Psychology,* 1:275–276 (1956).

41. "Das hypothetisch-konstruktive Denken: Zur Methodologie der Naturwissenschaft," *Deutsche Universitätszeitung,* 23/24:8–13 (1956).

42. "Levels of Scientific Inquiry," *University of Minnesota Medical Bulletin,* 28:90–97 (1956).

43. *Minnesota Studies in the Philosophy of Science, Volume I: The Foundations of Science and the Concepts of Psychology and Psychoanalysis* (co-editor with M. Scriven). Minneapolis: University of Minnesota Press, 1956.

44. "Comments," in R. Lepley, ed., *The Language of Value.* New York: Columbia University Press, 1957.

45. "Empiricism versus Theology," in A. Pap and P. Edwards, eds., *A Modern Introduction to Philosophy.* Glencoe, Ill.: The Free Press, 1957.

46. *Minnesota Studies in the Philosophy of Science, Volume II: Concepts, Theories, and the Mind-Body Problem* (co-editor with M. Scriven and G. Maxwell). Minneapolis: University of Minnesota Press, 1958.

47. "The 'Mental' and the 'Physical,'" in H. Feigl, M. Scriven, and G. Maxwell, eds., *Minnesota Studies in the Philosophy of Science, Volume II: Concepts, Theories, and the Mind-Body Problem.* Minneapolis: University of Minnesota Press, 1958.

48. "Other Minds and the Egocentric Predicament," *Journal of Philosophy,* 55:978–987 (1958).

49. "A Note on Justification and Reconstruction," *Philosophical Studies,* 9:70–72 (1958).

50. "Philosophical Embarrassments of Psychology," *American Psychologist,* 14:115–128 (1959). Reprinted in *Psychologische Beiträge,* 6:340–364 (1962).

51. "Critique of Intuition According to Scientific Empiricism," *Philosophy East-West,* 8:1–16 (1958).

52. "Mind-Body, Not a Pseudoproblem," in S. Hook, ed., *Dimensions of Mind.* New York: New York University Press, 1960. Reprinted in Jordan Scher, ed., *Theories of the Mind.* New York: The Free Press of Glencoe, 1962.

53. *Current Issues in the Philosophy of Science* (co-editor with G. Maxwell). New York: Holt, Rinehart, and Winston, 1961.

54. "Philosophical Tangents of Science," Vice Presidential Address, Proceedings of Section L of the American Association for the Advancement of Science, 1959, published in H. Feigl and G. Maxwell, eds., *Current Issues in the Philosophy of Science.* New York: Holt, Rinehart, and Winston, 1961.

55. "On the Vindication of Induction," *Philosophy of Science,* 28:212–216 (1961).

56. "Why Ordinary Language Needs Reforming" (with G. Maxwell), *Journal of Philosophy,* 58:488–498 (1961).

57. "The Meaning of Positivism" (reprint in part of No. 13 above), in R. N. Beck, ed., *Perspectives in Philosophy.* New York: Holt, Rinehart, and Winston, 1961.

58. "Matter Still Largely Material" (symposium paper written for the St. Louis meeting of the American Philosophical Association, May 5, 1961), in *Philosophy of Science*, 29:39–46 (1962). Reprinted in E. McMullin, ed., *The Concept of Matter*. Notre Dame, Ind.: University of Notre Dame Press, 1963.
59. Review of A. J. Ayer, ed., *Logical Positivism*, in *Contemporary Psychology*, 6:88–89 (1961).
60. *Minnesota Studies in the Philosophy of Science*, Volume III: *Scientific Explanation, Space, and Time* (co-editor with G. Maxwell). Minneapolis: University of Minnesota Press, 1962.
61. "Modernized Theology and the Scientific Outlook," *The Humanist*, 23:74–80 (1963).
62. "The Power of Positivistic Thinking, An Essay on the Quandaries of Transcendence," in the *Proceedings and Addresses of the American Philosophical Association*, 36:21–42 (1963).
63. "Towards a Philosophy for Our Age of Science," in *Proceedings of the XIIIth International Congress of Philosophy* (Mexico City), 4:101–110 (1963).
64. "What Hume Might Have Said to Kant," in M. Bunge, ed., *The Critical Approach*. New York. The Free Press, 1964.
65. "From Logical Positivism to Hypercritical Realism," in *Proceedings of the XIIIth International Congress of Philosophy* (Mexico City), 5:427–436 (1964).
66. "Everybody Talks about the Temperature: Satirical Theme and Variations on the Nature of Value Judgments," in *Festschrift for Jørgen Jørgensen*. Copenhagen: Munksgaard, 1964.
67. "Philosophy of Science," in Richard Schlatter, ed., *Humanistic Scholarship in America*. Englewood Cliffs, N.J.: Prentice-Hall, 1964.
68. "Physicalism, Unity of Science and the Foundations of Psychology," in P. A. Schilpp, ed., *The Philosophy of Rudolf Carnap*. La Salle, Ill.: Open Court, 1964.
69. "Some Remarks on the Logic of Scientific Explanation," in *A Broader View of Research in the University*. Mimeographed. Minneapolis: Department of Chemical Engineering, University of Minnesota, 1964.
70. "Logical Positivism after Thirty-Five Years," in *Philosophy Today*, 8:228–245 (1964).
71. "Modernisierte Theologie und Wissenschaftliche Weltanschauung" (translation of No. 60 above), in *Club Voltaire: Jahrbuch für Writische Aufklärung*. Munich: Szczesny Verlag, 1965.
72. "Models of Man," *The Humanist*, 25:260–261 (1965).

NAME INDEX

Name Index

NAME INDEX

Democritus, 298, 503
Descartes, René, 98, 382
Dewey, John, 241–242
Dirac, Paul M., 427
Donagan, Alan, 397n
Dreyer, J. L. E., 424–426
DuBois-Reymond, 126
Duhem, Pierre, 273–276, 282–295
Duncker, Karl, 79
Dyson, F. J., 449n, 450, 462

Eckart, Carl Henry, 418
Eddington, Arthur S., 118, 167n, 185, 270–271, 456, 483
Ehrenfest, Paul, 437–438
Eilstein, Helena, 10
Einstein, Albert, 8, 61, 283–295, 371, 449, 452, 460, 461n, 462–463, 466–467, 485, 494, 500, 502
Ellis, Albert, 10
Ellis, Brian, 295n, 299, 304
Empedocles, 93, 495
Euclid, 421, 463, 492, 494–495
Eveling, H. S., 262

Fajans, Kurt, 6
Fechner, Gustav T., 224–225, 499
Feigl, Herbert, 3–9, 7n, 11–13, 17–38, 45n, 60–61, 65, 68, 70, 74–75, 80, 90, 92–93, 95–96, 99, 101–103, 108–109, 112, 120–121, 136, 140, 142–143, 151, 153–154, 161, 165, 168–172, 173n, 174–176, 178, 181, 185, 191, 215–216, 218–220, 306, 309–317, 319, 326, 328–332, 334–337, 341–342, 354–355, 358, 377, 379, 381, 389, 391–392, 404, 413
Février, Paulette, 456
Feyerabend, Paul, 10, 12, 108n, 126, 153–154, 178, 306n, 378
Feynman, Paul, 447, 450
Finetti, Bruno de, 257
Flew, Antony, 10
Fliess, Robert, 63
Fock, U., 462, 471–474
Fraenkel-Brunswik, Else, 10
Frank, Philipp, 8, 60, 462, 473
Frege, Gottlob, 486
Freud, Sigmund, 59, 63–66, 68, 128
Fricke, H., 502
Fromm, Erich, 246
Fuller, Margaret, 187

Galileo, 40, 48
Gauss, Karl, 493, 499

Geach, Peter, 393
Gehrcke, E., 502
Gel'fand, I. M., 447
Gellner, Ernest, 261–262, 265, 271, 377n
Gödel, Kurt, 486–488
Gomperz, Heinrich, 343
Goodman, Nelson, 216, 357, 375
Gotlind, Erik, 10
Goudge, T. A., 377n
Graetz, Leo, 6
Groddeck, Georg, 68
Grünbaum, Adolf, 10

Hahn, Hans, 6
Hall, A. R., 424–426
Hallowell, A. Irving, 242–243
Hamilton, William R., 443, 464
Hanson, Norwood Russell, 10
Harré, R., 262n
Hathaway, Starke, 10
Hawkins, David J. B., 397n
Heisenberg, Werner, 184, 427, 441–442, 457, 503
Helmholtz, Hermann von, 79
Hempel, Carl G., 10, 209n, 321, 354, 357, 364–365, 367–368
Henderson, L. J., 216
Hering, Ewald, 79–80
Hesse, Mary B., 322
Hilbert, David, 421, 463, 486, 492
Hill, E. L., 10, 442, 449n
Hipparchos, 417
Hobart, R. E., 385–386
Hocking, William E., 215
Hollitscher, Walter, 4
Homer, 93, 97, 101
Hook, Sidney, 66, 68
Hospers, John, 63
Howells, T. H., 133
Hume, David, 260n, 297n, 385, 392, 395n
Huntington, E. V., 216
Hurst, C. A., 379n
Huygens, Christiaan, 423

Ignatowsky, W. von, 462, 473
Inhelder, Bärbel, 496, 498
Ingarden, Roman, 10

Jacobi, Carl G. J., 443
James, William, 99, 184, 220
Jeffrey, Richard C., 260n

Kandinsky, Wassily, 8

NAME INDEX

Kant, Immanuel, 213, 392–393, 493
Kaplan, Abraham, 10
Kendler, Howard, 10
Keynes, John M., 251
Klee, Paul, 8
Klein, Melanie, 65
Kneale, William K., 399
Koch, Sigmund, 10, 246–247
Kraft, Julius, 343
Kraft, Victor, 3–4
Kraus, O., 502
Kris, Ernst, 62–63
Kubie, Lawrence, 246–247
Külpe, Oswald, 7
Kuhn, Thomas, 424–426

Lachs, John, 143
Landé, Alfred, 10
Laudan, Laurens, 274, 281–282
Laue, Max von, 6
Lazerowitz, Morris, 268
Leibniz, Gottfried W., 33, 100, 421, 484–486
Leith, G. O. M., 262
Lenard, Phillipp, 502
Leucippus, 503
Lewis, C. I., 147, 215
Lindzey, Gardner, 10
Linton, Ralph, 240
Locke, John, 48–49
Luce, R. David, 230
Luria, S., 298n

MacCorquodale, Kenneth, 10
Mack, J. D., 230
MacLane, Saunders, 216
Malcolm, Norman, 262–263, 266–271, 416, 417
Margenau, Henry, 10, 284
Maslow, Abraham, 246
Maxwell, Grover, 10, 11, 108n, 261
Maxwell, James C., 453, 472
Meehl, Paul E., 10, 103, 125, 132
Mehlberg, Henryk, 10
Menger, Karl, 494, 502
Meyer, Max, 218
Meyerson, Émile, 451
Michelson, Albert A., 449
Mill, John Stuart, 198, 311
Milne, E. A., 455, 461
Minkowski, Hermann, 469, 484, 494
Mises, Richard von, 8, 216
Mohorovičić, A., 502
Montaigne, M., 492

Moore, G. E., 262, 263, 265, 415–416, 419, 421–423, 427–428
More, Henry, 493
Morf, M. A., 496
Morgenstern, Oskar, 216
Münzer, Egmont, 6

Nagel, Ernest, 10, 59, 238
Neumann, John von, 371, 373, 442, 456–457, 464, 489
Neurath, Otto, 8, 248
Newton, Isaac, 297, 421, 423, 432, 484, 493
Nietzsche, Friedrich, 61–62
Northrop, F. S. C., 275–276, 284
Nowell-Smith, P. H., 385

Oppenheim, Paul, 10
Oppenheimer, J. Robert, 67

Pap, Arthur, 3–5, 10
Parmenides, 495
Pasquinelli, Alberto, 10
Pauli, Wolfgang, 8, 444, 462, 471–474
Peano, Guiseppe, 463
Peirce, Charles S., 401
Peirce, John R., 411
Pepper, Stephen, 10
Perry, Ralph Barton, 215
Pfänder, Ludwig, 6
Piaget, Jean, 496, 497, 498
Pieri, Mario, 463
Place, U. T., 381
Planta, E. de, 496
Poincaré, Henri, 283, 499, 502
Polya, George, 216
Popper, Karl R., 4, 7, 10, 248–251, 256, 319–320, 324–326, 399, 402–403, 412n
Price, Derek, 424–426
Price, H. H., 70
Ptolemy, 418, 424
Putnam, Hilary, 10, 279

Quine, Willard V. O., 8, 215, 276–281, 288, 359, 368, 374

Ramsey, Frank P., 257
Rapaport, David, 65
Reichenbach, Hans, 209n, 283–284, 292, 304, 307–317, 358, 366, 371n, 456, 459–461
Reid, S. R., 10
Reik, Theodor, 68
Révész, Geza, 496–499

[523]

NAME INDEX

Richards, I. A., 8, 216
Richman, R. J., 262n, 268, 270
Riehl, Aloys, 7
Riemann, Bernhard, 297, 299–301, 304, 504
Ritchie, Benbow F., 10
Robb, Alfred A., 461
Robertson, H. P., 460–461
Rogers, Carl, 246
Rohrmoser, Günther, 12
Rothe, H., 462, 473
Rozeboom, William, 10
Rugg, Harold, 246
Runyon, Damon, 264
Russell, Bertrand, 8, 128, 421, 451, 486
Ryle, Gilbert, 10, 27, 101

St. John, 97
Salmon, Wesley, 322
Sarton, George, 216
Schachtel, Ernest G., 243, 246
Schlegel, Richard, 10
Schlesinger, George, 11, 295–297, 299, 302–305, 322
Schlick, Moritz, 6–7, 62, 371, 451
Schrödinger, Erwin, 418, 427, 464, 500, 503–504
Schumpeter, Joseph A., 215
Schwinger, Julian, 450, 454
Scriven, Michael, 11
Sellars, Roy Wood, 213n
Sellars, Wilfrid, 11, 28–29, 103, 108n, 125, 128, 130–131, 143n, 167n, 177, 420
Shakow, David, 62–63
Sheffer, H. M., 215, 421
Skinner, B. F., 25–26, 89, 145, 189–190
Smart, J. J. C., 393–394, 396–397
Smoluchowski, Maryan von, 409–412
Socrates, 494
Sommerfeld, Arnold, 6
Spence, Kenneth W., 11
Spinoza, Baruch de, 186–187
Stebbing, L. Susan, 270–271
Stevens, J. C., 230

Stevens, S. S., 8
Strawson, Peter F., 11, 382
Szilard, Leo, 410–411

Tarski, Alfred, 8, 216, 344–345, 347–348, 350, 351, 486–488
Thales, 495
Thirring, Hans, 6
Thistlethwaite, Donald L., 11
Thomson, J. J., 409
Tolstoi, Leo, 183, 187–188
Trapold, Milton, 133n

Urmson, J. O., 262, 268, 270

Veblen, Oskar, 463
Vigier, J. P., 378

Waismann, Friedrich, 6, 7, 501
Wartofsky, M., 273n
Watkins, J. W. N., 261, 262, 265, 270–271
Weber, Ernst H., 499
Weizsäcker, C. F., 456
Wentzel, G., 449n
Weyl, Hermann, 285, 462, 467, 469–470, 504
Whitehead, Alfred North, 215, 451, 486
Whyte, L. L., 11, 461, 503
Wien, Willy, 6
Wigner, Eugene P., 449n, 453
Williams, Donald C., 232
Wisdom, John, 419
Wittgenstein, Ludwig, 4, 7, 8, 377, 382, 388, 414–417, 421–422, 428
Woodruff, Peter, 297n

Xenophanes, 97

Yaglom, A. M., 447
Yennie, Donald R., 11
Yourgrau, Wolfgang, 11

Zener, Karl, 11
Zilsel, Edgar, 6
Zipf, G. K., 216